Introduction to Social Welfare

Introduction
to Social Welfare

WALTER A. FRIEDLANDER

Associate Professor of Social Welfare
University of California at Berkeley

PRENTICE-HALL, INC.

1955

PRENTICE-HALL SOCIOLOGY SERIES

Herbert Blumer, Editor

HV
91
.F 7

L.C. Cat. Card No.: 55-6209

Preface

In our modern industrial society, social welfare has become such an important part of our life and our culture that an understanding of its fundamental philosophy, structure, and functions becomes necessary for every educated citizen. It is generally accepted that government agencies and private citizen groups, organized in religious charities or humanitarian philanthropy, are indispensable in order to relieve suffering, poverty, sickness, and delinquency and counteract a waste of human capacities. This book explains how social welfare concepts and services have developed by tradition, experience, and sociological changes. We need an historical and a philosophical perspective in order to comprehend the complicated present system of social welfare, its principles, its legal framework, and its effect on our fellow citizens.

The aim of this book is to serve particularly three groups of readers: (1) those citizens who wish to serve as volunteers or board members in the field of health, education, or social welfare; (2) those who are looking forward to, or are employed in, positions in the fields of public assistance, social insurance, recreation, group work, public employment services—plus those in correctional, institutional, probation, and parole services, or related activities for which graduate professional training is not always required; (3) and those who plan to take up, or are engaged in, studies of graduate social work, or who are working in responsible positions and want to inform themselves through this survey of the development, the basic ideas, and the present system of social welfare.

The fundamental concepts, the historic perspective, and the main phases of social welfare organization are presented in nontechnical language; professional jargon is avoided as much as possible. References are given predominately to books and journals available in most college and university libraries and in many public libraries.

v

The author is greatly indebted for the reading of the entire manuscript and for many constructive suggestions to his wife, Li B. Friedlander, and to Professor Herbert Blumer, editor of this series and chairman of the Department of Sociology and Social Institutions, University of California, Berkeley. He also wishes to acknowledge his appreciation for the encouragement, advice, and assistance in the preparation of the volume to Dean Milton Chernin, Miss Gertrude Wilson, Miss Ruth Morgan, Mrs. Eliot Studt, and Professor Ernest Greenwood of the School of Social Welfare, University of California, Berkeley. The writer owes gratitude to Mrs. Dorothee F. Mindlin, Mrs. Beverlee Filloy, Mrs. Wanda McNeill, Mrs. Sally T. Severance, Mr. Ray Studt, Mrs. Madeline Tikijian De Antonio, and Mrs. Mary Y. Tyler, who have kindly helped in the preparation and improvement of the book.

The author finally wishes to indicate his debt, for many ideas and contributions, to his colleagues on the faculty of the School of Social Welfare, University of California; his students; social workers in this country and abroad; and to the authors and publishers of the professional publications from which materials have been used.

WALTER A. FRIEDLANDER

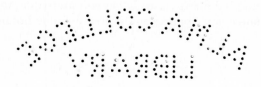

Table of Contents

vii

*Part II. The Present System and Organization
of Social Welfare*

I. The Nature of Social Insurance. II. Old-Age and Survivors
Insurance; Coverage; Eligibility; Benefits; Financing Old-Age
and Survivors Insurance; Administration; Procedure; Un-
solved Problems. III. Unemployment Insurance; Concept and
Organization; Legislation and Administration; Covered Employment; Benefits; Disability and Insurance Benefits; Experience Rating. IV. Railroad Workers Insurance; The Railroad
Retirement System; The Railroad Unemployment and Temporary Disability System; Administration of Railroad Insurance. V. Workmen's Compensation; Principles and Coverage;
Compensation Benefits; Administration of Workmen's Compensation. VI. Gaps in Our Insurance Program; Health Insurance; Maternity Insurance; Permanent Disability or Invalidity
Insurance; Family Allowances.

I. Family Service Agencies. II. Fee-Charging in Family Service
Agencies. III. Principles of Family Service. IV. Special Service
in the Family Welfare Field; Services to the Aged; Homemaker Services; Services to Travelers and Migrants; Legal Aid
Service.

I. Children's Needs for Special Services. II. Welfare and
Health Services for Children; Maternal and Child-Health
Services; Services for Crippled Children; Child Welfare Serv-
ices. III. Foster Family Care; Adoption; Children of Unmar-
ried Parents; Guardianship; Children in Institutions; Day
Nurseries and Child Care Centers; School Lunches. IV. School
Social Work. V. Child Labor Protection.

I. Cost of Medical Care. II. Medical Care for Needy Patients.
III. Medical Social Work.

I. History and Functions of Mental Hygiene. II. Child Guidance Work. III. Psychiatric Social Work.

Part III. Social Welfare Administration

Illustrations

Charts

Tables

PART I. *The Development of*
Social Welfare in England
and the United States

1. Introduction: The Concept of Social Welfare

The concept and the term "social welfare" in the sense of a scientific program have only recently developed in connection with the social problems of our industrial society. Poverty, sickness, suffering, and social disorganization have existed throughout the history of mankind, but only the industrial society of the nineteenth and twentieth centuries had to face so many social problems that the older human institutions—family, neighborhood, church, and local community—could no longer adequately meet them. The need for a broader system of social services resulted. In the following chapters we shall briefly analyze how human society dealt with destitution, maladjustment, and physical and mental ills and how the family and the tribe, the church, private philanthropy, and the community, under the influence of humanitarianism, in turn assumed the responsibility for satisfying people's needs. But it was only about a hundred years ago that the magnitude of social problems made it necessary to organize, under private and public initiative, activities to achieve aid to the needy. Since that time government has taken an increasingly greater responsibility for the well-being of the citizens. In addition to the increase in humanitarian ideas with emphasis on our responsibility for others, the development of the biological and social sciences provided new tools for investigating the causes of poverty, of human deficiencies, and of dissatisfaction with the aim to cure or to alleviate social problems.

A number of studies have tried to establish a concise terminology for the concepts of "social welfare," the "social services," "social

3

work," "social security," and so on. It has been difficult, however, to reach an agreement which is universally accepted.[1]

For this study the author suggests the following as a definition: "*Social welfare* is the organized system of social services and institutions, designed to aid individuals and groups to attain satisfying standards of life and health. It aims at personal and social relationships which permit individuals the development of their full capacities and the promotion of their well-being in harmony with the needs of the community." "Social work" is a professional service, based upon scientific knowledge and skill in human relations, which assists individuals, alone or in groups, to obtain social and personal satisfaction and independence. It is usually performed by a social agency or a related organization. The term "social welfare" has a broader implication than professional social work. Gertrude Wilson characterizes social welfare as an organized concern of all people for all people.[2] Finally, the term "the social services" is often used in a very broad sense; Harry M. Cassidy[3] defined it as "those organized activities that are primarily and directly concerned with the conservation, the protection, and the improvement of human resources" and includes as social services: social assistance, social insurance, child welfare, corrections, mental hygiene, public health, education, recreation, labor protection, and housing.

Education and labor legislation contribute to people's well-being and physical and mental growth, but they have not been included in our definition of social welfare. Social welfare services are administered by public or private organizations, and the structure and functions of these services will be discussed. The objective of social welfare is to secure for each human being the economic necessities,

[1] Karl de Schweinitz, *The Art of Helping People Out of Trouble* (Boston: Houghton, 1924); Helen L. Witmer, *Social Work: An Analysis of a Social Institution* (New York: Farrar & Rinehart, 1942), pp. 3-10; Alice Cheyney, *Nature and Scope of Social Work* (New York: American Association of Social Workers, 1926); Harry M. Cassidy, *Social Security and Reconstruction in Canada* (Boston: Humphries, 1943), pp. 13-17; Helen I. Clarke, *Principles and Practice of Social Work* (New York: Appleton-Century-Crofts, 1947), pp. 3-16; Arthur Fink, *The Field of Social Work* (New York: Holt, 1949), pp. v, vi, 3; Herbert Stroup, *Social Work: An Introduction to the Field* (New York: American Book, 1948), p. 1; Joseph P. Anderson, "Social Work as a Profession," *Social Work Year Book*, 1945, p. 446.

[2] Gertrude Wilson and Gladys Ryland, *Social Group Work Practice* (Boston: Houghton, 1949), p. 16.

[3] *Op. cit.*, p. 13.

a high standard of health and decent living conditions, equal opportunities with his fellow citizens, and the highest possible degree of self-respect and freedom of thought and action without interfering with the same rights of others.[4]

By "social security" we understand a program of protection provided by society against those contingencies of modern life—sickness, unemployment, old age dependency, industrial accidents, and invalidity—against which the individual cannot be expected to protect himself and his family by his own ability or foresight.[5] This general goal of social protection, as a rule, is secured through the various forms of public assistance, social insurance, and frequently preventive health and welfare services. In general use, the term social security does not embrace private social welfare activities, which are, however, an important part of the system of social welfare in most countries. Our Social Security Act includes public child welfare and health services, public health, and vocational rehabilitation as part of the program of social security.[6]

The social philosophy which has led to the origin of the concept of social welfare as one of the most essential cultural characteristics of modern society has fundamentally changed during the centuries of human history. We shall trace its essential elements in the following chapters in order to understand the present-day meanings and the reactions of the public toward the question of social welfare.

This book does not attempt to teach the methods and professional skills of social work. They are based upon knowledge of human behavior and motivation, the dynamics of human relationships, the sociological, economic, and political structure of our society, knowledge of the community and of the organization and function of the social services, and upon the practical application of social work techniques in supervised field work. This study will present an analysis of the structure and functions of those activities which serve the aim of social welfare in their evolution up to the present time, and of the underlying social philosophy.

Social work is both a science and an art and is carried on in its

---

[4] Robert Kelso, *The Science of Public Welfare* (New York: Holt, 1928), p. 22.

[5] Maurice Stack, "The Meaning of Social Security," William Haber and Wilbur J. Cohen (editors), *Readings in Social Security* (New York: Prentice-Hall, Inc., 1948), pp. 41-45.

[6] See Chapters 5, 8, 9, 11, 12 and 13; also Helen L. Witmer and Ruth Kotinsky, *Personality in the Making* (New York: Harper, 1952), pp. 357-367.

practical application in six different forms, which are all based upon a common core of knowledge and skill which we call "generic social work."[7] The six processes of social work are: (1) *social case-work,* which helps by counseling the individual client to effect better social relationships and a social adjustment that makes it possible for him to lead a satisfying and useful life; (2) *social group work,* which helps people to participate in the activities of a group for their intellectual, emotional, and physical growth, and for the obtainment of desirable goals of the group; (3) *community organization,* the process of planning and developing social services in order to meet the health and welfare needs of a community or larger unit; (4) *social welfare administration,* the process of organizing and directing a social agency; (5) *social welfare research,* inquiry into the validity of the structure and applied methods of social work; and (6) *social action,* the organized group process solving general social problems and furthering social welfare objectives by legislative, social, health, or economic progress.

Social work has drawn its knowledge and insight from political science, psychology, sociology, economics, medicine, psychiatry, anthropology, biology, history, education, and philosophy, but by synthesis it has developed into a science of its own. As a profession social work depends upon the body of knowledge based upon these other social sciences, the specific structure and function of social welfare activities, and the skill and responsibility which is required for each professional performance. As a helping process social work assists people with problems of social and emotional adjustment and helps them to achieve greater social and personal satisfaction and independence.

SELECTED BIBLIOGRAPHY*

*Abbott, Edith, *Social Welfare and Professional Education,* 2nd ed. Chicago: University of Chicago Press, 1942.
Barnes, Harry Elmer, *Social Institutions.* New York: Prentice-Hall, Inc., 1942.

[7] The official interpretation of social work by the Armed Forces is narrower: "Social work is that process which deals directly and differentially with persons who have problems relating primarily to their social situation and which endeavors, individual to individual, to understand what help is needed, and to assist the individual to find and utilize the help indicated." *Social Work Journal,* January, 1951, Vol. XXXII, No. 1, p. 43.

* Publications of particular value for the reader in this and the following bibliographies are marked with an asterisk (*).

———, and Oreen Ruedi, *The American Way of Life*, 2nd ed. New York: Prentice-Hall, Inc., 1950.

———, and H. Becker, *Contemporary Social Theory*. New York: Appleton-Century-Crofts, 1940.

*Bisno, Herbert, *The Philosophy of Social Work*. Washington, D.C.: Public Affairs Press, 1952.

Bruno, Frank J., *The Theory of Social Work*. Boston: Heath, 1936.

Cassidy, Harry M., *Social Security and Reconstruction in Canada*. Boston: Humphries, 1943.

Chapin, F. Stuart, *Contemporary American Institutions: A Sociological Analysis*. New York: Harper, 1935.

Cheney, Alice, *Nature and Scope of Social Work*. New York: American Association of Social Workers, 1926.

*Clarke, Helen I., *Principles and Practice of Social Work*. New York: Appleton-Century-Crofts, 1947.

Cuber, John F., and Robert A. Harper, *Problems of American Society: Values in Conflict*. New York: Holt, 1948.

*de Schweinitz, Karl, *The Art of Helping People Out of Trouble*. Boston: Houghton, 1924.

———, Jr., and Kenneth W. Thompson, *Man and Modern Society: Conflict and Choice in the Industrial Era*. New York: Holt, 1953.

Ellwood, Charles A., *A History of Social Philosophy*. New York: Prentice-Hall, Inc., 1938.

*Fink, Arthur E., *The Field of Social Work*, 2nd ed. New York: Holt, 1949.

Kelso, Robert W., *The Science of Public Welfare*. New York: Holt, 1928.

Lee, Porter R., *Social Work as Cause and Function*. New York: Columbia University Press, 1937.

MacIver, Robert, *The Contribution of Sociology to Social Work*. New York: Columbia University Press, 1931.

Merrill, Francis E., and H. Wentworth Eldridge, *Culture and Society*. New York: Prentice-Hall, Inc., 1952.

*Miles, Arthur P., *An Introduction to Public Welfare*. Boston: Heath, 1949.

Myrdal, Alva, *Nation and Family*. New York and London: Harper, 1941.

Queen, Stuart Alfred, *Social Work in the Light of History*. Philadelphia: Lippincott, 1922.

Quinn, James A., *Human Ecology*. New York: Prentice-Hall, Inc., 1950.

Rosenquist, Carl M., *Social Problems*. New York: Prentice-Hall, Inc., 1940.

*Stroup, Herbert Hewitt, *Social Work: An Introduction to the Field*. New York: American Book, 1948.

*Witmer, Helen L., *Social Work: An Analysis of a Social Institution*. New York: Farrar & Rinehart, 1942.

2. The Emergence and Growth of Social Welfare Problems in Europe

I. SOCIAL PROBLEMS

Modern anthropology and sociology have shown that with the beginning of human society in its primitive stages the feeling of belonging, the readiness to mutual protection, were just as essential forces as the selfish desire to dominate other weaker human beings. From this early phase of human development this willingness to mutual assistance can be called one of the fundamental drives which effectively compensate the demand for destroying or enslaving fellow men. It first was felt among the members of the family or tribe, and the role of the head or chief was mainly that of protector against human enemies as well as against wild animals or natural disasters. Mutual aid served as self-protection for family or tribe against a hostile world. However, the weak, old, and sick, the crippled, and the handicapped were sometimes killed or abandoned by the tribe since they were a burden or thought to be under a curse of evil ghosts.

With the growth of tribes and the beginnings of religion, the priests assumed leadership in providing protection for the helpless, widows and orphans, and the sick. Religious devotion became the most powerful incentive for benevolence and charity. We find this motive in almost all ancient religions, the Vendidad and Hindu philosophy, in Assyrian, Babylonian, and Egyptian codes, in Greek and Roman customs—particularly, however, in Jewish and Christian religious teachings.[1] Charity was motivated primarily by the desire

[1] Amos G. Warner, *American Charities*, 3rd ed. (New York: Crowell, 1919), pp. 4-6; and Stuart A. Queen, *Social Work in the Light of History* (Philadelphia: Lippincott, 1922), pp. 267-307.

9

to receive the grace of God or to secure the merits of good deeds for eternal life, but a genuine feeling of pity for the widows and orphans may well have been a reason that the demands of the churches for the relief of the poor were willingly followed. To relieve the distress of the unfortunate became, in Jewish and Christian concepts, an important religious duty. It was essential to the church as the dominant moral force, to the giver as a means of satisfaction and hope, to the destitute as a welcome aid, and to the community as an important cultural and ethical action. The teaching of the prophets in Israel and of St. Paul, St. Augustine, St. Francis, and St. Thomas Aquinas in the Christian church gave the recipient of alms dignity and religious flavor, whereas almsgiving enobled the generous donor. The early Christians helped one another when facing poverty and persecution but the medieval church entrusted the administration of charity to the bishops, the local priest, and the deacons. With the growing influence of the church and the acceptance of Christianity as state religion, institutions for the poor were established in the monasteries, serving as orphanages, as homes for the old, the sick, and the handicapped, and as refuge for the homeless, continuing the tradition of the Greek *xenodochia* (guest houses). Particularly active in distributing alms to the poor, the hungry, and the naked were the Franciscans, founded by Saint Francis d'Assisi, and the Hospitallers, established by Guy de Pontpellier. They devoted their main activity to missionary preaching, collecting alms, and distributing relief to the sick and the destitute. Under these circumstances mendicancy grew throughout Europe since asking for alms was not only an easy way of making a living but was also socially respected because it was shared with the missionaries and monks, with students of the universities, and with the Crusaders on their way to the Holy Land. Although the church praised charity and almsgiving, the state did not take the same attitude. Beginning with the statute of Charlemagne in 800, secular authorities issued decree after decree prohibiting mendicancy and threatening fines to citizens who would give alms to able-bodied beggars. These decrees aimed to force serfs and rural laborers to stay on the manors, and to protect peasants and travelers against robbery by vagrant beggars. This conflict between church and state existed until the end of the Middle Ages.

The older church institutions in which charity was rendered—monasteries, abbeys, and convents—were partly replaced by the "hospitals" (*hôtels de Dieu*) which administered to old and sick persons, orphans, abandoned children and pregnant women and became the main agency of medieval charity. Hospitals were founded with the help of donations from kings, dukes, and members of the aristocracy. However, only some of the destitute found shelter and refuge in these institutions; many wandering beggars remained on the roads and were a curse with which local and state governments were unable to cope. The difference in ideology regarding beggars was not the only conflict in the field of charity between the church and the secular authorities. Another conflict arose from frequent mismanagement of church institutions and hospitals and the abuse of funds, which led to criticism from the citizens, measures of control, and the setting up of boards of supervision by the states.[2] In order to stop vagrancy and mendicancy, many European states enacted repressive statutes imposing brutal penalties, but none really succeeded in wiping out vagabondage. The secular authorities were thus compelled to force cities and local communities to take charge of relief wherever the religious institutions refused to accept their principles.

Still more violent became the conflict between church and state in the sixteenth century, during the period of the Reformation. In Germany, Martin Luther appealed in an open address, "Appeal to the Christian Nobility of the German Nation" (1520), to the princes to forbid begging and to organize in all parishes a "common chest" for the receipt of money, food, and clothes to assist the needy. Luther requested that regular contributions in addition to voluntary gifts be made to these chests. A similar plan for relief was proposed in Zurich, Switzerland, by the Protestant Reformator Ulrich Zwingli, in 1525. Other communities in France, Austria, and the Scandinavian countries developed programs which resembled the Lutheran concept; the responsibility for the collection of funds and the distribution of relief to destitute, sick, and handicapped persons and orphans was assumed by local authorities, but the church wardens played the leading role in relief administration.[3]

Although these methods recognized the legal responsibility of the community for the maintenance of the poor, they did little to change the social conditions of destitute families. The idea that the fate of

[2] A. Warner, *op. cit.*, pp. 8-10.
[3] Karl de Schweinitz, *England's Road to Social Security* (Philadelphia: University of Pennsylvania Press, 1949), pp. 36-38.

the individual poor deserved attention was first conceived by the Spanish philosopher Juan Luis Vives in the sixteenth century. Vives was educated in Paris and lived most of his life in Belgium. A friend of Erasmus of Rotterdam and of Sir Thomas More, he was one of the noted scientists of his time. He was invited to teach at Oxford University, and he developed a concise program of poor relief for the Consuls and the Senate of the city of Bruges in Flanders under the title *"De Subventione Pauperum."*[4] He proposed dividing the city into parish quarters, assigning two senators with a secretary to each quarter in order to investigate the social conditions of every pauper family, and providing for aid through vocational training, employment, and rehabilitation, instead of through the customary distribution of alms. For the aged and unemployable Vives asked commitment to a hospital (almshouse). These excellent, foresighted ideas were not practiced, however, in Continental Europe for a long time, though they were discussed at the Sorbonne University in Paris, together with a similar relief plan developed at Ypres in Belgium in 1536.

It was two and a half centuries later that the methods of Vives' plan were applied in practice. This was done in Hamburg in 1788, where a reform of poor relief introduced a district system of investigation and distribution of relief to individual paupers through volunteer committees appointed by the Senate. The city was divided into sixty quarters following a plan suggested by Professor Busch, city senator and commissioner of public relief. Each quarter had about the same number of poor families. Each commission consisted of three respectable citizens who offered their service without compensation. The investigations were directed by regulations of a central board composed of five senators and ten other citizens. The board established the basic principles of the program. The sixty commissions acted at the same time as agents of the "central poor house," interviewed the poor, inquired about their health, earnings, and morals, and determined the individual needs of each family. Children and adolescents were trained in elementary courses and in an industrial school attached to the central orphan asylum.[5]

[4] Juan Luis Vives, *Concerning the Relief of the Poor or Concerning Human Need*, A Letter Addressed to the Senate of Bruges. Translated by Margaret M. Sherwood, New York School of Philanthropy, 1927.

[5] K. de Schweinitz, *op. cit.* pp. 91-99; and Walter Friedlander and Earl Dewey Myers, *Child Welfare in Germany Before and After Naziism* (Chicago: University of Chicago Press, 1940), pp. 39-44.

A similar system of relief was used in Munich in 1790. It was inaugurated by Benjamin Thompson, later Count of Rumford, who became chief of the general staff of the Bavarian army. In order to prevent the begging of sturdy paupers, who had become a threat to the citizens, he founded a "military workhouse" which manufactured the clothing for the army. With the help of volunteer district commissions, all able-bodied beggars were recruited for this workhouse. It also provided raw materials for home industry to persons in poverty who wanted to earn their living. Both the Hamburg and the Munich relief systems were financed by taxation and by collections of voluntary gifts. Although the system was actually used first in Hamburg, it was called the *Elberfeld system*. The city of Elberfeld introduced the same plan in 1853 and financed it exclusively from public taxation. The volunteers of the Elberfeld commissions lived in the same quarter as the poor whom they supervised, and thus were closely acquainted with their conditions. Later a large number of other European cities accepted this program.

The most important reformer of the charities of the Catholic Church was Father Vincent de Paul in France during the seventeenth century. This young priest had a dramatic experience when he was captured by Tunisian pirates and sold as a galley slave. Sharing for a number of years the fate of the most unfortunate, he devoted his life after his escape to the improvement of charities, especially for prisoners and their families, orphans, illegitimate children, and the sick and hungry. He succeeded in arousing serious interest among the aristocracy and at the royal court, and obtained large foundations for the establishment of hospitals, orphanages, and foundling asylums. Not satisfied with such spectacular success, he persuaded the ladies of the court to devote themselves to personal services for the destitute and sick. He organized a lay order, the "Ladies of Charity," whose members visited the poor in their homes, distributing food and clothes. In order to improve the methods of nursing the sick and handicapped, in 1633 Father Vincent founded another order, the "Daughters of Charity," composed of simple young women of the peasant class who wanted to devote themselves to charitable work. They were trained in nursing and in attending to the poor and became the forerunners of the modern social worker. The ideas of Father Vincent introduced important reforms in the entire charity program under Catholic auspices, not only in France, but also in other Catholic countries.

The social concepts, legislation, and customs of England were of decisive importance in the development of charities in the United States for they were the cultural background upon which this country was built. Therefore, in this chapter, we shall survey the British background.

II. EARLY CHARITIES IN ENGLAND

In medieval England, as in other European countries, care of the poor was an activity of the church. To give alms to the destitute, blind, and lame was a religious duty and considered a means of salvation from the threat of divine punishment after death. Religious rules required the faithful to offer alms to the needy, to feed the hungry, to nurse the sick and invalid, and to aid poor widows and orphans. Since the main motive for almsgiving was the salvation of the soul of the donor, he usually had little concern for the human being who received his charity. Beginning in the fourteenth century, however, some distinction was made between two classes of the poor: the able-bodied poor who could earn their living, and the impotent poor who were unable to work—the blind, the lame, the aged, the sick, young children, and pregnant women. For the care of the poor the church devoted from one-fourth to one-third of the tithes and offerings collected from its parishioners.

Relief to the destitute was first distributed by the priest of the parish, sometimes with the help of the churchwardens and deacons. In the thirteenth and fourteenth centuries, religious orders and church institutions relieved the parish churches from most of the duties of caring for the poor and the sick. In the fifteenth century their number had grown so that more than a thousand monasteries, convents, hospitals, and abbeys provided shelter, alms, food, and clothes for the poor of neighboring villages or for wandering beggars. Many of these religious institutions were maintained by endowments that were donated for charitable purposes by members of the royal house and the aristocracy. Every charitable institution attracted beggars and destitute persons who hoped for support. Although daily distributions of food were made at the convent gate and shelter was granted to the homeless, little was done to change the social conditions of the poor so that they might become self-supporting again.

Whereas the church with its monasteries, abbeys, and convents was by far the most important charitable institution of this period,[6] its work was supplemented from the twelfth to the fifteenth century by the relief activities of the guilds. Craft and merchant guilds, rural fraternities, and social or church guilds were organized primarily for the purpose of mutual self-help, brotherhood, and fellowship. Therefore, they supported first their own sick or needy members, and their widows and orphans, but they also organized charities for the poor of the town. Particularly in times of droughts and famines, they distributed barley and corn to the destitute, fed them on certain feast days, and offered free lodgings to poor travelers.

Until the fourteenth century the King and Parliament did not concern themselves with the charities of the church and the guilds. With the slow disappearance of feudalism and the social changes resulting from a new economic order which freed the serfs and employed agricultural labor for wages, the King and his nobles faced the problem of how to maintain order among the laborers and prevent vagrancy. The emancipation of the rural laborer from serfdom on the manor created new problems. Formerly the serf and his family were fed and clad by the lord, and the lady cared for the old and the sick. Emancipation gave the laborer and his family the freedom to wander, but it deprived him of his former security. In times of unemployment, sickness, old age, and invalidity, he was forced to go begging. At the beginning of the Industrial Revolution the manufacture of wool opened some work to the laborer but resident workers were hired first. During the summer, workers migrated from one part of the country to another in order to find work in harvesting the crops. Soldiers returning from the wars in France often preferred to live in the towns rather than to go back to their hard, low-paid work and dependency on the manor. These social conditions increased the danger of poverty.

The first poor law in England was based upon a national catastrophe.[7] In 1348, the plague or "Black Death," brought in from the Levante on ships carrying infected rats killed two-thirds of the entire English population within two years. It caused a very severe shortage

[6] Charles Richmond Henderson, *Modern Methods of Charity* (New York: Macmillan, 1904), pp. 165-167, 556-557.

[7] The description of the development of social welfare in England during the past six centuries presented in *England's Road to Social Security, 1349 to 1947* (Philadelphia: University of Pennsylvania Press, 1949) by Karl de Schweinitz is recommended for further study.

of labor on the manors and resulted in a steep rise in wages. Urged by the landed gentry, King Edward III issued the *Statute of Laborers* of 1349. It ordered that able-bodied laborers without means must accept employment from any master willing to hire them and forbade them to leave their own parish. Citizens were not allowed to give alms to able-bodied beggars. The Statute of Laborers became the first of many laws and decrees designed to prevent vagrancy and begging, and to force the rural worker to stay on the land. Cruel punishment such as being put into the stocks, being whipped, branded, or mutilated by cutting off the ears and the nose, being condemned to the galleys, and finally hanged was ordered for beggars and vagrants. The growing woolen industry made sheep raising for the gentry more profitable than grain crops. This led to the conversion of tilled land into pasture. Comparatively few shepherds replaced large numbers of rural laborers. New unemployed families joined the ranks of former soldiers, sailors, the handicapped, and the sick who were unable to find work.

The first constructive measure taken by government for relief of the poor was the statute of Henry VIII in 1531. It provided that mayors and justices of the peace should investigate applications of the aged and paupers unable to work who were maintained by the parish. They were to be registered and licensed to beg in an assigned area. This law was the beginning of a recognition of public responsibility for the poor, but it still threatened brutal punishment for other beggars and vagrants.

The Reformation brought a fundamental change in the entire system of charities and relief for the poor in England. One of its features was the secularization of the monasteries and hospitals which until that time had been the primary source for the relief of the destitute, the aged, and the sick. The influence of the guilds had vanished during the fifteenth century. Other benevolent foundations which formerly provided aid to needy groups no longer did so, and with the confiscation of church property by Henry VIII it became necessary to provide otherwise for the care of the poor. Therefore the statute of 1536 established the first plan of public relief under the auspices of the government in England. It ruled that paupers be registered in their parishes but only after they had resided for three years in the county. The parish had to maintain the "impotent poor" and the means for the relief came from voluntary contributions of the parishioners through church collections. Able-bodied beggars were forced to work, and idle children from five to fourteen years of age were taken away from their parents and assigned to masters for training. In 1562 the *Statute of Artificers* regulated wages and hours of labor and sought to increase the skill of artisans by an apprentice system. It required that vagrants and vagabonds be forced to hard labor and that unemployed beggars between twelve and sixty years of age be hired out as servants. However, voluntary collections proved to be insufficient for the support of the poor. Their ranks had been swelled by disbanded monks, nuns, and by thousands of families formerly sheltered or employed in monasteries and convents. As work became scarce and the price of food rose, vagrancy and begging increased. In 1563 Parliament had to adopt compulsory measures to finance parish poor relief. Each householder was compelled by law to make a weekly contribution based upon property and income.

In 1572, Queen Elizabeth signed a statute of Parliament that introduced a *general tax* to provide funds for *poor relief* and established overseers of the poor to administer the new law. The Statute of 1572 marked the final recognition that the government was responsible for providing aid to people who could not maintain themselves. In 1576 "houses of correction," supplied with wool, hemp, flax, and iron, were established in which the able-bodied poor, particularly young persons, were forced to work.

Another Statute of 1597 confirmed that the churchwardens and four substantial householders were to be appointed as overseers of the poor by the justices of the peace. It also ordered that almshouses should be erected for the impotent poor, the old, the blind, the lame, and those unable to work, and that parents and children were legally liable for each other's maintenance.

III. THE ELIZABETHAN POOR LAW OF 1601

The *Poor Law of 1601*, often referred to as "43 Elizabeth," was a codification of the entire precedent poor relief legislation. Its only new feature was the establishment of liability for support to grandparents as well as to parents in need. The statute represented the final form of poor law legislation in England after three generations in which public opinion had been greatly excited about the necessary provisions for the poor in a period of political, religious, and economic changes that required government action. The law confirmed the responsibility of the parish—the local community—for the maintenance of the poor who were not supported by their relatives. The parish's responsibility to aid the destitute was limited to persons who had been born there or who had at least lived in the parish for the last three years. This question of "residence" or "settlement right" as one of the important requirements for the receipt of public relief has remained a vital issue in public assistance up to the present time.

The Poor Law did not permit the registration of a person as in need of charity whenever his relatives, husband or wife, parents or children were able to support the distressed person. The "principle of relatives responsibility" or "family responsibility" means that relatives have to assume the primary obligation for supporting the poor, and that public relief authorities aid the destitute only if the family cannot maintain him. This question of family responsibility has persisted in being a serious problem in public assistance because people do not want to spend tax money for the support of distressed persons who can be maintained by their own relatives. The law distinguished three classes of the poor:

1. *The Able-bodied Poor.* They were called "sturdy beggars" and were forced to work in the "house of correction" or "workhouse." Citizens were forbidden to give them alms, and paupers who arrived from other parishes were returned to the place where they had last dwelt for a year. A beggar or "valiant vagabond" who refused to work in the house of correction was put in the stocks or in jail.

2. *The Impotent Poor.* These were people unable to work—the sick, the old, the blind, deaf-mute, and lame, the demented, and mothers with young children. They were to be placed in the almshouse where they were to help within the limits of their capacities. If the impotent poor had a house or a place to live and it seemed less expensive to maintain them there, the overseers of the poor could grant them "outdoor relief," usually "in kind," giving them food, clothes, and fuel in their own homes.

3. *Dependent Children.* These were orphans, foundlings, and children who had been deserted by their parents or whose parents were so poor that they could not support them. These children were to be placed out to any citizen who was willing to take them

without a charge. If no such "free home" was available, the child was to be given to the lowest bidder. Children of eight years and older who were able to do some domestic and other work were indentured with a townsman who took the child without charge and supported him. Boys were taught the trade of their master and had to serve until their twenty-fourth birthday. Girls were brought up as domestic servants and remained in indenture until they were twenty-one years of age or married.

If children could stay with their parents or relatives who were poor, such materials as hemp, yarn, or wool were provided so that the children could earn their living by home industry for a crafts-man or a merchant in town. If neither way was suitable, the child was to be placed in the poorhouse.

The "overseers of the poor" administered the poor law in the parish. They were appointed by the justices of the peace or magis-trates. Their function was to receive the application of the poor person for relief, to investigate his condition, and to decide whether he was "eligible" for relief. The overseers decided whether the ap-plicant and his family should be placed in the workhouse or alms-house, were to be "sold out," or should receive aid in their own home. As a rule, an old relinquished building which was not used for other purposes served as almshouse and workhouse. In the latter section the inmates were forced to do hard labor, under the super-vision of a superintendent who was appointed by the overseers of the poor. The overseers had to collect the poor tax assessed upon land, houses, and tithes of all inhabitants, and to register assessment and payments. The poor tax was the main source for the financing of poor relief. It was supplemented by private donations and be-quests, and by the use of fines for the violation of certain statutes.

The Poor Law of 1601 set the pattern of public relief under gov-ernmental responsibility for Great Britain for three hundred years. It established the principle that the local community—the parish—had to organize and finance poor relief for its residents, providing sustenance to the unemployable and to children and work to the able-bodied. It still maintained many of the earlier features of repres-sion and disdain for the destitute, but it also accepted an obligation for the aid of people who could not provide for themselves. The fundamental provisions of the Elizabethan Poor Law were incor-porated into the laws of the American colonies and have remained an important element even in the present concepts of public assistance and in the considerations of the public in regard to social legislation.

A. THE SETTLEMENT ACT OF 1662

Since each parish was responsible for the maintenance of its own poor, it wanted to protect itself against an additional burden by the moving in of poor persons from other communities who might ask for relief. The gentry, on the other hand, were anxious to retain on the land those rural laborers who were still needed for the cultivation of the estates. Following the pressure of both the parishes and the gentry, Charles II enacted in 1662 the *Law of Settlement*. It empowered the justices of the peace to return to his former residence any newcomer who, in the opinion of the overseers of the poor, might at some future date become a public charge. Within forty days after arrival the overseers had to investigate and might request from the justice of peace that the newcomers be expelled. However, if the new family was able to rent property for ten pounds sterling a year or to deposit this sum, it was exempted from the threat of removal.

This statute was the expression of an extreme parochialism. It discriminated against the common laborer who could not afford a deposit or a rent of ten pounds sterling a year. It represented a post-feudal attempt to force the rural workers to stay in their villages, although the industrial development of the towns offered greater promise for them. Difficulties arose in some towns when the overseers, eager to get rid of paupers, offered them bribes to go clandestinely to another parish. Therefore, in 1686, King James II ruled that the prescribed forty days for investigation should be counted only from the date on which the newcomer sent a written report on his abode and his family to the overseers or the churchwardens. A few years later, in 1691, King William III required that an announcement of the arrival of newcomers be posted in the church. Despite these legal amendments, frequent disputes between townships arose over the question of whether or not laborers had gained settlement in a parish. Litigation before the courts and useless transportation of families and witnesses cost the country a great deal of money. Furthermore, the statute prevented workers from going during harvest time to other counties where they were badly needed. These economic conditions during the eighteenth century made necessary further changes in the administration of the settlement law. Mobility of labor was finally achieved by the introduction of the "certificate," a document issued by the parish authorities which guaranteed that the township would pay the cost of maintenance of the bearer if he should be in need. Thereafter each community requested such a certificate from newcomers. It was not until 1795 that the Act of 1662 was amended so that a newcomer could not be sent back to his former residence until he actually had applied for relief. Even so vagabonds, "disorderly persons," and unmarried pregnant women could still be forcibly expelled immediately.

B. WORKHOUSES AND OUTDOOR RELIEF

During the second half of the seventeenth century, the English were in fierce commercial competition with the Dutch, who had succeeded in developing an efficient industry and trade. English economists admired the absence of beggars in the streets and the productive operation of the Dutch almshouses, in which inmates manufactured goods for export. The desire to keep raw materials, wool and mining iron, in England and thus to produce finished goods for export led to the training of the poor for industry. Following the *Workhouse Act* of 1696, workhouses in Bristol and other cities instructed the inmates, adults and children, in spinning, knitting, linen weaving, lace work, and in the manufacture of nets and sails. However, these experiments had no economic success since the unemployed poor had no particular skill or adaptability and could not compete with workshops employing skilled foremen and laborers. In 1722, the overseers were authorized to make contracts with private manufacturers who employed the paupers, and relief was refused to any person not willing to enter the workhouse. This "workhouse test" forced entire families to give up their homes and to live in the workhouse as in a prison, the men separated from their wives and children. The establishment of workhouses by manufacturers throughout England led to savings in local taxes, because many paupers preferred to live in utmost poverty with their families rather than to move to the workhouse or "house of correction." Workhouses conducted by private contractors attempted to make profits by spending as little as possible for equipment and repair and for the food and clothing of the inmates, but in some instances the work of the tired and hungry inhabitants was so inadequate that the contractors still operated at a loss. Sometimes they even discouraged paupers from entering the overcrowded workhouse, bribing them to stay out, to leave the institution, or to move to another parish.

The mistreatment of the inmates, the lack of air and proper sanitation and the immorality in the overcrowded wards aroused serious criticism among ministers and social reformers such as Jonas Hanway, Joseph Townsend, Richard Burn, John Scott, and Thomas Gilbert. The first of the crusaders for a reform of the workhouse, Jonas Hanway, spent several years in the study of these institutions. He exposed the appalling rate of infant mortality in the workhouses where sometimes 82 per cent of all babies under one year of age died. In 1761, on the incentive of Hanway, Parliament attempted to improve these conditions by ordering the registration of all infants in workhouses, and in 1767 the removal from the workhouse of all children under six years and their placement with foster families was ruled.

One of the most persistent reformers of the workhouse was Thomas Gilbert. As a magistrate he knew the failures of the poor laws, but as member of the House of Commons he could appraise them with more effect. The Poor Law Amendment of 1782, known as the "Gilbert Act," abolished the "contractor system" of the workhouse, replaced the honorary overseers of the poor by salaried "guardians of the poor," and reversed the principle of "indoor relief" by the provision that persons able and willing to work should be maintained in their own homes until employment was procured.

Economic changes in England during the eighteenth century, however, were a continuous source of increasing poverty. For centuries the poor man had used the "commons" of the village. He had grown vegetables, potatoes, barley, and wheat for his family, had grazed his sheep, geese, pigs or cows, and had thus supplemented the meager earnings from his small field or from working as a tenant farmer. The "enclosure movement" enlarged the holdings of the landed aristocracy, but took away from the poor peasant the small livestock and products that had made it possible for him to maintain his family. Moreover, many peasants lived on the common land and thought they owned it. With the "enclosure," they became "squatters," landless poor, and were forced to move. In industry, the invention of power machinery, driven by wind or water, removed production from villages and small towns to larger cities where water transportation was available. The place of manufacture shifted from the home of the craftsman to the larger workshop and mill. The growth of industry tended to increase the number of workers, but the new machinery in the mills replaced many of the hand weavers, thus creating new unemployed paupers and vagrants.

C. PARTIAL RELIEF

The war with France from 1793 to 1815, following the French Revolution, increased the cost of living. Disabled war veterans refused to go to the poorhouse with their families and insisted upon receiving poor relief in their own homes. Magistrates and guardians became concerned with the suffering of the poor and considered means to increase wages or to secure a minimum wage. In May 1795, a conference of poor-law officials of Berkshire County at Speenhamland decided to establish "a table of universal practice," which determined the amount of relief on the basis of the local cost of bread needed for the sustenance of the family. This so-called "bread scale" was to be used also to supplement wages of laborers whose earnings were less than this minimum subsistence. The new practice spread to other places and was approved by Parliament by the *Speenhamland Act* of December 24, 1795. The statute authorized relief allowances in the homes of the poor, according to the size of the family, either for their support or to supplement low wages. It led to widespread use of outdoor relief for old, infirm, and handicapped persons.

As a result of these measures, wages and the general standard of living were lowered. More and more persons received full or partial relief and, therefore, contributed to the need for higher poor tax rates. Employers became accustomed to paying substandard wages and to referring workers to the guardians of the poor. Relief destroyed the worker's incentive to do a good job and tended to keep wages down to the bread scale.

It is not difficult to understand why such a system was severely criticized. The opposition centered on the granting of relief to persons in their own homes, that is, "outdoor relief." This practice was held responsible for the economic and moral failure of the program.

In reality, it was not just the method of "direct" or "outdoor" relief which caused undesirable effects, but rather the failure to secure minimum wages that would maintain the worker, and the lack of administrative ability for constructive use of poor relief. With the increasing cost of the poor rate dissatisfaction among taxpayers was aggravated by the uneven distribution of this burden. Communities with a large number of paupers frequently had few wealthy merchants so that the poor tax had to be collected from householders of modest income. Another criticism of poor law practice was based upon the economic theory of "laissez-faire," as presented in Adam Smith's *Wealth of Nations.*[8] It postulated that the state should not interfere with private economy so that the manufacturer could reap the profits of production. Supporters of Smith's doctrine, like Jeremy Bentham and Reverend Joseph Townsend, suggested a gradual decrease and finally the elimination of public poor relief. The most influential representative of this theory was another clergyman, Thomas R. Malthus. In his famous *Essay on Population,* which appeared in 1798, he explained that the food supply increased only in arithmetic progression, the population in geometric progression, and that agriculture, therefore, was unable to feed a steadily increasing population—a situation, he claimed, that made war, famine, and pestilence necessary to stem this dangerous growth. Malthus disapproved of poor relief because it tended to encourage paupers to have more children in order to get relief for them, and tended to raise the price of food, which again impoverished the entire working class.

Although the opposition of the classical economists to public relief had a theoretical, financial, and commercial basis, objection of another group to the poor law practices was founded upon humanitarian and moral considerations. Reverend Thomas Chalmers (1780-1847), a parish minister in the small community of Kilmany, Scotland, organized a program of private charity on the principle of neighborly aid. An eloquent preacher, he was called to Glasgow in 1814, and found there an expensive system of poor relief, financed from public taxes and from church collections. Chalmers opposed the impersonal character and inefficiency of this charity. At Kilmany he had visited each home of the parish, and he resumed this custom at the large Tron parish in Glasgow with its 11,000 members. His visits revealed numerous personal and health problems which had

[8] *An Inquiry Into the Nature and Causes of Wealth of Nations,* published in 1776.

been unknown before. After four successful years, Chalmers was called to organize the St. John parish in a very poor section of Glasgow. He accepted on condition that he would be given full control over the administration of relief. He divided this parish into twenty-five districts, with about 400 parishioners each, under the guidance of a deacon who investigated relief applications. The surprising result was that during four years only twenty new applicants, from a parish population of 8,000, were found in need.

Based upon this experience, Chalmers proclaimed that the prevalent practice of public and church relief was wasteful, demoralized the pauper, destroyed his will of self-support; that it eliminated the will to help in his relatives, friends, and neighbors; and that it failed to use the readiness of philanthropists to aid the poor. Chalmers, on the other hand, suggested the following procedure: (1) Each case of distress be carefully investigated, the cause of destitution determined, and the possibilities of self-maintenance of the pauper developed; (2) if self-support was not possible, relatives, friends, and neighbors be encouraged to care for orphans, the aged, the sick and handicapped; (3) if the need of the family could not thus be met, some wealthy citizens be found to maintain the family; (4) only if none of these measures succeeded, the deacon of the district should ask for the help of the congregation.

Chalmers' important contribution to the field of charity was his philosophy of personal, parochial relief. He developed the principle of investigating each case of destitution on an individual basis and of attempting a solution of the cause of distress. Chalmers, like his contemporaries, considered personal failures as the main cause of poverty and overlooked the economic and social factors outside the power of the individual. Nevertheless, his concept that a personal interest in the fate of the destitute is essential, was important to the progress of relief work. Fifty years after Chalmers' pioneer work, the London Charity Organization Society organized a program of relief that was, in the main, based upon Thomas Chalmers' ideas. They laid the first foundation for the individual approach in social work which today we call "case work."

IV. POOR LAW REFORM OF 1834

Severe opposition to the poor law practice, the rising flood of pauperism, and the heavy increase in the poor tax burden (which in 1818 had become six times the amount of the tax in 1760), led in February

1832 to the appointment of a "Royal Commission for Inquiring into the Administration and Practical Operation of the Poor Laws." Its chairman became Professor Nassau W. Senior, a noted economist, and its secretary, Edwin Chadwick, a brilliant young lawyer, who had studied under Jeremy Bentham. The Commission undertook for two years in every county of England an extensive survey of poor law administration and rendered its report in 1834. The report emphasized that the prevailing practice of poor relief had failed to bring children and able-bodied adults to work and had made them "permanent paupers" instead of self-supporting citizens, particularly through the introduction of "partial relief." Poor tax rates were used as subsidies to farmers, landlords, storekeepers, and manufacturers. The six main recommendations of the report were (a) to abolish "partial relief" as provided under the Speenhamland system; (b) to place all able-bodied applicants for relief in the workhouse; (c) to grant "outdoor relief" only to the sick, the old, the invalid, and to widows with young children; (d) to coordinate the administration of relief of several parishes into a "poor law union"; (e) to make the conditions of poor relief recipients less desirable than those of the lowest paid worker in the community: *Principle of "Less Eligibility"*; and (f) to establish a central board of control to be appointed by the King.

These recommendations were enacted August 14, 1834, a statute known in England for one hundred years as *The New Poor Law*.

"Poor Law Unions" were formed by neighboring parishes. They were administered by a Board of Guardians, composed of representatives of each parish with a paid staff, and managed a common workhouse and almshouse. In order to develop a uniform poor law policy, a Permanent Royal Poor Law Commission was appointed with three commissioners; Edwin Chadwick was its first secretary and George Coode, assistant secretary. Fifteen assistant commissioners visited poor law unions, attended meetings of the boards of guardians, and inspected workhouses and almshouses.

The application of the legal principle of less eligibility meant that poor relief was granted to the destitute in such a meager amount and in such a derogatory way that its receipt put the poor in a condition less desirable than that of the lowest paid laborer in the community. By maintaining this principle the boards of guardians thought to force relief applicants to accept any type of labor rather than asking for public support. This concept has persisted in public assistance in many parts of the world. The public is afraid that destitute persons would prefer to receive poor relief to exerting themselves in unpleasant manual work; the amount of assistance, therefore, should be less than the wage earned by a low-paid worker and should not provide a higher standard of living than can be earned by honest work. In fact, even today most public assistance payments are considerably lower than normal wages or income. But in cases of large families the maintenance of the children might require a higher amount than some underpaid workers earn, and here the old idea of "less eligibility" is a controversial issue up to today.

From the point of view of financial economy, the reform of 1834 was a success. It reduced the cost of poor relief between 1834 and 1837 by more than one-third; two hundred workhouses were constructed and old institutions improved. Able-bodied poor were forced to go to the workhouse with their families as a test of their economic need. No separate buildings for almshouses and workhouses were established, however, as had been recommended by the Commission in 1834. Old and young people, sturdy and ill, feeble-minded, insane, and cripples were placed into the same institution. Families were broken up, because women, young boys and girls, the aged, crippled, and infirm were assigned to separate wards of the workhouse. Mothers were permitted to care for their young children in the so-called "nursery" only at prescribed hours. Under a rigid discipline, inmates were forced to hard labor as much as their physical strength permitted and were treated not much differently than in a jail or prison. No wonder that the workhouse was very unpopular, hated by the working class. Disraeli said in a famous address that the reform bill of 1834 pronounced that to be poor in England was a crime.

The Reform of 1834 meant a resumption of the rigid, repressive measures of the Poor Law of 1601. They reduced the expenditures for poor relief, but they made relief in the workhouse so unbearable for the poor that the destitute would ask for relief only when there was no other way to survive. These methods also did not consider the danger of mass poverty in periods of unemployment and economic depression. Therefore some poor law unions introduced "a work test outside the workhouse," which permitted the poor to receive outdoor relief in their homes. In order to maintain uniform practices, the "Outdoor Relief Regulation Order" of 1852 upheld the principle of "less eligibility." It warned the poor law unions that relief recipients should not be given as much as the wage of the independent laborer. These measures were violently resented by the working class who called the workhouse the "bastille." The interest in the poor was awakened by humanitarians, such as Charles Dickens who published his "Oliver Twist" with its description of workhouse life in 1837 and 1838, and by members of Parliament who disliked the power entrusted to the poor law commissioners. The Poor Law Commission also had internal difficulties. Edwin Chadwick was an energetic, aggressive reformer, not content with the cautious actions of the commissioners. Chadwick's zeal for improving social and health conditions and his uncompromising character made work hard for the Commission. In 1847, the Commission was replaced by a *Poor Law Board* whose president had a seat in the House of Commons. The four other members of the Board were appointed by the Crown. Edwin Chadwick became General Commissioner of the Poor and supervised investigations into the causes of poverty and the means of an effective social reform.

Earlier surveys made by the poor law commissioners with the assistance of medical inspectors, especially Dr. Southwood Smith, had revealed that widespread prevalence of disease among the lower classes was a major cause of destitution. Disease deprived the laborer and his family of the means of livelihood and made them dependent upon public poor relief. Disease among the poor was caused mainly by unhealthy housing and living conditions and by malnutrition. In urban slums people lived in overcrowded quarters, and often adolescents and children of both sexes slept in one bed. This led to promiscuity, quarrels, delinquency, immorality, and rapid spread of contagious diseases. Many workingmen as boarders lived with families in the same room. Often seven to ten used one sleeping room, or lived in damp, dark cellars without any ventilation. All over England the poorer quarters were without water supply and drainage; drinking water was often polluted in rivers or deficient pipelines. There were usually no outside toilets and no sewers in the streets. The refuse was thrown into the public gutter, and there existed no scavenger service or regular street cleaning, although occasionally this was done by inmates of the workhouse. Another cause of epidemics was the long delay of the burial for deceased paupers, that is, until the poor law guardians assumed the cost of the funeral. The general practice of having cemeteries in the midst of cities resulted in further pollution of the water. The high window taxes prevented the slum owners from equipping tenements with windows and made ventilation impossible.

On the initiative of Edwin Chadwick the Poor Law Board brought these conditions to the attention of Parliament. Chadwick thus became the first pioneer of public hygiene. He developed a program of protection against contagious diseases by sanitary provisions for water systems, sewage, and drainage. He also advocated the establishment of parks and flower gardens for the recreation of the population. Due to his insistence, free public vaccination against cholera, typhus, and smallpox was introduced in 1840. The *Public Health Act* of August 31, 1848, established a General Board of Health, and Edwin Chadwick served as one of its members. The Board supported local authorities in the fight against epidemics, in the improvement of housing conditions in the slums, and in the establishment of sanitation. In spite of his devoted service, Edwin Chadwick again found severe opposition. After six years he was dismissed because the House of Commons felt that he entrusted too much power to a central health authority, and because the physicians complained that "he infringed upon vested interests of the medical profession."[9] Undertakers and water-supply companies also complained that their profits were curtailed by the regulations of the Board of Health.

Chadwick was a prophet far ahead of his contemporaries. It took many decades until his vision of a system of government providing under central direction decent aid to the poor, a sound public health protection, adequate housing, recreation, and public schools for the entire population became an accepted concept of society.

V. CHILD LABOR AND FACTORY LEGISLATION

Until the beginning of the nineteenth century, social policy in England had been used to suppress the laboring classes in the in-

[9] Frank Bruno, *Trends in Social Work* (New York: Columbia University Press, 1948), p. 249. See also, J. L. Hammond and Barbara Hammond, *Lord Shaftesbury* (London: Longmans, 1923), pp. 166-167; Dorsey D. Jones, *Edwin Chadwick and the Early Public Health Movement in England* (University of Iowa Studies, Vol. IX, No. 3), 1931, pp. 126-130; and S. E. Finer, *The Life and Times of Sir Edwin Chadwick* (London: Methuen, 1952), pp. 453-474.

terest of the land owners, the manufacturers, and the merchants. Pauper children were set to work by "selling" them to farmers, by indenture to craftsmen, or by hard labor in almshouses. The development of the textile mills in the nineteenth century, however, offered an unprecedented opportunity to use the poorhouse children. They were offered to textile manufacturers as cheap labor. The fate of these children became deplorable. Some were as young as four, five, or six years of age, and there was no legal limitation of their working hours. So-called "slappers" held them awake by whipping them when they fell asleep. A typical day of such a poor child leased out to a textile mill was as follows:[10] The children got up at four to five in the morning. The younger ones had to pick up cotton waste from the factory floor all day. Children of six or seven years were put to the spinning wheel or to the loom where their small, deft, flexible fingers could throw the thread quicker than adults. The children usually had half an hour for a frugal breakfast and an hour for a lunch of similar quality. During working hours they had to stand and were not allowed to leave their work place, outside of the meals, to go to the toilet or to get a drink of water. The latter was strictly prohibited, and if it did occur, the hapless child was brutally punished by whipping. As a rule, the child's labor was completed after five or six in the evening, often hours later, so that the working day was sometimes sixteen to eighteen hours long. The lack of sleep, of fresh air and sunshine, of rest and of any vacation made many of these children undernourished, weak, and sick. Many died in their teens, when they had worked themselves to death.

The first step in the direction of their protection was taken by the *Health and Morals Act* of 1802, passed on the initiative of Sir Robert Peel, who objected to the use of young poor children in labor camps at the textile mills. The statute of 1802 restricted the working hours of "pauper apprentices"[11] to twelve hours a day, between 6 A.M. and 9 P.M., and forbade night work for children. The law applied, however, only to pauper children leased out from the poor houses. Cotton mill owners, however, hired children directly from their parents and continued to exploit them without any limit of working hours.

[10] Grace Abbott, *The Child and the State* (Chicago: University of Chicago Press, 1938), Vol. I, pp. 138-152.

[11] Some boards of guardians went even as far as to pay the mill owners an additional sum from the poor tax rate because these "apprentices" presumably were taught spinning and weaving.

Concerned about these conditions, Sir Robert Peel, Robert Owen, John Wood, and John Fielden pursued the demand for a protection of working children against mistreatment and overwork which was so destructive to their health. In 1819, they succeeded in obtaining an amendment that forbade the employment of children under nine years of age, and restricted to twelve hours the daily working hours of children under sixteen years. It covered, however, only the cotton industry, not the other trades. In Parliament Michael Sadler, Anthony Ashley Cooper (later the Earl of Shaftesbury), R. Cobden, and James Graham became the advocates of child labor legislation. This movement led to the enactment of the *Factory Act of 1833*, which prohibited the employment of children under nine in the textile industry and limited daily working hours to nine hours for children up to thirteen years, and to forty-eight hours during a week. At the suggestion of Edwin Chadwick the law introduced the appointment of factory inspectors under a central, national office. An amendment of the *Factory Act of 1847* ordered a daily maximum of ten working hours for women and children under eighteen years. This endeavor to protect children against overwork and health damage prepared the way for general social legislation, the aim of which was to safeguard the working class. It also attempted health protection through sanitation, low rent housing projects, and the provision of general education for children.

The industrial development of England and the economic crises which accompanied the introduction of modern machinery led to several periods of unemployment and distress. Local boards of guardians were forced to borrow money in order to maintain the workhouses or to provide public works in times of widespread unemployment. Even so, the conditions in numerous workhouses were unbearable. These conditions were exposed by officials of the Poor Law Board, particularly by Louisa Twinning (a field inspector) and by Dr. Joseph Rogers (a medical officer). Their findings revealed that most workhouses had inadequate sanitary facilities, poor ventilation, and lack of medical and nursing care for the sick and the aged. The beds were so short that inmates were unable to sleep well. Above all, superintendents and attendants were, as a rule, ignorant and callous people. Legislative reforms led to an expansion of the supervisory powers of the Poor Law Board. In 1871, the Local Government Board was founded, and took over the functions of the Board of

Health and of the Poor Law Board. The new board maintained the policy of advocating the workhouse test and of warning the boards of guardians against a liberal granting of outdoor relief. The Local Government Board failed to recognize that such stern treatment usually fell upon broken down, depressed, and feeble persons who could not obtain employment and needed encouragement and help for their rehabilitation.

<h3 style="text-align:center">VI. PRISON REFORM</h3>

Since the Middle Ages prisons had been the place of severe human suffering. The medieval dungeons, often situated without light and air in the deep, humid cellars of old castles, were not much different from the prisons used during the seventeenth to the nineteenth century. The convicts suffered from hunger and cold, neglect and brutal beatings. Queen Elizabeth's Poor Law of 1601 ordered that the county had to pay 20 shilling a year for the maintenance of a prisoner. However, this provision was never carried into effect since the county treasurers were anxious not to waste money for "wretched criminals."

The prison population did consist not only of offenders convicted for crime but included numerous persons who could not pay their civil debts. Nevertheless, all inmates were forced to pay the jailer for their upkeep since he and his assistants lived off the money they extorted from the prisoners and their families and friends. Since the seventeenth century some charitable donations and bequests provided prisoners in certain jails with bread, beef, and broth on Sundays and holidays, but these small favors did not change the miserable conditions in the prisons and on the floating jail-hulks on the Thames.

In 1681, Thomas Firmin began to free hundreds of unfortunate debtors from prison by paying their small debts and the jailers' fees, and other philanthropists followed his example. In 1700, a meeting of the Society for Promoting Christian Knowledge advocated that jailers found guilty of extortion and mistreatment should be dismissed, although they had bought the management from the authorities.

The demand for a reform of the prisons was rising throughout the eighteenth century. Among the early reformers who became deeply concerned about the inhuman treatment of the victims of penal

institutions was General Oglethorpe. One of his friends, young archi-
tect Castell, had been imprisoned for debt in the London Fleet
prison, in 1728; after he was forced to spend all his money for his upkeep, he was sent to the "sponging house" in spite of his plea that
he would die there because it was infected with smallpox. His fear
proved justified because he contracted the disease and died. The
House of Commons appointed a committee of inquiry with Oglethorpe as chairman. The investigations led at least to some improvements, especially the prohibition of sale of liquors in prisons and
houses of correction.

The work of prison reform found its strongest advocate in another
philanthropist, John Howard. He was born 1726 as son of a well-
to-do London tradesman, lost his mother early, and was educated as
a Calvinist dissenter. He was of delicate health, a quiet, self-enclosed,
deeply religious young man without ambitions for honors and conformity. The death of his father left him at the age of sixteen heir
to a considerable fortune. He traveled through France and Italy and
became interested in the relief of the people of Lisbon, which had
been destroyed in the earthquake of 1855. He decided to investigate
the conditions in Lisbon in order to organize a relief action. The
ship on which he was sailing was captured by a privateer, and together with other passengers and the crew he was brought to Brest
and confined to a filthy, dark dungeon as a prisoner of war. During
the following months Howard and his companions were dragged
through several other prisons along the French coast, and he discovered that everywhere the conditions were the same—unhealthy,
cold quarters (without light and air), insufficient food, no bedding, no blankets, and brutal treatment. Howard finally succeeded
in being released under his pledge to find an exchange in England.
There he began telling of his horrible adversities and procuring help
for prisoners of war. This experience became the root of Howard's
life work for prison reform. During the following decade, he improved housing conditions of his tenants, on his estate, whom he
encouraged by low rent and active support in the reconstruction of
their homes, in the education of their children, and in church and
recreational activities. After making studies of prisons in France,
Italy, Switzerland, and Holland, Howard was nominated Sheriff of
Bedford, in 1773, at the age of forty-six. In general the office was a
post of honor, but Howard took his assignment seriously and de-

voted his time fully to its duties. He sat in the courts during the trials and visited all prisoners in the jails of the county. His conscience was aroused when defendants accused of crimes, but not found guilty, were often dragged back to jail, after already having suffered months of unjust imprisonment before trial because they could not pay the fees to the jailer. In surrounding counties, John Howard found the same conditions of prisons that had shocked him when he was incarcerated in France. Debtors who could not pay their debts were treated like felons who had committed serious crimes, and men were hanged as certainly for stealing a pair of shoes as for arson or murder. The job of feeding the prisoners was farmed out to the highest bidder. Tap selling of beer and liquor induced the jail-keeper to encourage drunkenness and orgies under his eyes. Because no separation between the sexes was properly secured, temptation and vice were the consequence. The prisoners were kept in idleness, whereas Howard had observed that in continental countries the prison inmates were put to work. The jailers and their helpers were coarse and ignorant men, selected for their brutality and insensibility to human suffering. The decayed, insecure buildings led to the use of irons, clubs, and whipping to prevent escape.

Many prisons had no water supply, and the excrements of a large mass of prisoners accumulated in heaps of poisonous feculence within the precincts. The prisoners were forced to sleep upon muddy floors and a rotten mass of litter in their cells while the stench of the manure oozed into them. No wonder that prisoners died from cold and from the "gaol-fever." No ventilation nor light was available in the overcrowded cells. The prisoners did not receive religious or moral comfort, since most of the prison chaplains were rough, idle men who preferred to drink and gamble with the debtors. They spent little time during their rare visits to the jail in gabbling a short prayer among the felons. These were the conditions which John Howard found on his visits to many jails in England. His sense of justice was aroused, and he recorded his distressing observations with the conclusion that a more searching investigation was necessary. In his travels, Howard did not overlook any jail, bridewell, sponging-house, or other place of detention. In the House of Commons, John Howard was invited to speak as an expert on prison questions. He continued his studies on travels to the European continent and published, in 1777, his work, *On the State of the Prisons in England and Wales, with Preliminary*

Observations and an Account of Some Foreign Prisons and Hospitals, written with the aid of his friend Reverend Densham and of a Dr. Price. The book was received with unusual interest by the public and was highly praised because of its revelation of the horror, cruelty, and inefficiency of the prisons. Although it led to improvements in English prisons, to better food and ventilation, to the cleaning of cells, to the supply of bedding and blankets, and to medical care in cases of "gaol-fever," John Howard was not satisfied, so he continued his travels to the European countries and the Near East in order to help other countries in prison reform. On such a journey he died in Russia, in 1789.

Another pioneer in prison reform was Elizabeth Fry (1780-1845). As a Quaker she followed her religious inspiration to visit the infamous Newgate prison, known as "hell upon earth." Using the influence of her wealthy banker husband, she succeeded in starting a school for the children in the prison and in employing one of the women convicts as teacher. She then introduced, for the adult women, knitting and lace embroidery work, which improved their morale and created new hope in their lives. Her interest in the personal fate of the inmates brought a new spirit of order, industry, and religion into their habits. Her methods inspired other philanthropists to make similar attempts in other penal institutions in England.

Despite some improvements brought about by the reformers, jails and prisons remained backward in England as long as they were under local administration. It was not until 1877, when the *Prison Act* transferred the administration of penal institutions to a central organization—the National Prison Commission—that reform of the entire correctional system started. Until this time most jails and prisons did not separate young offenders from hardened criminals but operated as "schools of vice" where the youngsters as novices were introduced into the skills of crime. The lack of segregation and of protection by the jailers had often calloused the young delinquent against the feeling of responsibility for his fellow men, while his greed for money and his drives for violence and lust were developed. In 1894, a parliamentary committee investigated the penal institutions and requested the separation of young offenders from older convicts, and their special treatment with vocational training. One of the committee members, Sir Evelyn Ruggles-

Brise, visited the United States, in 1897, and studied the youth reformatory at Elmira, New York. Stimulated by his observations, the first separate institution for the treatment of young delinquents in England was established at the Rochester Prison near Borstal. From this school, the entire new program of special correction of young offenders received the name "Borstal System." Volunteers were enlisted for the supervision of youngsters after they had been released from the school and placed in families.

For a long time, the Courts of Chancery in England had jurisdiction of neglected and dependent children. In criminal cases, however, children over seven years of age were treated as adults. The first legal protection for delinquent children was created by the *Juvenile Offenders Act of 1847*, which limited the criminal persecution of children under fourteen years of age and of adolescents under sixteen years to specific cases of crime. Special children's courts which replaced the criminal courts were introduced in England only in 1912, after the previous experience of juvenile courts in the United States had been studied.

VII. SOCIAL REFORM AND CHARITY ORGANIZATION

Three main factors influenced the social philosophy and practice of poor relief in England during the nineteenth century: the social reform movements, the Charity Organization Societies, and methods of social research. These three developments were possible through the initiative of individuals deeply devoted to philanthropy and human progress.

A. SOCIAL REFORM

The most important elements in the development of social reform caused by the rapid industrialization of England were the Chartist, Christian Socialist, and the trade union movements.

At the turn of the century, the *Combination Laws of 1799 and 1800* prohibited workers under the threat of severe penalties from forming trade unions in order to obtain higher wages or better working conditions. It was not until 1824 that on the initiative of Francis Place this legislation was repealed. Even with this advance, however, political discrimination against the working class remained effective. Laborers were excluded from suffrage when this civic privilege, in 1832, was extended to the middle class and the professions. The Chartist movement, beginning in the 1830's as the political voice of labor, attempted to obtain suffrage and secret vote by ballot for all citizens, but it failed in spite of riots and petitions to Parliament with millions of signatures. Thereafter, the disappointed workers turned their interest from political aims to more practical methods of improving their economic conditions. In 1844, the Chartists opened the first cooperative store owned by the workers themselves at Rochdale. The example for consumers' cooperatives had been presented by the philanthropist Robert Owen in his textile mills at New Lanark. Owen started his career as a poor boy, but gained a large fortune as a manufacturer in the textile industry. He recognized that decent wages and sanitary working conditions attracted the best workers and made the industry profitable. He established a model industrial community, providing low cost, healthy housing with gardens, sanitation, and playgrounds; cooperative stores selling at cost; and a library and recreation facilities for workers and their families. Several other manufacturers in various parts of England followed the example of Robert Owen.

Another approach for the improvement of social conditions of the workers was taken when trade unions began to organize mutual benefit plans for their members, providing aid in case of sickness, accidents, unemployment, invalidity, and old age. The success of cooperative and mutual aid enterprises led to the establishment of the Trades Union Congress as a national federation. Under the leadership of Richard Cobden and John Bright the congress campaigned for the extension of suffrage to laborers, which was granted to urban workers by parliament through the *Reform Bill of 1867*. After the first trade union representatives had been elected to the House of Commons in 1874, agricultural workers, rural householders, and miners were enfranchised in 1884. An amendment to the poor law of 1894 made elective officers the members of the boards of guardians, which administered poor relief. Women as well as labor representatives became eligible for membership. The influence of the social reform movement freed workers from the continuous threat of destitution, and the trade union movement made labor a new participating force in government, rather than a mere object of pity and poor relief.

In regard to poor law practice, another element that influenced public opinion was the movement of the Christian Socialists. After the collapse of the Chartists, in 1848, a group of religious and intellectual reformers under the guidance of Frederick Denison Maurice, Charles Kingley, and J. M. Ludlow pursued the idea of improving social conditions of the working class through education and spiritual development of the workers. They appealed to the church to assist the masses in their desire for cultural and social emancipation. The Christian Socialists sponsored cooperative associations among the workers of various industries, and they developed night classes for adult education for which they found idealistic teachers among clergymen and university faculties. The Christian Socialist movement laid the groundwork for a sympathetic understanding between labor and the church, which is still characteristic of England. The "Working Men's College" in East London, founded by F. D. Maurice in 1854, was the most famous of these adult schools.

British socialism had its roots in the ideas of the social reformers, particularly those of Robert Owen. In addition to his work in connection with his own factories, Owen had conceived a general plan to establish cooperative rural communities in which agricultural and industrial products would be exchanged to make their population self-supporting. He proposed that educational and cultural facilities be included in such an organization. Robert Owen appealed to his friends and other wealthy citizens to assist the working class in its attempt to gain self-respect, education and independence. The socialist philosophy contained in his thinking was further developed by Karl Marx and Friedrich Engels, who lived in exile in England. Marx's influence as a theoretical philosopher was profound, but his political and economic ideas were not widely accepted among British labor. Of the groups interested in social reform, the most influential became the Fabian Society, which was founded in 1883. Among its leading members were Bernard Shaw, Sidney and Beatrice Webb, Sidney Olivier, and Graham Wallas. The Fabians did not, in contrast to Marx's philosophy, advocate a revolutionary socialist action in order to achieve a classless society; they rather embarked upon practical reforms, such as women's suffrage, wage and hours legislation, housing projects, and educational reforms. Their influence upon the practice and legal background of poor relief was, however, delayed until the social legislation at the beginning of the twentieth century accepted their basic concepts.

B. HOUSING REFORM

Since the beginning of the nineteenth century, the expanding industries had attracted hundreds of thousands of workers and their families from the villages to the towns. It was obvious that this rapidly growing urban population could not be easily housed in the cities unless construction was stepped up to increase the housing facilities available to the industrial workers. Several philanthropists exposed the serious danger to the health and morale of the working class from unsatisfactory housing conditions. Old mansions left by wealthy owners of mills and factories were split up into tenements with small apartments or single rooms for the workers' families. Near the mills, gardens and open spaces were quickly filled with shoddy constructions, erected without regard to lack of sanitation, ventilation, or security against fire hazards. In order to make the maximum of profits, the builders in new industrial areas were bent on squeezing the largest possible number of dwellings on to every acre of land. In contrast to this general practice, a few model cottages were established by some philanthropic employers. At their initiative, the Metropolitan Association for Improving the Dwellings of the Industrious Classes was founded in 1842, in London. Following suggestions of Edwin Chadwick, several cities enforced the clearance of the worst slums in order to avoid the grave danger of cholera and typhus. The interest of the public in housing reform was aroused by the writings of John Stuart Mill, Thomas Carlyle, John Ruskin, and Charles Dickens who were concerned about the poverty and degradation of the working masses. Thus Parliament also became aware of the need of social reform.

Outstanding in the fight against unhealthy housing and the exploitation of the workers in the slum tenements was Octavia Hill, an admirer of John Frederick Denison Maurice and a member of the Christian Socialists. With the help of her friend, the philosopher John Ruskin, Octavia Hill started, in 1864, a philanthropic project of rebuilding slum tenements in London. She changed them into sanitary, decent living quarters and rented them at low prices to working families who could not afford to pay higher rents. In this project she enlisted a number of ladies as volunteers, who collected the monthly rent from the residents, and, at the same time, advised the families in economic home management and sound leisure time activities. Octavia Hill was convinced that the personal influence of these volunteer rent collectors encouraged the workers and their families to better training, to self-respect, and to an education of their children which would secure them the skills of higher paid trades and regular jobs. In 1865, Octavia Hill was also one of the founders of the Commons Society in London, which began to build recreational facilities, parks, and gardens in various districts of London.[12]

C. THE CHARITY ORGANIZATION SOCIETY

The Poor Law Reform of 1834 had reduced the cost of poor relief and had led to a more efficient relief administration, but it did not stem the widening gulf between the growing wealth of the manufacturers and mill owners and the severe pauperization of the steadily increasing masses of industrial workers. Philanthropists became concerned in saving either individuals whom they personally knew or certain groups of the poor, such as the children, and the blind, lame, or crippled people, from the degradation and cruel treatment of the mixed almshouse.

In periods of economic crises and unemployment public concern became particularly strong, and many charitable societies with various purposes were endowed and organized. In newspapers donations for the poor were solicited, and a large number of philanthropic agencies were established. In the 1860's several business crises occurred, and the importance of private charities was now felt in the entire population. In London almost all churches and about one hundred charitable agencies distributed alms in money, food, clothes, and fuel tickets. Private charity societies began to face the usual criticism of waste of money and that by their alms and gifts they induced people to become beggars. The societies were accused of discouraging the poor to make an effort toward supporting themselves, which Thomas Chalmers had emphasized as the first step needed in their rehabilitation. Private charities still considered poverty as a personal fault of the poor, just as did the boards of guardians in public relief.

[12] Lord William Beveridge, *Voluntary Action* (London: G. Allen, 1949), p. 133.

In order to overcome the chaos and lack of coordination between the many charitable church groups and philanthropic societies, the Reverend Henry Solly recommended, in 1868, establishing a board coordinating the activities of private and public charities. In 1869 the Society for Organizing Charitable Relief and Repressing Mendicity was founded in London, to be renamed soon after the Charity Organization Society, (frequently abbreviated, C.O.S.).[13] The leading spirit of the Society was Sir Charles Stewart Loch, who served from 1875 to 1915 as its secretary. Among other well-known members of the Society were the Reverend Richard Green, Edward Denison, Octavia Hill, and the Reverend Samuel Barnett. In its principles the Charity Organization Society was guided by the theories of Thomas Chalmers. The Society accepted Chalmers' idea that the individual was responsible for his poverty and that acceptance of public relief destroyed the self-respect of the pauper and led him to subsist on alms. The Society also followed Chalmers' thought that the pauper be asked to exert all his abilities for maintaining himself. To carry out these principles, the Charity Organization Society set up an inquiry department where the poor law guardians, charity societies, and individual philanthropists were given information about an applicant for relief. This innovation caused the unmasking of many "professional beggars" and people who received aid from several relief agencies. The Charity Organization Society used the German method of the "Elberfeld System." It divided the city into small districts, each of which was administered for relief distribution by a group of citizens serving as volunteer commission. Great confidence was bestowed upon the activities of well-to-do volunteers, who would take a strong personal interest in the poor families assigned to them. They were to assist the families with money, clothes, and food, but the main emphasis was placed on their moral influence that would change the way of life of the poor. In larger districts, the direction of the work of these volunteers was entrusted to a paid "agent" of the Charity Organization Society.

The Society was opposed to an extension of public poor relief and supported the tendency among its members to reduce government expenditures for the poor. It encouraged, on the other hand,

[13] Lord W. Beveridge, *op. cit.*, pp. 143-149; and K. de Schweinitz, *op. cit.*, pp. 147-150.

the growth of private charities, the giving of donations and bequests in their behalf, and the initiative among the volunteers for bringing individual aid to families in distress.

The example of the London Charity Organization Society of 1869 was followed in other large cities in England and Scotland,[14] and nine years after the foundation of the Society in London, this movement reached the United States. It developed cooperation between poor relief and private charities and succeeded in the elimination of some fraudulent setups. It prevented duplication of support, and strengthened the concept of rehabilitation of the poor. The value of prevention of pauperism and the need for a careful administration of private as well as public relief funds were emphasized.

D. THE SETTLEMENT HOUSE

Among the active members of the Christian Socialists, Edward Denison took a new approach in the endeavor to help the underprivileged toward education. As a volunteer of the Society for the Relief of Distress in London, in 1867, he became convinced that the mere distribution of alms was futile. He abandoned his comfortable life and moved to Stepney, a poor quarter in East London, in order to live with the people in this slum district. There Denison taught Bible classes, history, and economics. The inhabitants of Stepney found him reluctant to give them the customary meat and coal tickets unless he was certain they were in dire need, but he was generous with time spent in listening to their personal problems and offered his counsel when he felt they were oppressed.

The idea of living among the people who needed help was most effectively demonstrated by Canon Samuel Augustus Barnett. Born in Bristol, 1844, he had studied theology at Oxford and accepted in 1873, the post of Vicar of St. Jude's Church in Whitechapel in East London, one of the poorest parishes in the diocese. Barnett was encouraged by his fiancee, Henrietta Rowland, who had worked under Octavia Hill. After their marriage Henrietta became her husband's co-worker. In Whitechapel the Barnetts found a great proportion of the 8,000 parishioners unemployed or sick, and living

---

[14] Since 1873, all charities in Liverpool presented their claims for support on one sheet and made their collections through one office (*The Survey Midmonthly*, June, 1948, p. 181).

in filthy, overcrowded tenements. Colleges in Oxford and Cambridge had inquired from Barnett whether students interested in social studies could do something to help the poor. The Barnetts went to Oxford and Cambridge and discussed with university students the conditions they had encountered in St. Jude's. They invited them to come to live with them in Whitechapel in order to study the life of the underprivileged, to help in their education, and to render personal aid. Among those who followed Vicar Barnett's invitation was Arnold Toynbee, an enthusiastic and gifted young Oxford graduate. He was outstanding among his colleagues by his devotion and by the warm, personal contact he had established with the families of the parish. Unfortunately he was of poor health, contracted tuberculosis, and died in 1883, before reaching his thirtieth birthday. In his memory, a number of his friends built, in 1884, a university settlement in the Whitechapel district and called it "Toynbee Hall." It was the first settlement house in the world.

Canon Barnett was elected the first warden of the settlement house. Toynbee Hall had three main objectives: (1) education and cultural development of the poor, (2) information for the students and other residents of the settlement regarding the conditions of the poor and the urgent need for social reforms, and (3) a general awakening of popular interest in social and health problems and in social legislation. The basic purpose of the settlement was the contact of educated men and women with the poor for their mutual benefit, so that by common work and studies they could exercise a cultural influence beyond the teaching of special subjects. The settlement offered not just classes for children and adults. Toynbee Hall brought to the people in this quarter heretofore inaccessible educational opportunities. The attitude of a superior "lady bountiful" which still prevailed in charity societies was replaced with honest cooperation and learning on the part of both instructors and workers attending lectures and discussion groups.

E. SOCIAL RESEARCH

Social research was a third important factor that influenced the social philosophy and the practice of poor relief in England. The first of a long series of social studies was undertaken by Edwin

Chadwick when he was secretary of the Poor Law Commissioners; it dealt with health and sanitary conditions of the working classes. The report was published in 1842, and became the start of the public health movement. Another stimulus to public concern and philanthropic endeavor was found in the articles of Henry Mayhew on "London Labour and the London Poor," published in 1849 in the London *Morning Chronicle*. These articles made a deep impression on people like Octavia Hill and awakened their social conscience, and contributed to the rise of the movement of the Christian Socialists. The most important social survey, however, was made by a wealthy businessman, Charles Booth. He hired, in 1886, a staff of interviewers and conducted the research as his private enterprise. The study investigated people by trades, their living and labor conditions, working hours and wages, and unemployment. Booth was determined to get the true facts, and his staff worked systematically and with precision. The study was not limited to destitute people. It covered thousands of employed workers' families. The results of Booth's study, which was published yearly, showed that one-third of the London population was living on, or below, the "poverty line." The findings of Booth's studies disproved the previous theory of poverty always being the fault of the individual. They also showed that the deterrent features of the poor laws were no solution, and that human suffering from destitution was often created by insufficient wages, environment, inadequate housing, and unhealthy sanitary equipment. The results of this research were supported by another study, *Poverty, A Study of Town Life*, conducted by R. Seebohm Rowntree in the city of York and published in 1901. It revealed that in the small city of York 27.84 per cent of the entire population were living in poverty. Through these findings of social research the necessity of introducing more effective measures of social reform became evident.

SELECTED BIBLIOGRAPHY

*Abbott, Grace, *The Child and the State*. Chicago: The University of Chicago Press, 1938.

Aschrott, P. F., *The English Poor Law System*. London: Knight & Co., 1888.

Barnett, Henrietta O., *Canon Barnett, His Life, Work, and Friends*. London: J. Murray, 1918 and 1921.

Bell, E. Moberly, *The Life of Octavia Hill*. London: Constable, 1938.

Bellows, Reverend H. W., *John Howard, His Life, Character and Service* (with a Foreword by Joseph E. Ragen). Chicago: John Howard Association, 1948.

Booth, Charles, *Life and Labour of the People of London* (10 vols). Longmans, 1900-1911.

Bosanquet, Helen, *Social Work in London, 1869-1912*. London: J. Murray, 1914.

Chalmers, Thomas, *The Christian and Civic Economy of Large Towns* (abridged and edited by Charles R. Henderson). New York: Scribner, 1900.

*de Schweinitz, Karl, *England's Road to Social Security, 1349-1947*, 3rd rev. ed. Philadelphia: University of Pennsylvania Press, 1947.

Finer, S. E., *The Life and Times of Sir Edwin Chadwick*, London: Methuen, 1952.

Gray, B. Kirkman, *A History of English Philanthropy: From the Dissolution of the Monasteries to the Taking of the First Census*, 2nd ed. London: P. S. King & Son, 1905.

Hammond, J. L., and Barbara Hammond, *The Village Labourer, 1760-1832*. London: Longmans, 1912.

Hill, Octavia, *Homes of the London Poor*. London: Macmillan, 1883.

———, *Our Common Land and Other Short Essays*. London: Macmillan, 1877.

Hovell, Mark, *The Chartist Movement*. Manchester, England: The University Press, 1925.

Jones, Dorsey D., *Edwin Chadwick and the Early Public Health Movement in England*. Iowa City: University of Iowa Studies in the Social Sciences, Vol. IX, No. 3, 1931.

Loch, Sir Charles S., *Charity and Social Life: A Short Study of Religious and Social Thought in Relation to Charitable Methods and Institutions*. London: Macmillan, 1910.

———, *Charity Organization*. London: Sonnenschein, 1890.

Pimlott, John A. R., *Toynbee Hall, Fifty Years of Social Progress, 1884-1934*. London: Dent, 1935.

*Queen, Stuart A., *Social Work in the Light of History*. Philadelphia: Lippincott, 1922.

Rowntree, B. Seebohm, *Poverty, A Study of Town Life*. London: Macmillan, 1903.

Slater, Gilbert, *Poverty and the State*. New York: Richard R. Smith, 1930.

Smith, Adam, *An Inquiry into the Nature and Causes of Wealth of Nations* (2 vols.). London: Strahan & Cadell, 1776.

Traill, H. D., *Social England*. London: Cassell, 1897.

Warner, Amos G., *American Charities*, 3rd ed. New York: Crowell, 1919.

Watt, Hugh, *Thomas Chalmers and the Disruption*, 2nd rev. ed. Edinburgh: Nelson, 1943.

Webb, Beatrice, *My Apprenticeship*. London: Longmans, 1926.

Webb, Sydney, and Beatrice Webb, *English Local Government: English Poor Law History*. Part I, The Old Poor Law, 1927; Part II, The Last Hundred Years, 1929. London: Longmans.

Whitney, Janet, *Elizabeth Fry, Quaker Heroine*. London: Harrap, 1937.

3. British Social Security in the Twentieth Century

I. THE POOR LAW COMMISSION OF 1905

At the beginning of the twentieth century the people of England faced the grave threat of unemployment. It was most serious in the coal mining regions. Due to technical superiority of the United States mines and more favorable production and transportation conditions in the European continental coal industries, a number of British mines were unable to compete and were forced to discontinue operations. Others needed fewer workers, and some closed because their coal supply was exhausted. When masses of unemployed coal miners and their families asked for relief, it was not possible to put entire communities into the workhouse, as required by the Poor Law of 1834. Some mining towns applied to Parliament for aid. Private charities found themselves unable to meet the needs of tens of thousands of jobless families for unlimited periods, and national emergency funds had to be appropriated. The Liberal Party, in 1905, promised a reform of the poor laws and aid to the unemployed. After its victory the new government embarked upon a policy of social reform. On the day when the Tory government resigned, December 4, 1905, a "Royal Commission on the Poor Laws and Relief of Distress," with Lord George Hamilton as chairman, was appointed. Among its eighteen members were Sir Charles Loch, Octavia Hill, and Helen Bosanquet, but only four composed an aggressive, able minority: Mrs. Beatrice Webb (representing the Fabian Society), George Lansbury (Trade Unions and Labour Party), Francis Chandler (Trade Unions), and the Reverend Prebendary, later Bishop H. Russell Wakefield. In press discussions, the meetings of the Commission were cited as "The Webbs

Against the Poor Law." Beatrice Webb was morally supported by her husband although he was not a member of the Commission.

Sidney Webb's father had served on one of the London boards of guardians, and his son inherited from him a concern for the fate of the workers and the poor. From the time he was sixteen years of age, Sidney Webb worked for a living. He became an official with the London City Council and accepted the role of economic analyst[1] with the Fabian Society. In 1890 he wrote his treatise on the reform of the poor law. His wife, Beatrice Potter Webb, came from a wealthy London business family. During her studies she became interested in social problems from the viewpoint of economic and political theory. After serving some time as a visitor for a district committee of the London Charity Organization Society and as a rent collector in a philanthropic housing project, she assisted Charles Booth as an investigator in his study on the conditions of workers at the docks and in the "sweat" industries of London. In 1890, she undertook on her own a study of the cooperative movement and, during its preparation, met Sidney Webb, who advised her in this research. After the completion of the work, they decided to study together the trade union movement; they were married in 1892. Together they completed many studies in the field of labor conditions, economics, political science, and social legislation.

Beatrice Webb insisted upon a critical investigation of the poor law philosophy and its results. The extent of economic distress which the investigation revealed was appalling. The official statistics showed that 928,621 persons were receiving public relief, among them 300,-000 children living under most unfavorable conditions.

The Poor Law Commission agreed upon the following recommendations: (1) poor law unions and boards of guardians should be replaced by county councils, reducing the number of local relief administrations by three-quarters; (2) the punitive character of poor relief should be abolished in favor of a humane public assistance program; (3) mixed almshouses should be abolished, mentally deficient and mentally ill patients should be treated in hospitals, and children placed in foster homes or residential schools; and (4) national pensions for the aged, free hospital treatment for the poor, gratuitous public employment services, and a program of so-

[1] See Chapter 2.

cial insurance with unemployment and invalidity benefits should be introduced.

However there were fundamental differences of opinion between the majority and minority of the Commission. The majority wanted a mild reform of the old poor law and advocated close cooperation with private charities. The minority demanded the abolition of the poor law.

As a result of the work of the Commission the way for fundamental progress in social legislation was opened. Sidney and Beatrice Webb founded a "Committee for the Prevention of Destitution," which worked with the trade unions for social reform.

Already during the sessions of the Royal Commission social legislation had started. The *Provision of Meals Act of 1906* organized free school lunches in the elementary schools; the *Education Act of 1907* provided medical examinations of school children; the *Old Age Pensions Act of 1908* secured a weekly pension of five shillings for deserving poor persons over seventy years of age. The pension was thought of as a reward for virtuous living, not as the care of the community for its enfeebled citizens. Disqualified were persons who had been loath to work, had not supported their families, lived in almshouses, or had criminal records within the last ten years. If an applicant had been convicted of habitual drunkenness, the court decided whether or not he should receive the pension. Only after World War I, in 1919, disqualifications for moral reasons were eliminated.

A. EMPLOYMENT SERVICES AND SOCIAL INSURANCE

Large-scale unemployment forced Parliament to pass the *Unemployed Workmen Act of 1905*. For unemployed workers it provided relief administered by local distress committees which tried to find jobs for them. Following the proposal of the Royal Commission of 1909, the *Labor Exchange Act* of September 20, 1909 empowered the Board of Trade (comparable to the Department of Commerce in the United States) to set up labor exchanges (employment services) in order to bring employers and workers together. The labor exchanges helped employers find competent workers, helped workers find jobs, and increased the mobility of labor.

In the field of *social insurance legislation*, the urgent need for protection of injured workers led in 1897, to the enactment of the *Workmen's Compensation Act*.[2] Earlier legislation, the *Fatal Accidents Act of 1846* and the *Employers' Liability Act of 1880*, had proved insufficient to help the injured worker and his family. The statute of 1897 recognized the principle of family protection and established the legal right of compensation for the injured worker independent upon any fault of the employer or his crew. No machinery for public administration, however, was provided. The injured workers and the widows and orphans of those killed in industrial accidents were forced to sue the employer before the courts. This led to long delays and high expenses, which the workers could not afford, or to agreements which deprived the injured worker or his survivors of most of his compensation.

During the investigations of the Royal Commission of 1905, the vital need of protection of the workers in periods of unemployment proved to be the most urgent problem. The report of 1909, therefore, proposed the setup of a system of compulsory unemployment insurance. On a visit to the European continent, in 1908, David Lloyd George was impressed with the operation of the German sickness insurance plan, so Parliament proposed national insurance with unemployment and health benefits. This twofold program was enacted by the *National Insurance Act* of December 16, 1911. The bill had been prepared under the direction of Winston Churchill, with the assistance of Sir Hubert Llewellyn-Smith and William H. Beveridge.

Beveridge was the son of a Scotch judge, had been born in India, and studied law and economics at Oxford where he was a brilliant student. Greatly influenced by the work and the ideas of Sidney and Beatrice Webb, he left a successful law practice after one year

---

[2] The first compulsory social insurance legislation had been enacted in Germany. On the initiative of Chancellor Bismarck who pursued political as well as economic goals, the German parliament had passed a sickness insurance law in 1883, an industrial accident insurance law (corresponding to workmen's compensation) in 1884, and old age and invalidity insurance in 1889. The German program did not include an unemployment insurance law because the problem of unemployment was not of major importance during the 1880's in Germany. Many other countries in Central and Northern Europe followed the German example. Some of them chose instead of the German system of compulsory insurance the way of voluntary insurance legislation. Denmark enacted 1891 an old age pensions act which did not require contributions from the insured workers nor from the employers.

of activity at the London Bar in order to accept the position as sub-warden at Toynbee Hall. There he lived among the East London workers and studied particularly the conditions of the unemployed families. In 1909, he published his first book *Unemployment—A Problem of Industry.*

After the enactment of the Labor Exchange Act of 1909, Churchill appointed William Beveridge to organize the labor exchanges. When the National Insurance Act was passed, it was natural that Beveridge was called upon to take responsibility for the setup of the unemployment insurance plan.

Following the practice of medieval guilds, the "friendly societies" and some trade unions in England paid benefits in times of sickness and unemployment to their members. However these groups represented only a small section of the working population. The National Insurance Act of 1911 established compulsory health insurance for workers of modest income. The program was financed by contributions of the insured workers and their employers, and grants from Parliament. The health insurance program was administered by "approved societies," nonprofit organizations established either by trade unions, mutual aid societies, employers, or commercial insurance companies. The latter were interested in carrying health insurance because their agents could sell other policies, particularly accident and death insurance, to families when they collected health insurance contributions. The insured worker received only medical treatment, from a practitioner, and prescribed medicine,[3] but no hospital care or treatment by a medical specialist and no insurance for his family. Cash allowances during the time of sickness were limited to twenty-six weeks, after this period a reduced disablement benefit was paid. Maternity benefit was given at confinement to insured women workers and to the wives of insured men.

In the beginning, ten million persons were covered by health insurance, but only about two and one-quarter million by unemployment insurance. Subsequent amendments increased the coverage so that in 1945, about twenty-two million people were protected by health insurance, and fifteen million by unemployment insurance.

[3] The medical benefits and the contracts with physicians were administered by the "insurance committees" established by the counties; for more details of the organization and operation of the health insurance law, see David Marsh, *National Insurance and Assistance in Great Britain* (London: Pitman, 1951), pp. 28-38.

Contributions for the unemployment insurance plan were paid by the employers. Rates were classified for age groups, males and females, and differed between a general and an agricultural scheme. The employment exchanges administered unemployment benefits.

In 1925, the *Widow's, Orphans' and Old Age Contributory Pensions Act* extended the principle of social insurance to men over sixty-five, women over sixty years of age, and widows, to orphans, and dependent children under fourteen (or under sixteen years of age when in school). Contributions from the insured workers and their employers were collected by the "approved societies," together with health insurance contributions. Local post offices paid the benefits, and the claims were adjudicated by local branch offices of the Ministry of Health. For both contributions and benefits a "flat rate system" was used so that uniform amounts were paid throughout the country, with different classification for men and women.[4]

The program of social insurance was fundamentally different from poor relief. Its contributions and benefits were determined by law. Payments were made upon the arrival of contingencies—old age, sickness, widow- and orphanhood, unemployment—without regard to the financial situation of the individual, insured person. There was no disgrace in receiving benefits from funds to which the insured himself or the husband or father had contributed. Psychologically, people were stimulated to save money, because they were anxious to have funds in addition to the social insurance benefits which merely covered basic necessities. Thus the initiative toward economic independence of the insured persons was not suppressed. They were rather encouraged to use their savings and other earnings for a decent living, in addition to the insurance benefits. Under poor relief the applicant asked the state to care for his needs; under social insurance the beneficiary remained responsible for his social and economic conditions and retained his self-respect and personal freedom.

B. CHANGING SOCIAL POLICY

World War I absorbed the unemployed and even created a labor shortage. Toward the end of the war, the *Representation of People*

[4] An analysis of the provisions and schedules is to be found in Joan Simeon Clarke, "Widows', Orphans' and Old Age Pensions," in William A. Robson, *Social Security*, 3rd ed. (London: G. Allen, 1948), pp. 156-172; and in D. Marsh, *op. cit.*, Chap. VI, pp. 54-59.

Act of 1918 abolished the disfranchisement for recipients of poor relief. In 1919, the central poor law agency, the Local Government Board was replaced by the Ministry of Health, which administered poor relief, public health, sanitation, health insurance benefits, as well as public housing and town planning. The *Housing and Town Planning Act of 1909* with provisions for slum clearance and low rent housing for workers' families marked the beginning of government participation in public housing in England. With financial aid of the government, over one and one-half million dwellings were constructed in England between 1919 and 1939. The majority were suburban cottages with gardens, hot and cold water, and bathroom. In large cities modern apartment houses were built with low-rent flats. One-third of the new buildings with public subsidies were constructed by private firms, two-thirds by local government agencies.

The *Blind Persons Act of 1920* provided old-age pensions to unemployable blind people, already at the age of fifty, and in 1948 this age was further reduced to forty years. Consultation centers for expectant and young mothers and babies became a public service, after voluntary activities had pioneered in this field, in 1918. The consultation centers employed health visitors for follow-up care and provided free midwives and hospitalization when needed.

The *Local Government Act* of March 27, 1929 led to a fundamental reform of the public relief structure. It abolished the poor law unions and boards of guardians and assigned public relief to the *county councils* and in metropolitan areas to borough councils, concentrating the administration in 145 counties. Public assistance committees were appointed that were composed of members of the county councils and other citizens. In each county, a "guardians committee" acted as voluntary investigators of relief applications. The *National Economy Act of 1931* introduced a new type of aid under the title "Unemployment Assistance"; it provided payments from the Exchecquer (the national treasury) to unemployed persons who had exhausted, or were not eligible for, unemployment insurance benefits.

The administration of all programs of assistance was placed under the *Unemployment Act* of June 28, 1934, in a new national agency, the Unemployment Assistance Board. It established 300 local offices with advisory volunteer committees to recommend policies and decide disputes.

II. SOCIAL WELFARE DURING WORLD WAR II

At the outbreak of the war in 1939, the Unemployment Assistance Board was charged with payment of war victim allowances. In 1940, the name of the Board was changed to National Assistance Board, an indication of its broader jurisdiction.

The *Determination of Needs Act* of March 26, 1941 strengthened the liberal trend of public assistance policy. The responsibility of grandparents for their grandchildren and of grown-up children for their parents was abolished.[5]

The *Old-Age Pensions Act of 1940* provided for additional pensions upon individual need, particularly for medical care.

In the field of health services, the war demand increased efforts for the treatment of tuberculosis, cancer, and venereal diseases. Important changes were made in the coordination of hospital facilities. The voluntary or private hospitals had been the pioneer institutions in England; before World War II more than 1,000 private hospitals cared for one and one-half million "in-patients" per year, and six million patients received clinical services. Private hospitals were also the only training facilities for the medical schools. Public hospitals in cities and counties provided nearly three-quarters of all hospital beds, but suffered from the close affiliation with poor law authorities, lack of funds, and the large number of chronic sick patients. When the outbreak of the war seemed imminent, in 1939, Parliament approved an "Emergency Hospital Scheme" and coordinated the entire facilities of voluntary and public hospitals and clinics. Modern health treatment centers, consultation services, and rehabilitation clinics were set up, and an extension of medical research and an expanded program of training of young physicians were achieved.

Serious problems were created in England during World War II, by the necessity of evacuating hundreds of thousands of women, babies, young children, and school children and the old, infirm, and sick persons from the large cities. School children were evacuated together with their teachers, so that school could be continued in rural schools or in hostels and children's homes. Mothers and young children were placed in foster homes, and the old and sick persons

---

[5] For other members of the household a reasonable rent payment was to be deducted.

in rural hospitals or institutions. Many difficulties arose from the different habits of urban and country children, living customs, and diets. Other problems were caused by the changing conditions of the war, with heavy bombings at certain periods and lulls at other times, which induced women and children to return to the endangered cities.[6]

The population in England found it hard to be aware of the many regulations regarding air raid protection, rationing, shelters, war damage compensation, family allowances for wives and children of men in the Armed Forces, rent control, taxes, and evacuation schedules, so that reliable information became necessary. Following London's example, over 1,000 Citizens' Advice Bureaus were established to meet this need, especially for information for servicemen on furlough regarding the whereabouts of their evacuated families. The bureaus rendered free advice on questions arising out of the war, gave legal opinion, and issued forms for applications. The Citizens' Advice Bureaus did not dispense assistance but referred applicants for material help to social agencies. Their staff consisted of trained social workers, lawyers, administrative officials, and volunteers borrowed from both public and voluntary social agencies. The services of the Citizens' Advice Bureaus proved to be so valuable, and were so widely used, that a large number now has been maintained as community information services.

III. THE BEVERIDGE REPORT

In a dramatic hour of the war, when in June, 1941 bombs were continuously falling near Westminster Hall, England began a revolutionary reform of her entire social welfare program. Arthur Greenwood, Labour Minister of Reconstruction, appointed with the unanimous consent of Parliament an Interdepartmental Committee on Social Insurance and Allied Services under the chairmanship of Sir (now Lord) William Beveridge,[7] in order to survey the

[6] An interesting account of the practice of evacuation is given in Amy S. Strachey's *Borrowed Children* (New York: Commonwealth Fund, 1940); and in Martha Eliot's report, *Civil Defense Measures for the Protection of Children* (Report of Observations in Great Britain, February, 1941), U.S. Children's Bureau, Publication No. 279, 1942.

[7] See pp. 50-51, D. Marsh, *op. cit.*, pp. 65-71; and M. Penelope Hall, *The Social Services of Modern England* (London: Routledge and Kegan Paul, 1952), pp. 26-49.

structure and the efficiency of the British social services and to make recommendations for necessary reforms. After World War I, Beveridge was Director of the London School of Economics, and in 1937 he became Master of the noted University College at Oxford. This explains why the challenging task of a re-examination of the entire social insurance and welfare program was entrusted to him. The Beveridge Committee included representatives of all ministries and organizations of public assistance, social insurance, pensions, health, and economic affairs. The committee's investigations included hundreds of hearings of citizen's groups, ranging from chambers of commerce, manufacturers' associations, and commercial insurance companies to labor unions, consumers' cooperatives, and the Fabian Society. Sir William's report attempted to find a way to "Freedom from Want" because personal and economic suffering in modern industrial society was, as a rule, caused by interruption or loss of earning power. It emphasized that in addition to "want," four other "giants" also prevent human well-being: "disease," "ignorance," "squalor," and "idleness."

The Beveridge Report devised a system of social security in which the program of social insurance is only one, although the most important of several measures. Without losing a bold look ahead into the future, recommendations were based on past experience in England. The goal of social security was to guarantee a basic level of income for every citizen with his own cooperation, so that his initiative to secure for himself and his family more than a mere subsistence minimum should not be stifled.

It inaugurated a comprehensive system of social security based upon five programs: (1) a unified, comprehensive, and adequate program of *social insurance;* (2) *public assistance* as a national program for aiding people who were not sufficiently protected through social insurance benefits; (3) *children's allowances* (now called "family allowances") providing a weekly benefit for each child after the first; (4) comprehensive free *health and rehabilitation* services for the entire population; and (5) the *maintenance of full employment* through public works measures in order to prevent mass unemployment in economic crises.

The project was aimed to protect the entire population, not just the working class. It was conceived as a unified plan, to be administered by one single national agency (now called Ministry of

Pensions and National Insurance) integrating the vast number of un-coordinated, overlapping efforts that had been made in the past. Six basic principles were suggested for the procedure: (1) unified administration, (2) comprehensive coverage, (3) flat rate of contributions, (4) flat rate of benefits, (5) adequacy of all benefits to meet basic needs of the recipients, and (6) classification of the population.[8]

Lord William emphasized that the underlying social philosophy of his plan was to secure the British people against want and other social evils, and that social security could be rendered while preserving the personal freedom, enterprise, and responsibility of the individual for his family. The Beveridge Report became the foundation of the modern social welfare legislation of Great Britain and a model for other countries.

IV. ENGLAND'S MODERN SOCIAL SECURITY PROGRAM

The structure of the present British social security program follows the recommendations of the Beveridge Report, although certain changes have been made. The *Ministry of Pensions and National Insurance*, created in 1944, coordinates the unified plan and its administration. It includes as one division the *National Assistance Board*, which is in charge of public assistance. The four main sections of the program are (1) a comprehensive *social insurance scheme*, based upon the *National Insurance* (Industrial Injuries) *Act* of July 26, 1946, and upon the (general) *National Insurance Act* of August 1, 1946; (2) a system of *family allowances* created by the *Family Allowance Act* of June 15, 1945; (3) a supplementary program of *public assistance* on the basis of the *National Assistance Act* of May 13, 1948; and (4) *public health services* founded by the *National Health Service Act* of November 6, 1946.

[8] The Report suggested six groups: (1) employees; (2) employers and self-employed persons; (3) housewives; (4) adult persons who are not gainfully employed, e.g., cripples, invalids, insane; (5) retired persons above working age; and (6) children below working age. The National Insurance Act of 1946 (see below) reduced the classification scheme to three groups: (1) employed persons, gainfully occupied in Great Britain under a contract of service; (2) self-employed people, gainfully occupied, but under no control of an employer; and (3) nonemployed persons. See D. Marsh, *op. cit.*, p. 83; and M. Hall, *op. cit.*, pp. 31-38.

The family allowances have been in effect since August 1, 1946, and the other parts of the program since July 5, 1948.

The backbone of the entire social security plan is the *social insurance system*. It includes health insurance, unemployment insurance, old-age (superannuation) and invalidity insurance, workmen's compensation, and special grants for marriage, child birth, and funeral expenses. It protects over thirty million people against the dangers of sickness, unemployment, old age, invalidity, death of the breadwinner, and industrial injuries. The insured population is divided into three categories: (a) employed persons (over nineteen million); (b) the self-employed (three million)—employers, members of the professions, independent artists, and artisans; and (c) nonemployed people (over 10 million)—mostly married women in their own household.

Contributions for the social insurance program are paid by purchasing a weekly stamp for an insurance card. They are classified according to three categories for men, women, and boys and girls under eighteen years of age. The benefits are uniform weekly flat-rate cash payments[9] for a single person in case of old-age retirement, invalidity, unemployment, and sickness; higher benefits for a married couple and for the first child. Other children are covered by family allowances. For partial or total incapacity, workers who have suffered industrial injuries receive higher insurance benefits with supplements for their dependents.

A married woman receives special benefits: a *marriage grant* for every forty weekly social insurance contributions paid prior to her wedding, in order to ease expenses for the establishment of a new home; a *maternity grant* which enables her to make the necessary purchases for the new baby; and if she was gainfully employed an additional weekly *maternity allowance* for a period of eighteen weeks (provided she leaves her job for this time), and an additional *home confinement grant*. After the death of her husband, a widow has a claim to a widow's allowance for an adjustment period of thirteen weeks. After this time, she receives a weekly guardian's benefit for each of her dependent children, as long as they are under sixteen

---

[9] The rates of contributions may be reduced or increased by order of the treasury in order to assist in the maintenance of employment or to combat inflation in accordance with the economic needs of the country. The law provides also for a review every five years to adjust the rates of benefits.

years of age. Orphans who have lost both parents receive the same orphan's benefit. Death benefits are given in case of the loss of either husband or wife to the survivor, so that funeral expenses can be met.[10]

The administration of the social insurance benefits is carried out through the Ministry of Pensions and National Insurance and its regional and local offices, with the help of local advisory committees. Medical boards and medical appeal tribunals decide questions of health damage and capacity to work. Independent local appeal tribunals hear grievances of the insured persons. Social workers employed by the National Assistance Board and workers of private social agencies offer personal advice and counseling to beneficiaries of the social insurance plan.

The second part of the British social security system is *family allowances*. They are paid upon application to every family with two or more children under sixteen years of age, without regard to the financial condition of the family. The allowance is paid to the mother, until the year after the child's sixteenth birthday, if he is in school or in apprenticeship. The family allowance is based upon the consideration that in our industrial society wages are paid for the work rendered, so that families with several children barely earn enough for a decent living, whereas a single worker might well go along with the same earning. The family allowance represents, therefore, a mutual sharing between society and parents in the expenses for the upbringing, the education, and the preservation of health of children. The family allowance of 8 shilling a week does not cover the entire cost of the rearing of the children. All children receive free school lunches or dinners and recreation and health services, such as in a free day camp or summer vacation home. Family allowances are financed from national taxation; over four and one-half million children in over 2,750,000 families receive family allowances in Great Britain.

The third part of the social security system is *public assistance*. Public assistance, under the National Assistance Act of May 13, 1948, replaced the poor law through two new schemes: (1) financial assistance to persons in economic need, administered by the National

[10] The various grants also are adjusted to changing living standards. See also Alan Peacock, *Income Redistribution and Social Policy* (Oxford: Blackwell, 1953).

Assistance Board and its twelve regional and 350 local offices; and (2) institutional and individual services, administered by the county councils. In urgent cases the local office may immediately grant emergency relief. Old, blind, deaf, crippled, and disabled persons are encouraged in their efforts to earn a part of their living. National assistance is granted according to general regulations, but the applicant's individual conditions are considered. The applicant has a right of appeal against the decision of the local office to the National Assistance Board. The Board assumes financial responsibility for vagrants and "casual poor persons" who formerly were supported by the local authorities. In 1952, over one million recipients of social security benefits received supplementary aid through public assistance. About one and one-half million families were at this time clients of the National Assistance Board.

County councils as local authorities provide *welfare services* as distinct from financial aid. These services include old people's homes and hostels for infirm, blind, deaf, mentally deficient, crippled, and handicapped persons. The residents pay their board from their own income or insurance benefits. If their income is insufficient, the National Assistance Board pays the difference, including a small amount for pocket money. The county provides instruction, workshops, vocational training, and cultural and recreational activities, and it employs the staff of the hostels as well as social workers who give casework service to the residents. Private social agencies may be asked by the county to accept old and handicapped people into their institutions and to provide individual care by their social work staffs and volunteers.

The care of orphans and neglected and deserted children remains the responsibility of the county councils. The children are placed either in foster families or in children's institutions. Under the provisions of the *Children Act of 1948*, each county council appoints a Children's Committee as the authority for child care with a Children's Officer as head of its staff. The children remain under the protection of the committee until they are eighteen years of age. The court may appoint the county council to serve as legal guardian of the child. The central supervisory authority for the care of dependent children is the Home Secretary who is assisted by an Advisory Council on Child Care. Private agencies and children's institutions that receive children or place them in foster homes are registered with the Home Office, and have to meet established standards of care.

A Central Training Council in Child Care has organized two types of special training. The first developed in cooperation with the universities for the training of the "boarding-out officers"—social workers who explore suitable foster homes and supervise the children placed in these families. The second type, establishd with the help of local education authorities, trains house mothers, house fathers, and other resident workers for children's homes.

The county councils use facilities of voluntary social agencies for the accomodation of children and adults who need institutional placement, special treatment, vocational training, recreation, and skilled social work service.[11] The counties may grant subsidies to private organizations which provide welfare services. Each county council has an advisory committee with whom the area officer meets, usually every second month, in order to ask advice and help for individual cases. Adoption was introduced as a legal measure in 1926; the *Adoption Act of 1950* regulates the process of adoption and the protection of the child, of his mother, and of the adopting parents.

The shortage of manpower in England, during World War II, led to the employment of many old, blind, deaf, and crippled persons, who proved to be reliable, conscientious workers. Based upon this war experience, the *Disabled Persons (Employment) Act of 1944* requires from industrial or commercial enterprises with a regular working force of twenty or more workers the employment of one, or more, disabled veteran or civilian. The quota is assigned annually by the Minister of Labor; it is usually 3 per cent of the working force of the plant. No disabled person is forced to register, but the law entitles the registered disabled worker to attend adult education and vocational training courses, without charge, to complete his interrupted apprenticeship and to receive vocational counsel and guidance. He also has the claim for reinstatement in private industry and priority in the employment in occupations designated as appropriate for disabled workers by the Minister of Labor,

---

[11] Of four "re-establishment centers" for vagrant young people, three were administered, in 1951, by voluntary social agencies. See also D. Marsh, *op. cit.*, Chap. XII; and D. V. Donnison, *The Neglected Child and the Social Services* (Oxford: Blackwell, 1953).

for example, car park attendant or electric elevator operator. Forty-four "re-employ factories" provide jobs for severely disabled persons under particular legal protection, with safety measures and special production methods. Twenty-three other factories voluntarily offer employment to registered, severely handicapped workers.

Special care is given by the National Assistance Board to "persons without a settled way of life," who need assistance by one single agency. Until the reform, wandering people in England were sheltered under primitive conditions in hostels and "casuals" for just a few days and then forced to move on. The new policy segregates the unsettled persons into two groups: (1) those able to work and (2) the unemployables, particularly the invalid, aged, and sick. *Reception centers* permit individual observation and diagnosis and separate the unsettled from the customary climate of the life on the road or of the city slums. After the diagnosis has been made, a treatment plan is developed. The treatment is provided in *re-establishment centers*, with adjustment to regular work, vocational training, and workshop facilities. The centers combine strict discipline with a sympathetic approach to the individual's problems and attempt to bring the unsettled person back to normal life and work. The second category of the unsettled, old, sick, and invalid vagabonds are cared for in *casual wards* where they receive medical and custodial treatment; many of these wards are affiliated with hospitals.

THE PUBLIC HEALTH SERVICE

Among modern British social legislation, none has provoked so much attention and heated controversy as the National Health Service Act of November 6, 1946, which came into force on July 5, 1948. The statute marks a fundamental change in the attitude toward health. It provides medical care free of charge to all British citizens who apply for this public service. Already, during the war, in 1942, the Medical Planning Commission established by the British Medical Association had recommended a program of medical care for the entire people. The Churchill government, in 1944, first introduced the plan, which was enacted in 1946 under Prime Minister Atlee.

The National Health Service system is not "socialized medicine." The patient is not compelled to use the service; if he takes advantage of the service, he may choose his family doctor, dentist, hospitals, and specialists. Physicians, dentists, pharmacists, and nurses are not forced to work for the Health Service, either; they may also continue private practice. Under the former National Insurance Act of 1911, the insured workers could only get medical treatment by a general practitioner. They had to pay for hospitals and specialists, and their families were not insured.

Now the Public Health Service is separate from the benefits under the Health Insurance Program. The health insurance fund pays to the insured worker a cash allowance during his sickness and thus protects the patient and his family against economic destitution. The National Health Service plan provides medical examination, diagnosis, and treatment free of charge in the doctor's office or at the patient's home, and hospitalization. The health service supplies the necessary medicines, artificial limbs, and appliances. Services are obtained through the family doctor with whom the patient has registered, if he wants to use the health service. A change of the family physician is possible any time, and the physician also may remove a patient from his list when he no longer wishes to serve him. The family doctor prescribes medicines, hearing aids, and appliances, which the patient receives at the pharmacy.[12] Since the Amendment of 1951, one-half of the cost of dentures and eyeglasses is charged to patients who are able to afford this contribution. Prescriptions for old age pensioners and ex-servicemen are free of charge. The family physician refers the patient whenever necessary to specialists, hospitals, and clinics. If a patient is taken sick while away from home, he may consult any doctor in the Health Service for free treatment as a "temporary resident."

Dental treatment does not require previous registration and includes fillings, removing infected teeth, and repairing dentures. For more complicated and expensive dental work to be done under the health plan, the patient needs an approval by the local Dental Esti-

---

[12] The statute of 1946 did not provide a fee for medicines and appliances. The introduction of a fee, however, was felt necessary in 1949 to avoid the abuse of drugs and medicines and to prevent too heavy expenditures under the health service. The Minister of Health is authorized to regulate the fees. Patients have to pay for replacement of appliances which have been lost or damaged by lack of care. See M. Hall, *op. cit.*, pp. 69, 81; and Derek H. Hene, *The British Health Service* (London: Shaw, 1953).

mate Board.[13] Under the auspices of the local public health authorities, priority in preventive and curative dental clinics is given to
expectant mothers and young children.

The Public Health Service Plan is widely used in England. Ninety-
six per cent of the population have registered with a family physician in the Service. About 88 per cent of all general physicians,
95 per cent of the dentists, and nearly all medical specialists, opticians, and pharmacists offer their services under the health plan.
The list of local physicians, general practitioners and specialists,
dentists, optometrists, and pharmacists is available to the public for
its information at the post offices and at public libraries. Among the
citizens registered for the Service are, of course, many people of
means who expect from the family physician the same medical attention which they formerly received as private patients. This will
not be possible always, with regard to the larger number of patients,
but this fact is expected to assist in the maintenance of high standards of medical care.[14]

The compensation of doctors under the Health Service is regulated by two schemes among which the physicians had a choice
when the plan started to operate: (1) by "capitation fees," remuneration based on the number of patients enrolled in the doctor's register;
or (2) by a combination scheme which comprises a basic, fixed
annual payment of £300 plus capitation fees at a lower rate. Now
the second type is applied to newly accepted physicians only when
justified by special local conditions. Medical services which require unusual effort and time, such as maternity care or long-distance
home calls in rural districts, are remunerated by increased fees, and
supplements are granted to doctors working in difficult and unpopular areas. The general practitioner may accept no more than

[13] In order to prevent the individual dentist accepting more patients than he
can take care of properly, the Minister of Health ruled that the dentist's fees
under the Health Service Plan are reduced by one-half after the dentist's annual
income reaches £4,800 ($17,200). The heavy load in dental care has been
caused by the fact that dental treatment of the low income population had been
badly neglected until the new health plan went into effect.

[14] American observers criticize that the English medical practitioner often has
too many patients so that they do not receive complete examinations and effec-
tive treatment (see Dorothy V. Whipple, "Health Care—England and the
USA," *The Survey*, September, 1950, pp. 403-407; and D. Marsh, *op. cit.*, Chap.
XIII); but this might be objected to in health insurance plans in the United
States also.

4,000 patients on his list, but the average of patients is between 2,000 and 3,000.[15] Dentists, ophthalmologists, opticians, and pharmacists are paid, according to their individual services, on the basis of an approved fee schedule. Medical specialists receive their remuneration on a part-time or full-time salary basis, with special awards for qualified professional services. Government grants are available for physicians who attend medical postgraduate refresher courses, who accept young assistant doctors for training, and who are engaged in medical research.

The administration of the National Health Service is organized, according to the three branches of the Service, into (a) general medical and dental services, (b) hospital and specialist services, and (c) local government services. The general medical and dental services are administered by 138 Executive Councils established by the counties as local health authorities. They review the patients' lists of the physicians, allocate patients whom no doctor wants to accept, and refuse in "over-doctored areas" the admission of new general practitioners until there is need for them.

Hospital and consultant physicians' services are administered by fourteen Regional Boards, whose areas are designated by a Central Medical Practices Committee. After consultation with the medical executive councils, the local medical associations, and senior staffs of the hospitals in the area, the Regional Board appoints "management committees" for hospitals in the region, takes measures for coordination of hospitals, and develops regional health policies and public health planning.

Each of the fourteen regions is connected with a university medical school which uses one or several "voluntary teaching hospitals" for the training of medical and dental students. The university teaching hospitals retained their legacies, gifts, and endowments for research and fellowships. Endowments of other hospitals are pooled in a Hospital Endowments Fund. Hospital management committees and regional medical boards use the fund for the development and improvement of hospital facilities, equipment, and research. The broad representation of noted members of the medical, dental, and pharmaceutical professions on these boards enables them to give

---

[15] The fee does not include earnings from private patients, compensation for clinical and hospital services, obstetric treatment, and other special services. The capitation fee varies from area to area.

leadership in the planned expansion of hospitals and clinics throughout the entire country and to work toward higher standards and effective health policies. Under the new health plan, 2,688 voluntary and public hospitals with over 500,000 beds were transferred to the Public Health Service Plan. Professional and technical improvements and an amalgamation of small and inefficient hospitals were achieved.[16] Two hundred and seven denominational hospitals have been "disclaimed," and continue to operate under private management. The regional hospital boards negotiate the contracts with specialists (medical consultants). The urgently needed eye services are temporarily administered by the "executive committees" in the counties, but will ultimately be directed by the regional hospital boards.

The local health authorities provide for maternity and child welfare services, midwifery, home nursing, health visiting, and after-care of the sick. They arrange for domestic help in time of confinement and sickness, for vaccination and immunization, and for ambulance services for emergency transportation to hospitals or clinics. Domestic help under the Home Help Service is free to families who cannot afford to pay for a homemaker, whereas other families pay a moderate weekly charge. The local health authority employs a medical officer and his staff under the direction of a "health committee." In cases of home confinement, free midwife service and a maternity outfit is granted, and in the cases of home nursing, such comfort articles as crutches and wheel chairs for the sick room and for convalescence. Tubercular patients receive medical care and public assistance benefits. After the patient returns from the hospital or tuberculosis sanitarium, a social worker or a visiting nurse assumes after-care. By the establishment of child guidance and mental hygiene clinics, local health authorities also help in the prevention of mental diseases.

Special attention is given to expectant and nursing mothers, infants and young children under five years of age. The maternity

[16] An increasing number of British hospitals have "almoner's departments," staffed by medical social workers. Mental hospitals and psychiatric clinics employ psychiatric social workers. Two public medical services have not been incorporated: the Schools Medical Service, controlled by the Minister of Education, and the Industrial Medical Service, under the Minister of Labor. See also Emory S. Bogardus, "Social Aspects of the British National Health Service," *Sociology and Social Research*, Vol. 35, July-August, 1951, pp. 428-433.

and child welfare services of the counties provide free antenatal and postnatal care with obstetric and pediatric examination and treatment. Expectant mothers and young children are entitled to milk, cod-liver oil, and orange juice at a reduced price, but free of charge to mothers who cannot afford to pay for it.

In schools, free medical inspections, dental treatment, and special attention to blind, visually handicapped, epileptic, and crippled children are provided. Some counties employ medical social workers under the title "welfare officer" for services for children, the aged, and the handicapped.

When the National Health Service was established in 1948, it faced very difficult conditions. There still is a serious shortage of hospitals, clinics, and health centers; of medical specialists, dentists, nurses, and midwives; and a lack of modern technical equipment. Broad masses of the population had never had eye examinations, spectacles, or dental treatment. It was not surprising that a heavy demand of new patients burdened doctors, dentists, clinics, and hospitals. Certain abuses of the new, free service, particularly for obtaining eye glasses, medicines, and appliances, were unavoidable. Doctors have not been flooded by hypochondriacs, but in some areas they have to work hard in order to treat the large number of patients (especially children) whose medical and dental care had been neglected.

The cost of the National Health Service is high. Funds contributed by the social insurance program to the health service cover about 13 per cent of the entire health service budget. The remainder is financed by national and some local taxes. Administrative cost of the National Health Service amounts to only 2½ to 3 per cent of the expenditure.

The final success of the health service will depend upon the understanding and cooperation of the public and of the professions. The statute provides for the future establishment of Health Centers by the counties, when financial and technical conditions permit. At these centers, family doctors, medical specialists, and dentists will have their offices for both the health service and their private practice, with laboratory and pharmaceutical facilities. Nurses and midwives will be stationed at the centers.

The public in England often regards the health service still as part of the social insurance plan and as a return for the weekly social insurance contribution. In fact, the health service is available to everyone independent of his coverage under the social insurance program. The health service is no "charity." But the health service cannot, in a few years, overcome the long prevailing shortages in doctors, nurses, clinics, and hospitals as well as their maldistribution.

V. PRIVATE SOCIAL SERVICES IN ENGLAND

For centuries England has been noted for the important role that private charities have played as pioneers of the various kinds of social services, and for the high number of volunteers active in the field of social services. The recent broad expansion of public welfare and the social insurances have accepted insurance benefit and financial assistance as the responsibility of the entire community, not of private, benevolent organizations. But this development has still left wide opportunities for the activities of private social agencies. The public authorities encourage voluntary agencies to continue their work in personal aid and counseling to old, sick, handicapped, and young persons and to nurseries and community centers. Characteristic examples for present social services under the auspices of voluntary agencies are maternity and old-age Homes, health visiting, home nursing, midwives' services, ambulances and transportation aid; care of mothers and babies; clinics and sanitariums for tubercular patients; hostels for mental defective children and adults; and after-care service for the sick. Other activities of private social agencies include probation and parole work for juveniles and adults; social clubs for adolescents, the aged, and the unemployed; marriage guidance councils; child guidance clinics; disaster relief; visiting old people in their homes or in institutions; and providing "village halls" (rural cultural and education centers).

The essential functions of private social agencies in these fields in England today are (1) carrying on new experiments and developing new forms of social work which may later be taken over by public agencies when they have proved successful; (2) supplementing public social services when certain persons or particular needs are not covered, as public services are limited by funds and legal provisions, and by individual care and counseling; (3) interpreting social work to the public, particularly through citizens' advice bureaus and by informing legislators and public agencies of the special problems which have escaped their attention; and (4) performing social surveys in order to determine the social and health needs of a community and the quest for social legislation—plus providing the stimulation of public authorities to take the necessary action.[17]

Volunteers play a very essential role in private social agencies in Great Britain, particularly in youth groups, advisory bureaus, child care work affiliated with the schools, and probation, but they often work under instruction and supervision of trained professional workers. Volunteers are particularly active in work with aged and handicapped persons. Subsidies to private agencies are widely granted by the counties and the various ministries of the national government. Most advisory and administrative committees of the counties' public assistance and health programs are composed mainly of volunteers. Nearly all voluntary social agencies are represented in the National Council of Social Service, which was founded in 1919. More than 100 national organizations are members of the Council, among them the Family Welfare Association (successor to the Charity Organization Society), the Women's Voluntary Services, the Standing Conference of Voluntary Organizations, the National Old People's Welfare Committee, the National Association of Mental Welfare, the Women's Group on Public Welfare, the Standing Conference of National Voluntary Youth Organizations, the Central Council for the Care of Cripples, and the National Council of Associated Children's Homes. The national Council encourages the setup of local "councils of social services" and "rural community councils" with the aim of coordination and cooperation between local agencies. It has been difficult, however, to finance some of the local private agencies because endowments and contributions are scarce, due to the economic conditions of postwar England. Fear that private social agencies would be no longer needed when public social services were expanded has not proved justified.

The recent extension of public social services has, however, led to a certain duplication of work and overlapping between public and private social work activities. The English citizen dislikes regi-

[17] As an example we may mention the "Community-Center" movement in England which started with voluntary agencies and enlisted the assistance of municipal authorities. See Eyre Carter, "The Partnership Between the Statutory and the Voluntary Social Services in Postwar Britain," *The Social Service Review*, Vol. XXIII, No. 2, June, 1949, pp. 158-175; and Hilda Jennings, *The Private Citizen in Public Social Work* (London: G. Allen, 1930).

mentation and is skeptical towards organization; for this reason no community chests have been established so far. Some private social agencies still maintain a critical attitude, and sometimes express even hostility against the growing public social services, with the argument that private organizations have a superior social philosophy and practice based upon the old principle of "voluntary action" for which there is at present scarcely any proof.[18] In the interest of economy and efficiency, it seems desirable to achieve an elimination of overlapping services and a coordination of public and private activities to meet the social needs of the population.

Persons who are recipients of public assistance payments are entitled to be members of advisory councils, grievance committees, and appeal tribunals. The broad participation of laymen and of members of the working population, as well as of the professions, secures an understanding of the social problems in the carrying out of social services in England and serves as a control against the danger of bureaucracy together with the activities of the voluntary social agencies. These are able now to concentrate on their real task, on the difficult, intangible problems of bringing aid to human beings in need of understanding, encouragement, and respect, especially in prevention of juvenile delinquency.

VI. TREATMENT OF JUVENILE DELINQUENCY

In 1908, the *Prevention of Crime Act* had authorized the courts to order special treatment of young delinquents and their detention up to three years. It introduced the *Borstal System* as part of the national penal program. When the *Children's Act of 1912* (inspired by the example of juvenile court laws of the United States) established juvenile courts and probation services, Borstal institutions grew further in number and became more specialized in the nature of their methods of education, vocational guidance, and occupational training. The age of young offenders who might be adjusted in Borstal institutions was raised to twenty-three years, and the maximum time of institutional treatment in Borstal schools to four years.

---

[18] See Emmeline W. Cohen, *English Social Services, Methods and Growth* (London: G. Allen, 1949), p. 152; Lord William Beveridge, *Voluntary Action* (London: G. Allen, 1948), pp. 303, 308, and 319-324; Eileen Younghusband, *Report on the Employment and Training of Social Workers* (Edinburgh: Constable, 1947), p. 82.

The Commissioner of the Borstal institutions is a member of the National Prison Commission. He decides, upon the recommendations of his staff, how long the individual young offender shall remain in the institution. Education is entrusted to teachers, housemasters, and matrons who, under a cottage system, live together with the youngsters. Disciplinary officers are separated from the other educational staff. A preliminary observation of each offender in a clinical setting enables the governor of the Borstal institution to select the specific school, the type of vocational training, and the personnel which promise the most effective adjustment of the juvenile delinquent. The Borstal schools use the volunteer assistance of the surrounding communities. A "visiting committee" of interested citizens gets acquainted with the boys and maintains contact with them. Youth groups in the towns visit the schools and invite the boys for sport games and recreation. Other volunteers in the surrounding communities teach technical skills and handicraft and arrange for such recreational activities as musical performances and dramatic plays. The vocational training in Borstal schools is directed toward practical skill with no makeshift work. Competition with free labor on the general market has been avoided by manufacturing goods approved by labor unions. After the young offender is released, he remains under parole supervision which is carried out by trained parole officers or by volunteers organized and instructed by the Borstal Association.

After World War II, England has shared with most other countries a considerable increase in juvenile delinquency. Its main causes have been broken homes, neglect of supervision of children in their homes or at play, the influence of juvenile gangs, and boredom of children without proper guidance. The lack of real interest in school activities and the negative influence of certain types of movies and crime books are often blamed in England for the violation of the law by children and youngsters. The largest number of offenses committed by children and adolescents are theft and sex delinquencies.

The Juvenile Courts, first created by the *Children's Act of 1912*, have helped in the restraint of juvenile delinquency. In 1920, the *Juvenile Court Metropolis Act* provided that the Home Secretary may select, for the juvenile courts, magistrates with previous experience and special qualifications for dealing with young offenders, so that in the courts higher standards of procedure and more effective adjustment of youth may be obtained. In England, the juvenile court consists of the magistrate as presiding judge and of two lay justices (often teachers, physicians, social workers, or members of charitable agencies), one of whom must be a' woman. The *Children and Young People Act of 1933* emphasized the need of action toward the welfare of the young offender. The court may remove the young delinquent from his home or from undesirable surroundings and secure his effective education and training. The court's sessions are not open to the public or to the press; only persons immediately concerned, including parents or guardian of the child and the probation officer or investigating social worker, are admitted.

In their work of protection and adjustment of children and young persons the juvenile courts depend upon the aid of public and private child welfare agencies, child guidance clinics, and probation services.[19] Probation for minors is widely used in Great Britain. If it is necessary to remove the child from his own family, foster homes are selected and supervised by child protective agencies or by chapters of the Borstal Association. There are also "hostels" and "probation homes" for young offenders who, for special reasons, cannot be placed in a foster family. For the adjustment of difficult and seriously delinquent children and adolescents the Borstal institutions and 182 "approved schools"[20] are used. Of these approved schools, 143 are private institutions maintained by voluntary social agencies, and 39 are public schools of the counties. The value of preventive services, such as recreation and youth group activities, is well recognized, and these clubs and recreation groups receive financial support from private organizations, the counties, and the national government. The "approved schools," on the other hand, are classified according to their special training equipment and their staff skills. They are separate for girls and boys and consider the various age groups and particular difficulties of the children.

[19] Probation is supervision of the youth in his own home by a probation officer, in lieu of his commitment to an institution.

[20] The "approved schools" correspond to licensed training schools or industrial schools in the United States. For an analysis of the Borstal institutions, see William Healy and Benedict Alper, *Criminal Youth and the Borstal System* (New York: The Commonwealth Fund, 1941); and Lionel W. Fox, *The English Prison and Borstal Systems* (London: Routledge and Kegan Paul, 1952).

SELECTED BIBLIOGRAPHY

*Alper, Benedict S., "The English System of Borstal Schools," *National Probation Association Yearbook*, Vol. XXXV, 1941, pp. 260-276.

Armstrong, Barbara Nachtrieb, *Insuring the Essentials*. New York: Macmillan, 1932.

——, *The Health Insurance Doctor*. Princeton: Princeton University Press, 1939.

Attlee, Clement Richard, *The Social Worker*. London: G. Bell, 1920.

Ball, F. N., *National Insurance and Industrial Injuries*. Leigh-on-Sea, Essex: Thames Bank Publishing Company, 1948.

Benjamin, Zoe, *The Emotional Problems of Childhood*. London: University of London Press, 1948.

*Beveridge, Sir William, *Social Insurance and Allied Services*. New York: Macmillan, 1942.

*——, *Voluntary Action: A Report on Methods of Social Advance*. London: G. Allen, 1949.

Bosanquet, Helen, *The Poor Law Report of 1909* (A Summary Explaining the Defects of the Present System and the Principal Recommendations of the Commission, so far as relates to England and Wales). London: Macmillan, 1909.

Bourdillon, A. F. C., *Voluntary Social Services, Their Place in the Modern State*. London: Methuen, 1945.

Brady, M., *Children's Health and Happiness*. London: Health-for-All Publishing Co., 1948.

Burt, Sir Cyril, *The Young Delinquent*. London: University of London Press, 1948.

Carter, Eyre, "The Partnership Between Statutory and the Voluntary Social Services in Postwar Britain," *The Social Service Review*, Vol. XXIII, No. 2, June, 1949, pp. 158-175.

*Cohen, Emmeline W., *English Social Services, Method and Growth*. London: G. Allen, 1949.

Cole, Margaret, *Beatrice Webb*. New York: Harcourt, 1946.

*de Schweinitz, Karl, *England's Road to Social Security*, 2nd ed. Philadelphia: University of Pennsylvania Press, 1943.

Donnison, D. V., *The Neglected Child and the Social Services*. Oxford: Blackwall, 1953.

Eliot, Martha M., *Civil Defense Measures for the Protection of Children*. Washington, D. C.: U. S. Children's Bureau, Publication No. 279, 1942.

Fox, Lionel W., *The English Prison and Borstal Systems*. London: Routledge and Kegan Paul, 1952.

Frazer, W. M., *A History of English Public Health, 1834-1939*. London: Baillière, 1950.

Gordon, J. W., *Borstalians*. London: Hopkinson, 1932.

Grunhut, Max, *Penal Reform—A Comparative Study*. Oxford: Clarendon Press, 1948.

*Hall, M. Penelope, *The Social Services of Modern England*. London: Routledge and Kegan Paul, 1952.

*Healy, William, and Benedict S. Alper, *Criminal Youth and the Borstal System*. New York: The Commonwealth Fund, 1941.

Hene, Derek H., *The British Health Service*. London: Shaw, 1953.

Hill, A. C. C., and Isador Lubin, *The British Attack on Unemployment*. Washington, D. C.: The Brookings Institution, 1934.

Hill, C., and J. Woodcock, *The National Health Service*. London: Christopher Johnson, 1949.

Hobman, D. L., *The Welfare State*. Oxford: Blackwell, 1953.

Hohman, Helen Fisher, *The Development of Social Insurance and Minimum Wage Legislation in Great Britain*. Boston: Houghton, 1933.

Isaacs, Susan, *Childhood and After*. London: Routledge and Kegan Paul, 1948.

James, Thomas E., *Prostitution and the Law*. London: Heinemann, 1951.

Jameson, Sir Wilson, "Britain's New Health Law," *Survey Graphic*, Vol. XXXVII, No. 5, May, 1948, pp. 259-261.

Jegar, Lena M. (editor) *Illegitimate Children and Their Parents*. London: National Council for the Unmarried Mother and Her Child, 1951.

Jones, D. C., *Social Surveys*. London: Hutchinson, 1949.

King, C. M. (editor), *Advising the Citizen* (A Handbook for Workers in Advice Services). London: National Council of Social Service, 1948.

Lesser, Henry, *The Health Services*. London: G. Allen, 1951.

Levy, H., *National Health Insurance*. Cambridge: Cambridge University Press, 1945.

*Macadam, Elisabeth, *The Social Servant in the Making*. London: G. Allen, 1945.

Manson, Julius, *The British Health Service*. New York: League of Industrial Democracy, 1952.

*Marsh, David C., *National Insurance and Assistance in Great Britain*. London: Pitman, 1951.

Mendelsohn, Ronald, *Social Security in the British Commonwealth*. Oxford: Blackwell, 1953.

Mess, Henry A., *Voluntary Social Services Since 1918*. London: Routledge and Kegan Paul, 1948.

Morris, Charles (editor), *Social Case Work in Britain*. London: Faber, 1950.

Moss, John, *Health and Welfare Services Handbook*. London: Hadden, Best, 1949.

———, *The Duties of Local Authorities Under the National Assistance Act, 1948*. London: Hadden, Best, 1948.

Mueller, G. W., and E. C. Robertson, *Fundamentals of Health and Safety*. London: Macmillan Co., 1949.

National Council of Social Service, *Voluntary Social Services. Handbook of Information and Directory*. London: The Council, 1948.

Newsholme, H. P., *The Illegitimate Child: A Challenge to Society*. London: National Council for the Unmarried Mother and Her Child, 1946.

Nuffield Foundation, *Training for Social Work*. London: Oxford University Press, 1946.

Owen, A. D. K., *The British Social Services*, 2nd ed. London: Longmans, 1943.

Pringle, Rev. J. C., *British Social Services*. London: Longmans, 1933.

Rathbone, Eleanor, *Family Allowances*. London: G. Allen, 1949.

*Robson, William A., *Social Security*, 3rd ed. London: G. Allen, 1948.

Rowntree, B. Seebohn, and G. R. Lavers, *English Life and Leisure: A Social Study*. London: Longmans, 1951.

Ruggles-Brise, Sir Evelyn, *The English Prison System*. London: Macmillan, 1921.

Sheldon, J. H., *The Social Medicine of Old Age*. London: Oxford University Press, 1948.

Speller, S. R., *National Health Service Act, 1946*. London: H. K. Lewis, 1948.

Stevenson, Allan C., *Recent Advances in Social Medicine*. London: Churchill, 1950.

Strachey, Amy Simpson, *Borrowed Children* (A Popular Account of Some Evacuation Problems and Their Remedies). New York: The Commonwealth Fund, 1940.

Tillyard, Sir F., and F. N. Ball, *Unemployment Insurance in Great Britain*, 1911-1948. Leigh-on-Sea, Essex: Thames Bank Publishing Co., 1949.

Unger-Meier, Gitta, "The British Home Help Service," *The Social Service Review*, Vol. XXIV, No. 1, March, 1950, pp. 108-109.

Utting, F. E. G., *Social Accounts of Local Authorities*. Oxford: Blackwell, 1953.

von Caemmerer, Dora, *Probation*. Munich: W. Steinebach, 1952.

Watson, John, *British Juvenile Courts*. London: Longmans, 1948.

Webb, Beatrice, *British Poor Law Will Endure*. London: Oxford University Press, 1928.

———, *The Abolition of the Poor Law*. London: The Fabian Society, 1918.

Webb, Sidney, *The Break-up of the Poor Law* (Being Part One of the Minority Report of the Poor Law Commission). London: Longmans, 1909.

Webb, Sidney, and Beatrice Webb, *English Poor Law Policy*. London: Longmans, 1910.

———, *The Prevention of Destitution*. London: Longmans, 1912.

*Wickwar, H., and M. Wickwar, *The Social Services: A Historical Survey*, Rev. ed. London: Lane, 1949.

Wilson, R., *Social Work in a Changing World*. London: Family Welfare Association, 1950.

*Younghusband, Eileen L., *Report on Employment and Training of Social Workers*. Edinburgh: Constable, 1947.

*———, *Social Work in Britain*. (A Supplementary Report on the Employment and Training of Social Workers). Edinburgh: Constable, 1951.

4. Local Government and Private Charities in the United States Before 1900

I. EARLY DEVELOPMENT: LOCAL CHARITIES

As early as in the beginning of the seventeenth century, the colonists (most of them coming from England) brought with them the customs, laws, and institutions of the mother country. In general, they were vigorous persons, who came to the New World in order to gain freedom to worship, better economic opportunities, or to seek adventure. They found a vast land of forests, fertile valleys, an abundance of wild game, and fish in the lakes and rivers. Few of the new settlers had substantial means—most had only meager belongings—but they were willing to work hard for their living as farmers, hunters, or traders. The isolated settlements of the new frontier were subject to the dangers of Indian assaults, of wild animals, and of natural disasters.

A wide variety of cultural backgrounds have influenced American approaches to welfare problems, particularly English Puritan, Scotch, English Catholic, Anglican, Dutch, and French, as well as the Quaker traditions. The majority of the newcomers were followers of the social philosophy of Calvinism and disapproved of drinking, gambling, and other vices. They demanded thrift and industrious work and tested religiosity by demonstration of material success. The Puritans had a horror of laziness and poverty because they considered idleness a sin and the source of unhappiness and crime, and poverty a proof of low moral quality. They were also anxious about avoiding the heavy taxes common in England where some parishes spent as much as a third of their total revenues for poor re-

77

lief. From the English tradition the colonists inherited the concept that paupers, beggars, and vagrants were criminals, and this accentuated their contempt for those who asked for support from the parish.

Most paupers, however, were widows and orphans and the sick, old, and invalid persons. But there was another category of involuntary immigrants that the mother countries, especially England, wanted to get rid of. At the order of English courts, demented and maimed persons and convicted offenders were deported, because the mother country wanted to be rid of them; they were sent as "involuntary servants" to work for a number of years. Others were kidnapped by traders and sea captains and sold as servants to colonists. Under the apprenticeship laws, dependent children were also deported from the poorhouses to the Colonies. The majority of the involuntary servants became self-supporting, law abiding citizens, but some of them were weak, sick, or unwilling to work.

In contrast to the thickly populated European countries from which they emigrated, the settlers lived in scattered places as farmers and hunters on the ragged edge of existence, and struggled hard to wrench a bare living from the soil and the woods. They were so involved in their own problems of survival that they gave little thought to the needs of others unable to face the hardships of frontier life. Since land was cheap and labor scarce, beggars able to work were not given alms. Still, the aged, the sick, and women with young children needed help. The traditional resources of the mother country, such as church institutions, endowed charities, hospitals and almshouses did not exist in the settlements. The local parish had to take care of its destitute. As in England, the colonists were eager to prevent from entering the settlement those who might become a public charge or who seemed objectionable for religious, political, or moral reasons. Such persons were deported, and the Colonies sometimes even paid the passage back to Europe when the individual settlement could not afford the expense.

In accordance with the Elizabethan Poor Law, overseers or supervisors of the poor were appointed in the parish or township. They had to assess and to collect a poor tax, to investigate the resources of relief applicants, and to dispense relief to the paupers. Frequently the overseer held other functions, too, such as councilman or town treasurer; later his position became a full township office.

The Colonies adopted the Elizabethan Poor Law, at least in principle. Every town made provisions for the maintenance of the poor, supplying food, clothing, firewood, and household essentials to persons with legal settlement. They had to be residents for a statutory period, varying between three months and five years. Following English tradition, newcomers often were "warned out," i.e., ordered to leave the community unless they could provide security by bond of a resident in good standing. If members of such a family were found begging, they were whipped in the market place and forcibly returned to their former residence. Since many immigrants arrived without means, ship masters who brought them over had to deliver passenger lists and to deposit bond in order that no passenger would become a public charge for five years. Residents responsible for the arrival of paupers had to indemnify the town.

Poor relief was given mainly in two forms: (1) either as "outdoor relief" in kind (food, clothes, fuel) in the home of the poor, or (2) by "farming out" or "selling out" the pauper to the lowest bidder. A special type of farming out was the placement of widows and infirm and aged paupers, for short periods, from house to house. Older children were "indentured"; the town did not pay for them as they worked for their maintenance.

The cost of poor relief was met by the poor tax and certain fines that were imposed for refusal to work at harvest time, for selling bread or butter at short weight, for not attending public worship, or for illegally bringing a pauper into the Colony. If a town failed to make appropriations for poor relief, the county courts assessed the town and disposed of the funds.

Whatever the cause of his distress the pauper was treated as a morally deficient person. He had to swear to the "pauper's oath" and his name was entered on the "poor roll" exhibited in the city hall or in the market place. Local newspapers published the names of all paupers, with the amount of their relief allowances. In Pennsylvania, all members of a pauper family had to wear the Roman letter "P" on the shoulder of the right sleeve. Old and invalid indigents who had resided for a long time in the parish were considered "worthy poor," if they complied with the moral standards of the neighborhood; all others, particularly strangers and newcomers, were considered "unworthy poor." Disfranchisement of paupers prevailed everywhere. The repressive, punitive character of poor relief, as it had developed in England, was maintained in the New World.

Especially harsh was the treatment of "wanderers" or vagabonds; they were adjudged "rogues" to be "stripped naked from the middle upward, be openly whipt on his or her naked body, not exceeding the number of fifteen stripes"[1] and ordered to leave the parish. If they refused to leave, the court might order them to be sold out of the county in servitude. Idlers and beggars were often confined to the jail, the "bridewell," or the house of correction. The main purpose of this practice was to spare the citizens of the Colony high taxes for poor relief.

Unlike the other New England Colonies, poor relief in New York was first administered by the Dutch Reformed Church. Its volunteers, "siecken troosters," visited the poor and the sick and brought them food and medicine. In 1661, the Netherlands enacted a poor law for New York in order to protect the Colony against the entrance of paupers. A provincial law of 1683 regulated poor relief to conform to the English practice.

In the southern states (Virginia and North Carolina) under the English parish system, churchwardens and vestrymen acted as overseers of the poor, levied pauper taxes, distributed relief, and farmed out the indigent. The first *Virginia Poor Law* was enacted in 1646. In 1785, county overseers of the poor were appointed as a consequence of the separation of church and state after the Revolution. In Louisiana, a French Colony, religious charities according to French tradition took care of the poor. Louisiana did not follow the Elizabethan pattern; children were cared for in orphanages, the sick and the aged in hospitals. Institutional care was preferred to outdoor relief.

Orphans and abandoned and illegitimate children remained a major problem of the southern states; many were born to Negro, Indian, and mulatto women and others to white servants who were not permitted to care for the child. In the eighteenth century, impoverished Negro slaves and freed mulatto servants became another group requiring poor relief. Illegitimate children and orphans were "bound out" in order to save poor relief expenses.

There were two fundamental differences between the English and the American poor law practice in the seventeenth and eighteenth

---

[1] Marcus W. Jernigan, *Laboring and Dependent Classes in Colonial America, 1607-1783* (Chicago: University of Chicago Press, 1931), p. 201.

centuries. In England the general method of poor relief was to place the paupers into poorhouses and workhouses; in the Colonies only in some larger cities were a few almshouses and houses of correction established. In England, legacies, endowments, and bequests provided substantial funds for the support of the poor in hospitals, asylums, and orphanages; in the Colonies, private charities played an insignificant role until the end of the eighteenth century.

The first almshouse was established as early as 1657 at Rensselaerswyck, New York, where the Lutheran pastor was a resident. Plymouth Colony ordered the construction of a workhouse in 1658, and Boston set up an almshouse in 1660. The legislature of Massachusetts ruled in 1699 that vagabonds, beggars, and disorderly persons should be put to work in houses of correction. During the eighteenth century some other Colonies began to use almshouses and workhouses in large cities, instead of boarding out the paupers with families. Connecticut used county jails as houses of correction in 1713 where the jail keeper had to "set the inmates to work." At Newport, Rhode Island, an almshouse was instituted in 1723, and the first poor farm was organized in Philadelphia in 1773. Most smaller towns continued, however, to farm out the poor by "auctioning them off" to the lowest bidder. Other towns "contracted" with a resident so that he would take care of all paupers in town for a stipulated sum. This method secured the taxpayers against unexpected expenses for poor relief but did not protect the poor against brutal treatment, inadequate care, hunger, and exploitation.

Besides public poor relief, church charities during the Colonial period played a certain role but limited their aid to members of the congregation, especially in cases of death or illness. The minister and his wife and some deacons visited the sick, widows, and orphans. Assistance was denied to people who neglected admonitions of the minister or whose moral behavior, laziness, drinking, or gambling were criticized in the parish. Churches financed their charity by collections among their members, offerings at the religious services, and appeals for funds in cases of emergency.

A second characteristic type of private charities in America were the National Benevolent Societies, fraternal orders of various nationality groups. The first was founded in Boston among Scottish immigrants in 1657. Other benevolent societies for the English (St. Andrew's Societies), the Irish, the French, the Dutch, and the Germans were organized in the eighteenth and nineteenth centuries.

A third type of private charity was the *philanthropic association* founded in order to aid groups in special need. Examples are the Philadelphia Society for Alleviating the Miseries of Public Prisoners, founded in 1787; the Massachusetts Charitable Fire Society of 1794, for the victims of fire; and the New York Society for the Relief of Poor Widows with Small Children, founded in 1798. Some endowments to charities were made in the eighteenth century, but they became important only during the nineteenth and twentieth centuries. Founders of private charities assigned in their bequests or wills the administration of endowed funds to a board of trustees who incorporated the foundation according to state laws.

II. THE ALMSHOUSE PERIOD

During the first decades of the nineteenth century, the parishes and counties complained about rising expenses for poor relief. In Massachusetts and Connecticut, the state governments had at least assumed the cost for those paupers who were "unsettled" or were "warned out." In New York, "Laws on the State Poor" provided state funds for refugees fleeing from the Indians, or from the British armies. In general, the maintenance of the poor remained the responsibility either of the local community (town or township) or of the county. Some midwestern and the western states made the counties responsible for the administration of the poor laws, whereas in New England and the eastern states the township continued to be the government unit which had to provide poor relief.

The growing burden of the expenses for poor relief on local government resulted from two causes: (1) The number of the "impotent poor;" the old, sick, blind, and handicapped persons; and the orphans and illegitimate dependent children grew with the total increase of population. (2) In times of failure of crops and lack of suitable employment, other "able-bodied persons" also applied for poor relief, often granted them by the overseer of the poor as a political or personal favor. This "spoil system of poor relief" led to the support of families who might have been able to maintain themselves but had become accustomed to living off public charity.

Large cities in several states—Rhode Island, New Hampshire, New York, Virginia, Connecticut, Delaware, Virginia, and Pennsylvania

—had established some poorhouses and considered them the most economic and effective method of care for the poor. In 1821, the General Court of Massachusetts appointed a committee to investigate the pauper laws of the Commonwealth. Under the chairmanship of Josiah Quincy, the committee suggested to the legistlature the adoption of five principles: (1) that outdoor relief was wasteful, expensive, and destructive to the morals of the poor; (2) that "almshouses" were the most economic mode of relief, because in a "house of industry" each pauper was set to work according to his ability so that the able-bodied earned their maintenance and contributed to the support of the impotent group; (3) that the poor be employed in agricultural work; (4) that a board of citizens should supervise the almshouse; and (5) that intemperance was considered the most powerful and universal cause of pauperism.

Two years later, in 1823, the New York legislature instructed Secretary of State J. V. N. Yates to collect information on the expense and operation of the poor laws. The Yates Report, rendered in January 1824, divided the poor into two classes—those under permanent support and the "temporary poor." Among the first class, 35 per cent were unable to work because of age, infirmity, blindness, and physical and mental handicaps; 38 per cent were children under fourteen years of age. The remaining 27 per cent, however, were considered able to earn their living if proper arrangements were made. The Yates Report criticized that sturdy beggars and "profligate vagrants" were encouraged to become "pensioners of public relief" because overseers granted them aid without careful examination. The Report found that the complicated system of legal settlement led to expensive litigation between towns and counties; that paupers suffered by the cruel removal from one town to another; and that the "farmed out" paupers were mistreated and "tortured" by their keepers. Education and morals of the children were neglected, and they grew up in filth, idleness, ignorance, and disease "to become early candidates for the prison or the grave." No adequate provisions were made for setting the paupers to work. On the basis of these findings, the Yates Report recommended the following measures: (1) to establish in each county a "house of employment," providing a farm for agricultural work and education of the children; (2) to procure a workhouse (or "penitentiary") for sturdy beggars and vagrants, with enforced hard labor; (3) to levy an excise tax on whisky distilleries in order to raise the funds for poor relief; (4) to rule that one year's residence in a county of New York constitutes a legal settlement; (5) to abolish "the orders of removal" and the appeals in poor law litigation; (6) to order that no healthy male between eighteen and fifty years of age be placed on the pauper list; and (7) to punish street begging and the bringing of paupers into the state.[2]

Following the Quincy and Yates Reports, Massachusetts, New York, and most states of the Union established almshouses and workhouses and placed relief applicants into these institutions. Immediately after the release of the Yates Report, the state of New York passed, in 1824, the *County Poor House Act*, which transferred the management of the almshouse from the township to the county.

Unfortunately, the introduction of almshouse care in all the states did not have the effect of improving the conditions of the poor which the legislators had hoped for. The first almshouses had sheltered the old and the sick. Now the poor families who had been supported in their own homes, and persons who were boarded out to families, were forced into the rapidly increasing number of almshouses. There the old and sick were thrown together with tramps and vagabonds of all ages, with blind, deaf-mutes, cripples, idiots, epileptics, and insane people. Children, orphans, foundlings, unmarried mothers with their children, prostitutes, and criminals were put in these houses, often without separation of the sexes and age groups. There were no sanitary facilities, and old cots and straw were used instead of beds. The almshouse usually was a delapidated building, bequested to the town or cheaply bought at auction. Its management frequently was assigned to a jobless political supporter of the overseer or to an old farm couple unable to continue regular work and unqualified for the care of children and adults. For the education of the children in the almshouse there were no funds nor personnel able to teach. Sometimes, 20 to 25 per cent of the inmates were idiots or insane. The almshouses became a "human scrap heap" and did not fulfill the hope that had been raised in a reform of the care of the poor.

[2] The text of the Quincy and Yates Reports may be found in Sophonisba P. Breckinridge, *Public Welfare Administration in the United States* (Chicago: University of Chicago Press, 1935), pp. 30-54.

A. MEDICAL CARE FOR THE POOR

From the beginning of American Colonial history, the hardships of frontier life, unwholesome situations on immigrant ships, climatic conditions, natural disasters, and battles with Indians caused injuries and illness among the settlers. Because doctors were few and lived long distances from their patients, their services were expensive. Under these circumstances, it became necessary for the towns to provide for the medical treatment and maintenance of the indigent sick. Such statutory provisions were enacted in Rhode Island in 1662, in Connecticut in 1673, and in New York in 1687. If a destitute patient needed medical care the overseer of the poor or the justice of peace arranged for the service of a physician. Sometimes an annual contract was made between the overseer and a physician to care for all assigned paupers. In New York, pauper patients were boarded out to families, and the city paid for their maintenance and nursing.[3] During the seventeenth century, there were no hospitals in the Colonies, and it was not before the second half of the eighteenth century that the first private hospitals were built. Because the poor law authorities were reluctant to spend money for paupers, they assumed the responsibility for payment of surgical treatment for poor patients, only after they had approved the expense or had been ordered to do so by the court. In emergencies, especially when the patient's life was endangered, physicians cared for him and later sued the poor law authorities for their fees.

In some Colonies physicians were engaged by the Colony, not by the individual towns, to "attend upon the poor generally in the county."[4] Pauper patients had no free choice of a physician. These doctors frequently were not very competent because the contracts granted them rather low compensations and because they were sometimes engaged for political and personal favoritism. Poor law physicians, however, were pioneers in the field of public health in the New World.

Mentally disturbed and feeble-minded patients—children as well as adults—were usually left with their families and without special care.

[3] David M. Schneider, *History of Public Welfare in New York, 1609-1866* (Chicago: University of Chicago Press, 1938), p. 84.

[4] Edith Abbott, *Public Assistance; American Principles and Policies* (Chicago: University of Chicago Press, 1940), p. 358.

The violently insane and the deformed were considered to be possessed by the devil. One attempted to drive out the "evil spirit" by whipping the unfortunate victim, by shackling him to stakes at the market place, or throwing him into coarse pens, leaving him to hunger and cold. Other mental patients were locked up in attics, basements, and outhouses; were put into straight jackets; chained to a wall of their homes; or confined to the local jail. When the family could not pay for the maintenance of an insane patient, the overseers farmed the "lunatic" out to people willing to take him, just as was done with lame, blind, and crippled indigents.

The first hospitals for indigent patients in the Colonies were the infirmaries or sick wards of the almshouses.[5] When the city of New York established, in 1736, its Public Workhouse and House of Correction, a physician was engaged as medical officer for the infirmary. Bellevue Hospital in New York was started, in 1794, as a "pesthouse"; and a "fever hospital ward" for patients suffering from contagious diseases was added in 1825. When most counties established almshouses during the period following the Quincy and Yates Reports, they became also the typical place of care for the indigent sick. Medical treatment and nursing were, however, inadequate in these institutions. Only in some larger almshouses were the sick paupers separated from other inmates and placed into a "sick bay" or infirmary, and even there medical care was limited to emergency operations and rare visits of the doctor. In general, sick inmates of the almshouse were left to the attention of the matron, and more often the nursing was left to other inmates. No reliable, competent nursing could be expected under such circumstances. It was not until the end of the nineteenth century that Massachusetts and Rhode Island set up special "almshouse hospitals," and that special wards in almshouses were set aside for the medical care of sick paupers. As a rule, the almshouses were neither equipped nor staffed to provide suitable medical attention to the sick inmates, because most of the houses were without water and sanitary facilities and did not separate the sick from other inmates.

The first hospitals were established as private charity institutions e.g., the Almshouse and Infirmary of the Society of Friends in Philadelphia, but after some time it became necessary for cities,

[5] Bernhard J. Stern, *Medical Services by Government* (New York: Commonwealth Fund, 1946), p. 15.

counties, or the states to grant subsidies to the hospitals. During the eighteenth century, the almshouse and hospital in some cities developed as one institution. During the nineteenth century, the separation of the hospital from the almshouse became necessary. In the western states (Washington, Oregon, Nevada, and California) the lack of almshouses caused many counties to set up hospitals. The rapid development of medical and sanitary science in the nineteenth century contributed greatly to the improvement of medical facilities in the county hospitals. An important stimulus to the raising of standards was the beginning awareness of the dangers for the entire community, of epidemics and contagious diseases.

B. CHARACTERISTICS OF PUBLIC POOR RELIEF

The deplorable conditions in the poorhouses led to three major changes in poor relief during the nineteenth century: (1) Private charity societies took the initiative in establishing orphanages and asylums, because they objected to the placement of children and helpless invalid and old people in mixed almshouses where they were forced to live with vagrants, rogues, prostitutes, mentally disturbed patients, and criminals. Private relief societies were often affiliated with churches, fraternal orders, or national benevolent associations, and they became the leading, progressive element in American social welfare during the past century. (2) The states themselves assumed responsibility for certain classes of the poor, such as the insane, the feeble-minded, and convicted offenders for whom there were no adequate local facilities. (3) Some local public relief authorities, under the influence of state boards of charity, began to question the old concepts of poor relief with their humiliating, deterrent treatment of the poor. As a whole, however, public poor relief was still following the pattern of the Elizabethan poor law.

Changes of the underlying principles and improvements in the practice of poor relief were rather slow and sporadic as a result of sociological and economic factors.

C. SOCIAL PHILOSOPHY OF POOR RELIEF

The spirit of the English poor laws dominated most of the Colonial laws, whether or not they used degrading terminology in speaking of "paupers." The public, with few exceptions, maintained its resentment against the poor tax burden and its contempt for people unable to take care of themselves in a society which identified economic prosperity and success with efficiency and virtue. Some of the most cruel forms of treatment of the poor, such as the whipping after the "warning out" and the posting of the poor roll at the market place, were gradually abandoned, but there remained the spirit of unwillingness to recognize the aid for the poor as socially necessary and justified.[6] The abuses of corrupt local politicians to maintain their positions with the help of poor relief as a matter of political expediency did not make it popular with the people. On the other hand, indigent families were still subject to such humiliation that they would rather starve than go on relief. An example of this attitude[7] is the case of a Kansas farmer's family. A severe drought that caused a failure of the crop, in 1878, forced them to ask for county relief when both husband and wife fell ill. When the family with their two children was put into the poor farm, the husband left, after he recovered from his illness, in order to take a job as a farm hand and his wife with the two children remained at the poor farm until he could earn money. The superintendent of the poor farm bound out the eight-year-old son of the couple for ten years, against the child's will and without the consent of his parents. When the parents asked for the boy, the courts refused to release the child. This treatment of parents and child characterizes the disregard of their human rights and their feelings in the practice of the old poor laws.[8]

D. INADEQUATE RELIEF FUNDS

Due to the principle of local responsibility for general poor relief, the towns, parishes, or counties had to raise from local taxes the funds for the care of the poor. The various states differed in their legislation regarding the tax power of municipalities and counties, but generally the "general property tax" on real estate was the sole source of revenue for the local government. Small towns and

[6] See Frank Bruno, *Trends in Social Work* (New York: Columbia University Press, 1948), pp. 136-137.

[7] See E. Abbott, *op. cit.*, pp. 125-179.

[8] See Grace Browning and Sophonisba P. Breckinridge, *The Development of Poor Relief Legislation in Kansas* (Chicago: University of Chicago Press, 1935), pp. 130-133.

thinly populated rural counties, therefore, were unable to raise sufficient funds for poor relief.

E. SETTLEMENT AND REMOVAL

In order to protect the taxpayers against the financial burden of additional indigents, settlement laws made elaborate provisions limiting the eligibility for public relief to lawful residents who had been in the community, county, or state for a prescribed period. Nobody could acquire legal settlement when he had been "warned out" or had applied for public or private aid during this period. The required time of settlement varied widely, but, as a rule, it was between one and five years.

Persons without legal settlement applying for poor relief were sent back to the last place of residence because they had no means of support. Since there was frequently no agreement on who was responsible for the support of a destitute person, wasteful litigation between townships and counties and between counties and states resulted.

F. FAMILY SUPPORT

Parents and adult children were legally obliged to support one another if in need, and in some states even grandparents, grandchildren, brothers, and sisters had to support their relatives. The legal enforcement of this obligation often led to the prosecution of unwilling relatives with little income, which usually brought about open hostility between destitute old parents and their children.

G. UNSKILLED ADMINISTRATION

The lack of skilled personnel was a serious obstacle to an efficient administration of the poor laws. We have already discussed the influence of the spoils system on the selection of poor law officials. Complaints of corruption and mismanagement were often justified because of the incompetence of these officials.

The practice of the poor law was incompatible with the principles of American economic development. The rapid growth of agriculture, industrial production and manufacturing enabled the masses of the population to purchase the goods of the country. The deterrent, restrictive treatment together with the lack of rehabilitation of the destitute failed, however, to enable them to become self-respecting and self-supporting citizens.

III. SOCIAL SERVICES UNDER STATE AUSPICES

The legal principle of town or county responsibility for poor relief and the development of private charities within the community explain that institutions for relief and charity were local in character. For certain groups of the poor, however, the resources of the community or the county were insufficient, so a more powerful authority had to assume responsibility. These groups were the insane, the feeble-minded, the blind, the deaf-mute, the criminal, and the delinquent. The states, therefore, had to establish the necessary provisions for the care and treatment in special institutions. This change developed gradually during the eighteenth and nineteenth centuries.

The various state institutions were administered by separate boards of directors or trustees, and at first there was no cooperation whatever between these boards nor a unified plan in using the available facilities. Finally, for financial and practical reasons, the states coordinated the use of their institutions and developed uniform standards of care in hospitals, asylums, and correctional institutions.

A. THE CARE OF THE INSANE

Mentally disturbed patients, since 1732, had received hospital care in the almshouse of Philadelphia and later, in 1753, in the Pennsylvania Hospital. But the first institution to be established especially for the mentally ill was the Eastern State Hospital at Williamsburg, Virginia, founded in 1773. With the progress of medicine and natural science, physicians became optimistic about the possibility of curing mental diseases.

Ten years after the opening of the hospital at Williamsburg, the outstanding psychiatrist of this period, Dr. Benjamin Rush, joined the medical staff of the Pennsylvania Hospital in Philadelphia and became a member of the medical faculty of the University of Pennsylvania. Dr. Rush had visited England and France and was greatly impressed by the work of Philippe Pinel at the Bicêtre Hospital in Paris. Instead of the cruel method of chaining the insane to the walls in the dungeon-like basements and the whipping of unruly patients, he advocated their humane treatment, blood-letting, and occupation of the patients in the hospital. Inspired by these ideas Dr. Benjamin Rush, in 1783, introduced the new methods to the Pennsylvania Hospital and taught them to medical students at the university. In thirty years of devoted service to the mentally ill he won the title of "The Father of American Psychiatry." Recognizing the importance of the diseases of the mind, Dr. Rush insisted that mental patients should no longer be considered incapable of human reactions and left in cold, dark, and windowless wards. He introduced cold and hot baths, placed the patients in heated and ventilated rooms, assigned them simple work as "occupational therapy," and trained male and female attendants to nurse the patients with kindness. He separated the sexes and the violent from the quiet patients, as well as the chronic from acute cases of mental illness. He removed the iron rings which had been used for chaining the patients to the wall, and changed the attitude of giving mere custodial care to giving active cure.

The Eastern State Hospital at Williamsburg, Virginia remained for nearly half a century the only hospital exclusively reserved for mental patients. In 1817, the Friends Asylum at Frankford, Pennsylvania followed as a private institution, and in 1824 the state of Kentucky opened the Eastern Lunatic Asylum at Lexington. Maryland, Massachusetts, Pennsylvania, Connecticut, Ohio, and New York followed in building institutions for the mentally ill and deficient. These mental hospitals, however, could accommodate only a small fraction of the mentally ill. Many dependent insane and feeble-minded remained neglected, and often poor law commissioners failed to commit insane paupers to the state hospitals that charged the county higher rates. They preferred to keep the insane, who could not remain with their families, in local jails, houses of correction, and almshouses.

The great pioneer for the care of the mentally ill was a woman without medical training, Dorothea Dix.[9] Born in 1802, she left her

[9] Dorothea Dix's life and work is described in Edith Abbott, *Some American Pioneers in Social Welfare* (Chicago: University of Chicago Press, 1937); Helen E. Marshall, *Dorothea Dix, Forgotten Samaritan* (Chapel Hill: University of North Carolina Press, 1937); and Francis Tiffany, *Life of Dorothea Lynde Dix* (Boston: Houghton, 1890). Dorothea Dix published several books for children, among them, *Hymns for Children* (Boston: Munroe & Francis, 1825), and *American Moral Tales for Young Persons* (Boston: L. Bowles & Greene, 1832).

parents after an unhappy childhood to live with her wealthy grandmother in Boston. At the age of fourteen she opened a school at
Worcester and, after completing her education, the Dame School
(in Boston, in 1821), which became a famous institution for girls
under her direction. Miss Dix became acquainted with the leading
citizens of New England who sent their children to her school. In
1836 health reasons forced her to take a rest in England. After her
return to Boston, in 1841, a young divinity student asked her help
in speaking at a Sunday service to women convicts at the East
Cambridge jail. Miss Dix was deeply shocked to find the women in
their cells, many of them mentally deranged, and in bare, filthy,
and unheated quarters. This caused her to enlist the help of influential friends—the statesman Charles Sumner and the physician Dr.
Samuel G. Howe—to investigate the jail with her and to mobilize
the Boston press. Her findings aroused Dorothea Dix's suspicion that
conditions in other institutions might be similar. Without any public authority Miss Dix visited every almshouse, workhouse, jail, and
prison in Massachusetts. After talking with the inmates and with
the keepers, she explored possibilities of improvements. On the advice of her friends, Miss Dix submitted in 1843 a memorial to the
state legislature[10] in which she described the shocking conditions
which she had found. Insane patients and idiots were chained to the
walls in cold cellars, beaten with rods, lashed, and confined in cages
and pens. One man was in a close stall for seventeen years, and a
young girl, naked in a barn, was the prey for the boys of the village. Another patient had been chained in an outhouse in winter so
that his feet had been frozen. Although some politicians and overseers tried to obstruct Miss Dix's survey, public indignation and the
influence of Charles Sumner, Horace Mann, Dr. Samuel Howe, and
Dr. Luther Bell led the legislature to pass a bill providing for immediate relief of the insane and the enlargement of the state lunatic
hospital at Worcester. After this success, Dorothea Dix decided to
continue her investigations of the conditions of the insane and feeble-
minded in other states. In Rhode Island, she received large donations from two philanthropists, Cyrus Butler and Nicholas Brown,

---

[10] Dorothea L. Dix, *Memorial to the Legislature of Massachusetts, 1843* (Boston: Old South Leaflets, 1889), Vol. VI, pp. 1 and 6; see also Albert Deutsch,
The Mentally Ill in America (New York: Columbia University Press, 1946),
p. 179.

for an asylum. In New Jersey, Miss Dix convinced the legislature of the necessity of building a mental hospital at Trenton. She traveled many thousands of miles in her stage coach and inspected hundreds of almshouses and jails. By her accurate, reliable reports of the suffering of mental patients she convinced eleven state legislatures of the necessity of constructing or increasing the capacity of mental hospitals. She became the crusader for the mentally ill.

Her observations convinced Dorothea Dix that with the growth of industrialization, mental diseases would increase, and that it would be necessary to obtain federal grants from Congress for the future care of the insane. In 1848, she submitted a memorial to Congress and pleaded that five million acres of land be given to the states for the care of indigent insane. When her proposal was rejected, she repeated her request in 1849, suggesting the land grant should be used also for blind and deaf-mute persons. After much delay, Congress passed the bill in 1854. The bill provided for 10,000,000 acres of land for care of insane persons and 2,250,000 acres for maintenance and training of blind and deaf-mutes (*12¼ Million Acre Bill*). However, President Pierce vetoed the bill on constitutional grounds because "the power for relief of the needy or otherwise unfortunate members of society" was vested in the states and not conferred upon the federal government. There was bitter debate in Congress, but the veto was not overruled, and it established for eighty years a principle of abstention by the federal government from the field of social welfare. But Dorothea Dix's life work had made the public aware of the sufferings of the mentally disturbed patients and had caused the building of thirty-two hospitals in our country.

B. CARE FOR THE MENTALLY DEFICIENT

For a long time the feeble-minded (idiots, imbeciles, and morons) shared the fate of the psychotic (insane). They were kept at home without proper care or were committed to jails or poorhouses whenever their families were unable or unwilling to keep them. The first attempt to educate a feeble-minded child was made in France, in 1799, when Dr. Jean Marc Gaspard Itard in Paris trained an idiot boy found by hunters exposed in the woods. In 1837, Dr. Edouard Seguin opened a private school for feeble-minded children in Paris. His work found recognition throughout Europe, and in 1848, he followed an invitation to the United States to address legislatures and medical societies in several states. In the meantime, studies of the conditions of the mentally deficient had been made in Massachusetts and New York, and the first state School for Idiots and Feeble-minded Youth was opened in South Boston, Massachusetts, in 1848. Dr. Samuel Gridley Howe, who was appointed its director, had studied the treatment of mentally deficient children in Paris.[11] The Massachusetts school developed new methods of training of feeble-minded children under Dr. Walter E. Fernald. New York built a state school for feeble-minded children at Albany in 1851. Pennsylvania granted state subsidies to a private school for idiots in Germantown in 1854, and Ohio and Connecticut followed in 1857 and 1858. Other states established state mental institutions during the following decades. Many private institutions were first supported by state grants, and later were taken over by the state when private funds were insufficient.

Other provisions for mentally deficient children were the establishment of separate classes in elementary schools and of special schools in larger cities. These schools taught subnormal children who were mentally so retarded that they could not profit by the regular school program. In order to enable the mentally deficient to become self-supporting, the states also have organized programs of vocational education, guidance, and placement services.

C. CARE OF THE BLIND

Indigent blind persons had been objects of private and public charity for a long time, and the almshouses sheltered many blind children and adults. The first attempt to educate blind children was made in Paris, in 1784, by Valentin Haüy. His school set patterns for other European institutions. A Boston physician, Dr. John D. Fisher, visited the school for the blind in Paris and aroused interest in Boston for an institution for blind children. In 1832, the Massachusetts Asylum for the Blind, under the direction of Dr. Samuel Gridley Howe, was opened.

Samuel G. Howe (1801-1876) graduated from Harvard Medical

[11] For information on Samuel Howe's life and work, see Julia W. Howe, *Reminiscence* (Boston: Houghton, 1900), and Laura E. Richards, *Samuel Gridley Howe* (New York: Appleton-Century-Crofts, Inc., 1935).

School in 1824 and joined the Greeks in their fight for independence. Before returning to the United States, Dr. Howe observed in France new methods of teaching the blind and mentally deficient. Before opening the school in Boston, Dr. Howe returned to Europe to study the methods of education of the blind in England, France, and Germany and to recruit experienced teachers for the new asylum. The school soon became too small for the growing number of blind students and moved to a mansion donated by Colonel Thomas H. Perkins. The institution later was named Perkins Institute and Massachusetts School for the Blind.

Dr. Howe's outstanding success became Laura Bridgman, a seven-year-old blind and deaf girl; she was brought to Dr. Howe as a hopeless idiot. Dr. Howe taught her, in years of patient work, to read, speak, and become an intelligent, thoughtful woman. She became, after Dr. Howe's death, one of his biographers. Together with his friend, Horace Mann, Dr. Howe achieved a reform of the Boston school system, the training of teachers, and the education of deaf-mute children.[12]

The Perkins Institution offered training of the blind in academic studies, in music, and gymnastics and developed mechanical and domestic skills for vocational preparation. Under Michael Anagnos the Howe Memorial Press, a Reference Library on Blindness and the Blind, and a kindergarten for blind children were established.

In 1832, a second school, the New York Institution for the Blind, was set up under the direction of Dr. John D. Russ, and was later known as The New York Institute for the Education of the Blind. There, in 1863, a modification of the French Braille system of raised print was introduced.

The third pioneer institution for the blind was established in Philadelphia, in 1833, by Dr. Julius Friedlander, with emphasis on industrial training and vocational guidance. These three schools served as examples for most other states. In 1837, Ohio had opened the first public institution for the blind that was financed entirely by taxation. The first school for the blind in California was combined with a school for the deaf and opened in San Francisco as a

[12] Berthold Lowenfeld, "The Blind," *Social Work Year Book, 1949,* p. 60; M. Robert Barnett and Helga Lende, "The Blind," *Social Work Year Book, 1954,* pp. 55-60; Thomas D. Cutsforth, *The Blind in School and Society; A Psychological Study* (New York: American Foundation for the Blind, 1951).

private institution, in 1860, to be financed by the state a month after its establishment.[13]

In day schools for blind children (the first one started in Chicago, in 1900), they are taught together with sighted children, but the blind ones receive special instruction in reading, writing, and arithmetic. Now all states have developed schooling for blind children, either in special classes or by home teachers.

The prevention of blindness was first stressed by Dr. Park Lewis in New York. There, the State Commission for the Prevention of Blindness, organized under Miss Louise Schuyler in 1908, primarily spread the knowledge of prophylaxis to prevent ophthalmia neonatorum, an eye infection at childbirth. The Commission, now named the National Society for the Prevention of Blindness, extends its program to the entire country, includes other diseases which may lead to blindness, and promotes safety programs in industry for the protection of eye sight.

The first state to enact special legislation for the financial maintenance of the blind was Indiana, which passed a statute on the indigent blind as early as 1840. Other states followed—Ohio in 1898, Illinois in 1903, and Wisconsin in 1907. Before the enactment of the *Social Security Act* in 1935, twenty-nine states had passed special statutes on blind relief. There was, however, among social workers and among the blind themselves differences of opinion whether special relief was not undermining the initiative of the blind in their attempt to learn a trade or a profession and thus to become self-reliant citizens. This desire of the blind to be respected as normal human beings deserves recognition, appreciation, and encouragement. The number of blind persons in the United States is estimated at about 300,000.

D. THE CARE OF THE DEAF AND DEAF-MUTE

Different from the blind, the deaf and deaf-mute have found in human society less sympathy and willingness to help them. Their inability to understand the world around them has been a source of irritation or ridicule to others. If the deaf were poor, they were

[13] Frances Cahn and Valeska Bary, *Welfare Activities of Federal, State and Local Government in California* (Berkeley: University of California Press, 1936), pp. 114-121; see also Hector Cheoigny and Sydell Braverman, *The Adjustment of the Blind* (New Haven: Yale University Press, 1950).

treated as idiots, left to their families, or placed in poorhouses. Some attempts to teach the deaf were made by Spanish and French monks in the sixteenth and seventeenth centuries. But the first scientific training of deaf-mute children came in the eighteenth century and was the life work of Jacob Rodriges Pereire of Bordeaux, France. Based upon Pereire's method the first school for deaf-mute children was founded in Paris, in 1760, by the Abbé Charles Michel de l'Epée. Students of his school founded other institutions for the deaf and deaf-mute in Europe. At the same time, John Braidwood opened a school for the deaf in Edinburgh, Scotland which for generations held a monopoly in instruction of the deaf in Great Britain.

An attempt to teach the deaf in the United States was made in New York when, in 1810, Dr. John Stanford, a minister, found a number of deaf children on his visits to the almshouse and offered them religious education. In 1812, John Braidwood, Jr., a grandson of the founder of the Edinburgh institution, came to America and tried to open schools for the deaf in Virginia, New York, and Baltimore. He had no success since the public was apathetic to the fate of the deaf, and Mr. Braidwood was not familiar with American customs.

When at Hartford, Connecticut in 1815 Alice Cogswell, the deaf daughter of a physician, was in need of education, friends of the family took up a collection and sent Dr. Thomas H. Gallaudet to Europe in order to study the methods of teaching the deaf. In England the disillusioned Braidwood family prevented him from observing their work, but in Paris Abbé Sicard, director of the Paris school for the deaf, instructed him in the art of training the deaf. He also sent one of his best teachers, Lautent Clerc, with Dr. Gallaudet to America where both opened the first American Asylum for the Deaf at Hartford, in 1817.

The first *public*, residential school for the deaf was the Central College at Danville, Kentucky, organized in 1823. Other states followed the Kentucky pattern—Ohio in 1829, Virginia in 1838, Indiana in 1844, Tennessee in 1845, Georgia in 1846, and California in 1861. Private as well as public institutions for the deaf, in their early development, had the character of charities and were primarily devoted to the education of poor deaf children. The first day school for deaf children was opened in New York, in 1869, under Mr. Fuller. In the beginning, sign language was taught, more recently the oral method and lipreading have been emphasized. Frequently both methods are combined. In 1864, Congress granted funds for the organization of the Columbia Institute for the Deaf and Dumb in Washington, D. C. Thus, of all the handicapped groups, the federal government first assumed responsibility for the education of the deaf. Today, fourty-four states have residential schools for the deaf; Delaware and Wyoming operate day schools; and New Hampshire and Nevada send their deaf children to the schools of neighboring states.

The deaf are no longer treated as charity cases, but as people of normal intelligence permitted to participate in such occupations as they can perform. There are about 90,000 deaf and 10 million hard-of-hearing persons in the United States, and emphasis is laid upon their education, not on public assistance.[14]

In California, for example, the supervision of all educational measures for children and adults with defective hearing is coordinated in the State Department of Education's Bureau for the Deaf and Hard-of-Hearing. The training program includes a residential state school at Berkeley, special classes and day schools for deaf and hard-of-hearing children, and evening classes for hard-of-hearing adults.

Private societies, such as the American Society for the Hard-of-Hearing, support the work for the prevention of deafness by information of the public about the danger of scarlet fever. They procure hearing aids for people who cannot afford to buy them, and urge the medical examination of preschool children, so that medical treatment and education may start early.

E. THE "STATE POOR"

Since local poor relief was granted only to residents who had acquired legal settlement, towns refused to take care of other paupers who had recently arrived, or were "warned out." The urgent needs for food and medical care of such unfortunates, however,

---

[14] Stanley S. Stevens and Hallowell Davis, *Hearing: Its Psychology and Physiology* (New York: Wiley, 1938); George William Bachman, *Health Resources in the United States; Personnel, Facilities, and Services* (Washington, D.C.: Brookings Institution, 1952); Hallowell Davis (editor), *Hearing and Deafness; A Guide for Laymen* (New York: Rinehart, 1947); and Minnie M. Hill, "The Deaf and the Hard of Hearing," *Social Work Year Book, 1954,* pp. 162-165.

could not fully be denied. For this reason the Colonial legislature of Massachusetts assumed the payment of the necessary expenses for these "state paupers" as early as 1675. Other Colonies took similar measures, particularly in such periods of emergencies as attacks by Indian tribes, inundations, and other natural disasters. In New York State relief at the expense of the state treasury was granted those refugees who fled in the wars against the Indians and, in 1778, to the survivors of veterans in the War of the Revolution.

The assumption of state responsibility for persons without legal settlement and without an earlier residence to which they could be returned became a necessity, because the township or county refused to care for such persons in need.[15] The beginning of industrial production in the New England states attracted agricultural workers from the farms to look for jobs in the towns. If they lost their job the period of legal settlement often had not been attained, so that the number of "state poor" greatly increased during the nineteenth century and sometimes was almost as high as that of the resident poor under township relief.

Another group of needy persons who were considered a responsibility of the Colonies and later the states, rather than of local government, were the disabled veterans. For the veterans, various provisions were enacted during the Colonial period. Immediately after the Revolution the federal government became the main source of their support, while the states continued to grant veterans and survivors of veterans additional pensions and special privileges.

F. CRIME AND DELINQUENCY

During the Middle Ages and up to the sixteenth century, many crimes were punished by death or exile. Prisoners were detained, usually tortured before sentence, and incarcerated, often for life, in dungeons of castles or towers. No consideration was given to their health, and they lived or died under the worst conditions. In the Colonial period a large number of crimes against persons or property was punished by hanging or by banishment from the Colony. Persons arrested were held by the sheriff or his deputies in

[15] The states paid a lump sum for the relief of these "state poor" to the town, which delegated its poor relief to a contractor. Frequently, both the town and the contractor wanted to profit from this appropriation so that very meager care resulted for the poor.

the local jail. This frequently was not a safe place because outbreaks of desperate criminals and attacks by gangs of friends of the convicted person were not rare, but no other facilities existed until the later part of the eighteenth century.[16] The growing population, the deportation of convicts from Australia and England to America, and the changing economic structure of our country led to an increase in serious crimes. On the other hand, the influence of French humanitarianism made it difficult to continue the death sentence as punishment for minor crimes. As the number of convicted offenders became larger, the communities were looking to the states for protection. Pennsylvania was the first to establish a state penal institution. In 1790, the legislature decided to convert the local jail at Walnut Street in Philadelphia into a state prison. Since its founding by William Penn, Pennsylvania lived under the influence of the philosophy of the Religious Society of Friends (Quakers). They were convinced that the divine power in every human being could achieve his reformation and that the sinner left to meditation would repent and give up his sin. In accordance with this philosophy, prisoners in the state prison in Philadelphia were segregated into two groups. Those convicted for such serious crimes as murder, arson, adultery, burglary, and manslaughter were confined to solitary cells without communication with other prisoners. Others who had committed minor offenses were lodged in dormitories, and lived in groups. The new method meant a classification of the prisoners according to the nature of their offense; it was a step toward differentiation of treatment and rehabilitation. Under this Pennsylvania System of prisons, which was accepted by other states (New York, Virginia, Massachusetts, Vermont), more humane treatment and less corporal punishment were exercised. The system was optimistic in hoping for an inner reformation of the convict. However, the lack of qualified and devoted personnel, due to low wages of the warden and guards, overcrowding of the institutions, idleness of the convicts, lack of sufficient funds for proper management, and

---

[16] The typical jail was a "catch-all" for dangerous criminals, minor offenders, debtors, and destitute people. There was no separation of prisoners by crime, age, or sex. Debauchery and promiscuous intercourse were frequent. The jailers demanded fees from all prisoners, regardless whether they had been acquitted by the court. See Orlando Lewis, *The Development of American Prisons and Prison Customs* (New York: American Prison Association, 1922), p. 13.

political scandals, led to a failure of this type of prison management.

A second type of state prison was introduced at Auburn, New York, in 1816. It differed from the Pennsylvania plan inasmuch as the prisoners were confined only at night to solitary cells, but had to work during the day in congregate prison workshops. The plan of reformation by isolation was abandoned; confinement to a single cell was used only as a disciplinary measure. Following the example of the prison at Ghent (Belgium), the Auburn prison was built in a star shape with cell blocks opening to a gallery which could be easily watched by one single guard in the center of the building at each floor. The Auburn System was widely accepted, and well-known prisons, such as Sing Sing in New York (1825) and San Quentin in California (1852), followed its pattern.

Prison reform in the United States, the introduction of humane treatment of the convicts, and the use of work as a means of rehabilitation was influenced by experiences of the English reformers (particularly John Howard)[17] and by the penal philosophy of Beccaria and Lombroso. In this reform it proved important to segregate young offenders from hard-boiled criminals; this resulted in the establishment, in 1876, of a special institution in Elmira, New York. The reformatory was used for young convicts between sixteen and thirty years of age, and later also for older first offenders. Its main purpose was to prevent the "habitual criminals" from infecting younger offenders. The first prison for women was established at Sherborn, Massachusetts, in 1879, and most states followed by building separate penal institutions for women.

In prisons and penitentiaries, as well as in reformatories, modern industrial machinery is now used for the work of the convicts in workshops, in addition to agricultural employment and road building. The present method, therefore, is called the Industrial Prison System. The production of goods in prisons or by prison gangs hired by farmers, mill owners, and manufacturers presented serious competition with free labor. Employers, workers, and particularly labor unions objected to this competition so that federal and state legislation finally limited the use of prison labor (discussed in Chapter 15), but modern industrial machinery in penal institutions is necessary in order to train the prisoners for useful work.

[17] See Chapter 2.

IV. STATE BOARDS OF CHARITIES

The increasing number of state institutions for the handicapped groups in the nineteenth century, such as hospitals, insane asylums, schools for the blind and deaf, prisons and penitentiaries, asylums for the mentally defective, and reform schools for delinquent boys and girls, created a chaotic state of administration. Each of these institutions was based upon special state legislation and was placed under the administration of a different board of directors. Each board requested annually higher appropriations from the legislature. There was no uniform policy in principles of management, treatment of inmates, and budgets or personnel standards in institutions even within the same state. The lack of coordination of the various institutions and of intelligent use of their facilities was badly felt.

The first state to create a central agency for the supervision of all state charitable institutions was Massachusetts, which organized a State Board of Charities in 1863. The Board had an able secretary in Mr. Frank S. Sanborn, and Dr. Samuel Gridley Howe[18] served from 1864 for ten years as its president. He initiated a survey of the existing statutes and regulations of the lunatic asylums, state hospitals and almshouses, industrial schools, and charitable institutions for which Massachusetts granted annual subsidies. Dr. Howe recommended methods for humane treatment of the poor in all these institutions and for efficient management; these were published, in 1866, under the title *Principles of Public Charities*. They emphasized the family system in placing children and adults in the community whenever it was not absolutely necessary to keep them in almshouses, hospitals, or asylums. Members of the Massachusets Board of Charities inspected not only the state almshouses, lunatic asylums, reform schools and prisons but also local almshouses and jails. Information and data collected from the inspections were summarized and submitted to the legislature. In five years, the State Board of Charities succeeded in reducing substantially the number of "state paupers," in introducing a plan of classification for all inmates of state institutions, and in establishing order in the administration of all state charity institutions. In 1869, a "state visiting agent" was appointed to attend the trials of juvenile delinquents before the

[18] For Samuel Howe's other achievements, see pages 94-95.

courts in order to assume care for the children who were not committed to reform schools. The state agent became a forerunner of the juvenile probation officer.

The advantages of a central state charity agency were soon recognized in other states. They followed the example of Massachusetts, in that each established its own State Board of Charities and Correction. In the meantime Massachusetts had added, in 1869, an agency of coordination in the field of public health—the State Board of Health. Its example stimulated other states to organize such boards, first California in 1870 and then the District of Columbia in 1871.

The main results of the activities of the State Boards of Charities were (1) better care and protection of dependent children who were removed from the poorhouses, placed in licensed children's asylums or in foster homes with standards set by the state boards; (2) more uniform and more efficient administration of local public relief; (3) decrease of pauperism and economic suffering in industrial districts by control and protection of immigrants; (4) improvement in the care of the mentally ill; (5) progress in criminal reform and rehabilitation of prisoners; and (6) the foundation, in 1871, of the National Conference of Charities and Correction, now the National Conference of Social Work.

In the western states the historical sequence of local and state responsibility for poor relief differed from the development in eastern and midwestern states. In California, for example, counties or cities were unable to face the serious social problems of the Gold Rush of 1850, when tens of thousands of immigrants arrived after long, strenuous travels. Mining towns had no facilities for medical care nor public relief of any kind. Thus, for the first years of California's statehood the state government was forced to assume the sole responsibility for the maintenance of the sick and of orphans. Orphanages founded by religious societies were first partly maintained by municipal subsidies, later by the state. In 1853, the counties under the Boards of Supervisors assumed the responsibility for the care of the aged and the sick, which was regulated by a state *Poor Law of 1855*.

Upon the requests of various citizens' groups and social agencies under the leadership of Katharine Felton, Director of the Associated Charities of San Francisco, the legislature established a State Board of Charities and Corrections, in 1903, for the supervision of the charitable, correctional, and penal institutions of the state, the counties, and cities. In 1913, Children's Agents in the State Board of Control were appointed to supervise children's institutions and children in foster care for whom state aid was paid; their activities were, in 1921, assigned to the Bureau of Children's Aid in the Department of Finance. Finally, in 1925, the functions of supervision and control of state agencies were consolidated in the Department of Public Welfare which was renamed, in 1927, the State Department of Social Welfare. This illustration of the California development[19] is characteristic of the haphazard legislation and the slow development of systematic organization of welfare functions in the western states.

V. PRIVATE SOCIAL AGENCIES AND THE CHARITY ORGANIZATION

The inadequacies of the mixed poorhouses that were harmful to the poor, and especially to children and young people who were forced to live with vagrants, criminal elements, prostitutes, and sick and mentally disturbed persons, were the main incentive for the foundation of private social agencies during the nineteenth century. As we have seen, religious charities and philanthropic relief societies were already in existence, but their activities were limited to aid for some special local groups. One of the first organizations which attempted to find a constructive remedy for people in economic distress was the New York Society for the Prevention of Pauperism, created in 1817. Its aim was to determine scientifically what were the causes of poverty and to develop means of rehabilitation instead of the mere palliative of financial relief. In a survey under the auspices of the Society, the following causes of poverty were found: ignorance; idleness; intemperance; lack of thrift; imprudent, hasty marriages; lotteries; pawnbrokers; houses of prostitution; gambling; and the large number of charitable institutions. The Society divided the city of New York into districts and assigned to each district two or three volunteer "visitors of the indigent" as its agents. It introduced bills in the city council in order to prohibit street begging and to restrict saloons, which were considered a primary cause of destitution. The Society established an employment bureau and a savings bank and encouraged the foundation of mutual aid and mutual life insurance

[19] See F. Cahn and V. Bary, *op. cit.,* pp. XIII-XX.

groups to protect their members against economic hazards. For home industrial employment of women supplies were provided. The activities of the Society revealed the lack of cooperation between the various charitable organizations and the need for constructive rehabilitation of the poor families.

In Boston, the Reverend Joseph Tuckerman, a Unitarian minister and city missionary, was appointed by the Massachusetts legislature, in 1832, to conduct a survey of the conditions of the poor. His investigations showed the influences of low wages and unemployment, which did not permit the unskilled worker and his family to buy the bare necessities of life. He recommended securing better housing facilities for the poor, compulsory school attendance for all children, and providing an individual consideration of the conditions and needs of each family in distress.

After a severe winter in 1843, which included large-scale unemployment in New York, the Association for Improving the Condition of the Poor was founded in order to coordinate the disorganized relief measures of the large number of church and other charitable societies which had been set up to give relief. The Association, under the able leadership of Robert Hartley, criticized the indiscriminate almsgiving without knowledge of the individual needs of the applicants and the lack of constructive measures which helped to make the poor families self-supporting. The Association requested that each applicant for relief be visited in his home by either a volunteer or an employee of the charity society so that the family could be counseled.

The city was divided into twenty-one districts with 225 sub-districts, each of them assigned to one "friendly visitor." The Association did not grant money, but the visitor might enlist financial aid from relatives or friends of the poor, or from relief societies. The Association attempted to restrict lotteries, gambling, and drinking, and it organized the foundation of the New York Juvenile Asylum in 1851, the Society for the Relief of the Ruptured and Crippled in 1853, and the New York Children's Aid Society in 1854. Similar associations were established in other cities.[20] These associations had certain success in the line of social reform, but they did not accomplish the desired cooperation between the numerous relief and

[20] Frank D. Watson, *The Charity Organization Movement in the United States* (New York: Macmillan, 1922), pp. 80-87.

charity societies. These agencies jealously guarded the favor of wealthy citizens for contributions to their own institutions and refused to cooperate in a systematic plan for relief and rehabilitation.

A. THE CHARITY ORGANIZATION SOCIETIES

In the economic depression of 1873, the public again became aware of the inadequacy and disorganization of public and private relief, and its interest in the work of the London Charity Organization Society was aroused.[21] The Reverend S. Humphreys Gurteen who had been previously in London and was acquainted with the Charity Organization Society, organized, in 1877, in Buffalo, New York the first society of this type in the United States. Its aim was to help the poor more effectively and to avoid waste of funds, competition, and duplication of work among the relief societies. Within ten years, twenty-five charity organization societies were founded. Among their leaders were Josephine Shaw Lowell in New York, Robert T. Paine and Zilpha D. Smith in Boston, Amos G. Warner in Baltimore, and the Reverend Oscar McCulloch in Indianapolis. The main principles of the Charity Organization Societies (C.O.S.) were (1) cooperation of all local charity agencies under a board of their representatives; (2) a central "confidential register" in order to avoid duplication of work, fraud, and waste of money; and (3) a social investigation of every applicant by a "friendly visitor" in order to determine the need and the individual measures necessary in each individual case.

The founders of the societies represented the "bourgeois benevolence," wealthy citizens who felt morally obligated to alleviate the suffering of the poor and hoped thus to minimize political unrest and industrial strife. The members of the board, manufacturers, bankers, and merchants wanted to be respected in their communities as religious and philanthropic benefactors and civic leaders. Their economic and political philosophy influenced the attitude of the visitors. They believed that poverty was caused by personal fault, idleness, negligence, mismanagement, waste of wages by drinking, gambling and vice. It was hoped that friendly advice of the visitor would strengthen the moral fiber of the indigent and encourage them

[21] *Ibid.,* p. 211; the London Charity Organization Society was more fully treated in Chapter 2.

to become self-supporting, by help in procuring employment and sometimes with the aid of a loan.

Although this doctrine was originally the accepted social philosophy of the C.O.S., the visitors found that there were other factors that caused destitution, when they became more intimately acquainted with the conditions of "their families." They recognized that unhealthy neighborhood and housing conditions prevented the maintenance of health and morals, that low wages did not allow the purchase of adequate food and clothes even with careful housekeeping and thrift. Jobs were scarce in periods of economic depressions, and it was not the fault of the unemployed worker that he could not find a new position. In times of sickness or unemployment, families became the victims of "loan sharks" who caused them to be in debt for years by high interest and heartless pressure. Others lost their meager savings by fraud. The practical experiences of the visitors thus revealed that the concept of individual fault did not stand the test of honest analysis. They began to ask for measures which would fundamentally change those social conditions, and became advocates of social reform. In order to implement the findings of their members, Charity Organization Societies became active in promoting social legislation for improvement of housing, clearance of slums, and better enforcement of housing and tenement legislation, as well as in measures for prevention and treatment of tuberculosis wide-spread among the poverty stricken classes. Some societies established employment bureaus, loan societies, workshops, laundries, lumberyards, wayfarers' lodges and shelters, and legal aid bureaus. Training centers were set up for the rehabilitation of handicapped people, the blind, the deaf and crippled, and for domestic training of girls. Hospitals, dispensaries, and visiting nurses' services, recreation and summer camps, nurseries for young children, fresh air playgrounds and related facilities were organized under the auspices of Charity Organization Societies. They supported the movement for child labor legislation and the organization of special courts for children and adolescents. Many active workers and volunteers of the Charity Organization Societies felt the need for a deeper understanding of the behavior of individuals and of social and economic problems and asked for special training for social work. Such study was first suggested by Anna Davis of Pittsfield, Massachusetts, in 1893, and Mary Richmond, in 1897, formulated the plan for the establishment of a Training School for Applied Philanthropy, which led to the organization of the first social work courses in New York in 1898.[22] Out of these requests within the Charity Organization Societies grew the recognition of the need of professional education for social work. Another characteristic of the Charity Organization Societies was that their members desired for themselves, and for the public, reliable information on social and health conditions and on the activities of the societies. The result was the publication of a new magazine, *Charities Review*, in New York in 1891, which later merged in 1910 with several other related journals and became one of the leading professional publications under the title, *The Survey*. This was published until 1952, and has greatly contributed to the theoretical and practical development of social work.

The Charity Organization Societies did not attempt to reform public poor relief. They followed Thomas Chalmers' belief that receipt of public poor relief weakened the initiative and moral strength of the indigent. In several cities—Brooklyn, New York, Baltimore, Philadelphia, Washington, St. Louis, Kansas City, Missouri, and San Francisco—the Charity Organization Societies convinced the city councils that public outdoor relief could be abolished and might be dispensed by private relief agencies. Some societies received public subsidies, for several years, for saving the municipal treasury the expense for public outdoor relief.

In their programs the Charity Organization Societies faced two conflicting tasks: They had been organized to achieve better coordination and integration of the existing relief societies and to achieve a constructive development of the health and social resources of the community. On the other hand, vested interests among member agencies often resented recommendations for changes of methods of work, so that some of the societies were forced to establish themselves new divisions for service to families in need. These divisions conflicted with the activities of other relief societies, which objected because the C.O.S. had not been founded to set up rival organizations. Therefore at the suggestion of Francis H. McLean, Director of the Russell Sage Foundation, a separation of functions of the Charity Organization Societies was performed. In 1908, in

[22] Edith Abbott, *Social Welfare and Professional Education*, Rev. ed. (Chicago: University of Chicago Press, 1942), pp. 20-21; and Frank J. Bruno, *Trends in Social Work* (New York: Columbia University Press, 1948), pp. 138-140.

Pittsburgh, Pennsylvania, a Council of Social Agencies was founded as the social welfare coordination and planning body. It was composed of representatives of all member social agencies, and The Associated Charities of Pittsburgh was organized as a family welfare society. This pattern was applied in most of the C.O.S. They assumed the title Council of Social Agencies for their planning and coordinating activities,[23] while United Charities, Federated Charities, and so forth were established as nondenominational family and children's services. The Council of Social Agencies had difficulties in raising its operating funds from the public because administrative functions do not appeal to the donors. Thus in 1913, in Cleveland, the need for joint financing of all private charity work, including the activities of the Council of Social Agencies, was recognized, and led to the establishment of a Community Chest as the organization for collecting private contributions and donations and for their fair distribution to the social agencies.

One of the main arguments that C.O.S. had used in their criticism of public relief was that they were able to operate cheaper than poor law authorities and would save taxpayers' money. Local governments, states, and even Congress had for a long time supported the work of private charities by subsidies for institutions, schools, hospitals, and for relief services to children and adults. Examples have been already mentioned. In Pennsylvania, in 1889, almost one-third of the public expenses for charities and corrections was spent in subsidies to private charities, and in New York City, in 1890, the percentage of expenditure for support of private charities from public taxes was still higher. This practice was widely used throughout the country.[24]

The main point in favor of public subsidies to private relief societies was that they were more economic. They used endowments, donations, voluntary contributions and often had only minor expenses for salaries and wages, particularly in sectarian agencies which

[23] Councils of similar nature had been set up before in New York City, Rochester, and Elmira, New York (Frank Bruno, *op. cit.*, p. 194.) See also Wayne McMillen, *Community Organization for Social Welfare* (Chicago: University of Chicago Press, 1949), pp. 320-321; and Chapter 21.

[24] Amos G. Warner, Stuart A. Queen, and Ernest B. Harper, *American Charities and Social Work* (New York: Crowell, 1930), pp. 185-189; Arthur P. Miles, *An Introduction to Public Welfare* (Boston: Heath, 1949) p. 148; and F. Bruno, *op. cit.*, pp. 67-69.

used the service of volunteers and religious orders. Another argument was that private charities had a wholesome moral influence upon the clients, and were directed by devoted people, not by "bureaucrats" or political appointees. The "spoils system" in public service had indeed caused mismanagement and inadequacies in public relief. Some philanthropists also thought that relief from private charities would not burden the poor with the stigma of pauper relief and was less degrading.

On the other hand, there were valid arguments against tax-supported subsidies to private charities: the objection that public funds should not be spent for denominational or private purposes; that private charity encouraged pauperism and frequently duplicated public efforts; and, that public subsidies would weaken the willingness of sponsors to contribute to private charities. From the point of social philosophy the subsidy system had definite weaknesses. Our country's characteristics are self-reliance, pride of independence, and neighborly aid to people in distress, so it seemed inconsistent for private charity to ask for the help of the same government that was criticized in its relief administration as corrupt and inefficient.

The new concept of public subsidy to private agencies made it necessary that certain safeguards were introduced whenever public tax funds were used to subsidize private social work. The formula "public control must go where public money goes" expresses this trend. This principle requires the following measures: (1) The methods and standards of the private agency have to be approved by the public organization granting the subsidy; (2) the private agency and institution has to permit inspections by government representatives; (3) the organization has to keep accounts, has to allow their auditing and has to render reports; (4) the admission policy of the private institution needs approval by the public subsidizing agency; and (5) the private agency agrees to ask for a uniform rate of subsidy for each needy client or patient per month or day. The general trend seems toward limiting the use of public funds for public social welfare activities, leaving the maintenance of private social agencies to their own membership, to donations and foundations, and to financial campaigns through Community Chests.[25]

[25] An analysis of the principles involved in public subsidies in social work is to be found in Arlien Johnson, *Public Policy and Private Charities* (Chicago: University of Chicago Press, 1931).

B. THE SETTLEMENT HOUSE MOVEMENT

The development of modern industry brought masses of workers and their families into the cities. They lived in overcrowded quarters, without comfort, sufficient space for their children and without relatives and friends whom they had left in rural villages or towns from which they had come. Even more forlorn were the large numbers of immigrants, arriving in the United States, who increased the masses of industrial labor and who were living in slums and in unsanitary surroundings of overcrowded flats or shabby shacks around the factories, railroad yards, docks, or stock yards. Little of promise from an educational or cultural standpoint could be expected in neighborhoods where poverty went hand in hand with sickness and ignorance. There was little mutual understanding among the poor who came from different racial and religious backgrounds and spoke different languages. The need for the creation of a new sense of neighborhood spirit in order to make good citizens out of underprivileged families in slum conditions had first been felt by Canon Samuel Barnett and his friends at Toynbee Hall in London.[26] Toynbee Hall gave the inspiration to American visitors that educated persons living in such a neighborhood together with the poor and sharing life with the underprivileged would be a valiant factor in overcoming dangers of social and spiritual disorganization. Stanton Coit and Charles B. Stover were the first Americans to transplant the idea of the settlement house to this country. After a study of Toynbee Hall and European experiments, they founded, in 1887, the Neighborhood Guild of New York City, later changed to the University Settlement House. One of the most important social settlements in the United States became Hull House in Chicago, founded by Jane Addams and Ellen Gates Starr, in 1889.

Jane Addams, one of the great pioneers in American social work, was born in Cedarville, Illinois, in 1861. Since her childhood she had wanted to live among the poor. Her travels with Ellen Starr in Europe, the observation of living conditions in Italy and London, and the remarkable success of the Barnetts at Toynbee Hall strengthened Miss Addams' desire to create a similar cultural center in Chicago. They did not plan a new charity, but they built the settlement house

[26] See Chapter 2, pages 42-43; and Jane Addams, *Twenty Years at Hull House* (New York: Macmillan, 1910), pp. 121-127.

as a place for the working people (particularly new immigrant groups of various nations and religions), where they might enjoy life in the new country with its opportunities, in order to develop those higher moral and intellectual qualities upon which depend values of living in a democracy.[27] Hull House, the settlement on the West side of Chicago, on Hallsted Street, was open to large groups of foreign immigrants in the neighborhood: Bohemians, Italians, Germans, Greeks, Polish and Russian Jews, and Irish newcomers. Among the residents who joined Jane Addams in devoted work at Hull House were Florence Kelley, Julia Lathrop, Edith and Grace Abbott, Mrs. J. T. Bowens, Graham Taylor, and Alice Hamilton. Although at first the neighborhood was distrustful of the aims of the newcomers, some people accepted the invitation to visit the settlement house, began to ask for advice and came to work with the residents. Deserted women, injured workmen, widows, families unable to pay their installments on furniture asked for counsel. To meet the needs of the neighborhood, a day nursery and kindergarten were established, followed by various clubs for boys and girls. An art gallery was donated by a Chicago merchant. Discussion and study groups, a school of music, dramatics and arts, classes in rhythm and dancing, and workshops for children and adults developed. Later Hull House organized playgrounds, summer camps, and recreation for children and adults. The residents became active in promoting factory legislation, better housing, adequate wages and working hours, arbitration of labor disputes, free employment services, and other social reforms. Jane Addams and her co-workers lectured to civic groups in order to convince them of the need of social legislation, child labor protection, prohibition of night work for women and children, juvenile courts, and probation services. Playgrounds and summer camps for children and recreational and school reforms were other activities which grew from the experiences of Hull House.[28]

[27] Jane Addams, "A Function of the Social Settlement," *The Annals of the American Academy of Political and Social Science*, Vol. 13, May, 1899, pp. 323-345; and *Twenty Years at Hull House* (New York: Macmillan, 1910), Chapters VI and VII.

[28] In this connection the leading role of Jane Addams as a pacifist, in the international women's movement, in the fight for women's suffrage and for civil liberty, in foreign relief for the children after the end of World War I, for school reform, tolerance in religious and racial questions can only be indicated. Among her books are the following: *Democracy and Social Ethics* (1902), *Newer Ideals of Peace* (1907), *The Spirit of Youth and the City Streets* (1909), *Twenty Years at Hull House* (1910), and *The Second Twenty Years at Hull House* (1930). Jane Addams died May 21, 1935.

The experiences of Hull House helped in the development of other settlement houses. We might mention here College Settlement for Women in New York (1889), Andover House in Boston (later called South End House), founded by Robert A. Woods in 1892, and Chicago Commons organized by Professor Graham Taylor in 1894. Lillian Wald and Mary Brewer founded Henry Street Settlement in New York in 1894; Mary Kingsbury Simkhovitch, the Cooperative Social Settlement (later, Greenwich House) in New York; Mary McDowell, the University of Chicago Settlement near the stockyards. Other early settlement houses were Gaylord White Union Settlement attached to Union Theological Seminary in New York; Goodrich House in Cleveland; the Irene Kaufman Settlement in Pittsburgh, Pennsylvania; and Telegraph Hill Neighborhood House in San Francisco (1903).

Residents of settlement houses became champions of social reform. Living among the poorest classes of industrial workers and immigrants, they recognized the damage done by unsanitary housing conditions, overcrowded flats, low wages, night work for women and children. No wonder that among their ranks were pioneers for social action. From the settlement houses came the call for slum clearance, for special juvenile courts to deal with young offenders, and for the organization of the Consumers' League in order to help the housewife and to protect the health of the family. They requested housing legislation, supported the prevention of tuberculosis, and organized child labor committees.

SELECTED BIBLIOGRAPHY

*Abbott, Edith, *Public Assistance. American Principles and Policies*, Vol. I. Chicago: University of Chicago Press, 1940.
*———, *Some American Pioneers in Social Welfare: Select Documents with Editorial Notes*. Chicago: University of Chicago Press, 1937.
*Abbott, Grace, *The Child and the State: Select Documents with Introductory Notes*. 2 vols. Chicago: University of Chicago Press, 1938.
*Addams, Jane, *Twenty Years at Hull House: With Autobiographical Notes*. New York: Macmillan, 1910.
———, et al., *Philanthropy and Social Progress*. New York: Crowell, 1893.
Benton, Josiah H., *Warning Out in New England*. Boston: Clarke, 1911.
*Best, Harry, *Blindness and the Blind in the United States*. New York: Macmillan, 1934.

————, *Deafness and the Deaf in the United States.* New York: Macmillan, 1943.

Bosworth, Francis, "Settlements and Neighborhood Centers," *Social Work Year Book, 1954,* pp. 470-474.

Breckinridge, Sophonisba P., *Public Welfare Administration in the United States,* 3rd impression. Chicago: University of Chicago Press, 1935.

Browning, Grace, and Sophonisba P. Breckinridge, *The Development of Poor Relief Legislation in Kansas.* Chicago: University of Chicago Press, 1935.

*Bruno, Frank J., *Trends in Social Work: As Reflected in the Proceedings of the National Conference on Social Work, 1874-1946.* New York: Columbia University Press, 1948.

Cahn, Frances and Valeska Bary, *Welfare Activities of Federal, State, and Local Governments in California, 1850-1935.* Berkeley: University of California Press, 1936.

*Clarke, Helen I., *Principles and Practice of Social Work.* New York: Appleton-Century-Crofts, Inc., 1947.

Coit, Stanton, *Neighborhood Guilds: An Instrument of Social Reform.* London: Sonnenschein, 1841.

Corner, George W., *The Autobiography of Benjamin Rush.* Princeton: Princeton University Press, 1950.

Creech, Margaret D., *Three Centuries of Poor Law Administration.* Chicago: University of Chicago Press, 1936.

*Deutsch, Albert, *The Mentally Ill in America: A History of Their Care and Treatment from Colonial Times.* New York: Columbia University Press, 1946.

Devine, Edward J., *When Social Work Was Young.* New York: Macmillan, 1939.

Dix, Dorothea L., *Memorial to the Legislature of Massachusetts, 1843.* Boston: Old South Leaflets, Vol. VI, 1889.

Duffus, R. L., *Lillian Wald: Neighbor and Crusader.* New York: Macmillan, 1938.

Frampton, Merle, *Education of the Blind.* New York: World Book Co., 1940.

French, Richard Slayton, *From Homer to Helen Keller: A Social and Educational Study of the Blind.* New York: American Foundation for the Blind, 1932.

Greer, Thomas H., *American Social Reform Movements: Their Pattern Since 1865.* New York: Prentice-Hall, Inc., 1949.

Hayes, Samuel Perkins, *Contributions to a Psychology of Blindness.* New York: American Foundation for the Blind, 1941.

Henderson, Charles R., *Introduction to the Study of the Dependent, Defective and Delinquent Classes and Their Social Treatment.* Boston: Heath, 1893.

————, *Modern Methods of Charity.* New York: Macmillan, 1904.

———, *Social Settlements.* New York: Lentilhon, 1899.

Howe, Julia W., *Reminiscences (1819-1899).* Boston: Houghton, 1900.

Jernegan, Marcus W., *Laboring and Dependent Classes in Colonial America, 1607-1783.* Chicago: University of Chicago Press, 1931.

Johnson, Arlien, *Public Policy and Private Charities.* Chicago: University of Chicago Press, 1931.

Kelso, Robert W., *The History of Public Relief in Massachusetts, 1620-1920.* Boston: Houghton, 1922.

*———, *The Science of Public Welfare.* New York: Holt, 1928.

Kennedy, Albert J., Kathryn Farra, and Associates, *Social Settlements in New York City—Their Activities, Policies, and Administration.* New York: Columbia University Press, 1935.

Klein, Alice Campbell, *Civil Service in Public Welfare.* New York: Russell Sage Foundation, 1940.

*Lee, Porter, *Social Work as Cause and Function.* New York: Columbia University Press, 1937.

Lende, Helga (editor), *What of the Blind?* New York: American Foundation for the Blind, Vol. 1, 1938; Vol. 2, 1941.

Lewis, Orlando, *The Development of American Prisons and Prison Customs, 1776-1845.* New York: Prison Association, 1922.

Linn, James W., *Jane Addams: A Biography.* New York: Appleton-Century-Crofts, Inc., 1935.

McMillen, Wayne, *Community Organization for Social Welfare.* Chicago: University of Chicago Press, 1945, (1949).

Mangold, George, *Problems of Child Welfare,* 3rd ed., New York: Macmillan, 1936.

Marshall, Helen E., *Dorothea Dix: Forgotten Samaritan.* Chapel Hill: University of North Carolina Press, 1937.

*Miles, Arthur P., *An Introduction to Public Welfare,* Chap. 4. Boston: Heath, 1949.

———, *Federal Aid and Public Assistance in Illinois.* Chicago: University of Chicago Press, 1941.

*Pintner, R., J. Eisenson, and M. Stanton, *The Psychology of the Physically Handicapped.* New York: Appleton-Century-Crofts, Inc., 1931.

*Queen, Stuart Alfred, *Social Work in the Light of History.* Philadelphia: Lippincott, 1922.

Richards, Laura E., *Letters and Journals of Samuel Gridley Howe,* 2 vols. Boston: Dana Estes & Co., 1909.

———, *Samuel Gridley Howe.* New York: Appleton-Century-Crofts, Inc., 1935.

Sanborn, Franklin B., *Doctor Samuel Gridley Howe, The Philanthropist.* New York: Funk, 1891.

Schneider, David M., *History of Public Welfare in New York, 1609-1866.* Chicago: University of Chicago Press, 1938.

Shaffer, Alice, Mary W. Keefer, and Sophonisba P. Breckinridge, *The*

Indiana Poor Law: Its Development and Administration. Chicago: University of Chicago Press, 1936.

Simkhovitch, Mary K., *Neighborhood: My Story of Greenwich House.* New York: Norton, 1938.

Stern, Bernhard J., *Medical Services by Government.* New York: The Commonwealth Fund, 1946.

*Stroup, Herbert Hewitt, *Social Work. An Introduction to the Field.* New York: American Book, 1948, 1953.

Sunley, Emil W., *The Kentucky Poor Law, 1792-1936.* Chicago: University of Chicago Press, 1942.

Teeters, Negley K., and John Otto Reinemann, *The Challenge of Delinquency.* New York: Prentice-Hall, Inc., 1950.

Thurston, Henry W., *The Dependent Child: A Story of Changing Aims and Methods in the Care of Dependent Children.* New York: Columbia University Press, 1930.

Wald, Lillian D., *The House on Henry Street.* New York: Holt, 1915.

———, *Windows on Henry Street.* Boston: Little, 1934.

Warner, Amos G., *American Charities* (revised by Mary Roberts Coolidge), 3rd ed. New York: Crowell, 1919.

Watson, Frank Dekker, *The Charity Organization Movement in the United States.* New York: Macmillan, 1922.

Wisner, Elizabeth, "The Puritan Background of the New England Poor Laws," *The Social Service Review.* Vol. XIX, No. 3, September, 1945.

Woods, Robert A., and Albert J. Kennedy, *The Settlement Horizon— A National Estimate.* New York: Russell Sage Foundation, 1922.

5. Development of the American Public and Private Social Services

I. FEDERAL PARTICIPATION IN THE SOCIAL SERVICES

Until the end of the nineteenth century social services under private and public auspices maintained their local character. Only to a very limited extent state-wide systems for a few special groups of people were established, which we discussed above. One of the new trends in social welfare in the twentieth century was the recognition of the need to consider problems of social welfare on the national scale, using the experience of all local and state organizations in order to introduce the most effective measures throughout the country.

This development was not a rapid one. It faced the traditional resistance of local and state interests, which insisted on their autonomy, asserting that democracy required the exclusion of federal interference. Until the Depression of 1930 the participation of the federal government was only a half-hearted and partial one. The leadership in nationwide organization was taken by private welfare organizations, particularly the National Child Labor Committee (1904) and the National Consumers' League (1899). Other national agencies had already been founded, such as the American Association on Mental Deficiency (1876), the American Humane Association (1877), the American Prison Association (1870), the National Association of the Deaf (1880), and the National Society for the Study of Education (1895).

The Constitution of the United States did not contain a specific principle regarding the responsibility of the federal government with respect to social welfare. The power of Congress to provide for the "general welfare of the people" (Article 1, Section 8) was a rather general clause and did not refer especially to the setup of public social services. This fact explains the veto of President Pierce against Dorothea Dix's suggestion of federal land grants to the states for mental hospitals.[1] For certain categories of persons, however, the federal government could not refuse to accept responsibility, and these five groups were sometimes called the "Federal Wards." They are the Indians, the immigrants, passengers and crews of seagoing vessels, the veterans, and offenders of federal laws. Before the twentieth century, the federal government established services for these five classes, which we shall now investigate.

A. SOCIAL SERVICES FOR THE INDIANS

The Continental Congress founded, in 1775, departments of Indian affairs in order to improve the relations with the Indian tribes and to protect their land against seizure without treaty. In 1789 a Bureau of Indian Affairs was organized in the War Department, which regulated treaties for land purchase, schools for Indian children, and some medical care.[2] In 1849, when the Gold Rush in California lured large masses of migrants to the West, the Bureau was reorganized as the Office of Indian Affairs, under the Department of Interior in order to placate the Indian tribes. After the War Between the States, a Board of Commissioners was appointed, which arranged for reservations on which the Indians might live without interference from the whites. These reservations would include schools and health facilities. In 1887, the *Allotment Act* provided for a distribution of land to Indian families to be held in trust by the United States so that it could not be sold. Unfortunately the aims of the law were not fulfilled. The land was largely "rented" to white men, and the Indians lost nearly 60 per cent of their original property. The Indian Service of the Department of the Interior, meanwhile, employed experts on land use to help the Indians in the reservations to more effective agricultural production and husbandry, and a medical supervisor to improve the health services.

In 1924 all Indians received United States citizenship, but the poverty of the tribes continued with a few exceptions. On the basis

[1] See Chapter 4.
[2] Through the *Indian Removal Act of 1830* the Indians were forced, however, to leave all their lands east of the Mississippi, although they met in the West hostile native tribes unwilling to let them in.

of Lewis Meriam's survey of 1928, the appropriations for education of Indian children were increased, and in 1934, the Indian Reorganization Act[3] provided increased protection for the Indian tribes by incorporation of the land and support of agricultural training and production, schools, and medical care. The Act attempted to secure the Indians civic and cultural freedom, to restore their own management of their affairs, to prevent further depletion of natural resources in the reservations, and to develop a sound economy which would make the Indians independent of outside support. With the help of this program under the Bureau of Indian Affairs in the federal Department of the Interior, the number of Indians is now increasing and has grown from 1933, when it was only 200,000, to more than 400,000. However the average income of an Indian farm family in most reservations is still only about one-third of that of a white farm family. Some tribes, such as the Navahos and Hopis, whose grazing lands were insufficient for their growing population, have been in such serious emergencies for the past years that federal appropriations and private relief actions through citizens' groups, the American Red Cross, the American Friends Service Committee, and other religious and philanthropic societies were necessary in order to avoid starvation and disaster.[4]

The 238 schools for Indians on the reservations (144 boarding schools, 94 day schools) are still not adequate to secure education for all Indian children, and nearly 30 per cent of the present population of the reservations is illiterate. The death rate among the Indians is far above the national average. Although the Indians are entitled to receive free medical service throughout their lives, available hospitals, tuberculosis dispensaries, and sanitation and health centers need further expansion. The funds allocated for relief administered to Indians are too low to meet the need of the many indigent people among the Indians. Social services are rendered in the states through the Indian Agency set up by the Bureau of Indian Affairs for each tribe. The payment of public assistance to the Indians in the states is frequently

[3] The Indian Reorganization Act was advocated by Harold Ickes, Secretary of the Interior, and John Collier, Commissioner of Indian Affairs. Unfortunately Congress has been less sympathetic to the health, social, and economic needs of the Indians than was the Bureau of Indian Affairs.

[4] See Preston Valien, "Racial Programs in Social Work," *Social Work Year Book, 1949*, p. 418; and Haven Emerson, "Indian Health—Victim of Neglect," *The Survey*, Vol. 87, No. 5, May, 1951, pp. 219-221.

difficult because their economic need and their legal eligibility are not proved; in Arizona and New Mexico the Federal Indian Service pays 65 per cent of the public assistance expenditure for the Indians. The lack of adequate salaries for the personnel of the Bureau of Indian Affairs makes it difficult to attract well-qualified physicians, teachers, nurses, and social workers needed for medical care, preventive health work, education, and counseling on the reservations.[5] In order to create self-maintaining Indian tribes, the irrigation of unproductive and arid land, the introduction of productive home industries and other industrial manufacturing, and native crafts will be necessary. Experiences on the reservations prove that with patient education and with industrial and technical training the Indians will be able to become self-supporting, maintaining their native culture and dignity, but as long as the tribes remain on the reservations, special educational, health, and social services will be absolutely needed. For Indians who leave the reservations to live in urban communities, the Bureau of Indian Affairs offers relocation and placement services.

B. THE IMMIGRANTS

With regard to new immigrants, the Colonies and later the states assumed measures of control primarily to protect their citizens against health and moral dangers and financial burdens which the newcomers might engender. Supplementing many state statutes, the federal *Passenger Act* of 1819 was the first national law which required medical inspection of all arriving immigrants, in order to control their health status. In 1882, the federal government assumed the main control of immigration (thus replacing the states), introduced a head tax for immigrants, and prohibited the naturalization of foreign-born Orientals. In 1891, the Bureau of Immigration in the Treasury Department became the administrative federal agency. It was transferred to the Department of Commerce and Labor in 1903 and was called Bureau of Immigration and Naturalization, in 1906. Under changing laws and regulations, admission of immigrants became more difficult. Persons considered of immoral character, likely

---

[5] Voluntary organizations working in the interest of the Indians include the Indian Rights Association, the Association on American Indian Affairs, the Institute on Ethnic Affairs, various Indian native organizations, and the American Friends Service Committee.

to become public charges, and contract laborers hired abroad were excluded. In 1917 the *Burnett Bill* introduced a literacy test. After the end of World War I, in a period of intense isolationism, the so-called *Quota System Law* of 1921 and the *Immigration Act* of 1924 were passed. They limited the annual number of immigrants to a total of 153,774; for each nationality group, however, to a maximum of 3 per cent of the estimated number of this national background residing in the United States in 1910, with a minimum of 100 for each country. The new policy towards immigration was discriminatory and restrictive. Immigrants from England, Ireland, and northern and western Europe were favored over those from southern and eastern Europe, where pressure to emigrate was high. The *Oriental Exclusion Law* of 1924 virtually stopped immigration from the Far East. As a consequence, immigration which had averaged, in the decade before 1914, over one million per year fell during the decade preceding World War II to a yearly average of 53,000. In 1940, the Bureau of Immigration and Naturalization was transferred to the Department of Justice under a Commissioner for Immigration and Naturalization.

The federal immigration services have been mainly legal control and administration of naturalization procedure. When the *Alien Registration Act* of 1940 required the registration of all immigrants and alien residents, the Bureau of Immigration and Naturalization developed an Educational Services Division, which helped in preparation for naturalization by textbooks, pamphlets, and home study courses. Most language and citizens' classes are conducted by local boards of education and voluntary social agencies. Recently the naturalization of Chinese nationals was permitted (1943), as well as that of East Indians (1946) and Philippinos (1946), but the annual immigration quota of these countries is small: China, 105; India, 100; Ceylon, 100; the Philippines, 100; Japan, 185; and Korea, 100.[6]

Social work for immigrants in the form of counseling, immigration aid, case work and group work is rendered by private social agencies, particularly the International Institutes; Protestant, Catholic, and Jewish family welfare agencies; the International Social Service (formerly International Migration Service); Travelers' Aid

[6] Marian Schibsby, "Aliens and Foreign Born," *Social Work Year Book, 1949,* pp. 53-59; F. Campbell Bruce, *The Golden Door: The Irony of Our Immigration Policy* (New York: Random House, Inc., 1954); and Frank L. Auerbach, *The Immigration and Naturalization Act: A Summary of Its Principal Provisions* (New York: Common Council for American Unity, 1952), pp. 18-23.

Societies; the United Service for New Americans; settlement houses; American Red Cross chapters; the American Friends Service Committee, the YWCA's, and other voluntary groups. The Department of State and the American Consulates administer immigration procedure abroad.

After World War II, the *Displaced Persons Act* of 1948 permitted the admission of 415,744 refugees and victims of Nazi forced labor camps, of whom actually 370,000 came to this country. The Act also allowed 15,000 refugees who were already in the United States for temporary asylum, as well as war orphans, to remain here. The first version of the Act of 1948 was severely criticized for its religious and ethnic discrimination, but an amendment of 1950 corrected some of its faults. Displaced persons were admitted only on assurance that they would have employment and housing, and would not become public charges. Politically undesirable persons were excluded. A three-man Displaced Persons Commission administered the Act, working closely with accredited voluntary social agencies. Private agencies, through their state and local committees, were providing assurances of housing and employment, affidavits of support, and placement with relatives and friends. Several states organized special commissions for resettlement of displaced persons, conducted surveys on employment opportunities, and coordinated the resettlement work carried on by public and private agencies.[7]

Since the enactment of the *Immigration Act* of 1917 immigrants could not apply for public assistance within five years after their arrival without being faced with deportation. More recently, however, immigration authorities have interpreted the provisions of the laws that displaced persons and other immigrants are not subject to deportation if they become ill, develop a mental disability, lose a job and are forced to apply for public assistance. Physical or mental ill-

[7] Frank L. Auerbach, "Aliens and Foreign Born," *Social Work Year Book, 1954*, pp. 47-55, particularly pp. 50-52. The private agencies engaged in immigration work formed, in 1950, the National Committee for Resettlement of Displaced Professionals in New York. It attempted to facilitate the immigration of professional persons among the displaced persons who received priority if they possessed special educational, scientific, technological, or professional qualifications, and to help in their employment and social adjustment. Since 1951, the Displaced Persons Commission itself was authorized to issue affidavits for immigrants in order to permit their emigration to this country. See U.S. Displaced Persons Commission, *The DP Story* (Washington, D. C.: Government Printing Office, 1952).

ness must not have existed prior to the immigrant's entry to the United States. After the displaced person applies for public assistance, he has to show that the cause of his need for public aid did not prevail before his immigration to this country.

On January 1, 1953, the President's Commission on Immigration and Naturalization submitted a thorough study and recommendations, evaluating the immigration and naturalization policies. All major religious creeds had asked the President to appoint the Commission. The Commission expressed its conviction that immigration has given strength to this country not only in manpower, new industries, and prosperity, but also in new ideas, inventions, and new culture that have enriched our nation. An outstanding characteristic of our country is its great cultural diversity, but such differences do not mean the existence of superior and inferior classes. It is contrary to the traditional American spirit to view every alien with suspicion or even with hostility. Although immigrants certainly need the United States, we also need immigrants.

We cannot be true to the democratic faith of our own Declaration of Independence in the equality of all men, and at the same time pass immigration laws which discriminate among people because of national origin, race, color, or creed. Nor can we ourselves really believe, or persuade others to think that we believe, that the United States is a dynamic, expanding, and prosperous country if our immigration law is based upon a fear of catastrophe rather than a promise and hope for greater days ahead.[8]

On the basis of these considerations the Commission believed that our present immigration laws flout fundamental American traditions and ideals, display lack of faith in America's future, damage American prestige and position among other nations, and ignore the lessons of the American way of life. It recommended that our present immigration law should be completely rewritten.

The *Internal Security Act* of 1950 ordered that aliens report their present residence each year between January 1 and 10 to the Federal Immigration and Naturalization Service. They receive an Alien Registration Receipt Card which is added to their visa so that they may prove their legal admission to employers in industries in which such legitimation is required for security reasons. Displaced

[8] President's Commission on Immigration and Naturalization, *Whom Shall We Welcome* (Washington, D. C.: Government Printing Office, 1953), pp. XIV-XV.

persons receive on arrival a provisory registration card for their legitimation.[9] The *McCarran-Walter Act* of 1952, which was passed over a veto of President Truman, excluded alien members or affiliates of the communist or other totalitarian parties and those who advocate the doctrines of world communism or totalitarianism. It maintains the outdated quota system for immigration. Its discriminatory nature was severely criticized by Protestant, Catholic, and Jewish religious groups as unfair to ethnic and religious minority groups, an attitude that is foreign to fundamental American principles. The law went into effect in 1952. The U. S. Department of Labor expressed the opinion that our country needed yearly more than 155,000 immigrants permitted to enter the United States under the law of 1950. It may be hoped that the Act will be amended so that its discriminatory character and its legal ambiguities might be removed.

A new *Refugee Immigration Act* was passed by Congress in 1953 at the request of President Eisenhower. Its purpose was to offer refugees (most of whom fled from communist countries) asylum in the United States, in addition to the regular immigration quota. The total maximum of refugees who might be admitted until the end of 1956 was 214,000, but no aliens shall be encouraged to immigrate to this country unless they have the sincere desire to become United States citizens. This statute is no revision of the Immigration Law.

Each refugee who wants to come to the United States must be sponsored by an individual resident in this country who has to give the assurance that the refugee can get a job and housing without displacing someone else. The sponsor has to take the initiative, but he may use the services of a relief or refugee organization. Preference is given to parents, children, brothers, and sisters of United States citizens, to relatives of lawfully admitted aliens residing in this country, and to refugees (such as engineers, scientists, tool makers, and farm workers) whose skills are valuable to this country.

The travel cost to this country has to be paid by the refugee himself, his future employer, or a relief organization. The Secretary of the Treasury may make loans to public and private agencies to pay

[9] See Charles Gordon, "The Immigration Process and National Security," *Temple Law Quarterly*, Vol. 24, January, 1951, pp. 302-319. Total immigration from Oriental countries is limited to 2,000 a year, in contrast to the British quota of 65,000. Negros of Trinidad, Jamaica, and other West Indian colonies are limited to one hundred from each colony.

for refugee traveling cost inside this country, however the loans must be repaid within ten years.

The refugee immigration law specifies the maximum admissions regarding several national groups. Admitted may be 100,000 Germans (55,000 expelled from communist areas, 35,000 who escaped from the Russian Zone, and 10,000 other escapees); 45,000 Italian refugees and 15,000 relatives; 15,000 Greek refugees and 2,000 relatives; 15,000 Netherlands refugees and 2,000 relatives; 2,000 Polish ex-soldiers; 3,000 Asian refugees and 2,000 non-Asian refugees from the Far East; 2,000 Chinese approved by the National Chinese Government; and 2,000 Arab refugees. In addition to these refugees, 4,000 orphans are to be admitted. Finally, 5,000 refugees who already are in the United States may receive immigrant status. For the adoption of an orphan written assurance must be given that the child will be adopted and properly cared for. Adoption of more than two orphans is prohibited unless it is necessary to prevent the separation of brothers and sisters.

The security provisions of the McCarran-Walter Act are applied to refugees. Each refugee is thoroughly investigated and a visa is granted only if there is no doubt of his eligibility. However, for this reason, the operation went very slowly. From August 7, 1953, when the Act went into effect, until March, 1954, just seven refugees were admitted to the United States of the 214,000, although more than $600,000 already were spent for the administration of the refugee immigration law.

C. FEDERAL PUBLIC HEALTH SERVICE

The first federal program in the field of public health was the Marine Hospital Service, which in 1798, provided medical care and hospitalization for American seamen. In 1878 foreign quarantine was made a responsibility of the Marine Hospital Service. Emergency funds for the prevention of epidemics were appropriated in 1883, and a hygienic laboratory added in 1887. Foreign and interstate quarantine became the full responsibility of the federal service in 1893. Its name was changed to Public Health and Marine Hospital Service in 1902, when cooperation with the states and responsibilities of the service were expanded and the Pan American Sanitary Bureau was established. The research activities of the agency were broadened and the name changed again to United States Public Health Service in 1912. Venereal disease control was added in 1918, two hospitals for narcotic drug addicts and a Mental Hygiene Division in 1930. At the same time the National Institute of Health was developed as an expanded research and laboratory division of the Public Health Service.

Under the Social Security Act of 1935, the Public Health Service became first a part of the agencies under the Social Security Board, and its activities in grants-in-aid to the states, in cancer research, and in control of venereal diseases were expanded. With the establishment of the Federal Security Agency, in 1939, the Public Health Service became an independent, operating agency under the supervision of the Federal Security Administrator and is now a major part of the Department of Health, Education and Welfare. During World War II it assisted in emergency services for war production areas through the establishment of hospitals and sanitation. In 1944 the *Public Health Service Act* codified the provisions on federal public health activities, and expanded research and tuberculosis control. Under the *Hospital Survey and Construction Act* of 1946 the U.S. Public Health Service allocates grants-in-aid to the states for determination of medical needs and for construction or expansion of hospitals, health centers and clinics. Special attention has recently been given to research and development of facilities for prevention and treatment of mental diseases, cancer, heart diseases, and for dental care.

Research activities of the U. S. Public Health Services are conducted through the National Institutes of Health, which now comprise cancer, mental health, heart, dental, experimental biology, and microbiology research. The Bureau of Medical Services includes the Divisions of Hospitals, Mental Hygiene, Foreign Quarantine, and Federal Employee Health. The Bureau of State Services administers the grants-in-aid programs to the states; its divisions are State Relations, Venereal Disease and Tuberculosis Control, Industrial Hygiene, Hospital Facilities, Communicable Diseases Center, and offices of Public Health Nursing, Health Education, and Administrative Management.

Other federal health activities are administered by the U.S. Children Bureau, the Social Security Administration, and the Food and Drug Administration (under the Department of Health, Education and Welfare), the Department of Agriculture, and the Veterans Administration.

D. WAR VETERANS

Already in the New England Colonies pensions for war veterans disabled in their military service and for their survivors were an accepted practice which followed the English tradition established under Queen Elizabeth. The Continental Congress, in 1776, continued this custom in providing pensions for invalid veterans and the widows of soldiers who had died in the Revolutionary War, and the federal government accepted this concept after the adoption of the Constitution. After the War Between the States, the benefits granted to the veterans as "federal wards" were limited to pensions, land grants, and the care of severely mutilated veterans in The National Asylum for Disabled Volunteer Soldiers and Sailors. Since 1833 the federal Bureau of Pensions took over the veterans pensions which had been paid by the Secretaries of the Army, Navy, and the Treasury. Under the impact of World War I the benefits of war veterans were supplemented by hospitalization, vocational rehabilitation, and government life insurance after the *War Risk Insurance Act* of 1917 established an insurance compensation in case of death and disability caused by war injuries. The administration of federal veterans benefits still was spread among many agencies which led to "red tape" and delay in the operations. In order to create a more efficient organization the Veterans Bureau was established in 1921, and in 1930 the Veterans Administration as a further step in the consolidation of federal activities for veterans. The Veterans Administration coordinated the work formerly done by the Bureau of Pensions, the War Risk Insurance Bureau, the Board of Vocational Education, and the National Home for Disabled Volunteer Soldiers.

During World War II, a new social philosophy regarding the duties of the nation for its veterans developed. Until this time it was assumed that pensions for the disabled and the survivors of those who lost their lives in the war was the main task. The new concept expanded this program by the goal of assisting all veterans to regain a position in the community after their return equal to that which they would have obtained without their absence in military service. Vocational rehabilitation, medical care, and educational benefits were strengthened or newly added for the returning veterans. The veterans of the Korean War are entitled to similar privileges as those of the two world wars.

In addition to these federal services for veterans, the states also established benefits for veterans who had been residents of the state for a certain period, and during World War II these supplementary state plans were enlarged.[10]

E. OFFENDERS AGAINST FEDERAL LAWS

Federal wards of a different nature were those persons who had violated federal laws and were sentenced to prison by federal courts. Because the federal government first had no facilities for the convicted offenders, they had to be boarded out at state prisons and penitentiaries for which the federal courts paid. In 1890 the establishment of federal prisons was enacted by Congress; they were expanded and improved after prison riots at Leavenworth in 1919. The U. S. Department of Justice introduced parole services for discharged prisoners and under the *Federal Probation Act* of 1925 a system of probation. In 1930, the federal Bureau of Prisons was organized, which developed pioneer methods in effective care and rehabilitation of the inmates of the federal prisons, under the leadership of Sanford Bates and his successor, James V. Bennett. This was stimulating to all penal institutions in the country. Vocational training (with the aim of preparing the prisoner for a job after his release), recreational and educational facilities, medical and dental care, and religious and cultural activities in the federal prisons and penitentiaries became goals for other institutions. Under the Bureau of Prisons the federal penal institutions were classified into six penitentiaries for serious crimes with separation of intractable, older improvable offenders from habitual, but tractable offenders; four reformatories, three for men, one for women; eight correctional institutions for short-term offenders, one of them for younger, improvable offenders; one medical center for mentally and physically maladjusted convicts; one National Training School for Boys; two detention headquarters, and five federal prison camps.[11] The federal

[10] For more details, see Chapter 16.

[11] Arthur P. Miles, *An Introduction to Public Welfare* (Boston: Heath, 1949), pp. 255-256; and the United States Bureau of Prisons, *Federal Prisons, 1949* (1950).

government is also active in the field of probation through the United States Probation System, which is attached to the Administrative office of the United States Courts. It investigates the social condition and background of an offender appearing before a federal court and supervises those offenders selected for probation and persons released from federal correctional institutions on parole or on "conditional release." It also refers juvenile delinquents to local juvenile courts for probation services.[12]

II. THE WHITE HOUSE CONFERENCES

Another important evidence of the trend in the social welfare scene, in the twentieth century, to recognize the need for a national policy instead of local efforts and piecemeal state legislation occurred in the field of child welfare. It began in 1909, when President Theodore Roosevelt, at the suggestion of a New York lawyer, invited leading workers of child welfare agencies from all over the country to Washington to the White House for a "Conference on the Care of Dependent Children." The Conference adopted a platform that children should not be taken away from their family for reasons of poverty, and that normal children who had to be removed from their own families should be placed in foster homes rather than in children's institutions. If children, for special reasons, had to be placed in orphanages or other children's institutions, these should be operated on the cottage plan with small units for the children instead of the large dormitories often used until this time. Children's agencies should need state licenses for their work and should be inspected by state authorities. Two recommendations of the Conference were of special importance: first, that the states should enact mothers' pension laws in order to enable widows and deserted women to keep their children; and second, that the federal government establish a federal children's agency. The first recommendation led, in 1911, to state legislation of mothers' pensions or allowances laws; Illinois was the first to do this.[13]

[12] See Chapter 12. Negley K. Teeters and John Otto Reinemann, *The Challenge of Delinquency* (New York: Prentice-Hall, Inc., 1950), pp. 627-628.

[13] The White House Conference of 1909 had suggested that state funds for mothers with children should be administered by private agencies, but the Illinois law and most others following it assigned the distribution of the mothers' pensions to such public agencies as juvenile courts or public welfare departments.

The second proposal of the Conference of 1909 resulted in the creation of the Children's Bureau by Congress in 1912. This idea had been conceived by Lillian Wald and Florence Kelley and was vigorously endorsed by social agencies and citizens' groups. President Taft nominated Julia Lathrop, prominent social worker and close friend of Jane Addams at Hull House in Chicago as the first chief of the Bureau. The Children's Bureau was the first active participation of the federal government in social welfare as distinguished from education and public health. The purpose of the agency was to act as a clearing house for the entire country, "to investigate and report upon all matters pertaining to the welfare of children and child life among all classes of our people," especially the questions of infant mortality, birth rate, orphanages, juvenile courts, child labor, and social legislation on children. The Children's Bureau's investigations released to Congress and to the people greatly influenced the practice of child care and legislation for the protection of children. A third administrative function was assigned to the Bureau by Congress through the federal child labor laws, the "Maternity and Infancy Act" of 1921 (*Sheppard-Towner Act*), the Social Security Act (1935) and the *Fair Labor Standard Act* (1939).[14] The Children's Bureau was first placed in the Department of Commerce and Labor, in 1913, in the newly separated Department of Labor; in 1946 it was transferred to the Federal Security Agency, and it is now one of the operating bureaus of the Social Security Administration in the U. S. Department of Health, Education and Welfare.

Another suggestion of the White House Conference of 1909 was the establishment of a voluntary nationwide organization for the development of standards for child care and protection. This organization was founded, in 1920, under the title, Child Welfare League of America. Its membership consists of voluntary and public child welfare agencies and institutions which meet the standards set by the League, and of individual members; it publishes a monthly journal, *Child Welfare*.

The second White House Conference, held in 1919 upon invitation of President Woodrow Wilson, was prepared by the U.S. Children's Bureau and called "The Children's Bureau Conference on

[14] See Chapter 9; also Frank J. Bruno, *Trends in Social Work* (New York: Columbia University Press, 1948), pp. 152-159; and Grace Abbott, *The Child and the State* (Chicago: University of Chicago Press, 1940), Vol. II, pp. 611-620.

Child Welfare Standards." It discussed problems of child labor, juvenile delinquency, and dependent children that had been aggravated by World War I, plus the topics of the health of mothers and young children, needs of the preschool and school child, and child welfare legislation. This Conference led to the enactment of the "Maternity and Infancy Act" in 1921 and to the setup of child welfare divisions in many states.

The third "White House Conference on Child Health and Protection," called by President Herbert Hoover, convened in 1930. It centered around the health needs of children, with special emphasis upon the physically and mentally handicapped child, education, medical care, and health protection of children. The principles of the Conference were announced as "The Children's Charter,"[15] asking for every child spiritual and moral training, understanding of his personality, a home with love and security, protection from birth through adolescence, proper schooling, recreation, and preparation for citizenship and parenthood. For rural children the Conference demanded equal services for urban children; for blind, deaf, crippled, and mentally handicapped children special care, treatment and training; and the establishment of necessary health and welfare services.

President Franklin D. Roosevelt called the fourth "White House Conference on Children in a Democracy" under the theme "Our Concern—Every Child." After thorough preparation (by numerous study and research groups) of the broad topics—the child in the family, religion in the life of the child, protection against child labor, youth and their needs, children of religious and racial minorities, and children of migratory families—the Conference met in January, 1940. The war in Europe was raging and the Conference studied the effects of the democratic and fascist philosophies on child care and education. It affirmed the interdependence of social and economic security, tolerance, health education, and opportunity for personal growth for the welfare of children. To follow up its recommendations, the Conference formed a voluntary National Citizens Committee, which remained active during World War II for the protection of children. The rejection of many young men for physical and mental defects demonstrated that more attention needed to be given to the health of all children.

[15] Reproduced in N. Teeters and J. Reinemann, *op. cit.*, p. 626.

The "Midcentury White House Conference on Children and Youth" held in December, 1950 was the fifth in the series of the conferences. It was invited to the capital by President Harry Truman and prepared by several committees under the leadership of Katherine Lenroot, Chief of the Children's Bureau, and Melvin Glasser.[16] The conference had the motto "For every child a fair chance for a healthy personality," but it was held under the shadow of the Korean War, and children of the 1940 Conference were dying on the icy mountains of Korea. The Conference emphasized the emotional factor in the development of children and the specific aspects of adolescence rather than those of younger children. It was aware that the child and adolescent should be regarded as a whole personality and not be treated as separate entities. In introducing President Truman, Oscar R. Ewing, then Federal Security Administrator, formulated the goals of the Conference as the furtherance of the development of a healthy personality through the contributions of family life, church, school, public health and social services, vocational guidance, and placement services. The Conference stated that social work as a profession could not stand alone, and that a planful cooperation between the various professions and between private and public organizations was necessary to secure the full understanding and the promotion of all potentialities for children and youth.[17] Characteristic of this fifth White House Conference was that young delegates as representatives of youth organizations participated with full rights.

Among the findings of the Conference were the following statements on the phases of child development: (1) The changing needs of each child depend upon his individuality, his environment, and particularly his relationship to his parents; (2) the feelings for children on the part of parents and professional people are more important than the techniques they use; (3) attitudes in giving advice are more important than the advice given; (4) both boys and girls need to be close to men and women for good emotional development; (5) a general healthy personality is not established once and for all at any age period, but can be strengthened or weakened at any stage in life.[18]

---

[16] In 1951, Dr. Martha M. Eliot became Chief of the Children's Bureau.
[17] Kathryn Close, "Youth in Today's World: Conference Report," *Survey*, Vol. LXXXVII, No. 1, January, 1951, p. 19.
[18] *Ibid.*

In the platform adopted by the 1950 Conference it was proclaimed that children require for their fullest development (1) regard for their individual worth and sensitive respect for their feelings; (2) loving care and guidance from mothers and fathers, who have a sense of the privilege and responsibility which parenthood involves, and who have confidence in their own capacity to rear a child; (3) a secure home that is free from want and dread of want and provides a satisfying physical, aesthetic, social, and spiritual environment; (4) a community dedicated to the task of making life meaningful and abundant for children of all colors, creeds and customs; (5) full access to health, educational, recreational, social and religious services and programs, directed toward the well-being of all they serve; (6) concern on the part of citizens for children; and (7) devotion to the pursuit of knowledge and its application. Under such conditions children would grow in trust to themselves and others, in independence and initiative, in satisfaction with their achievements, in responsibility for their future roles of citizens, workers, and parents, in family love and understanding of all mankind, in creative force and integrity.

Based upon these principles the Conference made recommendations for the use of research and professional skills, for education for parenthood, and for the strengthening of the parents' confidence in their educational abilities; for broader opportunities for children to gain knowledge of nature and social experiences; and for better training in the professions regarding human behavior and cultural influences, and an intensification of studies and preparation for child services. Other recommendations were local health services, hospitals and schools without racial discrimination, free college and university education, school lunches, nursery schools, and guidance and counseling in schools and social agencies.

The Conference expressed its firm belief in the principle of separation of church and state and its opposition to the use of public schools for religious education, which remains an important task of the family. Also suggested were expansion of recreation with participation of youth in its planning, extension of social insurance and public assistance, the use of social and psychological knowledge in the treatment of children before courts, and coordination of preventive services for children among private agencies and public authorities. Improvement of methods in child labor protection, adoption and foster care, and special care of handicapped children and children in migratory families were demanded. Emphasis was given to the needs of children under the defense program, particularly to adolescents, and to progress in social legislation and housing reform. The television industry was asked to recognize its great influence and responsibility for educational and cultural purposes. For the realization of the recommendations of the Conference, communities and states were requested to apply the principle of self-help and of broad participation of all groups without any discriminiation, to support both public and private social agencies, and to invite active representation of young people in the development, planning, and direction of youth programs.[19]

The Midcentury White House Conference finally adopted a "Pledge to Children," promising the following:

From your earliest infancy we give you our love, so that you may grow with trust in yourself and others.

We will recognize your worth as a person and we will help you to strengthen your sense of belonging.

We will respect your right to be yourself and at the same time help you to understand the rights of others, so that you may experience cooperative living.

We will help you develop initiative and imagination, so that you may have the opportunity freely to create.

We will encourage your curiosity and your pride in workmanship, so that you may have the satisfaction that comes from achievement.

We will provide the conditions for wholesome play that will add to your learning, to your social experience, and to your happiness.

We will illustrate by precept and example the value of integrity and the importance of moral courage.

We will encourage you always to seek the truth.

We will provide you with all opportunities possible to develop your own faith in God.

We will open the way for you to enjoy the arts and to use them for deepening your understanding of life.

We will work to rid ourselves of prejudice and discrimination, so that together we may achieve a truly democratic society.

We will work to lift the standard of living and to improve our economic practices, so that you may have the material basis for a full life.

We will provide you with rewarding educational opportunities, so that you may develop your talents and contribute to a better world.

[19] "Recommendations of the White House Conference on Children and Youth," *Social Security Bulletin*, Vol. 14, No. 2, February, 1951, pp. 10-14.

We will protect you against exploitation and undue hazards and help you grow in health and strength.

We will work to conserve and improve family life and, as needed, to provide foster care according to your inherent rights.

We will intensify our search for new knowledge in order to guide you more effectively as you develop your potentialities.

As you grow from child to youth to adult, establishing a family life of your own and accepting larger social responsibilities, we will work with you to improve conditions for all children and youth.

Aware that these promises to you cannot be fully met in a world at war, we ask you to join us in a firm dedication to the building of a world society based on freedom, justice, and mutual respect.

So may you grow in joy, in faith in God and in man, and in those qualities of vision and of the spirit that will sustain us all and give us new hope for the future.[20]

III. THE REVOLUTION OF THE SOCIAL SERVICES IN THE DEPRESSION

The economic depression which started with the crash of the New York Stock Exchange in October, 1929 marked a complete change in the methods of American social welfare, particularly in poor relief. Until this period, public relief had been managed mainly by political appointees in cities or counties, overseers, or supervisors of the poor. They identified poverty with vice or idleness, and distributed relief on a starvation level, ranging from ten cents to seventy cents per day. Only in forty large cities, trained social workers were on the staff of public relief agencies. Private family welfare agencies existed in about four hundred larger cities, and self-respecting families in financial need went to those voluntary agencies, which "protected them" from the disgrace of applying for "pauper aid." Public expenditures for poor relief had slowly increased during the two preceding decades, but private agencies emphasized that their methods in preventing destitution and in rehabilitation were more economic and, therefore, justified subsidies from taxation.

When due to the panic of the Depression the number of unemployed increased from 2,860,000 in spring 1929 to over four million in January, 1930, the public in the larger cities looked to the voluntary welfare agencies as the main source of financial support for the steadily growing mass of unemployed. The local private welfare agencies attempted to aid the new applicants who never before had

[20] "Pledge to Children," *The Child* (now *Children*), Vol. 15, No. 6, February, 1951, p. 119.

asked for relief. Many used up their savings whenever they could get payments from the banks that had not closed; others tried to borrow money from relatives, friends, the grocer, and baker, but credit was quickly exhausted and did not keep the family fed and rent or mortgage paid. In a few months the private social agencies spent the entire annual budget, exhausted their reserves, or incurred debts in order to continue their activities, but in the spring of 1930 all private agencies (as well as public relief offices) were deeply alarmed. The public expected that the private agencies would meet their obligation, but this trust did not fill the exhausted coffers. The Association of Community Chests and Councils issued frantic appeals to industry and to local chests to secure the necessary funds by a special emergency campaign. However the results of this effort were spent again in a few months, and unemployment increased in the spring of 1930 to over 4,600,000. Several severe droughts which afflicted Arkansas, Kentucky, Louisiana, Mississippi, Oklahoma, and Texas aggravated economic conditions.

President Hoover refused to consider federal aid to states which applied for help. He emphasized the American way of handling the emergency, which might be of only short duration, was through private charities, supported by voluntary donations—not by tax money. In August, 1930, he called a conference of governors and appointed an Emergency Committee for Employment, under the chairmanship of his personal friend, Colonel Arthur Woods.[21] This Committee followed Hoover's philosophy and appealed to community chests, private industry, and the public to supply the needed money for the support of the unemployed. It also requested free services from hospitals and dispensaries, and that child care and recreation agencies accept more children. These well-meant admonitions, however, had as little success as the Committee's slogans, "Spread the work" (suggesting that persons should be employed on part-time work) and "Give a job." In April, 1931, Colonel Woods resigned and his successor was Fred C. Croxton, an experienced social worker.

During this time the number of unemployed increased; by September, 1930 it exceeded five million, and all over the country municipal and county relief offices had to support a larger and larger amount of

[21] Josephine C. Brown, *Public Relief, 1929-1939* (New York: Holt, 1940), pp. 63-71.

unemployed families. Public relief was slowly taken out from its "Cinderella" role and became one of the principal functions of government.[22] Many states were at first reluctant to assume themselves financial responsibility, since their own taxes decreased due to losses in business, tax delinquencies, and lower production. But in 1931 Massachusetts, New York, Oklahoma, California, New Hampshire, and Maryland were forced to provide state unemployment relief in order to avoid starvation of the unemployed families. In December, 1930, the unemployed numbered seven million; in the spring of 1931, over eight million, and their number steadily increased. An investigation of the Federal Bureau of Census during January to March, 1931 revealed that outdoor relief expenditure had grown from $22,338,114 in 1929 to $73,757,300 in 1931. Most of this money was public tax funds. Not only employees and industrial workers lost their jobs; with the decreasing purchasing power of a large proportion of the entire population, over 750,000 farmers went bankrupt between 1930 and 1933, and 54.1 of every 1,000 farms were forcibly sold in 1932, because the farmers were unable to pay their mortgages or tax returns.[23]

President Hoover maintained his belief that private charity should continue in meeting distress, and, encouraged by his pronouncements, private social agencies still hoped that with a decrease in unemployment they would be able again to take care of the unemployed and their families. They stated the emergency required a combination of the resources of private philanthropy, government, and business. Because their hesitancy delayed the urgently needed appropriations for relief from state legislatures eager to avoid higher taxation for relief funds, counties and cities saw no way of further accepting the responsibility for mass relief in behalf of local government.[24] The Depression, however, grew more severe, and the repeated appeals of Community Chests and private charities did no longer raise the funds necessary to maintain the unemployed. In New York the first Temporary Emergency Relief Administration was organized, with Harry L. Hopkins as executive director. He was a trained social

---

[22] F. Bruno, *op. cit.*, p. 300.

[23] U.S. Department of Agriculture, *Historical Statistics of the United States, 1789-1945* (1949), pp. 95, 98, 233.

[24] J. Brown, *op. cit.*, pp. 78-80; E. P. Hayes, *Activities of the President's Emergency Committee for Employment, 1930-1931* (Washington, D. C.: Government Printing Office, 1936), pp. 2-4, 96, 115.

worker with experience in settlement house work, family welfare, Red Cross, and health services under the New York State Charities Aid, and immediately established highly successful uniform policies and standards of relief for the entire state.[25] Other states soon followed the example of New York, so that at the end of 1932 twenty-four states had granted appropriations for disaster relief or emergency relief for the unemployed.[26]

The means of private charities became exhausted. Local and state funds proved to be inadequate to protect the growing millions of unemployed against hunger, cold, suffering, and despair, and the requests for federal action were heard more frequently every month. Families were broken up in the vain, hectic attempt of the husband and father to find work. Disease increased, and sick people did not receive medical care. Children were passed around among neighbors because the parents had no food or were looking for jobs. The number of suicides mounted. Tuberculosis and malnutrition in children grew dangerously, and most savings of the middle class had been lost. In Congress, Senators Edward Costigan and La Follette introduced bills for federal aid to provide emergency relief, and the governors of several states claimed the unemployment problem could not be solved without federal support. But the opposition of the Hoover cabinet, the chambers of commerce, and some citizen's organizations remained firm. Several bills providing federal funds for relief were passed, but vetoed by President Hoover. Finally, he consented to sign the *Emergency Relief and Construction Act* of July 21, 1932. It authorized the Reconstruction Finance Corporation (RFC) to loan the states, counties, and cities $300,000,000 for relief and public work relief projects.[27] Numerous applications from states, counties, and cities immediately made it necessary that an expert should determine the real need of the various states, so Mr. Fred Croxton was appointed head of the Emergency Relief Division of the Corporation. Loans were given on an emergency basis, not exceeding the expenses for one month, so that neither adequate machinery could be set up nor projects developed to secure employ-

---

[25] *Relief Today in New York State*, Report of TERA, October, 1933, p. 11.
[26] National Resources Planning Board, *Security, Work and Relief Policies* (1942), p. 29.
[27] The loans of the RFC were to be refunded by 1935, but legislation in 1934 and 1938 repealed this provision.

ment of large numbers of people out of work or to be of permanent
value to the community. The local administrators never knew what
funds for work relief would be available for the next month, so that
no planning was possible in an operation from hand to mouth, which
only supplied bare subsistence to the unemployed.

When Franklin D. Roosevelt was elected President in November,
1932, the economic depression and widespread despair had reached
its peak. The people hoped that the new President would be able to
cope with an unemployment of fifteen million workers, and with
the situation which was depriving thousands of families of their
homes and farms and forcing them to live on meager relief without
a real hope for recovery. In his inaugural address, on March 4, 1933,
President Roosevelt analyzed this economic breakdown:

> Values have shrunken to fantastic levels; taxes have risen; our ability
> to pay has fallen; . . . the withered leaves of industrial enterprise lie
> on every side; farmers find no market for their produce; the savings of
> many years in thousands of families are gone.
> More important, a host of unemployed citizens face the grim problems
> of existence, and an equally great number toil with little return. . . .
> The only thing we have to fear is fear itself—nameless, unreasoning, un-
> justified terror which paralyzes needed efforts to convert retreat into
> advance.

In some states 40 per cent of the total population were receiving
relief, in some counties even as much as 90 per cent.

The first major legislation under President Roosevelt in the fight
against depression, unemployment, and economic apathy was the
Federal Emergency Relief Act of May 12, 1933. It represented a
radical change in federal relief policy. It abolished the principle of
short loans to the states and substituted for it a new concept of
federal responsibility for human welfare, because under our economic
system the individual has little control and influence upon the national production in periods of crisis. Federal grants to the states
were provided to assist the states in meeting the urgent needs of their
citizens.

The administration of the new law was assigned to the Federal
Emergency Relief Administration (FERA), and President Roosevelt
appointed Harry L. Hopkins its administrator. FERA was an independent agency directly under the President. The initial appropriation of Congress was $500,000,000, one-half of which sum was to be

given as grants to states on a matching basis (25 per cent federal, 75 per cent state and local funds), the other half without matching provision to states whose resources were depleted or whose unemployment was so grave that no matching could be expected. Congress appropriated later additional funds, so that until the end of FERA in 1936 the amount of $3,088,670,625 was allocated for this program. Since October, 1933 FERA was authorized to grant the funds to the states without a matching requirement at the discretion of the administrator. The two main functions of FERA were (1) to administer the grants to the states for unemployment relief and (2) to control proper use of the federal grants and to establish satisfactory relief standards in the interest of the unemployed.

The organization of FERA was divided into five divisions:

(1) The *Federal Work Division* provided grants to the states for work relief projects conducted by states or communities. They were approved, supervised, and, in special instances, administered by FERA, which advised in engineering problems, labor relations, working conditions, and safety measures. An Emergency Education Program for unemployed teachers and the Surplus Commodities Distribution were administered by the Work Division.

(2) The *Division of Relations with States* supervised the state relief programs through field representatives and regional offices in cooperation with the State Emergency Relief Administrations. A Social Service Section[28] in the Division supervised the standards of relief. Each local relief administrator had to employ at least one experienced social worker on his staff and a qualified supervisor for every twenty workers, in order to make social investigations of need and to assure a reliable and nonpolitical administration of federal funds.

(3) *Division of Special Programs*—the particular needs of the tens of thousands of migratory workers who were looking for work in other states made it necessary to establish the Federal Transient Bureau. This supervised the policies and standards of relief to migratory workers who had no legal residence and, in some states with numerous migrants, the setup of migratory labor camps with sanitary facilities.

(4) *The Division of Research, Statistics, and Finance* conducted

---

[28] In 1934, a separate Social Service Division in FERA was established to supervise the social service divisions in each state which, in turn, controlled local offices in cities and counties.

surveys and investigations, collected accurate data on the relief population, and issued regular relief statistics to provide the necessary information for a fair administration of the vast grant-in-aid program to the states.

(5) *The Rural Rehabilitation Division* provided aid to farmers, agricultural workers, and tenants; rehabilitation on the farm by grants for livestock, seeds, farm equipment, repair, and debt adjustment; resettlement of farmers removed from submarginal land; homesteads for tenants and farm workers.

A special service of the Work Division stimulated the voluntary organization of "self-help cooperatives" among farmers to improve methods of buying and selling, common use of expensive tractors and agricultural machinery, and the organization of prepaid medical and dental treatment programs. Free advice by agricultural specialists and home economists was made available to the farmers.

Among the first rules issued by FERA was that all federal grants were to be administered only by public agencies. It was prohibited, therefore, to delegate distribution of federal relief to private charities, a wide-spread custom until this period. All state plans were carefully reviewed, and the insistence of FERA on employment of trained social workers and qualified personnel helped in an efficient control of the entire program.[29]

The FERA program had as its objective the providing of work for the unemployed and the use of the appropriations exclusively for persons who were able to work but had lost their jobs through the Depression. Local authorities attempted to place their unemployables—sick, old, and infirm persons and mothers with young children—on the federal relief rolls, but the surveys of the Research Division revealed this practice and led to the elimination of unemployable people from FERA grants. The standards for relief developed by FERA required consideration of money for adequate rent and medical care and for relief that should be given by cash instead of by the commissary system, which had been frequently used by local relief offices. Useful public work was considered superior to direct relief, which endangered the self-respect and technical skill of the recipient.

[29] This change of policy, however, created serious difficulties for some private social agencies, which earlier had received large public subsidies for their relief distribution activities because they no longer could claim to have a monopoly on trained personnel.

In order to provide jobs for the unemployed, FERA immediately began to cooperate with the U.S. Employment Service and the Federal Emergency Public Works Administration. Under the U.S. Employment Service a special National Re-employment Service was organized. It was supported by FERA funds, and tried to find jobs for as many unemployed as possible. The work relief projects in most states were not too satisfactory and employed only about a million (mostly unskilled) workers. In order to introduce more adequate possibilities for the unemployed, the President created the Civil Works Administration by Executive Order of November 9, 1933 as a means of promoting recovery through the employment at regular wages of four million people who were at present unemployed. It was thought of as "a shot in the arm" for the economic system by means of a rapid increase of purchasing power which would set normal production and consumption again in motion. The main difference between the FERA program and the Civil Works Administration (CWA) method was that CWA was exclusively operated by the federal government; it used many skilled workers in teaching and supervision, and it paid union wages. The administrator of CWA was also Harry Hopkins, a setup which guaranteed close cooperation with FERA. One-half of the workers in CWA were taken from the emergency work relief rolls; the other half were people in general need of jobs. The program went into effect with remarkable speed and employed at its peak, in January, 1934, 4,260,-000 persons. But it was so costly that Congress was afraid of its high expenditures which amounted for the six months program to $863,-965,000 and decided to liquidate the plan when it had just started. The liquidation was completed in July, 1934 so that the Civil Works Administration functioned only four and one-half months. The workers were transferred again to the FERA program, which took over many unfinished projects of the CWA.[30] The period of CWA operation was too short to draw reliable conclusions regarding its economic, social, and psychological effect.

With the close of the work projects of the Civil Works Administration, the FERA organized a threefold program of employment. The first was an Emergency Work Relief Program in urban communities with over 5,000 population; the second, the Rural Rehabilitation Program for farmers to assist them to become self-supporting

[30] J. Brown, *op. cit.*, pp. 159-160.

again; and the third, a resettlement plan for landless rural workers, the beginning of a land utilization program to be continued later under the Department of Agriculture. In addition to these work relief programs, direct relief was granted to people who could not be employed on work projects.

The administration of this huge unemployment relief program under FERA faced extraordinary difficulties. It was carried on as a new venture in a confused and disturbed economic situation in which state and local authorities, as well as private social agencies, had to orient themselves to new principles and methods. It is not surprising, therefore, that severe criticism of the FERA operations was mixed with recognition for its unusually effective policies in the field of public welfare.[31] Its strict separation from the regular activities of state and local public welfare agencies unfortunately prevented the immediate influence of the new concepts of public responsibility on the policies of cities and counties that social workers had expected. But the acceptance of government responsibility for the relief of economic distress was definitely established as social philosophy during this period, and it was also recognized that people had a right to such an assistance without losing thereby the respect for their dignity and their worth as human beings.

A. THE WORKS PROJECTS ADMINISTRATION

As the FERA had been set up only as a temporary measure and the federal government felt that it should not assume responsibility for direct relief to people unfit for employment, President Roosevelt decided in May, 1935 to liquidate FERA. He substituted an exclusive work relief program within centralized federal control under the title Works Progress Administration (WPA), later (in 1939) to be named Works Projects Administration. The Emergency Relief Appropriations Act of 1935 provided the necessary funds. Originally it was hoped that private industry and the Public Works Administration would be able to absorb most of the unemployed people, but it soon became evident that the Works Progress Administration (WPA) would have to supply the jobs itself.[32] Its objective was to

[31] See Edith Abbott, *Public Assistance*, Vol. I (Chicago: University of Chicago Press, 1940), pp. 669-690; and Donald S. Howard, *The WPA and Federal Relief Policy* (New York: Russell Sage Foundation, 1943).

[32] D. Howard, *op. cit.*, p. 108.

employ three and one-half million people on relief. The WPA established the policies, administered the program, approved the projects presented by local and state governments, and reviewed the certifications of workers on the projects to ascertain whether they were in economic need and employable. The state and local governments selected useful work projects which were of value to the communities and provided funds for materials and supervision. The WPA paid the wages of the workers, which amounted to an average of $54.25 a month.[33] Congress excluded certain types of projects, such as military production, slum clearance and demolition work, and theater production projects, in order to avoid competition with private industries.

The wages in WPA were different from the earlier FERA method of family budget; they were a "security wage" without relation to family size and dependents. The wage provided a "minimum security income" which varied according to local standards and the skill of the worker. The workers were divided into four categories: unskilled work, intermediate work, skilled work, and technical and professional work. At least 120 hours of labor were required per month. An unfortunate limitation for WPA was that every worker had to be taken from public relief rolls, and small communities had not sufficient skilled workers to be hired as foremen and supervisors to set up valuable work projects. The fact that in one family only one member might be employed under WPA was also a hardship on large families. An amendment of the Emergency Relief Appropriations Act of 1939 increased the working hours to a minimum of 130 a month, regardless of skill, but allowed not more than eight hours per day or forty hours per week.

The administration of WPA was assigned to Harry L. Hopkins without a federal board. Mr. Hopkins established the WPA as a federal agency immediately under the President. Six regional field representatives approved and supervised local projects. In 1939 the agency was called Works Projects Administration and was merged with the Federal Works Agency. With exception of some federal projects under the auspices of federal agencies, such as the Office of Education, WPA projects were prepared and sponsored by cities, counties, and states. During its entire function, WPA furnished jobs for 7,800,000 individuals who had been unemployed.

[33] Florence Peterson, *Survey of Labor Economics* (New York: Harper, 1947), p. 170.

The WPA projects have greatly contributed to the improvement of economic, health, welfare, and cultural facilities of our country. The construction work provided 470,000 miles of highways, bridges, roads and streets; and 90,000 public buildings, among them 132 new, and 1,500 enlarged hospitals, medical and dental clinics, visiting nursing stations, libraries, schools, and museums. Three and one-half million acres of swamp land were drained to eliminate the danger of malaria, 12,000 water mains constructed and repaired, and 18,000 miles of storm and sanitary sewers built. A large number of play-grounds and parks, sport fields and swimming pools for recreation, airports for national defense, soil and water conservation works, and flood control and reforestation projects were part of the WPA activities. Unemployed professional persons, artists, sculptors, painters, musicians, teachers, day-nursery teachers, nurses, librarians, and recreation leaders were given jobs in their own fields for the benefit of communities. They taught classes and courses which could not have been offered, due to the lack of local funds or initiative. The arts projects brought new cultural stimulation, and the theatre and concert projects gave enjoyment to the people. Valuable research projects for unemployed writers and scientists created such books as the *American Guide Series.*

In spite of these achievements the WPA was not able to overcome severe criticism. The great costs of a public works program, the lack of conscientious labor on some projects, and the fact that WPA took away some private business were the main sources of complaint. As WPA never had sufficient funds to give work to all unemployed, those unable to get WPA jobs were among its opponents. Contractors were dissatisfied because they wanted to do construction work themselves; organized labor was uneasy because it feared that the low WPA wages would keep down union wages. The WPA was accused of engaging in political activities, particularly in the plays of the theatre projects and in paintings and murals of some artists. Much of this criticism may have been rather factional and biased, but the legal limitations and the lack of certainty about the continuation and financing of the projects made it impossible to develop the program in an ideal form. Since 1940 most projects were devoted to the defense effort, and in 1942 the President ordered the liquidation of the Works Projects Administration when industries and production absorbed all available labor. The WPA was closed in 1943.

Social workers in the Works Projects Administration program applied their case work skill in interviews with applicants asking for emergency employment. They had objected earlier to the punitive policies of the poor law authorities, which tended to degrade the poor and to create a demoralized pauper class. In the principles of the work program, they found an opportunity to treat the applicant with respect, to maintain his human dignity and his feeling of usefulness, and to use the work relief assignment as a means for his economic rehabilitation.[34]

B. WORK PROGRAMS FOR UNEMPLOYED YOUTH

Even in normal times it is not always easy for youth in a highly industrialized society to obtain work without special education, training, and experience, but the Depression aggravated this problem. Under the New Deal two programs were developed in order to aid youth in preparation for satisfactory employment and to prevent enforced idleness and unhappiness. The first of these programs was the Civilian Conservation Corps, the other the National Youth Administration.

The law on the Civilian Conservation Corps(CCC) was the first social legislation enacted under President Franklin D. Roosevelt, who signed the bill on March 31, 1933. It authorized the President to establish a nationwide chain of forest camps for unemployed youth. Their aim was to supply healthy surroundings, adequate food, training and vocational education, and at the same time to assist in the conservation of our country's national resources. Unemployed youth between the ages of seventeen and twenty-five (later twenty-three) years who were unmarried, in need of work, out of school, and physically and mentally fit for vigorous work could enroll for a CCC camp. In addition, war veterans and Indians were entitled to enroll; they usually were employed in the administration of the camps or in supervision of the work. Campers received thirty dollars a month, of which twenty-five dollars was sent home for the support of their families; in 1939 this compensation was reduced to twenty-two dollars. Many enrollees removed their families from public relief rolls through their work. The camps of

[34] Dorothy Kahn, "What Is Worth Saving in This Business of Relief?" *Survey Midmonthly*, Vol. LXXVI, No. 2, February, 1937, pp. 16-18.

wooden barracks and tents (mostly army material) were set up in national and state forests and parks. The boys and young men built fire towers and fire breaks, forest nurseries, truck and hiking trails, and emergency airfields. They worked in forest insect and tree disease control and planted over three billion new trees. They constructed roads in parks and rural areas, built dams to forestall soil erosion, cleared forests from blister rust and tree beetles, cleaned the streams for fish and fowl, and drained mosquito infested marsh land.[35] They assisted in flood control by irrigation, drainage and construction of ditches and dams and helped to create recreational facilities by the development of trails, picnic grounds, and vacation camps. The young men applied for CCC at the local welfare office. Most of them came from relief families, but this was no condition for their eligibility.

The President appointed Robert Fechner, general vice-president of the International Association of Machinists and lecturer on labor problems at Harvard University, as director of the emergency conservation work. He was assisted by representatives of the Department of Labor in the selection of the enrollees, by the Departments of Agriculture and the Interior in the organization of the work projects, and by the War Department in the setup of the camps, transportation, feeding, and clothing. The boys received in 1,500 camps medical care and preliminary training, conditioning them for forest work, education in subjects from elementary to high school studies, and vocational and technical training. In 1939 the admission requirement of having to be in financial need was abolished, and the Civilian Conservation Corps was placed under the Federal Security Agency.

Among the criticism voiced against the CCC program were the lack of integration with other federal agencies, the secondary role of the educational activities, and the competition with local training programs better fitted for urban youth. In fact, the Corps improved greatly the physical and mental health and the fitness of its members, their education and vocational skill, maturity, morale, and self-confidence. It employed during its operation 2,662,000 men, of whom 2,209,000 were young persons. Fourteen thousand Indians were employed on Indian reservations, doing work on drainage and improvement of land. About 260,000 enrollees were war veterans for whom

[35] John D. Guthrie, *Saga of the* CCC (Washington, D. C.: American Forestry Association, 1942), pp. 5-7.

no age limit was imposed. The normal time of enrollment was for six months, with the possibility of re-enrollment up to two years. During the last years of its operation, in 1940 to 1942, the CCC shifted to defense and industrial training and installation of public utilities systems. In 1942, contrary to the advice of the President, Congress decided to terminate the CCC program because it was too expensive and rural districts needed young agricultural workers. During the nine years of its work the CCC had been an effective buffer to the dangers of unemployment and economic suffering of youth caused by the Depression.

The second work program for youth was the *National Youth Administration* (NYA). Already in 1934 a student-aid plan had been financed by the Federal Emergency Relief Administration, which also had set up a few resident camps and schools for unemployed women.[36] When in 1935 almost three million young people received emergency relief from public funds, President Roosevelt felt it imperative to establish a special program which would preserve the energy and skill of unemployed young women and men. He created the National Youth Administration by executive order of June 26, 1935 as an independent unit within the Works Progress Administration. Two main programs were established: (1) a *student-aid* plan of part-time work with financial assistance to needy high school, college, and graduate students sixteen to twenty-four years of age, to enable them to continue their education, and (2) an *out-of-school* work program consisting of part-time employment on work projects designed to give experience and training to unemployed youths of eighteen to twenty-five years of age. In addition to these two main activities, the NYA established junior guidance and placement services in cooperation with the public employment services, training courses for recreational leaders, some resident projects for experience in cooperative living between rural and urban youth, and health examinations for its members.

The administration of NYA was headed by Aubrey Williams as executive director, assisted by an executive committee under Miss Josephine Roche, and by a National Advisory Committee representing labor, business, agriculture, education, and church and welfare groups under Charles Taussig. The organization was decentralized

---

[36] Palmer O. Johnson and Oswald L. Harvey, *The National Youth Administration* (Washington, D. C.: Advisory Committee on Education, 1938), pp. 6-7.

through five regional offices, a state youth administrator in every state with a volunteer advisory committee, and district and local directors and advisory committees to meet local needs. In 1939 the NYA was transferred to the Federal Security Agency, and in September, 1942 to the War Manpower Commission. In July, 1943 Congress withdrew the appropriations and ordered the liquidation of the NYA. In its eight-year work NYA had served 4,800,000 young men and women in continuing their education or training them for employment. It closed its operation January 1, 1944.[37]

The student-aid program provided 1,514,000 students in secondary schools with monthly allowances between three and six dollars, which covered carfare, shoes, and incidental expenses. College students received up to twenty dollars (graduate students up to thirty dollars) a month. They were selected by the schools on the basis of economic need and scholarship. Their activities in school ranged from maintenance and clerical help to tutoring, library, and research work. The out-of-school program aimed primarily at giving youths between eighteen and twenty-five years of age experience and confidence in their ability to work. It helped 2,700,000 youths by employment on projects, such as the construction of community centers, playgrounds, tennis and basketball courts, parks, and swimming pools; the making of furniture for children's institutions and schools and the repairing of fire equipment. All projects were devised and co-sponsored by public authorities, who provided materials, equipment, and supervision. The allocation of federal funds of the NYA was made on the basis of the total youth population of every state. Projects were approved by the State Youth Administrator; only projects with high material cost or complicated technical problems were submitted to the national administration. All youths were registered with the public employment services which, in some instances, were assisted by vocational guidance and placement through a special junior employment section.

In the central office of the NYA, a Division of Negro Affairs protected the particular interests of the Negro minority and secured their full share in educational and training facilities.

The main objections to the NYA came from the school authorities, who protested that a federal agency controlled the education program, that the activities of the regular schools were duplicated, and

[37] Federal Security Agency, *Final Report of the NYA* (1944), p. 234.

that NYA was too costly. In fact, the funds allocated to NYA were never adequate to meet the need for continued schooling, so that it was forced to limit the allowances to modest supplements. One of the valuable fruits of NYA and CCC work was the introduction of work experience into the educational program of American schools.[38]

C. RURAL REHABILITATION

In rural regions with poor soil, or under the one-crop system, the Depression brought disaster to the small farmers. They lost their part-time jobs in industries, their unemployed children returned from industrial centers, and they could not meet their installment rates nor buy feed and seed. Many lost their land to the mortgage holder and became tenants, sharecroppers, farm hands, and/or finally migrant laborers. The Federal Emergency Relief Administration, following examples in Texas and Alabama, first offered loans to farmers as well as some subsistence homesteads.

In 1935, President Roosevelt established the Resettlement Administration in order to continue the agricultural program of the FERA,[39] which was succeeded, in September, 1937, by the Farm Security Administration. It provided two programs, "rehabilitation" and "social services." The first included (1) loans to farmers, tenants, and sharecroppers on easy terms for the purchase of land, farm equipment, seed, feed, and livestock, with counseling on efficient farm management; (2) purchase of farms or homesteads with payment in installments running as long as forty years; (3) setup of farm cooperatives for the joint purchase of tractors, elevators, or purebred sires and for common use of the equipment; and (4) a "debt adjustment service," including legal advice and economic aid. The social services program organized voluntary prepaid medical and dental care at an annual cost, varying from fifteen to forty-five dollars per family. It provided cash grants in emergencies, such as sickness and accidents, and set up migrant camps (partly permanent and partly mobile) with sanitation, medical, and dental service. In the national defense program the Farm Security Administration resettled farm families whose land was used for army needs, established emergency housing for

[38] Warren C. Seyfert and Paul A. Rehmus, *Work Experience in Education* (Cambridge: Harvard University Press, 1941), p. 1.

[39] U.S. Department of Agriculture, *History of the Farm Security Administration* (1940) pp. 2-4.

war workers in dormitories and trailers, and erected public housing projects in defense areas.

In November, 1946, the Farmers Home Administration in the U.S. Department of Agriculture became the successor of the Farm Security Administration. The new agency grants three types of credit to farmers: (1) *farm ownership loans* amortized over 40-year period, to enable the farmer to purchase a family-size farm or to improve, enlarge, or repair the farm; (2) *insured mortgages* to guarantee for a period of forty years the loans of private lenders so that farmers may purchase and/or improve farms; and (3) *production and subsistence loans* (up to $3,500) to allow farmers to purchase on reasonable rates and terms, seed, livestock, feed, fertilizer, and farm equipment and to refinance debts and bolster family subsistence in emergencies. Loans carry no more than 5 per cent interest, and veterans and disabled veterans receive preference. The field staff of the Farmers Home Administration is so small that the agency could no longer assist in the organization of prepaid county medical care plans. However, the field staff still gives individual advice in farm management to farmers who ask for loans or help.

IV. A PERMANENT SOCIAL SECURITY PROGRAM

While temporary emergency measures for relief and work projects under the FERA were carried on, it became evident that a permanent organization of the welfare system of the country with the federal government sharing in its expenditures was necessary. In his message to Congress on June 8, 1934, President Roosevelt announced that a bill would be presented to provide security against the great disturbing factors in life, especially unemployment and old age. On June 29, 1934 he appointed a Committee on Economic Security consisting of Miss Frances Perkins, Secretary of Labor, as chairman and the secretaries of the Treasury, of Agriculture, the Attorney General, and the Federal Emergency Relief Administrator as members. In the preparation of legislation the Committee enlisted the help of a Technical Board of Economic Security, consisting of government experts in federal, state, and local public agencies with Arthur J. Altmeyer as chairman. The Committee also was aided by an Advisory Council on Economic Security, composed of experts who were not connected with public agencies and under the chairmanship of President Frank Graham of the University of North Carolina. He had a professional staff, with Professor Edwin E. Witte as executive director.[40]

On January 15, 1935 the Committee on Economic Security submitted its report to President Roosevelt, who transmitted it, under the title *Economic Security Bill*, to Congress. After certain amendments and changes the *Social Security Act* became law on August 14, 1935. Thus the fundamental federal law in the field of social welfare in the United States was created. The Social Security Act introduced three main programs: (1) a program of *social insurance*, consisting of a federal old-age insurance system and of a federal-state system of unemployment compensation, (2) a program of *public categorical assistance* supported by federal grants-in-aid for three groups, including Old-Age Assistance, Aid to the Needy Blind, and Aid to Dependent Children, to which a fourth category, Aid to the Permanently and Totally Disabled, was added in 1950, and (3) a program of *health and welfare services*, providing for Maternal and Child Health Services, Services for Crippled Children, Child Welfare Services, Vocational Rehabilitation, and Public Health Services. The last two systems were based on different legal foundations through the *Vocational Rehabilitation Act of 1943* and the *Public Health Service Act of 1944*.

The Social Security Act placed the federal administration or supervision of the most essential operations of the three programs under a new agency, the Social Security Board. The three members of the Board were appointed by the President of the United States for terms of six years, but not more than two could belong to the same political party. The Board consisted first of John Winant (Chairman), Altmeyer, and Miles; later of Arthur J. Altmeyer as chairman, Mrs. Ellen Woodward and George Bigge. The Board, in 1935, was established as an independent agency under the President, but an amendment of 1939 placed the Social Security Board, together with other agencies, under the newly created Federal Security Agency. At this time the U.S. Public Health Service was grouped together in one agency with other federal units concerned with health problems, but child welfare services remained under the administration of the U.S. Children's Bureau. In 1946, a reorganization

[40] Social Security Board, *Social Security in America* (1937), pp. III-V, 515-517.

of the Federal Security Agency abolished the Social Security Board and replaced it by the Social Security Administration under a single Commissioner for Social Security; Arthur J. Altmeyer served as commissioner until 1953,[41] when John W. Tramburg was appointed commissioner, who was replaced in 1954 by Charles J. Schottland.

This development meant that the federal government assumed a limited responsibility in the field of public welfare by its participation in the cost of three (later four) selected programs of public assistance and by the support of a group of services in the protection of health and the well-being of children and certain handicapped persons. Congress was not inclined to accept a full modernization of the entire poor relief system of the country nor to provide federal grants to all types of public assistance, which would have led to a unified support, supervision, and control of all public welfare activities. The President's Committee on Economic Security did not follow a proposal for such legislation by the Committee on Public Employment and Relief, appointed by Secretary of Labor, Frances Perkins, in November, 1934. This Committee of experts was composed of outstanding social workers and public relief administrators under the chairmanship of Miss Dorothy Kahn. The change of the Federal Security Agency into a cabinet department was suggested in various bills and recommended by professional organizations of social work. In 1953 the first Reorganization Plan of President Eisenhower realized this plan and established the Department of Health, Education and Welfare with Mrs. Oveta Culp Hobby as the first Secretary (see Chapter 7).

The amendments to the Social Security Act, particularly those of 1950, 1952, and 1954, greatly increased the numbers of people eligible for old-age and survivors' insurance and unemployment compensation. These amendments strengthened the operations of the public assistance programs and the various health and welfare services and indicated modern society's increasing recognition of responsibility for the preservation of the welfare of all people.[42]

The role of private social agencies fundamentally changed during the Depression. At the start of the Depression, private agencies soon exhausted all their funds and were forced to abandon the dispensation of economic aid that was considered until this date as one

---

[41] For the present organization see Chart 2, Chapter 7.
[42] J. Brown, *op. cit.*, pp. 304-305, and Chapters 7, 8, and 9.

of their main functions. Public welfare departments in cities and counties took over the main responsibility for the relief of the financially distressed. Private social agencies still are granting economic aid at a moderate level to persons who are not eligible for public assistance, and if it is necessary in order to make casework and counseling services effective; they are rendering such financial help as cannot be given by public agencies. The basic distinction between the present functions of public and private agencies is that private social agencies emphasize casework services for personal and behavior questions, adjustment in family and environmental problems, and the providing of group work and recreational facilities not supplied by public authorities. Private agencies no longer assume the main responsibility for economic support of people in financial need but rather supplement the assistance given by public welfare agencies. Private agencies still engage in health services for tuberculosis, cancer, venereal diseases, heart ailments, infantile paralysis, and rheumatic fever and in children's services, particularly for adoption and child placement, institutional care for children and adults, vocational guidance, and training. Often these services are coordinated with those offered under public auspices.

V. WAR AND POSTWAR PROBLEMS

The main problems which social services faced during World War II were family separation caused by the absence of husbands, fathers, and fiancés in the armed services or in war industries, and children left without proper care and supervision by working mothers. There also were general community, health, and moral difficulties caused by mass living in military training and inadequate conditions in war industries areas. Often, public and private agencies had to meet these increased problems with inadequate personnel, depleted by the call of social workers to service with the armed forces at home and abroad. Finally, war services endangered the maintenance of regular peace-time programs for the aged, the handicapped, the sick, and children.

In order to solve these problems, a nationwide effort of coordination of all available resources was attempted under the guidance of the Office of Community War Services, which was organized under the Federal Security Agency.[43] The Office was guided by an Inter-departmental Advisory Council, with representatives of all federal agencies engaged in health and welfare work. Five central committees dealt with (1) health and medical care, (2) family security, (3) nutrition, (4) social protection, and (5) community organization for health and welfare. The twelve regional offices of the Federal Security Agency established a similar coordination, their regional directors serving at the same time as directors of community war services. State and local defense councils in cooperation with public and private social agencies carried programs and suggestions to the people. In the new defense industrial areas, medical and dental facilities, sanitation, water supply, hospitals, clinics, schools, and housing often were lacking or inadequate, so that a tremendous effort was imperative to provide these public utilities.[44] The funds for the construction and operation of these institutions were made available through the so-called *Lanham Act* (Community Facilities Act) of October 14, 1940. They enabled communities to build housing for war workers and families of service men, hospitals, schools, water and sewage systems, and child care centers so that mothers working in war industries could leave their children with adequate care and protection.

A serious problem was the lack of leisure time and recreational facilities for service men on furlough and for war workers in cities in which the population suddenly increased to many times its former size. The recreation sections of the regional offices of the Community War Services joined their efforts with state and local defense committees and with the United Service Organization (USO). This agency was created in 1941 by six private social agencies—the YWCA, YMCA, the National Catholic Community Service, the Jewish Welfare Board, the Salvation Army, and the National Travelers Aid Association. Their cooperation resulted in the establishment

[43] In 1940, the Council of National Defense had set up an Office of the Coordinator of Health, Welfare, and Related Defense Activities; it was transferred in September, 1941 to the Federal Security Agency under the title Office of Defense, Health, and Welfare Service, until the final shorter name was selected in 1943.

[44] Federal Security Agency, "Health, Welfare, and Related Aspects of Community War Services," October, 1942; Helen R. Wright, *Social Service in Wartime* (Chicago: University of Chicago Press), 1944.

of centers for servicemen with facilities for social activities, music, dramatic performances, dances, hobby clubs, discussion groups, libraries, and reading and writing rooms. They arranged for invitations to servicemen for family dinners, concerts, and theatres. In addition to these recreational services, USO agencies and particularly Travelers Aid offered counseling and casework service to servicemen, war workers, and transients who had personal problems. More than 1,000 USO centers were operating during the war. The American Red Cross provided medical and casework services in military camps and assisted the families of the servicemen through its Home Service Division. Private social agencies, together with public welfare departments and others in the field of health, family, and child welfare, cooperated with the defense councils in instruction on civil protection, improvement of nutrition during rationing and war shortages, and (with the support of public health authorities) in "social protection" against venereal diseases. We shall discuss the services for war veterans and their survivors later in Chapter 16.

A. THE JAPANESE EVACUATION

One event during World War II deserves discussion from the point of view of social welfare: the evacuation of the population of Japanese descent from the states at the West Coast. The Japanese are one of the small minorities (about 127,000 persons) in our country. Almost 120,000 of them lived in California, Oregon, and Washington. Immediately after Pearl Harbor a wave of suspicion, hatred, and fear against persons of Japanese ancestry engulfed the Pacific Coast. Military leaders were afraid of sabotage and the danger of support of an enemy attack. Racial prejudice was combined with dislike of economic competition. Truck farmers, merchants, laundrymen, and restaurant, fruit, and vegetable market owners, and fishermen urged the removal of Japanese from the West Coast. Others argued that an evacuation would be necessary in order to protect the Japanese-Americans against harm from mob violence. After the President authorized the evacuation of military zones, Japanese-Americans were asked to move voluntarily from the Pacific Coast inland. Of 100,000 in California 10,000 followed this suggestion, hastily sold their business, land, and property, and tried to settle in the neighboring states. But they found difficulties as Utah, Nevada,

Wyoming, and Arizona prevented them from entering their territory because they considered them "dangerous." On March 2, 1942 General De Witt ordered their removal from the Western Coast areas. President Roosevelt created the War Relocation Authority on March 18, 1942 as a civilian agency to carry out the evacuation. Social workers with other citizens were concerned about the constitutionality of this measure, since 75,000 of the group were American citizens. However they assisted in the relocation process at the registration centers. They did their best to advise the Japanese about the disposal of their property, the storage of furniture and equipment, and the safekeeping of valuables, but many Japanese were so upset that they sold everything at great loss and patiently accepted being placed behind barbed wire in ten relocation centers, which were established by the evacuees themselves, in desert regions under the command of the army engineers. The War Relocation Authority sought to make life in these centers as bearable as possible. Crowded army barracks (without sufficient privacy for families with many children), lack of constructive work, limited and inadequate wages, and shortage of health and sanitary facilities and teachers for the schools in the camps were serious handicaps. The anxiety about the future and the hostility of the press—and sometimes of the guards and surrounding population—created problems and led, in a few instances, to riots. Japanese who were considered "disloyal" were segregated in Tule Lake, California, while in the other relocation camps an intensive outplacement program was carried out.

With the help of local committees on which members of the American Friends Service Committee, of the YWCA, the YMCA, and the Federal Council of Churches of Christ were particularly active, 41,000 persons left the centers and worked in communities all over the country. Life in the relocation centers was trying, especially for adolescents who lost the traditional oriental respect for their helpless and often embittered parents. Juvenile delinquency, family discord, and political strife were rampant. The removal of families to outside communities served to solve many difficulties which social workers in the centers tried to alleviate. When Japanese-Americans were permitted to volunteer for army service, the spectacular record of their combat units, particularly in Italy, helped to restore their own self-respect and caused a change in public opinion. The War Relocation Authority encouraged the return of the evacuees to their old communities or to places of their own choice as soon as it was permitted by Presidential order in 1945. Many older evacuees had suffered under the internment and had lost their initiative so that they first preferred to stay in the camps, a typical damage of "institutionalization." But with the aid of placement officers of the War Relocation Authority and local committees the difficulties of finding housing, jobs, and acceptance in the communities were finally solved.[45]

B. HEALTH AND WELFARE IN CIVIL DEFENSE

The *Federal Civil Defense Act* of January 12, 1951 prepares the country for emergency action in case of an enemy attack and organizes a Federal Civil Defense Administration. Among the civil defense measures which are considered in case of an air attack or atomic bombardment are warning systems, preparation of citizens for the best bodily protection, restoration of communications and medical, health and sanitation services, and emergency welfare activities.[46] The possibility of an atomic bombing has greatly aggravated the danger of mass destruction of human life and of entire communities. However, the abhorrence of people for a suicidal modern war makes it difficult for the public to develop realistic awareness of this danger and creates an atmosphere of apathy which does not secure an effective protection against disaster situations.

It is anticipated that in case of such a disaster many families will be left without a home, without food, clothing, without a place to eat, sleep, and rest, and without money. In order to preserve civilian morale in such a situation, efficient welfare services are necessary. Social workers may have to evacuate families or children, to place refugees in other households and other communities, and they may

---

[45] U.S. Department of the Interior, War Relocation Authority, *WRA: A Story of Human Conservation* (Washington, D. C.: Government Printing Office, 1947); Dorothy S. Thomas and Richard S. Nishomoto, *The Spoilage* (Berkeley: University of California Press, 1946); Alexander H. Leighton, *The Governing of Men* (Princeton: Princeton University Press, 1945); Dorothy Swaine Thomas, *The Salvage: Japanese American Evacuation and Resettlement* (Berkeley: University of California Press, 1952).

[46] Wilbur J. Cohen and Evelyn F. Boyer, "Federal Civil Defense Act of 1950: Summary and Legislative History," *Social Security Bulletin*, Vol. 14, No. 4, April, 1951, pp. 11-16; Ralph E. Pumphrey, "Social Work and National Defense," *Social Work Year Book, 1954*, pp. 500-505; and Raymond T. Schaeffer, "Disaster Relief," *Social Work Year Book, 1954*, pp. 166-170.

have to provide mass feeding, clothing, shelter, and financial aid to destitute people.

It is desirable to give such emergency help as rapidly as possible. The victims of an enemy attack should immediately receive medical aid, material assistance, and advice until they can again take care of themselves and can resume their normal work and life. Necessary emergency welfare services have to include information centers, field hospitals, shelter, canteens, and a registration service. The existing hospitals, clinics, and dispensaries would be used for emergency health measures, but supplementary facilities might have to be established if necessary. In each state the chief health officer takes charge of all civil defense health and medical services. Social workers advise evacuees and refugees about locating relatives and friends and refer them to public assistance, medical care, and child care services. They would also counsel them regarding their legal rights for insurance benefits and other allowances, employment services, retraining and vocational rehabilitation facilities, and preparing temporary settlement for uprooted families.

The social and health problems created by the establishment of new plants and installations in many defense communities, some of them in isolated areas, also require serious attention. Workers and their families in congested areas with defense factories are seriously threatened by hardships and inadequate housing and health provisions and lack of hospitals and schools. In 1953, in one trailer camp, 2,000 children were left without any playground or supervision, forced to crawl under the wheels of automobiles and trailers. In a southern community, a trailer camp was set in rigid rows under the blazing sun, like cell blocks in a prison compound, endangering the health of women and children. An open ditch served as the sewage system near a large concentration of huts as dwelling places for defense workers' families. Defense housing projects sometimes are full of dust and flies. Their inhabitants are without decent recreational facilities, lonely, and frustrated, and frequently in need of schools, health centers, nursing facilities, water supply, sewage disposal, and recreational and cultural life.

In many communities, classified as "critical defense housing areas," there are no Community Chests or Councils of Social Agencies. Often the social agencies are understaffed and not able to assume the additional responsibilities of meeting the problems created through large defense industries, military encampments or training centers, and of preparing for the people's protection in case of an atomic attack.

Under the auspices of the National Welfare Assembly as the nationwide coordinating body of private social welfare agencies, the main funds for the civil defense needs of the country are raised in a unified campaign by the United Defense Fund which, at the local level, is coordinated with the activities of the Community Chests (see Chapter 21). The United Defense Fund (UDF) is composed of six organizations: (1) The United Community Defense Services, (2) The United Service Organizations, (3) The American Social Hygiene Association, (4) The National Recreation Association, (5) The United Seamen's Service, and the (6) American Relief for Korea.

Recreation and welfare activities, including personal and family counseling for members of the armed forces, are the responsibility of the United Service Organizations (USO). USO, which had been very active during World War II, suspended its activities following the demobilization, then was reactivated and merged, in 1951, with the Associated Services for the Armed Forces. USO is now composed of the YMCA, YWCA, Salvation Army, National Catholic Community Service, National Jewish Welfare Board, National Travelers Aid Association, and "Camp Shows, Inc." These coordinated agencies provide wholesome leisure-time activities for military personnel to meet the religious, spiritual, social, cultural, and welfare needs of men and women in the Armed Forces. USO shares these services with the American Red Cross, whose field directors and staffs offer individual counseling and assistance to military personnel in camps and hospitals and supplement recreation programs overseas. The American Red Cross maintains preparation for disaster relief in cooperation with the Armed Forces; federal, state, and local governments; and private organizations. It assists in the planning and preparation of emergency relief measures.

The Air Force organized in 1951 an Office of Community Services in order to make available recreational and social welfare resources of the communities to members of the Air Force and their families.

The United Community Defense Services, in cooperation with the American Red Cross, provide defense programs for civilian welfare and health, which supplement the preparations of state and local governments for disaster relief in case of an emergency. United Community Defense Services (UCDS) is a federation of 15 nonprofit national organizations[47] founded, in 1951, at the suggestion of the National Welfare Assembly and the Community Chests and Councils of America. UCDS offers advice to defense communities by fact-finding surveys which determine the health and welfare needs of the population and enable the community to organize and finance an effective civilian defense social welfare program. It assists the community in the establishment and temporary financing of emergency programs, including health services, child care and recreation, where community resources cannot meet these needs. UCDS is engaged in the recruitment of nurses, social workers, and volunteers for defense service and emergency preparations. UCDS pays particular attention to the development of the resources of underprivileged minority groups and to the establishment of interracial cultural cooperation. Finally UCDS conducts research in order to discover the scope of the defense impact and to interpret to the public the importance of preparedness for emergency action.

Separate defense programs are carried on by (1) the American Social Hygiene Association for the prevention and cure of venereal diseases, (2) the National Recreation Association in the field of physical education and recreational activities, (3) the United Seamen's Service at ports for members of the merchant marine, and (4) the American Relief for Korea for the rehabilitation of the country which has so severely suffered during the war.

In the field of civil defense neither Congress nor the majority of States have yet taken the full-hearted action which secures the most available protection to the population. In the area of welfare service, the public welfare departments, with the support of the social agencies coordinated under the United Defense Fund and with the aid of the American Red Cross, are expected to provide the main social services in an emergency. In California, a Defense Mobilization Com-

---

[47] These are (1) American Social Hygiene Association, (2) Child Welfare League, (3) Committee on Careers in Nursing, (4) Family Service Association, (5) YWCA, (6) Catholic Community Service, (7) Committee on Social Work in Defense Mobilization, (8) Federation of Settlements and Neighborhood Centers, (9) Organization for Public Health Nursing, (10) Probation and Parole Association, (11) Recreation Association, (12) Travelers Aid Association, (13) Urban League, (14) AFL, and (15) CIO Community Services Committee.

mittee has been established as a coordinating agency under the Department of Veterans Affairs, and the State Recreation Commission attempts to secure recreation facilities in local communities. Civil defense and disaster protection is financed mainly through private contributions and state and local funds and is left to local initiative. It seems doubtful whether this arrangement provides the necessary preparedness and sufficient security under present conditions.

SELECTED BIBLIOGRAPHY

Abbott, Edith, *Historical Aspects of the Immigration Problem; Select Documents.* Chicago: University of Chicago Press, 1926.
Abbott, Grace, *The Child and the State: Select Documents with Introductory Notes.* 2 vols. Chicago: University of Chicago Press, 1938.
Adams, Grace, *Workers on Relief.* New Haven: Yale University Press, 1939.
Addams, Jane, *Forty Years at Hull House.* New York: Macmillan, 1935.
Auerbach, Frank L., "Aliens and Foreign Born," *Social Work Year Book, 1954,* pp. 47-55.
Bakke, E. Wight, *Citizens Without Work; A Study of the Effects of Unemployment Upon the Worker's Social Relations and Practices.* New Haven: Yale University Press, 1940.
Brown, Francis J., and Joseph S. Roucek, *One America; The History, Contributions, and Present Problems of Our Racial and National Minorities,* Rev. ed. New York: Prentice-Hall, Inc., 1945.
*Brown, Josephine C., *Public Relief, 1929-1939.* New York: Holt, 1940.
Bruce, J. Campbell, *The Golden Door; The Irony of Our Immigration Policy.* New York: Random House, 1954.
*Bruno, Frank J., *Trends in Social Work.* New York: Columbia University Press, 1948.
Clarke, Helen I., *Social Legislation.* New York: Appleton-Century-Crofts, Inc., 1940.
Davie, Maurice R., *World Immigration; With Special Reference to the United States.* New York: Macmillan, 1936.
———, et al., *Refugees in America: Report to the Committee for the Study of Recent Immigration from Europe.* New York: Harper, 1947.
*Deutsch, Albert, *The Mentally Ill in America.* New York: Columbia University Press, 1946.
Douglas, Paul H., *Social Security in the United States.* New York: McGraw, 1936.
Fechner, Robert, "The Civilian Conservation Corps Program," *Annals of the American Academy of Political and Social Science,* Vol. 194, November, 1937, pp. 129-140.
Feder, Leah, *Unemployment Relief in Periods of Depression.* New York: Russell Sage Foundation, 1936.

Fisher, Dorothy Canfield, *Our Young Folks*. New York: Harcourt, 1943.

Fosdick, Harry Emerson, *On Being a Real Person*. New York: Harper, 1943.

Glick, Frank L., *The Illinois Emergency Relief Commission*. Chicago: University of Chicago Press, 1939.

Guthrie, John D., *Saga of the CCC*. Washington, D.C.: American Forestry Association, 1942.

Handel, Alexander F., "Public Assistance and Displaced Persons," *Social Work Journal*, Vol. 31, No. 2, April, 1950, pp. 84-85.

Harper, Charles Price, *The Administration of the Civilian Conservation Corps*. Clarksburg, West Virginia: Clarksburg Publishing Co., 1939.

Haynes, Fred E., *The American Prison System*. New York: McGraw, 1939.

Hopkins, Harry L., *Spending to Save*. New York: Norton, 1936.

Howard, Donald S., *The WPA and Federal Relief Policy*. New York: Russell Sage Foundation, 1943.

Jacobsen, Paul B. (editor), *Youth and Work Opportunities*. Chicago: University of Chicago Press, 1943.

Johnson, Palmer O., and Oswald L. Harvey, *The National Youth Administration*. Washington, D.C.: Advisory Committee on Education, 1938.

Key, V. O., *The Administration of Federal Grants to States*. Chicago: Public Administration Service, 1937.

Kieley, James F., *Account of Origin, Growth and Work of the CCC*. Washington, D. C.: Department of the Interior, National Park Service, 1938.

Kluckhohn, Clyde, and Dorothea Leighton, *The Navaho*. Cambridge: Harvard University Press, 1946.

Lane, Marie D., and Francis Steegmuller, *America on Relief*. New York: Harcourt, 1938.

Leighton, Alexander H., *The Governing of Men*. Princeton: Princeton University Press, 1945.

Lindley, Betty, and Ernest K. Lindley, *A New Deal for Youth*. New York: Viking Press, 1938.

Lorwin, Lewis L., *Youth Work Programs, Problems and Policies*. Washington, D. C.: American Youth Commission, American Council of Education, 1941.

Macmahon, Arthur W., *The Administration of Federal Work Relief*. Chicago: Public Administration Service, 1941.

———, John D. Millett, and Gladys Ogden, *The Administration of Public Relief*. Chicago: Public Administration Service, 1941.

McWilliams, Carey, *Prejudice: Japanese Americans*. New York: Little, 1944.

———, *What About Our Japanese Americans?* New York: Public Affairs Committee, 1944.

Meriam, Lewis, *et al.*, *The Problem of Indian Administration*. Baltimore: Johns Hopkins Press, 1928.

Millspaugh, Arthur C., *Public Welfare Organization*. Washington, D. C.: Brookings Institution, 1935.

President's Commission on Immigration and Naturalization, *Whom Shall We Welcome*. Washington, D. C.: 1953.

Schmeckebier, Laurence F., *The Office of Indian Affairs, Its History, Activities, and Organization*. Baltimore: Johns Hopkins Press, 1927.

Schneider, David M., and Albert Deutsch, *The History of Public Welfare in New York State, 1867-1940*. Chicago: University of Chicago Press, 1941.

Thomas, Dorothy S., *The Salvage: Japanese American Evacuation and Resettlement*. Berkeley: University of California Press, 1952.

———, and Richard S. Nishomoto, *The Spoilage*. Berkeley: University of California Press, 1946.

U.S. Department of the Interior, War Relocation Authority, *WPA: A Story of Human Conservation*. Washington, D. C.: Government Printing Office, 1947.

U.S. Displaced Persons Commission, *The DP Story*. Washington, D.C.: Government Printing Office, 1952.

U.S. National Resources Planning Board, *Security, Work and Relief Policies* (Report of the Committee on Long-Range Work and Relief Policies). Washington, D.C.: Government Printing Office, 1942.

Weber, Gustavus, and Lawrence F. Schmeckebier, *The Veterans Administration, Its History, Activities and Organization*. Washington, D.C.: Brookings Institution, 1934.

Williams, Edward Ainsworth, *Federal Aid for Relief*. New York: Columbia University Press, 1939.

Wilson, Howard E., *Mary McDowell: Neighbor*. Chicago: University of Chicago Press, 1928.

Wise, Winifred E., *Jane Addams of Hull House; A Biography*. New York: Harcourt, 1935.

*Witmer, Helen Leland, *Social Work; An Analysis of a Social Institution*. New York: Farrar & Rinehart, 1942.

*Wright, Helen R., *et al.*, *Social Service in Wartime*. Chicago: University of Chicago Press, 1944.

PART II. *The Present System and Organization of Social Welfare*

6. Methods of Social Work

Social work activities are classified into six major types: social casework, social group work, community organization, social action, social welfare research, and social welfare administration. All types of social work require certain common skills and abilities which may be called generic social work qualifications, but the methods applied in the six categories differ.

The first two methods, social casework and social group work, consist of activities in direct contact with human beings who use these services. Helen L. Witmer's definition of "social work" applies to these types: "to give assistance to individuals in regard to the difficulties they encounter in their use of an organized group's services or in their own performance as a member of an organized group."[1] The methods of community organization, social action, research, and social welfare administration are used in order to establish, maintain, and operate social agencies which provide social casework and group work services. Although there is theoretical dispute whether all these methods are to be classified as social work,[2] we consider them an integral part of the tools in our modern social welfare program.

I. THE DEVELOPMENT OF SOCIAL CASEWORK

During the last quarter of the nineteenth century, the workers of the Charity Organization Societies were influenced in their ideas

[1] Helen Leland Witmer, *Social Work: An Analysis of a Social Institution* (New York: Farrar & Rinehart, 1942), p. 121.

[2] *Ibid.*, p. 123; another classification is suggested by Herbert H. Stroup, *Community Welfare Organization* (New York: Harper, 1952), p. 126: social casework, group work, and community organization as basic processes, and social research, social administration, and social action as auxiliary processes.

and practice by the recognition of the widespread economic and spiritual distress among the masses of low paid manual laborers, the sick, and unemployed in the industrial large cities. They realized the lack of helpful, constructive relief and the apathy toward the suffering of the destitute by the poor law authorities. They also became aware of the waste of energy and funds through the lack of cooperation and information, the confusion and duplication of effort among private charitable agencies. The Charity Organization Societies were convinced that help could not come from public poor relief, but that emphasis should be placed on private initiative and the "rehabilitation of the individual client." They hoped to make it unnecessary that the poor law commissions give monetary relief to paupers in their own homes and proposed that the Charity Organization Societies would rehabilitate the individual clients so that they might support themselves and their families.[3] Following the social philosophy of Thomas Chalmers, they thought that moral defects, idleness, drinking, and gambling were the essential causes of poverty. Their attempts of rehabilitation, therefore, were directed in the first place toward a behavior reform of the destitute individual in order to save him from "the sin of poverty." They sought to achieve this goal by personal visits to the poor, advice, admonitions, and financial aid. In each case the rehabilitation of the poor person was to be carried on after a careful investigation of his conditions and discussions with the applicant and the people in his surroundings.[4] This was the beginning of casework.

In their method of finding a social solution for the personal and economic problems of a client, the Charity Organization Societies spent money for vocational training, tools and equipment, rent for setting up a workshop or a small business, for food, clothes, and rent of a room or an apartment for the maintenance of the family. These measures were, however, merely incidental to the real purpose of rehabilitating the client. The volunteers and agents of the relief societies considered themselves representatives of society; they visited the applicant and collected facts on his conditions, family relations, experiences, and abilities. The findings were submitted to a com-

[3] See Chapter 4.
[4] Elizabeth de Schweinitz and Karl de Schweinitz, "The Contribution of Social Work to the Administration of Public Assistance," *Social Work Journal*, Vol. XXIX, No. 3, July, 1948, pp. 108-110.

mittee representing the local charities that decided which action should be taken, with the aim of restoring the client to self-support. In this task the "friendly visitor" continued the personal contact with the client, gave him advice and directions to become independent. It was expected that the client followed the suggested plan. The necessary funds for rehabilitation, however, were solicited from well-to-do citizens by employed agents of the Charity Organization Society. The personal contact of the volunteer was thus separated from the measures of financial assistance because the societies thought that the mixing of both would impair the moral and educational influence and the personal relationship between the friendly visitor and the client.

The approach of the "friendly visitors" still was based upon their social and economic superiority, higher education, and the assumption that the client was in his precarious condition due to some fault in his behavior. This moral and social foundation of the early casework approach became questionable when the "friendly visitors" began to realize that frequently the cause of distress was not a character defect of the poor, but the social conditions in which he lived. Such conditions were illness of the client or of his family, numerous children, unsanitary, overcrowded housing, low wages, debts, undernourishment, inadequate education and training, which sometimes led to acts of despair. This new recognition of the environmental influence on the individual was supported, at the turn of the century, by the scientific findings of the so-called "school of environmental determinism" in anthropology, biology, sociology, and economics. Novelists, sociologists, and political scientists exposed the social evils of industrial society and emphasized the need for fundamental social reforms in working conditions and wages, in the establishment of schools, housing, hospitals and clinics, in the prevention of communicable diseases, and the abolition of night work of women and children.

The effect of these experiences was that the Charity Organization Societies became concerned with finding ways of achieving social reforms and of advocating social legislation that would prevent destitution, disease, and social disorganization. But though measures of social reform were in various respects improving the living conditions of the poverty stricken and the low income group, there were still many families in dire want and distress. They needed understanding help, people to listen to them and to advise them so that they might make the right use of such community services as clinics, hospitals, employment bureaus, legal aid, training facilities, and adult education. Under these circumstances, social agencies continued to carry on casework in recognition of the fact that social reform did not solve all individual problems. Social workers also became aware that their interest should not be limited to the individual applicant, especially the breadwinner of the family, but that each member of the family deserved their full attention and should be considered in relation to his environment.

This change in emphasis was expressed during the first and second decade of this century in the term "family welfare work," replacing the older terminology of "charity organization." The American Association for Organizing Charity changed its name to American Association for Organizing Family Social Work, and is now called "Family Service Association of America."

The experiences of social workers also revealed a serious conflict of values in our civilization. Modern industrial society was inclined to embrace a theory of "Social Darwinism" that its unfit members should be eliminated as a natural process, and that interference with such elimination was harmful to a healthy society. On the other hand, religious thought and humanitarian philosophy respect the divine nature of man and demand that every human being should be assisted whatever his failures might be. These two value systems are strict contradictions. Social workers have accepted the "Humanitarian Ethos" as their concept of responsibility of society for the welfare of individuals in the community. Our general public, however, often is still ambivalent about following one or the other of the two conflicting concepts and is uncertain whether to accept rugged individualism or humanitarian philosophy.[5]

In 1911, Porter R. Lee, director of the New York School of Social Work, stated that social casework is "the method of effecting the understanding of the needs, resources, and reactions of individuals."[6] But there still remained at this time a paternalistic, domineering at-

[5] H. Witmer, *op. cit.*, pp. 55, 167-169, 172; Barrows Dunham, *Man Against Myth* (Boston: Little, 1947), pp. 59-60, 64-65; Herbert Bisno, *The Philosophy of Social Work* (Washington, D. C.: Public Affairs Press, 1952), pp. 30-41; and Ernest Greenwood, *Toward a Sociology of Social Work* (Los Angeles: Welfare Council of Metropolitan Los Angeles, 1953), pp. 7-9.

[6] Porter R. Lee, "Social Function of Case Work," *National Proceedings of Conference of Charities and Corrections, 1911*, pp. 260-266.

titude in the relation of the social worker toward the client who came to ask for advice and help. Although in theory it was proclaimed "casework must work with and not for the individual," in practice the caseworker considered herself the best and the only objective judge in what was the right solution for the client, because of her experience in social questions. Another factor in social casework practice at this period before World War I strengthened the domineering role of the social worker. Social agencies took advantage of the growing number of experienced persons who received training either in special courses or in the newly established schools of social work and employed those professionally trained workers instead of using untrained volunteers and a few administrative agents. This meant that the paid social worker assumed most functions in the agency: the initial interview with the applicant, social investigation at his home and with regard to his environment, the social diagnosis of the facts found in this investigation, and the development of a plan for treatment or rehabilitation of the applicant and his family. In 1917, Mary E. Richmond, director of the Charity Organization Division of the Russell Sage Foundation, described this method in her book, *Social Diagnosis*, the first classic description of the casework process.[7] Social agencies no longer submitted the findings of social investigations to a local committee of executives, so that the social caseworker became the decisive element in the process of aiding the client.

On the other hand, social agencies found that their aim of rehabilitation of children and adults could not be achieved by counseling alone. Frequently substantial financial assistance was needed in order to maintain families during the period of readjustment, retraining, and rehabilitation, and in some instances for long periods. Family welfare and child protective agencies still aimed at supporting people who were not in need of institutionalized care in hospitals, orphanages, or homes for the aged or invalid, by funds collected from private donors and contributors. They prevented, by this practice, the public from being aware of the necessity of improving the facilities of public relief authorities, of providing adequate budgets, and competent administration of public relief.

[7] New York: Russell Sage Foundation, 1917. See also Gordon Hamilton, *Theory and Practice of Social Case Work* (New York: Columbia University Press, 1947), pp. 11-12, 19.

Mary Richmond and the early practitioners of social casework required a thorough investigation of the facts and data of the life of the individual who was in need of help. They seemed necessary in order to arrive at an accurate diagnosis. Social diagnosis was the attempt to analyze these findings and to determine the underlying causes for social and personal difficulties of the client. After this critical examination followed the interpretation of the specific conditions for the behavior and the reactions of the client, based upon his individual personality. The therapy was planned upon the preceding investigation and the social diagnosis; it was frequently directed toward external improvements in the environment, living conditions, and type and location of work, which were considered of primary importance in the initial period of casework practice.

Methods and practice of social casework were also deeply influenced by the scientific development of and the growing interest of the general public in psychology and psychiatry in this country.[8] There were a number of important contributions from the social sciences, such as the studies of child growth by G. Stanley Hall, the investigations of sex problems by Havelock Ellis, and the invention of intelligence tests by Binet and Simon in France and their introduction in the United States by H. H. Goddard. Another decisive influence was the foundation of the mental hygiene movement by Clifford Beers after the publication of his experiences as a mental patient in his book, *A Mind that Found Itself*, in 1908. These ideas shifted the fundamental interest of social work from economic and sociological emphasis toward psychological and emotional problems of the client. Important factors in this development were the discoveries of Sigmund Freud, the findings of psychoanalysis and dynamic psychology, and the work of Freud's followers, Alfred Adler, Otto Rank, and C. G. Jung and others who founded their own analytic schools.[9]

Before this period, only a few social workers had been employed in mental hospitals, especially in children's wards; they helped the psychiatrists in securing information about the case history and the family conditions of the patient, and took care of the patient after his discharge. As early as 1905 some general hospitals felt the need to employ social caseworkers to assist the physician in his diagnosis and

[8] G. Hamilton, *op. cit.*, pp. 30-33, 139-142.
[9] H. Witmer, *op. cit.*, pp. 170-171, and Chapter 13.

treatment through collecting the data on the patient's earlier experiences and reporting on his social and economic conditions. These social workers were aware of the necessity to make use of the resources of the patient's family as well as of the facilities of the wider community, of social agencies, employers, and friends in order to preserve and strengthen the results of medical treatment.[10]

During World War I the interest of social workers took a further turn from environmental factors to the psychological aspects of human behavior for which psychiatry, psychology, and biology had laid the groundwork. The immediate reason for this intensified psychological concern of social workers was the establishment of "home service divisions" through the American Red Cross where social workers assisted families whose husbands were serving with the armed forces. These families were different from former clients of the Charity Organization Societies and of the poor relief agencies; most of them had never before been in contact with social agencies. These families, whose husbands served overseas, were typical American people, a cross section of the entire country. Because the Red Cross is maintained by voluntary contributions of the population, its job was to be of service to these families, and the old "lady bountiful" attitude was out of place for servicemen's families.[11] The same was true for Red Cross workers serving in hospitals and field stations with the fighting armies in Europe. The large number of neuropsychiatric patients suffering from "shell-shock" created a heavy demand for trained psychiatric social workers. Because of the war shortage of psychiatrists, psychiatric social workers were given for the first time substantial responsibility in the treatment of psychoneurotic patients and worked in close contact with the psychiatrists in the armed forces. In this work emphasis was placed on the fact that human behavior is not arbitrarily chosen or accidental but is the result of a lifelong development, as well as of family and surroundings upon the organism and the emotions of the individual.

In our society some people have serious difficulties in the conflicts between their own desires and the demands of society. Frequently the patient is not conscious of the motivations for his be-

---

[10] The development of medical and psychiatric social work is discussed in Chapters 12 and 13.

[11] Virginia Robinson, *A Changing Psychology in Social Work* (Chapel Hill: University of North Carolina Press, 1930), p. 53.

havior and attempts to conceal by rationalizations the true motives for his actions. The findings of Sigmund Freud about "the unconscious" have shown that emotions govern our behavior more than reason. Freud emphasized that the experiences in early childhood frequently determine the basic personality structure of the adult. This gave new insights to social workers who tried to incorporate psychiatric theories into their concepts.

The first implication of psychiatric theories for casework was the demand that the caseworker had to secure more detailed facts in order to understand the personality, the motivations, and the emotional needs of the client. This task, however, required more knowledge and skill than the average caseworker mastered and also more time for the work on each individual case. For this reason, after World War I, family and children's agencies began to employ trained psychiatric social workers to help clients with difficult emotional maladjustments. Under these circumstances, caseworkers had to sacrifice again the concept of working with the entire family as a unit, because the problems of the family group were not identical with the specific emotional and personality problems of the individual client, whether child or adult. On the other hand, in order to rehabilitate the family, it became necessary to cure or at least to alleviate the mental conflicts of one or more members of the family.

With a better psychological understanding of human behavior and a more realistic evaluation of economic problems, social casework changed its approach to the client. The full respect of the caseworker for the personal dignity and worth of the client as a human being represents the process of "democratization" of casework. The caseworker accepts the client as he is; she does not attempt to mold him as she would like him to behave. The change in approach led, in the beginning, from an active influence of the caseworker upon the client to an attitude of pronounced "passivity." For some time caseworkers barely spoke to the client, merely listened to his explanations and tried to accept his statements as well as his motivations which they revealed. The silence of the caseworker forced the client to speak but often did not give him sufficient help in making his own decisions.[12] The progress in casework technique was that the caseworker saw that effective help to the client is achieved only by the full understanding of his ideas and feelings, which are made the core

[12] G. Hamilton, *op. cit.*, pp. 68-69.

of the diagnosis and therapy. The client is enabled to work out his emotional and external problems in a way he chooses himself. He has the "right of self-determination" in how much he likes to accept the advice of the caseworker and to use the aid of the social agency or of other community resources.[13]

Since the late 1930's casework has attempted to avoid the extremes of domination and of passivity in relation to the client, and to achieve an equilibrium between these opposite approaches. Caseworkers have learned that social, economic, psychological, and cultural factors influence each individual, and that the concern of casework is not only the client as an individual, but in his relation to his family and community. As the capacity for self-help varies among human beings, the caseworker has to assume the responsibility for helping the client to find satisfactory solutions for his individual problems. The caseworker refrains from moral judgments of the client's behavior, but this does not imply that she approves of attitudes which are harmful to the client himself or to others and which lead to asocial or criminal action. Certain limitations are given by social and cultural standards, sometimes unwritten laws, which may not be violated in our society or in the setting of a religious welfare agency or a cultural society. The reactions of the community toward ethnic and religious minority groups, toward Negroes, Mexicans, Orientals, Indians, or toward recent immigrants require understanding and special consideration by the caseworker.

In social casework we deal with human feelings and human behavior. For this reason, professional training of social workers includes the study of motivations, the dynamics of human behavior, and the application of psychology in working with people. There are two basic orientations in social casework today which use such a dynamic psychological approach: the "diagnostic" or "dynamic school" and the "functional school." Both schools apply psychological knowledge in order to understand the client, relate their work to the individual needs of the client, and use the dynamics of relationship in order to help the client in his development. They differ from each other fundamentally, however, in the psychological

[13] Bertha C. Reynolds, "Between Client and Community," *Smith College Studies in Social Work*, 1934, Vol. V, pp. 98-99; Grace Marcus, *Some Aspects of Relief in Family Case Work* (New York: Columbia University Press, 1947), p. 70; H. Witmer, *op. cit.*, pp. 170-179; and Anita J. Faatz, *The Nature of Choice in Casework Process* (Chapel Hill: University of North Carolina Press, 1953).

scheme which they use. In the following paragraphs the psychological scheme of each of these two approaches is sketched briefly. The student who wishes to understand more fully and more clearly the complicated differences between these two approaches should consult the references in the footnote.[14]

The *diagnostic casework theory* derives its philosophy and methods from the theory of personality which was created by Sigmund Freud and his followers and applies the principles of "dynamic psychiatry" in the social casework approach. Diagnostic casework accepts personality organization as a composite of differentiated and interacting elements which react on each other but which also are influenced by the people in one's environment and by the social and economic conditions in which one lives. Conscious as well as unconscious influences are regarded as determining our human values, behavior, and self-control. Social workers need to comprehend the effects of emotional experiences on human behavior, especially the emotions in early childhood, the feelings of anxiety, frustration, guilt, and tensions caused by the conflict between the "id" (the primitive drives for gratification of all needs) and the "ego" (the socialized force of the individual that becomes aware of its part in human society and of the values of religion, ethics, and civilization).

The relationship to parents, siblings, and persons in the environment play an important role in the life experiences of the individual. In Freudian psychology the ego holds the key position in the psychic structure. It performs the most important functions of maintaining a balance between the inner drives and the superego. The superego is the ideal that a person forms of a human being that is usually absorbed from the child's experience with his parents, particularly from the father. It represents the highest mental evolution. It consists of a synthesis of the rules of desirable conduct, of prohibitions and inhibitions impressed upon the child by his parents and his environment. The development of the superego creates the human conscience. The ego reconciles the psychic, emotional needs of the individual with the demands of reality and society. The ego is influenced by inner emotions and external factors, and it functions

[14] Cora Kasius (editor), *A Comparison of Diagnostic and Functional Casework Concepts* (New York: Family Service Association of America, 1950), pp. 7-13; G. Hamilton, *op. cit.*, pp. 258-262; and Grace Marcus, "Family Casework in 1948," *Journal of Social Casework* (now called *Social Casework*) Vol. 29, No. 7, July, 1948, pp. 261-270.

in self-preservation, perception, reality testing, organization, planning, and judgment. An understanding of the human personality structure, of intrapsychic conflicts and their influence upon behavior, is required in order to achieve change and improvement in attitude. Deviations from normal psychic functions may be recognized, classified, and changed by therapy. The type and intensity of therapeutic action necessary depends upon the nature and the extent of the psychosocial disturbance of the individual client. Therapy attempts to remove the disturbance caused by the interrelationship between the individual's emotional needs and the facts of his physical and social environment, and helps the client to change and to increase his ego capacity. Diagnostic casework encourages the client to discuss his difficulties and develops a planned treatment directed to the goal of helping the client to resolve his inner conflicts, to mobilize his ego strength, and to lessen environmental pressures by social planning. The diagnostic caseworker assumes the responsibility for evaluating the client's problems and for establishing either self-developing or supportive measures which help him to adjust according to his individual needs. Some proponents of the diagnostic approach are Gordon Hamilton, Charlotte Towle, Dorothy Hutchinson, Annette Garrett, Harriett Bartlett, Florence Sytz, Fern Lowry, Irene Josselyn, Grace Marcus, Eleanor Cockerill, Eileen Blackey, Florence Hollis, Leah Feder, Helen Pearlman, Henrietta Gordon, Sybil Foster, Helen Ross, Hyman Lippman, Ruth Gartland, Adelaide Johnson, Frances Upham, and Robert Gomberg.

Functional casework is taught primarily at the School of Social Work of the University of Pennsylvania in Philadelphia and is based upon the theory of "will therapy," developed by Otto Rank. This theory centers around the assumption of an organizing force, the "will," in the human personality, and unknown to Freudian concepts. It concludes that the interaction of inner instinctual drives of the individual and environmental influences is directed by the individual's autonomous yearning for his "self." This self is the result of transcendental forces composed of inner and environmental experiences by means of the will. Personality growth is achieved by relationships with others, primarily between mother and child, through "projection" of one's needs upon the other person. Because such projection cannot lead to complete union in reality, limitations are either accepted or frustration results because of refusal to recognize reality. The client is considered able to overcome his disturbances and anxieties by his will to solve a psychic problem. The functional caseworker attempts to help the client in response to his feelings in order to release his innate capacity. Because psychic disturbances are seen to be caused by a destructive use of the relationships of the client, functional casework seeks to replace it by new relationships conducive to constructive use of his "self" and of other people. In this process the client directs himself toward his change of attitude whereas the functional caseworker only helps him to release his energies toward self-responsibility and self-acceptance. Functional casework calls its function the "helping process" and does not use the diagnostic term "treatment." It is convinced that the client's use of his "self" toward his own goals and in accordance with his free choice are his right, but also the client's own responsibility. The functional approach does not refer to general norms as does the diagnostic school. The "helping process," according to the functional approach is limited by the agency setting. The needs of the client can be met only within the framework of agency function, which is considered the primary keynote. The "client must find his own satisfying solution and ultimate adjustment" among the services which the social agency offers.[15]

The diagnostic casework approach attempts to help the client adjust to normal behavior. It measures success in terms of how far the client approaches normal behavior. This approach aims at more effective treatment through the use of increasing scientific knowledge of the forces affecting human behavior and social adjustment; it seeks objective criteria for measuring and predicting casework results.

The functional theory operates on the assumption that the client himself must determine his goals and choices within the framework of agency services. Its measure of progress is how far the client achieves this self direction through the helping process. Some representatives of the "functional school" are Virginia Robinson, Kenneth Pray, Jessie Taft, Helen Wessel, and other members of the Pennsylvania School of Social Work.

The two schools of social casework are so different in their theo-

15 See Kenneth Pray, "A Restatement of Generic Principles of Social Casework Practice," *Journal of Social Casework* (now *Social Casework*), Vol. 28, October, 1947, p. 288.

retical philosophy that some of the proponents of each sincerely believe that only its own concepts make a full understanding of the client's personality, motivations, behavior, and need for change possible.

Social workers have been concerned whether social casework might use Carl R. Rogers' *client-centered therapy* as the psychological basis for a particular functional approach. Professor Rogers characterizes his method as "self-directed therapy," which permits the client to gain full confidence in the therapist or counselor and complete awareness of his own personality, so that the client himself can overcome his anxieties and feel able to cope with his problems.[16]

In fact, some social workers use an "eclectic theory" in applying elements of various schools of psychology (Freud, Alfred Adler, Jung, Rank, and others) as the basis of their approach to the client. The discussion about the specific values of the various schools of psychology in their application for social work has not been closed. An analysis of their essential elements for the practice of social work permits hope that in the future still some synthesis between the two psychological methods may be worked out. Such a synthesis might develop new effective skills of social work in helping the client.

The modern casework agency offers special, well-defined services to the client. The caseworker explains these services clearly and discusses with the client in what way he wants to use the agency's facilities and how they may best help him in a solution of his problems. No aid is imposed upon the client. He has to decide whether or not he wants to accept the agency's help. The caseworker explains to the client what his own abilities of solving his problems are, and what the agency may contribute. Thus the client gains an understanding of the economic and emotional elements which cause his problems. Casework attempts to awaken the strength for self-help in the client and to restore his ability for self-support, thus maintaining his self-respect and human dignity.

Present-day social casework is facing a number of serious prob-

[16] The reader may find more information on this specific type of psychotherapy in Carl R. Rogers, *Counseling and Psychotherapy, Newer Concepts in Practice* (1942), and *Client-Centered Therapy, Its Current Practice, Implications, and Theory* (Boston: Houghton, 1951).

lems.[17] Casework skills are required in all social agencies, in work with families and children, with delinquents and adult offenders, whereas many workers, particularly in public welfare agencies and probation and parole services, have no adequate professional training and competence for it. Some social agencies that want to employ caseworkers with full graduate training and supervised field work experience find it difficult to hire them, because their working conditions, salaries, supervision, or local situation are not attractive. The education of sufficient graduate social work students is impeded by the lack of good field work agencies with qualified supervisors and technical facilities.[18]

Another problem of casework is the lack of highly skilled and experienced caseworkers in social agencies where there is a heavy turnover and loss of trained workers to marriage and family life or to agencies which prove to be more attractive.

The question of research as to the validity of present casework methods has only recently been raised. There is need for research studies which attempt to evaluate the successes and failures of casework to determine the situations in which casework is helpful and where it does not operate with effect. Many caseworkers are inclined to look at each client as a new, unique phenomenon, but fail to recognize the types of human needs and reactions from which a general professional experience can be drawn. Examples of research studies in evaluation of casework efficiency are presented in Florence Hollis, *Women in Marital Conflict, A Casework Study* (New York: Family Service Association of America, 1949), and J. McV. Hunt, *et al., Testing Results in Social Casework; A Field-Test of the Movement Scale* (New York: Family Service Association of America, 1950).[19]

[17] Helen Harris Perlman, "Generic Aspects of Specific Casework Settings," *Social Service Review,* Vol. 23, No. 3, September, 1949, pp. 293-301; Fritz Redl, *Controls from Within* (Glencoe, Illinois: Free Press, 1952); Florence Hollis, "Social Casework," *Social Work Year Book, 1954,* pp. 474-480; and Herbert H. Aptekar, "Evolving Concepts in Casework and Counseling," *Social Service Review,* Vol. 28, No. 1, March, 1954, pp. 74-82.

[18] See Ernest V. Hollis and Alice L. Taylor, *Social Work Education in the United States* (New York: Columbia University Press, 1951), pp. 105-108, 241-247; and Florence Sytz, "Social Casework," *Social Work Year Book, 1951,* pp. 464-466.

[19] See Section V, "Social Work Research," of this chapter; also, Jane Hanford, "Maximum Use of Casework Service," *Selected Papers in Casework, 1951,* pp. 8-10. Case illustrations of social casework practice are discussed in Chapters 8, 10, 12, and 13.

Technical methods of casework recording need simplification, clerical operations need streamlining, and the practice of conferences and consultations needs concentration and more concise action.

Casework services still need to be interpreted to the public, in fact more than health or recreation services, in order to gain fuller understanding of their value in the community and increased moral and material support.

The following are certain trends in present casework practice: (1) Caseworkers gain a sharpened concept of the function of social diagnosis and treatment in relation to the facilities of the social agency; (2) caseworkers develop increasing skill in relating their understanding of the client's tensions, fears, and frustration to his social environment and economic conditions; (3) social agencies, particularly private agencies, show a growing awareness of the need for trained, skilled caseworkers in an adequate relation to the number of clients who need their services, and demonstrate an understanding for the importance of individual and family counseling to help early with problems of adjustment; (4) in this period of many social changes, casework is willing to apply its skills to new problems and to work in a team relationship with other professional groups whenever this is essential to help the clients.

II. SOCIAL GROUP WORK

Social group work as a method of social work is centered around a "group," not on the individual alone. It emphasizes the education, development, and cultural growth of the members of the group, frequently carried on in voluntary activities during leisure time, with the guidance of a group worker. Although work with groups has been a part of agencies identified with the social welfare movement for many years, the first recognition of such work as a social work process occurred in the second decade of this century.[20] The social group work process emphasizes the possibilities for the development and social adjustment of the individual through voluntary group action and the use of an association with others in a group as a means of furthering socially desirable objectives. This process is determined by the objectives of the agency, the dynamic forces and adjustive

[20] The history of social group work is discussed in Chapter 14. An enlightening analysis of social group work is presented in Gertrude Wilson and Gladys Ryland, *Social Group Work Practice; The Creative Use of the Social Process* (Boston: Houghton, 1949).

efforts within the group itself, the group worker's skill of observation and interpretation of adjustive and formative efforts within the group, and in the selection and application of an effective group work technique toward constructive results.[21]

This process was first used in such recreational activities as group discussions, physical education, sports, games, and festivals, often in connection with religious services. It spread under the influence of the settlement houses to the field of adult education in classes in language, art, history, labor laws, economic and social conditions, and such practical topics as crafts, home-making, cooking, sewing. On the other hand, it was used in work with young children in day nurseries, kindergartens, and supervised play indoors and on playgrounds.

The orientation in some of the early settlement houses and in other group work agencies founded by various organizations was first of religious and missionary nature, with the purpose of encouraging church participation and Sunday schools and protecting their members from the moral dangers of city life. But the young people who joined the groups and the classes of the settlement houses were often more attracted by the type of activities from which they hoped either material advantage, education, or pleasure. Similar motives frequently induced children and adolescents in poor quarters to join other group work agencies. When, in the beginning of the twentieth century, Boy Scouts and other groups for boys and girls were founded which no longer centered in underprivileged neighborhoods but appealed to middle and upper class children as well, the nature of some new group work organizations and their methods changed. A different use of the group work process was made when mental hospitals and child guidance clinics began to introduce recreational programs as a method of therapy for mentally ill, mentally defective, and nervous patients.[22] In other group activities, the emphasis changed from the content of these activities, whether in physical education, sports, crafts or learning and discussions, to the effect they had on the individual members for their personal growth and ability to participate in the collective life of the group. The learning to share experiences with others, to give

21 William I. Newstetter, "What Is Social Group Work " *National Conference of Social Work, 1935*, pp. 291-300.

22 Neva L. Boyd, "Group Work Experiments in State Institutions," *National Conference of Social Work, 1935*, pp. 339-346.

and take, to clarify differences of opinion and judgment without hostility and frustration, to yield in good spirit to decisions of the majority is even more important for the development of personality than the learning of special skills. The process changed from routine direction of activities to conscientious consideration of the desires and needs of the individuals in the group and of those factors which would make the group as a whole the educational and cultural experience the members hoped for, gaining a feeling of belonging together and of mutual solidarity.

Group work is a process through which group life is affected by a group worker who consciously directs the interacting process in which the members of the group develop into emotionally balanced, intellectually free, responsible, and physically fit persons and in which the group attempts to achieve goals desirable in an economic, social, and political democracy.[23] The group work process includes scientific, critical elements in measuring the interaction among group members, the results of guidance and mutual stimulation within the group, and the forces which determine the action of gangs and related groups which earlier had strongly opposed direction toward socially accepted goals and outside leadership.

Group work process attempts to achieve the following objectives: to provide experiences which integrate the essential needs of the individuals who form the group; to encourage wholesome mental and social attitudes on the part of each participant toward his place in the group and in society; to achieve skill and a kind of mastery in some leisure time pursuit; and to provide an opportunity for experience in acceptable, social behavior, and in collective, positive activities rather than useless or destructive ones.

We mentioned that the group worker as professional leader needs the understanding of attitudes and feelings of other people; he must know how to work with others, but also how groups are organized and function, how the group members are most effectively stimulated, how differences among them are straightened out, and how the creative potentialities of the individuals and of the group are released. The worker must know himself so that he can fully use his professional skills in the interest of the group, of its members, and in carrying out the functions which the program of the agency entails which the group worker represents. The group worker also

[23] This definition is derived from G. Wilson and G. Ryland, *op. cit.*, p. 61.

needs a thorough familiarity with the community and its resources, organizations, churches, social agencies, playgrounds, and recreation facilities so that he may enable the group to use, according to their needs, these resources as a group or as individuals.

The main skill in the social group work process is to stimulate the initiative, the group consciousness, and the self-direction in the group. The group worker in this process does not assume the initiative himself but makes the group members the active, creative forces. The program in group work, whether it includes sports, dramatics, games, music, craft work, hobbies, discussions, or dancing and social getting together, is the framework within which the group experience occurs. The interaction between the group members, the learning to be a member of a society, the understanding of different opinions and values, the acceptance of majority decisions as a good sport are important factors with creative values for personality growth especially in the development of young persons. The social group worker needs a knowledge of individual and group behavior and of social conditions as well as the ability to work efficiently with groups of people. His skill of leadership requires that he be able to awake in the members of the group their creative abilities and to develop constructive, socially acceptable activities in the group. The group worker knows how groups are organized, how the interest of the members may be stimulated and new members won, how conflicts may be settled and programs worked out. But the task of the group worker is to let the group members find these activities as their own desire and to lead them to establish their own program and activities. His function is to help each individual in the group gain satisfaction and enjoyment through the group relations and activities, and to assist the group as a social unit to find its objective and vitality.[24] He has to observe the group in its operation and to watch that it meet the needs of all its individual members. Of vital importance in the group work process is the feeling of unity and belonging which the individuals in the group develop among themselves with the aid of the group worker. Each member of the group experiences the awareness that he shares interests and work with others toward a common objective and that he has to adjust to the other members and

[24] Grace L. Coyle, "Social Group Work," *Social Work Year Book, 1951,* pp. 466-472; *Social Work Year Book, 1954,* pp. 480-486; Audrey Trecker and Harleigh B. Trecker, *How to Work With Groups* (New York: The Woman's Press, 1952).

to participate in group activities, even while maintaining his personality and his own opinion and values. The group work process provides for the individuals who compose the group the essential advantage of belonging to a group which accepts its members and gives them the opportunity to express their feelings and thoughts. It provides for the members the satisfaction of being with other sympathetic fellowmen, of developing social attitudes and skills, of having creative outlets for their cultural, artistic, or social abilities, which frequently would never have been noticed without such group stimulation.

The group worker has to know the skills and weaknesses of himself as a professional person, the behavior of human beings, and the functions and dynamics of groups, as well as the special conditions and forces of the community in which he is active. He has to be thoroughly familiar with the local community, its economic and political structure, its social agencies, their cooperation and facilities, the recreational and cultural resources of the community, its schools and churches, and its essential social problems.

The development of recreational and leisure time organizations— their organization and structure—and the current problems in social group work practice and its present trends are presented in Chapter 15.

The following sample case of group work in practice illustrates this social work process.

KIDS IN TROUBLE[25]

Roberto

Roberto, a boy of slight build and dark complexion, looks older than his 15 years. He has gone in gangs with older boys for several years, and consequently, when he was 12, he appeared before Juvenile Court, charged with stealing. Since, he has had a probation officer and has been taken in by the police twice, but not on charges serious enough to bring him before the court again. The probation officer reports that Roberto's home is small and physically inadequate, but that the family relations are pleasant enough.

When Roberto was in the seventh grade, his gang started going to a community center in the neighborhood. They had a weekly recreation program of sports, swimming, and dancing, but even here most of the

[25] The author is indebted to Miss Gertrude Wilson, Professor of Social Welfare, University of California, Berkeley, for this case illustration.

boys were older than Roberto. Much destruction of the building took place, and the solution for the Center, a year later, was to divide the group and form a smaller club for boys and girls who were Roberto's age, many of whom also had juvenile court records.

From the beginning, Roberto was loyal in attendance, but very moody, showing enormous distrust of the club leader, who was a woman. For several months he would not talk with the leader, but took great delight in mocking the way she spoke. He seemed to hope that she would be angry about this, but when she only laughed with him, he dropped this mockery. During this sullen, quiet period with Roberto, the leader always invited him to join in activities, but never insisted that he do so.

His favorite activity was to listen to bop records, and occasionally he danced, usually alone. While the other club members planned parties, played ping-pong and basketball, had crafts and dramatic groups, he sat, saying nothing, by the record player. Only once, however, did he outwardly cause trouble, this being on a day when his phonograph records were not available. He got a gang of boys together and they wandered around restlessly, eventually throwing a table down the stairs. When the club leader pointed out that club groups must pay for damage to the building, Roberto admitted that he was responsible and would pay himself, rather than have the whole group pay.

In planning their club program, the group asked to have dancing lessons. With this activity, the club leader saw a change in Roberto's attitude. He received a great deal of recognition from the club leader, the members and the dancing teacher, because he was the best dancer, and learned new steps very quickly. When complimented about this, he dropped his tough outward appearance and was more like a shy, modest kid.

Recently, Roberto was elected an officer of the club, and he takes his responsibility very seriously. He personally tried to see that all the members' behavior was good at the last dance, and everyone reported that it was the best party the club had had.

III. THE PROCESS OF COMMUNITY ORGANIZATION

The concept of "community organization for social welfare," "social welfare planning," or "social welfare organization" in its present meaning has its background in the Charity Organization Societies of the nineteenth century. Their interest in rehabilitating the individuals and families whom they were helping led to the development of "casework." Their concern about the lack of cooperation between the numerous private relief societies and welfare agencies, their attempts to avoid indiscriminate almsgiving, duplication of effort, waste of funds, encouragement of fraud, and pauperization were the source of community organization as a process of social work. It is distinct from other types of community activities, such as water works and public utilities, transportation, housing, parks and playgrounds, sanitation, schools, and churches, because it is directly related to social welfare. But community organization for social welfare should be well aware of other essential needs of organizing the community and should attempt to achieve close cooperation with other organizations which are active in related fields, such as the city council, board of supervisors, labor unions, educational boards, political parties, civic citizens groups, chambers of commerce, city planning commissions, housing authorities, public utilities, and transportation commissions.

Community organization for social welfare may be defined as the social work process of establishing a progressively more effective adjustment between the social welfare needs and the community welfare resources within a geographic area. This area in general is a community, city, or county, but recently community organization is also applied to the territory of entire states, nations, and even in the international field. The adjustment between social welfare needs and community resources is achieved through the cooperation of social agencies, other groups, and individuals in the community with the help of social workers; this joint endeavor provides the necessary and most efficient social and health services.

As a "process" community organization for social welfare encompasses, in the main, the following phases: (1) knowledge of the community welfare structure, its social agencies and their functions; (2) coordination of the existing facilities of public and private social agencies in order to give the best possible service to the population; (3) improvement of standards of private and public agencies; (4) the use of social research and surveys to determine the prevailing unmet human needs; (5) analysis of these needs compared with the available resources; (6) synthesis of data, testing of facts, and determination of priorities according to urgency and importance of needs; (7) the elimination or adjustment of outlived services and the development of new services as needed; (8) interpretation of the need for the expansion of existing, or the creation of new, services to all groups that may be willing to help and to the public; (9) the mobilization of financial and moral support for social welfare activities; and (10) the creation of community understanding of social welfare needs by education, information, and the securing of the active participation of the public.

The main social agencies in the field of community organization are councils of social agencies or community welfare councils, community chests, and neighborhood and coordinating councils.[26] However, other public and private agencies, such as city welfare departments, family and child welfare societies, health organizations, and state-wide or national social welfare and health agencies, are also actively engaged in community organization work. In this process the knowledge of research, the skill of establishing constructive public relations, and the ability to convince people of human needs and to gain their support for supplying the means to meet such needs are essential. In smaller agencies the work of community organization often is assumed by the executive or a case supervisor, sometimes by members of the board of directors. In large agencies, a special staff for the task of community organization is employed, and persons with professional training in social work and special skill and experience in community organization are recently more frequently engaged in this process.

Their skill is different from that of social caseworkers and group workers because the "client" in the community organization process is the entire community or the county, not an individual person or a specific social group. The community organizer is therefore concerned with the various forces in the community. He has to understand their ideas, motives, and desires and has to accept their real wishes, in order to help the community forces to clarify their insight into social problems and to stimulate their willingness to find a constructive solution which will meet important human needs of the entire community. In order to achieve this goal, the participation of all elements, groups, and interests in the process of community organization should be achieved as an essential factor. Since human needs are constantly changing in our society, community organization is not a static process, but rather a dynamic one which partici-

26 The structure and function of these agencies are discussed in Chapter 21; for the discussion of the process of community organization see Wayne McMillen, *Community Organization for Social Welfare* (Chicago: University of Chicago Press, 1946), pp. 19-27. Chapter 21 includes an illustration of community organization at work, its problems and present trends, and a case study on community organization is presented in the Appendix.

pates in social changes and develops new approaches in order to find solutions for social problems. To assure a continuing community progress, knowledge of "generic social work"—its methods, skills, and social values—is an important requirement for effective work in community organization,[27] as well as the understanding of individuals and groups in their behavior and its effect upon others.

IV. SOCIAL ACTION

Within the category of community organization the process of *social action* or *social reform* plays an essential role. Social action may be defined as an organized group effort with the aim of securing social progress and of solving mass social problems by influencing social legislation or the administration of social services.

There are various opinions on whether social action should be classified as a method of community organization or as a separate process in social work,[28] but for the purpose of our study this theoretical difference is of no importance. Essential elements in social action are that (1) group action is necessary though the initiative may be taken by one or a few individuals; (2) the movement must be concerted; (3) the movement is attempting to achieve social changes in the interest of the people; and (4) the action is taken in accordance with law, not by violence.

Social action involves public pressure by influencing public opinion through information or educational publicity in newspapers, pamphlets, lectures, radio broadcasts, television, or public meetings. The promotion of social legislation by pressure upon the legislators is one, but not the only, form of social action, and it may aim at social advance in the practice or interpretation of social work and at the improvement of conditions of child and women labor, housing, slum clearance, or other socially desirable objects. The activities of most social settlements and other social agencies during the period from

[27] C. F. McNeil, "Community Organization for Social Welfare," *Social Work Year Book, 1951*, pp. 122-128; Mildred C. Barry, "Community Organization Process," *Social Work Journal*, Vol. XXXI, No. 4, October, 1950, pp. 157-163.

[28] Mary E. Richmond, *What is Social Case Work?* (New York: Russell Sage Foundation, 1922); Harry L. Lurie, "Social Action; A Motive Force in Democracy," *National Conference of Social Work, Proceedings 1941*, pp. 631-641; Kenneth L. M. Pray, "Social Work and Social Action," *ibid., 1945*, pp. 348-359; John G. Hill, "Social Action," *Social Work Yearbook, 1951*, pp. 455-456; and Arthur E. Fink, *The Field of Social Work* (New York: Holt, 1949), p. 515.

1890 to 1915 included social action on a large scale.[29] Social action or social reform often seem indispensable if general economic and health conditions cause illness, suffering, and destitution which cannot be remedied by social agencies on an individual basis.

In the public, as well as among social workers, there is often fear of social action because they are afraid that "radicals" or "communists" may pull the wires. In fact, however, such social reform movements frequently initiate from rather conservative groups in neighborhood councils, churches, or group work agencies which are concerned about the well-being of the citizens, endangered by juvenile delinquency, fire hazards, or health damage which may come from lack of medical facilities, or lack of parks and playgrounds. Social action by its emphasis on social change attempts to prevent social maladjustment, illness, and social disorganization, but it is directed by the same concern for the well-being, the self-respect, and the dignity of the individual as are casework and group work.[30]

In its operation social action applies social research in order to find and present reliable and convincing facts and prepares a plan for social legislation. It enlists as much public support as possible by meetings, the press, radio, television, pamphlets, and similar means of publicity and presents its suggestions to those bodies, authorities, or individuals who are responsible for the legislative or administrative measures which require change. The follow-up of legislation or administrative rules is an important task of social action in order to assure that the aims of the movement are actually achieved. Social workers have for a long time considered the participation in social action as one of their professional duties with regard to their intimate knowledge of those social conditions which require reform or change. Many social workers have been pioneers in social action in the period of social reform and of the Depression (1930 to 1935). Social workers as a profession have been frequently accused, however, of not exercising the influence in social policy and social reform which could be expected from them on the basis of their experiences, because they are exclusively interested in individualized treatment. On the other hand, social workers who are actively engaged in social

29 See Chapter 4.
30 J. Hill, *op. cit.*, pp. 456 and 458; and Helen R. Wright, "Social Work Education—Some Questions," *Social Service Review*, Vol. XXIII, No. 1, March, 1950, pp. 74-83.

action have been criticized for confusion of their civic and professional obligations.

These criticisms suggest that a careful rethinking of the social worker's role in social action based upon the fundamental professional philosophy of social work is desirable.

V. SOCIAL WORK RESEARCH

Research in social work is the critical inquiry and the scientific testing of the validity of social work organization, function, and methods in order to verify, generalize, and extend social work knowledge and skill.

With the growth of social welfare services, their organization by government and private societies, with increasing numbers of persons benefiting from these services and of workers employed in these agencies, questions are raised about the efficiency and cost of the methods of social welfare. Professional social workers showed serious interest in the develoment of social work research, but there is still among rank-and-file workers some hesitation because of the time consumed for research investigation and because of doubts of whether it would produce tangible results.

At the 1948 National Conference of Social Work, Professor Philip Klein suggested five types of social research studies: (1) to establish, identify, and measure the need for social service; (2) to measure the services offered; (3) to test, gauge, and evaluate results of social work operation; (4) to test the efficacy of specific social work techniques; and (5) to develop a methodology of social work research.[31]

Professional organizations of social work, the schools of social work, and public and private welfare organizations have recently shown the desire to provide reliable data in order to carry on the necessary research studies and to overcome the reluctance of agencies and individuals to support research. There is now an increasing number of research workers in federal agencies, state departments of social welfare, in many national and regional private organizations, and in advanced public and voluntary agencies.

(1) *Social surveys* are conducted in order to explore the social needs of the population, how adequately these needs are met, and

[31] Philip Klein and Ida E. Meriam, *The Contribution of Research to Social Work* (New York: American Association of Social Workers, 1948).

what changes are necessary to achieve the goal of effective health and welfare protection. The first major social research project of comprehensive nature in the United States was the Pittsburgh Survey of 1907, carried on by Professor Philip Klein and his associates.[32] Other investigations of health, housing, nutritional, and other social problems of various selected groups of the people, such as children and women in agriculture, in certain industries, and migratory workers, were conducted by such federal and private organizations as the Social Security Administration, the Children's Bureau and the U.S. Department of Labor and by councils of social agencies and community chests.[33]

(2) Social research (as regards the *adequacy of social services*) reflects the major social problems, as well as the measures taken to meet those needs, of the changing historical scene: health and child welfare needs; mass unemployment; economic distress; special needs of the aged, the blind, the crippled, and other handicapped groups; the quest for social and economic security and recreation and leisure time activities. Topics of research have been the history and structure of social welfare systems, the changing concepts of principles applied in social work, statistical studies describing operations and cost of social welfare, extension and distribution of social services, the methods of social work education, and the professional characteristics of social work.

The following publications are examples of such research studies and indicate the great variety of their objectives:

1. Hilda C. M. Arndt, "An Appraisal of What the Critics Are Saying About Public Assistance," *Social Service Review*, Vol. XXVII, No. 4, December, 1952, pp. 464-475.
2. Jean M. Arsenian, "Psychiatric Social Work and Research," *Social Service Review*, Vol. XXVI, No. 1, March, 1952, pp. 15-29.
3. Citizens' Committee on Children of New York City, *Children Absent from School* (1949).
4. Community Chests and Councils of America, *Community Health and Welfare, 42 Urban Areas, 1946*, (New York, 1948).
5. Community Chest of Metropolitan Detroit, *Community Survey, 1948.*
6. Leonard S. Cottrell, Jr., "New Directions for Research on the Ameri-

[32] Philip Klein, *et al.*, *A Social Study of Pittsburgh: Community Problems and Social Services of Allegheny County* (New York: Columbia University Press, 1938).
[33] See Chapter 21.

can Family," *Social Casework*, Vol. XXXIV, No. 2, February, 1953, pp. 54-60.

7. Grace L. Coyle, "New Insights Available to the Social Worker from the Social Science," *Social Service Review*, Vol. XXVI, No. 3, September, 1952, pp. 289-304.

8. Sheldon and Eleanor Glueck, *Unraveling Juvenile Delinquency* (New York: Commonwealth Fund, 1952).

9. Greater Boston Community Council, *Greater Boston Community Survey* (1949).

10. A. A. Heckman and Allan Stone, "Forging New Tools," *Survey Midmonthly*, Vol. 83, No. 10, October, 1947, pp. 267-270.

11. Ernest V. Hollis and Alice L. Taylor, *Social Work Education in the United States* (New York: Columbia University Press, 1951).

12. Lillian Johnson and Joseph H. Reid, *An Evaluation of Ten Years Work with Emotionally Disturbed Children* (Seattle: Ryther Child Center, 1947).

13. Katherine A. Kendall, "A Conceptual Framework for the Social Work Curriculum of Tomorrow," *Social Service Review*, Vol. XXVII, No. 1, March, 1953, pp. 15-26.

14. L. J. Lehrman, H. Sirluck, B. J. Black, *et al.*, *Success or Failure of Treatment in Child Guidance Clinics of the Jewish Board of Guardians* (New York, 1949).

15. Edwin M. Lembert and Judy Rosberg Tarnopol, *The Administration of Justice to Minority Groups in Los Angeles County* (Berkeley: University of California Press, 1948).

16. Henry Maas, "Collaboration Between Social Work and the Social Sciences," *Social Work Journal*, Vol. 31, July, 1950, pp. 104-109.

17. Pauline Smith McClay, "Use of Recurring Statistical Data in Maine Public Assistance Program," *Social Service Review*, Vol. XXIII, No. 4, December, 1949, pp. 477-484.

18. Edward B. Olds and Jane E. Bierdeman, *Day Care Attitude Survey of St. Louis* (Social Planning Council of St. Louis, 1949).

19. Edwin Powers, "An Experiment in Prevention of Delinquency," *Annals of the American Academy of Political and Social Science*, Vol. 261, January, 1949, pp. 77-88.

20. Edwin Powers and Helen L. Witmer, *An Experiment in the Prevention of Delinquency: The Cambridge-Somerville Youth Study* (New York: Columbia University Press, 1951).

21. Ellery F. Reed, "How Shall a Community Measure the Adequacy of Its Welfare Program?" *Social Service Review*, Vol. XXVI, No. 1, March, 1952, pp. 53-58.

22. Albert J. Reiss, Jr., "Social Correlates of Psychological Types of Delinquency," *American Sociological Review*, Vol. 17, No. 6, December, 1952, pp. 710-718.

23. John Otto Reinemann, "Research Activities in the Probation Department," *National Probation Association Yearbook, 1946*, pp. 196-217.

24. Ann W. Shyne, *Distribution of Professional Staff Time in Six Private Family Service Association of America Member Agencies* (New York: Family Service Association of America, 1949).

25. Shirley A. Starr and Helen M. Hughes, "Report on an Educational Campaign: The Cincinnati Plan for the United Nations," *American Journal of Sociology*, Vol. 55, 1950, pp. 389-400.

26. Olive M. Stone, "What Can Social Case Work Contribute to the Social Sciences?" *American Sociological Review*, Vol. 15, February, 1950, pp. 66-73.

27. Dorothy Swaine Thomas, "Experiences in Interdisciplinary Research," *American Sociological Review*, Vol. 17, No. 6, December, 1952, pp. 663-669.

28. Charlotte Towle, "Selection and Arrangement of Case Material for Orderly Progression in Learning," *Social Service Review*, Vol. XXVII, No. 1, March, 1953, pp. 27-54.

29. Robin M. Williams, Jr., "Application of Research to Practice in Intergroup Relations," *American Sociological Review*, Vol. 18, No. 1, February, 1953, pp. 78-83.

30. Helen Leland Witmer, "Judging the Results of the Cambridge-Somerville Youth Study," *Smith College Studies in Social Work*, Vol. XX, No. 1, October, 1949, pp. 1-15.

Some of the research studies on the objectives of social welfare have covered the history, structure, and organization of welfare programs. The growing number of private and public welfare agencies created the desire to conduct statistical research in order to obtain uniform, comparable data for purposes of legislation, fund raising campaigns, budgeting, and public information.

(3) Studies that attempt to *test and to evaluate the results* of the operation of public and private social agencies often use records of these agencies or interviews in order to measure the accomplishments against social needs in the community. Community Chests and Councils are publishing annually a list of local research projects that during recent years amounted to about two hundred studies.

Another new trend in social work research is studies of international character. Stimulated by the statistical experience of the U.S. Children's Bureau and of the United Nations Relief and Rehabilitation Administration (UNRRA) during World War II, research studies abroad are undertaken by the Economic and Social Council of the United Nations, the Department of Social Affairs of the United Nations Secretariat, the International Labor Organization (ILO), and the World Health Organization.

The field of international comparative research has been stimulated by the International Conference of Social Work and by the International Congress of Mental Health, which first met in London in 1948, in Mexico City in 1951, and in Toronto in 1954. Research studies by social workers and students in foreign countries are encouraged by fellowships under the United Nations exchange program and in the United States through the Fulbright Act of 1946.

(4) *Research on social work skills* in casework, group work, and community organization is the latest development as to research objects. Statistical methods, in order to measure the efficacy of the casework process, have been first applied by the Institute of Welfare Research of the Community Service Society of New York under John McVicker Hunt and his associates. As criteria for "movement in casework," changes in efficiency of the client, in disabling habits, in attitude or understanding, and in the environment are used. There is among social workers some question whether it might be possible to find criteria that could not only be rated but also really measured. Studies in related fields, in social group work, and community organization methods are also conducted in growing numbers.

As illustrations of research studies of this type, we refer to the following publications:

1. Laura Ault, "Implications of Detroit Job Load Study for Professional Practice," *Selected Papers in Group Work and Community Organization, 1951*, pp. 68-73.

2. S. Axelrod, J. Frings, and E. Heizog, *A Study of Short Term Cases* (New York: Jewish Family Service, 1951).

3. R. G. Barker, T. Dembo, Kurt Lewin, and E. Wright, "Experimental Studies of Frustration in Young Children," *Readings in Social Psychology* (New York: Holt, 1947).

4. Kenneth D. Benne and G. E. Swanson, "Values and the Social Scientist," *Journal of Social Issues*, Vol. 6, No. 4, 1950.

5. Margaret Blenkner, "Obstacles to Evaluative Research in Casework," *Social Casework*, Vol. XXXI, Nos. 2 and 3, February and March, 1950, pp. 54-60, 97-105.

6. J. Dollard and O. H. Mowrer, "A Method of Measuring Tension in Written Documents," *Journal of Abnormal and Social Psychology*, Vol. XLII, No. 1, 1947, pp. 3-32.

7. Leon Festinger, "Current Developments in Group Dynamics," *Social Work in the Current Scene* (New York: Columbia University Press, 1950).

8. David G. French, *An Approach to Measuring Results in Social Work* (New York: Columbia University Press, 1952).

9. J. R. P. French, Jr., "Retraining an Autocratic Leader," *Journal of Abnormal and Social Psychology*, Vol. 39, No. 2, 1944.

10. ———, A. Kornhauser, and A. Marrow, "Conflict and Cooperation in Industry," *Journal of Social Issues*, Vol. II, No. 1, 1946.

11. A. A. Heckman, "Measuring the Effectiveness of Agency Services," *Journal of Social Casework*, Vol. XXIX, 1948, pp. 394-399.

12. Milton W. Horowitz, Joseph Lyons, and Howard V. Perlmutter, "Induction of Forces in Discussion Groups," *Human Relations*, 1951.

13. J. McVicker Hunt, "A Field-Test of the Movement Scale," *Social Casework*, Vol. XXXI, 1950, pp. 267-277.

14. ———, "A Social Agency as a Setting for Research," *Journal of Consulting Psychology*, Vol. XIII, No. 1, 1949, pp. 69-81.

15. ———, "Measuring Movement in Casework," *Journal of Social Casework*, Vol. XXIX, No. 8, 1948, pp. 343-351.

16. ———, "Measuring the Effects of Social Casework," *Transactions of the New York Academy of Science*, Vol. IX, 1947, pp. 78-88.

17. ——— and Leonard S. Kogan, *Measuring Results in Social Casework: A Manual on Judging Movement* (New York: Family Service Association of America, 1950).

18. ———, Margaret Blenkner, and L. S. Kogan, *Testing Results in Social Casework: A Field Test of the Movement Scale* (New York: Family Service Association of America, 1950).

19. David Jenkins, "Feedback and Group Self-Evaluation," *Journal of Social Issues*, Vol. 4, No. 2, 1948.

20. L. J. Johnson and J. H. Reid, "Hope for Three Out of Four," *Survey Midmonthly*, Vol. 83, No. 10, October, 1947, pp. 271-273.

21. Leonard S. Kogan, "The Discomfort-Relief Quotient (DRQ) in Verbatim and Dictated Social Casework Interviews," *Journal of Abnormal and Social Psychology*, Vol. XLVI, 1951, pp. 236-239.

22. ———, "Evaluative Techniques in Social Case Work," *Social Service Review*, Vol. XXVI, No. 3, September, 1952, pp. 305-309.

23. ——— and J. McV. Hunt, "Problems of Multi-Judge Reliability," *Journal of Clinical Psychology*, Vol. VI, No. 1, 1950, pp. 16-19.

24. Kurt Lewin, "Frontiers in Group Dynamics—Concept, Method, and Reality in Social Science; Social Equilibrium and Social Change," *Human Relations*, Vol. I, No. 1, 1947.

25. ———, R. Lippitt, and R. K. White, "Patterns of Aggressive Behavior in Experimentally Created 'Social Climates,'" *Journal of Social Psychology*, Vol. 10, No. 2, 1939.

26. Ronald Lippitt, "Techniques for Research in Group Living," *Journal of Social Issues*, Vol. II, No. 4, 1946.

27. ———, "The Morale of Youth Groups," *Civilian Morale* (New York: Reynal, 1942).

28. ——— and R. K. White, "An Experimental Study of Leadership and Group Life," *Readings in Social Psychology*, Rev. ed. (New York: Holt, 1952), pp. 340-355.

29. Davis McEntire, *Leisure Activities of Youth in Berkeley, California* (Berkeley: Council of Social Welfare, 1952).
30. Robert Plank, "An Analysis of a Group Therapy Experiment," *Human Organization*, Vol. 10, Nos. 3 and 4, 1951, pp. 5-21, 26-36.
31. Norman Polansky, Ronald Lippitt, and Fritz Redl, "An Investigation of Behavioral Contagion in Groups," *Human Relations*, Vol. 3, No. 4, 1950.
32. Fritz Redl, "Diagnostic Group Work," *American Journal of Orthopsychiatry*, Vol. 14, No. 1, 1944.
33. ———, "Group Resistance Techniques in Group Therapy," *Human Relations*, Vol. I, No. 3, 1947.
34. ———, "Leadership and Group Emotion," *Psychiatry*, Vol. 5, 1942, pp. 573-596.
35. Kermit T. Wiltse, *Social Casework in Public Assistance* (Sacramento: California State Department of Social Welfare, 1952).

(5) The study of *research methodology* in social work has found increasing attention in professional associations and in the literature of social welfare. Examples have been included in the two lists of publications above. At the 1949 National Conference of Social Work, the Social Work Research Group was organized in order to function as a channel of communication for its members, to publish a *Newsletter*, to collect material, and to publish abstracts of projects conducted by its members.

An example of an interesting social welfare research project conducted by Professor Ernest Greenwood, *Echo Park: A Pilot Study of a Social Area in Los Angeles*, will be found in the Appendix as an illustration of methods and procedure applied in social welfare research.

SELECTED BIBLIOGRAPHY

I. CASEWORK

American Association of Social Workers, *Social Case Work, Generic and Specific, an Outline*. New York: 1929.
Aptekar, Herbert, *Basic Concepts in Social Casework*. Chapel Hill: University of Carolina Press, 1941.
Benedek, Therese, *Insight and Personality Adjustment*. New York: The Ronald Press Company, 1946.
Breckinridge, Sophonisba P., *Family Welfare Work in a Metropolitan Community: Selected Case Records*. Chicago: University of Chicago Press, 1924.
de Schweinitz, Karl, *The Art of Helping People Out of Trouble*. Boston: Houghton, 1924.

Dixon, E. S., and Grace A. Browning, *Social Case Records: Family Welfare.* Chicago: University of Chicago Press, 1938.

French, Thomas M., and Ralph Ormsby, *Psychoanalytic Orientation in Case Work.* New York: Family Welfare Association of America, 1944.

*Garrett, Annette, *Interviewing: Its Principles and Methods.* New York: Family Welfare Association of America, 1942.

*Hamilton, Gordon, *Theory and Practice of Social Case Work.* New York: Columbia University Press, 1947.

Hester, Mary C., "Educational Process in Supervision," *Social Casework,* Vol. XXXII, No. 6, June, 1951, pp. 242-250.

*Hollis, Florence, *Social Case Work in Practice: Six Case Studies.* New York: Family Welfare Association of America, 1939.

Kardiner, Abraham, *The Individual and His Society.* New York: Columbia University Press, 1939.

*Kasius, Cora, *Principles and Techniques in Social Casework.* New York: Family Service Association of America, 1950.

*Lowry, Fern, *Readings in Social Case Work.* New York: Columbia University Press, 1939.

Mac Iver, R. M., *The Ramparts We Guard.* New York: Macmillan, 1950.

Paradise, Viola, *Toward Public Understanding of Casework; A Study of Casework Interpretation in Cleveland.* New York: Russell Sage Foundation, 1948.

Perlman, Helen H., "The Basic Structure of the Case-Work Process," *Social Service Review,* Vol. 34, No. 3, September, 1953, pp. 308-315.

Reynolds, Bertha Capen, *Learning and Teaching in the Practice of Social Work.* New York: Farrar & Rinehart, 1942.

*Richmond, Mary E., *Social Diagnosis.* New York: Russell Sage Foundation, 1917.

———, *What Is Social Case Work? An Introductory Description.* New York: Russell Sage Foundation, 1922.

*Robinson, Virginia, *A Changing Psychology in Social Work.* Chapel Hill: University of North Carolina Press, 1930.

Rogers, Carl R., *Counseling and Psychotherapy.* Boston: Houghton, 1942.

Taft, Julia, *Counseling and Protective Service as Family Casework: Functional Approach.* Philadelphia: University of Pennsylvania Press, 1946.

———, *Family Casework and Counseling.* Philadelphia: University of Pennsylvania Press, 1948.

Witmer, Helen Leland, *Social Work: An Analysis of a Social Institution.* New York: Farrar & Rinehart, 1942.

II. GROUP WORK

Bales, Robert F., *Interaction Process Analysis.* Cambridge: Addison Wesley, 1950.

Baxter, Bernice, and Rosalind Cassidy, *Group Experience: The Democratic Way*. New York: Harper, 1943.

Blumenthal, Louis H., *Administration of Group Work*. New York: Administration Press, 1948.

Cartwright, Dorwin, and Alvin Zander, *Group Dynamics: Research and Theory*. Evanston: Peterson, 1953.

*Coyle, Grace L., *Group Experience and Democratic Values*. New York: Woman's Press, 1947.

——, *Group Work With American Youth*. New York: Harper, 1948.

*Hendry, Charles E. (editor), *A Decade of Group Work*. New York: Association Press, 1948.

*Kaiser, Clara (editor), *The Objectives of Group Work*. New York: Association Press, 1936.

Klein, Alan F., *Society, Democracy and the Group*. New York: Woman's Press, 1953.

*Lieberman, Joshua (editor), *New Trends in Group Work*. New York: Association Press, 1938.

Meyer, Harold D., and Charles K. Brightbill, *Community Recreation*. Boston: Heath, 1948.

Philips, Helen U. (editor), *Achievement of Responsible Behavior Through Group Work Process*. Philadelphia: University of Pennsylvania Press, 1950.

Schulze, Susanne, *Creative Group Living in a Children's Institution*. New York: Association Press, 1951.

Simkhovitch, Mary K., *Group Life*. New York: Association Press, 1940.

Slavson, S. R., *Creative Group Education*. New York: Association Press, 1937.

—— (editor), *Practice of Group Therapy*. New York: International Universities Press, 1947.

*Sullivan, Dorothea F. (editor), *The Practice of Group Work*. New York: Association Press, 1941.

——, *Readings in Group Work*. New York: Association Press, 1952.

*Trecker, Harleigh B., *Group Process in Administration*. New York: Woman's Press, 1946.

*——, *Social Group Work: Principles and Practice*. New York: Woman's Press, 1948.

Wilson, Gertrude, *Group Work and Case Work*. New York: Family Welfare Association of America, 1941.

*—— and Gladys Ryland, *Social Group Work Practice*. Boston: Houghton, 1949.

III. COMMUNITY ORGANIZATION[34]

Cohen, Lillian, *Statistical Methods for Social Scientists*. New York: Prentice-Hall Inc., 1954.

Colcord, Joanna C., *Your Community: Its Provisions for Health, Educa-*

[34] See Chapter 21.

tion, Safety, and Welfare. New York: Russell Sage Foundation (3rd revision by Donald S. Howard), 1947.

*Hillman, Arthur, *Community Organization and Planning.* New York: Macmillan, 1949.

*Howard, Donald S. (editor), *Community Organization: Its Nature and Setting.* New York: American Association of Social Workers, 1947.

King, Clarence, *Social Agency Boards and How to Make Them Effective.* New York: Harper, 1938.

*McMillen, Wayne, *Community Organization for Social Welfare.* Chicago: University of Chicago Press, 1946.

Metcalf, Henry C., and L. Urwick, *Dynamic Administration.* New York: Harper, 1942.

North, Cecil C., *The Community and Social Welfare: A Study in Community Organization.* New York: McGraw, 1931.

Routzahn, Mary B., and Evart G. Routzahn, *Publicity for Social Work.* New York: Russell Sage Foundation, 1928.

Sanderson, Dwight E., and Robert A. Polson, *Rural Community Organization.* New York: Wiley, 1939.

Steiner, Jessie F., *Community Organization: A Study of Its Theory and Current Practice.* New York: Appleton-Century-Crofts, Inc., 1930.

Stroup, Herbert H., *Community Welfare Organization.* New York: Harper, 1952.

*Withers, Gertrude V., *Effective Rural Social Work Through Community Organization.* Chicago: American Public Welfare Association, 1942.

IV. SOCIAL ACTION

Bisno, Herbert, *The Philosophy of Social Work,* Chapter VI. Washington, D.C.: Public Affairs Press, 1952.

*Hill, John G., "Social Action," *Social Work Year Book, 1951,* pp. 455-460.

*King, Clarence, *Organizing for Community Action.* New York: Harper, 1948.

Lurie, Harry L., "Social Action; A Motive Force in Democracy," *National Conference of Social Work, Proceedings 1941,* pp. 631-641.

Odgen, Jean C., and Jess Odgen, *Small Communities in Action.* New York: Harper, 1946.

Pray, Kenneth L. M., "Social Work and Social Action," *National Conference of Social Work, Proceedings 1941,* pp. 348-359.

V. SOCIAL WELFARE RESEARCH

(See also literature quoted as illustrations in this chapter.)

Ackoff, Russell L., *The Design of Social Research.* Chicago: University of Chicago Press, 1953.

American Association of Schools of Social Work, *Research in Social Work.* New York: 1950.

Blumer, Herbert, "What Is Wrong With Social Theory?" *American Sociological Review*, Vol. 19, No. 1, February, 1954, pp. 3-10.

*Brown, Esther Lucile, *Use of Research by Professional Associations in Determining Program and Policy*. New York: Russell Sage Foundation, 1946.

Chapin, F. Stuart, *Experimental Designs in Sociological Research*. New York: Harper, 1947.

*————, *Social Science Research; Its Expanding Horizons*. Minneapolis: University of Minnesota Press, 1953.

Chein, Isadore, "On Some of the Difficulties of Doing Social Welfare Research," *Jewish Social Service Quarterly*, Vol. XXVI, No. 1, September, 1949.

Cockerill, Eleanor E., Louis F. Lehrman, Patricia Sacks, and Isabel Stamm, *A Conceptual Framework for Social Casework*. Pittsburgh: University of Pittsburgh, 1953.

Community Chests and Councils of America, *The Use of Research Techniques in Determining Need for Health and Welfare Services*. New York, 1950.

Duncan, Otis D., et al., *Social Research on Health*. New York: Social Science Research Council, 1946.

Fletcher, Ralph Carr, "Research and Statistics in Social Work," *Social Work Year Book, 1949*, pp. 435-446.

French, David G., *An Approach to Measuring Results in Social Work*. New York: Columbia University Press, 1952.

Glueck, Eleanor T., *Evaluative Research in Social Work*. New York: Columbia University Press, 1936.

Goode, William J., and Paul K. Hatt, *Methods of Social Research*. New York: McGraw, 1952.

*————, *Toward Basic Research in Social Work*. St. Louis, Missouri: Washington University, 1951.

Gordon, William E., "The Research Project; Its Educational Value and Its Contribution to Social Work Knowledge," *Social Work Journal*, Vol. XXXI, No. 3, July, 1950, pp. 110-116.

*Greenwood, Ernest, *Experimental Sociology: A Study in Method*. New York: Columbia University Press, 1944.

Herzog, Elizabeth, "An Approach to Family Agency Research," *The Social Welfare Forum, 1952*, pp. 152-160.

Jahoda, Marie, Morton Deutsch, and Stuart W. Cook, *Research Methods in Social Relations*. New York: Dryden Press, 1951.

Johnson, Arlien, "Science and Social Work," *National Conference of Social Work, Proceedings 1947*, pp. 3-18.

*Klein, Philip, and Ida E. Merriam, *The Contribution of Research to Social Work*. New York: American Association of Social Workers, 1948.

Lippitt, Ronald, "Socio-Psychological Research and Group Work," in Charles Hendry, *A Decade in Group Work*. New York: Association Press, 1948, pp. 166-177.

Lundberg, George A., *Social Research: A Study in Methods Gathering Data.* New York: Longmans, 1951.

*McMillen, Wayne, *Statistical Methods for Social Workers.* Chicago: University of Chicago Press, 1952.

Maas, Henry S., and Edith Varon, "The Case Worker in Clinical and Sociopsychological Research," *Social Service Review*, Vol. 23, No. 3, September, 1949, pp. 302-314.

Morgan, John S., "Research in Social Work: A Frame of Reference," *Social Work Journal*, Vol. XXX, No. 4, October, 1949, pp. 148-154.

Queen, Stuart A., "Research and Social Work," *Social Service Review*, Vol. XXVI, No. 1, March, 1952, pp. 1-14.

Schwartz, Edward E., "Social Work Research," *Social Work Year Book*, *1951*, pp. 500-512.

Shyne, Ann W., *Handbook on Statistical Recording and Reporting in Family Service Agencies.* New York: Family Service Association of America, 1947.

Stouffer, Samuel A., "Some Observations on Study Design," *American Journal of Sociology*, January, 1950.

*Towle, Charlotte, "Some Basic Principles of Social Research in Social Casework," *Social Service Review*, Vol. XXV, No. 1, March, 1951, pp. 66-80.

Turner, Ralph H., "Statistical Logic in Social Research," *Sociology and Social Research*, January-February, 1948, pp. 697-704.

*Witmer, Helen L., "Basic Conceptions in Social Work Research," *Mental Hygiene*, Vol. 33, January, 1949, pp. 108-114.

Young, Donald, "Limiting Factors in the Development of the Social Sciences," *Philosophical Society, Proceedings 1948*, pp. 325-335.

*Young, Pauline V., *Scientific Social Surveys and Research; An Introduction to the Background, Content, Methods, and Analysis of Social Studies*, Rev. ed. New York: Prentice-Hall, Inc., 1949.

Zander, Alvin, "Current Research in Group Work," in *Toward Professional Standards, American Association of Group Workers.* New York: Association Press, 1947.

7. Social Welfare Agencies

Organizations that provide social services may be classified into four main groups: (1) agencies designed primarily to give social services to clients, either as individuals or in groups (for example, social welfare departments, family and children's societies, adoption agencies, YWCA, YMCA, Girl Scouts, Boy Scouts); (2) organizations which offer social services as well as other services (for example, American Red Cross, settlement houses, recreations and park departments, International Institutes, Girls' Service Leagues, Salvation Army, Urban League); (3) organizations which are basically designed to offer other services, but which maintain an auxiliary department of social work (for example, hospitals, clinics, schools, juvenile courts, public housing authorities, vocational rehabilitation services, research foundations); and (4) organizations that are not rendering direct services to individuals or groups but are set up to assist other social agencies (for example, community welfare councils, community chests).[1]

The structure of welfare organizations differs in those agencies established under public auspices from those which are of voluntary or private nature. Public agencies are based upon law or statute, administered within the framework of local, state, or federal government, and financed by taxation. Private agencies are established by philanthropic, religious, fraternal, or humanitarian groups or individuals; their management is the responsibility of a board of directors, and they are supported mainly by contributions, donations, endowments, trust funds, and often by participation in the distributions of the Community Chest.

[1] See Helen L. Witmer, *Social Work* (New York: Farrar & Rinehart, 1942), pp. 184-186ff; Harry M. Cassidy, *Social Security and Reconstruction in Canada* (Boston: Humphries, 1943), pp. 13-17. The last group of organizations concerned with community organization will be discussed in Chapter 21.

I. PUBLIC SOCIAL AGENCIES

Our historical survey has shown that government has gradually assumed the basic responsibility for the maintenance of the social welfare of the people. For a long time in the United States, this responsibility had been assumed by charitable, voluntary organizations. But the Depression of the 1930's brought evidence that government could no longer avoid its fundamental obligation to protect the social welfare of the citizens. This change occurred on all three levels of government—local, state, and federal.

The strength of public welfare agencies lies in their structure: They are established by law; they must continuously provide designated services for all needy people (who are eligible according to legal conditions) and without discrimination against race, faith, and color.

Because public welfare agencies are government institutions, their programs and services need to be understood and appreciated by the public. Public welfare agencies need the approval and support of the citizens, because they depend upon legislation to appropriate the funds for their services and their administration.[2]

A. LOCAL PUBLIC WELFARE AGENCIES

The largest number of public social agencies operate on a county, city, and township basis. Their structure differs according to state and local statutes. Frequently, a county or city welfare department is directed by a board of commissioners or board of supervisors. In rural counties the elected officials sometimes administer public welfare services themselves, or they appoint a director or commissioner to be responsible for the administration. In other instances, a city or county welfare department may be managed by a board or a commission of lay citizens appointed by county or state officials; one or several members of the county board of commissioners or supervisors may be members and one of them chairman of the welfare board. This board appoints an executive and controls the operation of the public agency. Although the functions of the public welfare agencies

[2] See Wayne McMillen, *Community Organization for Social Welfare* (Chicago: University of Chicago Press, 1949), pp. 75-76.

differ widely, there is a trend to consolidate the various activities in one local welfare agency and to coordinate the different assistance and child welfare programs. Other local public agencies which deal with programs of influence to social welfare are the public health department, the board of education, the juvenile court, the park and recreation commission, the police department, the city planning commission, and the housing authority.[3] An example of the organization of a typical public welfare department is presented in Chart 1.

B. STATE DEPARTMENTS OF PUBLIC WELFARE

Among the states there are substantial differences in the organizational setup of their public welfare organization. The large majority of states has concentrated most, or all, of their public welfare programs in a single agency (Department of Public Welfare, of Social Welfare, of Social Security), but Illinois and Pennsylvania still maintain two different state administrations in public welfare.

As a rule, the State Department of Public Welfare is administered by a board whose members are appointed by the governor, and by a "Director" or "Commissioner," who also is appointed by the governor. The majority of states leaves the immediate administration of general assistance (indigent aid), of the categorical public assistance programs,[4] and of child welfare and health services to counties, cities, townships, and towns, but some states have assumed the entire responsibility for the direct administration of these programs through local state offices. All state departments of public welfare are responsible for the administration of categorical public assistance and child welfare services for which they receive federal grants-in-aid, but in several states the administration or the supervision of other state institutions, such as mental hospitals, training schools, schools for the blind and deaf, or correctional programs, probation, and parole services, also falls under their jurisdiction.[5] The question whether it is desirable to combine all public welfare services under one single department, depends upon the size and the population of

[3] In this chapter only the structure of social agencies is under consideration. The basic problems of administration are analyzed in Chapter 20, the possibilities of common planning of various agencies in Chapter 21.

[4] See Chapter 8.

[5] See Ellen Winston, "Public Welfare," *Social Work Year Book, 1954,* pp. 429–439, and R. Clyde White, *Administration of Public Welfare,* Chap. IV (New York: American Book, 1952).

CHART 1: ORGANIZATIONAL STRUCTURE: PUBLIC WELFARE DEPARTMENT (CITY AND COUNTY OF SAN FRANCISCO)

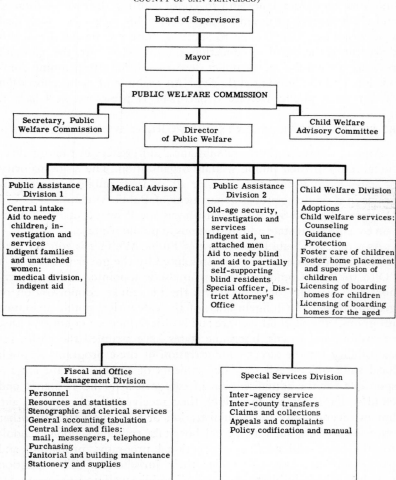

the state, and the number of its institutions. The author favors such a coordination, but some students of public administration believe that in a large state such a department may be unwieldy. Delegation of authority to qualified division heads and the setup of area offices, such as those operating in California, would secure effective administration.

C. FEDERAL PUBLIC WELFARE AGENCIES

The main federal agency in the field of public welfare is the Department of Health, Education and Welfare. It was created as the tenth major executive department on the basis of President Eisenhower's Reorganization Plan No. 1 of 1953, after several similar proposals by President Truman had been rejected by Congress. The organization of the Department of Health, Education and Welfare is illustrated by Chart 2. Its predecessor was the Social Security Board, which was established by the Social Security Act of 1935. The board was abolished in 1939 when the Federal Security Agency replaced it as an independent federal agency, with the Federal Security Administrator as head executive. At this time the Social Security Administration became one of the major branches of the Federal Security Agency; the others were Public Health Services, Office of Education, and Office of Special Services, under which the Bureau of Vocational Rehabilitation and the Food and Drug Administration were of particular importance for social welfare. The Social Security Administration was directed by the Commissioner for Social Security and had four operating bureaus: (a) the Bureau of Public Assistance, (b) the Bureau of Old-Age and Survivors' Insurance, (c) the Children's Bureau, and (d) the Bureau of Federal Credit Unions.

This organizational pattern, in its main phases, has been transferred to the new Department of Health, Education and Welfare. The Secretary of the Department has full Cabinet rank. An Under-secretary and two Assistant Secretaries of Health, Education and Welfare share with the Secretary the responsibility for the entire area of work, but another Special Assistant Secretary is in charge of health and medical affairs. As in the former Federal Security Agency, a Commissioner of Social Security, a Surgeon General, and a Commissioner of Education are the head executive officers of the three branches of the new Department. All these leading officials of the Department are appointed by the President with the confirmation of the Senate.[6]

Among the social welfare programs, only Old-Age and Survivors' Insurance is directly administered by the Department of Health,

---

[6] See *Social Security Bulletin*, Vol. 16, No. 4, April, 1953, p. 1; and U.S. Congress, Committee on Government Operations, *Creating a Department of Health, Education, and Welfare*, Report No. 166, March 17, 1953.

CHART 2: ORGANIZATIONAL STRUCTURE: U.S. DEPARTMENT OF HEALTH,
EDUCATION AND WELFARE

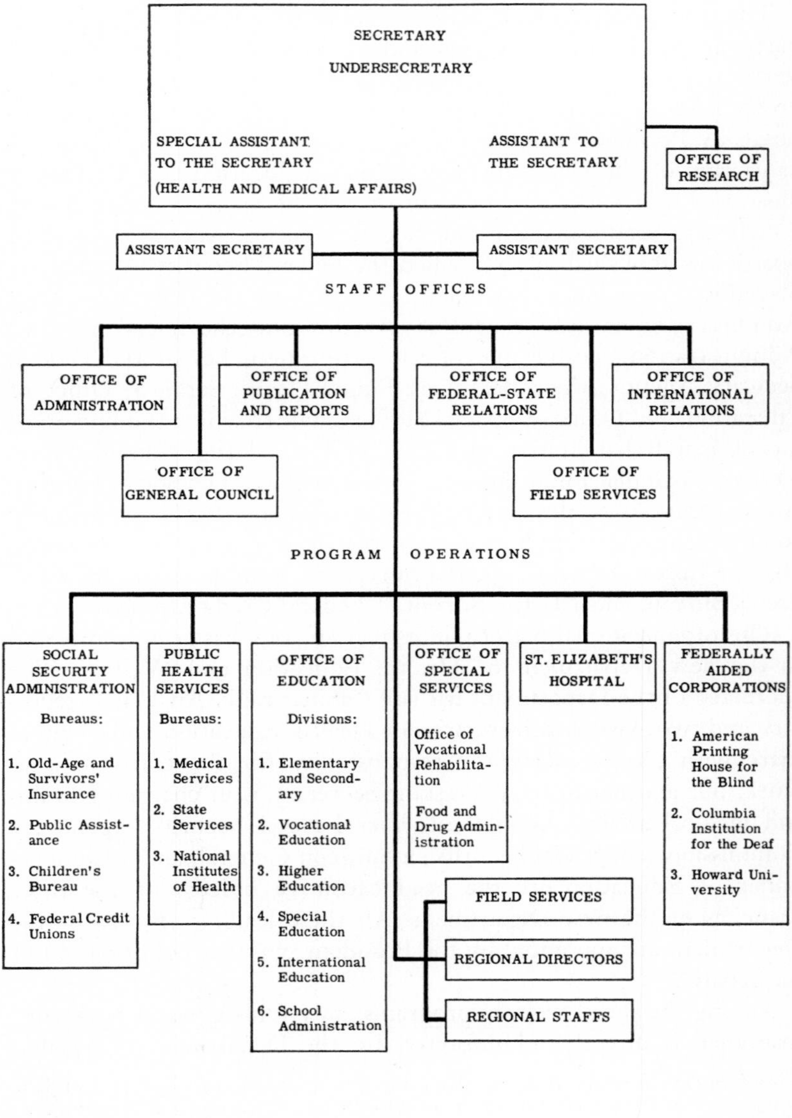

SECRETARY

UNDERSECRETARY

SPECIAL ASSISTANT
TO THE SECRETARY
(HEALTH AND MEDICAL AFFAIRS)

ASSISTANT TO
THE SECRETARY

OFFICE OF
RESEARCH

ASSISTANT SECRETARY   ASSISTANT SECRETARY

STAFF OFFICES

OFFICE OF
ADMINISTRATION

OFFICE OF
PUBLICATION
AND REPORTS

OFFICE OF
FEDERAL-STATE
RELATIONS

OFFICE OF
INTERNATIONAL
RELATIONS

OFFICE OF
GENERAL COUNCIL

OFFICE OF
FIELD SERVICES

PROGRAM OPERATIONS

SOCIAL SECURITY ADMINISTRATION	PUBLIC HEALTH SERVICES	OFFICE OF EDUCATION	OFFICE OF SPECIAL SERVICES	ST. ELIZABETH'S HOSPITAL	FEDERALLY AIDED CORPORATIONS
Bureaus:	Bureaus:	Divisions:	Office of Vocational Rehabilitation		1. American Printing House for the Blind
1. Old-Age and Survivors' Insurance	1. Medical Services	1. Elementary and Secondary	Food and Drug Administration		2. Columbia Institution for the Deaf
2. Public Assistance	2. State Services	2. Vocational Education			3. Howard University
3. Children's Bureau	3. National Institutes of Health	3. Higher Education			
4. Federal Credit Unions		4. Special Education			
		5. International Education			
		6. School Administration			

FIELD SERVICES

REGIONAL DIRECTORS

REGIONAL STAFFS

Education and Welfare. In all other instances, the federal government only approves state plans, establishes rules and standards (based upon federal legislation), supervises the operation of the programs in the States, and shares the expenses of the operation by grants-in-aid according to statutory provisions.

There are, however, important phases of social services administered or supervised by other federal agencies. The Veterans Administration, an independent organization under the President, administers veterans' services directly throughout the country (see Chapter 16). The Department of Labor is in charge of the United States Employment Service and of the Bureau of Employment Security that cooperate with the states in the administration of employment services and unemployment compensation (see Chapters 9 and 17) and in the protection of child labor (see Chapters 5 and 11).

The Bureau of Indian Affairs, United States Department of the Interior, provides educational and medical services as well as land rehabilitation aid, hospitals, schools and clinics for Indians on the reservations. Immigration and naturalization services for newcomers to this country are administered by the United States Department of Justice. The Women's Bureau of the United States Department of Labor conducts research and disseminates information on working conditions.

II. PRIVATE SOCIAL AGENCIES

Private or voluntary social agencies have been the pioneers in creating modern social services. In contrast to public social welfare departments, which serve all parts of the states, including the rural regions, private social agencies operate mainly in urban areas. Often they also serve the territory which immediately surrounds the cities, but they are rare in remote rural communities. This fact explains that the federal program of grants-in-aid to the states for the development of child health and welfare services and for hospitals and medical care gives priority to the needs of rural communities in order to compensate for the lack of private social and health facilities.[7] As we have seen, the Charity Organization Societies have helped to integrate and to improve the organization and working methods of private social agencies and the quality of services to the public, whether

[7] See Chapters 8, 10, 11, 12, and 13; also, H. Witmer, *op. cit.*, pp. 187-191.

to individuals or to groups. The efficiency and the standards of private social agencies have been greatly enhanced by the formation of national organizations of either sectarian or functional character, such as the National Lutheran Council, the National Council of the Protestant Episcopal Church, the Presbyterian Church, the National Conference of Catholic Charities, the National Catholic Welfare Conference, the National Conference of Jewish Communal Service, the Child Welfare League of America, the Family Service Association of America, the National Committee for Mental Hygiene, the National Travelers Aid Association, the National Board of the YWCA, the National Council of YMCA, and the Salvation Army. These national organizations, which are themselves members of the National Social Welfare Assembly as a coordinating body, assist their member agencies in planning, organizing, and budgeting; in the development of professional standards of work and personnel; and in research and participation in the total program of health and welfare services in their community. They share the experiences of other local and regional organizations with their member agencies through conferences, institutes, workshops, consultation and field services.[8]

The foundation of private social agencies and the continuation of their activities is based upon the recognition of the need for this service in the local community. Originally, philanthropists, a group of interested citizens, or a church society became aware of the need for some type of social service, such as a family welfare agency, a children's protective society, or an organization to aid unmarried mothers or crippled children. More recently the social and health needs of the various groups of the population are considered by the Council of Social Agencies or Community Welfare Council. There is a careful investigation into what resources exist in the community and what institutions or facilities are missing before the establishment of a new social agency is encouraged and supported. But still, individuals or groups of citizens concerned with social and health conditions in the community may take the initiative if they are able to secure the necessary moral and financial support for a new enterprise in health and welfare work, such as a mental hygiene association or a vocational guidance clinic.

[8] See Robert E. Bondy, "National Associations in Social Work," *Social Work Year Book, 1951,* pp. 336-342; and George W. Rabinoff, "National Organizations in Social Welfare," *Social Work Year Book, 1954,* pp. 360-369.

A. NONSECTARIAN PRIVATE AGENCIES

According to the variety of social and health needs, voluntary organizations have been organized to meet particular problems of family disorganization, orphans and neglected children, truancy, juvenile delinquency, recreational needs of children or adults, unmarried mothers, problems of emotional disturbances, care for aged people, tuberculosis, crippled children, blind people, heart diseases, or infantile paralysis. As a rule, the interest of one, or a few persons, is the motivating factor for the establishment of such an organization. After a group of members has convened and financial funds have been donated or collected, usually a constitution and bylaws are set up, which determine the goal and the place of operation of the agency that may be incorporated according to statutory provisions of the state where it is organized. In general, the approval of the project in an early stage is asked from the community welfare council and the Community Chest if their support is expected.

The responsibility for the management of the agency is entrusted to a board of directors. It is usually composed of persons who had taken the initiative for the foundation of the organization or who had helped in gaining the financial support for it. Typical members of the board of directors are bankers, well-to-do businessmen, physicians, lawyers, a representative of the local welfare and health department, a member of the board of education, and one or two representatives of organized labor and consumers groups. The board also should represent in a nonsectarian agency the major religious groups in the community and the larger racial minorities. In most social agencies women form a substantial proportion of the board. It is important to include some women who represent influential women's organizations, such as the League of Women Voters, the Federation of University Women, the Junior League, and business women's clubs. Similarly, the board should have prominent members of men's service clubs and fraternal societies, such as the Masons, Rotary, Shriners, Kiwanis, Elks, American Legion, and Chamber of Commerce. The representation of these different groups in the community is essential in order to demonstrate to the public and the authorities the broad interest in the goals of the agency and to testify to its integrity and responsibility in carrying out its purpose. Agencies which receive part of their support from the annual drive of the Community Chest are under some obligation to have representatives of different economic levels on their board of directors that formulates the policies of the agency and controls its work and expenditures.[9]

The board of directors appoints a number of committees which take charge of different administrative functions, because the board usually limits its own tasks to the establishment of the general policy of the organization, the appointment of the executive, and the control of the total agency operation. The *executive committee* supervises the current activities and represents the board of directors during the time when the board is not in session. A *nominating committee* prepares suggestions for the election of new board members; sometimes it also proposes suitable persons for the appointment as executive, assistant-director, legal counsel, medical consultant, or similar responsible positions in the agency in cooperation with the executive secretary or director.

The *financial or budget committee* controls the expenditures of the agency, prepares the budget for the approval of the executive committee and for the board of directors, and often develops plans for raising additional funds or enlisting bequests and donations for the agency. If the agency owns real estate property, such as a school, a hospital, or an administrative building, a *committee of buildings and maintenance* assists the executive in its management. Frequently, there are other "standing committees" on which members of the board, representatives of the professional staff, and lay persons of the community serve. They include a *committee on personnel practice*, which determines the salaries of the staff, recruitment, and promotion policy; and the regulations for staff employment, vacation, sick leave, and working conditions. By cooperation with newspapers, radio, television, and civic and religious societies in the community, a *public relations committee* informs the public about the activities of the agency. Some agencies that provide services to children, families, unmarried mothers, and handicapped or aged people have a "case committee" with which the professional staff discusses experiences in particularly significant cases in order to keep the board aware of the specific problems which the agency faces, of the methods and

[9] See Chapter 21; W. McMillen, *op. cit.*, pp. 68-75; H. Witmer, *op. cit.*, pp. 188-191; and Sidney Dillick, *Community Organization for Neighborhood Development—Past and Present* (New York: Woman's Press, 1953).

changing aspects of the professional work, and of the needs of innovations in policy or practice which seem necessary.

The task of interpreting the agency's work to the citizens is not limited to the committee on public relations; in fact, it is an essential function of all members of the board of directors, of the other committees, and of the entire staff of the agency. Because most private social agencies depend financially upon the current contributions to the Community Chest, continuous information should be given to the public about the necessity and the value of the agency's activities in order to convince the citizens that its services are needed and worthy of their contributions. Still more important is the interpretation of a proposal to create a new welfare agency or to expand the service of an existing organization to new fields of operation.

The immediate services of a social agency to individuals or to groups are under the control of the executive-director, appointed by the board of directors, and are carried out by the professional and clerical staff. According to the character and the functions of the social agency, the social work staff may need special assistance by other professional persons, such as a physician, psychiatrist, lawyer, dietitian or home economist, nurse, psychologist, an accountant, and engineer. They may be employed on either a full-time or part-time basis. In casework and recreation agencies of large size, territorial districts are set up under the direction of an assistant executive, and most of them employ one or more supervisors who have the responsibility to work with several caseworkers or group workers, helping them in carrying out their assignment. This practice of working under a supervisor rather than as an independent professional practitioner as in medicine, teaching, and law has its roots in several facts: The core of social work is the relation of the worker with human beings which is based upon subjective understanding, individual values, and moral judgments. In the distribution of limited resources of private agencies, including financial support, the maintenance of an equal, fair policy is required. The professional training in schools of social work provides the beginning worker with the basic professional knowledge and skills, but the introduction of a supervisor in the practical process of operation of the specific agency is still necessary. Even more indispensable is the skilled supervision of workers in agencies that employ persons without professional social work education and rely upon the so-called "apprenticeship method" of training the staff at work in the agency.[10]

In contrast to public agencies, which according to statutory provision have to accept every client who meets the legal requirements for eligibility, voluntary agencies are not under obligation to serve every applicant. The social workers in private agencies have become convinced that their work will be most effective if the persons who come to the agency fully understand the conditions under which the agency can serve them, what the nature and limitations of the services are, and if the applicant himself decides whether or not he wishes to use these facilities. Where there is conflict between members of a family, such as in cases of marital discord or neglect of or cruelty against children, social agencies attempt to find measures of protection which are acceptable to the other side; only as a last resort a court order is asked for.

The possibility of the private social agency limiting its services to special groups, such as to persons suffering from handicaps, particular diseases, or the psychological effects of racial discrimination, enables the organization to offer intensive methods of aid or services and to interpret the importance of its program to the public.

B. SECTARIAN SOCIAL AGENCIES

In the Colonial period of our country, religious charities played a minor role because the settlers brought over from England the tradition of public parish poor relief. The parish, however, was often almost identical with its church. Thus it was not felt necessary to organize separate church charity activities. Not until the nineteenth century were denominational charities founded by the different religious congregations, primarily in order to care for orphans and deserted children, but also for recreational and educational activities with emphasis on youth and children. In addition to welfare aims, these charities pursued those of culture, religion and education. Religious social agencies are usually supported like nonsectarian voluntary welfare services through Community Chests. However, they also receive contributions, donations, and funds from their own membership, from churches, and from special campaigns since they often

---

[10] H. Witmer, *op. cit.*, p. 190; Charlotte Towle, *Common Human Needs* (Chicago: University of Chicago Press, 1945), pp. 95-122; and Chapters 20 and 22.

extend their charity work beyond the boundaries of the local community within the territory of a larger ecclesiastical unit, such as a bishopric, a diocese, or synod.

One type of sectarian social agency limits its services to the members of the founding denominational group as a part of an extension of its religious training and education. Another type offers welfare service to the entire community without this being thought of as part of the religious education program. However, the activities of the agency are still sectarian. A third type is the interdenominational agency, serving more than one denomination and transcending the narrow concepts of sectarianism.[11]

1. *Protestant Social Work.* As the dominant religious group in this country, Protestant churches have never been concerned about discrimination against their members by public institutions. Numerous humanitarian and philanthropic charities have been created and maintained by Protestants and their congregations. In addition to such services for the entire community the individual Protestant denominations have established such religious charities as orphanages, hospitals, homes for the aged and handicapped, settlement houses, reform schools for boys and girls, and agencies for the aid of prisoners and their families and destitute, runaway children. Some of these services were founded as expressions of religious concern with the fate of the underprivileged and needy, and were not closely attached to a particular Protestant denomination, but often some contact with one or several church groups is maintained. The social consciousness of the Protestant church was represented by such personalities as Washington Gladden, Josiah Strong, Lyman Abbott, Vida D. Scudder, George Davis Herron, John Graham Brooks, Walter Rauschenbusch, Francis Peabody, Charles R. Henderson, Bishop Scarlett, Bishop Francis McConnell, and Harry Emerson Fosdick.[12]

Lutheran, Episcopal, Baptist, and Methodist churches have organized home missions or city missions in New York and other large

[11] Nathan E. Cohen, "The Place of the Sectarian Agency in Services to Groups," *Social Welfare Forum, 1951,* pp. 271-280; and John A. Hutchinson, *Christian Faith and Social Action* (New York: Scribner, 1953).

[12] See Wade C. Barclay, *The Church and a Christian Society* (New York: Abingdon Press, 1939), p. 56; Dores R. Sharpe, *Walter Rauschenbusch* (New York: Macmillan, 1942), p. 12; Almon R. Pepper, "Protestant Social Work," *Social Work Year Book, 1945,* pp. 304-312; and F. Ernest Johnson, "Protestant Social Work," *Social Work Year Book, 1954,* pp. 377-387.

cities which led to the establishment of "houses of refuge" and temporary shelters for children and adolescents, industrial workshops, settlement houses, summer camps, immigrant services, and various health facilities. The Salvation Army and Methodist churches have been prominent in the development of "goodwill industries" for the employment and training of the handicapped who are able to earn their living in these "sheltered workshops." Episcopal and Lutheran seaman's missions and reception centers are available in several ports. Over 300 old-age homes are in operation alone under the auspices of six large Protestant denominations,[13] and more than 300 Protestant hospitals include 149 schools of nursing.

In Protestant social agencies emphasis is laid upon the postulate that religious life be nurtured, that religious ethics be integrated into the basic principles of social work under government and nonsectarian social agencies as well, and that the members of the Protestant churches as volunteers have a good deal to contribute to service for the community. Protestant social agencies are operating either under one of the denominations—a local church or a regional, diocesan, or synodical authority—or under a national mission board of the church. Coordinating bodies of Protestant churches for the entire country are, for instance, the Division of Welfare of the National Lutheran Council, the Board of Hospitals and Homes of the Methodist Church, the Department of Christian Social Relations of the National Council of the Protestant Episcopal Church, the Council on Christian Social Progress of the Northern Baptist Convention, and the Division of Social Education and Action of the Board of Christian Education of the Presbyterian Church. These agencies maintain contact with their institutions and local agencies through field secretaries, regional conventions, and information services. Metropolitan and state councils of churches combine the social welfare activities of the various Protestant denominations, and the Federal Council of Churches attempts to coordinate the national program of Protestant social work through its Department of Christian Social Relations and the Church Conference of Social Work which has its annual convention at the time of the National Conference of Social Work. For rural social work the Home Missions Council acts as coordinating body.

[13] See Beverley M. Boyd, "Protestant Social Work," *Social Work Year Book,* *1949,* pp. 359-360; and Henry J. Whiting, "Current Emphases in Casework Under Religious Auspices, Integration of Casework and Other Programs," *The Social Welfare Forum, 1951,* pp. 215-224.

The Young Men's Christian Association (YMCA), the Young Women's Christian Association (YWCA), and the Salvation Army are not church organizations in a sectarian sense, but have been founded upon religious principles, and most of their members are active in Protestant churches; they are not controlled by any Protestant denomination or any group of churches. Some YWCA and YMCA centers, as well as some Jewish community centers, have accepted young people of various creeds to their membership and have thus assumed intersectarian character. But there is controversy in the YWCA and YMCA over the amount of Christianity that is necessary and desirable in their work.[14]

The Salvation Army was founded in England, in 1865, and has been active in the United States since 1880. Its main interest is the religious needs of people. Its family and child welfare services are less important than its work with groups of people who are reached less by other churches or social agencies, such as provision of shelters for the homeless, alcoholics, "derelicts" and "bums," and maternity homes and placement services for unmarried mothers. Other activities of the Salvation Army include employment services for handicapped, social settlements, prison work, boys' clubs, and children's institutions.

The American Friends Service Committee, founded in 1917, and the Unitarian Service Committee, established in 1939, have not only been active in international peace work, social services for foreign relief and rehabilitation, and interracial cooperation but also in services for the mentally ill, young and adult prisoners, and community work camps.

For the victims of Nazi persecution, the American Christian Committee for Refugees was organized by the Federal Council of Churches in 1934, and in 1947 the Church World Service developed a large program of aid to displaced persons and refugees under its Committee on Displaced Persons. The Church World Service also carries on foreign relief and religious education abroad.

Protestant hospitals, sanatoriums, and institutions for the chronic sick maintain the American Protestant Hospital Association with over three hundred institutions as members, and since 1948 Confer-

[14] Paul Limbert, *Christian Emphasis in Y.M.C.A. Program* (New York: Association Press, 1951), p. 32; Shelby M. Harrison, *Religion and Social Work—Perspectives and Common Denominators* (New York: National Council of Churches, 1950); and Harvey Seifert, *The Church in Community Action* (New York: Abingdon-Cokesbury, 1952).

ences on Protestant Homes for the Aged are held in order to exchange experiences.

2. *Catholic Social Work.* The social services under the auspices of the Roman Catholic Church are inspired by the religious concepts of the Catholic faith, particularly the virtue of charity. Their main objective is the salvation of the human soul. Catholic social work serves primarily communicants of the Catholic Church, but other clients are not rigorously excluded from the aid of Catholic agencies if their funds and facilities permit caring for them without offense to religion and disadvantage of Catholic applicants. Catholic social workers consider the supernatural element of "charity" as an expression of divine grace, as love of man for the love of God; their religious philosophy is primarily based upon the teaching of Thomas Aquinas in the thirteenth century.

The structure of Catholic social work follows that of the church organization. The main unit of its services is the diocese. In most of the 118 dioceses of the United States, a director of charities, appointed by the bishop ordinary, coordinates all Catholic welfare activities. As a rule, he is a priest with training in social work. In metropolitan districts the heads of the various departments of the Diocesan Bureau of Social Services or The Associated Catholic Charities are also priests who have received training in social work. The diocesan charities are responsible for the establishment, planning, and financing of all Catholic charitable activities and for cooperation with other voluntary and public social agencies in the area. They are interested in the maintenance of high standards of service and in professional training of young workers in schools of social work. The program of the diocesan charities, in general, emphasizes child care in foster homes and children's institutions; family casework; cultural, educational, and recreational activities for children and young people; work with juvenile delinquents and endangered youth; and care of the aged and chronically ill.[15]

The national agency representing Catholic social work is the National Conference of Catholic Charities, which was founded in 1910.

[15] See James T. McDonnell, "Catholic Social Work," *Social Work Year Book, 1949,* p. 87; Thomas Gill, *op. cit., 1954,* pp. 74-81; Mary J. McCormick, *Thomistic Philosophy in Social Casework* (New York: Columbia University Press, 1948); Katharine E. Griffith, "Developments in Casework Programs Under Religious Auspices," *The Social Welfare Forum, 1951,* pp. 224-235; and Daniel McColgan, *A Century of Charity* (Mliwaukee: Bruce, 1951).

Its main task is the coordination of all organizations active in Catholic charitable programs and their cooperation with other private and public social agencies. The Conference arranges national and regional meetings for the exchange of points of view and experiences, conducts research, and encourages the publication of books and studies. It also issues a monthly journal, the *Catholic Charities Review*, in Washington, D.C. In the field of social philosophy and social action another organization, the National Catholic Welfare Conference, has been established under which the Family Life Bureau and the National Catholic Rural Life Conference operate for the interpretation of their philosophy. Under this Conference the War Relief Services was set up in 1943; for several years it administered foreign relief in cooperation with government agencies and the United Nations Relief and Rehabilitation Administration (UNRRA) in Europe and Asia. The National Catholic Resettlement Council and the Catholic Committee for Refugees provide immigration services for Catholic refugees and displaced persons with resettlement, placement, vocational training, legal advice, and emergency relief.

Volunteer organizations play an essential role in Catholic charitable work in the dioceses. The prominent societies among them are the Society of St. Vincent de Paul (founded by Frederic Ozanam in France in 1833 and transferred to the United States in 1845) and the Ladies of Charity. Others include the Sisters of the Good Shepherd, the Catholic Big Brothers and Big Sisters, the Christ Child Society, the Knights of Columbus, the Catholic Daughters of America, the Sword of the Spirit, The Legion of Mary, and the diocesan councils of Catholic men and women. Volunteer work is mainly devoted to the sick and poor in the parish; to the inmates of hospitals, mental institutions, and prisons; to child care and employment services; and to the maintenance of rest homes and residence clubs for young people and the aged and shelters for transients and homeless.

3. *Jewish Social Work.* From ancient times Jewish laws and traditions have made aid to the poor a fundamental religious obligation for the individual and the community. The Bible and Scriptures emphasized the duty of caring for the widow and orphans, the blind and the lame, of feeding the hungry, and sheltering the homeless. Slaves were freed after seven years of service. The consciousness of the need of solidarity grew during the Middle Ages when Jews suffered from cruel persecutions, mass murder, and expulsions. In the Jewish re-

ligion charity is called "justice," and has always been an essential part of Jewish ethics. Traditions of charity led to the establishment of Jewish orphanages in the United States as early as during the Revolutionary War.

Jewish social work is religious in origin and inspiration, but its agencies are secular; it is not administered by synagogues and congregations. It is mainly financed by the local religious community, but it lacks the centralization achieved in Catholic social services. Following the opening of some Jewish orphan asylums and hospitals, United Jewish Charities were founded in New York, Chicago, Cincinnati, Cleveland, and a few large cities where the bulk of the Jewish population lived. Homes for the aged, community centers, and group work agencies followed later. In 1895, Boston and Cincinnati organized the first "federations," which were later accepted by most larger Jewish communities, and became characteristic for the form of community organization of Jewish social welfare. Their function was the conduct of a unified financial campaign for all Jewish institutions and agencies, preceding the Community Chest movement, to organize central budgeting for all social agencies according to their need, and the coordination of social work within family welfare and children's services, health and tuberculosis work, hospitals, clinics, group work, and educational and recreational activities. The Jewish federations were instrumental in the creation of the first Community Chests, participated in the combined campaigns for funds, and became members of the councils of social agencies with which they shared their surveys of need, welfare planning for the entire community, and coordination of social services.[16]

Another type of Jewish community organization are the Jewish Welfare Funds, which raise contributions by a unified central drive and provide budgeting for domestic and foreign relief needs. They started in Columbus (Ohio), Indianapolis, and Oakland (California) in 1925 and have since spread to most larger cities. They appeal for contributions to maintain the various Jewish welfare and health services, particularly for Israel and foreign aid programs, and for such

[16] See Martin M. Cohn, "Jewish Social Work," *Social Work Year Book, 1954,* pp. 285-295; Maurice J. Karpf, *Jewish Community Organization in the United States* (New York: Block, 1938); George W. Rabinoff, "Jewish Social Work," *Social Work Year Book, 1945,* pp. 203-214; and Council of Jewish Federations and Welfare Funds, *1953 Yearbook of Jewish Social Services* (New York: 1953).

local services which cannot obtain Community Chest support as religious education, vocational training, and special employment services. As a central agency in larger communities the Jewish Community Council coordinates religious, cultural, fraternal, and social service activities, including the relations with other organizations.

Until the Depression of the 1930's Jewish family societies had assumed major responsibility for Jewish people in need, particularly for Jewish immigrants who were not eligible for public assistance. Since the change of public welfare policies under the influence of the Social Security Act, Jewish family and child welfare services continue to aid Jews for whom government aid is not available or whose special religious needs require particualr help. They grant small loans for setting up people in business, provide vocational training and scholarships, and conduct various children's services (including child guidance clinics) usually in cooperation with a Jewish hospital, and camps. Casework services of Jewish family agencies are used in determining eligibility of applicants for hospitals, old-age homes, tuberculosis sanatoriums, and other institutions which do not have a casework division of their own.

Services for immigrants and refugees were organized, since 1884, by HIAS (Hebrew Sheltering and Immigrant Aid Society), as emergency shelter and transportation aid. These services were rendered by other Jewish welfare agencies on a large scale since 1935. Resettlement work for Jewish refugees and displaced persons and their adjustment in American communities, since this period, is a major task of Jewish agencies particularly USNA (United Service for New Americans), now united with HIAS. Local family welfare agencies, children's bureaus, vocational services, women's organizations share the responsibility for the resettlement of newcomers.

The National Jewish Welfare Board was the representative of Jewish social work in the United Service Organizations (USO) during World War II, and now has charge of recreational and group work services for the members of the armed forces through its field staff and local community army and navy committees. It coordinates and develops the policies for the 321 Jewish Community Centers and the Young Men's and Young Women's Hebrew Associations (YMHA and YWHA) and arranges for recruitment and training of personnel for these recreational agencies.

The largest national organization of Jewish social work is the

Council of Jewish Federations and Welfare Funds, with headquarters in New York which maintains eight regional offices. It coordinates Jewish community resources in cooperation with local agencies. The National Conference of Jewish Social Welfare serves as a forum for the discussion of problems and experiences and publishes a periodical, *The Jewish Social Service Quarterly*. The Jewish Occupational Council is the clearing house for vocational guidance and placement services and formulates programs regarding Jewish economic problems.

Most national and larger local Jewish agencies employ a professionally trained staff, educated in schools of social work.

III. RURAL SOCIAL SERVICES

The rural population of the United States includes persons living on farms, in villages and towns with less than 2,500 inhabitants, and in the open country; it still is about 32 per cent of the total population.[17] Although the average income of farmers has substantially increased during World War II and the postwar years, there was a decline beginning in 1949. The problems of insufficient income from submarginal land, of difficulties in marketing farm products, and of long-term unemployment, low wages, and insecurity among the migratory farm workers set special needs in the case of certain sections of the rural population. These problems differ in the various agricultural areas of our country, but are most urgent in those states where economic and health conditions are less favorable than in New England, the middle East and the far West.[18]

Under these circumstances, a strong national leadership has developed in order to improve social conditions in rural communities and to develop social services which have long been taken for granted in urban settings. The U.S. Children's Bureau, now under the federal Department of Health, Education and Welfare, is the oldest federal agency particularly concerned in its maternal and child health services with rural welfare and health. The Bureau of Indian Affairs in

17 *U.S. Census of Population, 1950: General Characteristics*, U.S. Summary, (1952), pp. 1-105, Table 58.
18 Grace Browning, "Rural Social Programs," *Social Work Year Book, 1949*, pp. 446; Benson Y. Landis, "Rural Social Programs," *Social Work Year Book, 1954*, pp. 455-463; and Carle C. Zimmerman and Nathan L. Whettan, *Rural Families on Relief*, Chap. 3; and Marjorie J. Smith, *Rural Case Work Service* (New York: Family Welfare Association, 1943).

the U.S. Department of the Interior is another long established agency in this area. In the U.S. Department of Agriculture the most important programs for rural communities are administered through the Extension Service in the form of free consultation and demonstrations of scientific methods in farming, crop cultivation, and home economics. A broad adult education program and the development of the so-called 4-H Clubs for teen-age boys and girls and of clubs of older rural youth develop agricultural and home economics skills, and appreciation of rural life and culture, as well as an understanding of child care and health preservation. The Extension Service is supported by the Bureau of Home Nutrition and Home Economics, the Bureau of Agricultural Economics, and the Farmers Home Administration, the latter providing loans, a farm housing plan, and a limited medical care program.

Aid to rural communities in recreation, adult education, and rural health protection is stimulated by the American Country Life Association, which attempts to coordinate rural youth services; the Farm Foundation; the National Education Association; several farm organizations, such as the National Grange of the Order of Patrons of Husbandry, the American Farm Bureau Federation, the Farmers' Union; and others.

Prior to the Depression of the 1930's, needy persons in rural communities depended upon uncertain neighborly help or meager, local poor relief. The inadequacy of this relief became evident when in the Depression years mass unemployment made it difficult to sell agricultural products and droughts and floods increased the suffering of the rural population in many states. The federal Emergency Relief Administration and the Farm Security Administration provided financial aid and special measures of assistance in rural communities.

In this period, the rural county public welfare departments developed for the first time an effective program of financial assistance. With the support of federal and state funds under the Social Security Act for aid to needy aged, to needy blind, and to dependent children (and lately for disabled persons), rural welfare departments became able to give more adequate economic aid to these groups of people. Family and child welfare services also were made possible through federal grants-in-aid, which were allocated primarily for rural communities.[19] Professionally trained child welfare workers, supervisors,

[19] See Chapters 10 and 11.

and consultants are now employed in rural regions for maternal and child care services, for crippled children, and for casework and group work with difficult, endangered, and delinquent children. In the rural communities where these services are not yet available, there are few qualified, trained social workers or sufficient financial resources. Often, the county welfare department is the only social agency in such a region. A number of state departments of public welfare supplement the forces of the local county welfare agency by sending field supervisors, consultants, and itinerant clinics to provide medical and psychiatric examinations and guidance.

Among voluntary social agencies, the local chapter of the American National Red Cross is best known to rural communities. A limited number of other private agencies, such as the Salvation Army, the National Tuberculosis Association, the National Travelers Aid and some child-placing and adoption agencies, have field services which serve rural regions.[20]

Social services in the rural community are influenced by its cultural pattern, particular customs, and traditions. The comparative simplicity of the rural village has its bearing upon attitudes toward assistance expenditures and restricts allowances for education and recreation. Rural relief applicants frequently are accustomed to living on a low economic scale, are shy or apathetic about presenting their requests, and are seemingly grateful to accept meager relief. Relationship between the client and the visiting social worker is more intimate than in the city—more informal and less professional. This is particularly true if the social worker is employed in her home county. If the social worker is not familiar with the rural county, she is forced first to get thoroughly acquainted with its form of government and its health, recreational, and community facilities.

The rural population often is more rigid in its moral values and attitudes toward illegitimacy, desertion, birth control, divorce, and sometimes toward drinking and gambling. Social work with the unmarried mother, a nonsupporting husband or father, or an alcoholic is made more difficult in a rural setting through these rigid attitudes and the closeness of relationships. The high value placed upon thrift

[20] See G. Browning, *op. cit.*, pp. 448-451, and *Rural Public Welfare* (Chicago: University of Chicago Press, 1941), pp. 95-98; and Arthur Hillman, *Community Organization and Planning* (New York: Macmillan, 1950), pp. 38-55.

and frugality leads easily to refusing aid to families who do not fully conform to the moral standards of the community. The social worker has more difficulty in obtaining information and keeping it confidential, due to the pressure of the neighborhood. In her work, she relies heavily upon her own initiative and resourcefulness (more than in the city) and usually cannot turn to a specialist or supervisor for advice.

Medical care, hospitals, and public health services in rural counties are poor compared with those in urban regions. There is no complete, paid public health staff with medical officer, sanitary engineer, laboratory assistant, public health nurse, and medical social worker in about 40 per cent of the rural counties, and about one-third of them do not even employ a public health nurse.[21] Most public health nursing in rural sections is carried on through maternal and child health centers. With the aid of federal funds, granted under the Hospital Survey and Construction Act of 1946, new hospitals in rural areas have been built, but preventive mental health services are still almost nonexistent in rural counties. Medical care in isolated areas is very expensive so that the inhabitants call a doctor only in severe cases, preventing early and quick cure. Dental care and lack of proper diets are sometimes special problems for the social worker in a rural community.

Recreational activities and sports in rural regions are conducted under the auspices of high schools, church groups, the 4-H Clubs, and the Extension Service of the federal Department of Agriculture;[22] often also through the YWCA, YMCA, Boy Scouts, and Girl Scouts.

SELECTED BIBLIOGRAPHY

Abts, Dorothy M., *Some Religious and Ethical Problems in the Practice of Catholic Social Workers.* Washington, D.C.: Catholic University of America Press, 1945.

Balmford, Edith F., "The Church as the Conscience of Social Work," *Christian Social Welfare*, Vol. 1, No. 1, October, 1953, pp. 10-11.

Barclay, Wade C., *The Church and a Christian Society.* New York: Abingdon-Cokesbury Press, 1939.

Bogen, Boris D., *Jewish Philanthropy.* New York: Macmillan, 1917.

[21] David E. Lindstrom, *American Rural Life* (New York: The Ronald Press Company, 1948), pp. 38-39; and President's Commission on the Health Needs of the Nation, *Building America's Health—Findings and Recommendations*, Vol. 1 (1952).

[22] B. Landis, *op. cit.*, pp. 456-457, 461.

Bonthius, Robert H., *Christian Paths to Self-Acceptance.* New York: King's Crown, 1948.

*Boyd, Beverley M., "Protestant Social Work," *Social Work Year Book, 1949,* pp. 358-366; and *Social Work Year Book, 1951,* pp. 350-359.

*Boylan, Marguerite T., *Social Welfare in the Catholic Church.* New York: Columbia University Press, 1941.

Brown, Josephine C., *Rural Community and Social Case Work.* New York: Little & Ives, 1933.

*Browning, Grace, *Rural Public Welfare: Selected Records.* Chicago: University of Chicago Press, 1941.

———, "Rural Social Programs," *Social Work Year Book, 1949,* pp. 446-453.

Bryson, Lyman, Louis Finkelstein, and Robert MacIver, *Approaches to Group Understanding.* New York: Harper, 1947.

Chaplin, Dora P., *Children and Religion.* New York: Scribner, 1948.

Clarke, Helen I., *Principles and Practice of Social Work.* New York: Appleton-Century-Crofts, Inc., 1947.

Cohen, Nathan E., "The Function of Social Group Work Agencies in a Democracy," *Social Work in the Current Scene, 1949.* New York: Columbia University Press, 1950.

*———, "The Place of the Sectarian Agency in Services to Groups," *The Social Welfare Forum 1951,* pp. 271-280.

Cohn, Martin M., "Jewish Social Work," *Social Work Year Book, 1951,* pp. 260-269.

de Schweinitz, Karl, *People and Process in Social Security.* Washington, D.C.: American Council on Education, 1948.

Dicks, Russell L., *Pastoral Work and Personal Counseling.* New York: Macmillan, 1945.

Edidin, Ben M., *Jewish Community Life in America.* New York: Hebrew Publishing Co., 1947.

Fuller, Varden, *No Work Today!* New York: Public Affairs, 1953.

Gill, Thomas, "Catholic Social Work," *Social Work Year Book, 1951,* pp. 81-88.

Groves, Ernest R., *Rural Problems of Today.* New York: Association Press, 1918.

Hiltner, Seward, *Religion and Health.* New York: Macmillan, 1943.

Jorns, Auguste, *The Quakers As Pioneers in Social Work.* New York: Macmillan, 1931.

*Karpf, Maurice J., *Jewish Community Organization in the United States.* New York: Block Publishing Co., 1938.

Kavanaugh, John, *The Quaker Approach.* New York: Putnam, 1953.

Landis, Benson Y., "Rural Social Programs," *Social Work Year Book, 1954,* pp. 455-463.

*———, *Rural Welfare Services.* New York: Columbia University Press, 1949.

Landis, Paul H., *Rural Life in Process.* New York: McGraw, 1948.

*Lauerman, Lucian L., *Catholic Education for Social Work.* Washington, D.C.: Catholic University of America Press, 1943.

*Lurie, Harry L., "The Approach and Philosophy of Jewish Social Welfare," *The Jewish Social Service Quarterly,* Vol. 19, No. 3, March, 1953.

McCormick, Mary J., *Thomistic Philosophy in Social Casework.* New York: Columbia University Press, 1948.

McDonnell, James T., "Catholic Social Work," *Social Work Year Book, 1949,* pp. 85-92.

McMillen, Wayne, *Community Organization for Social Welfare,* Chap. II-IV. Chicago: University of Chicago Press, 1945.

Maves, Paul B., and J. Lennart Cedarleaf, *Older People and the Church.* New York: Abingdon Press, 1949.

Miles, Arthur P., *An Introduction to Public Welfare.* Boston: Heath, 1949.

*Mott, Frederick D., and Milton I. Roemer, *Rural Health and Medical Care.* New York: McGraw, 1948.

Nelson, William Stuart (editor), *The Christian Way in Race Relations.* New York: Harper, 1948.

*Niebuhr, Reinhold, *The Contribution of Religion to Social Work.* New York: Columbia University Press, 1932.

O'Grady, John, *Catholic Charities in the United States.* Washington, D.C.: National Conference of Catholic Charities, 1930.

———, *The Catholic Church and the Destitute.* New York: Macmillan, 1929.

Pickett, Clarence E., *For More Than Bread.* Boston: Little, 1953.

Rabinoff, George W., "Jewish Social Work," *Social Work Year Book, 1954,* pp. 203-214.

———, and Martin M. Cohn, *The Setting and Rationale for the Jewish Communal Agency.* New York: Training Bureau of Jewish Communal Service, 1949.

Roberts, David E., "Theological and Psychiatric Interpretations of Human Nature," *Christianity and Crisis,* Vol. 8, February 3, 1947, pp. 3-7.

Schwer, William, *Catholic Social Theory.* London: Herder, 1940.

Sharpe, Dores R., *Walter Rauschenbusch.* New York: Macmillan, 1942.

Sheed, F. J., *Society and Sanity.* New York: Sheed & Ward, 1953.

Stidley, Leonard Albert, *Sectarian Welfare Federation Among Protestants.* New York: Association Press, 1944.

Tillich, Paul J., "The Relation of Religion and Health," *The Review of Religion,* Vol. 10, May, 1946, pp. 348-384.

*Williams, Meloin J., *Catholic Social Thought.* New York: The Ronald Press Company, 1950.

Winston, Ellen, "Public Welfare," *Social Work Year Book, 1951,* pp. 402-412.

Withers, Gertrude V., *Effective Rural Social Work Through Community Organization.* Chicago: American Public Welfare Association, 1942.

Zimmerman, Carle C., and Nathan L. Whettan, *Rural Families on Relief.* Washington, D.C.: U.S. Printing Office, 1938.

8. Public Assistance

I. PRINCIPLES OF INCOME SECURITY

In modern industrial society the majority of the population is dependent for their livelihood upon their current wages as laborers, workers, and employees, or upon their income as self-employed persons. Whenever the breadwinner is unable to work due to illness, injuries, physical and mental handicaps, when he cannot obtain work, or when his death leaves the family in need, social legislation is necessary to provide economic protection. In the industrial countries, no longer can we rely upon relatives, friends, or neighbors to support people in need of financial aid, nor upon religious or philanthropic voluntary charities to assume the responsibility to supply the funds for maintaining the indigent and their families. There are two main systems of achieving this goal of economic security: (1) a program of *public assistance* (or social assistance), which is financed by taxation, and (2) a program of *social insurance,* financed by contributions of the beneficiary and of his employer.[1] Public assistance may be provided by payments based upon the economic and social needs of the applicant, "which are determined by a means test," or they may be granted as a "flat rate allowance" legally fixed with regard to recognized average needs of families of a specific size. Assistance payments may be rendered in money so that the recipient is able to purchase the necessities of life, or in kind, such as food, clothing, fuel, and medical supplies. Public assistance may be offered either by accepting the destitute into an

[1] This chapter deals with public assistance; the programs of social insurance will be discussed in Chapter 9, and the health and welfare services in Chapters 11 to 13. Discussion of the important contribution of public education to human welfare is beyond the scope of this book. In some of the economically less developed countries, public assistance and social insurance programs are just beginning to be organized and are different according to their cultural, religious, social, and economic conditions.

institution, such as an orphanage, a hospital, a home for the aged, or by granting aid to the applicant in his own home. Because public assistance is granted only to individuals who are in economic need, this fact must be established through some kind of a means test. Modern programs of public assistance characterize the receipt of the payment as a right of the applicant, provided that its legal requirements are fulfilled. The amount of assistance is usually limited by statute and adjusted to the recipient's social and economic conditions whereby his income, all resources, and property are taken into consideration. The administration of public assistance determines the extent of need, and the amount of assistance often cannot be predicted in advance.

In contrast, social insurance benefits are fully predictable. They are based upon legal provisions which provide statutory benefits either on a flat rate system or in relation to earned wages, or income, length of work, or loss of working capacity in cases of industrial injuries. Insurance benefits are not dependent upon the financial status or the economic need of the insured person. They are provided to the insured who has a legal claim to receive these benefits without arbitrary interference of government authorities. Insurance benefits are financed by contributions of employers and self-employed persons, and of workers. In other countries often the government shares contributions for social insurance with the insured and their employers.

Between these two main methods of providing economic security, there is a *third approach* to income security: a *pension system* based upon statute. In our country veterans' pensions to disabled veterans and to survivors of veterans, and allowances to dependents of military personnel are examples of such pensions which are granted as a matter of legal right to the claimant. Foreign countries have other programs of this nature such as family allowances, flat pensions to persons over sixty-five or seventy years of age, or to certain qualified handicapped groups.

In order to provide economic protection, we use in the United States a dual system, consisting of public assistance on the basis of individual need, and of social insurance programs in which benefits are paid to the insured persons as their legal claim in predetermined, specific contingencies of life (old age, death of breadwinner, unemployment, industrial accident). These two main programs of economic security are supplemented by a system of health and welfare services which provides social services, protective and preventive measures, such as child welfare services, recreation, medical and psychiatric care (particularly for mothers and children and certain handicapped groups), occupational guidance, and vocational rehabilitation, which are of greatest importance for the welfare of the population.

Other public programs, such as public employment services and correctional treatment of juvenile and adult offenders, also may be classified as public welfare measures in a broader sense.

These public activities are often strengthened and augmented by the work of private social agencies, which contribute to the economic security of the population. This work is carried on under the auspices of religious or nonsectarian philanthropic organizations or of industries and labor unions.

The system of public welfare in the United States has its principal legal foundation in the Social Security Act of 1935 and its subsequent amendments. As we mentioned in Chapter 5, the Social Security Act deals with all three programs: social insurance, public assistance,[2] and health and welfare services. It provides federal funds for the development and the improvement of standards in specific programs of public assistance and health and welfare services. However, the Social Security Act does not establish a comprehensive system of public welfare services in all these fields but rather sets up programs for federal aid in selected and specified types of assistance and welfare services. The social insurance programs of the Old-Age and Survivors Insurance and Unemployment Compensation are until now financed exclusively by contributions of employers and the insured persons without the use of general tax funds.

The cost of public welfare is shared by the federal government, by the states, and counties and cities. This circumstance has contributed to the fact that the importance of public welfare has been recognized by an increasing proportion of the population. The public is, at the same time, more critical toward the expenditure of huge sums of money, which necessitate higher taxes, and has become conscious of the marked differences in the amount of benefits received under the various programs in states and counties, and in the standards and methods of their administration. In general, it is now accepted that

[2] Public assistance may be characterized as financial aid given by government with regard to individual need and resources of the recipient.

government on its various levels has to assume responsibility of caring for the people who have no means of support. But there is, so far, no unanimity of social philosophy as to how this responsibility should be met, what seems an adequate aid to persons in need, and what government agencies should administer the public welfare services.

An application of a person in need of material assistance is, as a rule, made by the person himself (or if a child is in need, by his parent or guardian), at the local department of public welfare. A blind or disabled person may send a relative or friend to submit the request for assistance to the agency. If for special reasons the needy person cannot go to the welfare department, he may write a letter that he wants to apply for aid or he may phone the agency. If the application is made in person, the social worker explains how the application form is to be filled out and what information is needed. The applicant may have to include documents for proof of age, data regarding his income and property, or medical certificates about blindness or disability. If the applicant has not come to the welfare office but has written or phoned, a social worker visits the home and gives the explanation about the form of application and the required data and documents at the home of the applicant. The social worker also checks the facts presented in the application and attempts to make certain that the applicant is eligible for the assistance he is asking for. If further investigations are necessary (for example, about relatives who may support the applicant, or about income and property), these are made within a reasonable time which differs within local welfare departments, and a notice is sent to the applicant telling him whether or not he has been accepted for public assistance and how much he will receive monthly. The amount of aid is based upon the applicant's individual needs and resources and is often limited by rules of state or local authorities. If the applicant is eligible, he receives a check at regular intervals, usually once a month. If assistance is denied, the applicant is informed about his right to ask for a hearing or to appeal to another authority, as much as the categorical types of public assistance are concerned. In general assistance there is possible, as a rule, only the request for a reconsideration through the county board of supervisors or the city council, but no formal appeal.

Decisions of the public welfare department must be given in

writing so that misunderstandings may be avoided, and so that the applicant is able to take his steps after consulting friends, relatives, or legal counsel, within the period legally provided for.

In all forms of public assistance the applicant is required to report promptly to the public welfare department any change in income, economic conditions, address, or other important facts which are essential for the granting of assistance. The social worker often may be able to help the applicant in other matters regarding his living conditions, health problems, personal questions, and plans for change of his dependent situation.

II. CATEGORICAL ASSISTANCE

The goal of public assistance is to provide minimum economic protection to persons who have no other means of supporting themselves by work or from their property, nor are adequately maintained by relatives, private social agencies, or other sources. Public assistance is granted only to people in financial need, distinguished from social insurance benefits which are not dependent upon economic need.[3] Before the enactment of the Social Security Act in 1935 less than half of the states had special relief systems providing more adequate care than general poor relief for the aged, for blind persons, or for children. Under the Social Security Act the federal government shares in the expenses of four major types of *categorical assistance:* old age assistance, aid to the blind, aid to dependent children, and aid to the permanently and totally disabled.[4] For the residual part of public assistance, which is called *general assistance* (or indigent aid), no federal standards exist, and no federal money is provided for, so that this field remains the sole responsibility of state or local governments. We shall discuss first the categorical forms of public assistance, and then the field of general assistance.

The question whether public assistance should bear the major burden in providing income security to those persons who need such protection is highly controversial. Whereas public assistance before the enactment of social insurance legislation into the Social Security Act was the only means of public aid to people in distress in the

[3] Public welfare agencies provide in addition to financial aid other services, such as casework, which we shall discuss below.

[4] The last category was created by the Amendment of 1950.

United States, it is now only one, but no longer the largest, program within the framework of social security. The number of people protected by the categorical forms of public assistance are now by far more numerous than the recipients of general assistance. For example, in April 1953 there were 2,604,341 persons receiving old age assistance; 98,434, aid to the needy blind; 2,011,-389, aid to dependent children; and 170,152, aid to the permanently and totally disabled—altogether 4,884,336 persons; whereas only 395,000 were supported by general assistance payments.[5] Under the amendments of the *Social Security Act of 1950*, Congress decided to emphasize that the payments of the old-age and survivors' insurance program shall become the main bulwark against destitution in our country and that, therefore, public assistance will play a less important role in the maintenance of income security for the entire population.[6] The reduction of the financial burden of taxation for public assistance payments is effected by more substantial contributions and benefits and by an increase in the number of insured persons covered by the old-age and survivors' insurance plan.

The federal government shares the cost of categorical assistance, but it does not administer these programs. It pays one-half of all state expenditures for the proper and efficient administration of approved categorical public assistance programs. The Social Security Act allows the states wide latitude in the legal provisions and administrative setup of the categorical assistance plans. Only the following conditions must be met everywhere by the state plan in order to meet with the approval of the Department of Health, Education and Welfare:

1. The program must be statewide; it must be effective in all political subdivisions of the state, such as counties and townships.

2. The state must participate in the financing of the categorical assistance plans. The law does not specify how large the state's contribution has to be, which is regulated in the state's statute, but the state is not permitted to transfer all financial responsibility beyond the federal grant-in-aid to the county, town, or township.

[5] See *Social Security Bulletin*, Vol. 16, No. 7, July, 1953, pp. 24-28.

[6] U.S. Senate: *Recommendations for Social Security Legislation*. Reports of the Advisory Council on Social Security to the Senate Committee on Finance, Document No. 208, 80th Congress, 2nd Session, 1949. In 1953, for the first time, the number of recipients of public assistance was less than the number of beneficiaries of old-age and survivors' insurance.

3. The state must secure methods of administration which guarantee proper and efficient operation of the categorical assistance plan and which include the establishment and maintenance of a *merit system* of personnel standards (see Chapter 20 for more details). This last provision of the Amendment of 1939 is of particular importance because only competent personnel enables the public welfare department to aid effectively people in need.

4. The state has directly to administer the program or to supervise it by a single state agency, usually the state department of social welfare.

5. The state agency has to submit all required reports to the U.S. Department of Health, Education and Welfare.

6. The state has to give an opportunity for filing of applications for categorical assistance with the provision that action is taken with reasonable promptness. The specific regulations have to be made in each state.

7. The state must provide opportunity for a *fair hearing* for a claimant whose application is fully or partially denied or not acted upon with reasonable promptness, as well as the right of *appeal* to the state agency for the claimant.

8. The state must take into consideration all income and resources of the recipient in determination of his need and of the amount of the assistance payment. An exception is made for earned income of blind persons, which is disregarded up to $50 a month in order to encourage the blind to maintain themselves as far as possible. For other needy persons, however, income may not be ignored as it was in several states, particularly in California, before the Amendment of 1939 prohibited this practice.

9. A state agency, frequently the State Department of Public Health, must be designated as responsible for the establishment and maintenance of standards for public and private institutions (such as hospitals, nursing homes, infirmaries), in which residents may receive categorical public assistance payments.

10. The state plan must provide safeguards which restrict the use or disclosure of information concerning applicants and recipients to purposes directly connected with the administration of public assistance. This provision requiring confidential treatment of categorical assistance records was added by Congress in the Amendment of 1939.

The so-called "Jenner Amendment" under the *Federal Revenue Act of 1951* prevents the Department of Health, Education and Welfare from withholding federal grants-in-aid from a state (or territory) which enacts legislation giving public access to information concerning assistance disbursements, providing such legislation prohibits the use of any list of names obtained for commercial or political purposes. Thus the requirement of the Social Security Act to keep public assistance records confidential is, as a rule, maintained, but the states are now entitled by statutory measures to give access to people who seek information on assistance disbursements.

In addition to the ten requirements which have to be met in each state plan in order to get it approved, the plan may not include:

(a) any residence requirement more restrictive than five years of state residence in the last nine years and one year preceding application, and in the case of aid to dependent children only a maximum of one year residence;

(b) any citizenship requirement barring a citizen of the United States who is otherwise eligible for aid. This does not, however, force the state to require citizenship as a condition to receive categorical assistance;[7] non-citizens may be included in the state provisions.

Categorical assistance is rendered in the form of money payment to needy persons or of payment for medical or remedial treatment for needy persons to doctors, hospitals, clinics, and pharmacists.[8] Categorical assistance usually does not issue vouchers or supply food, clothes, or fuel in kind to needy persons as was formerly frequently the case, but it may pay the medical expenses for an individual or for all recipients of public assistance through local or state-wide pre-payment medical care plans. The categorical assistance plans with federal grants-in-aid favor and encourage applicants to live in their own homes, but since 1950 federal payments are also made to share the expenses for medical and remedial care of needy persons (except dependent children) in public medical institutions (hospitals and sanatoriums), except for psychotic or tubercular patients.[9]

The federal share in the expenses for categorical public assistance differs between the payments for adults and those for dependent children and their caretaker. For adult recipients—needy aged, blind, and permanently and totally disabled persons—the federal government pays monthly four-fifths of the first $25 assistance payment and one-half of the balance between $25 and $55. Thus the federal

[7] Anne E. Geddes and Charles E. Hawkins, "Public Assistance," *Social Work Year Book, 1954*, pp. 396-398; and Elizabeth Wickenden, "Confidentiality of Assistance Records," *Social Work Journal*, Vol. 33, No. 2, April, 1952, pp. 88-93.

[8] This is one of the important changes caused by the Amendment of 1950; for the Amendment of 1952, see Wilbur J. Cohen, "Social Security Act Amendments of 1952," *Social Security Bulletin*, Vol. 15, No. 9, September, 1952, pp. 8-9.

[9] The exclusion of tuberculosis and mental diseases from the program was based upon the high cost for these illnesses, which frequently last very long periods. The federal government no longer shares the categorical assistance expenses for needy tubercular or psychotic patients in private hospitals and sanatoriums.

share is limited to a monthly maximum payment of $35 per person.[10]

In the aid to dependent children program, the federal share amounts to four-fifths of the first $15 paid monthly for the first dependent child and for the mother or other caretaker, such as an older sister, plus one-half of the balance between $15 and $30. The federal payment for the first child and his caretaker cannot exceed $19.50 per month for each. The federal share for the second and other children in the same family eligible for aid to dependent children is four-fifths of the first $15 and one-half of the balance between $15 and $21. The federal monthly payment thus cannot exceed $15 for each additional child.

The establishment of these ceilings for federal grants-in-aid means that the share of the federal government covers only a modest proportion of the actual assistance payments in those states which have higher standards of assistance. They cover a greater proportion of the assistance cost in the states whose assistance standards are low. For the former group, only rarely will it be possible to use the federal contribution to cover the cost of medical treatment, but in states with low assistance payments some federal money is used for the payment of medical care which was paid from general assistance before 1950. In order to secure a minimum standard of health and decency it seems necessary that the federal grants be increased in order to encourage the states and local governments to provide adequate funds for people in need.

The Social Security Act does not define the concept of "need," which is a requirement for granting of public assistance, so that each state has to determine what property or resources an individual or a family may have and still be eligible for public assistance. The statutes and regulations of the states regarding home ownership, cash reserves, savings, and insurance policies which shall not exclude an applicant from eligibility vary greatly. Many states, counties, and cities impose liens on real estate in order to secure the refund of public assistance payments after the death of the recipient or in case of his economic independence. In order to avoid hardship, some of these provisions require the refund only after the death of the

[10] The increased federal contribution enacted by the "McFarland Amendment" of 1952 expires on September 30, 1956, unless extended. This would reduce by $5 a month the federal grant-in-aid for each recipient of old-age assistance, of aid to the blind, and aid to the permanently and totally disabled, and by $3 a month for an individual recipient of aid to dependent children.

spouse of the assistance recipient. The establishment of these policies means that an applicant for public assistance has first to use up his reserves, income, and property (except a limited amount) before he is granted public assistance, in order that chiselers be discouraged. This is often hard to understand for an honest applicant who has saved for a "rainy day"—such as for times of chronic disease or of acute serious illness, or just for his own or his spouse's burial.

Most state laws require that not only must the applicant almost fully exhaust his resources before he may receive assistance, but that also his close relatives remain first responsible for his support and assistance be given only when the applicant does not receive such support. This "relatives' responsibility" is usually limited to the spouse, parents toward their minor children, and adult children toward their parents, but the state laws show differences in their approach. In some states the requirement of the support of family members is limited according to sliding scales, which are classified according to income and number of dependents of the responsible relative. An example of this type is California where the "Relatives' Contribution Scale" requires a contribution of $5 a month from a relative without other dependents if he has a monthly net income of $201; a son who has a wife and two young children has to contribute to the maintenance of his widowed mother only if he has an income of $351 per month. With higher incomes the monthly support increases, but a businessman earning $600 monthly would have to contribute $30 to the support of his mother if he has a wife and three children in his family.[11]

The effect of family responsibility is disputed. Some statutes base these provisions on the assumption that by requiring the support of close relatives the family ties are strengthened. In fact, however, the demand for support often is a serious strain on the budget of relatives with modest income, and leads to a hostile attitude against the old parents that may cause a breakup of friendly relations and serious emotional suffering of the parents. In some states the contribution which relatives owe to the applicant for assistance is deducted from the assistance payment, even if it is not given. This policy leads to hardship for the poor and most states deduct the relative's support only if it is in fact rendered.

The amount of public assistance which is given to the individual

11 California Welfare and Institutions Code (1953), Section 2181.

person or to the family is, as a rule, determined upon a budget consisting of the cost figures for food, shelter, fuel, utilities, and clothing. Most states have developed standard budgets which include several of these items, but leave consideration of rent, nursing, and medical cost to the county or city. For the categorical forms of public assistance, frequently a flat sum is given which represents the average budgetary needs from which the income of the recipient is deducted, but special expenses for medical care, appliances, and medicines may also be considered. The financial situation of a number of states sometimes makes it difficult to grant the full budgetary needs, so that payments are cut because of the lack of adequate appropriations for assistance funds.

Although mobility of labor has been a characteristic of American life, and migrations enabled agricultural and industrial development, communities and states have refused to support "strangers" in need of financial help. We have already discussed the settlement laws of the Colonies, but they still persist in most of the states. They mean that public assistance authorities are not obliged to support indigent nonresidents and may return them to the community where they belong. The length of residence required to obtain "legal settlement right" varies from a period of one year in most states to a maximum of five years, frequently with different provisions for categorical and general assistance. Rhode Island was the first state to abolish all settlement requirements in 1943, and New York followed in 1946, requiring only presence in the state at the time of application. Pennsylvania refuses public assistance to nonresidents, except those who come from states which have no settlement requirements. The majority of states, however, still maintains their settlement laws and frequently special provisions for counties within the state. Often a family moving to another state loses its settlement rights in the old place without gaining new settlement status in the second state. Usually settlement cannot be gained while a person lives in a public institution (county farm, hospital, and so on), nor if he receives private or public relief. The hardships which migrants and their families suffer under these conditions have led to a more liberal policy in some states, permitting residents to receive public assistance payments outside of the state; some reciprocal agreements between states permit mutual assistance to their residents. The Social Security Administration and the principal professional organizations in social work are in favor of the abolishment of these anachronistic settlement laws, but have found little response in the majority of states. Other proposals for remedy are the enactment of uniform settlement legislation in all states, general reciprocal interstate agreements, or a federal program for the financial support of needy nonresidents, but none seems to offer much hope for realization. Therefore, the demand for the establishment of a new general assistance category with federal grants-in-aid which would give special consideration to aid for nonresidents might be the best possible solution to this problem.

CHART 3: RECIPIENTS OF PUBLIC ASSISTANCE UNDER THE SOCIAL SECURITY ACT, 1936-1954. (THE DATA REFER TO THE DECEMBER STATISTICS OF EACH YEAR.)

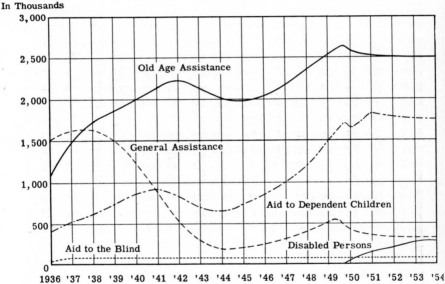

In Thousands

Source: *Social Security Bulletin,* Vol. 14, No. 3, March, 1951, pp. 34-36; Vol. 15, No. 9, September, 1952, p. 49, Table 36; and Vol. 17, No. 7, July, 1954, pp. 30-33.

The development of the public assistance categories since the enactment of the Social Security Act of 1935 is shown in Chart 3. Until this time general assistance was the common form of public relief, and under the impact of the Depression it still represented during the years 1936 and 1937 the program that served the largest numbers. In 1937 the new category of old-age assistance reached the

CHART 4: ASSISTANCE PAYMENTS PER INHABITANT (DOLLAR AMOUNTS EXPENDED
AND ACTUAL PURCHASING POWER REPRESENTED, FISCAL YEARS 1939-1952)

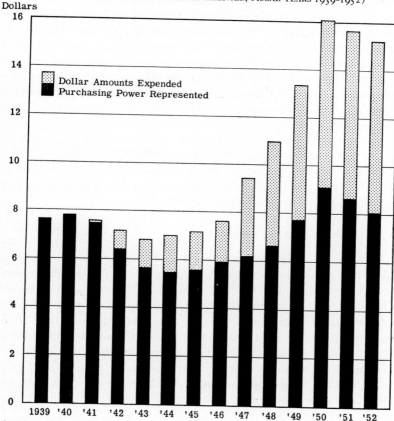

Source: Social Security Administration, Bureau of Public Assistance, *Public Assistance, Graphic Representation of Selected Data,* January, 1953, Chart 2, pp. 4-5. The chart includes payments for old-age assistance, aid to dependent children, aid to the blind, aid to the permanently and totally disabled, and general assistance. Dollar amounts are adjusted to actual purchasing power.

same level as general assistance and since has been increasing in numbers by far outweighing all other assistance categories. In 1950 the number of old-age assistance recipients was seven times that of recipients of general assistance. During the war years of 1941 to 1945 the number of recipients in both programs decreased due to the labor shortage and the opportunities of employment of older and handicapped persons. In the period after World War II the number of old-age assistance recipients has steadily grown while in general assistance a decline has taken place since 1950 when the new defense program again absorbed part of the employable group.

The increasing importance of the financial payments under "Aid to Dependent Children" becomes evident in the chart. During the war years aid was decreasing when many mothers and adolescents were employed, but in the subsequent years the number of dependent children has steadily increased. Supplementary aid to mothers and caretakers, which began in 1950, has made this program still more important. Compared to these large programs the number of persons supported under the aid to the blind, and the new program of aid to the permanently and totally disabled, is not huge, but the social significance of aid to these persons should not be underrated. The expenses for public assistance in our country per inhabitant and their purchasing power are illustrated in Chart 4. In 1952, they amounted in total to nearly $2,500,000,000.

A. OLD-AGE ASSISTANCE

The old-age assistance program is an important source of income to retired or unemployable old people over sixty-five years of age. It is in effect in all states, the District of Columbia, Alaska, and Hawaii,[12] but the proportion of the aged population assisted by this categorical program varies widely among the states. In 1951 about one-fourth, and in 1953 about one-fifth, of the entire population of the aged over 65 years in the United States were in receipt of old-age assistance; in Louisiana, nearly 80 per cent, in 1951, and 63 per cent, in 1953, as the highest proportion; and in New Jersey, 5 per cent, and Delaware, only 6 per cent as the lowest. The average monthly payments on January 1, 1953 varied from $98.19 in Colorado to $25.38 in Virginia. Federal grants-in-aid have not been able to raise the level of assistance in some low income states to a really adequate standard, but in the majority of states the payments are securing a subsistence on a "health and decency level." Many states have

---

[12] Colorado is the only state which grants old-age assistance already to people of sixty years (about four thousand in number); the federal government does not participate in the cost for this group under sixty-five. The important question of work for older citizens is analyzed in a stimulating article by Albert J. Abrams, "Discrimination in Employment of Older Workers in Various Countries of the World," in Thomas C. Desmond, *Age Is No Barrier*, New York State Joint Legislation Committee on the Aging, 1952, pp. 69-85. Statistical data are based upon *Social Security Bulletin*, April, 1953, p. 26, Table ii.

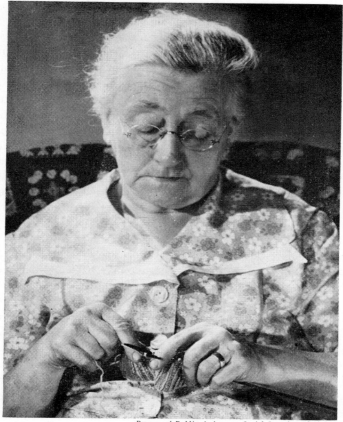

Bureau of Public Assistance, Social Security Administration
PEACEFUL RETIREMENT

monthly maximum payments, e.g., in 1952-1953 Alaska, $80; Arkansas, $50; California, $80; Illinois, $65; Michigan, $60; Minnesota, Nebraska, Nevada, and Ohio, $55; Utah, $45 for one person and $90 for two persons in one household; Wyoming, $68; and other states, $50 or $60. Some states require citizenship; others do not. In some states persons are not eligible if they are found begging, have failed to support their minor children, or have committed a felony within the past ten years. Frequently, additional payments with regard to medical needs, chronic diseases, or surgical and dental care are permitted, even when the regular maximum is exceeded.

Old-age assistance makes it possible in general for aged men and women to go on living in their own homes, either alone or with their families, and to receive regular monthly cash allowances for their maintenance. If they are unable to manage their own households they may live in boarding homes or in private homes for the aged. Most states provide that old-age assistance is paid to aged persons residing in nonprofit homes for old people, many of them under the auspices of religious or philanthropic charities or fraternal orders or lodges, if the residents have not paid for their maintenance for life, or if the standards of the home are not luxurious. Federal grants are denied to old people in such public institutions, as almshouses or county farms, but a necessary period of treatment in a hospital does not interrupt the receipt of old-age assistance. During recent years a good many county almshouses were converted into hospitals for the chronically ill, and patients over sixty-five may therefore receive old-age assistance in these medical institutions.

The state laws determine how much property and other resources an applicant for old-age assistance may have and still receive aid.[13] The amounts of property vary in the states. For example, California, which calls old-age assistance "Old Age Security," grants this aid to needy aged who own real property up to an assessed value of $3,500, and personal property of $1,200 for one person and $2,000 for a couple. Usually, transfer or assignment of property in order to qualify for old-age assistance makes such old persons ineligible for aid. Frequently residence of the last year before application and of five years within the last nine years is required. At the local welfare department the applicant receives help in filling out the required application forms and signs his statements under oath. Then a social investigation at his home is made in which the resources of the applicant and the ability of his relatives to contribute to his support are explored.[14] Emergency aid is given during this investigation if absolutely necessary. The decision by the county or city authorities is made in writing so that the applicant may request a hearing and

[13] For an analysis of the specific features in the states, see "Characteristics of State Public Assistance Plans Under Social Security Act," Federal Security Agency, Bureau of Public Assistance, Report No. 18, 1950. In our comparison, the territories—particularly Puerto Rico and Virgin Islands—have not been included because social conditions there vary widely from those on the continent.

[14] In California, in December, 1952, the medium time elapsed between the signing of the application for old-age assistance and the payment was 62.8 days.

reconsideration if he is not satisfied. He is entitled to attend the hearing and to be represented by an attorney, and he may appeal to a commission or board of the State Department of Social Welfare for another hearing and a final decision. Court suit is usually possible only if the applicant feels himself aggrieved by misinterpretation of the law.

Old-age assistance payments beyond the federal share are paid either by the states in full or partly by counties and cities. (For example, in California the state pays six-sevenths, the county one-seventh of the remaining cost.) Payments are made without discrimination. The federal and state administrations encourage the preservation of the client's self-respect, dignity, self-reliance, and of his feeling of being a useful "senior citizen"—at least in theory—but the lack of well-trained personnel sometimes causes failure to live up to these principles.

Each state designates an authority which has to establish and maintain standards for the types of public and private institutions in which recipients of old-age assistance may live. This supervision shall eliminate such inadequate conditions in nursing and convalescent homes as poor service, untrained personnel, fire hazards, and lack of proper medical and dietary care.

B. AID TO THE BLIND

The second categorical assistance program for which the federal government shares expenses with the states is aid to the needy blind. State laws determine which persons are considered "blind," and the designation is usually totally blind or with an impairment of sight which prevents competitive industrial work.[15] A practical definition of "needy blind" is presented in an Oregon statute: "an individual whose vision is so defective as to prevent the performance of ordinary activities for which eyesight is essential." The states also decide whether this category shall be limited to a minimum and maximum age, for example, over sixteen years, and sometimes under sixty-five. In the beginning of 1953 over 98,000 persons received aid to needy blind in the United States. The average monthly payments differed from a maximum of $85.96 in California to a minimum of $28.06 in

[15] Missouri and Pennsylvania administer special pension plans for the blind; Nevada, a limited assistance plan without federal grants.

Alabama, with a total average of $53.55 per month. Average payments in Washington were $83; in Minnesota, $59; in Oregon, $72; in Illinois, $49; in Pennsylvania, $49; in New York, $67. Only a few states require citizenship,[16] but a number require residence, as in old-age assistance, for persons who became blind outside of the state. In order to receive federal grants, states may not specify more stringent residence requirements than five years out of the last nine in the state, of which the year immediately preceding the application is one. The procedure of application is the same as in old-age assistance. The states decide in their legislation how much property and other resources a person may have in order to receive aid to the blind. Fifty dollars monthly earned income is disregarded in determining the need of the blind person and of other recipients of public assistance in the family. An applicant for aid to the blind is examined by a medical eye specialist (ophthalmologist) or an optometrist, and federal grants are used for the remuneration for their services to the blind.

A few states have set up special state-financed programs in order to encourage blind persons to become self-supporting. An example is the California program of Aid to Partially Self-Supporting Blind Residents which encourages blind persons to achieve self-support by establishing themselves in business, farming, regular trade, employment in industry or commerce, or the operation of a vending stand. This is done by permitting them to earn up to $1,000 a year without reducing their standard monthly aid of $85.

In many states additional services for the prevention of blindness are provided for, such as free medical examination and treatment, special education of children in schools for the blind or classes for visually handicapped children, usually under the auspices of the state department of education. Rehabilitation services render occupational counseling, vocational guidance, and training for employment or special trades, such as for piano tuning, broom making, handicrafts, or professional work. Rehabilitation services are administered by a State Bureau of Vocational Rehabilitation, which serves the blind as well as other handicapped people. Federal grants-in-aid for rehabilitation work are allocated by the Department of Health, Education and Welfare, Office of Vocational Rehabilitation on the

16 District of Columbia, Indiana, Iowa, North Dakota, and Texas; source of data *Social Security Bulletin*, April, 1953, p. 26, Table 12.

basis of the *Barden-La Follette Act* (Vocational Rehabilitation Act) of 1943. Rehabilitation includes medical treatment, surgery, hospital care, artificial appliances, adult training centers, placement services, and assistance in providing occupational equipment. Federal grants-in-aid for the needy blind may be used for medical care to remove cataracts by surgery or to conserve vision in cases of glaucoma. Earlier and more effective medical treatment, including eye surgery, is unfortunately still a goal far from being generally achieved for persons with limited means who might be saved from blindness.

Private organizations play an important role in supplementing the services for the blind offered under public auspices. Some of them strengthen educational and rehabilitation work for the blind. Since 1921 the American Foundation for the Blind in New York has served as coordinating agency for all nationwide interests of the blind. In all states, local private groups of the blind and organizations interested in helping the blind are making valuable contributions in the field of social and recreational life of the blind. They assist them in finding employment and organizing cultural and recreational activities, and pioneering in new adventures for the blind. They promote a better understanding of the public for the needs of the blind and of the importance of more adequate services and legislation for them.

C. AID TO THE PERMANENTLY AND TOTALLY DISABLED

The Amendment to the Social Security Act of 1950 added a new public assistance category for permanently, totally disabled persons in economic need. Until this time, many of them had been meagerly supported by counties and cities under general relief provisions without help from state or federal funds. The new category includes adults over eighteen years who have serious physical or mental handicaps; children and adolescents under eighteen years are not cared for under this category. The Social Security Act does not give a definition of "permanently and totally disabled" but allows the states to define the terms and the conditions of need which entitle one to apply for this categorical aid. The program provides either money payments to adult, invalid persons under sixty-five who are not eligible for old-age assistance, or medical and remedial care for them.

The group of persons under this category consists mainly of people who suffer from physical or mental impairment, which in medical judgment offers no indication of a substantial improvement, and which prevents the invalid person from gainful employment, from independent work for profit, and from normal homemaking. The program, however, is not limited to completely helpless people. Economic assistance to these disabled persons resembles the aid to needy blind people. Standards of assistance and special requirements in the states vary. In general, the administration is carried out by the state and local agencies which also are in charge of the other categorical assistance programs, such as the department of social welfare. The average payment, in August, 1953, in this category of 184,768 recipients was $53 per month per person, slightly less than average aid for the needy blind. It is hoped that medical care and rehabilitation for these invalids will be intensified by more adequate financial support with the help of federal grants-in-aid for this group. Now the categorical assistance may be used for cash payments, remedial care, hospitalization, and medical treatment. The physicians and hospitals may be paid directly by the welfare authorities in behalf of the patients.

In its present form the categorical assistance for disabled needy persons is given to persons who have some physical or mental impairment, disability (such as arthritis, heart disease or paralysis) or a loss of a limb that substantially precludes them from engaging in useful occupations within their competence. The element of disability depends partly on medical findings and partly upon the social and emotional ability of the individual to carry out his responsibilities, for example, as a wage-earner or homemaker. A permanent mental or physiological impairment, confirmed by medical statement, may exist from birth or may be later acquired by illness or accident. It must be permanent (a condition likely to continue for life) and not likely to improve or disappear spontaneously unless special remedial or therapeutic measures are applied. The possibility of recovery or of vocational rehabilitation does not prohibit categorical aid for the disabled person. According to a 1953 statement of the Secretary of Health, Education and Welfare, there are two million physically handicapped persons in the United States who need rehabilitation in order to work; among this number are many permanently and totally disabled in economic need. In 1954, forty-two states and territories had established this type of public assistance.

Students of social economics and professional associations of social workers have suggested, for many years, that Congress create a permanent disability insurance program against the risk of invalidity. But in 1950 Congress decided to limit the help for invalids to a categorical program of public assistance for needy disabled persons only. This program seems no substitute for a disability insurance plan which would protect the entire population against the risk of permanent disability.

D. AID TO DEPENDENT CHILDREN

Destitute children have always constituted a large proportion of the poor. In Colonial times they were indentured or placed in foster families; during the nineteenth century, they were brought into almshouses and later into orphan asylums until criticism of institutional care again led to the wider use of boarding homes, particularly in rural families. The first White House Conference in 1909 endorsed the principle that children should be helped to remain in their own homes whenever possible and should not be removed for economic reasons. Their mothers should receive "mothers allowances" or "pensions" so that they would not have to give their children to institutions while they worked as domestics or in factories. Out of this tenet grew the program of Aid to Dependent Children as a categorical form of public assistance under the Social Security Act. The Social Security Act's definition of a dependent child is "a child under 18 years of age who has been deprived of parental support or care by reason of the death, continued absence from the home, or physical or mental incapacity of the parent, and who is living with his father, mother, brother, sister, grandmother, grandfather, stepmother, stepfather, stepbrother or stepsister, uncle or aunt in a place of residence maintained by one or more of such relatives." This does not include all needy children. It excludes orphans who have no close relatives and, therefore, cannot live with them, and who are placed in foster families or in children's institutions; the law does not grant federal aid for the maintenance of such children.[17]

[17] The number of full orphans is rather small. Many of them are adopted either by relatives or by other adoptive parents; full orphans, therefore, are only an insignificant proportion of all needy children.

Children over sixteen years of age receive this aid only if they are not earning their living because they regularly attend school. The payment is usually made to the mother or to the relative who takes care of the child. Upon application, aid has to be given with reasonable promptness. The time which elapses between application and payment of aid differs among the states.

In order to receive federal grants, the states cannot impose a residence requirement of more than one year or any special county residence for aid to dependent children.[18] The states determine in their laws and regulations the requirements for eligibility to receive ADC (Aid to Dependent Children) and how much shall be paid. Frequently the need of the child is caused by the desertion of the father; many statutes require a certain period of absence. Usually aid is given on a standard budget basis which considers the elementary needs of the child and of the mother or the caretaker with regard to local conditions. On January 1, 1953 the average payment was $82 per family and $23 per recipient, but these payments varied greatly between the states. The lowest average payment per family in Mississippi with $27 per month contrasted with the highest average of $123 in Washington. The lowest monthly average payment per recipient of $7.17 in Missouri differed substantially from the highest average of $37.17 in California.[19] The proportion of the entire child population receiving aid also varies between 1.1 per cent in New Jersey to 7.8 per cent in Louisiana. Only one-fifth of the children receiving help under this program, in 1951, lost their fathers through death; in about one-fourth of the cases the fathers were insane, crippled, chronically ill, or committed to prison; and in the cases of more than one-half of these dependent children, the father had deserted the family, or was divorced and did not support the child.

Aid to dependent children is not the only social security program to help needy children. An increasing number of children receive support under Old-Age and Survivors Insurance and some under Workmen's Compensation laws,[20] but at present ADC supports a

[18] All states but Nevada have federal-state plans for dependent children, and Puerto Rico and the Virgin Islands receive federal grants based upon the 1950 Amendment of the Social Security Act.
[19] *Social Security Bulletin*, April, 1953, p. 27, Table 13.
[20] See Chapter 9.

Courtesy National Child Labor Committee
CHILDREN IN A MIGRATORY LABOR CAMP

larger number than all other measures through which children receive economic aid.[21]

Whenever aid to dependent children is given to a child who has been abandoned by a parent, the state agency has to report the case promptly to the law enforcement authority—usually the district attorney. The purpose of this regulation, added by the 1950 Amendment, is to facilitate legal action against the father who has deserted the family in order to force him to assume his financial responsibility for the support of his child. From the psychological point of view there are hardships created by this involvement of the district attorney in a categorical public assistance program. Mothers some-

[21] On January 1, 1951, 1,632,236 children and 563,076 adults received ADC payments, and 699,653 children received child or orphan benefits in the Old-Age and Survivors Insurance program; however, the respective figures on January 1, 1953 were 1,503,692 children and 506,773 adults under Aid to Dependent Children, and 950,134 children under Survivors Insurance (*Social Security Bulletin*, April, 1953, p. 22, Table 5).

times are afraid that court action may prevent their husbands from returning to the family, making them hostile and seeking divorce rather than reconciliation. On the other hand, the public resents deserting fathers relinquishing their moral and legal responsibility for the support of their children, and insists that they should be discouraged from unburdening their own obligations upon public welfare agencies. It is hoped that district attorneys will use trained social workers for the social investigations and negotiations in cases of desertion and nonsupport.

As we have seen, the federal government shares the expenses of the states for aid to dependent children and pays one-half of the total administrative cost of this program. The federal share amounts to four-fifths of the first $15 ($12) and in addition one-half of the exceeding payment up to $30 ($9), together making $21 maximum each for the first child and for his mother or another caretaker; for the second and further children to four-fifths of the first $15 ($12) and one-half of the balance up to $21 ($4.50), together making a maximum of $16.50 for each additional child under eighteen years of age.[22] The states either meet the entire residual cost for ADC[23] or divide it in various percentages between the state and local units of government (counties, cities, and townships).[24]

Since some children in economic need cannot live with relatives and have to be placed in foster families, or in orphanages or other children's institutions for which federal grants-in-aid are not available, the states support these children either in the same way as "dependent children" or under their general assistance plans. For example, California administers categorical assistance under the title "needy children" to all children who are deprived of parental support. These children live in their own families or with close relatives with the help of federal grants-in-aid. Those in other foster families or children's institutions are supported without federal assistance

---

[22] See page 237.

[23] The full residual expense for ADC is assumed by Arizona, Arkansas, District of Columbia, Florida, Hawaii, Idaho, Illinois, Kentucky, Louisiana, Mississippi, Missouri, New Hampshire, New Mexico, Oklahoma, Pennsylvania, Rhode Island, South Carolina, South Dakota, Texas, Utah, Washington, and West Virginia.

[24] Equally shared are the expenses in Alabama, Delaware, Iowa, Kansas, Minnesota, New Jersey, North Carolina, North Dakota, and Wyoming; in California and Montana, two-thirds by the state, one-third by the county.

from state and local funds; but less than seven per cent of needy children live outside of their own families.

The American Public Welfare Association conducted an interesting study in order to determine whether the program of aid to dependent children is successful in conserving the human resources of our nation upon which the future depends.[25] The results of this research show that it is necessary to expand and to improve financial assistance and social services to children and young people deprived of sufficient support by their parents. The study reveals that since the beginning of this program in 1936 more than six million children received valuable help under this federal-state system. One of its most important achievements has been the keeping together of the families and enabling the children to remain with their mothers. Through this program child neglect, illegitimate births, delinquency, and crime have occured less frequently than it would have happened in this endangered and stress-ridden group without such aid. It was found that one-fourth of the families were still in economic need when the assistance under this program had to be terminated under its legal provisions, such as age of the children, other income, and return of an absent father. But the study also proved that the assistance payments in many parts of the country are still so low that they barely reach minimum subsistence standards. The study covered 6,500 families whose receipt of aid to dependent children was terminated in 1951. It made it clear that it is very important that children are secured not only financial aid but also casework service, educational opportunities, protection of their health, and decent housing conditions.

III. GENERAL ASSISTANCE

General assistance is public relief to needy persons who are not eligible for one of the four categorical public assistance programs or whose needs are not sufficiently met by them. Among the recipients of general assistance are young and old, children and adults, handicapped and sick people. The rigid limitations of our public assistance categories which are analyzed above explain why numerous persons are not encompassed by this categorical approach; general

[25] Gordon M. Blackwell and Raymond F. Gould, *Future Citizens All* (Chicago: American Public Welfare Association, 1952).

assistance, as a rule, is their only recourse. The principles of restriction of public assistance, such as legal settlement, family responsibility, requirement of exhaustion of all resources and savings, which we have discussed, apply to general assistance even more rigidly than to the categories of public assistance. One reason for this practice is the fact that general assistance is financed more than any other economic relief program by the cities, townships, or counties which have the weakest tax power.[26] In other states the cost of general assistance is shared between the state and the community or county, frequently the state paying one-half or more of the expenses. In only ten states was the entire financial burden of general assistance in 1952 met by the state without a contribution from the communities and counties.[27] Since the federal government does not share the cost of general assistance, the poorer states and communities are inclined to spend as little as possible for the recipients of this type of aid.

The uneven treatment of the persons in need under general assistance in the various states is characterized by the following facts: In June, 1952, 293,000 families were supported by general assistance with an average of 2.1 persons per family and an average monthly payment of $45.95. This average monthly payment per family varied between the states from $12.79 in Mississippi to $73.32 in New York. Other examples of California with $46.39, Minnesota with $46.56, Wisconsin with $54.29, and Washington with $54.21 show that local cost of living alone cannot explain the difference between the highest and lowest standards in the various states.[28]

"Work-relief" may sometimes still be required as a condition for the receipt of general assistance, although it is seldom applied even when state and local statutes authorize this method of determining the willingness of an applicant to work. The assignment of "relief clients" to useless types of work, such as leaf raking and wood piling, is rare today.

In some states, the administration of general assistance is integrated into the public assistance program at the local level; in other

---

26 In 1954, the entire financial burden of general assistance in fifteen states was laid on the counties or other local authorities.

27 A. Geddes and C. Hawkins, *op. cit.*, p. 403.

28 See *Social Security Bulletin*, September, 1952, p. 24, Table 17.

states, it is still administered separately. Whenever the state pays the entire cost or shares the expenses for general assistance, the state welfare agency sets the standards of the program, supervises the administration, or carries it out itself. Where no financial aid for general assistance is given to community or county, the local authority determines the methods and form of general assistance, sometimes still using relief in kind, by vouchers or tickets, which is no longer permitted in categorical assistance. Frequently persons who seem employable are denied relief in order to force them to work regardless of whether or not a job is in fact available, and the spending of the last penny often is required before county or township might give help under general assistance.

General assistance has been called "a patchwork" because each state handles it in a different way, and principles, standards, administration, and financing vary even within the counties and cities of the same state.[29] Frequently the treatment of needy persons depends upon the local community in which they fall sick or find themselves unemployed without the protection of unemployment insurance. For many years the professional associations in social work have advocated that the federal government share the expenses for general assistance as a special category or combine all public assistance categories into one which would be supported by grants-in-aid of the federal government. But Congress and the conscience of the people have not, as yet, been ready to translate this proposal into reality. There is still too much suspicion that an unemployed, able-bodied person asks for relief because of willful idleness, whereas he could find a job and support himself and his family. The public is afraid that public assistance might be made too easy, and too generous, and the anxiety of the taxpayers that their burden might be still heavier is understandable in a time of high taxes. Despite these facts, however, the need for integration of all types of public assistance into one unified program, administered by the same

[29] Marietta Stevenson, "Public Welfare," *Social Work Yearbook, 1949,* pp. 411, 412. In 1952, seven states did not require a specific time of residence as condition for an application for general assistance. Two states required six months of residence, twenty-six states required one year of residence, four states two years of residence, eight states three years of residence, one state four years of residence, and five states required five years of residence (American Public Welfare Association, *Public Welfare Directory, 1952,* pp. 342-350).

agency, and staffed with trained social workers remains a goal which cannot be given up.

IV. CASEWORK IN PUBLIC ASSISTANCE

Until the period of the Depression of the 1930's it had been questioned whether public relief agencies were able to provide suitable casework service. At that time most poor law authorities employed untrained personnel, although their supervisors were partly professional social workers. Many relief workers attempted to help the applicants, but the official policy in many poor law offices was to discourage people from applying for public assistance, and to disregard their needs beyond financial support. Since the changes in public welfare during the Depression, however, which we discussed in Chapter 5, methods and skills of casework have been utilized in public welfare agencies in a steadily increasing measure. Even today many county welfare departments rely upon nonprofessional personnel in the administration of their assignments, but the number of such agencies slowly decreases, and more professionally trained social workers are employed. The basic philosophy of public assistance agencies is also undergoing progressive change. It is more and more recognized that public assistance is rendered to persons in need as a right, not as a "handout" of a "benevolent" worker, and that the material help granted to people in financial distress often requires an understanding of the applicant in his entire personal, economic, and social conditions, his feeling about asking for assistance, and his fear of humiliation by this situation.[30] Casework in public assistance agencies attempts to avoid pauperization of the client, so that he does not become permanently dependent upon public relief, but tries to make use of his own resources in order to maintain himself again. The large case load of most public assistance agencies and the pressure of work in the investigation of legal data for eligibility require different methods in casework from those applied in a private family welfare or child care agency

---

[30] An excellent analysis of the application of casework skills is presented by Professor Charlotte Towle (University of Chicago) in her *Common Human Needs, An Interpretation for Staff in Public Assistance Agencies* (Chicago: University of Chicago Press, 1945). This is recommended for reading on this subject. See also Kermit T. Wiltse, *Casework in Public Assistance* (Sacramento: California State Department of Social Welfare, 1952).

with a small case load for each worker. The basic principles of case-work, however, which we discussed in Chapter 6, remain the same for private and for public agencies.[31] The personal needs of the individual client have to be considered as well as the preservation of his dignity and self-respect, which are essential to his rehabilitation. Jane Hoey characterized the work in public assistance as follows:[32]

The central purpose of a public assistance program is to assure adequate money payments to each eligible individual promptly and in a constructive manner, so that his legal rights are protected, his self-respect and dignity as a person are maintained and strengthened, and so that he may live in the community in the same way as other individuals.

The caseworker in a public welfare agency has to be sincerely convinced of the fact that an individual in economic need has a rightful claim on society for public assistance. By explaining clearly legal requirements and the policy of the agency, the worker will then be able to help the client present the necessary data and facts for establishing "eligibility" for public assistance. This has to be done in a way which expresses the confidence of the worker in the client and her respect for him, rather than using a hostile attitude which tries to prevent the client from getting aid. The worker has to understand how vitally important money is for everyone in financial stress in our society. In general, clients come to social agencies in times of want and anxiety, and they often are emotionally disturbed. They naturally are more sensitive to their treatment than the average citizen, and they react differently to the kind of approach used by the caseworker.

Casework in public welfare, therefore, requires professional skills. The caseworker in his job must have: (1) skill in personal interviewing; (2) skill in establishing a positive, constructive relationship with the client; (3) training in perception and observation of human beings and interpreting documents; (4) ability to distinguish be-

[31] Grace F. Marcus, "The Nature of Service in Public Assistance Administration," Federal Security Agency, Washington, D. C., 1945; and Rosa Wessel (editor), *Method and Skill in Public Assistance* (Philadelphia: Pennsylvania School of Social Work, 1938).

[32] Edith B. Elmore, "The Public Assistance Job," *Tennessee Public Welfare Record*, Vol. XIV, No. 3, March, 1951, p. 44; see also K. Wiltse, *op. cit.*, which describes the constructive possibilities in rehabilitation by skillful case-work.

tween pertinent facts that are essential for the application and confidential, casual, personal information not needed for the decision
on assistance or service in which the client is interested; (5) skill
in recognizing distress and emotional unbalance, which requires
help from such other sources as a mental hygiene clinic; (6) skill in
technical administration, communication, recording, and reporting;
(7) ability to comply with the prescribed policy and procedure of
the agency; (8) awareness of the client's social, health, and personal
needs and ability to encourage the client to use other community
resources by referral; (9) ability to evaluate the policy and practice
of the agency regarding its effect in fulfilling its legal obligation;
(10) ability to plan and organize his own work load efficiently; and
(11) ability to accept and use supervision with intelligence in the
interest of the client.[33] In the framework of these activities the professional relationship between the worker and the client remains of
greatest importance.

Although the establishing of eligibility, the provision of financial
assistance, and the observation of continued eligibility are primary
functions of the worker in public assistance, they are not the only
aspects to which the worker has to give attention. He also has to
be aware of personal needs in which the client may require help.
This may be illustrated by the two following cases:

An old-age assistance applicant refers to dizzy spells as a reason for
decreasing ability to support himself by odd jobs. In discussing his needs,
he does not mention medical care. He has not been in the habit of consulting a doctor and, in his losing struggle to remain independent, he has
neither the energy nor the freedom of mind to consider his health. When
the worker asks whether he has gone or wishes to go to a doctor, his
response is casual and indifferent. He must straighten out his financial
affairs before he can attend to anything else. The worker's responsibility,
however, is to let him know that the agency does take care of medical
needs or that it can refer him to a source that does provide them, if and
when he so desires.

A father applies for aid to dependent children on the eve of going to
a hospital for an indefinite period. He explains that he should have gone
a year ago, and that he is still uncertain about remaining any length of
time. Neither he nor his wife can bear the thought of his separation from
the family. The worker realizes that it is important to discuss the possibility of the family's visiting him at the hospital and the possible need
for money for transportation. She also notes the father's anxiety about

[33] E. Elmore, *op. cit.*, pp. 44-45.

the welfare of his wife and children. The interview is planned to provide him with opportunity to satisfy himself that in his absence both he and his wife can count on the agency for practical consideration of need and a reliable interest in enabling the wife to meet it.[34]

Both examples show that financial needs of clients often are connected with emotional and psychological questions beyond the payment of money. In larger cities, public assistance agencies may refer difficult problems of this nature to private family welfare or child welfare agencies if the client is willing to consult them.

However, in rural areas frequently no private social agencies are available for casework services, so that the county welfare department is the only source of help for the client. The caseworker in the urban public agency needs to have accurate knowledge of the services and policies of the agencies in the community, in order to refer clients who will receive more effective aid to another social agency if they want to request its help. The caseworker in public assistance has to be careful not to use the client's economic helplessness to force upon him an undesired change in attitude or way of life, even if the worker is convinced that such change is in the interest of the client or of his family. If the caseworker acts upon request of an authoritative agency, such as a court, a parole board, or a youth authority, the source of any specific request has to be clearly explained to the client.

Several state welfare laws require the departments of social welfare to study the causes of dependence of the needy and to encourage them to support themselves, if possible. In order to achieve this goal, social workers of public welfare agencies have to make and to carry out plans for the rehabilitation of needy persons so that they may cease to be a charge of the community.[35] Unfortunately, however, state budgets often do not provide the funds for an adequate staff to carry out this assignment, nor for salaries which are sufficient to attract professionally trained personnel. Public welfare workers are frequently required to have a car. Their starting salary in some states is as low as $200 a month, an amount completely out of line and far below what is offered for work in industry or other

[34] Grace F. Marcus, *The Nature of Service in Public Assistance Administration* (Washington, D. C. Federal Security Agency, 1946), p. 21.

[35] As an example, we refer to the experience of the Florida State Department of Public Welfare, Report 1951-1952, pp. 14-15.

public services requiring similar training. The heavy turnover in public welfare work resulting from such practice is detrimental to the people receiving help, but it is unavoidable as long as social workers leave their agencies for private employment, business, or other state or county positions where salaries meet present living costs.

The following case describes casework in public assistance:

THE THOMAS CASE[36]

In January 1951 the Public Welfare Department in S. received a letter from the King County Welfare Department that Mrs. Thomas had applied for assistance. It requested that we interview Mr. Thomas, the woman's husband, to ascertain whether he is able to contribute to his wife's support. The letter informed us that the Thomases have been separated for several years. Mrs. Thomas had spent two years as a patient in a state mental hospital and since her discharge had been living with her parents who supported her. Since her father had lost his job and the sole income of the family is his old-age assistance allowance, they are unable to support Mrs. Thomas who applied at the Public Welfare Department for aid. The Thomases have one child, a six year old girl, who is being supported in a foster home by Mr. Thomas.

February 1, 1951 I telephoned Mr. Thomas. After giving my name and our agency, I told him that I was calling in regard to a letter of the King County concerning his wife. His voice immediately assumed a belligerent tone, as he demanded to know what the letter was about. I replied that it concerned his wife's application for public assistance which I would like to discuss with him. He interrupted to demand to know what they expected him to do about it. I said that I thought it would be easier for both of us to discuss the matter in a personal interview rather than over the telephone. Rather grudgingly Mr. Thomas agreed that he would come to the office during his lunch hour that day.

When Mr. Thomas walked into the office at noon I noted that he was a tall, well-groomed man, probably in his early forties, who appeared worried and a bit angry. His greeting was curt, and again he demanded to know "what this is all about?". As I had expected from the telephone conversation his attitude was hostile. I felt that he thought I was trying to force him to do something he didn't want to do, and possibly that he expected me to condemn him for the fact that his wife was applying for public relief. Both hostility and defensiveness seemed inherent in his attitude. As clearly and briefly as I could, I told him of the request of the letter and explained the responsible relatives clause in general relief cases. I told him that we were interested in finding out whether or not he felt he was able and willing to contribute to his wife's support.

[36] Adapted from "Case Syllabus for Social Case Work," School of Social Welfare, University of California, pp. 4-5.

A good deal of Mr. Thomas' belligerence seemed to leave him while we talked. The defensiveness remained, however, and he said he didn't see what he could do about it. He was maintaining two households now, his own and his daughter's. Furthermore, he'd moved out to P., where his daughter lived with her foster family just to be near the girl, and it was pretty difficult getting back and forth to the city to work since he didn't have a car, and it cost a lot too. I said that I knew from the letter that he was supporting his child in a foster home, and that I recognized maintaining two households presents many problems. He replied that it won't be easy, but he was trying to do what was best for the girl. Spontaneously he went on to tell me a good deal about his daughter and the friends with whom she was living, what he paid for the girl's care, and his difficulties in meeting that obligation in past years. My part in this discussion was confined to indicating interest by asking him a few questions about the girl.

The memory of past difficulties in meeting his obligations seemed to recall the matter in question to Mr. Thomas' mind, and angrily he said that "this damn State" had certainly never done anything for him but try to get money out of him. Why, he'd only been in the state a couple of months when his wife was committed to the state hospital, and the state started charging him for her care although he'd just come out of the hospital after a serious illness, was in debt, and earning very little. I said that his wife's illness must have been hard on him too. "Rough" he exclaimed, "I'll tell the world it was . . . especially when she tried to kill me once!" His hostility toward his wife was evident, and he obviously wanted to tell me about the situation, so I simply said "Really?" and looked interested. He went on to say that he had been in the hospital when his wife became seriously disturbed, and a few days after he got out of the hospital, he woke up one night "to find her coming at me with one of my own razors!" That had been enough for him, he said; he never wanted to have anything to do with her again. But that hadn't been all. If it wasn't for her, his mother would be taking care of his girl, but she refused to do so, because his wife had threatened to kill her if she ever saw her taking care of her daughter. "She'd do it too," he added, referring to his wife.

I said that under the circumstances I could understand how he felt about his wife. "Oh hell," he said, "I know she was sick and maybe she couldn't help it. . . . But what gets me is that I can't do anything to straighten the situation out, so I can make a home and a decent life for myself and the girl." He was obviously referring to a divorce although he didn't use the word. I was surprised and said so. "Sure," he said, "I've tried everything but the lawyers tell me there isn't a thing I can do about it." He added he had attempted everything without success . . . and what sort of life did that leave him . . . living in hotels and eating in restaurants. "Maybe I'd feel differently about sending her some money if I could straighten things out," he mentioned. I said that I could see how he might feel that way. He went on to say that he didn't want charity; he'd always been able to take care of himself and his family. And he wanted to do what was right . . . he knew her family also were having a rough time. "I won't make any promises," he decided, "but I'll try and see what I can do for her."

I said that I would write to King County Welfare Department explaining what he had just told me. They would want to know about his income and expenditures and I wondered how he felt about giving me that information to send them. "That is O.K. with me," he said, and he proceeded to give the information readily. I told Mr. Thomas it was possible that King County might write directly to him but mentioned that they had requested that he send any contributions he felt he could make directly to Mrs. Thomas' residence. He replied he'd send it to his wife's father, since he never knew what she did with it when he sent her money.

As Mr. Thomas prepared to leave, I thanked him for his cooperation and for giving up his lunch hour to come to the office. "Oh, that was all right," he answered, "he'd been glad to come." As he left he said again that "he'd see what he could do about it."

This case study illustrates a simple casework interview which secures information but, at the same time, brings out feelings and ideas which have gravely bothered the client. The case does not describe what the further development in the relationship among the members of the family may be, but the interview accomplished a more objective attitude on the part of Mr. Thomas toward his wife because of a discharge of hostility in an accepting atmosphere. It might be necessary to do more intensive casework or to refer Mr. Thomas to a suitable family service agency in order to clarify his future relation to his wife and the financial arrangements for her support.

In concluding our discussion of public assistance, we might well look at the two conflicting philosophies about the best method of aiding people in financial need which we have observed in the development of public relief and in the new modern concept of public assistance. The old, traditional policy was the "punitive approach." In England and during the two first centuries of American history under the impact of Puritan theory this practice made the receipt of poor relief as unbearable and intolerable as possible, with the hope that these conditions would induce people in need to avoid asking for support, and that the humiliations connected with poor relief, the swearing of the pauper oath, and the posting of pauper lists on the market place, in church, and at the city hall would deter most indigent people from applying for poor relief. One expected they would attempt every other way, such as asking relatives and neighbors for help, accepting underpaid work and substandard labor conditions, or even begging, to sustain themselves. Recently some inclination to revive this punitive method has shown itself in the "Jenner Amendment," and legislation in twenty-three states desires to deter people in economic need from asking for assistance by opening the assistance rolls for public inspection.[37] The experience in those states has not led, so far, to any larger reduction in public assistance cases than in other states which continue to keep the names of recipients of public assistance confidential. This is evidence of the fact that the number of chiselers and swindlers of public assistance is small, and that the vast majority of recipients are in such urgent need of economic help that at the cost of their self-respect and pride they must apply for assistance, even if their name is exposed to public humiliation. There are some exceptions, such as an old, respectable man who committed suicide a few days after the state in which he lived had announced it would make the names of all assistance recipients public. Not only social workers are convinced that the punitive approach is placing an unwarranted humiliation upon human beings who are mostly in need without a personal fault, and that it will not really reduce the expense of public assistance. A well-known newspaper editor called the publication of the assistance rolls "a disgrace and a shame" at the National Conference of Social Work, in May, 1952.[38]

Other reflections of this punitive approach are the measures of some states of denying aid to dependent children of a mother whose husband has deserted her and the children, before she has exhausted all legal efforts to force support from the father. Because these measures disregard hope for the return of the father to the family, a reconciliation of the parents may be destroyed in enforcing them. Certainly there should be no encouragement of desertion in the interest of the family, the mother, and the children, but careful, conscientious counseling of the mother is needed in order to advise her about the

[37] See pages 235-236; also, Jane M. Hoey, "Our Common Goals," an address to the Home Economics Association in June, 1952, published in *Rhode Island Welfare*, Vol. XII, No. 11, November, 1952, pp. 115-122.

[38] Jane M. Hoey, *loc. cit.*, p. 116; and Margaret Greenfield, *Confidentiality of Public Association Records* (Berkeley: University of California Press, 1953), p. 25.

right efforts to induce her husband to support the children. The same experiences have been frequently made with unmarried mothers who did not want to destroy the chance of a marriage by hostile enforcement of support from the father of the illegitimate child.

In regard to the treatment of unmarried mothers, some have suggested another punitive measure: demanding the denial of economic aid to children in order to prevent the mother from promiscuous behavior. Advocates of this method seem to believe that women have been induced to become pregnant and bear illegitimate children in hope of getting from $10 to $20 a month from ADC as some states pay on an average. Social workers have found little evidence of this claim. In fact, vital statistics prove that only 3 to 4 per cent of births in our country occur out of wedlock, and about one-half of these babies are born to teen-age girls who scarcely in their adolescent status speculate about such a doubtful financial basis for their lives. Most of those women who have several illegitimate children are retarded, feeble-minded, or disturbed persons with serious personal mental problems. It also should not be overlooked that in depriving the mother of an illegitimate child of public aid, the child is hurt most.

Another hostile, punitive treatment of parents is found in the attitude of some social agencies to refuse aid because housing is not considered suitable. It is true that child welfare workers will insist that children should not be endangered by living in vermin-infested, unsanitary places whenever the parents can get better, healthier quarters. But the amounts of ADC in many states are still so low that it will be difficult for widows or unmarried mothers to avoid living in substandard housing conditions. Judges and social workers aware of the findings of child psychology do not want to take the responsibility for removing children from their mother as long as she loves the children and does not endanger them in extreme cases. Then, however, the denial of public aid leads to hunger, sickness, and suffering of the children, and to a delinquent behavior which is destructive to them and a burden to society.

Thus, the punitive approach by restrictive, harsh treatment does not produce substantial savings of assistance funds but creates deep human suffering, bitterness, delinquency, and humiliation. In contrast to this punitive attitude stands the *philosophy of rehabilitation*, or *constructive aid*. Practice of this approach has found less attention in newspapers, radio, and public discussions than the rare incidences of chiseling, abuse of public aid, and the demands for harsh treatment. Particularly important have been measures of rehabilitation for persons with physical handicaps who have been helped by vocational training, placement, and equipment to become financially self-supporting. By rehabilitation services these families are not only removed from public assistance rolls, but they gain the satisfaction of becoming respected members of their community. Often some hundred dollars spent on rehabilitation save, in the long run, thousands on relief and transform the former relief clients into happy, proud, self-supporting citizens. The same approach has been encouraged by Congress in the establishment of the categorical assistance program for disabled adults with federal grants-in-aid so that more adequate and effective medical and orthopedic treatment, vocational guidance, occupational training, and psychological and social casework help might assist them to take care of themselves and of their families again.

In this rehabilitative approach, preventive services play an important role, because they protect vulnerable groups so that they do not become destitute, desperate, or hostile toward society. Such concept includes the establishment of reasonable standards of public aid which permit the underprivileged to live on a level of decency so that they are not threatened by hunger and cold, contagious diseases and emotional upset, and may rear their children to become responsible citizens.[39]

The future trends in public assistance depend upon two major factors: the social and economic conditions of our country and the amount of economic security granted the population under the expanded system of social insurance.[40] In times of depression and unemployment both general and categorical assistance will have to assume larger responsibility for those persons and families who find no, or insufficient, protection through unemployment insurance benefits. There are still many people who are not covered by insurance schemes—casual workers, migratory labor, and other unprotected groups. The categorical assistance to totally and permanently disabled is not yet operating in many states and leaves numerous disabled citizens who suffer from disabling diseases which are not

[39] *Ibid.*, pp. 119-122; K. Wiltse, *op. cit.*, pp. 28-35.
[40] See Chapter 9.

permanent to general assistance. Thus a substantial responsibility remains with the public assistance program to protect people against destitution and to help them to become self-supporting again as much as their health and capacities permit.

SELECTED BIBLIOGRAPHY

*Abbott, Edith, *Public Assistance*, Vol. I. Chicago: University of Chicago Press, 1940.
*Abbott, Grace, *From Relief to Social Security*. Chicago: University of Chicago Press, 1941.
Ashton, Elma H., *Money-Giving in Social Work Agencies—In Retrospect and in Prospect*. Washington: Federal Security Agency, Public Assistance Report No. 11, 1947.
Blackey, Eileen, "Case Work Services in an A.D.C. Program," *The Family*, Vol. 23, No. 5, July, 1942, pp. 185-191.
*Breckinridge, Sophonisba P., *Public Welfare Administration in the United States: Select Documents*, Rev. ed. Chicago: University of Chicago Press, 1938.
Cohen, Wilbur J., "Social Security Act Amendments of 1952," *Social Security Bulletin*, Vol. 15, No. 9, September, 1952, pp. 3-9.
Cox, Cordelia, and Ella W. Reed, *Interviews and Case Studies in Public Welfare*. Chicago: American Public Welfare Association, 1945.
Elmore, Edith B., "The Public Assistance Job," *Tennessee Public Welfare Record*, Vol. XIV, No. 3, March, 1951, pp. 43-46.
Fauri, F. F., "Public Assistance," *Social Work Year Book, 1949*, pp. 370-381.
Geddes, Anne E., "The Changing Role of Old-Age Assistance," *The Social Welfare Forum, 1953*, pp. 238-249.
Gentile, Felix M., and Donald S. Howard, *General Assistance with Special Reference to Practice in 47 Localities of the United States*. New York: American Association of Social Workers, 1949.
Glassberg, Benjamin, *Across the Desk of a Relief Administrator*. Chicago: American Public Welfare Association, 1938.
Greenfield, Margaret, *Permanent and Total Disability Aid*. Berkeley: University of California, Bureau of Public Administration, 1953.
Harrison, Shelby, *Attacking on Social Work's Three Fronts*. New York: Russell Sage Foundation, 1942.
*Kurtz, Russell H. (editor), *The Public Assistance Worker; His Responsibility to the Applicant, the Community, and Himself*. New York: Russell Sage Foundation, 1938.
La Barre, Maurine (editor), *Practice of Case Work in Public Agencies*. New York: Family Welfare Association of America, 1940.
Lally, Dorothy, "The Interrelationships of Merit Systems and the Quality of Public Welfare Personnel," *National Conference of Social*

Work, Proceedings 1942, pp. 553-562. New York: Columbia University Press, 1942.

Lane, Marie Dresden, and Frances Steegmuller, *America on Relief*. New York: Hartcourt, 1938.

Linford, Alton A., "Public Assistance Categories, Yes or No?" *Social Service Review*, Vol. XXII, No. 2, June, 1948, pp. 199-210.

Loomis, Charles P., and J. Allan Beegle, *Rural Social Systems*. New York: Prentice-Hall, Inc., 1950.

Marcus, Grace F., *The Nature of Service in Public Assistance Administration*. Washington, D.C.: Federal Security Agency, Public Assistance Report No. 10, 1946.

Meriam, Lewis, *Relief and Social Security*. Washington, D.C.: Brookings Institution, 1946.

Perlman, Helen H., "Are We Creating Dependency Through Our Public Assistance Programs"? Madison: Wisconsin Welfare Council, 1951.

Russell, Elizabeth, *Professional Growth on the Job: A Guide for the Public Assistance Worker*. New York: Family Service Association of America, 1947.

Schottland, Charles J., "California Plans for Its Aging Population," *Public Welfare*, Vol. 10, No. 4, October, 1952, pp. 103-106.

Smalley, Ruth, *et al.*, *Meaning and Use of Relief in Case Work Treatment*. New York: Family Welfare Association of America, 1941.

Street, Elwood, *The Public Welfare Administrator*. New York: McGraw, 1940.

Taylor, Alice L., *Case Recording in the Administration of Public Assistance*. Washington, D.C.: Federal Security Agency, 1950.

*Towle, Charlotte, *Common Human Needs*. An Interpretation for Staff in Public Assistance Agencies. Chicago: University of Chicago Press, 1945.

Van Driel, Agnes, "Staff Development in the Public Assistance Programs," *Social Service Review*, Vol. XIV, No. 2, June, 1940, pp. 224-236.

Weaver, Mary S., "Improving Services to the Permanently and Totally Disabled," *Social Welfare Forum, 1952*, pp. 144-157.

Wessel, Rosa (editor), "Method and Skill in Public Assistance," *Journal of Social Work Process*, December, 1938.

Wiltse, Kermit T., *Social Casework in Public Assistance: Testing Method and Skill Applied to a Selected Case Load*. Sacramento: California Department of Social Welfare, 1952.

*Witmer, Helen Leland, *Social Work: An Analysis of a Social Institution*, pp. 211-245. New York: Farrar & Rinehart, 1942.

9. Social Insurance

Social security in our American form of democratic government is based upon three types of services: (1) a program of *social insurance*, which primarily aims to establish a minimum standard of health and decency by providing insurance against the loss of earning capacity; (2) a program of *public assistance* to aid persons in individual economic need; and (3) a program of *welfare and health services* devised to prevent ill health and maladjustment and to meet individual and social needs. In this chapter we shall discuss only the first of these three forms of services—social insurance.

The historical background of social insurance is found in the functions of the medieval craft and merchant guilds beginning in the twelfth century. They organized among their members mutual aid societies, based upon the exercise of the same occupation, which provided benefits in cases of severe sickness and invalidity of their members, and burial expenses and pensions to widows and orphans after the member's death, in return for regular contributions to the fund. What the required contributions lacked in accuracy of actuarial precision was compensated by the warm and sympathetic spirit in the benevolent administration of the funds by fellow members in small, closely knit societies.

In the industrial age of the nineteenth century, a more comprehensive system of governmental social insurance was first established in Germany under Chancellor Bismarck. The program included sickness and maternity insurance (1883), workmen's compensation (1884), and old-age and invalidity insurance (1889). In England, workmen's compensation was enacted in 1897, and unemployment and health insurance was established by the National Insurance Act of 1911.[1]

---

[1] For the social significance of the social insurance system in England and its recent modern development, see Chapters 2 and 3.

I. THE NATURE OF SOCIAL INSURANCE

The mutual aid societies of the guilds preserved their members from destitution and from the humiliation of charity or pauper relief. Modern programs of social insurance were established in order to protect the insured workers against the greatly increased contingencies of life in an industrial society: unemployment, old-age dependency, industrial accidents, sickness, disability, and death of the breadwinner. Social insurance protection is based upon statutory provisions which determine precisely which persons are eligible, the conditions under which benefits are to be paid as a matter of legal right, and the amount and nature of these benefits. As in the practice of commercial insurance, the risk of loss of income or catastrophic expenses is spread by social insurance over large groups of people and over long periods of time. The few persons who suffer these losses in a given year could not meet this risk from their own means or providence. Social insurance benefits are financed either entirely or in part by contributions of the insured persons, by their employers in their behalf, or by both, so that the beneficiaries have a legal as well as an economic and moral claim to the benefits when the contingency occurs. Eligibility and benefits are predictable. Social insurance benefits are a legal right of the insured person without regard to his personal economic need or financial situation; no means test may be required in order to qualify the insured for benefits. The claim for social insurance is based upon former work of the insured person, whether independent or employed, not upon individual financial indigence. The insured or his survivors may use the benefits as they please. This fact implies that the claimants of social insurance benefits are less subject to the discretion of the agencies which administer the social insurance plan[2] than are the applicants for public assistance. As a social institution, social insurance provides income security on the basis of presumptive need, not of demonstrated want, and its benefits are determined by the principle of

[2] See Eveline M. Burns, *The American Social Security System* (Boston: Houghton, 1949), pp. 28-39; and William Haber and Wilbur J. Cohen, *Readings in Social Security* (New York: Prentice-Hall, Inc., 1948), pp. viii-xii.

average, common necessities of life rather than individual poverty.[3]

In cases of special, increased personal needs, social insurance benefits may have to be supplemented by public assistance payments.

Another difference between social insurance and public assistance is the method of financing. At least, in the United States social insurance is financed exclusively by the insured persons and their employers (but in many foreign systems taxes supplement these contributions), whereas public assistance is financed by taxes. Social insurance uses an actuarial base for determining contributions and benefits, but the operational principles of private, commercial insurance and nonprofit social insurance in this respect are not the same. Social insurance benefits in the United States and those other countries which do not apply a flat-rate system are related to the previous work and earnings of the insured. In public assistance this element is without importance, and merely the individual want of the applicant is considered.

Social insurance has been preferred to public assistance because social insurance recipients maintain a feeling of self-earned rights, independence, and self-reliance; they have built up social insurance funds by their own work; no connection with charity or poor relief exists; and the receipt of social insurance benefits does not impair their social status, the respect of their neighbors, nor any citizen's rights. From the standpoint of administration, social insurance provides income security under simple procedure without the requirement of detailed, individual social-economic investigation, because the benefits are not dependent upon personal want of the insured. It reduces the number of people who are in individual poverty and have to depend upon public assistance payments. In general, the principle of social insurance as a sound system of necessary basic economic protection against the dangers inherent in an industrial society is recognized in most countries of the world.

In the United States, the ideals of private enterprise and individual initiative, as well as the fear of government interference and of the

---

[3] E. Burns, *op. cit.*, pp. 30-32, 35-36; Karl de Schweinitz, *People and Process in Social Security* (Washington: American Council on Education, 1948), pp. 13-17; Arthur J. Altmeyer, "The Future of Social Security in America," *Social Service Review*, Vol. XXVII, No. 3, September, 1953, pp. 251-268; Donald S. Howard, "Current Issues in Social Security," *Social Security in 1953* (Columbus: National Conference of Social Work, 1953), pp. 13-16; and Carl T. Curtis, "Which Way Old Age Security?" *ibid.*, pp. 3-12, and "Some Basic Issues in Our Social Security Program," *Social Welfare Forum, 1953,* pp. 71-79.

financial burden of insurance taxes, have long delayed the introduction of social insurance. The first social insurance legislation,
which started on a state basis in 1910 in our country, was workmen's compensation for the protection of workers who were injured or killed by industrial accidents and for their families. The
Social Security Act of 1935 established old-age insurance as a federal
social insurance program and unemployment compensation as a federal-state program. Special social insurance systems have been created
for railroad workers and employees, including unemployment, disability, maternity, and retirement insurance benefits. No compulsory
health insurance and maternity insurance program has been enacted
in the United States nor any permanent disability or invalidity insurance which are operating in many countries.

The basic principle of social security itself, however, has been
fully accepted with the enactment of the Social Security Act and all
its amendments by both political parties in our country. President
Eisenhower confirmed this general conviction in his statement that
the premise of social security is a proper concern of the federal government, and that the social security program furnishes, on a national
scale, the opportunity for our citizens to build the foundations for
their security.

We shall discuss, first, the existing three types of social insurance
in our country—old-age and survivors' insurance and unemployment
compensation (both based upon the provisions of the Social Security
Act) and workmen's compensation established by state legislation.
Then the questions of health insurance, permanent disability insurance, and of family allowances will be taken up.

II. OLD-AGE AND SURVIVORS INSURANCE

The Old-Age and Survivors Insurance Program, created by the
Social Security Act of 1935, is the only federal and the most comprehensive social insurance system in the United States. About 86 per
cent of our population are covered, and more than six million people
already receive monthly benefits under its provisions. The purpose of
the system is to protect workers and self-employed persons and their
families against the economic hazards of old age and death. The law
provides for compulsory contributions from workers, their employers, and self-employed people throughout the period of gainful work;

and for benefits related to prior earnings to the retired, their families, and the dependent survivors after the death of the breadwinner. The original Social Security Act of 1935 protected the workers, but the Amendments of 1939 and 1950 changed the emphasis to a family basis. The covered groups were increased and benefits were made more adequate in the Amendments of 1950, 1952, and 1954, in order to compensate the insured population for a portion of the loss in income sustained in retirement or through the death of husband and father.

A. COVERAGE

Insured under old-age and survivors' insurance are workers in "covered employment," in industry, commerce, agriculture, domestic employment, federal employees not covered by special retirement systems, and self-employed persons including farm operators with yearly earnings of $400 or more. For employers and self-employed persons earnings are considered up to $4,200 a year.

The insurance coverage includes now, as a rule, most farm and domestic workers, and self-employed people, such as artisans, craftsmen, artists, store owners, businessmen, fishermen, persons employed in American firms abroad, life insurance and traveling salesmen, agent drivers, commission drivers, homeworkers, and farmers.

Excluded from coverage are (1) members of the armed forces; (2) railroad employees who receive benefits under a special plan; (3) independent farmers with net cash incomes of less than $400 a year; (4) other self-employed persons with annual incomes of less than $400; (5) specified agricultural workers, such as those employed in crude gum processing, and farm hands who are not regularly employed; (6) domestic workers who are not regularly employed; (7) a few self-employed, professional groups, mainly doctors, dentists and lawyers; (8) policemen and firemen covered by local or state retirement systems; and (9) federal civilian employees covered by staff retirement plans.[4]

Agricultural workers are covered only in regular employment, when they earn at least $100 a year for their labor from one employer for whom they have worked on a full-time basis. A frequent change of employer, therefore, makes the farm worker lose his status of regular employment. The employer has to report cash wages, to withhold

---

[4] Excluded also are certain foreign rural workers.

the worker's tax, and to pay the entire tax, but board, lodging, meals and pay in kind are disregarded.

Domestic servants are covered if they are paid cash wages of $50 or more by one single employer during one calendar quarter. Thus, a cleaning woman who works one full day a week for each of a number of employers is not "regularly employed" and is only protected if she receives from one employer at least $50 in a calendar quarter. For those domestic servants who are covered, the law permits that the husband of the employing couple add the domestic servant in his home to the social security report for his commercial employees in his business. Otherwise, the housewife reports the income of the domestic worker on a simple form to the Director of Internal Revenue. Casual domestic work is not included.

Professional self-employed persons who are excluded from the coverage under Old-Age and Survivors Insurance mainly at the demand of their own professions are lawyers, physicians, dentists, osteopaths, veterinarians, optometrists, Christian Science practitioners and related medical groups.

Voluntary Insurance. Several groups of employees are not compulsorily insured but may be covered by voluntary arrangements: ministers and members of religious orders, public servants in state and local government, and employees of non-profit organizations. Agreements have to be made with the Department of Health, Education, and Welfare.

1. Ordained ministers of all creeds and members of religious orders employed by nonprofit organizations may be insured under old-age and survivors' insurance if they elect to be covered. The ministers have self-employed status and pay contributions of one and one-half times the rate of an employee.

2. State, county, and city employees (other than policemen and firemen) may be insured under old-age and survivors' insurance through voluntary agreements between the state and the federal government if a majority of the employees vote in a referendum and a majority of the voting members favor coverage under social insurance. No referendum is required by public servants not covered by a retirement plan.

3. Other employees of nonprofit organizations, such as schools, hospitals, churches, social agencies, foundations for scientific, literary, educational or charitable purposes, who earn at least $50 a calender

quarter, may be insured under the following conditions: The employing organization voluntarily elects to insure its employees, to pay its portion of the contribution, to deduct the employees' share of the tax, and to pay the entire contribution; and at least two-thirds of the employees vote in favor of coverage. Only those members of the present staff who voted in favor of the insurance at an election are insured, but new workers engaged by the nonprofit organization are covered on a compulsory basis after the coverage of the employees has been certified.

Professor Eveline Burns illustrated at the National Conference of Social Work in 1951 how rather complicated this system operates in the case of social workers.[5] They are not protected if they work for a social agency which does not wish to pay taxes, but they are covered if the agency is willing to do so and two-thirds of the staff members desire to be insured. They are not covered by old-age insurance if a two-thirds majority is not obtained or if they belong to a minority that voted against coverage. Social workers are insured if they join the staff of an agency which has already secured coverage for its employees. If they work for a public welfare agency which does not want to insure its staff, they are not covered. But they are insured, if the public welfare agency is willing to insure its staff and secure a state agreement to this end. Workers engaged in private social work practice are covered as self-employed persons if earning over $400 a year.

B. ELIGIBILITY

Insurance status is acquired by a certain period of work with a minimum income. Employed and self-employed workers are classified according to the length of their work into two groups—the fully insured and the currently insured. "Fully insured" is a worker who on retirement at sixty-five years of age, or later, or at time of death, had worked either one-half of the calendar quarters (three month periods beginning January 1, April 1, July 1, or October 1) since December 31, 1950 or after reaching age twenty-one, whichever is later, but had at least six quarters of coverage, earning a minimum of $50 in each quarter. Self-employed persons under the same conditions must have had a minimum income of $100 a calendar quar-

---

[5] "Further Needs in the Social Insurances," *The Social Welfare Forum, 1951*, p. 183.

ter to be counted for fully insured status. Forty quarters of coverage make the covered person, employed or self-employed, "fully insured" for life. "Currently insured" is a person who has at least six quarters of coverage within the thirteen calendar quarters preceding his death. This enables his widow and children to receive benefits even if the deceased breadwinner was not fully insured, and had been frequently ill and unemployed. The status of being currently insured is important only for survivors; it does not suffice to secure retirement benefits for the insured person himself.

The following are examples:

(a) George Brass retired April 1, 1954 at the age of 67. He has worked as an auto mechanic most of his adult life, without any longer interruption through illness, earning monthly more than $200 all the time. He is eligible for retirement benefit because he has been employed more than one-half the calendar quarters since December 31, 1950.

(b) Glenn Sannon, a mill worker died June 17, 1954 at the age of twenty-four, due to an automobile accident. After working as a farm hand with various employers, he had been employed at the mill since February 1, 1952, earning over $50 every quarter. Glenn was born August 10, 1930; he completed his twenty-first year in 1951. His widow and his child, age fourteen months, are eligible for survivors' insurance because Glenn was currently insured by working in covered employment more than six calendar quarters during the last thirteen quarters before his death.

Eligible for insurance payments after retirement are (1) the insured person, (2) his wife if she is herself sixty-five years of age or (3) if she is younger but has in her care a child, under eighteen years, of the insured husband, and (4) a child of the insured wage earner under eighteen years of age. If the insured person is a woman, she is entitled to her own primary insurance amount, and her husband may claim benefits if he is over sixty-five, lives with his wife, and is at least half-supported by her, provided he is either not himself entitled to a primary benefit or only to one that is less than one-half of his wife's benefit.

After the death of the insured worker, the following survivors may be entitled to insurance benefits: (1) his widow aged sixty-five, or (2) his widow, who is younger but taking care of his child; (3) a divorced wife caring for a child under eighteen; (4) children under eighteen years of age; (5) a dependent widower of sixty-five years of age; and (6) dependent parents if no widow, widower, or child qualify for benefits.

The beneficiary may earn in covered employment or as a self-employed person $1,200 a year and still receive his full benefit. One month's benefit is withheld for each $80 of earning in excess of $1,-200 a year. Beneficiaries over seventy-two years of age receive their benefit even if they have higher earnings.

The claim for insurance payments ends when the retired worker under seventy-two years earns in covered employment over $100 a month or as a self-employed person renders substantial services in his own trade or business and earns in average for the year more than $100 a month. A wife or widow under sixty-five loses the right to receive benefit if she is divorced or remarried, or no longer caring for a child under eighteen; a child under eighteen loses his benefit rights by marriage.

Disabled Persons. Special provisions to preserve the benefit rights of workers who become disabled before reaching retirement age and are not already permanently insured were considered in the Amendment of 1952 and enacted in the Amendment of 1954. These provisions freeze the old-age and survivors' insurance status of the insured people during a period of extended total disability. This freeze is similar to a "waiver of premium" used in many commercial life insurance policies. It prevents the loss of the retirement and survivors' benefits of the stricken person. The individual person must be totally disabled by illness, injury, or other physical or mental impairment which is expected to be of long-continued and indefinite duration. Blindness also constitutes disability. The nature of the disability must be determined by a medical examination and must prevent the insured person from engaging in substantially gainful work. The disability must have lasted for six months before it may be considered so that temporary impairments are excluded. All efforts for the rehabilitation of the insured person are encouraged for his recovery or a substantial reduction of the symptoms of his impairment. During the period of total disability the insured is not required to have any earnings or to make contributions, and he retains the insurance status that he had acquired up to the time of his permanent disablement.[6]

[6] Fedele F. Fauri, "Recent Proposals Concerning Old Age and Survivors Insurance and Public Assistance," *Public Welfare*, Vol. 12, No. 11, April, 1954, pp. 46-49.

C. BENEFITS

The benefits to the insured person, his family, and his survivors are defined as percentages of the monthly "primary insurance amount" to which the insured person is entitled under the law. This amount may be found by two different methods. It may be determined by the average wages earned since January 1, 1937 until retirement or death, or by counting only the wages since January 1, 1951. The latter method, as a rule, is more advantageous as wages after 1950 usually were higher than those in the earlier years. This latter method must be used for persons who reach the age of twenty-two after 1950. Earnings before this age may be omitted; all other income in covered employment is added and divided by the total number of months since 1937 or 1950, or the attainment of age twenty-two. In order to raise the average amount of wages or income, particularly for newly insured persons, the four years of lowest earnings may be eliminated from the computation. If the insured has twenty quarters of coverage, a "dropout" of five years is permitted. Thus the basic income becomes higher, and retired workers do not lose benefits for periods in which their income was low.

The minimum payment to a single insured, eligible person is $30 a month; the maximum payment, $108.50 a month. The monthly primary insurance amount is found through the "benefit formula," by taking 55 per cent of the first $110 of the average monthly wage and by adding 20 per cent of the remainder up to $240.

A textile worker reaches age sixty-five in January, 1955. He claims his benefit and has earned between January, 1951 and December, 1954, in forty-eight months, $11,040. His monthly average income amounts, therefore, to $230. This monthly benefit is computed from 55 per cent of $110 = $60.50, plus 20 per cent of the remaining $120 = $24, making a total $84.50 per month.[7]

The monthly insurance benefits of the wife or of the dependent husband of a retired woman are computed as one-half of the primary insurance amount. But the minimum benefit of one survivor is $30. A single child under eighteen is entitled to three-quarters of the father's primary insurance amount, several children to an amount based upon this sum. The insurance benefits of a widow of sixty-five

[7] The benefit is computed upon the new formula enacted by the *Social Security Act Amendment of 1954.*

years, a widow with a child under eighteen, of a dependent widower and of a dependent parent are each three-quarters of the primary insurance amount. However, the total monthly payment to the family cannot be more than 80 per cent of the retired person's previous average earnings, and provided that the total family benefits shall not be reduced below one and one-half times the insured worker's primary insurance amount or $50, whichever is the greater, and no more than $200 a month as a maximum. If the percentages of the primary insurance amount exceed these limits, each dependent's payment is reduced to bring the total down to the maximum allowed. The monthly minimum payment to a family is $45. The Amendment of 1954 increased the insurance benefits of earlier retired workers and their dependents by an average amount of $6 per month.

After death of the insured person, a *lump sum* of three times the monthly primary insurance amount, but not to exceed $255, is paid for *burial expenses* to the widow or the widower or whoever paid for the funeral when no widow or widower survives.

D. FINANCING OLD-AGE AND SURVIVORS INSURANCE

The insurance plan is paid for by a contribution of the employee's wages and the self-employed person's earnings up to $4,200 a year. The employer and the employee each pay 2 per cent of the wage; the worker's part is deducted from his wage and sent together with the employer's share to the Bureau of Internal Revenue. Self-employed persons have to pay one and one-half times the rates of an employee up to $4,200 a year.

These tax rates are scheduled to increase, as follows:

Calendar year	Worker	Employer	Self-employed
1954-1959	2%	2%	3%
1960-1964	2½%	2½%	3¾%
1965-1969	3%	3%	4½%
1970-1974	3½%	3½%	5¼%
1975 and after	4%	4%	6%

The taxes are deposited in the federal Old-Age and Survivors Insurance Trust Fund whose managing trustee is the Secretary of the Treasury.

E. ADMINISTRATION

The Old-Age and Survivors Insurance Program is administered by the regional offices of the Bureau of Old-Age and Survivors Insurance of the Social Security Administration, Department of Health, Education and Welfare. The central office of the Bureau in Washington, D.C. and Baltimore maintains wage records of all insured persons, issues rules and regulations, and carries on research. The Field Operations Division of the Bureau is part of the Department, with six area offices, several hundred field offices, and over 2,000 field stations.

F. PROCEDURE

Everyone who is employed or self-employed in work covered by the Social Security Act receives a social security card. This card shows an account number under which the record of the worker's earnings is kept. No one should have more than one such card. It permits the insured person to check on his earnings and his resulting insurance rights. The card should be shown to each employer at the beginning of a job. For a lost card, a duplicate is issued by the Social Security office. If the owner of the social security card changes his name, the new name will be entered on the card under the same account number.

Before benefits can be paid, the entitled persons must file an application with the nearest social security field office, the address of which may be obtained from the post office. If the claim is denied or the applicant is dissatisfied with the benefit award, he may ask for reconsideration, or a hearing before a referee. If the applicant is still dissatisfied, he may request a review by the Appeals Council at the Social Security Administration. The decision of the Appeals Council may be contested by an action in the U.S. District Court.

G. UNSOLVED PROBLEMS

For older people, obviously, hospitalization is more frequently needed than for other age groups. The benefits under old-age and survivors' insurance are not high enough to allow the recipients to pay substantial hospital costs, and they badly need financial protection when they have to go to a hospital. In June, 1951, the Federal Security Administrator recommended the introduction of hospitalization insurance of up to sixty days a year for the recipients of old-age and survivors' benefits, including dependents of deceased insured people. Hospital benefits would be paid from the current contributions to the insurance plan without the use of general tax funds. Through a mutually acceptable schedule the expenses of hospitalization, at the request of a physician, for an insured person would be paid to the hospital out of the insurance fund. Hospital insurance within the framework of old-age and survivors' insurance would be particularly important because the recipients cannot obtain hospital insurance by private insurance companies, which do not accept people of such age or such physical conditions. Inclusion of hospital insurance would greatly enhance the emotional and social security of this group. Its costs could be met by the regular old-age and survivors' insurance contributions.[8]

The development of old-age and survivors' insurance has brought us a long way to the goal of this program: to provide protection against destitution and want for people working for a living when their income is cut off by major catastrophes in their lives. But certain aspects of this goal for all citizens have not been considered yet. If death of the breadwinner and old-age retirement constitute inevitable risks to personal and family security, so does the risk of long-term or permanent disability, which requires premature retirement. The want of the disabled person and his family is not different from that insured by old-age insurance.[9] The most critical deficiency is the lack of a social insurance program for meeting medical and maternity care costs, particularly the expenses for hospitalization.

In 1954, about 90 per cent of civilian workers in our country were under one or the other retirement protection. Eighty per cent were covered by old-age and survivors' insurance, and almost one-fifth of them had still some supplementary security under industrial, private annuity plans, which we shall discuss in Chapter 17.

III. UNEMPLOYMENT INSURANCE

A. CONCEPT AND ORGANIZATION

Unemployment has been called the scourge of modern industrial society. Through enforced idleness of millions of citizens it has

---

[8] Federal Security Agency, "Background Statement on Old Age and Survivors Hospitalization Insurance," June 25, 1951; the Amendment of 1954 has not acted upon this recommendation.

[9] Oscar C. Pogge, "Old Age and Survivors Insurance—The 1950 Amendments," *Social Casework*, Vol. XXXII, March, 1951, pp. 100-101; Arthur J. Altmeyer, *Your Stake in Social Security* (New York: Public Affairs Committee, 1954), pp. 5-7, and 13.

caused widespread deprivation. The idea of unemployment insurance is to secure an income to replace wages when they are interrupted by loss of employment. Insurance payment is secured for a defined period only, and in instances where loss of employment has occurred through no fault of the worker. At the same time, unemployment insurance attempts to reduce the period of unemployment by the procurement of jobs through public employment services.

When the Social Security Act established unemployment insurance in 1935, our country had just passed through an economic depression with its high rates of unemployment and severe suffering. Different than the federal program of old-age and survivors' insurance, "unemployment insurance" or "unemployment compensation" was established as a federal-state system. The federal law induced all states to adopt unemployment compensation laws by the so-called "tax offset device." This means that the Social Security Act levied everywhere a tax of 3 per cent of the payroll on employers of eight or more workers for wages up to $3,000 a year who were employed twenty weeks a year (except certain types of employment). The Amendment of the Social Insurance Act of 1954 extended the coverage to firms hiring four or more workers. Whenever a state employment insurance law has been approved, 90 per cent of the federal tax is credited to the state unemployment insurance fund, and becomes available for unemployment benefits in this state. Under these circumstances all states enacted unemployment compensation laws because without a law employers would have had to pay the federal tax, without possibility of a tax reduction, and the unemployed in their state would not have benefited. For the approval of a state unemployment compensation law, the following requirements have to be met: (1) All benefits must be paid through public employment offices; (2) taxes must be deposited into the Unemployment Trust Fund, which is administered by the Secretary of the Treasury; (3) the funds must be used only for unemployment compensation; (4) benefits must not be denied for refusal to accept work made available by a strike, lockout, or labor dispute, or for refusal of substandard wages; and (5) nobody must be forced to join a company union or to join or to resign from a labor union.

B. LEGISLATION AND ADMINISTRATION

All states, the District of Columbia, Alaska, and Hawaii passed unemployment compensation laws that meet the federal requirements; all provide that unemployed workers be registered by the public employment service, which tries to help them find suitable jobs. Each state administers its own unemployment compensation law, but the entire cost of administration is paid by the federal government out of the 10 per cent of the payroll tax that is reserved for this purpose and not credited to the state fund. It amounts to 0.3 per cent of the payroll, while the remaining 2.7 per cent are credited to the state. The states have to guarantee correct administration, in case of grievance a fair hearing before an impartial tribunal, and employment of personnel on a merit basis.

The federal administration is the responsibility of the Bureau of Employment Security in the U.S. Department of Labor. In the states either a special department or commission[10] or an agency in charge of administration of other labor laws is responsible for the administration of unemployment insurance. There are questions whether the arrangement is fortunate in that the federal government pays the entire administrative expenses but has little control of the laws which are administered.

C. COVERED EMPLOYMENT

In general, jobs in factories, mines, mills, offices, industry, business, and commerce fall under the state laws. Excluded in most states are agricultural labor; domestic service in private homes; family jobs; employment with nonprofit religious, charitable, scientific, and educational organizations; and casual employment. Several states, however, have covered one or the other of these groups, and many state laws protect employees in firms with fewer than four workers; seventeen states include even employment where only one worker is employed. Seamen are covered in forty-four states. The Amendment of 1954 added also about two and one-half million federal government employees to the groups covered by unemployment compensation laws.

The payroll tax is in most states paid by employers only, but Alabama requires also contributions from employees, and Rhode Island, California, New Jersey, and New York require such contributions for special temporary disability insurance benefits.[11]

Contributions and benefits are related to wages, with limits of

[10] E.g., in California, the Employment Stabilization Commission.
[11] See E. Burns, *op. cit.*, p. 130; and Wilbur J. Cohen, "Social Insurance," *Social Work Year Book, 1954,* pp. 489-492.

minimum and maximum benefits, and the large majority of states also determines the duration of unemployment compensation upon past earnings or employment. The establishment of a weekly maximum benefit limits—in fact the theoretical relation to former earnings —and the maximum period in which benefits may be received range from twelve to twenty-six weeks in a year. The benefit amounts vary substantially among the states dependent upon specific statutory provisions.

D. BENEFITS

Compensation is paid to workers who are able to work and are available for work. Before an unemployed worker may file a claim for unemployment compensation, he has to be registered with the public employment service. Usually the claim for compensation may be based upon loss of the job, for example, the closing down of a factory or dismissal of workers due to lack of orders, or partial loss of work. After filing his claim, the worker has to wait usually for one week in which he does not receive unemployment compensation ("waiting period").

In unemployment compensation laws, a worker who loses his job is entitled to receive compensation provided he has earned a certain amount or worked a certain number of weeks, or both, during a so-called "base period"—usually one year preceding his loss of the job with a one-calendar-quarter lag. These requirements aim to limit unemployment compensation to fairly regularly employed workers, but they discriminate against low-paid and migratory workers who may not earn enough during the base period to qualify for benefits.

The weekly minimum benefit in many states is $5 or $10; the maximum varies between $20 and $35 a week. Many state laws also determine a maximum amount which during a given year may be paid to an unemployed worker (for example, $468 in California). In January, 1954, the average weekly amount of unemployment insurance benefits in the United States was $24.34.

The maximum duration of benefits varies in the states from sixteen to twenty-six weeks a year. Unemployment compensation limits its protection to the short-period unemployed; it does not provide economic security to workers who exhaust their maximum period of compensation without finding a new job.

An unemployed worker may be disqualified for unemployment insurance benefit if he lost his job in a labor dispute, if he was discharged for misconduct on the job, if he left his work voluntarily without good cause, and if he refused suitable work without valid reason. Many states disqualify a worker who has not been "actively seeking work" beyond the registration with the employment service. In the majority of states disqualification postpones unemployment compensation for a certain number of weeks, but in others it reduces benefits or cancels them even entirely.

Dependents. In eleven programs, unemployment insurance benefits are supplemented by additional allowances for dependents ranging from $1 to $3 weekly per dependent, with maximum weekly benefits including dependents between $20 and $70.

Interstate Benefit Payment Plan. For workers who move from one state to another, reciprocal agreements between forty-five states make it possible that wages earned in several states may be combined in order to establish eligibility for unemployment compensation.

E. DISABILITY INSURANCE BENEFITS

In four states (California, New Jersey, New York, and Rhode Island) *Temporary Disability Insurance Laws*, combined with unemployment compensation, provide insurance benefits also for a specified period for wage loss due to unemployment caused by illness or disability (other than industrial accidents) in which the worker is not able to work. Disability insurance benefits are paid according to the same scale as provided under unemployment compensation and to the same workers. Temporary disability insurance is administered by the unemployment insurance agency in three states (e.g., by the Employment Stabilization Commission in California), but in New York by the Workmen's Compensation Board. Benefits are the same cash payment as unemployment compensation, but in California an additional hospitalization benefit for a maximum of ten dollars a day for twelve days in one year is also paid by the Disability Insurance Division. The contributions for disability insurance in California and Rhode Island, are made exclusively by 1 per cent of the payroll tax paid by the workers (not by the employers!). It is deducted from their wages; in New Jersey and New York both employer and worker contribute. Except in Rhode Island, employers may be insured under an approved "private plan."

F. EXPERIENCE RATING

The payroll tax of 3 per cent for unemployment compensation may be reduced for employers who were able to maintain regular employment so that few workers of their firms claimed compensation. The long period of high employment during and after World War II has greatly reduced the number of unemployed. "Experience rating" or "merit rating" means that the employer's tax is reduced from the 2.7 per cent of the payroll (up to $3,000 a year) credited to the state to a smaller percentage or even to nothing, dependent upon the ratio of benefits paid to his former workers during a "base period" of one year preceding the year of taxation. The federal proportion of the contribution of 0.3 per cent of the payroll is not involved in this reduction.

In 1952, the original contribution of employers of 2.7 per cent of the payroll had been reduced on the national scale to an average of 1.4 per cent. Students of economics have objected to this method of experience rating on the ground that it defeats the principle of collective responsibility. Stabilization of employment is not an achievement of the individual employer but depends upon the type of industry and production methods, so that experience rating favors large firms against small undertakings. It also drives employers to attempt to defy claims of discharged workers, and it increases administrative cost of unemployment insurance.[12] But the advantages of reduced taxes have induced all states to adopt "experience rating." The specific forms of "merit rating" have led to inequities among the states. They will require an increase of the contribution rates again at times of higher unemployment and economic depression when business will be less able to pay higher taxes. Provisions are made that federal advances may be paid when a state unemployment insurance fund approaches insolvency. This provision has not been used yet.

[12] See E. Burns, *op. cit.*, pp. 162-169, and for details about the various types of "experience rating," pp. 156-159; Charles A. Myers, "Experience Rating in Unemployment Compensation," in W. Haber and W. Cohen, *Readings in Social Security* (New York: Prentice-Hall, Inc., 1948), pp. 199-200. The question of fraud is discussed by Joseph M. Becker, *The Problem of Abuse in Unemployment Benefits* (New York: Columbia University Press, 1953). See also Alfred M. Skolnik, "Temporary Disability Insurance Laws in the United States," *Social Security Bulletin*, Vol. 15, No. 10, October, 1953, pp. 11-22.

IV. RAILROAD WORKERS INSURANCE

Two separate federal social insurance programs protect railroad workers with a unique comprehensive system. They provide benefits for retired workers and their survivors, for unemployed and disabled railroad men.[13]

A. THE RAILROAD RETIREMENT SYSTEM

This system has its legal foundation in the *Railroad Retirement Act of 1937* and its amendments (particularly the Crosser Act of 1946). It covers over eight million employees of railroad companies and connected associations and provides the following types of benefits: (1) pensions to retired railroad employees; (2) age annuities to retired workers at sixty-five, or at sixty years of age after thirty years of service; (3) permanent disability annuities; (4) survivors' insurance annuities to widows, orphans, and aged dependent parents; (5) lumpsum death insurance benefits for burial expenses; and (6) residual payments guaranteeing the full return of the worker's own tax payments plus an allowance in lieu of interest.

The retirement and disability benefits include a monthly compensation computed on the basis of the worker's wage with minimum and maximum amounts, and survivors' insurance annuities related to the last monthly remuneration of the worker. The program is financed by equal contributions from employers and workers of 6¼ per cent of the payroll up to $3,600 a year. The contributions are placed into a Railroad Retirement Trust Account.

B. THE RAILROAD UNEMPLOYMENT AND TEMPORARY DISABILITY SYSTEM

This system is based upon the *Railroad Unemployment Insurance Act* of 1938 with several amendments. Covered are railroad employees who received at least $150 in wages in the base year preceding the fiscal year in which unemployment or disability occurs. There is a waiting period of seven days for unemployment and disability benefits, both of which are divided into nine classes depend-

[13] See E. Burns, *op. cit.*, pp. 224-264; and W. Haber and W. Cohen, *op. cit.*, pp. 476-488.

ent upon the amount of annual earnings, ranging from daily benefit rates of $1.75 to $5.

The entire costs for this system are met by the employers whose annual contribution rate is determined by their account balance in the Railroad Unemployment Insurance Account.

C. ADMINISTRATION OF RAILROAD INSURANCE

Both railroad insurance programs are administered by the Railroad Retirement Board. It is composed of three members appointed by the President, with consent of the Senate, for five years with overlapping terms. One member is appointed upon recommendation of the railroad carriers, the second upon that of the railroad employees; the chairman is neutral. The staff is employed under civil service. Under the Board, nine regional offices and ninety-five branch and district offices receive the claims for the various benefits, determine eligibility, and pay the benefits.

V. WORKMEN'S COMPENSATION

Workmen's compensation is the first system of social insurance enacted in England and in the United States. With the development of modern industry the provisions of the common law on work injuries proved to be wholly inadequate. They were based upon old master-servant relations when incidents were rare, and they limited the claim for damage of the injured worker to cases in which the employer had neglected to provide reasonable protection for the safety of the worker. Worse than that, the employer was able to refuse damage recovery on the basis of three "common law defenses": (1) that the worker had assumed the risk of accidents at work and (2) also the risk of injuries caused by fellow-workers, and (3) that he must prove that he was not negligent when the injury occurred. The worker or his survivors had to sue before civil courts, had to pay court and attorney fees, and usually wait for years until a decision was reached. Thus, many never went to court as they had no means, or accepted whatever poor settlement was offered them. These legal provisions made an injured worker or his widow and orphans helpless victims. The condition was so appalling that many states introduced employers' liability laws, which prohibited the use of the common law defenses, particularly for the mining industry, the railroads, and the merchant marine where accidents were most frequent. But these laws offered still no adequate protection to the injured workers.

The movement for the enactment of legislation in order to eliminate in our country social injustice, the question of fault, and demoralization was started by social reformers, economists, and the American Association for Labor Legislation. In 1908 the first workmen's compensation law for federal employees was passed, and in 1911 a large number of states enacted this legislation with the others following. Now all states have workmen's compensation laws.[14]

A. PRINCIPLES AND COVERAGE

Workmen's compensation is based upon the principle that the risk of work injuries is an element of industry and that the cost of such injuries is to be considered a part of cost of production, not dependent upon a fault of either employer or injured worker. The aim of this program is to assure prompt medical aid, rehabilitation, and cash benefit to the injured worker and to his dependents regardless of who is at fault. But there are still many differences among the state laws. Only about 75 per cent of all workers are covered; certain groups of workers are excluded because they are not employed in "hazardous occupations," or because they work in agriculture, domestic service, or casual jobs. About one-half of the states have elective systems of workmen's compensation where the employer is permitted to refuse insurance of his workers if he prefers the risk of being sued for damage by an injured worker or his survivors. Thirty-one of the states cover all occupational diseases as well as industrial accidents; the other states, only some of these diseases. Eight states do not cover the damage caused by occupational diseases, such as lead poisoning and silicosis, but other systems treat occupational diseases like industrial accidents.

Because workmen's compensation was the pioneer among social insurance in our country, this legislation was enacted under a great variety of patterns in the different states, and no specific type of workmen's compensation has found adoption as the most effective system. In some states the "compulsory," and in others, the "elect-

[14] Walter A. Dodd, *Administration of Workmen's Compensation* (New York: Commonwealth Fund, 1936); and W. Cohen, *op. cit.*, pp. 487-489.

ive," method of covering workers and employment is used. As to organization, there are many states where private insurance companies compete with a public compensation fund, but in a minority of states exclusive private insurance or exclusive public insurance is in operation. In many laws there is the possibility of self-insurance, which is the employer's privilege of not insuring his workers, provided the employer is able to deposit securities, giving proof of his financial ability to carry his own risk.

In the majority of the states the employer has the choice whether he wants to (1) insure with a private insurance company, (2) insure with a state workmen's compensation fund, or (3) apply for self-insurance permission.[15]

Excluded from compensation are usually injuries that have been due to the injured worker's willful misconduct, gross negligence, intoxication, or intentional self-infliction.

B. COMPENSATION BENEFITS

Workmen's compensation laws provide two types of benefits—medical treatment and cash indemnities as compensation for loss of earning. Cash benefits provide for temporary disability, for total or partial permanent disability, and for the survivors in case of death of the injured worker.

1. Medical Benefits. In the majority of states full medical care, including first aid, medical and surgical treatment, hospitalization, medicines, and medical and surgical appliances, are provided free for the injured worker. This medical aid, however, is limited in seventeen states either by a certain time or by a maximum amount of expenses, but thirty-one states (for example, California, Illinois, Minnesota, Nebraska, Washington, and Wisconsin) provide no limit, neither in the period of medical treatment nor as to the amount of medical expenses.

As a rule, the employer or the insurance carrier arranges for medical care and hospitalization, but in some instances the injured worker has choice of physician and hospital. The quality of medical service, nursing care, and rehabilitation service differs widely among the states. Where medical treatment is limited to a certain period or to a

[15] Arthur J. Altmeyer, "Social Insurance," *Social Work Year Book, 1954,* pp. 474-475; and Arthur H. Reede, *Adequacy of Workmen's Compensations* (Cambridge: Harvard University Press, 1947).

definite expense maximum, sometimes extension may be granted.

2. *Indemnity Payments.* After a waiting period of usually seven days, the injured worker who had to leave his work due to the accident or the occupational disease is entitled to an indemnity payment. The amount of this indemnity is, as a rule, different for temporary disabilities and permanent impairments, such as loss of an arm, a leg, or of both eyes.

(a) Temporary Disability. This is compensated by a percentage of the last wage, that varies from 50 to 80 per cent—frequently 66⅔ per cent (for example, California, 61.75 per cent; Illinois up to 97½ per cent). Maximum weekly payments (for example, California, $35; New York, $32) lead to the result, however, that in the period of illness the worker often receives only a fraction of his regular wage, and has difficulty meeting high living costs. In a few states the rate of compensation is higher for married workers, and increased according to the number of dependent children.

There is usually, also, a maximum period for which temporary disability indemnity is paid (frequently five years) or a maximum sum, which amounts to the same limitation.

(b) Permanent Disability. In all states compensation is provided for permanent disabilities caused by industrial accidents, and different rates are scheduled for permanent total or partial disability.

Permanent partial disabilities. These are either classified as specific injuries, such as loss of an eye, a hand, or a foot, or as of general nature, such as disability caused by injury to the head or back. For such partial disability compensation is limited in the majority of states to a stated number of weeks, but in several states (e.g., Washington and Wyoming) the weekly payments are fixed sums. In California compensation is rated upon degrees of total disability as classified in a Rating Schedule in relation to nature of injury, occupation, and age of injured worker.[16]

The periods of compensation for specific injuries vary from state to state, which certainly is not logical; they are sometimes paid in addition to the indemnities during temporary disability.

Permanent total disability. If the injured worker is totally disabled by the injury, often defined as having lost 70 per cent or more of his

16 A. Reede, *op. cit.*, pp. 125-127; Edison L. Bowers, *Is It Safe to Work?* (Boston: Houghton, 1930), Chap. IV; and Max D. Kossoris, Warren H. Pillsbury, and John Petsko, "Workmen's Compensation in the U.S.," *Monthly Labor Review*, April, May, June, 1953, pp. 359-366, 480-483, 602-608.

working capacity, he receives an indemnity as a proportion of his wage with weekly and total maximum amounts. The periods range from 250 to 1,000 weeks, and the money maximum amounts from $5,000 to $12,000.

The federal compensation systems for civil employees and long-shoremen, and the laws of eighteen states (among them Arizona, California, Colorado, Illinois, Massachusetts, Nebraska, Nevada, New York, Oregon, Utah, and Washington) and the District of Columbia provide for lifelong benefits in case of permanent total disability, but often with reduced rates and dependent upon the severity of the disability (e.g., in California limited to 40 per cent of the last wage). In some states different rates are paid with regard to dependents (e.g., Idaho).

(c) Subsequent Injuries. The majority of compensation laws contains provisions to secure benefits for such workers who had been injured and lost a member of the body, but who suffer another injury which may involve total, permanent disability. Without legal provisions, handicapped persons might be refused employment because an employer or the insurance carrier would not take the risk of another injury. For this purpose "second-injury" or "subsequent injuries" funds have been established which, as a rule, secure full compensation for the actual disability to the injured worker without undue burden for the new employer.

(d) Death Benefits. If the injured worker dies, the economic security of his wife and his children often depends upon the death awards under workmen's compensation. In general they are based upon the average weekly wages of the deceased breadwinner, but Oregon, Washington, West Virginia, and Wyoming grant a flat pension. Only seven systems provide that death benefits be paid to the widow for life or until remarriage, but in the majority of compensation plans death benefits again are limited to payments for a specific period ranging from 260 to 600 weeks or up to a maximum amount ranging from $3,500 to $9,000. Weekly minimum and maximum payments usually are similar to those of permanent disability benefits. Neither as to the amounts of payments nor in regard to the limitations in periods and maximum sums may these laws be considered an adequate economic security for the survivors of the victim of the injury. In addition to survivors' benefits, funeral expenses are paid in many systems, usually not exceeding $300.

As an example of how necessary the protection of workmen's compensation is today, the following data may be cited from an experience in California in January, 1953: In this month, sixty-seven workers were killed in work accidents. Three construction workers fell to their death from scaffolds, a carpenter from a top deck of a highway bridge, an oil-well puller from a derrick onto the floor, and a water company laborer from a waste gate to rocks below. An airplane mechanic was killed when he fell from the main wheel well to the pavement. Transportation accidents involving trucks and automobiles caused the death of six farm workers. Three workers were fatally burned when one filled a tank truck with oil, another applied rubber cement to an automobile tire, and a third sprayed weeds with sodium chlorate powder; the last two accidents were caused by cigarette smoking. In a steel plant two laborers were killed by carbon dioxide gas. Two other workers, when prodding sand into the bottom chutes of bunkers, were suffocated when the sand pulled them down into the chutes.[17] These are some accidents which happened in just one month in one state, causing the death of the workers involved.

Not all state laws require that reports be made of all industrial accidents and occupational diseases. No reliable statistics of their total amount is available, therefore. There are estimates that the annual death rate caused by industrial injuries throughout the country averages 20,000, that about 100,000 workers suffer permanent total or partial disablement, and that about 1,700,000 persons are temporarily disabled by accidents and occupational diseases at work. But it is correct to state that workmen's compensation has increased the prevention of accidents by encouraging safety measures and has improved the social conditions of the victims of work accidents and occupational diseases and of their families.

C. ADMINISTRATION OF WORKMEN'S COMPENSATION

The main objective of the system is to guarantee a simple, fair, convenient, and inexpensive method of settling the claims of injured workers and their dependents. For this reason in most states an ad-

[17] State of California, Department of Industrial Relations, *Report to Governor's Council*, March, 1953, pp. A-B.

ministrative commission (e.g., Industrial Accident Commission) or board administers the program, but six states and Alaska still rely upon court administration.

State Compensation Insurance Funds are, as a rule, administered by a board of directors, which is independent and separated from the industrial accident commission. State funds are nonprofit and self-supporting, even when operating aside from private insurance carriers, and they have to use rates and classifications ordered for all insurance companies under state laws. Encouragement of prevention of industrial accidents and of occupational diseases by strengthening safety devices and instruction of workers is an important function of workmen's compensation, but not yet equally achieved in the various systems.

The federal programs of workmen's compensation for federal civil employees and for longshoremen are administered by the Bureau of Employees' Compensation, U.S. Department of Labor (until 1950 it was under the Federal Security Agency). The Bureau has twelve branch offices spread about the country.

The administration of workmen's compensation, as well as more recently unemployment insurance and old-age and survivors' insurance, has been carried on by personnel which has developed into a group of civil servants who have, during the past decades, gained substantial technical skill and knowledge in their activities. Workmen's compensation originally suffered under the frequent change of personnel dependent upon local and state political conditions. Recently, however, most of the staffs of industrial accident commissions and similar agencies in charge of administration of workmen's compensation have been placed under civil service and gained regular employment status. The same development has taken place in the organization of unemployment insurance in connection with state public employment services, and in the federal service of old-age and survivors' insurance.[18]

The competence of personnel in social insurance administration is in many respects related to the skill required in other fields of social

[18] For a very enlightening discussion of the question of personnel in social insurance administration, see Karl de Schweinitz, *People and Process in Social Security* (Washington, D.C.: American Council of Education, 1948), pp. 62-93.

welfare administration.[19] It requires good, general education for ability to understand laws, rules, and regulations and to explain them clearly and with sympathetic attitude to the public. It also includes an objective approach as a representative of a public agency, impartial and polite consideration for the applicants, and an awareness of the personality of the person for whom the social insurance program is set up. Beyond these general requirements and the skills connected with technical problems of legal and financial nature, accounting, and computation, the question has been frequently raised whether specific professional social work skills are required in the administration of social insurance. Under present conditions it is certain that the administration of the various social insurance systems does not require fully trained professional social workers for most of its functions.

The people who come to the social insurance offices in order to file their claims often incidentally express personal, emotional, or health problems. In our present setup of the social insurance administrations no one is prepared to cope with those needs which are not met by the cash benefits and medical care offered under the social insurance program. When claimants reveal psychological problems indicating health or emotional disturbance, anxieties, and fear, personnel not trained professionally is unable to recognize their needs and to refer them to social agencies which are equipped to help. It is under these circumstances of great importance that the various social insurance programs employ social workers as consultants who are fully acquainted with the social agencies of the community and their special facilities and services. These workers would be available for the insurance benefit recipients who need to be counseled regarding the facilities of other health and welfare services, family and children's agencies, child guidance and mental hygiene clinics, and recreational facilities. In interviews and discussions they could bring the resources of the community to the attention of the recipients of insurance benefits, who would greatly benefit from an expansion of the service offered.

It might be worth mentioning that in other countries, particularly France, Belgium, and England, a much closer integration of social

[19] See Chapter 22 below for discussion of professional skills in social welfare. With the expansion of social insurance programs it becomes more important to employ professional social workers.

insurance and family allowance benefits with the general system of welfare services has been highly beneficial and is accepted by the population.[20] The establishment of social work consultants in the field offices of the Social Security Administration, the state unemployment compensation, and workmen's compensation programs would be valuable progress in the interest of the public.

VI. GAPS IN OUR INSURANCE PROGRAM

A. HEALTH INSURANCE

The most spectacular gap in our system of social insurance is the lack of health insurance. Insurance against the hazard of ill health by the provision of medical care and cash allowances during the time of illness was the earliest type of compulsory, public social insurance in many other countries. In fact, the United States is the only great nation which has no public health insurance program today. Under auspices of the federal government, medical care is given to members of the armed forces, veterans, Indians, and seamen. Under state systems of workmen's compensation, medical care and cash indemnity are provided for workers injured by industrial accidents and occupational diseases according to specific statutes. In four states, unemployment insurance in the form of disability benefits, but no medical care, is given to insured workers who are unable to work due to illness for a limited time. Persons who receive various forms of general and categorical public assistance also, as a rule, receive a certain amount of medical care; recent legislation permits for these clients the use of federal grants-in-aid for the payment of doctors and hospitals. In spite of its limitations, it improves medical care for the recipients of public categorical assistance, but it does not protect the entire population.

The idea of a compulsory health insurance program has been vigorously opposed in our country. The main objections to such a program are presented by representatives of the medical profession, by some of the commercial insurance companies, by the Christian Science churches, and drug manufacturing companies. The princi-

[20] Walter A. Friedlander, "Coordination of Family Welfare Services in France," *Social Service Review*, Vol. XXVII, No. 1, March, 1953, pp. 62-66; and American Association of Schools of Social Work, *Education for the Public Social Services* (New York: 1953), pp. 12, 14-15, 17-18.

pal arguments of these groups are the following: medical societies fear that compulsory health insurance would lead to a lowering of standards of medical care by overcrowding of doctors, clinics, and hospitals; would subject the medical profession to bureaucratic control, red-tape paper work; and would decrease their income. Some commercial insurance companies are afraid that their own accident, hospitalization, and medical care policies would be cancelled and their profits might be lost. Drug manufacturing firms selling patent medicines feel that their products would no longer be bought by health insurance administrators and patients under a health insurance program which would standardize medicines and drugs. The Christian Science churches do not want health insurance because their members believe in cure through prayer, not through medical service. In public discussion, health insurance is often confused with socialized medicine, a system under which doctors and nurses are government employees, and patients have no free choice in selecting doctor, pharmacist, clinic, or hospital. None of these characteristics applies, however, to the concept of health insurance as it operates in most other countries.

The need of a large proportion of our population to protect themselves against the economic risk of heavy cost for serious illnesses, which strike every year about four million people in a way that they are ill for longer than six months, is obvious. Many families have attempted to solve this need by selecting a "medical care prepayment plan"—a voluntary health insurance program. Such plans are established either by nonprofit organizations, such as the "Blue Cross" which covers about twenty-five million people, the "Blue Shield" which is closely connected with the state medical societies, by some private foundations, labor councils, unions, fraternal societies, and business concerns,[21] or by commercial insurance companies.

The benefits under these plans vary considerably. Most of them offer either only hospitalization, or only medical care in the doctor's office, or a cash allowance for the patient to compensate for the loss of earning—frequently only a part payment toward the various expenses. Membership is often limited to persons of low income or to people within specific age limits, and some plans exclude persons who are suffering from various diseases. A recent analysis of the effect of voluntary insurance plans demonstrated that in 1951 under

[21] We shall discuss the health insurance plans in industry in Chapter 17.

such arrangements for the insured persons, 36.3 per cent of hospital costs and 17 per cent of costs of hospital, physician, and loss of income were provided; and for 17 per cent, medical expenses alone were covered.[22] Thus, only a small proportion of our population has comprehensive aid in case of sickness, including medical care at home, in the doctor's office, in the hospital, and the necessary medicines and medical appliances. The premiums for comprehensive health insurance coverage are frequently too high for persons in the low income groups, so that often patients most in need of this protection are not able to become members of voluntary plans.

In the discussion of a comprehensive compulsory health insurance legislation, the question has recently come up whether or not a general public health service, such as the programs in Great Britain, New Zealand, Australia and Chile, may be preferable to a health insurance plan.[23]

In 1954, at the suggestion of President Eisenhower health insurance bills were introduced in both Houses that would provide that the premium for health insurance be based on a percentage of the insured person's income. Federal and state grant-in-aids would make up the difference between the standard premium and what the individual could afford to pay on this basis. Primary responsibility for the development of adequate medical care was to be placed with the states, local communities, nonprofit private health groups, and the medical profession, but a federal reinsurance service with a capital fund of $25 million would serve as a guarantee. However, this legislation was not enacted.

B. MATERNITY INSURANCE

In many other nations, maternity insurance provides for insured women workers and for wives of insured men medical and maternity ward care, midwife aid, nursing, and medicines at the time of child-

---

[22] "Voluntary Insurance Against Sickness: 1948-1951 Estimates," *Social Security Bulletin*, December, 1952, pp. 3-7; and George W. Cooley, "The Potentials of Voluntary Health Insurance," *Building America's Health*, Vol. 4, (1952), pp. 76-82.

[23] E. Burns, "Further Needs in the Social Insurances," *op. cit.*, p. 188; W. Haber and W. Cohen, *op. cit.*, pp. 326-327; I. S. Falk, "The Need, Potential and Implications of Compulsory Health Insurance," *Building America's Health*, Vol. 4 (1952), pp. 66-75; Maurice B. Hamovitch, "History of the Movement for Compulsory Health Insurance in the United States," *Social Service Review*, Vol. XXVII, No. 3, September, 1953, pp. 281-299.

birth. Cash allowances of one-half of the actual or average wage are paid for periods from about four weeks before to six weeks after confinement. This insurance proves of considerable help to mothers and infants. No public insurance of this type is available in the United States, except to railroad workers.

C. PERMANENT DISABILITY OR INVALIDITY INSURANCE

Foreign social insurance programs combine permanent disability insurance with the old-age insurance scheme. In our country a good number of experts have requested such legislation. But Congress, in the Amendment of 1950 of the Social Security Act, only has set up a limited type of categorical public assistance to needy, permanently and totally disabled persons. There is little hope, at present, that a permanent disability insurance law will be enacted.

D. FAMILY ALLOWANCES

Family allowances have first been introduced in France and Belgium, on a voluntary basis, by employers for families with several children. Their goal is to alleviate the financial burden of rearing more than one young child for the parents, particularly the mother, and to secure a living standard of health and decency which could not be obtained by earning the normal wage alone. The individual and health needs of the worker and his family are not considered in the determination of wages and salary. A young bachelor may get along on his wage without difficulty, but his married fellow worker with five young children at home will have a hard time to make ends meet with the same wage. Organized labor originally was opposed to family allowances, but later it favored legislation which made the family allowances compulsory so that their payment is no longer dependent upon the discretion of the employer. At present, a large number of countries, including Canada and England, have enacted family allowance legislation. There seems, however, no indication that federal or state legislatures in our country are inclined to pass a compulsory family allowance law.

SELECTED BIBLIOGRAPHY

*Altmeyer, Arthur J., "Social Insurance," *Social Work Year Book, 1951,*
    pp. 472-482.
——, "The Future of Social Security in America," *Social Service Review,* Vol. XXVII, No. 3, September, 1953, pp. 251-268.

Armstrong, Barbara N., *Insuring the Essentials.* New York: Macmillan, 1932.

Atkinson, Raymond C., *The Federal Role in Unemployment Compensation Administration.* Washington, D.C.: Social Science Research Council, 1941.

Backman, George W., and Lewis Meriam, *The Issue of Compulsory Health Insurance.* Washington, D.C.: Brookings Institution, 1948.

Ball, Robert M., "Social Insurance and the Right to Assistance," *Social Service Review,* Vol. XXI, No. 3, September, 1947, pp. 331-344.

Becker, Joseph M., *The Problem of Abuse in Unemployment Benefits.* New York: Columbia University Press, 1953.

Breul, Frank R., "The Genesis of Family Allowances in Canada," *Social Service Review,* Vol. 27, No. 3, September, 1953, pp. 269-280.

*Burns, Eveline M., "Further Needs in the Social Insurances," *The Social Welfare Forum 1951,* pp. 181-189. New York: Columbia University Press, 1951.

——, *The American Social Security System.* Boston: Houghton, 1949, and Appendix, 1951.

——, *Toward Social Security.* New York: McGraw, 1936.

Cohen, Wilbur F., "Social Insurance," *Social Work Year Book, 1954,* pp. 486-495.

——, (editor), *War and Post-War Social Security.* Washington, D.C.: American Council on Public Affairs, 1942.

Dahm, Margaret M., "Temporary Disability Insurance: The California Program," *Social Security Bulletin,* February, 1953, pp. 15-20.

Davis, Michael M., *America Organizes Medicine.* New York: Harper, 1941.

——, and Dewey Anderson, *Medical Care for the Individual and the Issue of Compulsory Health Insurance.* Washington, D.C.: Brookings Institution, 1948.

Dawson, Marshall, *Problems of Workmen's Compensation Administration.* Washington, D.C.: U.S. Department of Labor, Bulletin No. 672, 1940.

——, *Second Injury Funds as Employment Aids to the Handicapped.* Washington, D.C.: U.S. Department of Labor, 1947.

*de Schweinitz, Karl, *People and Process in Social Security.* Washington, D.C.: American Council on Education, 1948.

*Dodd, Walter F., *Administration of Workmen's Compensation.* New York: Commonwealth Fund, 1936.

Douglas, Paul H., *Social Security in the United States.* New York: McGraw, 1936.

Epstein, Abraham, *Insecurity: A Challenge to America,* Rev. ed. New York: Random House, Inc., 1938.

*Ewing, Oscar R., *The Nation's Health.* Washington, D.C.: Federal Security Agency, 1948.

Falk, I. S., "Health Services, Medical Care Insurance and Social Se-

curity," *Annals of the American Academy of Political and Social Science*, Vol. 273, January, 1951.
York: Doubleday, 1936.
——, *Security Against Sickness: A Study of Health Insurance.* New
*Goldmann, Franz, *Voluntary Medical Care Insurance in the United States.* New York: Columbia University Press, 1948.
——, and Hugh R. Leavell, "Medical Care for Americans," *The Annals of the American Academy of Political and Social Science*, Vol. 273, January, 1951.
*Haber, William, and Wilbur J. Cohen,, *Readings in Social Security.* New York: Prentice-Hall, Inc., 1948.
Hamovitch, Maurice B., "History of the Movement for Compulsory Health Insurance in the United States," *Social Service Review*, Vol. 27, No. 3, September, 1953, pp. 281-299.
Harris, Seymour, S., *Economics of Social Security.* New York: McGraw, 1941.
Hobbs, Clarence W., *Workmen's Compensation Insurance.* New York: McGraw, 1939.
Huntington, Emily H., *Cost of Medical Care.* Berkeley: University of California Press, 1951.
Kingsbury, John A., *Health in Handcuffs.* New York: Modern Age Books, 1939.
——, *Health Security for the Nation.* New York: League for Industrial Democracy, 1938.
Linford, Alton A. (editor), *Social Security in 1953.* Columbus, O.: National Conference of Social Work, 1953.
Malmberg, Carl, *140 Million Patients.* New York: Reynal, 1947.
Matscheck, Walter, *Unemployment Compensation Administration in Wisconsin and New Hampshire.* Chicago: Public Administration Service, 1936.
Means, James H., *Doctors, People and Government.* Boston: Atlantic, 1953.
*Meriam, Lewis, *Relief and Social Security.* Washington, D.C.: Brookings Institution, 1946.
Millis, Harry A., *Sickness and Insurance.* Chicago: University of Chicago Press, 1937.
——, and Royal E. Montgomery, *Labor's Risk and Social Insurance.* New York: McGraw, 1938.
Mott, Frederick D., and Milton I. Roemer, *Rural Health and Medical Care.* New York: McGraw, 1948.
National Resources Planning Board, *Security, Work and Relief Policies.* Washington: Government Printing Office, 1943.
Palyi, Melchior, *Compulsory Medical Care and the Welfare State.* Chicago: National Institute of Professional Services, 1949.
*President's Committee on the Health Needs of the Nation, *Building America's Health*, 5 vols., Washington, D.C.: 1952.

Rathbone, Eleanor F., *The Case for Family Allowances*. London: Penguin Books, 1940.

Reed, Louis S., *Health Insurance: The Next Step in Social Security*. New York: Harper, 1937.

Reede, Arthur H., *Adequacy of Workmen's Compensation*. Cambridge: Harvard University Press, 1947.

Redl, Fritz, "Child Study in a New Setting," *Children*, Vol. 1, January, 1954, pp. 15-20.

Robbins, Rainard, *Railroad Social Insurance*. New York: American Enterprise Association, 1947.

Rubinow, Issac M., *The Quest for Security*. New York: Holt, 1934.

Schlesinger, Edward R., *Health Services for the Child*. New York: McGraw, 1953.

Simpson, Herbert, *Compulsory Health Insurance in the United States*. Evanston: Northwestern University, 1943.

Sinai, Nathan, Odin W. Anderson, and Melvin H. Dollar, *Health Insurance in the United States*. New York: Commonwealth Fund, 1946.

Skolnick, Alfred M., "Temporary Disability Insurance Laws in the U.S.," *Social Security Bulletin*, October, 1952, pp. 11-12.

Steinhaus, Henry W., *Financing Old Age*. New York: National Industrial Conference Board, 1948.

Stern, Bernhard J., *American Medical Practice*. New York: Commonwealth Fund, 1945.

——, *Medical Services by Government—Local, State and Federal*. New York: Commonwealth Fund, 1946.

Stewart, Bryce M., *et al.*, *Planning and Administration of Unemployment Compensation in the United States*. New York: Industrial Relations Counselors, 1938.

Stewart, Maxwell, *Social Security*. New York: Norton, 1939.

Witte, Edwin E., "Development of Unemployment Compensation," *Yale Law Review*, December, 1945, pp. 21-25.

Wunderlich, Frieda, "Social Insurance versus Poor Relief," *Social Research*, March, 1947.

10. Family Services

The family is the basic unit of our society in which individuals receive most of their personal satisfactions, and in which the personality of the child is formed. It is within the family that sexual relations are regularized; children are given nurture and education; and food, clothing, and the dwelling place for its members are provided. In illness or pregnancy, during childbirth, the family renders care. It is the center of warm affection among its members as long as normal, healthy conditions prevail. Regardless of the social changes of modern, industrial society, family life has values for most individuals that cannot be found elsewhere. So it is desirable in terms of these values, to the individual members of the family as well as in the interest of society, that family life be protected and strengthened.[1] Family service of social agencies has the purpose of preserving healthy family life; the aim of family casework is to assist the individuals in the family to develop their capacities to lead personally satisfying and socially useful lives in the family unit.

Social anthropology has shown the influence of tradition, habits, customs, and the pattern of social organization upon the behavior of human beings, and sociology recognizes these factors as essential determinants in human values, ambitions, and reactions. Knowledge of the decisive role of culture in the formation of the human personality is essential in family casework, because the individual may be understood at times in terms of his environment. The role of the family in society, however, is not static. In our predominantly industrial, urban society many features of the earlier rural family have changed. Mar-

[1] James S. Plant, *Personality and the Cultural Pattern* (New York: Commonwealth Fund, 1937); and Andrew G. Truxal and Francis E. Merrill, *Marriage and The Family in American Culture* (New York: Prentice-Hall, Inc., 1953), pp. 29-51, 349-374.

garet Mead went as far as to characterize the new pattern of the American family as follows:

The typical American couple is composed of two people with no common childhood associations or traditions, living apart from the relatives of either, without responsibilities for their family shared as in other countries and in earlier American society with other relatives and neighbors. Divorce has increased to its present rate for a variety of reasons related to the complexities of modern society, and is self-increasing in that prospective partners approach marriage with the tacit—often explicit —understanding that divorce is an acceptable way of "resolving" marital difficulties. The role of women is particularly demanding and unrewarding. The increased social and political freedom of women has led to the desire and expectation for a professional career relatively independent of their husbands, yet the desire for marriage and the demands of the household make this difficult or impossible despite technical facilities. If the woman tries to have both home and career, both are likely to suffer. If she gives up the career, she is constantly reminded of what she might have made of herself if she had not. If she fails to prepare for a career, she faces the likelihood that her marriage might fail and she will have to support herself and her children because of divorce without being equipped for earning sufficient money. The rewards of maintaining the household are less tangible than formerly. Schools, nurseries, and kindergartens have largely taken over the training of children. Canneries, bakeries, and factories have taken over the production of food and clothing. The complexities of keeping a home intact have increased in rough proportion to the decrease of visible achievement in accomplishing this.[2]

Whether we consider the essential changes of our pattern of family life a "progress" or a "decline," compared with the quiet satisfaction of earlier rural family life, these changes undoubtedly have created many serious disturbances which afflict the members of the families concerned. Margaret Mead explains: "To the extent that we continue to act as if the family were what it used to be, we compromise our capacity to understand its limitations, and also we delay the development of the community services, the education, and the counseling we need."[3] The community services which Miss Mead mentions are primarily family welfare services.

[2] Margaret Mead, "What Is Happening to the American Family?" *Journal of Social Casework* (now *Social Casework*), November, 1947, pp. 322-323; quoted by permission of the Family Service Association of America. See also, A. Truxal and F. Merrill, *op. cit.*, pp. 583-603.

[3] M. Mead, *op. cit.*, p. 327; see also A. Truxal and F. Merrill, *op. cit.*, pp. 267-272.

The difficulties which arise in the life of the family are of great variety. There may be lack of harmony between husband and wife, emotional instability of either, economic problems caused by failure of good home management, or small income; or they may be caused by unemployment, sickness, accidents, health problems, lack of support, or desertion of the breadwinner. We find problems in the relation to children, sometimes leading to neglect or cruelty, housing problems, financial need for the mother to obtain work and to place the children, or delinquency or other maladjustment of the children. Personal and family difficulties are usually caused by a combination of various elements, frequently involving several members of the family and comprising social, economic, emotional, and physical factors. Therefore an improvement in difficult family situations may be obtained by enabling the members of the family to understand the reasons for their difficulties and the need for changing their emotional reactions and behavior. Changes in the environment or in the economic conditions in which the family lives may help to improve relationships between its members.

In former times, family casework depended mainly upon the overt behavior of the people for both social diagnosis and cure. If a husband neglected his wife and children because he was devoted to drink, the social worker advised him to stop drinking and threatened with legal measures or with sending him to jail. At present, family casework attempts to explore the motives for his drinking and to find ways to convince him, by insight into his personality, of the necessity of changing his habits and of going to a clinic for therapy.

Some characteristics of the present form of American family life may be called "democratic"; husband and wife have a larger amount of equality than in former generations and are aware of their common, equal rights. In the choice of the mate greater freedom is granted the young couple than in other cultures. After its marriage the young couple seeks to obtain independence from the families of each partner and rejects interference from parents and relatives. In principle, decisions on their way of life are reached between the couple, sometimes with participation of adolescent children. The changes in the family pattern of the past to new forms of family living sometimes lead to conflicts, for those who cannot accept new customs, and require aid for adjustment. Progress in psychology and psychiatry, as well as in natural sciences, enables the caseworker to recognize difficulties in family life which formerly were not detected. The ability to diagnose their nature helps to find ways of solution. Social work is not the only source which attempts to help in such difficulties; other professional aid by the psychiatrist, the physician, the minister, or the nurse might be effective, but social casework remains one of the most important ways of helping to straighten out family problems.

I. FAMILY SERVICE AGENCIES

Both public and private social agencies frequently offer family services. In public welfare agencies, family casework, as a rule, is offered in connection with the granting of public assistance, particularly in the program of aid to dependent children. But only a few, well-organized public welfare departments have introduced a special family casework unit which aids applicants independent upon their economic need.[4] Financial help for the maintenance of a family in need is an accepted function of the public welfare department, provided that the family meets the legal eligibility requirements for assistance. Private family welfare agencies, therefore, frequently refer applicants who ask mainly for financial support to the public assistance agency. Private family service agencies are primarily concerned with personal problems and the emotional maladjustment of members of the family. Their casework attempts to help in the solution of such problems, by counseling in health, educational, and adjustment questions, to overcome disturbances to normal, healthy family living. Counseling may include advice on family budget and home management, and on vocational opportunities by referral to employment services and occupational guidance centers. Sometimes family casework includes premarital counseling when the social worker is consulted by the young couple or the parents. It is often concerned with marital disturbances—helping the couple to better mutual understanding and satisfaction—and with the adjustment of difficulties which have arisen between parents and children.

Most family welfare agencies are situated in urban areas, but surrounding rural communities are often included in their activities. Little family welfare service is available in most rural areas, which are remote from cities, except for social work rendered by the

[4] See Chapter 7, p. 256; and Clark W. Blackburn, "Family Social Work," *Social Work Year Book, 1954*, pp. 205-206.

county welfare department to persons receiving financial assistance, and occasionally by Red Cross chapters.

Many private family service agencies are nonsectarian and help families without relation to their creed and ethnic background. Family service agencies of high standards are organized in the Family Service Association of America. The Association accepts only such agencies that guarantee the clients a well-developed program of services, employing a qualified professional staff and having an adequate agency structure and a sound financial policy.[5] In 1954 the Family Service Association had 256 agency members; most of them are private social agencies, but a number of public welfare departments which provide family services and meet the requirements of the Association have also been accepted as members.

The staff of the family service agency depends upon the size and resources of the community. It consists usually of an executive director, one or more supervisors, and a group of caseworkers competently trained for family work. In private agencies, a board of directors must be active and responsible; a public agency needs an advisory board on family work in order to be accepted as a member of the Family Service Association. The executive is in charge of the organization, administration, and liaison work with the board and other agencies, but in a small community he also may serve as casework supervisor or even carry a case load himself. Funds for the private family service agency are provided from the annual campaign of the Community Chest, from contributions of members, interest on endowments, and other donations. Persons may come to the family service agency on their own initiative, informed by the radio or the press, on advice of friends, a minister, or neighbors. They may also come on referral by other social agencies, such as the public welfare department, a hospital or clinic, a children's agency, a probation service, or a group work agency. The Community Chest, a businessmen's club, a school, or any municipal agency may have sent a person to the family service agency.

The first interview usually takes place at the office of the agency. The applicant explains why he came to the agency, which difficulties have induced him to ask for help or advice, and what he expects from

[5] The Association formerly was named "Family Welfare Association of America," and its noted monthly journal, *The Family*, now is called *Social Casework*. See Frank J. Hertel, "Family Social Work," *Social Work Year Book, 1951,* p. 185.

the agency. The caseworker listens to the story of the applicant and helps him by friendly encouragement and sympathy to present his explanation. She will frequently discover that the reasons which the applicant presents are not the real core of his troubles and that he, in fact, wants help other than the things which he discusses first—such as legal advice, employment, and vocational training. The caseworker will clearly explain to the client what services the agency is able to offer, and under what conditions. She will leave him free to decide whether or not he wishes to use these services, but she may well help him in making a decision which lies in his interest and in that of his family. After the interview the caseworker records the client's description of his problems and of their causes in a "case history." If the client decides to make use of agency services, the caseworker attempts to help the client solve his problems by releasing his own resources, or his capacities, and by the use of such other facilities in the community as hospitals and clinics, employment services, schools, and training centers. The length of contact, the frequency of interviews, and the intensity of the helping relationship of the caseworker vary according to the circumstances.

Although private family service agencies are mainly asked for help in personal and emotional problems, the question of financial assistance also is frequently raised. The general practice is that financial aid is given to those clients where it is necessary to implement other services given by the agency (casework, counseling, legal advice), and where financial assistance is an integral part of the family casework process. Such support may be necessary with clients who feel unable to apply for public relief or who are not eligible for it. Money payment may be needed during a period of investigation by the public welfare department, whether financial support is unavoidable or whether the client should be referred to another agency. Financial help is given in emergencies for the maintenance of the household before public assistance can be obtained, and for recreational or educational purposes for which public funds might not be available.[6] Among the clients who need material help are particularly nonresidents, families who have not gained settlement rights and therefore are not eligible for public assistance, and new immigrants who cannot apply for material assistance to public welfare agencies unless

[6] Family Service Association of America, *Report of the Committee on Current and Future Planning* (New York: The Association, 1946), p. 9.

their economic need has been caused by events which could not be anticipated at the time of their immigration to the United States.

The following cases will illustrate the approach of family welfare casework:

CASE OF THE GRAY FAMILY[7]

Mr. and Mrs. Gray, both in their late twenties, had been married one year. They had met while attending college. Mr. G expected to complete his science course at a university at mid-year, and his wife was continuing her teachers' training. Mr. G requested help with their marital problem. He and his wife quarreled and were having difficulties in their sexual adjustment. He had previously had brief psychological treatment which he had found helpful. He discussed anxiety about finances and his insecurity in social and personal relationships. He immediately told about his parents, their standards, and how they played into his concerns. He brought out many positive elements in his marriage.

Mr. G is a slightly built man, pleasant in manner, not especially masculine in appearance. He is the oldest of five children. His father comes from an established old family and is a highly successful business man. He had expressed hope that Mr. G would later use his scientific knowledge in the business. Mr. G described his mother as an intelligent person who gave up her earlier interests and became absorbed in her family. His parents were upset when he married a girl of different religious faith and of lower social status.

Mrs. G, an attractive, well-dressed girl with a sweet and superficially poised manner, is the youngest of five. Her father was incapacitated during most of her childhood and died when she was in college. The members of her family were affectionate but had strict religious beliefs. They were always under considerable financial strain and Mrs. G had borrowed money for her college education. Mrs. G, too, expressed concern about her arguments with her husband and later was able to speak of her concern about herself. Mrs. G brought out her interest in boys who were "different" and thought Mr. G fitted this description.

In the early interviews both Mr. and Mrs. G told their respective caseworkers about their relationship and their increasing difficulty in their sexual adjustment. Mrs. G expressed reluctance to have intercourse. Their day-by-day discord arose largely over the use of money. Mr. G was particularly concerned about his wife's impulsive spending. Each gave considerable background material which indicated that Mr. G was preoccupied with his relationships with his parents; he had rebelled against

[7] This and subsequent case illustrations are quoted from Eleanor A. Moore, "Casework Skills in Marriage Counseling," *Social Casework*, Vol. XXXIV, No. 6, June, 1953, pp. 255-258, by permission of the Family Service Association of America.

them in many ways and felt considerable guilt. Mrs. G seemed also to have rebelled against her parents and seemed, in addition, to be reacting to the various deprivations.

In psychiatric consultation the treatment aims and techniques were discussed.

Mrs. G seemed to be somewhat hysterical in personality make-up and not able to gain much gratification from sexual relationships. She, however, was reacting with withdrawal to Mr. G's need to control, and to his obvious conflict about having married her without his family's approval. Although it was recognized that each partner had personality disturbances, it was agreed that treatment should be focused on their marriage relationship and their day-to-day difficulties, with the intent of increasing their emancipation from their parents and permitting them to feel less guilty about making their own choices, planning for themselves, and experiencing sexual gratification.

As both were helped in handling daily events and their reactions to each other, considerable improvement in their relationship took place. Mr. G began to plan for a job away from his father and to be less concerned about his parents' reactions. Mrs. G responded to his changed attitude and discussed more freely her aversions to sex. Their sexual adjustment also seemed to improve.

The treatment enabled the partners to improve the balance in their marital relationship and to become aware that their difficulties stemmed from personality disturbances. Either, or both, might later decide that psychiatric treatment would be advisable.

In some instances, one or both of the marital partners may be helped to gain some understanding of their specific behavior and feelings at the time of crisis, or of a shift in the family balance. The birth of a baby, for instance, may revive earlier conflicts about relationships with their parents or siblings. In some marriages, one partner's irrational wishes for excessive love and security, or his overdetermined need for prestige, may make overwhelming demands on the other partner which may culminate in "blow-ups." In treatment, the problems of adjustment are approached first from the standpoint of the couple's patterns of relationship and then gradually directed to the specific area of difficulty. The client must first develop confidence in, and a strong relationship with, the caseworker before he is able to engage in an examination of his part in precipitating the problem.

CASE OF THE WEBB FAMILY

Mr. and Mrs. W, a couple in their forties with three children, were referred by their minister because they had reached an impasse in their management of money. There was no real financial need. Just prior to the referral, Mrs. W had suddenly bought a new washing machine. This had upset Mr. W and he had threatened to leave home. The minister indicated that Mr. W was extremely thrifty, was a good workman, and had held his job for years. To the community, the church, and friends they appeared to be a substantial family.

Mr. and Mrs. W were interviewed separately. Mr. W stressed the need to save as much as possible for the family's future; he wanted his family to have more security than he had had as a child. Mr. W's preoccupation with money, his stubbornness, and his orderliness were all traits suggestive of a rigid personality pattern. Mrs. W was more anxious than her husband. She had been having various aches and pains which she attributed to her approaching menopause. She expressed a desire for outside activities and for a more attractive home.

Psychiatric consultation confirmed the caseworker's impression that Mr. W's capacity for change was limited. His defenses seemed effective and his activities, such as hoarding money, fishing, and hunting, were socially acceptable. Mrs. W, also controlling, used money as a tool to express aggression against her husband. Each capitalized on the other's vulnerability and used similar defenses of projection, denial, and rationalization.

Casework treatment was directed toward fortifying Mr. and Mrs. W's defenses and toward helping Mrs. W relate to her husband in a less aggressive way.

Because of Mr. W's absorption with his own needs, he did not realize that he was not providing some of the things that were important to his wife and to the management of the home. The caseworker pointed out that he could continue to manage the finances, but that he could also afford to spend more for certain items for the home; that this would enable his family to manage better and his children to get more enjoyment, and would be an investment for himself and his family.

Mrs. W was helped to realize that her earlier acceptance of her husband's ways of doing things made it difficult for him to accept her change of attitude and behavior.

The caseworker's acceptance of Mrs. W helped her to discuss the day-by-day events in order to see why she was now acting differently. She could bring out her need for more money than she was getting and was helped to realize that it was important for her to let her husband know what she wanted so that he could have a part in planning expenditures for things that were needed. Both Mr. and Mrs. W were able to make some modifications in their behavior. Through this treatment the marital balance was restored and the marital relationship improved.

The caseworker, in this type of treatment, attempts to help the martial partners clarify factors in the current situation and their reactions to them, with the aim of helping them achieve greater ability to meet social responsibilities. The aims of this method are to support existing strengths and to produce modification of adaptive patterns, but not to help the client achieve basic personality change.

CASE OF THE BROWN FAMILY

Mr. and Mrs. Brown were referred by the visiting nurse because Mrs. B was upset by her husband's recent severe injury to his hand and prolonged convalescence. The couple had been married five years and had a son three years of age. Mr. B, 29, had always been the dominant partner. Mrs. B, 22, a small, attractive person, seemed to have considerable maturity, despite the fact that her mother had died when Mrs. B was 12 and her father and grandmother, with whom she had lived, had given her little attention during her adolescence.

Mr. B had finished high school, had done well in his work as a shop foreman prior to service, and had a good service record. His accident precipitated much anxiety about whether he could resume his work and support his family. Because of the accident, Mrs. B, who enjoyed being a wife and mother, had taken a job for the first time. In addition, she had considerable responsibility for her husband's care.

The strains of working and the lack of time for her family responsibilities were making her increasingly nervous and irritable, especially with her husband. The caseworker recognized that this family had real strengths but, because of external pressures, needed immediate help in finding a day nursery, in handling expenses, and in clarifying Mr. B's prognosis and capacities for retraining. It was also clear that the reversal of roles was particularly upsetting to Mrs. B and that she needed help in understanding her many feelings of concern, frustration, inadequacy, and resentment. Through contact with the caseworker, Mrs. B was enabled to carry her responsibilities more comfortably during the months of her husband's convalescence and retraining. Mr. B gained reassurance from the doctor about his condition and was able to use vocational testing and retraining realistically. He subsequently found employment and assumed the role of wage earner, and as a result the marital balance was restored. Through the support and practical help of the caseworker the family's needs, both practical and personal, were met, and the possible destructive effects of this crisis on their marital relationship were averted.

Such supportive treatment is also appropriate in cases in which the problems are deep-seated. Often families of alcoholics, for example, are of real concern to the community because of frequent quarrels and separations and because of the severe deprivation to the children. These families may be able to use help during periods of crisis. In other families, where periodic absences are due to the husband's delinquent or emotionally disturbed behavior, the treatment aim is to help the wife accept the limits of the marital relationship, to help her get some satisfactions for herself, and to strengthen her in her role as mother. Even in cases in which problems are severe, treatment may result in a lessening of tension between marital partners, or a decrease in the problems of rearing the children. Use of community resources, such as camp and recreational groups, may supplement the direct treatment, providing opportunities for children to satisfy some of their growth needs.

II. FEE CHARGING IN FAMILY SERVICE AGENCIES

Although family welfare agencies, in general, provide their service to the clients without charge, it has been found for some time, with the wider acceptance of casework as an important, valuable help in personal problems and social difficulties, that some clients wanted to pay for casework service and counseling. They felt that they could afford to pay for such professional service in the same way as they pay their doctor or lawyer in consulting them, and they expressed their preference to pay for casework, rather than to have to ask for free service. Family service agencies which offer such paid service use a graduated scale so that the client pays a fee according to his financial ability. By this type of casework the agencies have made it possible for a type of client to use casework who never would have been willing to seek counsel from any charity agency before. Among them are bankers, merchants, factory workers, engineers, teachers, white-collar employees, artists, craftmen, and others.

There are about thirty-five fee-charging family service agencies in the country, most of them in large cities. Casework with paying clients includes all aspects of social problems, personal, emotional, and family difficulties, employment questions, placement of children in summer camps or in schools and of adults in rest homes, sanatoriums, old-age homes, and mental institutions. Most family service agencies are satisfied with their clients' reactions about fee charging and consider this form of service a real contribution to the needs of the public.[8] In a few large cities, some individual social workers, usually well-experienced and trained persons, are engaged in casework as a personal professional activity without connection with a social agency, sometimes under the title of "personal relations counselor." There is not yet sufficient experience to predict whether or not such an independent practice on a fee basis will have a future.

[8] See Alice D. Taggart, *et al., Fee Charging in a Family Agency* (New York: Family Welfare Association of America, 1944).

III. PRINCIPLES OF FAMILY SERVICE

The goal of family casework in social agencies is to aid the individual client and the members of his family in achieving harmonious relationships in their family life. In recent years there has been a growing emphasis on education as a process for strengthening the relationships of the members of the family, their mutual affection, and cooperation. Some of these activities have been called "family life education"[9] and have been carried on by social workers in family service agencies. These agencies share, however, the effort for family protection with programs of adult education, parent-teachers associations, discussion groups of young married couples, and church and mothers' clubs. The Family Service Association defines it as a "process by which people are helped, through group discussion, to broaden their understanding of family relationships." The specific role of the caseworker here is devoting full interest to the individual who is in anxiety or trouble, and knowing the sources of the community which may help in this process.

In our urban-industrial civilization, the family has assumed a highly individualistic pattern which often has not been conducive to the happiness of all its members. Marriage counseling is in most family service agencies one of the essential parts of the caseworkers' assignment. It regularly includes premarital guidance; the caseworker helps the two marriage partners to decide whether or not their plan promises happiness to both of them in their social, sexual, and cultural relationship, especially with regard to economic and occupational conditions, employment of the wife, relationship to parents and relatives of both partners, and health and behavior problems.[10] In both premarital and marital counseling regarding conflicts of husband and wife, the caseworker advises the consultation of clinics and physi-

[9] See Helen L. Witmer, *Social Work: An Analysis of a Social Institution* (New York: Farrar & Rinehart, 1942), pp. 246-247; and Gertrude K. Pollak, "Family Life Education: Its Focus and Techniques," *Social Casework*, May, 1953, pp. 198-203.

[10] See Judson T. and Mary G. Landis, *Building a Successful Marriage*, 2nd ed. (New York: Prentice-Hall, Inc., 1953) and *Personal Adjustment, Marriage, and Family Living* (New York: Prentice-Hall, Inc., 1950); Helen Witmer, *op. cit.*, pp. 257-263; A. Truxal and F. Merrill, *op. cit.*, pp. 730-735; and Luther E. Woodward, "Family Life Education," *Social Work Year Book, 1954*, pp. 197-203.

cians, whenever medical and psychiatric problems seem to be important in the decision of the partners. She suggests the use of a mental hygiene clinic or a psychiatrist if sexual maladjustment and behavior patterns make it advisable to explore the chances of successful therapy. Family casework covers conflicts between parents and children whereby the right of children to their own choice of play, companionship, and activities is recognized in accordance to their age. In some instances the family service agency shares the responsibility of premarital, marital, and child problems counseling with other community facilities engaged in this work.

The main element in family casework is the counseling of all members of the family in order to prevent individual and family disorganization, mutual hostility, unhappiness, and breakdown. If differences of opinion, apathy, or anxieties develop, the family caseworker tries to help the members of the family understand one another better and to create among them the desire of mutual assistance to overcome this threat to their successful family life. This service is given to people who are willing to use it constructively, whether or not they are in economic need.

Modern family service is convinced that most clients will make real use of a plan of rehabilitation only when they themselves share in the planning, and when their desire for self-support and responsibility for their life is fully considered. In order to carry on such a plan, the social caseworker frequently helps to straighten out differences and tensions within the family, and to change the environmental or health situation by arranging financial assistance, finding housing at reasonable cost, a satisfactory job, and securing necessary medical or psychiatric treatment through the use of community facilities, hospitals, and clinics.

This type of social casework includes so-called "supportive work" —encouragement and supervision rendered to parents in order to secure constructive relations to the children or other members of the family. Family casework requires that the social worker possess a full understanding of the client's personality, motivations, behavior, and his situation within the family. On this basis she[11] assists the client in developing his plans to meet his difficulties. The caseworker's task is

[11] We have been using the feminine form because the majority of family caseworkers are women, but the functions of male social workers are the same.

to inform the client which social institutions, such as the public welfare department, child welfare agencies, hospitals, clinics, and recreation services, are available that may be helpful in the solution of his problems, and she explains the nature and conditions of these services. If the client desires to use some of these facilities, the caseworker arranges for the necessary contact and referral. But the client himself makes his final decision; he uses his right of self-determination.

In her relationship with the client and with his family, the caseworker encourages all members of the family to use their thoughts and resources, their capacity and ingenuity, thus preserving and strengthening their energy and desire of independence. She helps the client to overcome his anxieties and confusions, which are a barrier to finding a way out of his difficulties. In enabling the client to make his own decision in his affairs, she strengthens his self-reliance and self-respect. She clearly explains to the client what the facilities and limitations of the family service organization are, so that the client knows what to expect from the agency according to its policies and resources, and what his own role has to be.

The characteristic problems which families face today are based upon economic, environmental, health, or psychological conditions. Economic suffering may result from illness in the family, unemployment, a change of jobs, and low wages, all of which frequently impair a normal, happy family life. After World War II, adequate housing was in many areas difficult to obtain, particularly for families of minority groups and families with several children and low income. Young couples sometimes were forced to live with parents and in-laws, and to give up their independence and privacy. The expectations and dreams of other families for a fine house, garden, car, or television set have been frustrated, and contribute to dissatisfaction and emotional disturbance.

Illness of one or more members of the family is one of the most frequent causes for anxieties, debts, economic insecurity, and personal difficulties. The achievements of medical science are not easily available for patients of modest means or low income.

Psychological conditions of family discord are sometimes caused by hasty marriages of young couples who are driven together by a short-lived passion and use marriage as a device to create a semblance of love and security. Counseling alone may not produce sincere affection, patience, and tolerance necessary for successful adjustment of married life, but it may well serve as a medium of understanding where both partners are able to strive for such an adjustment.

Solutions of problems in family life based upon physicial, social, or economic conditions are difficult, and cannot easily be found. The person asking for advice in the family service agency is assured that his information is kept confidential by the caseworker, and that other persons will share the discussion of his problems only with his permission. The caseworker's ability to help the client requires insight into the psychology of human behavior, into cultural, ethnic, and religious patterns, and into her personal feelings and reactions regarding all the elements involved in the client's asking for help which brought him to the family agency. The fact that the caseworker is the representative of the family service agency, not just an individual with professional skill, sometimes makes it easier for her to explain the policy and limitations of the organization. It also spares the client the feeling of humiliation to be forced to ask for sympathetic understanding and help from an individual who at the first visit is a stranger.

We discussed in the preceding chapters the fact that basic financial needs of families without income or resources are increasingly met by public assistance and social insurance payments. The role of the private family service agency under sectarian or humanitarian auspices has been primarily to help in emotional and personal troubles. However, families in financial distress frequently also suffer from dissatisfaction, frictions, and hostilities and need help in these problems as well. For this reason private family service agencies give temporary financial aid or supplement public assistance payments in order to make it possible for the client to re-establish normal family life. Family casework offered by trained, professional workers is available in a growing number of communities and has created a better understanding of the value of counseling service in the public, including the service to financially independent family circles.

IV. SPECIAL SERVICES IN THE FAMILY WELFARE FIELD

We shall discuss now a few activities of family service agencies which deal with special problems of clients who have particular needs.

A. SERVICES TO THE AGED

The growing number of aged people whose proportion in relation to the entire population is steadily increasing in all countries of Western civilization has called attention to their specific needs. In 1850, only 2.6 per cent of the population was sixty-five years of age or older; in 1950, 7.7 per cent. The average life expectancy has advanced from forty years in 1850 to forty-nine years in 1900, to sixty years in 1930, to sixty-three years in 1940, and to sixty-seven years in 1950. Improved living conditions and sanitation, easier and shorter work with the use of machinery, and advances in medical science, nutrition, and health education have contributed to these longer life spans. But our society has not yet succeeded in using sufficiently the lengthened life of older persons for useful activities and cultural satisfaction.

Our methods of public assistance and social insurance, industrial pension plans, and private insurance provisions[12] have emphasized securing economic protection for older people who cannot work any longer. But social workers become aware that the "senior citizens" living in enforced retirement often not only suffer from chronic diseases, frailties of their age, but also from the unhappiness caused by their feeling of uselessness, loneliness, or despair. In addition to methods of economic protection discussed above, family welfare and social group work agencies, therefore, are in full agreement that the communities have to pool all their resources in order to offer older persons more than the bare necessities of life—food, clothing, shelter, and medical care. "Senior citizens" need understanding, sympathy, companionship, and acceptance in the community in order to continue a way of life that gives them some amount of satisfaction.[13] When an old person loses the ability to take care of himself, and his own family is not able to care for him and nurse him, a protective en-

[12] See Chapters 7, 9, and 17; and Geneva Mathiasen, "Significant Trends in Aiding the Aging in This Country," in Senator Thomas C. Desmond, *Age Is No Barrier* (Albany: New York State Joint Legislative Committee on Problems of the Aging, 1952), pp. 47-51.

[13] Ruth Hill: "The Aged," *Social Work Year Book, 1949*, pp. 43-47; Charles I. Schottland, "California Plans for Its Aging Population," *Public Welfare*, Vol. 10, No. 4, October, 1952, pp. 103-106; and Senator Thomas C. Desmond, *Enriching the Years* (Albany: New York State Joint Legislative Committee on Problems of the Aging, 1953), with many practical illustrations of services to the aged.

vironment has to be found for him. The services of the community must be mobilized for helping the aged to meet their personal, economic, medical, and social needs, and to offer cultural, educational, recreational and vocational projects for the lonely and unemployed.

In the past, a "home for the aged" was considered the traditional place where an older person could find shelter when he could not live in his own home or with his family. At present social agencies consider institutions only one of several possibilities to care for old people. For the chronically sick, hospitals, special institutions for the chronically ill, homes for the aged, and family foster care with the support of medical and nursing services are beginning to be used. Other programs for the aged are special housing units or apartment projects equipped with easy housekeeping facilities and arrangements for collective use of kitchens, laundries, living rooms, library, or music room. The units provide medical and nursing supervision and special recreational centers for older citizens.

Family welfare agencies have noted that older people express the desire to be counseled by caseworkers with special experience, sympathy and skill in working with the aged and their families. If housekeepers are provided for older people, the family welfare agency plans to prepare them for a longer period of service than usually considered, and for taking care of the shopping, cleaning, and cooking, as well as giving some personal aid.

Family welfare agencies also develop placement services in private families and supervise boarding homes for older people, who either pay the monthly board themselves or receive aid from relatives, public assistance or the family agency. They assist older people in finding convalescent and nursing homes, sometimes supplementing private resources or old-age assistance payments in order to secure adequate medical and nursing care.

Clubs and community centers for the aged have been recently established in order to give older citizens the feeling that they are not unwanted, and to offer them opportunities to apply their experience and creative abilities, or to learn new skills with the satisfaction of accomplishment.[14] Recreational activities of the aged are not limited

[14] Ruth Hill, "Group Living for the Elderly," *National Conference of Social Work, Proceedings 1948*, pp. 410-418; and Oskar Schulze, "*Live Long and Like It*," Associated Lutheran Charities, 1947. See also, Alexander Simon, "Psychological Problems of Aging," *California Medicine*, Vol. 75, August, 1951, pp. 73-80.

to clubs and centers but are included also in modern homes for the aged and made available to older people in hospitals and homes for the chronically ill.

Private homes for the aged, frequently maintained by charitable organizations, sectarian agencies, and fraternal orders, are using increasingly the payments of social insurance and public assistance benefits of their residents. Since in old-age assistance the need of the individual old person has to be proved, most old-age homes have changed their former policies of requesting, when a resident is admitted, the payment of a lump sum in order to secure life-time care. Instead, they have introduced boarding contracts which include provision for monthly payments for the services rendered by the home. Advantages of this policy are that the institution is no longer compelled to keep a resident who cannot adjust to congregate living, and that the resident himself is not compelled to stay on when he does not like the conditions of the home. On the other hand, in periods of inflation the home is no longer obliged to continue care because the money paid has lost part of its value, and those residents who at the time of admission were able to pay their board may then become elegible for public assistance after their financial means have been used up.

B. HOMEMAKER SERVICES

In families, problems arise from the absence or sickness of the mother when no adult member of the family nor any relatives and friends are able to care for the children and the working father. Family service and child care agencies have found that in such instances the temporary break-up of the family, when the mother is too ill to manage the home, by placement of the children in institutions or foster families, may be avoided through providing the family with a "housekeeper" or "homemaker." Homemakers are carefully selected and trained in advance by social agencies which provide this type of service. When a family asks for homemaker service, the agency decides whether that family may receive this aid under the rules of the agency. The social worker clears the relationship and duties of the homemaker in the family and makes arrangements for the family's contribution to the salary of the homemaker. If circumstances allow, an interview between the mother and the homemaker is arranged so that the mother may explain her wishes for the care of the family and the special duties which the home management entails. This contact usually removes anxiety and feeling of jealousy from the mother, who has to let another woman take her place temporarily in the family.

Philip Bonn photo. Courtesy U.S. Children's Bureau.

THE HOUSEKEEPER AS MOTHER'S SUBSTITUTE

In general, homemakers are sent only for limited periods to a home, and try to continue the regular routine of home management, diets, and child care. The children have the advantage of remaining with their father in their own home with little change in their rhythm of life. If the family has no means for paying the homemaker, the social agency's budget often provides funds for assuming this expense. As a rule, the agency guarantees the payment of the salary to the homemaker and collects from the family according to its ability to pay. In 1954, eighty-eight family and child care agencies offered homemaker service, among them fifteen public welfare agencies. Most homemakers are employed on a full-time basis. The social agencies assume training and supervision of the homemakers, frequently by their own supervisors and caseworkers.[15]

C. SERVICES TO TRAVELERS AND MIGRANTS

Travelers who are on their way to another community and migrants who wish to settle in another part of the country (or arrive here from abroad) often encounter serious difficulties en route. They become stranded without means, are without funds for food or shelter, or need medical care. They face these difficulties in a strange environment where they do not know anyone and do not know what means of help may be available. Family welfare agencies, therefore, have been giving aid to transients for many years, but since they are often limited by policy to serve the resident population, specialized services became necessary. They are rendered primarily by the Travelers Aid Society. This agency, through its branches, is prepared to assist travelers and transients in need on a "short-contact" basis. The problems in travelers' aid vary from simple information on trains, planes, bus connections, and hotel accomodations, to the location of families and friends, vocational and employment opportunities, financial aid, medical or hospital assistance, and even serious personal difficulties. The services of the Travelers Aid Society usually are situated at railroad stations, bus terminals, and piers of ports where the persons arrive and need advice or help. The casework in the Travelers Aid Society requires a thorough knowledge of all community resources within the city where the agency is located, but also special contact with facilities in other cities, and the ability to refer the client to places where his needs are really met. Runaway children and adolescents without realistic plans are among the groups which frequently become the charge of the Travelers Aid Society. Wayward children may be cared for by a children's agency until the return to their own home is arranged. Then they might be put on a train or bus and agreements made with other social agencies en route to help in the safe return of the child, unless his problems require that a social worker or an attendant accompany

[15] Maud Morlock, "Homemaker Service," *Social Work Year Book, 1951*, pp. 225-229; U.S. Children's Bureau, *Homemaker Service; A Method of Child Care* (Washington, D. C.: 1946), Publication No. 296; and Rika MacLennan, "Homemaker Service," *Social Work Year Book, 1954*, pp. 253-257.

him all the way home. Other help might be necessary for aged or invalid, crippled, blind, or mentally disturbed people who have tried to travel alone but are found in need of direction.

The need for travelers aid is particularly great in periods of war, defense, or economic distress when many people are on the move in order to join the armed forces or to find new jobs. The society assists not only travelers who are just on their way, but also migrants looking for a new home and refugees and displaced persons who are not receiving help in the settlement and adjustment by other social agencies. Since 1917 the National Travelers Aid Association coordinates the local travelers aid societies, which have been established in 110 places, but which have enough representatives in other communities to allow about 1,500 cities to use their services.[16]

D. LEGAL AID SERVICE

Another service which is sometimes connected with family welfare agencies is called Legal Aid. It means that persons without sufficient money receive free, or for a nominal charge, legal advice and representation before a court. Trained caseworkers have some knowledge of certain legal questions, but are not equipped to give responsible legal advice on a professional basis. The need of special legal service developed first in New York, in 1876, and in Chicago, 1886, for large immigrant groups frequently victimized by swindlers, extortionists, and ruthless exploiters who refused to pay their wages. Arthur von Briesen, a New York lawyer, established the New York Legal Aid Society for German immigrants, and in Chicago the Protective Society for Women and Children was organized to aid immigrant women. Both agencies broadened their scope and developed into organizations which assisted persons without regard to origin, race, and creed. Among the pioneers of this movement Reginald Heber Smith (Boston), John S. Bradley (Duke University), and Harrison Tweed (New York) should be mentioned.

In many small communities lawyers give their service free to people who have no funds to pay for their professional service. In large cities the needs of the poor cannot be met by casual arrangements, since most lawyers are too busy to serve clients without a charge. Thus branches of the Legal Aid Society in larger cities are

---

[16] *Social Work Year Book, 1954,* p. 654.

necessary in order to allow the people without means the protection of the law, which would be denied to them if they had to miss professional counsel and representation in legal matters.[17] Since 1949 these legal aid societies have established the National Legal Aid Association in Washington, D.C. as their coordinating body, which develops standards and promotes the general aims of legal aid.

Local legal aid societies are organized, as a rule, in one of the following six types of organization: (1) as a division or branch of a *family welfare agency*, such as the Legal Aid Bureau of the United Charities of Chicago; (2) as an *independent legal aid society* under its own board of directors, supported by the Community Chest, and often with prominent lawyers as members of the board; (3) as a *bar association office* which employs paid personnel; (4) as a *law school clinic* of a university, where advanced law students provide legal service under supervision of faculty members; (5) as a government *legal aid bureau* where a lawyer is employed from tax funds, usually under the city authorities; or (6) as a *public defender office* where the accused receives free counsel when he is unable to pay an attorney in criminal cases.

To engage a lawyer they can afford, people are referred by legal aid societies to a list supplied by the local bar association. In cooperation with the bar association, the societies often make special financial arrangements for clients with moderate means. The problems brought before legal aid societies include family and personal legal questions (family discord, divorce, separation, adoption), which are the largest group; economic legal problems, such as eviction, debts, mortgages, sick pay, wage difficulties, budget collection, compensations, and insurance benefits; as well as some litigation on real estate or personal property, and other legal matters.

SELECTED BIBLIOGRAPHY

Beattie, Anna B., and Florence Hollis, *Family Case Work: A Good Profession to Choose*. New York: Family Welfare Association of America, 1945.

[17] See Frances Craighead Dwyer, "Legal Aid," *Social Work Year Book, 1951,* pp. 294-298. In 1951, legal aid was provided in 152 cities, and seventy-six had a centrally located office for this service with paid staffs. In addition to these services, certain courts—small claims courts, domestic and family relation courts—do not require fees (or only nominal fees) and allow the claimants to present their complaints and arguments without an attorney.

Beck, Joseph E., *et al.*, *Family Case Work Services for Refugees*. New York: Family Welfare Association of America, 1941.

Berkowitz, Sidney J., *et al.*, *Diagnosis and Treatment of Marital Problems*. New York: Family Service Association of America, 1949.

Bradway, John S., *Law and Social Work*. Chicago: University of Chicago Press, 1929.

Breckrinridge, Elizabeth, *Community Services for Older People: The Chicago Plan*. Chicago: Wilcox and Follett, 1952.

——, *Effective Use of Older Workers*. Chicago: Wilcox and Follett, 1953.

Brownell, Emery A., *Legal Aid in the United States*. Rochester, New York: Lawyers' Cooperative Publ. Co., 1951.

——, "Legal Aid," *Social Work Year Book, 1954*, pp. 320-322.

Burgess, Ernest W., and Harvey J. Locke, *The Family: From Institution to Companionship*. New York: American Book, 1945.

——, and Paul Wallin, *Engagement and Marriage*. Chicago: Lippincott, 1953.

Burns, Eveline M., "Economic Factors in Family Life," *The Family in a Democratic Society*, pp. 12-28. New York: Columbia University Press, 1949.

Clifton, Eleanor, and Florence Hollis (editors), *Child Therapy: A Casework Symposium*. New York: Family Service Association of America, 1948.

Creech, Margaret, "Migrants, Transients, and Travelers," *Social Work Year Book, 1954*, pp. 355-360.

Cuber, John E., *Marriage Counseling Practice*. New York: Appleton-Century-Crofts, Inc., 1948.

Davis, Allison, and R. J. Havighurst, *Father of the Man*. Boston: Houghton, 1947.

Desmond, Thomas C., *Age Is No Barrier*. New York State Joint Legislative Committee on Problems of the Aging, 1952.

——, *Enriching the Years*. New York State Joint Legislative Committee on Problems of the Aging, 1953.

French, Thomas M., "Personal Interaction and Growth in Family Life," *The Family in a Democratic Society*, pp. 29-40. New York: Columbia University Press, 1949.

Gilbert, Jeanne G., *Understanding Old Age*. New York: The Ronald Press Company, 1952.

Goldfarb, Dora, *Homemaker Service for the Aged*. Washington, D.C.: Social Security Administration, Bureau of Public Assistance, 1949.

Groves, Ernest R., *Conserving Marriage and the Family*. New York: Macmillan, 1944.

Gruenberg, Sidonic, *Our Children Today*. New York: Viking Press, 1952.

Hertel, Frank J., "Family Social Work," *Social Work Year Book, 1951*, pp. 183-190.

——, "The Aged," *Social Work Year Book, 1949*, pp. 43-47.

Hill, Ruth L., "Group Living for the Elderly," *National Conference of Social Work, Proceedings 1948*, pp. 410-418.

*Hollis, Florence, *Women in Marital Conflict: A Casework Study*. New York: Family Service Association of America, 1949.

Kaplan, Jerome, *A Social Program for Older People*. Minneapolis: University of Minnesota Press, 1953.

Karpf, Maurice J., *The Scientific Basis of Social Work: A Study in Family Case Work*. New York: Columbia University Press, 1931.

*Kasius, Cora (editor), *A Comparison of Diagnostic and Functional Casework Concepts*. New York: Family Service Association of America, 1950.

———— (editor), *Relief Practice in a Family Agency*. New York: Family Welfare Association of America, 1942.

Kimble, Grace E., *Social Work with Travelers and Transients: A Study of Travelers Aid Work in the United States*. Chicago: University of Chicago Press, 1935.

Kluckhohn, Clyde, "Variations in the Human Family," *The Family in a Democratic Society*, pp. 3-11, New York: Columbia University Press, 1949.

Koos, Earl, *Families in Trouble*. New York: King's Crown Press, 1946.

*Landis, Judson T., and Mary G. Landis, *Building a Successful Marriage*, 2nd ed. New York: Prentice-Hall, Inc., 1953.

————, *Personal Adjustment: Marriage and Family Living*. New York: Prentice-Hall, Inc., 1950.

————, *Readings in Marriage and the Family*. New York: Prentice-Hall, Inc., 1952.

Lansdale, Robert T., "Trends in Care of the Aged," in Senator Thomas C. Desmond, *Age Is No Barrier* (New York State Joint Legislative Committee on Problems of the Aging, 1952), pp. 109-111.

Lawton, George, *Aging Successfully*. New York: Columbia University Press, 1946.

Levy, John, and Ruth Monroe, Jr., *The Happy Family*. New York: Knopf, 1938.

Loomis, Charles P., and Allan Beegle, *Rural Social Systems*. New York: Prentice-Hall, Inc., 1950.

Manginelli, Madeleine K. H., *Homemaker Service: Meeting Crises in Family Life with a New Horizon in Child Care*. New York: Child Welfare League of America, 1941.

Maclachlan, John M. (editor), *Health in the Later Years*. Gainesville: University of Florida Press, 1953.

MacLennan, Rika, "Homemaker Service," *Social Work Year Book, 1954*, pp. 253-257.

McLean, Francis H., *The Family Society: Joint Responsibilities of Board, Staff, and Members*. New York: Family Welfare Association of America, 1927.

Mead, Margaret, "What Is Happening to the American Family?" *Journal of Social Casework*, November, 1947, pp. 322-329.

Morlock, Maud, "Homemaker Service," *Social Work Year Book, 1951,* pp. 225-229.

Mowrer, Harriet R., *Personality Adjustment and Domestic Discord.* New York: American Book, 1935.

*Plant, James S., *Personality and the Cultural Pattern.* New York: Commonwealth Club, 1937.

Reynolds, Bertha C., *An Experiment in Short Contact Interviewing. Smith College Studies in Social Work,* Vol. 3, No. 1, September, 1932.

Rogers, Carl R., *Counseling and Psychotherapy: Newer Concepts in Practice.* Boston: Houghton, 1942.

Smith, Marjorie J., *Rural Case Work Services.* New York: Family Welfare Association of America, 1943.

Smith, Reginald Heber, *Growth of Legal Aid Work in the United States,* Rev. ed. Washington, D.C.: Bureau of Labor Statistics, Bulletin #607, 1936.

———, *Justice and the Poor.* New York: Carnegie Foundation for the Advancement of Teaching, 1919.

Stein, Herman D., *Careers for Men in Family Social Work.* New York: Family Service Association of America, 1946.

*Taft, Jessie (editor), *Family Casework and Counseling.* Philadelphia: University of Pennsylvania Press, 1948.

Taggart, Alice D., *et al.,* *Fee Charging in a Family Agency.* New York: Family Welfare Association of America, 1944.

Taussig, Frances, *et al., Family Counseling: Practice and Teaching.* New York: Jewish Family Service, 1949.

Tibbitts, Clark (editor), "Social Contribution by the Aging," *The Annals of the American Academy of Social and Political Science,* January, 1952.

Towle, Charlotte, "The Social Worker and Treatment of Marital Discord Problems," *Social Service Review,* Vol. XIV, No. 2, June 1940, pp. 211-223.

Truxal, Andrew G., and Francis E. Merrill, *Marriage and the Family in American Culture.* New York: Prentice-Hall, Inc., 1953.

Wilson, R. S., *The Short Contact in Social Work: A Study of Treatment on Time-Limited Relationships in Social Work.* 2 Vols. New York: National Association for Travelers Aid and Transient Service, 1937.

Wolf, Anna W. M., *The Parent's Manual.* New York: Simon & Schuster, 1951.

Woods, James H., *Helping Older People Enjoy Life.* New York: Harper, 1953.

Young, Leontine, *Out of Wedlock.* New York: McGraw, 1954.

11. Child Welfare

I. CHILDREN'S NEEDS FOR SPECIAL SERVICES

Care for children who are without the protection of their families, and for orphans and abandoned children, is one of the oldest forms of charity. But the recognition that children are in need of a different type of care from adults is only a recent development. Helpless orphans were the object of ancient religious charity. The modern term of "child welfare" has assumed a broader meaning. It is not only concerned with the care for destitute, neglected, deserted, sick, handicapped, or maladjusted and delinquent children. It is understood that "child welfare" also incorporates the social, economic, and health activities of public and private welfare agencies, which secure and protect the well-being of all children in their physical, intellectual, and emotional development.[1]

Scientific progress in the fields of anthropology, biology, medicine, psychology, and social research during the past hundred years has changed the attitude of society toward the child. He no longer is treated as an adult person, only smaller in stature, but as a human being with his own, different rhythm of life, and with his own laws of biological and mental growth. We are aware that the child is following drives, social forces, and motivations which are basically different from those which govern adult behavior. In the child's mind the world is identical with his own personality; fantasy and reality are not yet separated. Only in the period of adolescence do reality and fantasy begin to part.

As we have seen, the Colonial period in the United States ac-

[1] Hazel Fredericksen, *The Child and His Welfare* (San Francisco: Freeman, 1948), p. 1; Elizabeth W. Deuel, "Child Welfare," *Social Work Year Book, 1951*, p. 88; and Helen L. Witmer & Ruth Kotinsky, *Personality in the Making—The Fact Finding Report of the Midcentury White House Conference on Children and Youth* (New York: Harper, 1952).

cepted methods of care for dependent children, which Queen Elizabeth had ordered in the Poor Law of 1601. Older children were indentured for many years and served as cheap labor. Young children were boarded out to foster families or were later placed in the almshouses which developed in the United States during the eighteenth and nineteenth centuries. The large stream of immigrants from many countries to the New World and the high rate of mortality among indentured servants left numerous children alone and destitute. The Colonies were ill prepared for their care. Relatives, neighbors, church members, and a few nationality groups or religious societies took care of some dependent children. But usually the overseer of the poor chose indiscriminately to place them out, which was the cheapest way for the community.

When more and more children were brought into the almshouses during the first half of the nineteenth century, they lived in dark, overcrowded, filthy rooms, without adequate food and clothing, herded together with adults suffering from various physical and mental diseases. The typical conditions in these almshouses were revealed in an investigation in New York in 1857.[2] The committee described the poorhouses as the most disgraceful memorials of public charity, "where the misfortune of poverty is visited with greater deprivations of comfortable food, lodging, clothing, warmth, and ventilation than constitute the usual penalty of crime." Children should never have been permitted to enter the poorhouses. Young children were forced to pass their most impressionable years in the midst of such "vicious associations as will stamp them for a life of future infamy and crime." The committee recommended that children should be removed from the poorhouses and be placed in orphanages or asylums in which they would be educated according to the needs of their age. The idea of saving destitute children from the dangers of the "mixed almshouse" was the first, but not the only, cause for the rapid growth of orphan asylums during the twentieth century. There was also the need to find a place for other children who were endangered in their health and morale through conditions in their own families, who were neglected, and who were roaming

[2] State Board of Charities of New York, *Annual Report, 1903*, Part I, pp. 795-820; Sophonisba P. Breckinridge, *Public Welfare Administration in the United States* (Select documents) (Chicago: University of Chicago Press, 1935), pp. 149-158; and Grace Abbott, *The Child and the State*, Vol. II (Chicago: University of Chicago Press, 1938), pp. 3-9, 51-54.

the streets in large cities. A special problem existed for Negro children for whom no other care could be found. Religious societies were desirous of placing children in orphanages where religious education would bring them up in the faith of their parents.[3]

Before the nineteenth century, only a few orphanages had been established in this country. The first was built by the French Ursuline Sisters in New Orleans, in 1729, to place homeless orphans whose parents had been killed by Indian massacres, and the first public children's asylum was the Charleston Orphan House, founded in 1790 in South Carolina.[4] In the large cities private orphanages and children's branches of public almshouses or asylums took care of an increasing number of dependent and neglected children. In smaller communities and rural counties the segregation of children from adults took a long time, and children remained exposed to the undesirable influence of adult rogues and vagabonds who as inmates still were used to managing the children's sections of almshouses and even some public orphan asylums. The Congress of State Boards of Charities, in 1875, challenged the legislatures in the states to remove all children from county poorhouses, city almshouses, jails, and from all associations with adult paupers and criminals, and to place them in families, asylums, reformatories, or other children's institutions.[5]

Child placement in families in the form of indenture, which had been the main type of care for destitute children in the Colonial period, lead, in most instances, to neglect of the child's needs for affection and education and to heavy overwork and exploitation of the child as cheap domestic labor. In fact, the almshouse at first seemed to promise better treatment and education when it was proposed as a method of relief in the 1820's. The disadvantages of the bringing up of children in almshouses, asylums, and orphanages, however, were recognized fairly early. Children reared in institutions became dull, without vigor and initiative. Other wayward children and young adolescents in the streets of the large cities run away from these institutions. It was primarily due to the initiative of Charles Loring Brace and the New York Children's Aid Society, founded by

[3] Henry W. Thurston, *The Dependent Child* (New York: Columbia University Press, 1930), p. 40.
[4] G. Abbott, Vol. II, *op. cit.*, p. 7.
[5] H. Thurston, *op. cit.*, p. 90.

him in 1853, that family homes in the country were located for neglected children.[6]

At this period hundreds of thousands of immigrants landed each year in New York, and the police complained that over 10,000 vagrant children were running loose in the streets, begging and stealing. The main activity of the newly founded Society became the organization of a "mass deportation" of underprivileged or homeless children to farmers and mechanics in rural communities of the midwestern states. Many of these children found homes in the rural families where they were placed, but others did not adjust to the unfamiliar country life and agricultural work. The majority of the farmers who asked for children were poor and wanted cheap labor, without being too deeply interested in helping in the rehabilitation of wayward children.[7]

In Baltimore, Boston, Brooklyn, and Philadelphia, children's aid societies followed the New York example. In Chicago, Martin Van Buren Van Arsdale founded, in 1883, the American Educational Society, the first state-wide child placing agency for Illinois, which later expanded its services as the National Children's Home Society with charters in other states. Several states began to place children in foster homes under the auspices of state boards of charities, later departments of social welfare. They tried to select foster homes in which the children were not treated as only an economic asset, and they provided a certain amount of supervision by their inspectors who visited the families from time to time. Since the children's aid societies, however, did not pay board to the foster parents, they felt unable to require higher standards of care which were desirable in the interest of the children. The placement in rural regions in other states, frequently far away from the former residence of the child, usually led to a permanent breakup of the child's ties with his family and made it difficult for the family to maintain contact or to take back the child.

Foster care was a decidedly progressive step compared with the shortcomings of orphanages and other children's homes in that period. Children's asylums did not meet any individual needs of the

[6] Emma Brace, *The Life and Letters of Charles Loring Brace* (New York: Scribner, 1894); and Edith Abbott, *Some American Pioneers in Social Welfare* (Select Documents) (Chicago: University of Chicago Press, 1937).

[7] Moving examples of the fate of such children are presented by H. Thurston, *op. cit.*, pp. 113-120.

children. They were mostly mass institutions with huge dormitories where the children lacked personal attention and understanding, received treatment as groups rather than individuals, and missed the feeling of belonging and the love of parents and family. It was only toward the end of the nineteenth century that some children's institutions recognized these deficiencies and introduced the "cottage plan." Large dormitories were replaced by small family-like groups living in a separate building with a housemother and a housefather who were to function as a substitute for a real family. Even with such improvements, care of children in institutions deprived them of growing up in the normal setting of the community, playing with the neighbors, going to school, and returning to "their home." This fact explains that the introduction of carefully selected and supervised foster homes seemed a better solution to the problem of caring for children dispossessed of their own families.

The latest step in the development of methods for child protection is the concept that the child, whenever possible, should be left in his own family. We have already noted that until the end of the nineteenth century many children were taken away from their parents because of their poverty, and because it was thought that a pauper family could not properly bring up a child. The findings of modern psychology and psychoanalysis, as well as the observations of the juvenile courts and social agencies dealing with difficult and maladjusted children, proved, however, that it would be advisable to enable children to remain at home with their mothers and their siblings. Economic aid granted to the mother would allow her to rear her children instead of forcing her to give the children away and work in a factory, on the farm, or as a domestic worker. It was the first White House Conference on the Care of Dependent Children, in 1909, which emphasized the need of financial help to mothers in order to preserve the family.

Originally, private agencies carried a major share of responsibility for maintaining the family in cases of death of the father, divorce, and desertion, but more and more public funds were made available for this purpose. As we discussed before, the function of aid to dependent children with the support of federal and state funds is, at present, the main factor in overcoming the economic problems of financial maintenance of 2 million children in 550,000 to 600,000 families in the United States.[8] This support enables these families to provide adequate shelter, food, clothing, medical care, education, and recreation for their children. Our public social welfare services thus contribute to the maintenance of family life for the entire population, but other measures, such as public health services, schools, minimum wages and hours, agricultural subsidies, low-rent housing, social insurance benefits, and recreation facilities, also play an important role to this effect.

Essential as economic deficiencies frequently are for the development of the child in his family, they are not the only problems which require child welfare activities. Children are often endangered not only by poverty, insufficient income or sickness in the family, but also by neglect or rejection, lack of understanding or love, or because the parents are unable to manage the child. For these reasons casework for children is a vital necessity, and private family and child care agencies as well as the child welfare divisions of city and county welfare departments have developed casework for children as an integral part of their programs.[9]

Child welfare services are rendered mainly in three forms: (1) as economic and personal aid to children living in their own homes, (2) by providing substitute families or an adoptive home for children who have no home or cannot remain with their own families, and (3) by institutional care in children's homes and orphanages when children for particular reasons cannot be in their own homes or in foster families. Casework for the child in his own home considers the individual needs of the child for his well-being and health. It also uses facilities of the community like day nurseries, recreation, organized childrn's and youth activities, and clinics. In general, casework with the parents or the foster parents is indispensable in the interest of the child. Still more vital becomes individual service to children who cannot remain in their own families and for whom, therefore, substitute care has to be provided, either in a foster home or in a children's institution.

[8] See Chapters 5 and 8.

[9] The author considers casework with children as the very core of social work in the child welfare field, whether it is rendered by public welfare departments in connection with aid to dependent children or general assistance, by public health agencies, or by private child care or family service agencies; Helen Witmer, *Social Work—An Analysis of a Social Institution* (New York: Farrar & Rinehart, 1942), pp. 283, 303, 312-314, questions the character of some phases of these activities as social work.

II. WELFARE AND HEALTH SERVICES
FOR CHILDREN

The Social Security Act encourages public child welfare activities in three fields by annual federal grants-in-aid to states which present plans for such services that are approved by the United States Children's Bureau of the Department of Health, Education and Welfare. These include maternal and child health services, services for crippled children, and "child welfare services"[10] for the protection and care of homeless, dependent, neglected, and pre-delinquent children. In these health and welfare activities for children private social agencies render valuable aid and supplement public services which are carried on through the states, counties, and cities.

A. MATERNAL AND CHILD-HEALTH SERVICES

For the promotion of the health of mothers and young children, especially in rural areas and in areas suffering from severe economic distress, these services are strengthened by annual federal appropriations, which in 1953 totaled $16,500,000. The states have to share the expenses and administer the program through the state health agency. Personnel standards on a merit basis and proper, efficient administration are required; reports must be rendered, and the funds must be used for improvement of local services. Cooperation with medical, nursing, and private welfare organizations is required, and demonstration services in deprived areas and for groups in particular need have to be arranged. The federal allotment is composed of a uniform rate to all states—a sum based upon the ratio of live births in the state to the total in the United States, and an amount based upon the individual need of the state for financial assistance in order to carry out its maternal and child-health program. The services include well-baby clinics for regular medical examinations of young children and advice to their mothers, and prenatal clinics; home delivery nursing; infant and child health conferences; school, dental, and mental health services; advisory and consultation services; and training programs for pediatricians, dentists, nurses, nutritionists, and social workers. The necessity for further improvement

---

[10] "Child welfare services" is a technical term used in the Social Security Act to designate these preventive and protective activities as distinguished from material aid under public assistance.

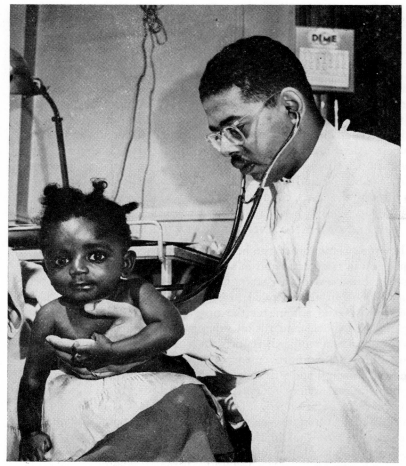

Esther Bubley photo. Courtesy U.S. Children's Bureau.

A CHILD HEALTH CONFERENCE

of specialized medical care for young children and school children in rural areas has been revealed by a nationwide study of child health by the American Academy of Pediatrics (1948).[11]

During World War II the federal government provided free "emergency maternity and infant care" to wives of service men of

[11] A. L. Van Horn, "Maternal and Child Health," *Social Work Year Book, 1951*, p. 301.

the lower ranks, including medical care for infants during their first year. The costs of this program were entirely met by federal funds, and its remarkable success showed the value of comprehensive medical care. During the period 1939 to 1948 the neonatal mortality rate (death of infants under one month) has decreased by 24 per cent, that of children under one year by 48 per cent, preschool mortality (ages one to four years) by 50 per cent, and maternal mortality by 71 per cent.[12]

B. SERVICES FOR CRIPPLED CHILDREN

These services are also administered at the federal level by the Division of Health Services of the Children's Bureau in the Department of Health, Education and Welfare. The Social Security Act defines these services as locating crippled children; providing medical, surgical, corrective, and other services and care; and facilities for diagnosis, hospitalization, and after care. They include provision of aids and prosthetic appliances, physiotherapy, medical social services, and maintenance of a state crippled children's registry. The federal grant of $15,000,000 annually is allocated by a uniform grant of $60,000 to each state, and a portion of $4,320,000 on the basis of the state's particular need for this program in relation to the number of crippled children; this amount must be matched by state, local, or private funds. The remaining $7,500,000 are allotted according to each state's need and in proportion to urban and rural child population without the requirement of matching funds. For the location of crippled children, the states use local public and private social agencies, public health nurses, physicians, midwives, hospitals, and nursery and kindergarten teachers, as well as elementary school teachers. In all states, diagnosis and treatment cover children with severe crippling conditions, such as clubfoot, harelip, cleft palate, and heavy deformities. Other diseases, such as rheumatic fever, heart diseases, cerebral palsy, eye and speech defects, ear diseases, epilepsy, and dental defects requiring orthodontia, are covered in some state programs (at present, frequently only on a demonstration basis). Usually the program is administered by the state and local health departments. In most states special classes for the instruction of crip-

[12] Children's Bureau, "Changes in Infant, Childhood, and Maternal Mortality Over the Decade 1939-1948" (Statistical Series, No. 6), 1950.

pled, deaf, and blind children are organized in urban areas, but they accommodate only a limited number of those children who need special education.

Private crippled children's agencies, established and supported by such fraternal orders as the Shriners, the Elks, and the Rotary Clubs, and also by religious and nonsectarian societies, have been the pioneers in this field. They built the first orthopedic hospitals and

Esther Bubley photo. Courtesy U.S. Children's Bureau.

HELP FOR A CRIPPLED CHILD

clinics and encouraged state legislation for crippled children preceding the Social Security Act of 1935. The first state orthopedic hospital was set up, in 1897, in Minnesota.[13] Despite the recently more

[13] Douglas McMurtrie, "Care of Crippled Children in the U.S.," *American Journal of Orthopedic Surgery,* Vol. 1912, pp. 3 and 5.

generous federal and state appropriations for crippled children, supplementation by private social agencies is still urgently needed, since most states do not yet provide adequate diagnosis, and particularly, the expensive treatment for many crippling diseases.[14]

C. CHILD WELFARE SERVICES

At the time of the enactment of the Social Security Act of 1935, nearly seven and one-half million boys and girls were "on relief," 300,000 children were dependent or neglected, and about 200,000 children annually came before the juvenile courts. Help and protection for these children was mainly left to private social agencies and to the inadequate powers of local communities. With the support of federal grants-in-aid, public services for the protection of the unfortunate homeless, orphaned, abandoned, dependent, or neglected children, and for children in danger of delinquency, have been greatly strengthened. Every state now has a child welfare division in its public welfare department, and local child welfare activities under city and county welfare departments are more efficiently operated. These public services include casework with parents and relatives for the improvement of unsatisfactory family and personal relationships of the child, and help in economic or social difficulties. Children with physical, mental, and emotional handicaps receive aid. Special attention is given to children born out of wedlock, and foster families or institutional care are provided for children who need to live away from their own homes. Public child welfare authorities are responsible for the supervision of foster homes and children's institutions. These child welfare services also provide assistance to courts which handle children's cases, to schools, and to child guidance and mental hygiene clinics, and other health agencies concerned with individual children.[15] Frequently they cooperate with group work agencies for the protection of children. The child caseworker also is concerned with the promotion of an understanding of the needs of children in the community, and with the encouragement and development of such public or private facilities as day

[14] Lawrence J. Linck, "The Crippled," *Social Work Year Book, 1951,* p. 144; and Donald V. Wilson, "The Crippled," *Social Work Year Book, 1954,* pp. 154-161.

[15] Spencer H. Crookes, "Child Welfare," *Social Work Year Book, 1954,* pp. 90-91.

care centers, nursery schools, group work agencies, community centers, and recreation places for children and adolescents.

The federal annual grant-in-aid for child welfare services has been increased from $1,500,000 in 1936 to $10,000,000 since 1950. Each state receives a flat amount of $40,000 and shares in the balance according to the proportion of its rural population under eighteen years to the total rural population in the United States under such age.[16] The emphasis on rural services is justified by the greater need of preventive and protective care for children in such areas, but neither are all urban regions well equipped nor are the states forced to use the funds exclusively for rural communities. These federal funds are not used for the care of individual children, but for the development and improvement of services for children. The cost of returning a runaway child under sixteen years of age to his home community in another state may be met from these funds if necessary, provided the return is in the interest of the child. The principal advantage of these child welfare services is the employment of trained child welfare workers and consultants for improving the work of local welfare departments, institutions, public and private child and family welfare agencies, clinics, and community centers. The facilities and the experience of voluntary organizations may be utilized. The states may authorize coordinated programs for child care and protection with private social agencies in the field of group work and casework and cooperate with probation departments of juvenile courts and police juvenile aid bureaus. Child welfare work is devoted to strengthening family life and permitting the child to grow up in his own family where he feels at home with his parents and siblings, and feels loved and secure. Children shall not be deprived of this emotional security based upon life with their own family because of economic need. In case of personal or emotional difficulties within the family, the child welfare worker will try to help in an adjustment by counseling the child and parents. She will assist in making available other facilities, such as participation in a children's or youth group, in recreational activities, or the use of a mental hygiene or child guidance clinic. Only if a child cannot remain in his own family, he may be placed in a foster home, or if this

[16] *Ibid.*, p. 90. The Social Security Act of 1935 considered the entire rural population ratio, but the Amendment of 1950 replaced this factor by the ratio of rural children and youth under eighteen years of age.

is needed for reasons of health, education or adjustment in a suitable children's institution.

The functions of Child Welfare Divisions of each State Department of Public Welfare include the development of standards for child care and for adoption procedure, licensing and inspection of children's institutions and foster families, and the promotion of legislation for child protection. In some states, the Child Welfare Division also administers state institutions for delinquent and mentally and physically handicapped children, e.g., in Wisconsin. In other states, a separate state agency is in charge of all institutions, or assumes the responsibility for prevention and treatment of juvenile delinquency, as for example the California Youth Authority.[17]

III. FOSTER FAMILY CARE

There are children who cannot live with their families, children who are orphans without relatives, abandoned children whose parents are unknown, children who have been deserted by their parents, children whose parents are unable to keep them because of illness or who have been committed to a prison. Some parents also may be a direct danger for their children. For such children, as a rule, placement in a foster home is considered. The social agency which handles foster family placement needs to know the child well enough to find the proper home for the individual child. The caseworker helps the child to accept the necessity for placement and to share, as much as his age permits, the plans for his placement. The caseworker also sustains the child in this inescapably anxious period. The child receives medical and psychological examinations, and the child placing agency considers his social and cultural background; his relation to all members of the family, the neighborhood, and school; his behavior, attitudes, and personal preferences, as well as the wishes of his parents (whenever this is possible). Working together with the parents, the child, and the foster parents in order to secure a mutually satisfactory solution for all persons concerned, the social agency attempts to find the foster home best suited to the individual child's needs.

[17] See Chapter 15. An instructive picture of state activities is presented by Loa Howard, *The History of Child Welfare in Oregon* (Portland: State Public Welfare Commission, 1951), and by John R. Ellingston, *Protecting Our Children from Criminal Careers* (New York: Prentice-Hall, Inc., 1948), Chapter 5.

In the selection of foster families, the social agency considers whether the individual foster family will provide the right home for a healthy and normal development of the particular child but also gives attention to the financial situation, housing conditions, neighborhood, and housekeeping standards. The educational, spiritual, and religious background of the foster parents deserve serious thought. Professional skill in foster placement is needed for fitting together the child's emotional, intellectual, and physical needs with the demands of foster parents to succeed in the best possible adjustment and satisfaction for both child and foster family.

In the foster family a normal and harmonious relationship between the parents is necessary, and if there are children or other relatives, the entire family group should be congenial. They also must have (particularly the foster mother) a sincere interest in children, because a child in a foster home requires, above all, love and understanding in order to adjust to a new family environment. The main motivation of families applying for a foster child should be their desire to rear such a child as if he were their own. Families who apply merely for financial reasons in order to have a greater income, or who want to get a child primarily for their own emotional satisfaction, without being able to give the child warmth and understanding, should not be accepted. It is often difficult for the child welfare worker to refuse applicants who want badly to be foster parents; sometimes it is necessary to refer such applicants to a family service agency in order to help them in their own personal problems.[18] As a rule, it is desirable that the foster parents be of about the same age as the natural parents of the child, but practical experience shows that older, well-suited foster parents often establish an excellent relationship with the child if he responds to their affection and understanding. Foster parents need to accept the fact that the child's ultimate security is with his own family, that he will return to them, and that his ties to his parents or other close relatives are not to be weakened or destroyed.

In general, the child placing agency assumes the supervision of the foster home after the child has been placed. Of course, the foster

---

[18] Dorothy Hutchinson, *In Quest of Foster Parents: A Point of View on Homefinding* (New York: Columbia University Press, 1943), pp. 13-15; Herbert H. Stroup, *Social Work* (New York: American Book, 1953), pp. 193-196; and Arthur E. Fink, *The Field of Social Work* (New York: Holt, 1949), pp. 178-184.

Philip Bonn photo. Courtesy U.S. Children's Bureau.

CHILDREN IN A FOSTER HOME

family has responsibility for the physical care of the child, his education, and training. The child caseworker helps the child and the foster parents to adjust in their mutual relations, and to solve difficulties and disappointments which rarely are missing in any family. The child frequently brings into the foster home his suspicions, anxieties, resistance, or hostility, and the caseworker aids the foster parents in their effort to overcome these problems and give the child the security he longs for. Whenever possible the caseworker attempts to preserve the child's interest in his natural family, and to keep alive the family's feeling of responsibility for the child, because in the majority of cases the child finally will return to his natural family. Sometimes visits of the parents with the foster family or of the child with the mother or siblings are arranged, but this has to be done with the full cooperation of the foster family. In cases of conflict, the caseworker will consider the welfare and happiness of the child as the decisive factor in such arrangements. The following case illustrates the effect of foster home care.

THE CASE OF BILLY[19]

The juvenile court judge didn't know what to do about Billy. At 11 years of age, the child had come before the court for the fourth time. In the past, he had been returned to his home under the supervision of relatives. His mother was in jail, his father had deserted years before, and the aunt with whom he lived was "tired of fooling with Billy." Obviously, the child had reason to feel unloved and unwanted. When he stole money, he used it to spend hours in the picture show. There was not any doubt about Billy's delinquency, but there was plenty of doubt as to what a suitable plan for him might be.

If Billy had been 12 years old, the juvenile court judge would have committed him immediately to the training school. Billy, however, was barely 11. As he had done in many other cases, the judge solved his dilemma by turning to the Department of Public Welfare. The agency agreed to try to provide the kind of boarding care that would fit Billy's needs and to offer supervision.

This happened over a year ago. Billy made his grade in school last year and gives promise of doing the same thing again. He is living out in the country with a firm but understanding foster father and a kind, jolly foster mother. He walks to school with the child of the foster parents, plays with the neighborhood children, and works with the foster father on the farm. The foster parents knew Billy's problems before he came to them. They accepted him as he was because they felt they could do something for him.

Everything has not been perfect. When Billy grew tired of a task assigned and quit before it was finished, he was made to understand that a chore must be completed. When he became frightened after an unfortunate episode at school, he found with his foster parents the security he had never had before. While he was packing his clothes to run away, he was discovered by the foster parents and, for the first time, knew that grown-ups could understand and that this was his home.

Some child welfare and family service agencies use temporary foster homes in order to place children in emergencies and to have enough time to find a more permanent family home in which the child will feel accepted and secure. During this period the child himself who in his own family has experienced the neglect, and domestic discord that leads to running away, stealing, or other maladjustments, has time to adapt himself to the idea of living with another normal and understanding family.

Among the various types of foster homes, only one plays a major role in present child care practice: the boarding home. Here the

[19] *Alabama Social Welfare*, Volume XVIII, No. 5, May, 1953, p. 11.

foster parents receive payment for their service, either by the parents, relatives, guardian of the child, juvenile court, or by the social agency which places the child. Free foster homes in which the foster parents do not receive any remuneration are rare today, because such families usually are not willing to submit to the standards, conditions, and supervision of the social agency or to the special needs of the child; however, there are sectarian agencies which still find free homes in some instances. Wage homes are scarcely used in child placing at present; in a wage home (or "work home") the older child is maintained in exchange for work he does for the family with which he is placed.

A different type of substitute care is the adoption home where the child is placed without payment of board and with the understanding that the adoptive parents will accept the child as a permanent member of the family if the placement of the child proves to be mutually satisfactory.

A. ADOPTION

Adoption is the legal, social, and psychological method of providing a family for children who have lost their natural parents or who cannot be reared by them under sound conditions as other children with their natural parents. Adoption as a legal proceeding of the court establishes the relationship of parent and child between persons who are not so related by nature.[20] Through adoption the child in effect becomes a permanent member of the adopting family. Often children are adopted by relatives or by a stepparent, but the legal and social safeguards of present adoption laws are designed to protect children who are not related to the adopting family.

Adoption was widely used in Roman law and was brought from France and Spain to Louisiana and Texas in the seventeenth century. The first state under common law to introduce adoption legislation was Massachusetts (1851), and at present each state has an adoption statute though they vary widely from one to another. One objective of adoption laws is *to protect the child* from unnecessary separation from his natural parents or mother who might give him love and good care if adequate help were available; from adoption

[20] Children's Bureau, Social Security Administration, *Essentials of Adoption Law and Procedure* (Publication No. 331), 1949, pp. 3-5; and Clyde Getz, "Adoption," *Social Work Year Book, 1954,* pp. 26-30.

by unfit parents; and from interference by his natural parents after a successful adoption has been arranged. Another objective is to protect *the natural parents*, particularly the unmarried mother, from unwise, hurried decisions made under emotional anxieties or economic pressure, which they might greatly regret later. Still another is *to protect the adopting parents* from taking a permanent responsibility for children whose health, heredity, or physical and mental capacities might lead to their disappointment, and also to protect them from disturbance of their relationship with the adopted child by threats or blackmail of the natural parents.

Typical features of adoption laws are that adult persons may adopt a child only with the consent of the natural parents or of the unmarried mother, that the adoptive parents must be at least 10 years older than the child, and that the child has to give his consent to the adoption if he is 12 or 14 years or older. The consent of the natural parent or parents has to be given before the court (frequently the juvenile court or the probate court), or before the state department of social welfare or a licensed adoption agency. In general, a social investigation by a public or private welfare agency is required so that the court be fully informed of all essential factors before its decision on the petition is made. As a rule, the child is placed in the adoption home for a trial period from 6 months to one year under supervision of a social agency until the final decision of the court on adoption is rendered. During this time the development of the child in his new environment is observed by the social worker, and the adoptive parents have an opportunity to find out whether they really want to have this child as a member of their family.[21]

Throughout the United States there is a large demand of childless couples for children to adopt, particularly babies. There are, on the other hand, not nearly enough children available for adoption to meet this demand. This discrepancy explains the public criticism that adoption agencies are too strict in their postulations, preventing people who wish to adopt a child from getting the desired child, and that a family is denied to homeless children. Social agencies are

[21] American Adoption laws of today do not in general require that only a married couple, or a couple that cannot have children, may adopt a child. But the practice of social agencies and courts has been to place children for adoption into "full families" to give the child the opportunity for normal development. Georgia alone of all states limits adoptions legally to married couples.

conscious of this widespread criticism and are trying to find ways to improve their service and to curtail the long waiting periods for adoption. They also are anxious to create better public understanding of the reasons for the time involved in this process. These conditions have caused the "black market in babies" in which unscrupulous employees of maternity wards, together with other "middle-men," abuse the anxiety of unmarried girls and the sentimental attitude of well-to-do childless couples desirous of receiving a baby. Arrangement is made for adoption placement before, or immediately after, the birth of the child in exchange for the payment of substantial amounts of money (sometimes from both parties), called "gratitude donation." This "selling of babies" results in handsome profits for the managers of this business, and no questions nor investigations delay the placement of such a baby. However, unhappiness for the child and the adopting parents often results.

Similar manipulations which are not exclusively based upon greed for profit are called "the gray market in babies." They are carried on by those people who attempt to please a couple, wishing to have a child, by persuading fearful unmarried mothers to give up the child immediately after birth. There is no competent method of determining whether this action will be really in the interest of the child and the mother. Trained workers of an adoption agency are the only ones professionally qualified to counsel with the mother, to acquaint her with alternatives to adoption placement, and to proceed with skillful study of the child's parental background and potentialities to suit him to the adopted home. Although child placements by unauthorized persons are prohibited in some states these "independent adoptions" are still very frequent, and the unmarried mother or the natural parents are usually entitled to place their child in a family of their choice. The danger in these "independent adoptions" is that the mother may not have time nor insight to form a clear opinion whether she really wants to give away her child. She may be unable to assess the qualities of the adoptive family. The child may unnecessarily lose his natural mother. This method also involves the risk for the adopting parents that the child in his mental and physical health, temperament, and personality may not fit into their family.

For these reasons, agency adoption offers greater security to the three parties concerned—the child, the natural parents, and the

adoptive parents. More than one-half of all adoptions concern illegitimate children, and nearly 98 per cent of children placed for
adoption are under one year of age. In some states a trend exists to
limit the adoption placements to licensed social agencies, but it is
questionable whether one should attempt to prevent parents from
placing their own child, particularly with relatives or friends. In
agency adoptions the natural parents (or the unmarried mother)
"relinquish" the child to a licensed social agency which then takes
full responsibility for the placement of the child in an adoptive
home not known to the natural parents. This decision is made only
after careful interviews. Many an unmarried girl comes to the
agency during her pregnancy and wants to relinquish her baby immediately. In general she is advised to wait with her final decision
until the baby is two or three months old. Frequently she is motivated by fear, shame, or feeling of guilt, and might be very unhappy
later about a hasty decision. She is counseled about all possibilities, such
as aid to dependent children, foster care, and other temporary arrangements, so that she may be able to keep her child for a time before making her decision of whether or not to rear him. According
to the experience of adoption agencies about 25 per cent of the
mothers who, when first known to the agency, want to relinquish
their child, come to the conclusion after the birth that they do not
wish to live without the baby. Adoption should be a free, well-con-
sidered plan, not a hasty decision of the mother under emotional and
economic pressure.

If the parents or the unmarried mother are determined to relinquish the child, the social agency makes a thorough study of the
child with medical examination, psychological tests, and information
about the social and health background of the child's mother and
father. Also, their hereditary, racial, and constitutional type is
studied. The agency attempts to find an adoptive home in which
these factors are similar, and this explains why outsiders frequently
comment on the resemblance of adoptive children to their adoptive
parents. Relinquishing of the child to the agency also insures that
the identity of both natural parents and adoptive parents is concealed
from each other so that embarrassment, jealousy, friction, interference, and blackmail are avoided. The role of the adoption worker
is a very responsible one. The adoption worker must be well aware
of her own feelings and attitudes in order to give an objective, but
warm-hearted, understanding to the needs of the three parties in

the adoption process, and to perform a service satisfactory to the community.[22]

In the selection of the adoptive parents the social agency looks for families who are in good physical and mental health and are emotionally and economically able to rear the child. After the child is placed with the selected adoptive family, the social agency generally maintains contact with the child and the adoptive parents for one year. This is done to give help in whatever adjustment difficulties might arise, and to observe whether the child satisfactorily takes roots in the new family. If the adjustment is satisfactory, the social agency recommends the granting of the adoption to the court.[23] In general the courts follow the social agency's suggestion, which is based upon its work with natural parents, child, and adoptive parents. In many states court hearings are not open to the public, but the older child is usually present in order to give his consent. The decree of adoption declares that the child is the child and legal heir of the adopting parents and acquires the same rights, privileges, and obligations as a child born to them.

There are two other types of adoption: the stepparent adoption and adoption of an illegitimate child by his natural father. Under stepparent adoption the child remains with his mother, whether she was not married before, widowed, or divorced. The petition for adoption is filed with the court by the stepfather, and requires the formal consent of the mother. It is done so that the child has the same legal status and name as other children in the family. In these cases social investigations are often carried out by the probation officer of the court. A father who wants to adopt his own natural child has to undergo different procedures in the various states. For instance, in California he has to acknowledge the child as his own before the court, has to receive him into his family, and treat him like a legitimate child. He needs the formal consent of the natural mother if she is alive, and also of his own wife if he is married.

B. CHILDREN OF UNMARRIED PARENTS

Programs to meet the needs of the unmarried mother and to offer care and protection to her child are among the most important services

[22] H. Fredericksen, *op. cit.*, pp. 205-211; Grace Abbott, *The Child and the State* (Chicago: University of Chicago Press, 1938), Vol. II, pp. 167-171.

[23] If the child does not adjust well, the social agency removes him and makes another arrangement, but such cases are rare due to careful selection.

organized by family and children's agencies. The unmarried mother often is living away from her home community in order to avoid the embarrassment and disdain which even today frequently is connected with this situation. The social agency may have to assist in arrangements for the confinement and for the care of the child. Obviously the illegitimate child needs just as much affection and feeling of belonging as any other child, and for this reason children's agencies usually attempt to permit the mother to stay with the baby until she decides what she wants done with the child. The child born out of wedlock fundamentally should not be treated differently than other children in need of protection and care, but his mother frequently needs intensive help and counseling by the caseworker in order to avoid unwise plans for herself and for the child. The unmarried father also should be included in the work of the social agency in order to meet his moral and financial responsibilities for the child.[24]

C. GUARDIANSHIP

Guardianship is the establishment of legal protection for children when the parents are dead, incapacitated, incompetent (e.g., insane), or have failed in their duty toward the children.[25] The guardian is a substitute for the parent, but he is not liable for the child's support. The guardianship ends with the child's majority or with his marriage. In case of death of the father, the mother is the *natural guardian* of the children, and the unmarried mother is the *sole guardian* of her child. Other types of guardianship are *testamentary guardians*, named in the will of the deceased parents, and often are relatives or friends of the family; *public guardians*, as a rule county officials, are provided in ten states for the protection of children; there are *guardians of estate* to manage property rights of the ward, and *guardians ad litem* who are appointed by the court for special purposes, mainly legal proceedings. The legal provisions for guardian-

[24] Some states have adopted the *Uniform Illegitimacy Law* drafted by the National Conference of Commissioners on Uniform State Laws in 1922, by which both the mother and the unmarried father are responsible for support, maintenance, and education of the illegitimate child (Arizona, Indiana, Iowa, Nevada, New Mexico, New York, North Dakota, South Dakota, and Wyoming).

[25] Irving Weissman *et al., Guardianship for Children* (Washington, D.C.: U.S. Children's Bureau, Publication No. 330, 1949), p. 19.

ship in most states are enacted in the laws on infancy and guardianship, but too much emphasis still is placed upon the management of estate rather than upon the protection of the child's. healthful placement, education, and guidance. Besides the testamentary guardianship, guardians are appointed by various courts, such as the probate court, the juvenile court, orphans', or surrogate court. In some states, e.g., California, the probation officer of a rural juvenile court is guardian for the wards of the court. The investigation of the fitness of guardians before their appointment and supervision of the activities of guardians are necessary for the protection of children, but these measures unfortunately are seldom carried out.[26]

D. CHILDREN IN INSTITUTIONS

Although in the nineteenth century care of children in orphanages and asylums was the customary way of provision for destitute and orphaned children, the trend has been away from institutional care. The main reason is that children's homes require from the child an adjustment to a large number of other children, educators, staff members of the institution, in an atmosphere unlike home. That children become "institutionalized," that they lose their personality in conforming to strict, general regulations, and that they have no opportunity to develop their individuality, their mental, physical and creative abilities, and are apt to become docile and dull have been the main arguments against institutional care. Life in an institution makes a certain routine necessary that often limits warm personal relationships with the personnel and other children in the home and easily leads to an overprotection of the child. On the other hand, the children's institution offers an opportunity for an experience in group living, regular physical care, a healthy diet, an atmosphere provided by friendly, interested, trained educators concerned with the well-being of the child, and medical (often psychiatric) aid and trained social work service.

Modern children's institutions have tried to overcome the problems of mass education and living in large dormitories by the es-

[26] Hazeltine Byrd Taylor, *Law of Guardian and Ward* (Chicago: University of Chicago Press, 1935), p. 5; and Mary Stanton, "The Administration of Guardianship by a Local Probate Court," *The Social Service Review*, Vol. XIV, No. 4, December, 1945, pp. 495-505. In Texas and Louisiana the search for the father of an illegitimate child is prohibited by law.

tablishment of the "cottage plan." This means the decentralization of the institution into a number of cottages, usually accommodating a group of about twenty girls and boys with a couple of cottage parents. Instead of dormitories, small sleeping rooms for two to four children, and living and dining rooms are used in which the children feel more like they are "at home."[27]

Which children need institutional care? Infants and preschool children who cannot remain with their own families are rarely placed in institutions, but into foster families. It also is an accepted principle that institutional care for children should be a temporary placement, and not planned until the child has fully grown up. The following groups seem in need of institutional care: (1) children who, because of severe illness or accident of the parents, have to leave their home and who are so strongly emotionally tied to the parents that they or the parents feel threatened by a placement in another family; (2) children who because of family disturbances, tensions, or divorce have become so difficult that they cannot remain in their family, but who also are unable to establish sound emotional relationship with a foster family; (3) children who have been so badly disappointed or so deeply hurt by previous foster placement that they are unfit to become, at this point, an integral part of a new family; (4) children presenting such difficult health or behavior problems that they are not acceptable to foster families, and are in need of professional observation and guidance, as well as medical or psychiatric treatment in a controlled environment; (5) large family groups of siblings who do not want to be separated, but who would have to be split up among several foster families; (6) older children and adolescents who are breaking away from their own families and for whom a foster home would repeat the features of the family authority which is no longer acceptable to them; and (7) adolescents who for various reasons within their own families need only short-term care and would profit more from the experience of group living during such a period.[28]

Placement of a child in an institution often seems easier for parents to accept than placement in a foster family because it does

---

[27] Examples of various types of children's homes and of the life of the children in such institutions are found in Howard W. Hopkirk, *Institutions Serving Children* (New York: Russell Sage Foundation, 1944).

[28] Henrietta L. Gordon, "Foster Care of Children," *Social Work Year Book, 1951*, pp. 206-207.

not endanger their social prestige in the community, which often interprets foster home placement of children as a failure of the parents. Effective treatment of children in an institution requires that the children receive a friendly, homelike reception in a small group according to the cottage system; that medical and, if necessary, psychiatric examination and service be available, and that the individual needs of the children be met by trained casework service. It is also necessary that educational, recreational, and vocational facilities be of high standard, and that the work in the institution be fully devoted to the development of the children into useful and happy members of the community.

Under such circumstances, the institution is able to care more successfully for children than their own inadequate home or a foster family. Recently the special merits of children's institutions have been recognized for certain types of difficult, disturbed, pre-delinquent children. Institutions have been used for a long time for the care of feeble-minded, blind, deaf, deaf-mute, epileptic, and crippled children in need of special education, and also for delinquent children who are so dangerous for the community and to themselves that placement in a family does not promise success. On the other hand, there is a new trend toward keeping blind and deaf children in their own or in foster families and to encourage them to take part in normal activities as much as possible. This trend has limited the setup of special classes for handicapped children in public schools to only such subjects in which their health makes it impossible to learn together with normal children. The number of institutions for seriously disturbed children and adolescents that offer intensive treatment with psychotherapy and skillful therapeutic group living experience is not sufficient.[29]

The number of children placed in public and private institutions is still substantial. The U.S. Children's Bureau estimated in 1950 the figure of children living in public institutions at 37,000, and it is assumed that about the same number reside in private children's institutions. As to the size of public children's institutions, the over-all median was forty-six for homes for neglected and dependent, and 110 for delinquent children.[30] The establishment of small, well-

[29] Susanne Schulze, *Creative Group Living in a Children's Institution* (New York: Association Press, 1951), pp. 158-186; and Marian G. Morris, "Juvenile Behavior Problems," *Social Work Year Book, 1951*, p. 281.

[30] I. Richard Pearlman and Jack Wiener, "Children Living in Selected Public Institutions" (Washington, D. C.: Children's Bureau, May, 1950).

staffed child institutions which give individualized, personal care to each child and provide understanding for young and disturbed children seems most desirable.

A special type of care which lies between an institution and a foster family is the "group home," which accommodates between six and ten children or adolescents in a house or spacious apartment. The housemother or the houseparents are in a position to let the children participate in such home management as required in a large family, and the personal contact between the parents and children is the same as in a foster family of substantial size. This type of care might well be used as a transition from institutional placement to a foster family or to the return of the child or adolescent to his own family.[31]

E. DAY NURSERIES AND CHILD CARE CENTERS

Day nurseries are institutions which provide care for young children (between two and five years) during the day while their mothers are at work. These nurseries have become necessary with the increasing employment of women in industry. At first only custodial care was offered, but more recently day nurseries have assumed broader responsibilities for the health and education of the children. These include social casework with parents and relatives, mothers' study groups, and cooperation with children's and family service agencies whenever the children require additional services or special treatment. Nursery schools are educational institutions for preschool children, age two to five, which attempt to develop the mental, physical, social, and emotional capacities of the children, and to help in the formation of desirable habits and behavior patterns. Not being limited to children of working mothers, these schools usually devote considerable effort to parent education through conferences, study groups, and mothers' participation in the nursery school activities and in discussions with the nursery school staff.[32]

The care of children of school age is frequently necessary if

[31] H. Gordon, *op. cit.*, p. 207; and Helen R. Hagan, "Foster Care for Children," *Social Work Year Book, 1954*, pp. 229-232. See also F. Fischer, *The Group Home: An Innovation in Child Placement* (New York: Child Welfare League of America, 1952).

[32] Examples may be found in *Day Nursery Care As a Social Service: A Discussion of Current Viewpoints with Case Material* (Philadelphia: Pennsylvania School of Social Work, 1943), pp. 21, 25.

their parents work late and cannot supervise the children after school. During the Depression of the 1930's "day care centers" for such extended school care were supported by the Federal Emergency Relief Administration, the Works Progress Administration, and the Farm Security Administration. Some of these centers were in connection with migratory labor camps.

When numerous women went into industrial work during World War II for patriotic, as well as for economic, reasons the establishment of new day care centers became imperative. For their organization and operation funds of the *Lanham Act*[33] were used, and after the war, state subsidies in several states have made the continuation of day care centers possible. Their number has decreased during recent years because frequently children are accepted in the centers only if the income of their parents does not exceed certain limits or if their parents are veterans. It seems desirable that day care centers be made a permanent part of child welfare services. They function as valuable substitutes for family care during the time when the mother is not available at home, improve the health, education, and social attitudes of the children, give them a healthy outlet for their energies in play, games, and leisure time activities, and above all an experience in group living (aside from the common school attendance) with other children of the same age. The potentialities of day care centers could be increased if trained social caseworkers are employed to serve as intake workers and establish the individual contacts with the children and their families which prove to be constructive in such relationships. Until now, few of the day care centers have been able to use caseworkers for this service, but some have made arrangements with family welfare or children's agencies for members of their staff to establish liaison work as "outposts" in the centers.[34]

F. SCHOOL LUNCHES

During the Depression and later during World War II, school lunches were provided in many schools in order to safeguard the health of children who frequently had no breakfast at home.

[33] See Chapter 5, p. 155.

[34] See Cathryn S. Guyler, "Social Work Responsibilities for the Development of Day Care," *National Conference of Social Work, Proceedings, 1942* (New York: Columbia University Press, 1942), p. 442.

The program was partly financed by the parents, partly by local communities and private social organizations, and was supported by Lanham Act funds. In 1946, the *National School Lunch Act* appropriated federal funds under the administration of the Department of Agriculture, because school lunches assist in the proper nutrition of children and, at the same time, encourage domestic consumption of farm products on a permanent basis. Under supervision of the various state departments of education, which finance an increasing proportion of the program, the schools make the lunch available to children regardless of their race, religion, and ability of their parents to pay.[35]

IV. SCHOOL SOCIAL WORK

Until the end of the nineteenth century, the concept prevailed that children with reasonable physical care would grow into normal, happy adulthood. But scientific investigation of psychological, sociological, and psychiatric principles regarding personality development has discovered the greater importance of the growing-up process and its lasting effects on the total human personality. The introduction of programs of social work in schools was felt necessary, almost at the same time, in Boston, Hartford, Connecticut, and New York City in 1906 and 1907. They were established under the title "visiting teachers' work" because difficulties which children had in schools frequently were caused by faulty relationships within the family or environment, or by the child's personal problems which could not be well handled by the teachers in school.

In Boston, the West End Neighborhood Association, a social settlement, and the Women's Education Association, a parent-teachers group, each engaged a social worker, called a "home and school visitor," in order to assist the schools in overcoming misunderstanding between the families and the schools. In Hartford the director of the Henry Barnard School Clinic, a psychological clinic, requested the employment of a "visiting teacher" in order to coordinate the work in school, family, and clinic and to prevent serious maladjustment of children.

In New York, two settlement houses, Hartley House and Greenwich Neighborhood House, each assigned a social worker to assist

[35] Charles C. Wilson, "School Health Services," *Social Work Year Book, 1949*, p. 455.

in the home-school relationships of children and to meet the social problems which seemed to cause trouble for children in schools. Other cities followed these examples, and in 1913, Rochester, New York, established the first public, municipal system of visiting teachers with the requirement that they have social work training.[36]

The program of school social work was greatly strengthened by funds granted by the Commonwealth Fund in New York, in 1921, which were aimed to serve in the prevention of juvenile delinquency. They were designed to develop four different, but coordinated, programs: (1) demonstration projects for visiting teachers in thirty communities; (2) child guidance clinics with the advice of the National Committee of Mental Hygiene; (3) psychiatric studies of difficult, pre-delinquent, and delinquent children in connection with schools and juvenile courts; and (4) the training of social workers, visiting teachers, and psychologists for competent work in the field of delinquency prevention.[37]

The Commonwealth Fund insisted that the communities which received allocations for visiting teacher work share, usually by one-third, the expenses during a demonstration period of five years and help for another three years in the training of personnel for the understanding of behavior problems. After this experience, many cities, including smaller and rural towns, developed school social work programs. The American Association of Visiting Teachers was organized in 1916 and renamed "National Association of School Social Workers" in 1945. In some states the employment of at least one school social worker in each community is required (Louisiana); in others, such as Michigan and California, state funds support the school districts or communities in school social work. In 1950 the cities with full-time school social workers were estimated at 450, but many more have part-time service.[38]

The school social worker helps individual children who have difficulties in making a satisfactory school adjustment. These difficulties may be expressed in truancy and failure in school subjects and

[36] Helen L. Witmer, *Social Work* (New York: Farrar & Rinehart, 1942), pp. 359-360.

[37] Herbert H. Stroup, *op. cit.*, pp. 272-274; and Negley Teeters and John Reinemann, *The Challenge of Delinquency* (New York: Prentice-Hall, Inc., 1950), pp. 598-600.

[38] Mildred Sikkema, "School Social Services," *Social Work Year Book, 1951*, p. 448; and Florence Poole, "School Social Services," *Social Work Year Book, 1954*, pp. 467-469.

in timid, fearful, withdrawing, or overaggressive behavior. Other indications may be stealing, fighting, sullenness, resentfulness, inability to get along with other children, to accept the authority of the teacher, or the demand for special attention. The classroom teacher will ask for the help of the school social worker for such children. She usually first observes the child in class, and then discusses his problems with the teacher and principal. Sometimes a discussion with the child changes his attitude. The school social worker in most instances contacts the parents, after the interview with the child, in order to understand his difficulties and seeks the parents' help to improve the child's adjustment in school.

The school social worker will also interpret the methods and philosophy of the school to the parents to enlist their active cooperation. In this way she helps the school to establish constructive parent-school relationships. She interprets the school program to parents' associations, civic groups and to the community, and participates in faculty meetings, school committees, and group projects.[39] The school social worker maintains an independent role in the interest of the child, so that the child trusts her and does not identify her fully with the school authority. She works with four parties: (1) the child, (2) the family, (3) the school staff, and (4) the community. She attempts to change attitudes of the child, the parents and teachers, and community groups if they are detrimental to the adjustment of the child and to the requirements of the school. The maladjusted child is often a serious handicap to other children in his class. The school social worker learns about the child's difficulties from the classroom teacher, from school records, the school nurse, the attendance or truant officer, the parents, and above all from the child himself.

Her functions vary in different communities. Whether the school social worker should also serve as a truant or attendance officer is questionable, but the execution of the compulsory school attendance laws is not limited to mechanical, police, or legal aspects. It is also debatable how much a school social worker may effectively prevent the development of mental disorders.[40] The practice has shown that the school social worker is frequently successful in solv-

[39] National Association of School Social Workers, "Would You Like to Do School Social Work?" (New York, n.d.).

[40] H. Witmer, *op. cit.*, pp. 360-361.

ing behavior problems and disciplinary questions, such as unruly behavior, unsatisfactory work due to disturbing influences at home, and minor delinquencies. Sometimes she is able through the use of other community resources, group work agencies, and family welfare services to improve the conditions in the family which caused the child's failure or maladjustment in school and thus change the child's behavior.

The school social worker should have professional training in social work and understanding of the educational process of the school, possess the ability to work with children and adults, and be able to operate in a team relationship with the school faculty. She needs humor, imagination, flexibility, and a good knowledge of the resources of the community.

V. CHILD LABOR PROTECTION

Children had been worked in the fields and the trades since the first settlements in our country had been established. They were cheap, willing, useful workers in a period when labor remained scarce. The philosophy of the Puritans and Quakers taught that labor was the right way in which children learned farming or craftwork so that they were trained to become thrifty and industrious. During the seventeenth and eighteenth centuries children were placed as apprentices with a farmer, craftsman, or merchant, and lived in the master's family. When the factory system developed in the nineteenth century, parents no longer apprenticed their children but sent them to factories where they earned higher wages.[41]

An apprenticeship did not seem necessary to learn factory work. The public was convinced that child labor was the natural way to accustom children, particularly those of the poor classes, to a life of thrift and toil. The first laws limiting daily working hours of young children to ten hours were enacted in some of the northern industrial states, beginning in Massachusetts (1842), Connecticut (1842), New Hampshire (1847), Maine (1848), Pennsylvania (1849), Ohio (1852), Rhode Island (1853) (eleven hours daily), and New York (1860); but the maximum age of the children covered by these laws differed from twelve to sixteen years. None of these statutes, however, required proof of age from working children, nor did they provide for

[41] Grace Abbott, *The Child and the State*, Vol. I (Chicago: University of Chicago Press, 1938), pp. 189-191.

inspectors who could enforce the observation of the laws,[42] so they were not effective. Children continued to be employed for long hours, at night, at dangerous work, and even in occupations in restaurants, music halls, bar rooms, and dance halls which damaged their morale.

In the beginning, child labor laws in the states applied to manufacturing shops and textile mills only. Children represented a large proportion (more than one-half) of the labor force at this period. The early trade unions complained of the excessive hours children had to work, and began, before 1860, to demand universal education, but they were fighting for their members' benefit as well as for that of children when they attempted to secure a shorter working day. When industries and the use of machine power increased after the War Between the States, the number of children working in factories and mines grew larger, and the demand for child labor legislation and means to enforce the statutes became stronger. The main arguments were the health damage to the child, interference with the child's education, and the depressing effect of children's work on the wages of adult workers. Another reason for the demand of restriction of child labor in factories was that they took the places of adults, a complaint which was raised particularly in periods of large-scale unemployment during the last two decades of the nineteenth century.[43]

Following the example of Massachusetts in 1836, the states enacted compulsory school attendance laws, but progress was slow due to stubborn opposition both from parents who did not want to lose the income from the labor of their children and from employers who preferred to use cheap labor. The industrial states began to introduce factory inspectors in order to supervise and to enforce child labor statutes, when social reformers, educators, and social workers showed their concern for the damage which excessive child labor did to the health and education of the children. Among the leaders of the movement for the protection of children were Jane Addams, Florence Kelley, (she became first factory inspector in the state of Illinois), Julia Lathrop, Edith and Grace Abbott, and Sophonisba P. Breckinridge. But public opinion was sharply divided

[42] *Ibid.*, pp. 260, 405. These laws were widely disregarded since children, parents, and employers were interested in child labor for profit, and fellow employees were either indifferent or scared to report violations of the laws.

[43] *Ibid.*, pp. 261-262.

over the question of child labor laws, and the influential groups which opposed this legislation earlier continued to do so for a long time. By the end of the nineteenth century most industrial states had enacted child labor legislation which limited the daily hours of work of children and young persons to ten or nine hours, prohibited work of children during school hours and at night between 10 P.M. and 6 A.M. This usually applied to children employed in manufacturing, mining, and industry. Employment in particularly dangerous occupations was, as a rule prohibited for children and adolescents under sixteen years of age, whereas child labor laws, in general, applied to children only up to twelve, thirteen, or fourteen years. Children working in agriculture and as domestic servants were not protected at all.

Although the provisions of these state laws were not well enforced, because the staff of factory inspectors was insufficient and many judges were not disposed to fine parents or employers for violating the laws, conditions in most southern states, such as North and South Carolina, were worse for they had almost no child labor legislation at all. In several states (North Carolina, Florida, Georgia, and Mississippi) children could be legally employed in the cotton mills as young as at the age of twelve. The exploitation of these children, their poor health, and the lack of school attendance led to the organization of the National Child Labor Committee in 1904, under the leadership of the Reverend Edgar Gardner Murphy and Reverend Alexander J. McKelway. The committee urged that the employment of the "poor white children" in the southern states be restricted as in the industrial states where at this time usually a minimum age of fourteen years was required for employment in manufacturing and mills. The southern millowners denounced the campaign for a federal child labor law which the Committee started as "the effort of northern agitators to kill the infant industries of the South"[44] and argued that due to the widespread poverty of the southern states the children were much better off in the mills than in their own homes.

The first proposals for a federal child labor law, the *Beveridge-Parsons Bill* and the *Lodge Bill* were submitted in 1906. In the following decade a number of similar bills to prevent the employment of children in factories and mines were introduced, without passing

[44] *Ibid.*, p. 462.

both houses of Congress.[45] With the moral support of President Wilson the *Owen-Keating Bill* finally was passed September 1, 1916, as the first federal child labor law. It was to take effect one year later. The law prohibited the interstate distribution of goods produced with the use of child labor and classified the violation of its provisions a misdemeanor. But the United States Supreme Court in its decision *Hammer* vs. *Dagenhart* of June 3, 1918, declared the law unconstitutional because it was not considered a legitimate exercise of Congress' power to regulate interstate commerce. In the meantime, the Child Labor Division of the United States Children's Bureau under Grace Abbott had administered the law and had, during nine months, proved that the law was an effective tool to protect children against health damage and industrial exploitation. The inspections were carried out in close cooperation with state factory inspectors and school authorities. The latter issued, in general, the age certificates for the children, and assisted the inspectors of the Children's Bureau in the supervision of mines, quarries, mills, canneries, factories, and workshops sending their products to other states or foreign countries. In the nine months of operation of the Act, 689 industrial establishments and twenty-eight mines were inspected; violations of the law were found in 293 mills and factories,[46] before the law was declared unconstitutional.

On recommendation of President Wilson, Congress enacted a second child labor statute, introduced by Senator Pomerene, as an amendment to the Federal Revenue Act—the *Child Labor Tax Law* of February 24, 1919, to become effective April 25, 1919. The law levied a tax of 10 per cent on the annual profits of an industrial establishment which employed children in violation of the legal minimum age of 14 years and of the maximum of 8 hours a day. The new law made it possible to pursue the inspections of factories and mills through federal and state inspectors, until it was also declared unconstitutional by the United States Supreme Court, May 15, 1922. The White House Conference on Children of 1919 advocated that standards for child employment be raised so that each child would have the opportunity for normal growth, development, and education.

The National Child Labor Committee, the Consumers' League, the American Federation of Labor, and many women's and civic groups

[45] The second attempt was the *Copley-Poindexter Bill* of 1912, the third the *Palmer-Owen Bill* of 1914.

[46] G. Abbott, Vol. I, *op. cit.*, p. 493.

formed a committee for a constitutional amendment which was introduced as the *McCormick-Foster Bill* (1923). The Child Labor Amendment was passed by both houses in Congress in 1924; it authorized Congress "to limit, regulate, and prohibit the labor of persons under 18 years of age."[47] The American Manufacturers Association and various trade journals and newspapers under its influence succeeded in misrepresenting the purposes and the nature of the amendment in local newspapers and in influencing state legislators to vote against the ratification of the child labor amendment. By January, 1938, only twenty-eight of the required thirty-six states had ratified the amendment, among them no southern state except Kentucky. Since that date no further ratification has taken place so that the amendment has not become effective.[48]

The practice of the two federal laws before they were declared unconstitutional, and the campaigns for the child labor amendment, however, had the effect of clarifying in the minds of the public the necessity for protection of children against excessive and damaging labor. Thus they led indirectly to important improvements in the child labor laws of most states and in raising the standards and methods of their operations. Other social forces that contributed to a decline in child labor were the growth of union strength, and a rise in the level of the national income which made education for more children possible. Pupils enrolled in high schools doubled from 2,200,000 in 1920 to 4,400,000 in 1930.[49] During the Depression years of 1930-1932 some children in factories were dismissed in order to employ adults who had lost their jobs, but in 1932 a reverse movement in industry started again to employ more children because they were cheaper labor. The *National Industrial Recovery Act* of 1933 required that no children were to be employed who were less than sixteen years of age in industries supported by the statute, but the Supreme Court, again, declared this provision unconstitutional in May, 1935. Thus in the following year the number of young children working in industries rose again.[50] The *Fair Labor Standards Act*

---

[47] Gertrude Folks Zimand, "Child Labor," *Social Work Year Book, 1943*, p. 99.
[48] See G. Abbott, Vol. I, *op. cit.*, pp. 467-468.
[49] Florence Taylor, "Child Labor Fact Book, 1900-1950" (New York: National Child Labor Committee, 1950), p. 10.
[50] Other federal laws affecting child labor were the *Walsh-Healy Act* of 1936, establishing a minimum age of sixteen years for boys and eighteen years for girls for employment in production under federal contract, and the *Sugar Act* of 1937, which prohibited federal subsidies to sugar growers employing children under fourteen—or children under sixteen longer than eight hours daily.

(so-called "Wage Hours Act") of 1938 prohibited the employment (during school hours) of children under sixteen years of age in industries engaged in interstate commerce and producing goods for shipment to other states, and (at any time) in mining, manufacturing, and processing industries. Agricultural work outside of school hours is not included in this law.

The U. S. Children's Bureau is authorized to permit the employment of children between fourteen and sixteen years of age in such work which would not interfere with their health, school attendance, and general well-being, but their employment in manufacturing or mining is absolutely prohibited. The Children's Bureau also may prohibit the employment of young persons between sixteen and eighteen years of age in hazardous occupations, such as the manufacture of explosives and gas, of motor vehicles, work in coal mining, logging and saw mills, work on wood-working machines and with power driven hoisting apparatus (like cranes and elevators), and work with radio active substances. In 1946 the Industrial Division of the U.S. Children's Bureau, which was in charge of child labor protection, was transferred to the Department of Labor. It is now the Child Labor Branch of the Wage and Hour and Public Contracts Division of the Department of Labor, which enforces the provisions of the Fair Labor Standards Act. Its small staff of inspectors, however, is able only to make sample inspections and on special complaint, so that merely a proportion of the establishments is reached which are covered by the Act. Inspections reveal that a serious tendency toward disregard of the federal child labor provisions is prevalent. In 1946-1947, 24 per cent of all minors under eighteen years employed in the inspected industries were found to be working in violation of the laws. The great majority of the violations consists in the employment of children under sixteen without special permit.

Certain progress in state child labor legislation has led to the enactment in twenty-three states of a basic sixteen-year minimum age for work in factories and to the prohibition of employment of young people during school hours. Twenty-two states do not permit gainful employment for children under fourteen years during school hours. But only six of these states (Illinois, Maryland, New Jersey, New York, Utah, and Virginia) protect agricultural labor and domestic services under these provisions.

CHART 5: EMPLOYED CHILDREN AND MINORS, 1900-1950 (CENSUS COUNTS OF FULL-
AND PART-TIME WORKERS IN INDUSTRY AND AGRICULTURE)

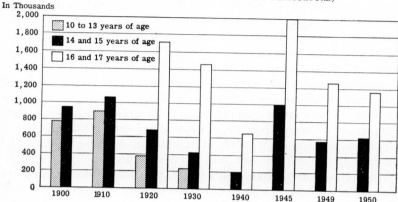

Source: Florence Taylor, *Child Labor Fact Book, 1900-1950* (New York: National Child Labor Committee, 1950), p. 12. The 1900-1940 figures are decennial Census counts. The later figures (April, 1945; February, 1949; and February, 1950) are Census estimates. Census counts prior to 1920 did not report employed minors sixteen and seventeen years of age. The 1940 Census count did not report child workers ten through thirteen years of age.

The present standards of child labor regulation in the states are the following:

1. Employment during school hours. A minimum age of sixteen years has been adopted by twenty-three states, a minimum of fifteen by two states, and a minimum of fourteen years by twenty-two states. Exceptions for some occupations, particularly for agriculture and domestic service, are frequent, and some states provide special permits for children in economic need.

2. Employment outside of school hours and during summer vacations. Minimum of fourteen years of age has been adopted by one-half of the states, with wide exemption of agriculture, domestic service, and street trades. Certain states have no minimum age limit for this type of employment.

3. Working hours for children and young persons. In forty-two states an eight-hour day has been set as maximum for most occupations, but twenty-seven of these states have limited this rule to adolescents under sixteen years. Twelve states have a forty-hour week for children up to sixteen years, but only five of these states extend the limit up to eighteen years. Seven states have ruled a forty-four-hour maximum week for children under sixteen years, and four of these states include young persons up to eighteen years. In twenty-four states a forty-eight-hour week is permitted for children under sixteen, and eight of these states have set this maximum also for young workers under eighteen years of age.

4. Part-time employment during school. No regulation exists in thirty-two states; sixteen states have limited the hours for children under sixteen, frequently to three or four hours a day, or to a combined school and work period of eight hours daily. Only five states have such limitations for young people under eighteen. Most school attendance laws contain exemptions permitting children to work after completion of the eighth grade, or because of family poverty.

5. Prohibition of night work. Most states prohibit night work for children under sixteen, but only twelve states require a rest of thirteen consecutive hours from 6 P.M. to 7 A.M. Some states prohibit night work for ten or eleven hours or only between 8 P.M. and 5 A.M. or 9 P.M. and 6 A.M. But eleven states prohibit night work after 10 P.M. for minors under eighteen years of age, some only for girls.

6. Work permits. Forty-four states require a work permit for the employment of adolescents under sixteen years of age; twenty-two states also for the employment of young workers under eighteen, but not for all occupations.

7. Hazardous occupations. In most states the employment of children under sixteen years of age for a substantial number of hazardous occupations is prohibited, but this protection is extended to young workers under eighteen in only a few states. In twenty states the child labor legislation authorizes the administrative agency to declare occupations dangerous for young persons under eighteen years of age.[51]

Eighteen states have not yet enacted adequate child labor legislation, and the extension of the sixteen-year minimum age to these states is one of the urgent tasks for future legislation.[52] Another essential problem which has not been solved is the extension of child

---

[51] F. Taylor, *op. cit.*, pp. 17-18; and Clara M. Beyer, "Labor Standards," *Social Work Year Book, 1954*, pp. 309-311.

[52] Since the Fair Labor Standards Act does not cover intrastate industries, children under sixteen are frequently employed in retail stores, bakeries, garages, beauty parlors, repair shops, hotels, restaurants, motels, bowling alleys, theaters, on merry-go-rounds, in offices, and domestic services without federal protection and often without state protection.

labor protection to agriculture, domestic services, street trades, and industrial homework. Child labor in agriculture is still the largest area of employment of children. In California, New Jersey, New York, Connecticut, and Hawaii special laws for the control of child labor in agriculture have been established, but in the other states much remains to be done. The Midcentury White House Conference on Children and Youth of December, 1950, emphasized the need of educational opportunities for all children and the improvement of vocational guidance, placement, and employment facilities. The number of young persons in formal apprenticeship is only about 250,000, but in recent years labor unions have begun to show increased interest in the apprenticeship program.

The exemption of agricultural work from the child labor provisions of most states causes children of sharecroppers and low-income farm families to be kept from school by farm work in rural areas and permits six-year-old children to work as cotton pickers. The enforcement of school attendance laws often is inadequate. The federal child labor law does not protect children employed in commercial agricultural work, neither during the long summer vacation nor after school hours. These children may have to work at an early age, sometimes for long hours under the hot sun and occasionally in backbreaking, monotonous labor. This is true not only for children of migratory farm workers whose miserable conditions frequently arouse public concern but also for other children of farm families, though their exploitation may be less known. This is scarcely to be regarded as "healthy farm work," which is good for the children, although some types of fruit picking are liked by children.

The selling and distribution of newspapers by small boys, classified as "independent little merchants," is of questionable value as business experience. Twenty-five states have no regulations of hours and working conditions for newsboys, and of the remaining twenty-three states only four have adequate protective legislation. The usual standards permit the employment of ten-year-old boys for newspaper delivery and of twelve-year-old children for street selling; they may begin their work at five o'clock in the morning and work until eight or nine o'clock at night in most of the states. The newspapers profit from the "little merchant system" by making the children responsible for uncollectible subscription rates and by escaping the payment of workmens' compensation contributions which would be due if the children were employed. Thus the children are not protected if they are injured on their jobs.

Changing economic conditions and technical progress induce employers to prefer high school graduates when there is no shortage of workers. Children who leave school early have little chance for satisfactory jobs and advancement. Uniform protection of children against damaging child labor, enforcement of compulsory education laws, federal aid to elementary and secondary schools, and scholarships to aid students in completing their secondary education will assist in educating children to become healthy, responsible citizens.

SELECTED BIBLIOGRAPHY

Abbott, Edith, "A Study of the Early History of Child Labor in America," *American Journal of Sociology*, Vol. IV, No. 2, July, 1908, pp. 15-37.

*Abbott, Grace, *The Child and the State*, Vol. I. Chicago: University of Chicago Press, 1938.

Addams, Jane, *Spirit of Youth and the City Streets*. New York: Macmillan, 1900.

Aldrich, Charles A., *Babies Are Human Beings*. New York: Macmillan, 1938.

Allen, Clara M., *Day Care Centers for School Children; Planning and Administration*. New York: Child Welfare League of America, 1947.

*Baylor, E. M., and E. D. Monachesi, *Rehabilitation of Children: The Theory and Practice of Child Placement*. New York: Harper, 1939.

Beck, Bertram M., "Juvenile Delinquency," *Social Work Year Book, 1954*, pp. 296-305.

Beer, Ethel S., *The Day Nursery*. New York: Dutton, 1942.

Bierman, Jessie M., "Maternal and Child Health," *Social Work Year Book, 1954*, pp. 323-327.

Bishop, Julia Ann, *et al.*, *Adoption Practice*. New York: Child Welfare League of America, 1941.

Blatz, William E., *Understanding the Young Child*. New York: Morrow, 1944.

Bossard, James H. S., *Parent and Child*. Philadelphia: University of Pennsylvania Press, 1953.

Brace, Emma, *The Life and Letters of Charles Loring Brace*. New York: Scribner, 1894.

Branscombe, Martha, "Basic Policies and Principles of Public Child Care Services," *Social Welfare Forum 1951*, pp. 335-348.

Brooks, Lee M., and Evelyn C. Brooks, *Adventuring in Adoption*. Chapel Hill: University of North Carolina Press, 1939.

Burmeister, Eva, *Forty-five in the Family: The History of a Home for Children*. New York: Columbia University Press, 1949.

Carson, Ruth, *So You Want to Adopt a Baby.* New York: Public Affairs Committee, 1951.

Coles, Jessie V., and Catherine Landreth, *Child Care Centers in California, 1947.* Berkeley: University of California, Bureau of Public Administration, 1949.

Crookes, Spencer H., "Child Welfare," *Social Work Year Book, 1954,* pp. 81-94.

Cruze, Wendell W., *Adolescent Psychology and Development.* New York: Ronald Press, 1953.

Dashiell, Alice T., *Health Program of a Day Nursery.* New York: Child Welfare League of America, 1944.

Fiedler, Miriam F., *Deaf Children in a Hearing World.* New York: Ronald Press, 1952.

Fink, Arthur E., *The Field of Social Work,* Rev. ed., Chaps. 5 and 6. New York: Holt, 1949.

Fredericksen, Hazel, *The Child and His Welfare.* San Francisco: Freeman, 1948.

Freud, Anna, and Dorothy I. Burlingham, *Infants Without Families; The Case For and Against Residential Nurseries.* New York: International Universities Press, 1944.

Friedlander, Walter, and Earl Dewey Myers, *Child Welfare in Germany Before and After Naziism.* Chicago: University of Chicago Press, 1940.

Fuller, Raymond Garfield, *The Meaning of Child Labor.* Chicago: McClurg, 1922.

*Gordon, Henrietta L., "Foster Care for Children," *Social Work Year Book, 1951,* pp. 204-210.

Hagan, Helen R., "Foster Care for Children," *Social Work Year Book, 1954,* pp. 225-232.

Hallowitz, David, and William Singer, *Discipline in the Child Care Institution.* New York: Child Welfare League of America, 1950.

Healy, William, Augusta F. Bronner, E. M. H. Baylor, and J. P. Murphy, *Reconstructing Behavior in Youth.* New York: Knopf, 1929.

Hopkirk, Howard W., *Institutions Serving Children.* New York: Russell Sage Foundation, 1944.

Howard, Loa, *The History of Child Welfare in Oregon.* Portland, Ore.: State Public Welfare Commission, 1951.

*Hutchinson, Dorothy, *In Quest of Foster Parents.* New York: Columbia University Press, 1940.

Ireland, Tom, *Child Labor: As a Relic of the Dark Ages.* New York: Putnam, 1937.

Klein, Earl E., *Work Accidents to Minors in Illinois.* Chicago: University of Chicago Press, 1938.

*Konopka, Gisela, *Therapeutic Group Work with Children.* Minneapolis: University of Minnesota Press, 1949.

Lesser, Arthur J., *Services for the Child Who Is Hard of Hearing.* U.S. Children's Bureau, Publ. No. 334, 1950.

Lockridge, Frances, *Adopting a Child.* New York: Greenberg, Publisher, Inc., 1947.

Lumpkin, Katharine DuPre, and Dorothy Douglas Wolff, *Child Workers in America.* New York: McBride, 1937.

*Lundberg, Emma O., *Unto the Least of These.* New York: Appleton-Century-Crofts, Inc., 1947.

Ma, Gioh-Fang Dju, *One Hundred Years of Public Services for Children in Minnesota.* Chicago: University of Chicago Press, 1948.

McWilliams, Carey, *Factories in the Field.* Boston: Little, 1939.

Mangold, George B., *Problems of Child Welfare,* 3rd ed., New York: Macmillan, 1936.

Meyer, Gladys (editor), *Studies of Children.* New York: King's Crown Press, 1948.

Poole, Florence, "School Social Services," *Social Work Year Book,* *1954,* pp. 463-470.

Prentice, Carol S., *An Adopted Child Looks at Adoption.* New York: Appleton-Century-Crofts, Inc., 1940.

*Reid, Joseph H., and Helen R. Hagan, *Residential Treatment of Emotionally Disturbed Children.* New York: Child Welfare League of America, 1952.

Sayles, Mary Buell, *Substitute Parents: A Study of Foster Families.* New York: Commonwealth Fund, 1936.

*Schulze, Susanne, *Creative Group Living in Children's Institutions.* New York: Assn. Press, 1951.

Simon, Abraham J., "Social and Psychological Factors in Child Placement," *American Journal of Orthopsychiatry,* Vol. XX, No. 2, April, 1950, pp. 293-310.

Slingerland, William Henry, *Child Placing in Families.* New York: Russell Sage Foundation, 1919.

———, *Child Welfare Work in California: A Study of Agencies and Institutions.* New York: Russell Sage Foundation, 1915.

Smith, William Carlson, *The Stepchild.* Chicago: University of Chicago Press, 1953.

Stroup, Herbert Hewitt, *Social Work: An Introduction to the Field,* Chaps. 4-6. New York: American Book, 1948.

Taft, Jessie (editor), *Day Nursery Care as a Social Service.* Philadelphia: Pennsylvania School of Social Work, 1943.

——— (editor), *Social Case Work with Children.* Philadelphia: Pennsylvania School of Social Work, 1940.

Taylor, Florence, "Child Labor Fact Book, 1900-1950," National Child Labor Committee, New York, Publ. No. 403, 1950.

*Thurston, Henry W., *The Dependent Child.* New York: Columbia University Press, 1930.

Truscal, Andrew G., and Francis E. Merrill, *Marriage and the Family in American Culture.* New York: Prentice-Hall, Inc., 1953.

U.S. Children's Bureau, *Essentials of Adoption Law and Procedure*, Publication No. 331, Washington, D.C., 1949.

Walker, Wilma (editor), *Child Welfare Case Records*. Chicago: University of Chicago Press, 1937.

*Weissman, Irving, *et al.*, *Guardianship: A Way of Fulfilling Public Responsibility for Children*. Washington, D.C.: U.S. Children's Bureau, Publ. No. 330, 1949.

White House Conference on Children in a Democracy, January 18-20, 1940. Washington, D.C.: U.S. Children's Bureau, Publ. No. 272, 1940.

Witmer, Helen Leland, *Social Work: An Analysis of a Social Institution*, Chaps. XII-XIV. New York: Rinehart & Company, Inc., 1942.

———, and Ruth Kotinsky, *Personality in the Making*. New York: Harper, 1953.

Young, Leontine, *Out of Wedlock*. New York: McGraw, 1954.

Zimand, Gertrude F., *Child Labor Facts, 1939-1940*. Washington, D.C.: Child Labor Committee, Publ. No. 379, 1939.

12. Health and Medical Care—
Medical Social Work

One of the most important aspects of social welfare is the maintenance of health. Health is the most precious asset in our society, and its preservation and restoration is one of the main goals of social welfare. Cure by a private physician has been available to the individual patient in the larger communities since Colonial times. For sick people who could not afford to pay a physician, the Colonies ordered the towns to provide medical treatment.[1] Indigent patients who were too sick to remain in their homes were placed in the infirmary of the poorhouse or of the house of correction. These were the forerunners of the hospitals of the United States, together with the "pesthouse" where patients with communicable diseases were confined in order to protect the citizens from contagious infection. The almshouse in Boston had some beds for paupers as early as 1662, and sick wards and infirmaries were set up in many institutions during the eighteenth century. Patients were treated by physicians under contract or engaged for the individual case of illness. Sick wards were poorly equipped and gave mainly custodial care.

With the development of medical science and skills, the need grew for specialized hospitals for the various types of diseases. At the same time the trend developed to replace small hospitals by larger institutions with better diagnostic equipment and with general surgical treatment as well as special medical facilities. In 1951, 6,637 hospitals with 1,529,988 beds were registered with the American Hospital Association, but in 1953 only 1,057,000 were classified as "acceptable"; other beds were available in rest homes, convalescent

---

[1] Edith Abbott, *Public Assistance* (Chicago: University of Chicago Press, 1940), p. 349; and Bernhard J. Stern, *Medical Services by Government* (New York: Commonwealth Fund, 1946), pp. 15-16.

homes, and old-age institutions.[2] Still there are not enough hospitals to meet the need of all patients who should be hospitalized. Most of the high standard hospitals have been set up in large cities in the industrial states, whereas rural areas are still short of hospitals and physicians. In order to assist in the provision of adequate hospital care for rural districts, the federal government is granting annual funds to the states under the "Hospital Survey and Construction Act" (*Hill-Burton Act*) of 1946. Programs have to be approved by the Surgeon General of the U.S. Public Health Service, and the funds are used for the construction of public or private nonprofit hospitals, but not for their maintenance. The danger is that communities and counties which cannot afford to build a hospital will later not be able to pay the maintenance costs either.

Hospitals are classified according to their *type of administration:* (1) governmental hospitals (federal, such as veterans hospitals and army hospitals; state; county; and city hospitals); (2) voluntary nonprofit hospitals (such as hospitals maintained by social agencies and charities, churches, fraternal orders); and (3) private proprietary hospitals which are financially self-maintaining, frequently owned by a group of physicians or a business concern. According to *type of service*, hospitals are classified as (1) *general hospitals* for general medical care and surgery; (2) *specialized hospitals* either for certain groups of patients (such as veterans, military personnel, and members of a religious sect or of a fraternal order) or for special diseases (such as heart, eye, ear, nose and throat, communicable diseases, cancer, maternity hospitals, drug addiction, and children's diseases); (3) *tuberculosis sanatoria;* (4) *mental hospitals*, including hospitals for the insane and for the mentally deficient; and (5) *hospitals of custodial type* (such as homes for the aged and infirm and convalescent and rest homes). (See Table I.)

It is generally accepted that the most effective form of medical care is provided by group practice of physicians in a hospital or a clinic (as in the Mayo Clinic), and that this form of treatment should become the method of care in the health center of a community, including curative and preventive care. At present, a great proportion of the population cannot pay for long hospitalization or is running in severe debt for such treatment. It seems necessary to increase

[2] Franz Goldmann, "Medical Care," *Social Work Year Book, 1951,* p. 303, and *1954,* p. 336.

TABLE I

HOSPITALS IN THE UNITED STATES (1951) *

I. HOSPITALS AND HOSPITAL BEDS, BY TYPE

Type	Hospitals	Beds	Percentage of Beds
Total	6,637	1,529,988	100.0
General hospitals	4,890	640,207	41.8
Special hospitals	341	31,421	2.1
Nervous and mental	596	728,187	47.6
Tuberculosis	430	88,379	5.8
Convalescent and rest homes	120	7,115	0.5
Other institutions	260	34,679	2.3

II. OWNERSHIP OF HOSPITALS AND HOSPITAL BEDS

Ownership	Hospitals	Beds	Percentage of Beds
Total	6,637	1,529,988	100.0
Federal	388	216,939	14.2
State	554	683,376	44.7
County and city	1,090	197,405	12.9
Nonprofit	2,121	225,903	14.8
Church	1,116	154,053	10.1
Proprietary	1,368	52,312	3.4

* Source: *The Journal of the American Medical Association*, Vol. 149, No. 2, May 10, 1952, pp. 150-151, Tables D and G.

federal appropriations for the construction of hospitals and to extend also federal and state support to their maintenance so that financial reasons will no longer constitute a barrier to medically required hospital care.[3]

The second type of institutional medical care is offered by *clinics*. They serve patients who do not need to be hospitalized (ambulatory patients) and are one of the most important means of preventing sickness by early medical examination, medication, and checkup. Clinics developed from "dispensaries" that were mainly for the care of the poor; the first clinic was established in New York in 1791. Medical and surgical treatment, medicines, drugs, and appliances were the help given in the dispensaries, which usually were

[3] Oscar R. Ewing, *The Nation's Health* (Washington, D.C.: Federal Security Agency, 1948), p. 17. About 70 per cent of all beds are situated in government hospitals (local, state, and federal), only 30 per cent in private hospitals, but 60 per cent of the beds in general hospitals are in voluntary institutions (F. Goldmann, *1951, op. cit.*, p. 303).

connected with hospitals. Home care was given only in emergencies. Most modern clinics are out-patient departments of hospitals and serve as diagnostic and treatment centers. They provide preventive care, sometimes serving also as district health centers in rural regions, through medical group practice. Clinics are still scarce in rural areas. They offer medical care free or for nominal, or at least reasonable, fees to those patients who cannot afford to pay much. The lack of dental clinics is particularly severe. A number of itinerary clinics, particularly for maternal, well-baby care, and some dental treatment of children have been developed with the aid of federal grants under the maternal and child health services which we discussed in Chapter 11.

Public medical services are extended in recent times to patients who are not indigent in the general sense of the word, are not supported by public assistance of any kind, but who still cannot afford to pay for the necessary expensive medical care. This group is called the "medically needy." County and city governments assume responsibility for the medical care of these otherwise self-supporting citizens. Several states encourage such medical services, partly by state participation in the cost of medical care, e.g., Tennessee in its law of 1937.[4] Other state laws recognize the social need for adequate medical care, such as the welfare statutes of Illinois, Indiana, Michigan, New Jersey, New York, and Rhode Island.[5]

Despite some progress, the expenses for medical treatment in time of severe illness are usually so high that numerous *voluntary health insurance plans* have been organized in order to provide either prepaid medical treatment, or hospital care, or cash allowances for the loss of income in case of illness, thus defraying at least a part of medical cost and loss of income. Voluntary health plans are administered either by commercial insurance companies or by private non-profit associations. They vary widely in their policies of admission of members and in type and quality of their services. Few of them furnish complete medical and dental care, medicines and hospitilization. The most noted of the voluntary hospital plans is the Blue Cross Plan, which serves over thirty-three million members. Among the medical prepayment programs, the Blue Shield Plan represents non-

---

[4] Bernhard Stern, *op. cit.*, p. 34.

[5] F. Goldmann, *op. cit.*, p. 306; Vlado A. Getting, "Unmet Needs in Public Health Services," *Building America's Health*, President's Commission on the Health Needs of the Nation, Vol. 4, 1952, pp. 83-89.

Courtesy of U.S. Public Health Service.

DENTAL CLINIC FOR CHILDREN

profit organizations under the auspices of state or local medical societies which permit insured patients to select a physician among a panel of doctors; but most of the plans limit the medical service under contract to patients with a modest annual maximum income, graduated according to the size of family.[6] Usually the plan excludes older applicants and requires substantial additional payments for persons of medium income that exceeds a stipulated amount.

Neither the increase in public medical services nor the present voluntary health plans have solved the problem of medical care for patients not eligible for free public medical treatment. Millions of self-supporting sick persons find themselves in the serious dilemma of having to pay the cost of medical treatment, operations, medicines, drugs, and hospitalization. Since the occurrence of illness and its cost are unpredictable for the individual family, it is usually impossible

[6] For more detailed information the reader is referred to Franz Goldmann, *Voluntary Medical Care Insurance in the U.S.* (New York: Columbia University Press, 1948), and to Chapter 17.

to budget these expenses. For this reason it seems necessary that some method be found to distribute the risks of sickness and medical costs among the total population. This can be done by a general system of health insurance, integrating existing effective voluntary prepaid group health plans, or by a substantial extension of supplementary tax-supported medical services for patients for whom special public responsibility is acknowledged (such as military personnel and veterans) and for those who are not protected by other facilities.[7] The idea of a compulsory system of health insurance has been opposed in varying degrees by commercial insurance companies, the patent medicine and drug industries, the American Medical Association, and the Christian Science movement. It is felt that some program of public health insurance or general public health service will be indispensable, in the long run, in order to secure adequate health protection for the part of the population which is, for reason of cost, now excluded from the full benefits of modern medical science.

An important role in the progress of health services is played by numerous voluntary health agencies. Among them are the National Tuberculosis Association, the National Foundation for Infantile Paralysis, the American Heart Association, the American Foundation for the Blind, the American Cancer Research Association, the American Hearing Society, the American Rheumatism Association, the United Cerebral Palsy Association, and others with state and local chapters. They emphasize in their work prevention, control, and treatment of such specific diseases as tuberculosis, cancer, and diabetes. Some devote their main efforts to research and health education, others to the development of higher standards of care and the provision of consultant or demonstration services.

Voluntary agencies derive their funds from membership fees, sales of seals, or from special fund raising campaigns. Research often is financed by foundations, private endowments, and public grants. Several voluntary health agencies have encouraged studies by grants

[7] For a fuller analysis of this question see Franz Goldmann, *Public Medical Care: Principles and Problems* (New York: Columbia University Press, 1945); Oscar Ewing, *op. cit.*, especially pp. 63-114; C.-E.A. Winslow, *Health Care for the Americans* (New York: Public Affairs Pamphlet No. 104, 1945); and Michael M. Davis and Dewey Anderson, *Medical Care for the Individual and the Issue of Compulsory Health Insurance* (Washington, D.C.: Government Printing Office, 1948).

and fellowships to universities and private scientists. They have done pioneer work in new fields of health education, prevention, and treatment and have stimulated the development of public health services. As a coordinating body of voluntary health organizations the National Health Council in New York is operating since 1921.

Public health services are devoted to the protection and improvement of health of the entire population. Their main object is prevention of diseases and elimination of environmental health hazards. Public health includes sanitation services, control of epidemics, sanitary disposal, and the protection of water supply and food. The functions of the federal government in this field are mainly the responsibility of the U.S. Public Health Service, under the Department of Health, Education and Welfare, the Veterans Administration, and the U.S. Children's Bureau, and were explained above.[8] The main responsibility in the area of public health lies with the city and county health departments. More recently district health departments combining several counties or city and county health units are considered the most effective type of administration. For a minimum staff of a public health department a full-time medical officer, a sanitary engineer, some part-time medical specialists, ten public health nurses, a medical social worker, and clerical personnel are recommended. The program includes in addition to the above-mentioned functions the compilation of vital statistics, maternal and child health services, laboratory services, and public health education.

In the states, the responsibility for public health usually is embodied in the several state departments of public health. Sometimes the health services are administered by a branch of the public welfare department. The functions of the state health authority are observation of health needs, coordination and supervision of local health services, preparation and enforcement of legislation and regulations, the establishment of an adequate collection of statistics, and informing the public on health protection.[9]

[8] See Chapters 5, 7, and 11—also 16.
[9] For more details see Haven Emerson and Martha Luginbuhl, *Local Health Units for the Nation* (New York: Commonwealth Fund, 1945); Wilson G. Smillie, *Public Health Administration in the United States* (New York: Macmillan, 1947); Leonard A. Scheele, "Public Health," *Social Work Year Book, 1951*, pp. 376-391; "Medical Care for Americans," *The Annals of the American Academy of Social and Political Science*, Vol. 273, January, 1951 (entire issue).

I. COST OF MEDICAL CARE

The total expenditure for medical care of the entire population, in 1951, ranged from $14 to $15 billion in the United States. Federal, state, and local government paid $3,170 million of this amount, which represented 1.04 per cent of the gross national product of the nation minus consumption of capital. Families spend a varying part of their income on health expenditures. The average figure is 4 to 5 per cent of all consumption expenditures of the family. But the proportion of medical expenses varies with the level of income. Health surveys show that in low income groups, earning less than $500 a year, the medical expenses averaged $48 or 17 per cent, while for people with income over $5,000 the average medical expense was $260 or 3.4 per cent. In the lowest income group 14.2 per cent of families account for only 4.7 per cent of medical outlays, while in the highest income group over $5,000, 0.9 per cent of the families spent 7.1 per cent of funds for medical care. The highest income group, therefore, spent 25 times as much for health per family than the lowest income group.[10]

The distribution of the main part of medical outlays for 1950-51 was the following:

Source of Payment	Million Dollars
Patients (Consumers)	8,918
Government	2,672
Private hospitals	419
Philanthropy	400
Industry	700
Total	13,109

It may be essential to state at this point the fundamental health principles formulated by the President's Commission on the Health Needs of the Nation, under the chairmanship of Paul B. Magnuson, M.D., as a guide to our health problem:

We Believe That
1. Access to the means for the attainment and preservation of health is a basic human right.

[10] Seymour E. Harris, "Medical Care Expenditures in Relation to Family Income and National Income," *Building America's Health*, President's Commission on the Health Needs of the Nation, Vol. 4 (1952), pp. 8 and 12.

2. Effort of the individual himself is a vitally important factor in attaining and maintaining health.

3. The physician-patient relationship is so fundamental to health that everyone should have a personal physician.

4. The physician should have access to proper facilities and equipment, affiliation on some basis with a hospital, and the help of trained personnel in order to fulfill his part in providing comprehensive health services.

5. Comprehensive health service includes the positive promotion of health, the prevention of disease, the diagnosis and treatment of disease, the rehabilitation of the disabled—all supported by constantly improving education of personnel and a continuous program of research.

6. Comprehensive health service is the concern of society and is best insured when all elements of society participate in providing it.

7. Responsibility for health is a joint one, with the individual citizen and local, State, Federal governments each having major contributions to make toward its fuller realization.

8. The American people desire and deserve comprehensive health service of the highest quality and in our dynamic expanding economy the means can be found to provide it.

9. The same high quality of health services should be available to all people equally.

10. A health program must take into account the progress and experience of the past, the realities of the present, and must be flexible enough to cope with future changes.[11]

II. MEDICAL CARE FOR NEEDY PATIENTS

The high cost of medical and hospital care explains that a large number of families and individuals are unable to get adequate care because they don't have the means to pay for it. For persons under public assistance, however, the provision of medical care, diagnosis, treatment, and rehabilitation was improved by the amendment of 1950 to the Social Security Act. It authorizes the use of federal grants-in-aid for the direct purchase of medical care for public assistance recipients and for the maintenance of patients in public or private medical institutions, except in mental hospitals and tuberculosis sanatoria.

Public assistance funds may be used to finance the cost of medical services in the following three ways:

1. Through direct money payments to assistance recipients, thus enabling them to pay the cost of medical care if the medical bill is small or in installments on larger bills;

[11] *Building America's Health*, Findings & Recommendations, Vol. 1 (1952), p. 3.

2. Through payment to physicians, group of physicians, or to a health prepayment plan in behalf of recipients of public assistance;

3. Through payments into a "medical cost pooled fund." This arrangement is in effect a prepayment arrangement with a group of doctors under the auspices of the public welfare agency (as a rule the county or city welfare department). A specified monthly amount is paid on behalf of each public assistance recipient into an account out of which all medical services rendered to any assistance recipient are paid. This method permits the use of grants-in-aid for the payments into the pooled fund for medical care. The arrangements with physicians and hospitals may be made by the public health department after agreement with the welfare department.[12]

The technical arrangements for securing medical care for the recipients of public assistance may be made in four different methods:

1. The welfare department may contract with individual physicians, a group of physicians, hospitals, and clinics to reimburse them on the basis of a fee schedule for the medical care of the recipients of public assistance.

2. The welfare department may employ physicians or a group of physicians who give medical treatment to the assistance recipients, and federal funds may be used for payment if the plan is financed through a "pooled fund."

3. Medical care may be arranged for assistance recipients through voluntary health insurance or physicians group practice plans. Prepayment plans have been reluctant to conclude such arrangement because assistance recipients are considered a poor risk.

4. The welfare department may contract with a medical society (e.g., the county medical association) to render medical treatment to the assistance recipients on the basis of an agreement about fees according to schedule.

In all forms of medical care for assistance recipients there are limitations because the federal maximum contributions for each individual are too low to support a completely adequate program of medical services.[13] No federal grants are available for patients who

[12] See "Tax Supported Medical Care for the Needy," *Public Welfare*, Vol. 10, No. 4, October, 1952, pp. 87-102; and Leon Lefson, "Rehabilitating Public Assistance Recipients," *Public Welfare*, Vol. ii, No. ii, April, 1953, pp. 47-50.

[13] See Chapter 8, p. 236-239. Michael Davis, "Problems and Present Methods of Financing Health Services," *Building America's Health*, President's Commission on the Health Needs of the Nation, Vol. 4, pp. 104-110.

receive general assistance but are not eligible for categorical assistance. For all groups, particularly the latter, substantial appropriations from states and local government will be necessary for medical care in order to secure adequate health protection of the needy.

III. MEDICAL SOCIAL WORK

Medical social work as a specialized method of social work is of recent origin. It involves the practice of social casework and sometimes group work in a hospital, a clinic, or another medical setting in order to make it possible for the patient to use the available health services most effectively. Medical social work is characterized by the emphasis on help in the social and emotional problems which affect the patient in his illness and his cure.

The development of medical social work is based on four main sources. The first start was the recognition in England, in the 1880's, that discharged patients of mental hospitals needed "after care" in their homes in order to avoid recurrence of their illness. "Visitors" went to the patient's home and advised family and friends about the necessary care of the patient after his discharge.[14] A second source of medical social work were the "lady almoners" in English hospitals; they organized upon the initiative of Sir Charles S. Loch in London, in the 1890's, served as volunteer receptionists, made social investigations, and decided whether the applicant should be admitted as a free patient to the hospital, and what charity organization might be asked to assume the patient's support.

Visiting nurses became the third precursors of medical social work. In 1893, Lillian Wald and Mary Brewster of the Henry Street Settlement House in New York began to visit the homes of sick people in the neighborhood who were too poor to pay for medical and nursing care. They found many social and personal problems which were caused by the illness of the patients. Some hospitals in New York learned from the experiences of the Henry Street Settle-

---

[14] Earlier "hospital visitors" had been used in France, in the seventeenth century, under the direction of St. Vincent de Paul and Louise de Merillac, as "Sisters of Charity," and following this example in other European countries. See Ida M. Cannon, *Social Work in Hospitals: A Contribution to Progressive Medicine* (New York: Russell Sage Foundation, 1930), pp. 5-15; Commonwealth Fund, Commission on Hospital Care, *Hospital Care in the United States* (New York: 1947), p. 429; and Ida M. Cannon, *On the Social Frontier of Medicine* (Cambridge: Harvard University Press, 1952), pp. 46-94.

ment House that visits in the home might greatly improve the effect of medical treatment; they sent nurses from the hospital staff for "after care" and supervision of discharged patients. The fourth source of medical social work was gained by the training of medical students in social agencies. Dr. Charles P. Emerson of Johns Hopkins University at Baltimore, in 1902, wanted to include the study of social and emotional problems into medical education and requested that his students serve as volunteers with charity agencies in order to understand the influence of social, economic, and living conditions on the illness of patients.

On the basis of these experiences, medical social work was established in 1905, at four different places almost at the same time. Social workers became members of the staff at Massachusetts General Hospital in Boston, at Bellevue Hospital in New York, at Johns Hopkins Hospital in Baltimore, and at the Berkeley Infirmary in Boston. Specialization in medical science made the physician in a hospital or dispensary a medical specialist. He no longer could be acquainted with the living conditions, income, environment, habits, and personality of the patient as was the old family doctor. Therefore, the medical social worker had to be the personal contact with patient and family, to investigate social and personal conditions of the patient, and to supply the factual background to the physician in order to help him in diagnosis and treatment. Dr. Richard C. Cabot of Massachusetts General Hospital was the first to recognize the need of a social worker who helped the patient after his return from the hospital to observe the orders of the physician, instructing the family in diets and the application of medical prescriptions. The social worker also interpreted the nature of the illness to the family and advised them about specific precautions in order to avoid recurrence of the disease.[15]

Medical social work often includes suggestions about the possibility of convalescent care, the influence of emotional strain upon the patient, the need of medical examination of other family members, and the provision of financial aid through social agencies. Questions

[15] The use of medical social work goes back to an experience of Dr. Cabot with a small boy cured of acute gastric conditions after careful medical treatment. A few days after his release, he was returned by his mother in the old, bad condition. When this happened again and once more, it became evident that observation in the family and instruction of the mother was needed to preserve the health of the child.

concerning the care of children during the mother's illness, arrangements for rest of the patient during convalescence, and finding a suitable job which would not jeopardize the results of medical treatment are among those problems which occupy medical social workers. An increasing emphasis is placed upon the social relationships of the patient, the attitude of spouse and children, and the patient's own reactions and feeling toward his illness.[16] The medical social worker operates in a team with the physician, the nurse, and the laboratory technician. Her particular contribution in this teamwork is enabling the patient to help himself to become well again. Although physician and nurse in hospital and clinic represent professional authority which easily makes the patient dependent upon their orders, the medical social worker strengthens the patient's self-confidence. She respects his natural feelings of worry about his illness and about social, economic, and personal implications for himself and his family and so tries to lessen his concern.

The medical social worker acquires an intimate knowledge of the personal and social situation of the patient, and she assists him in using the resources in the community which will help him most effectively to regain his health. The following is an example of this:

A farmer was treated in a hospital for heart trouble. The physician required that he rest after his discharge from the hospital. But the crops were to be harvested. So the doctor's advice would not let the patient rest while his mind was worrying about what to do about the crops. The social worker, therefore, contacted the Farm Bureau and got a crew for the patient which performed the agricultural work. She arranged with a family welfare agency to provide a place in a convalescent home and to make plans for the family until the patient could return and resume his work.[17]

Medical social work does not attempt to solve all problems of the patient but deals with those factors which are directly related to the

[16] Harriett Bartlett, *Medical Social Work: A Study of Current Aims and Methods* (Chicago: American Association of Medical Social Workers, 1934), pp. 98-103; and Frances Upham, *A Dynamic Approach to Illness* (New York: Family Service Association of America, 1949), pp. 8, 109. Examples for effective group work in a medical setting may be found in Helen L. Witmer and Ruth Kotinsky, *Personality in the Making* (New York: Harper, 1952), pp. 398-401.

[17] Ida Cannon, *Social Work in Hospitals,* 1st ed. (New York: Russell Sage Foundation, 1913), p. 136.

cause and nature of the patient's illness and its treatment and are called the "social component of illness." Medical social work has shifted its emphasis from the attention of the disease to the person of the patient with his anxieties, attitudes, and feelings.[18] The physician remains the highest authority in the team at the hospital and the clinic; the medical social worker as well as nurse, laboratory technician, psychologist, and physiotherapist must be able to cooperate wholeheartedly under the doctor's direction in this team relationship. The medical social worker interprets to the patient and his family requests and commendations of the physician. She helps the patient understand his disease and to make the best use of the medical treatment and the doctor's prescriptions. She thus extends the medical service of the hospital into the patient's home and into the community. Her work may be illustrated by the following example:

The Mills Case[19]

After treatment for tuberculosis in the hospital, Mrs. Mills was told that she should go to a sanatorium. She refused to go, however, so that the physician had to plan to continue medical treatment in her home. The doctor could not understand why Mrs. Mills, an intelligent woman, insisted on remaining at home, since she had carefully obeyed all orders in the hospital. The medical social worker after several home visits found that the husband of the patient who had been an excellent father to the two small children and an exemplary husband to the patient until this time had suddenly begun to come home intoxicated, at late hours, and without his salary. The social worker felt that such a change could not happen without some reason, and in a conversation with Mr. Mills learned from him that recently he had felt severe pains in his wrists at work which he had tried to ease by drinking. She persuaded Mr. Mills to go to the hospital for an examination which revealed that the pains were caused by an industrial poisoning which would become worse if he stayed in his job in the factory. The doctor recommended an out-of-door work. The Mills were discouraged because they had started to save money for building a home in the country, and Mr. Mills was sure that he could not continue to save if he left his factory job. With the advice of the medical social worker it was possible, however, to obtain a mortgage on three acres of land which permitted Mr. Mills to work in his trade in out-of-door work, and at the same time to build a small house

[18] Helen Witmer, *Social Work* (New York: Farrar & Rinehart, 1942), p. 428.
[19] American Association of Social Workers, *Vocational Aspects of Medical Social Work* (New York: 1927), p. 18.

and to grow a garden. After a period of one year, the city decided to expand the water system to the land of the Mills so that they were able to sell several lots, and with this income to complete the house and to accept work which was not harmful to Mr. Mills' health and which permitted Mrs. Mills to recover fully from her tuberculosis. This successful solution was due mainly to the intelligent cooperation and initiative of the patients, but was also reached through the understanding of the social worker.

The medical settings in which social work is practiced are private and public hospitals and clinics; voluntary health agencies; local, state, and federal health services; other public and private social welfare agencies; schools of social work, schools of nursing and medical schools. In most instances medical social work is casework with the individual patient, but it also encompasses administrative, supervisory, and consultant activities and community organization, teaching, group therapy, and research.[20] Particularly essential is the field of vocational rehabilitation in which the medical social worker plays a vital role in helping and encouraging the patient in his important adjustment for his future life and for his family responsibilities.

Medical social work is also concerned with social and economic conditions of the patient and his family, and with the interrelation of the physical and the emotional factors in illness. For some time medical science has recognized that there is an essential mutual influence between psyche and body, between the emotions of the patient and his organic well-being, and between organic disturbances, external factors and the patient's emotions and mental behavior. This is called the "psychosomatic approach." It emphasizes the consequence of the emotions of the patient and of his determination to become well again upon his cure. The rapid new scientific inventions in pathology, surgery, bacteriology, and biochemistry almost forgot about the patient as a human being. For the final success of medical treatment medical social workers are aware of the decisive role which is played by the patient's own attitude toward his illness and his desire to regain his health. Medical social workers attempt, therefore, to help the patient understand the nature of his disease, for instance tuberculosis or rheumatism, and the possibilities of its treatment, and to create in him a strong desire to participate in his recovery. The patient, under such conditions, will adjust his life

[20] American Association of Medical Social Workers, *Your Future Career* (Washington, D.C.: 1947).

in a way which makes his cure more probable and complete.[21] Modern medical social work accepts the concept of the functions of the human organism as a whole, not merely as a sum of various parts. Psychiatry, with its emphasis on the patient as a unique personality, and biology and psychology, with their findings that functions of the human body and mind are not localized, have contributed to this concept.

The number of medical social workers in the United States in 1953 was estimated at 3,285; in 1954, 2,293 were members of the American Association of Medical Social Workers. The Veterans Administration employs a large number of them; others work in hospitals, clinics, public health departments, private health agencies and organizations, and in rehabilitation services. The total number of medical and psychiatric social workers employed in hospitals alone in 1952 amounted to 5,062 but included workers who were not fully trained.

Among recent trends in medical social work is the growing recognition of the medical profession and of universities that social and psychological factors greatly influence diagnosis, treatment, and prevention of disease. This interrelationship is now taught in schools of medicine and of public health, and the student's attention is called to the influence of social environment, family, economic conditions, employment, and social adjustment on the patient's cure and the prevention of recurrence of his illness.[22]

Another trend is the continuous expansion of health programs outside of hospitals and clinics. In public school systems, vocational rehabilitation services, in state, county, and municipal health depart-

[21] H. Flanders Dunbar, *Mind and Body: Psychosomatic Medicine* (New York: Random House, 1947), pp. 65-66, presents characteristic examples for the influence of the patient's will for his recovery; see also Franz Alexander, "Psychosomatic Aspects of Medicine," *Psychosomatic Medicine,* Vol. 1, No. 1, January, 1939, pp. 7-18, and *Psychosomatic Medicine* (New York: Norton, 1950); Roy R. Grinker, *Psychosomatic Research* (New York: Norton, 1953); and Juergen Ruesch, "The Infantile Personality—the Core Problem of Psychosomatic Medicine," *Psychosomatic Medicine,* Vol. 10, February, 1948, p. 134 ff.

[22] Dora Goldstine, "Medical Social Work," *Social Work Year Book, 1951,* p. 319; *Hospitals* (The Journal of the American Hospital Association), April, 1952, p. 70; *Building America's Health,* President's Commission on the Health Needs of the Nation, 1952, Vol. 3 (Statistical Appendix), p. 221, Table 303; Elizabeth P. Rice, "Medical Social Work," *Social Work Year Book, 1954,* pp. 344-345; and Dora Goldstine, *Readings in the Theory and Practice of Medical Social Work* (Chicago: University of Chicago Press, 1954).

ments, in services for crippled children and for other groups of handicapped patients, medical workers find an increasing challenge to contribute their skill of integration in meeting social, emotional, and health needs.

Finally, medical social work is recognized in such community health planning bodies as municipal, county, or regional welfare councils and local health boards, and in coordinated programs of medical, health, and welfare projects. This also applies to the expanding area of health education in connection with schools and adult civic groups and to the use of medical social workers as teachers in medical schools and schools of public health. In these settings the medical social worker contributes her experience of the effect of the patient's insight into the nature of his illness for his full-hearted cooperation.

SELECTED BIBLIOGRAPHY

American Association of Social Workers, "Vocational Aspects of Medical Social Work," New York, 1927.
Bachmeyer, Arthur C., and Gerhard Hartman (editors), *The Hospital in Modern Society*. New York: Commonwealth Fund, 1943.
*Bartlett, Harriett M., *Medical Social Work: A Study of Current Aims and Methods in Medical Social Work*. Chicago: American Association of Medical Social Workers, 1940.
——, *Some Aspects of Social Case Work in a Medical Setting: A Study in the Field of Medical Social Work*. Chicago: American Association of Medical Social Workers, 1940.
Binger, Carl, *The Doctor's Job*. New York: Norton, 1945.
Cabot, Richard C., *Social Service and the Art of Healing*, Rev. ed. New York: Dodd, 1928.
Cannon, Ida M., *Social Work in Hospitals: A Contribution to Progressive Medicine*, Rev. ed. New York: Russell Sage Foundation, 1930.
*——, *On the Social Frontier of Medicine*. Cambridge: Harvard University Press, 1952.
Cannon, Mary Antoinette, and Harriett M. Bartlett, "Medical Social Work," pp. 38-81, in New York Academy of Medicine, *Medical Addenda*. New York: Commonwealth Fund, 1947.
Cannon, Walter B., *The Wisdom of the Body*. New York: Norton, 1932.
*Champion, William M., *Medical Information for Social Workers*. Baltimore: Williams & Wilkins, 1938.
Corwin, E. H. L., *Ecology of Health*. New York: Commonwealth Fund, 1949.
——, *The American Hospital*. New York: Commonwealth Fund, 1946.

Cressman, Edith M. (editor), *Functional Case Work in a Medical Setting.* Philadelphia: Pennsylvania School of Social Work, 1944.

Crothers, Bronson, *A Pediatrician in Search of Mental Hygiene.* New York: Commonwealth Fund, 1937.

Davis, Michael M., and Dewey Anderson, *Medical Care for the Individual and the Issue of Compulsory Health Insurance.* Washington, D.C.: Government Publishing Office, 1948.

*Dunbar, H. Flanders, *Emotions and Bodily Changes.* New York: Columbia University Press, 1946.

——, *Mind and Body: Psychosomatic Medicine.* New York: Random House, 1947.

Elledge, Caroline H., *The Rehabilitation of the Patient.* Philadelphia: Lippincott, 1948.

Ewing, Oscar R., *The Nation's Health.* Washington, D.C.: Federal Security Agency, 1948.

Falk, I. S., "Health Services, Medical Care Insurance, and Social Security," *Annals of the American Academy of Political and Social Science,* Vol. 273, January, 1951, pp. 114-121.

Faxon, Nathaniel W., *The Hospital in Contemporary Life.* Cambridge: Harvard University Press, 1949.

Frank, Marjorie H., *Volunteer Participation in Psychiatric Hospital Services.* New York: National Committee for Mental Hygiene, 1950.

Goldmann, Franz, "Medical Care," *Social Work Year Book, 1954,* pp. 327-339.

*——, *Public Medical Care: Principles and Problems.* New York: Columbia University Press, 1945.

——, *Voluntary Medical Care Insurance in the United States.* New York: Columbia University Press, 1948.

*Goldstine, Dora, "Medical Social Work," *Social Work Year Book, 1951,* pp. 315-320.

Halliday, James L., *Psychosocial Medicine.* New York: Norton, 1948.

Harris, Seymour E., "Medical Care Expenditures in Relation to Family Income and National Income," *Building America's Health,* (1952) Vol. 4, pp. 3-16.

Henry, Edna G., *The Theory and Practice of Medical Social Work.* Ann Arbor: Edwards, 1924.

Hinsie, Leland E., *The Person in the Body: An Introduction to Psychosomatic Medicine.* New York: Norton, 1945.

Jensen, Frode, H. G. Weiskotten, and Margaret Thomas, *Medical Care of the Discharged Hospital Patient.* New York: Commonwealth Fund, 1944.

Joint Committee on Medical Care of the American Public Health Association and the American Public Welfare Association, "Tax-Supported Medical Care for the Needy," *Public Welfare,* Vol. 10, No. 4, October, 1952, pp. 87-99.

Knott, Leslie W., et al., *Health Manpower Source Book: Medical Social*

Workers. Washington, D.C.: Public Health Service, 1953.

Plumley, Margaret Lovell, *Medical Social Work in Tax-Supported Health and Welfare Services.* Chicago: American Public Welfare Association, 1940.

*President's Commission on the Health Needs of the Nation, *Building America's Health.* 5 vols. Washington, D.C.: G.P.O. 1952.

*Rice, Elizabeth P., "Medical Social Work," *Social Work Year Book,* *1954,* pp. 339-346.

Richardson, Henry B., *Patients Have Families.* New York: Commonwealth Fund, 1945.

Robinson, George C., *The Patient as a Person: A Study of the Social Aspects of Illness.* New York: Commonwealth Fund, 1939.

Scheele, Leonard A., "Public Health," *Social Work Year Book, 1951,* pp. 376-391.

Shimberg, Myra E., *Health and Employment: A Study of Public Assistance Clients Attending Out-Patient Department Clinics.* New York: National Council on Rehabilitation, 1946.

Shirley, Hale F., *Psychiatry for the Pediatrician.* New York: Commonwealth Fund, 1948.

Sigerist, Henry E., *Medicine and Human Welfare.* New Haven: Yale University Press, 1941.

Smillie, Wilson G., *Public Health Administration in the United States.* New York: Macmillan, 1947.

Stephen, Karen, *Psychoanalysis and Medicine, A Study of the Wish to Fall Ill.* New York: Macmillan, 1939.

Stern, Bernhard J., *American Medical Practice in the Perspectives of a Century.* New York: Commonwealth Fund, 1945.

*———, *Medical Services by Government: Local, State, and Federal.* New York: Commonwealth Fund, 1946.

Thornton, Janet, and Marjorie S. Knauth, *The Social Component in Medical Care.* New York: Columbia University Press, 1937.

Turner, Clair E., "Public Health Education," *Social Work Year Book,* *1954,* pp. 415-418.

*Upham, Frances, *A Dynamic Approach to Illness: A Social Work Guide.* New York: Family Service Association of America, 1949.

Weiss, Edward, and O. Spurgeon English, *Psychosomatic Medicine.* Philadelphia: Saunders, 1943.

Witmer, Helen L., *Teaching Psychotherapeutic Medicine.* New York: Commonwealth Fund, 1947.

*———, and Ruth Kotinsky, *Personality in the Making.* New York: Harper, 1952.

Wright, John J., "Public Health," *Social Work Year Book, 1954,* pp. 405-415.

Yost, Edna, and Lillian M. Gilbreth, *Normal Lives for the Disabled.* New York: Macmillan, 1944.

Zapoleon, Marguerite W., "The Outlook for Women in Social Case Work in a Medical Setting," U.S. Department of Labor, Women's Bureau, Social Work Services, Bulletin No. 235-1, 1950.

13. *Mental Hygiene and Psychiatric Social Work*

The terms "mental health" and "mental hygiene" are sometimes used interchangeably, and there are many definitions of both terms. We want to conceive mental health as the desirable goal, and mental hygiene as one of the important means to preserve or to achieve the objective of mental health.

Mental hygiene has to fulfill many important functions. Mental hygiene is (1) a public health movement with the aim of preventing mental disorders through mental health education and freeing patients from external and internal conflict, anxiety, and emotional strain; (2) a science based upon psychiatry and psychology, applied to help people overcome inner conflicts and maintain or regain mental health, through psychiatric, psychological, and social treatment (frequently provided in mental hygiene or child guidance clinics); (3) a medical and psychiatric treatment in mental hospitals to aid severely disturbed mental patients; (4) a special orientation in education based upon recent developments in psychiatry and the social sciences; and (5) a philosophy of life and a concept of ethics that pursues the goal of healthy living in a democratic society.[1] Mental hygiene societies are groups of interested citizens, frequently including psychiatrists, public health officers, physicians, educators, psychologists, and social workers, that seek to secure adequate psychiatric services in the community and attempt to create the conditions for a healthy emotional climate.

[1] Joseph S. Kasanin, "Mental Hygiene," *Social Work Year Book, 1945*, pp. 267-268. James V. Lowry uses the definition: "the aggregate of measures designed to preserve mental health" ("Mental Hygiene," *Social Work Year Book, 1951*, p. 320); Ralph Kramer, "Attitudes and Actions in Mental Hygiene," *Beakon*, Spring, 1953, pp. 1, 3-8; and James V. Lowry, "Mental Health," *Social Work Year Book, 1954*, pp. 346-347.

The nature and causes of mental disorders were unknown until the end of the eighteenth century. Only recently man has acquired more knowledge of the origin, treatment, and prevention of mental disease. In ancient times people of disturbed mind were considered to be possessed by demons as punishment for their sins because they had offended the gods. The demented were tortured in order to drive out the evil spirits and were drowned, hanged, or burned at the stake for having allegedly practiced sorcery or witchcraft.[2] In the eighteenth century the ideas of humane treatment and the attempt of medical care for the mentally deranged were first conceived in France by Philippe Pinel, in England by William Tuke, and in Italy by Vincento Chiarugi. In the United States, Benjamin Franklin, the Quakers in Pennsylvania, and, particularly, Dr. Benjamin Rush became the pioneers of the movement to grant medical care and humane treatment to the mentally ill.[3] Toward the end of the nineteenth century scientific discoveries in medicine, psychiatry, biology, physiology, and psychology revealed the interdependence of mind and body and created a new outlook in the approach to mental disorders. Emil Kraepelin and Wilhelm Griesinger classified mental diseases upon their symptoms. Sigmund Freud, and his followers' studies of hysteria and neuroses, found the key to the knowledge of the unconscious and opened up new possibilities of cure through psychoanalysis.

Psychoanalysis caused a revolutionary change in the methods of psychiatry and psychotherapy all over the world. The psychiatric schools of Jung, Adler, and Otto Rank also contributed new elements to the methods of treatment of mental disorders. In the United States Dr. Adolf Meyer developed the psychobiological theory in psychiatry. Social psychiatry was taught by such leaders in this field as C. Macfie Campbell, William Healy, his wife Augusta Bronner, William Alanson White, Herman Adler, E. E. Southard, August Hoch, A. A. Brill, Arnold Gesell, Leo Kanner, Thomas W. Salmon, James S. Plant, Karl and Wilhelm Menninger, Karl Bowman, Lawson G. Lowrey, George Stevenson, and Fritz Redl. The scientific contributions of these pioneers in social psychiatry emphasized that mental disorders and emotional disturbances frequently are

[2] Albert Deutsch, *The Mentally Ill in America* (New York: Columbia University Press, 1946), p. 16.
[3] See Chapter 4.

not, or not exclusively, caused by biological and organic conditions, but also by social factors in family and environment. Therefore counseling and therapeutic treatment of the patient are necessary, and diagnosis of mental instability is not sufficient. Often social changes in the environment also are indispensable in order to prevent new illness and to help in the cure of the mental patient.

Until the beginning of this century, most hospitals for mental diseases offered scarcely more than detention and custodial care, with little insight into the personality of the patient and with limited facilities for treatment. As a patient in several mental hospitals, Clifford Beers had suffered under the usual brutal treatment and devoted his life after his release to the reform of mental institutions. He became the founder of the mental hygiene movement. In 1908, he published his diary, *A Mind That Found Itself*, with an introduction by the famous philosopher and psychologist, William James, and the noted psychiatrist, Adolf Meyer. Widespread public interest led to the foundation of a State Mental Hygiene Society in Connecticut in 1908, and, in the following year, to the establishment of the National Committee for Mental Hygiene, on which Clifford Beers served as its executive.[4]

The mental hygiene movement's first concern was the improvement of the inhuman methods of treatment in mental hospitals and institutions. There is at present a total of about 1,000 public and private mental hospitals in the United States, in which more than 1,000,000 patients are treated annually. About 70 per cent of these patients are in need of longer residential care.[5] In most mental hospitals there are well-kept grounds around their buildings, and an air of quiet peace, but inside frequently we find hundreds of silent, staring human beings who either polish floors or do nothing but sit in rocking chairs and wait endlessly. Sometimes weird screams are heard from the "violent wards." State hospitals are often overcrowded, and new building programs have been delayed by the war. Some states (California, Florida, Maryland, Minnesota, and Texas) have recently appropriated funds for the expansion and improvement of

[4] The term "mental hygiene" had been the title of a book of Dr. William Sweetser in 1843, but it had been forgotten until the mental hygiene societies brought it again to public attention. Since 1950 the National Association for Mental Health has united various organizations in this field.

[5] See Table II, and for the increase in hospitalized patients in mental hospitals and institutions for mental defectives from 1940 to 1949, Table III.

TABLE II

DATA FOR PATIENTS IN MENTAL HOSPITALS IN THE UNITED STATES, 1951*

	Number	*Percentage of Estimated Civilian Population*
Average daily patient population	515,108	0.34
First admissions	108,778	0.072
All admissions	146,506	0.097
Discharges	90,260	15% of patients
Deaths in hospital	42,027	6.4% of patients
Patients in mental hospitals at the end of 1951	610,458	
Patients at the end of 1950	598,000	
Maintenance cost per patient ..	$825.62 per year	$2.26 per day

* Derived from "Patients in Public Hospitals for the Prolonged Care of the Mentally Ill, 1951" in *Mental Health Statistics,* Current Reports, U.S. Department of Health, Education and Welfare, Public Health Service, National Institute of Mental Health, April, 1953.
An interesting analysis of the social structure and functions of mental hospitals is presented in S. Kirson Weinberg, *Society and Personality Disorders* (New York: Prentice-Hall, Inc., 1952), pp. 375-450.

mental institutions. It is frequently difficult to obtain a qualified staff—psychiatrists, attendants, nurses, psychologists, and psychiatric social workers—because of the isolation of most mental hospitals, lack of cultural facilities, and low salaries.

The incidence of mental diseases is indicated by Table III. As

TABLE III

SURVEY OF PATIENTS IN MENTAL HOSPITALS, 1940-1949*

Year	*Patients in Hospitals for Mental Disease at the Beginning of the Year*		*Mental Defectives and Epileptics at the Beginning of the Year*	
	Number of Patients	*Rate per 100,000 of Population*	*Number of Patients*	*Rate per 100,000 of Population*
1940	461,358	351.0	102,292	77.8
1941	480,741	362.4	103,288	77.9
1942	490,448	364.2	113,597	84.4
1943	498,828	365.4	112,449	82.4
1944	501,751	363.4	118,153	85.6
1945	510,661	365.8	117,783	84.4
1946	518,672	374.8	118,467	85.6
1947	530,255	371.7	122,605	85.9
1948	540,038	371.7	124,673	85.8
1949	554,372	375.2	129,402	87.6

* Derived from U.S. Bureau of the Census, *Statistical Abstract of the United States, 1952,* Table No. 89, p. 83.

in the case of illness in general, mental disorders have been found more frequent and more severe in the lower income groups in all surveys conducted during recent years. But obviously low income patients are less able to afford rest, vacations, psychiatric consultation, and therapy, so that free or low cost clinics are particularly needed. Among the approximately 1,200,000 patients placed on an average day in American hospitals, more than one-half are treated for mental disorders.[6] Among mental patients about 150,000 are admitted yearly to mental hospitals.

Besides patients in need of hospital care, there are an estimated total of eight million persons in our country suffering from some kind of mental disorder, and one in every twenty citizens will require psychiatric care at some time during his life.[7] Because the incidence of mental disease is heavier in old age than in younger age groups, the increasing proportion of our older population carries with it the probability of a further growth of mental illness unless we are able to provide efficient services of prevention, early diagnosis, and treatment. The practicing 4,500 to 5,000 psychiatrists are not sufficient to diagnose and treat all mental patients, particularly in rural regions and in the southern states, and the number of psychiatric nurses, psychiatric social workers, and clinical psychologists is also insufficient. Over 300,000 more hospital beds for mental patients and improvement in staffs, equipment, and facilities of hospitals as well as clinics are required.

The second concern of the mental hygiene movement is the prevention of mental disorders. To this purpose it pursues the establishment of mental hygiene clinics for diagnosis and therapy.

In 1953 there were thirty-four state mental hygiene societies which conducted programs of education and information about emotional conflicts and disturbances, promoted social legislation for the improvement of prevention and care of mental illness, and cooperated with public and private organizations in the setup of mental hygiene and child guidance clinics.

The main obstacle to the development of effective mental hygiene work was, and still is, the social stigma attached to mental

---

[6] Franz Goldmann, "Medical Care," *Social Work Year Book, 1951*, pp. 303-305.

[7] Oscar R. Ewing, *The Nation's Health* (Washington, D.C.: Federal Security Agency, 1948), pp. 115-118, 120-122; and Paul V. Lemkau, "Local Mental Health Services," *The Annals*, Vol. 286, March, 1953, pp. 116-125.

illness, caused by the lack of understanding of the nature of mental disturbances. It discourages mentally ill patients and their families from seeking early professional aid and is a retarding factor in public awareness of the large extent and urgency of the mental health problem. Other obstacles are the lack of financial resources for preventive mental hygiene clinics and the scarcity of well-trained personnel.

On the other hand, psychiatric experience proved that mental illness of many adult patients has its beginning in childhood, and so it becomes evident that helping children with their emotional problems would minimize serious mental diseases in later years. The need for psychotherapy of children was particularly felt by juvenile courts. Already in the first years of this century the juvenile court in Chicago found that it needed to know the causes of the child's troubles in order to decide about his treatment. A gift of Mrs. W. F. Dummer provided funds for the first child guidance clinic in Chicago, in 1909, known as the Juvenile Psychopathic Institute, under Dr. William Healy. Members of this clinic studied the wards of the juvenile court and suggested methods for their mental and social adjustment. The Institute in Chicago was renamed the "Institute for Juvenile Research" in 1917, when it was taken over by the state of Illinois. Other pioneer clinics were set up in Boston, Baltimore, Cleveland, and in Whittier, California.

An important expansion of child guidance therapy was made possible through the demonstration program developed by a grant of the Commonwealth Fund of 1921.[8] The first demonstration child guidance clinic was set up in St. Louis; it stressed necessary cooperation among psychiatrists, psychologists and social workers. This teamwork became a generally accepted basic principle in these clinics. The experience in the child guidance clinics brought out the importance of social work cooperation in therapy. Close working together of children's agencies, recreational programs, and school social work with the clinics and the juvenile courts proved to be essential in order to prevent further juvenile delinquency. Also, the teaching of mental hygiene principles to physicians, teachers, nurses, and social workers of juvenile courts and welfare agencies was emphasized.

[8] See Chapter 9; Helen L. Witmer, *Psychiatric Clinics for Children* (New York: Commonwealth Fund, 1940), p. 47; and George E. Gardner, "American Child Psychiatric Clinics," *The Annals*, Vol. 286, March, 1953, pp. 126-135.

Among the 650 psychiatric clinics in our country that provide child guidance services about four hundred are operating full time.

Child guidance clinics have now become part of community service in most larger cities. Difficulties which are brought to their attention cover a wide range from behavior problems and habit disturbances to personality maladjustments. Behavior problems include, for example, lying, running away, truancy, stealing, fire-setting, sex aggression, destruction of property, and cruelty to children or animals. Personality difficulties are often expressed by nightmares, anxiety, withdrawal, shyness, day dreams, and apathy. Under habit disturbances there are enuresis, excessive masturbation, nail biting, eating difficulties and thumb sucking. Children are referred to the clinic usually by their own parents, or by doctors, social agencies, schools, churches, parent-teacher associations, juvenile courts, or the public.[9]

The procedure of child guidance work usually starts with an application of both parents or just of the mother. In the "intake interview" they describe the child's difficulties to the social worker and what they expect from the treatment of the child. The social worker explains what services the clinic offers and the arrangements and financial obligations required if the child is accepted. In case of agreement, a medical and psychiatric examination of the child follows, and a clinical psychologist gives the indicated tests for proper diagnosis.

Usually mother and child come for treatment to the clinic once weekly for one hour. The young child engages in play therapy with the psychiatrist and thus reveals his feelings about his parents, siblings, teachers, and playmates. The psychiatrist gains a comprehension of the child's disturbance and personality. In the interviews with the mother, the social worker attempts to make her understand the causes of the child's difficulties and his behavior, her own attitude toward the child, and their relationship. Behavior change in mother and child leads to improvement of the original difficulties. Sometimes the mother becomes aware of her own emotional disturbance and asks for treatment for herself. There is also growing recognition of the importance of the father's role in the behavior of

[9] George Thorman, *Toward Mental Health* (New York: Public Affairs Pamphlet No. 120, 1946). For the important role of child guidance work in prevention and treatment of juvenile delinquency, see Chapter 15.

a difficult child. Several child guidance clinics now include fathers in the treatment process.

In the development of child guidance clinics, emphasis was first laid upon the advice to the parents about the child's education, later upon the direct treatment of the child. Finally, the concept has been accepted that the child's problems are usually a part of an emotional disturbance in the whole family pattern, and for this reason a co-ordinated treatment of child and parent now is considered the most effective method.[10]

Whenever social workers and clinical psychologists treat the child or his parents, they are working in consultation with a psychiatrist. Psychiatrist, social worker, and psychologist have conferences to coordinate their work. Representatives of other social agencies are invited for joint case conferences from time to time, if they have referred the child to the clinic.

It is no question that child guidance clinics are of great value for the early treatment of child behavior problems and for the prevention of some mental illness in adulthood. But only the larger cities in the United States have full time clinical services of this type. In small cities and in many rural areas such clinics are either missing or are only occasionally available as "itinerant clinics," so that several states are still without adequate psychiatric preventive facilities.[11] Other community services, such as prenatal and child guidance clinics have also incorporated into their work preventive mental hygiene concepts.

During World War I the large number of war neuroses exposed the need of intensive work in the cure of nervous and mental dis-

[10] See Genevieve B. Short, "Psychiatric Social Work in the Child Guidance Clinic," in *Education for Psychiatric Social Work* (New York: American Association of Psychiatric Social Workers, 1950), pp. 12-13; Carl R. Rogers, *Counseling and Psychotherapy* (Boston: Houghton, 1942); Leon Lucas, "Psychiatric Social Work," *Social Work Year Book, 1951*, pp. 359-365; Solomon E. Asch, *Social Psychology* (New York: Prentice-Hall, Inc., 1952), pp. 117 ff., 135 ff.; and S. Kirson Weinberg, *Social and Personality Disorders* (New York: Prentice-Hall, Inc., 1952), pp. 491-495.

[11] Robert H. Felix, "State Planning for Participation in the National Mental Health Act," *Public Health Reports*, Vol. LXII, August 15, 1947, p. 1,188. The vital importance of team work in mental hygiene and child guidance work is emphasized in *Mental Health and World Citizenship*, a statement prepared for the International Congress on Mental Health in London, 1948. It shows the value of cooperation among psychiatrist, physician, social worker, nurse, clinical psychologist, economist, minister, lawyer, and political scientist in releasing human potentialities for the common good.

orders. It led, in field stations and neuropsychiatric hospitals, to the use of social workers in order to assist the medical officers in obtaining information about personal, family, and community background of the patients for decisions about dismissal and after-care. World War II greatly aroused public concern over the increase of mental illness. The demand for physicians and psychiatrists was not only heavy in the armed forces, but also in the civilian population where the mental stress of war, caused by anxieties and the separation of families, and by the unusual demands of war work were the source of neuroses and exhaustion. The public became alarmed when it was informed that among fifteen million men examined under Selective Service procedure during World War II, 856,200 were rejected for neuropsychiatric disorders. They were by far the largest cause for rejection, exceeding all other diseases, and were also responsible for the majority of all medical discharges from the armed forces.

It is just as difficult, however, to obtain psychiatric examination, consultation, and treatment for adult patients as for children because mental hygiene clinics for adults are equally scarce in smaller cities and rural areas. The number of people in the United States who suffer from some sort of nervous or mental disorder is estimated at 8,000,000, about 6 per cent of the total population.[12] Of all hospital beds which are available in the United States one-half are used for mental patients, and of all hospitalized veterans even a larger percentage—60 per cent—are suffering from neuropsychiatric diseases.[13] These appalling figures have given considerable concern to legislators, psychiatrists, social workers, and psychologists. They finally resulted in the enactment of the *National Mental Health Act* of July 3, 1946. Its preamble says:

The purpose of this Act is the improvement of the mental health of the people of the United States through the conducting of researches, investigations, experiments and demonstrations relating to the cause, diagnosis and treatment of psychiatric disorders; assisting and fostering such research activities by public and private agencies, and promoting the coordination of all such results; training personnel in matters relating to

[12] R. Felix, *op. cit.*, p. 1,183.
[13] Another stirring fact is that since 1880 mental disorders have multiplied twelve times over in our country. (Walter B. Pitkin, "Facts 'The Snake Pit' Did Not Tell," *Illinois Welfare Bulletin*, Vol. 38, No. 1, January, 1947; and S. Kirson Weinberg, *op. cit.*, pp. 138-159, 160-180, 182-208).

mental health; and developing and assisting states in the use of the most effective methods of prevention, diagnosis and treatment of psychiatric disorders.

The Act is administered by the National Institute of Mental Health of the U.S. Public Health Service in the Department of Health, Education, and Welfare. Its governing body is the National Mental Health Council, with the Surgeon General as chairman and six members appointed by him (selected from outstanding authorities in the field of mental health) for three-year terms.

Three programs have been developed under the National Mental Health Act: (1) research, (2) training of personnel (psychiatrists, psychologists, psychiatric nurses, psychiatric social workers, and laboratory technicians), and (3) development of community services for mental health protection and treatment.

Research grants are appropriated to universities, hospitals, laboratories, other nonprofit institutions, and to qualified individuals engaged in mental health research. The National Institute of Mental Health maintains a hospital for clinical observations and research. Training grants are distributed to psychiatric centers; schools of social work, psychology, and nursing; and to medical schools for premedical studies. Grants-in-aid for the establishment of local diagnostic and treatment facilities and mental hygiene and child guidance clinics are distributed in each state by a State Mental Health Authority, which in most instances, is represented by the health departments or by the departments of mental hygiene, but in some states by the departments of public welfare. These funds cannot be used for services in mental hospitals and institutions or for the building of new institutions and clinics. The construction of hospitals and clinics remains the responsibility of states and local communities.

Since the federal grants-in-aid are allocated to the states on a matching basis, the success of the program depends upon the participation of states, counties, cities and of such private organizations as mental health societies. During the first two years of operation of the law, 106 new mental health clinics were opened and 184 clinics expanded. Important progress is made in the training of psychiatrists, psychologists, psychiatric social workers, and nurses.

The goal of the program is to make earlier diagnosis and more effective treatment available for adults and children, and to alleviate the present shortage of personnel by various grants for studies and research in the field of mental hygiene.

The trends in mental hygiene are the endeavors to strengthen psychiatric facilities and to establish sufficient, well-equipped adult and children's clinics in order to meet the large demand for examination, diagnosis, consultation, and treatment. Based upon experiences in military hospitals during World War II, treatment of small, selected groups has been introduced with success, and "group therapy" is now utilized for adults and children. Special attention is being given to the treatment and rehabilitation of alcholics, drug addicts, epileptics, and intellectually defective patients. The growing number of older people who are disoriented and disturbed, so that they require institutional care, is a serious problem in geriatrics. For the aged and senile who do not require care in a mental hospital, but rather in a proper old-age home, there are not sufficient facilities available at present.

PSYCHIATRIC SOCIAL WORK

Psychiatric social work is social casework undertaken in direct and responsible cooperation with psychiatry, practiced in hospitals, clinics, or under psychiatric auspices, with the purpose of helping patients with mental or emotional disturbances.[14] Recently group work and group therapy also are applied in psychiatric social work.

Its development is closely linked with the practice of mental hygiene. Psychiatric social work may be traced to four main sources: (1) the need for individual casework and after-care for patients in psychiatric wards and in mental hospitals; (2) casework with children and adolescents brought before juvenile courts and referred to child guidance clinics and social agencies for treatment and adjustment; (3) casework with adult patients in mental hygiene clinics; and (4) casework and group work with psychoneurotic patients in military and veterans hospitals and clinics.

After-care by social workers first was found necessary in state hospitals and neurological clinics in order to learn of the economic and environmental conditions of the patient in regard to the therapy plan and to preserve the effect of hospital treatment after the release of the patient. The first specific assignment of a social worker to a neurological clinic was made in 1905, at Massachusetts General

---

[14] Lois French, *Psychiatric Social Work* (New York: Commonwealth Fund, 1940), p. 12; Leon Lucas, "Psychiatric Social Work," *Social Work Year Book, 1951*, p. 359; and Ruth Ireland Knee, "Psychiatric Social Work," *Social Work Year Book, 1954*, p. 387.

Hospital in Boston. Then Bellevue Hospital, Manhattan State Hospital, and Cornell Clinic in New York employed social workers to take in account the patient's social and emotional life. The term "psychiatric social worker" was first used at Boston Psychopathic Hospital in 1913, under Dr. E. E. Southard.[15]

Of great importance for the development of psychiatric social work were the experiences during and after the two world wars. Because of the large number of patients suffering from war neuroses, psychiatric social work training facilities were extended in 1917, and a joint training project was organized by the National Committee for Mental Hygiene and Smith College School of Social Work. In 1953 there were thirty-six universities and colleges in the United States and Canada whose curricula had been approved for education in psychiatric social work.

Psychiatrists, psychiatric social workers, clinical psychologists, and psychiatric nurses were needed not only for the armed forces and for veterans, but also for the civilian population. Since 1945, psychiatric social workers in the Division of Neuropsychiatry in the Surgeon General's Office of the Army have received officer status. Special training programs for military social work have been set up. The largest number of psychiatric social workers in the United States is employed by the Veterans Administration in neuropsychiatric hospitals, in mental hygiene clinics in its regional and subregional offices, and in psychiatric wards of many general hospitals.

The function of the psychiatric social worker in child guidance and school clinics is, as a rule, the intake process and casework with the parents or relatives, while the psychiatrist treats the child. However, this pattern varies and sometimes the psychiatrist assumes the therapy of the more deeply disturbed adult patients—parents, or close relatives—while the psychiatric social worker sees the child. The activities of psychiatric social workers in mental hygiene clinics and out-patient departments of hospitals also include the in-take interview and casework treatment with the patient and his family. There is some controversy in the field as to what extent the psy-

---

15 E. E. Southard, *The Kingdom Of Evils* (New York: Macmillan, 1922), p. 521. For present conditions see Tessie D. Berkman, *Practice of Social Workers in Psychiatric Hospitals and Clinics* (New York: American Association of Psychiatric Social Workers, 1953); and Maurice F. Connery, "The Climate of Effective Teamwork," *Journal of Psychiatric Social Work*, Vol. 22, No. 2, January, 1953, pp. 59-60.

chiatric social worker is engaged in psychotherapy and shares the treatment with the psychiatrist.

New trends in psychiatric social work are the use of experienced workers as consultants in family and child welfare agencies, in schools, juvenile courts, hospitals, rehabilitation centers, and personnel divisions of industrial firms. Psychiatric social workers have been active in the development of new therapy techniques, particularly in group therapy with mental patients, the instruction and supervision of volunteers in clinics and hospitals, the expansion of family care for discharged patients of mental hospitals, and in research studies of the results of psychosurgical operations and shock therapy. Psychiatric social workers are teaching courses for students in medical, public health, and nursing schools, as well as in schools of social work.

Psychiatric social workers recently have given special attention to the placement of mentally deficient patients—children and adults —from state institutions in their own families or other types of family care. They have been able to help in the rehabilitation program for handicapped people, to interpret the necessary treatment to their families, friends, and to their employers, and they assist in the use of clinical out-patient services for the large number of mentally deficient, but not mentally ill (insane) patients.[16]

A professional organization, the American Association of Psychiatric Social Workers (AAPSW), was founded in 1926 in order to promote scientific development and professional standards in the field of psychiatric social work. Its membership, in 1953, was over 1,800 psychiatric social workers, but there were 2,253 persons employed in such positions in mental hospitals and clinics at this time.

Professional requirements for employment as psychiatric social worker, as a rule, include two years of graduate studies in an accredited school of social work with the specialty of psychiatric social work and the completion of the master's degree. The second year of graduate training must be carried on in the specialty of

---

[16] The reader is referred to a stimulating article of Winifred Wardell, "The Mentally Retarded in Family and Community," in Salvatore G. DiMichael (editor), *Vocational Rehabilitation of the Mentally Retarded* (Washington, D.C.: Federal Security Agency, Office of Vocational Rehabilitation, Publ. No. 123, 1950), pp. 64-78; S. Weinberg, *op. cit.*, pp. 340-357, 506-509; and *Building America's Health*, President's Commission on the Health Needs of the Nation (1952), Vol. 3, Table 306, p. 222.

psychiatric social work with supervised field work training in a psychiatric setting.

The following two case histories may illustrate psychiatric social work in a child guidance clinic.

Case of Michael[17]

Ten year old Michael was brought to the Berkeley Clinic by his mother in July, 1952, six weeks after he attempted to hang himself. In addition to describing Michael's periodic depressions, his mother described him as alternately bossy and withdrawn with other children and as having difficulty with his studies in spite of superior intelligence.

Michael was disturbed by his parents' divorce three years previously, and his mother noticed that he repeatedly displayed depression after his father's irregular visits. Psychological testing at the clinic showed Michael to be concerned mostly about his inability to control his strong aggressive impulses—his "badness," which he felt were responsible for his father's leaving the family.

Michael and his mother were seen weekly over a 10½ months period. Michael's sessions with the psychiatrists were marked at first by an inability to show any of his real feelings or to win at any competitive game. As he became more comfortable in the relationship he relaxed, began to win, and toward the end of therapy could occasionally express some of his fears of hurting others if he lost his temper. Meanwhile his mother reported that he was better able to play comfortably with other children and to assert his natural talents for leadership and also could show his anger toward her at times.

In the mother's visits to the social worker, she was helped to accept some of her own aggressive feelings and hence to become more tolerant of similar feelings in Michael. In time she and Michael came to the conclusion that they were ready to stop treatment.

Michael now appears to be a normally aggressive eleven year old who gets along well in school and at play. He has become less fearful of his angry feelings and is no longer compelled to turn them upon himself. His mother seems able to accept him this way and to foster his independence.

Case of Bobby[18]

Family's First Contact with the Clinic

Mrs. B, upon suggestion of the elementary school, telephoned the clinic asking for help with her son, Bobby. Upon the admission worker's

[17] Quoted from State Department of Mental Hygiene, California, *Report to Governor's Council*, September, 1953, pp. 3-4.

[18] The author is indebted to the California State Mental Hygiene Clinic in Los Angeles under the direction of Simon Conrad, M.D., Chief Psychiatrict, and to Mrs. Madeline De Antonio, psychiatric social worker, for the contribution of this case history.

inquiry she presented a brief picture of the behavior difficulties of the child at home and at school; he is nine years of age and an only child. The father is forty years old, she herself thirty-five. The family is of moderate means. There had been medical care but no previous psychiatric care. The admission worker's impression was that the clinic could be of service and informed the mother that she would be called for an appointment. In the meantime, she was asked to have the doctor and school send reports to the clinic directly.

Admission Interview (conducted two weeks later)

Mr. and Mrs. B were seen individually by a psychiatric social worker without the child because the total family constellation and relationships are important in the diagnosis and the therapeutic process.

The parents explained Bobby's difficulty. They told that he was unable to concentrate in school, had a reading and writing block, and that he was rebellious, negativistic, destructive, and overaggressive both at home and at school. He could not get along with his playmates, had been repeatedly transferred from school to school, and now again was faced with exclusion from school, pending the clinic's evaluation. Some history on the parents and the child was gathered to give a picture of the parents' adjustment and the development of the patient. The father, a businessman, described his own very unhappy childhood as an only child. He came from a broken home and had to work at an early age because of financial hardship. He thought of his eleven years marriage with Mrs. B as happy. He was unaware of internal conflicts, but seemed rather tense. He expressed interest in his son, engaged in activities with him, but was prone to occasional temper outbursts where he would reprimand Bobby severely. The worker's impression of Mr. B was that he was a somewhat passive man who was dominated by his wife.

Mrs. B said that she was oldest of four children. She had a sister and two brothers. She was very close to her mother, but was aloof toward her father. She felt competitive with her sister whom she described as more beautiful; and Mrs. B gained her recognition through scholastic achievement. She assumed much of the responsibility for the care of her siblings. She worked five years as a secretary before marrying at the age of twenty-four. The social worker's impression of Bobby's mother was that she was a tense, overconcerned woman with a great deal of drive; that she was a mother who forced Bobby to do many things he disliked or which were beyond what he could do. Mrs. B seemed to press Bobby toward achievement; Mr. B was inclined to discount the seriousness of his problem.

The parents described Bobby's infancy and early development as being normal. He was always a strong active child and was encouraged by his father to do gymnastics at an early age. The first signs of disturbance apparent to Mr. and Mrs. B was when Bobby entered school.

Report from Family Doctor

As Bobby had had considerable medical care, the clinic asked for a medical report upon the written permission of the parents. The doctor who had known Bobby and the family for some period of time reported that there were no significant medical problems. The patient had had many behavior problems since early infancy (in contrast to the parent's present report) and he was having steady difficulties in school. He also told that the boy had been masturbating the past three years. An electroencephalogram which was performed six months prior to therapy was normal for the patient's age.

School Report

A report from the school confirmed that Bobby was in the third grade, but had already attended four different schools. He was repeating his grade because his academic accomplishment was below average. A Stanford-Binet test given at the school showed an IQ of 113. School described Bobby as a nonconformist, as having a short interest span, as not being able to work up to his ability because of hypertension. They further stated that he was sweet-natured, accepted socially, but that he gravitated toward other boys with problems.

Psychiatric Examination

The diagnostic evaluation of the psychiatrist was adjustment reaction of childhood—conduct disturbances. Psychological tests showed the following results:

Rorschach: This youngster's record indicated considerable anxiety and a tendency to become disorganized and unrealistic under pressure. He is able to recover fairly readily, however, which is a good prognostic sign.

This is a child who is quite mixed up in his feelings and who seems to be making some cautious attempts at understanding himself.

He has a lot of dependency needs and wishes, yet is afraid to give in to them. He has the capacity to form satisfying relationships with others, yet is distrustful of others initially and tends to avoid getting close to anyone. He shows increased physical activity and wishful fantasy, is a rather controlling youngster, particularly in his use of negativism and opposition. Much of his behavior is in reaction to his environment, as well as to inner impulses.

The record suggests better than average intelligence, but patient is certainly not functioning up to capacity. He is erratic and inconsistent in both attention and performance and does not seem motivated to try for good achievement.

Bobby seems slightly less threatened by his mother than by his father, though neither relationship is adequate. He seems quite concerned about his masculinity, shows some castration anxiety, and some preoccupation with sexual material.

Without treatment, this child would almost certainly grow up to be a very unstable adult. With help at this time he has a very good chance of developing more mature ways of handling his inner feelings and better capacity for dealing with external pressures.

Drawing of family: This drawing does not contribute much to understanding of this patient. All of the figures seem rather vacuous and empty, as though they have little to give each other. There seems to be little open rejection, but a real inadequacy in both parents under the pleasant exterior. The drawing is quite immature and was done hastily and without particular effort, again showing patient's lack of concern with achievements.

Therapy

A month after the application interview, Mrs. B and Bobby began therapy. Mr. B was not seen for further therapy because he could not arrange to take time from work. Mrs. B and Bobby were treated once a week over a period of nine months with a total of thirty interviews each—the child by a child psychiatrist, the mother by a psychiatric social worker.

Mother's Interviews

The first hour. Mrs. B was upset and said that she did not know where to begin. Words tumbled out rapidly as she described numerous incidents indicating Bobby's destructiveness and ingenuity, hostility and aggressiveness. She had an urgency about her all the time as if she were exasperated and driven to the limit. She seemed to have a great need to "pour out," and probably expected answers to patient's problems in terms of "what to do," although the worker interpreted treatment as working jointly with children and parents toward self-understanding and getting along better, not as a directive, advice-giving process.

Second through seventh hour. Mother continued to be anxious, overwhelmed and extremely tense during the interviews, recounting many of the patient's activities and episodes with him. It became increasingly clear that she was rigid, punitive, restrictive, and controlling with the child and was seeking the boy's entrance into military school as a solution to the problem. She was concerned about what was going on in therapy with the boy and what he was doing. Mrs. B received from the worker recognition of her feelings, understanding, relief, and some beginning clarification of what was happening.

Eighth through twelfth interview. Mrs. B appeared more relaxed and was allowing Bobby to do more things alone. She was beginning to see her role in the difficulty and the implication of rejection in her relationship with the boy. She began to show more awareness of Bobby's behavior pattern rather than preoccupation with each episode. She began to express guilt over failure as a parent; yet at the same time expressed feelings that she had been helped. The psychological testing results were generally discussed with her and integrated into the findings of what was happening clinically.

Thirteenth through eighteenth interview. She began to report the first signs of improvement in Bobby, initially shown most markedly in his newly developed motivation. He still had many behavior problems, which worried Mrs. B, but she seemed better able to handle some situations more constructively and was able to maintain this attitude with the continued encouragement and clarification from the worker. Mrs. B was in better spirits, felt more relaxed, and spontaneously began to talk about herself. She ventilated pent-up feelings about the control of the paternal grandmother. She received understanding from the worker, and was given encouragement to diminish the grandmother's controls over the family.

Nineteenth through twenty-second interview. Although Mrs. B was feeling better and there was continued improvement with Bobby, he still had difficulty comprehending his school work and was very disturbed about the possibility of not passing again. Bobby had begun to express more of his feelings to his parents and told them, "I am afraid to read or write, almost as afraid as I am that you and daddy don't love me." It became clearer that whenever Bobby was frustrated in any endeavor, he became a behavior problem. It was apparent that part of this problem could be alleviated with special training, because the boy had no orientation in basic school subjects and now seemed more emotionally ready to learn. Therefore, arrangements were made for training in a special school during summer recess. The original contact was made by the social worker.

Twenty-third through thirtieth interview. Mrs. B continued to be in good spirits and was surprised that things were going so well. She reported that Bobby was calmer, more relaxed, accepted limitations more easily, was playing with other children more, and had lost some of his fears. He was able to remain in school, where he was making gradual and continued progress. Mrs. B continued to work out some of her own personal problems and conflicts and the difficulties which arise in the home. She was able to give Bobby more freedom and was not as overwhelmed or upset when he acted up, since she understood the cause of his behavior. She seemed tremendously encouraged, to have lost her sense of failure, and to be relaxed to the point of handling intelligently provocative situations when they arose. Bobby talked more to his mother about his feelings and was able to gain confidence for her reassurance. Both Bobby and his mother felt a lessened need to come to the clinic and began to express a desire to terminate their contacts. This was mutually agreed upon and the family was given the assurance that they could return to the clinic for help at any time.

Interviews with Patient

Therapy with Bobby was conducted in a playroom which had a variety of toys: a play house, a doll family, a punching bag, blocks, crayons, guns, a blackboard, finger paints, carpentry tools, wood, and a sink (for water play). This allowed Bobby an opportunity to express his feelings and conflicts through the media of play as well as through conversation.

First play interview. Bobby appeared as a tense youngster of slight build who had well-formed features, mildly slanting eyes, giving him a pixie-like expression and demeanor. He seemed friendly and interested and went into the playroom without difficulty but was mildly constricted. He showed direct and open interest in the therapist. He made tentative explorations of the playroom and listened tentatively to the discussion with the therapist of why he was coming to the clinic and the kinds of things that would help him. He was usually smiling but at times seemed very sad and forlorn. He showed no hyperactivity and instead concentrated intently on a quiet game of checkers. There were indications of competitiveness and anxiety in the game.

Second through seventh hour. He continued to be somewhat conforming and restricted his activity to checkers. It became apparent that he wished to alter rules drastically to win. He would express hostility toward the therapist playfully. Slight distrust, confusion and suspicion were noted, as well as more frequently frowning and scowling expressions.

Eighth through eighteenth interview. He brought out more of his underlying feelings, conflicts, and true behavior. He became increasingly hyperactive and destructive, and this showed itself more near the end of the hour; at the same time he showed repeated indication of marked attempts to reach out for affection and contact from the therapist. He strongly resisted limitations and at times would invite physical restraint. He expressed intense and bewildering confusion about himself and deeply ambivalent feelings toward the therapist when saying for instance in rapid fire succession, "I love you. I hate you."

He appeared to the therapist to be a deeply disturbed boy who was full of tense, anxious hostility, and who was reaching out desperately for a warm, close relationship both physically and psychologically with an adult, yet was deeply fearful of rejection. Much of his hyperactive and near destructive behavior appeared directly reactive to the disturbances at home as reported by his mother. It was evident that the environmental stress had to be lessened before Bobby could be helped.

Nineteenth through twenty-fifth interview. Bobby became quieter and began to play more constructively; destructive activity was minimized and at times ceased. Suspiciousness lessened. He was more relaxed. He began to discuss, with some interest, activities he engaged in when away from the clinic. He did not want to leave sessions and could talk about this rather than engaging in angry play and hyperactivity. An example of the patient working through his conflicts through play activity was shown as follows: On his own volition, Bobby said, "Let's build something." He built a large tower and knocked it down. He rebuilt the tower and put a man and baby into it and then bombed it. The therapist asked where his mother was, and he said that she died in the bombing. He had the father taking care of the baby, but always being bombed and killed. He built and rebuilt the tower several times. It would appear that he limited destructiveness to play and found acceptance for his feelings from the therapist.

An example of his working out his conflicts through discussion and interpretation was as follows: He told the therapist with pride of his acceptance into the special school. The therapist discussed with Bobby his reading and writing problem this way: "By the end of summer, you will have such a good time in school, you won't be afraid to read anymore." Bobby asked "What do you mean?" The therapist then explained that some boys who couldn't read, could not because they were frightened, that it was troublesome for him because he was scared, that when he felt better he would be able to read well. He did not make any comment, but his play became more organized after this.

Twenty-sixth through thirtieth interview: Bobby was more cheerful, smiled freely, and talked easily. He told how well he liked it in his special school and expressed directly his wish not to continue at the clinic. He could tell the therapist that he was feeling better and that the family was pretty busy. The therapist agreed with Bobby that he need not come in as he was feeling better and assured him that if anything came up, he should tell his mother and arrangements would be made to see him.

Results of Therapy

As a result of Mrs. B's and Bobby's active participation in therapy and the help received from the psychiatric social worker and the psychiatrist, there was a change in both the mother and the patient and in their relationship. Mrs. B became more relaxed, could understand and accept Bobby, could give up pressures, and felt comfortable and secure with her son. Bobby gained greater self-acceptance, was not as tense, angry or frightened, could accept limitations, had a longer span of attention, was more relaxed and happier. He was able to remain in school, improved in his school work, and used special training constructively. He was more secure with his mother and was making strides in his social relationships.

Follow-up

Four months later, a brief contact with Mrs. B and Bobby showed that the improvement had been sustained.

Summary

The picture presented was of a nine year old boy who was extremely fearful and anxious. He had coped with his internal conflicts and continual external pressures with immobilization as shown in his reading and writing block and with disorganization, hyper-aggressivity, and destructiveness as shown by his behavior. He was not able to grow emotionally because of problems in the familial relationships.

His mother was a chronically dissatisfied woman who was working out

her needs and unresolved conflicts through her child. Her earlier deprivation, anger and resentment toward having assumed responsibility before
she was ready, and the current frustrations in her marriage impeded
healthy relationship with her son. Through therapy, she could accept herself more readily and accept Bobby as an individual. As her attitudes changed, the boy could grow and the concurrent improvement
in both led toward stability and normal relationships.

SELECTED BIBLIOGRAPHY

Alexander, Franz, and Thomas French, *Psychoanalytic Therapy: Principles and Applications*. New York: The Ronald Press, 1946.

*Allen, Frederick H., *Psychotherapy with Children*. New York: Norton, 1942.

American Association of Psychiatric Social Workers, *Education for Psychiatric Social Work*, Proceedings of the Dartmouth Conference. New York, 1950.

American Psychiatric Association, *One Hundred Years of American Psychiatry*. New York, 1944.

Asch, Solomon E., *Social Psychology*. New York: Prentice-Hall, Inc., 1952.

Bassett, Clara, *Mental Hygiene in the Community*. New York: Macmillan, 1936.

Beck, Bertram M., and Lewis L. Robbins, *Short-Term Therapy in an Authoritative Setting*. New York: Family Service Association of America, 1946.

*Beers, Clifford W., *A Mind That Found Itself: An Autobiography*. New York: Doubleday, 1935.

Beyer, Clara M., "Labor Standards," *Social Work Yearbook, 1954,* pp. 308-320.

Bowlby, John, *Maternal Care and Mental Health*. New York: Columbia University Press, 1951.

Brill, Abraham A., *Freud's Contribution to Psychiatry*. New York: Norton, 1944.

Cabot, Richard C., *Social Work: Essays on the Meeting Ground of Doctor and Social Worker*. Boston: Hughton, 1919.

Cleckley, H., *The Mask of Sanity*. St. Louis: Mosby, 1941.

Clifton, Eleanor, and Florence Hollis, *Child Therapy, A Casework Symposium*. New York: Family Service Association of America, 1948.

Crutcher, Hester B., *A Guide for Developing Psychiatric Social Work in State Hospitals*. Utica: State Hospitals Press, 1933.

———, *Foster Home Care for Mental Patients*. New York: Commonwealth Fund, 1944.

*Deutsch, Albert, *The Mentally Ill in America: A History of Their Care and Treatment from Colonial Times*. New York: Columbia University Press, 1946.

Dysinger, Robert H., "Mental Health in the United States," *The Annals*, Vol. 286, March, 1953, pp. 1-174.

*English, O. Spurgeon, and Gerald H. J. Pearson, *Emotional Problems of Living: Avoiding the Neurotic Pattern.* New York: Norton, 1946.

Felix, Robert H., and Morton Kramer, "Extent of the Problem of Mental Disorders," *The Annals,* Vol. 286, March, 1953, pp. 5-14.

*French, Lois Meredith, *Psychiatric Social Work.* New York: Commonwealth Fund, 1940.

Gartland, Ruth, *Psychiatric Social Service in a Children's Hospital: Two Years of Service in Bobs Roberts Memorial Hospital for Children.* Chicago: University of Chicago Press, 1936.

Grinker, Roy R., and John P. Spiegel, *Men Under Stress.* Philadelphia: Blakiston, 1945.

Hamilton, Gordon, *Psychotherapy in Child Guidance.* New York: Columbia University Press, 1947.

Harms, Ernest, *Handbook of Child Guidance.* New York: Child Care Publications, 1947.

Hendrick, Ives, *Facts and Theories of Psychoanalysis.* New York: Knopf, 1946.

Horney, Karen, *Our Inner Conflicts.* New York: Norton, 1945.

———, *The Neurotic Personality of Our Time.* New York: Norton, 1937.

Klein, David B., *Mental Hygiene: Psychology of Personal Adjustment.* New York: Holt, 1944.

Knee, Ruth I., "Psychiatric Social Work," *Social Work Year Book, 1954,* pp. 387-394.

Krech, David, and Richard S. Crutchfield, *Theory and Problems of Social Psychology.* New York: McGraw-Hill, 1948.

Lee, Porter R., and Marion E. Kenworthy, *Mental Hygiene and Social Work.* New York: Commonwealth Fund, 1929.

Levy, David M., *New Fields of Psychiatry.* New York: Norton, 1947.

Levy, John, and Ruth Munroe, *The Happy Family.* New York: Knopf, 1938.

Lewis, Nolan D. C., and Bernard L. Pacella, *Modern Trends in Child Psychiatry.* New York: International Universities Press, 1945.

Lowrey, Lawson G., *Orthopsychiatry, 1923-1948, Retrospect and Prospect.* New York: American Orthopsychiatric Association, 1948.

*———, *Psychiatry for Social Workers.* New York: Columbia University Press, 1946.

Lowry, James V., "Mental Health," *Social Work Year Book, 1954,* pp. 346-355.

Menninger, Karl A., *Man Against Himself.* New York: Harcourt, 1938.

———, *The Human Mind,* 3rd ed. New York: Knopf, 1946.

*Menninger, William C., *You and Psychiatry.* New York: Scribner, 1948.

Moodie, William, *The Doctor and the Difficult Child.* New York: Commonwealth Fund, 1940.

Moustakas, Clark E., *Children in Play Therapy: A Key to Understanding Normal and Disturbed Emotions.* New York: McGraw, 1953.

National Committee for Mental Hygiene, *Mental Health and World Citizenship*. New York, 1948.

Phelps, Harold A., and David Henderson, *Contemporary Social Problems*, 4th ed. New York: Prentice-Hall, Inc., 1952.

*Plant, James S., *Personality and the Cultural Pattern*. New York: Commonwealth Fund, 1937.

Powdermaker, Florence B., and Jerome Frank, *Group Psychotherapy: Studies in Methodology of Research and Therapy*. Cambridge: Harvard University Press, 1953.

Preston, George H., *Psychiatry for the Curious*. New York: Rinehart, 1940.

———, *The Substance of Mental Health*. New York: Rinehart, 1943.

Rennie, Thomas A., and Luther E. Woodward, *Mental Health in Modern Society*. New York: Commonwealth Fund, 1948.

Rogers, Carl R., *Counseling and Psychotherapy*. Boston: Houghton, 1942.

———, *The Clinical Treatment of the Problem Child*. Boston: Houghton, 1939.

Saul, Leon J., *Emotional Maturity*. Philadelphia: Lippincott, 1947.

Small, S. Mouchly, *Symptoms of Personality Disorder*. New York: Family Welfare Association of America, 1944.

Southard, E. E., and Mary C. Jarrett, *The Kingdom of Evils*. New York: Macmillan, 1922.

Stern, Edith M., *Mental Illness: A Guide for the Family*, Rev. ed. New York: Commonwealth Fund, 1945.

Stevenson, George H., and L. E. Neal, *Personality and Its Deviations*. Springfield, Ill.: Thomas, 1947.

Teicher, Joseph D., *Your Child and His Problems: A Basic Guide for Parents*. Boston: Little, 1953.

*Towle, Charlotte, *Social Case Records from Psychiatric Clinics*. Chicago: University of Chicago Press, 1941.

Weinberg, S. Kirson, *Society and Personality Disorders*. New York: Prentice-Hall, Inc., 1952.

Wexberg, L. Irwin, "Psychodynamics of Patients with Chronic Alcoholism," *Journal of Clinical Psychopathology*, April, 1949.

Witmer, Helen Leland, *Pediatrics and the Emotional Needs of the Child*. New York: Commonwealth Fund, 1948.

———, *Psychiatric Clinics for Children*. New York: Commonwealth Fund, 1940.

*———, *Psychiatric Interviews with Children*. New York: Commonwealth Fund, 1946.

Wolf, Anna W., *The Parents' Manual*. New York: Simon & Schuster, 1945.

Zilboorg, Gregory, *Mind, Medicine, and Man*. New York: Harcourt, 1943.

14. Social Group Work and Recreation

Human beings live not alone; they grow up in a family, tribe, or other group. Each individual needs relationships with others, and he needs the assurance and conviction that he is part of a whole, of a collective that unites him with other persons, and that accepts him as a part. From ancient times, the philosophy has been maintained that the whole is more, is stronger and more important than merely the sum of its parts. The whole of human beings—society and the group as a distinct collection of people—have corporate needs which are not identical with those of their individual members but which are created by the interaction of the individuals who are the parts of this entity.[1]

Caseworkers devote their main attention to helping individuals, group workers to helping groups, in their activities. As we have seen, social group work as a process in social work may be defined as an educational process carried on with voluntary groups, mainly during leisure times, with the guidance of a group leader, directed toward the personal development of the individual members of the group and of the group as a whole, toward a socially desirable objective pursued by the group.

I. THE DEVELOPMENT OF SOCIAL GROUP
WORK AND RECREATION

Informal groups of people, particularly of young persons, have gathered together for religious services, sportive entertainment,

---

[1] See Gertrude Wilson and Gladys Ryland, *Social Group Work Practice* (Boston: Houghton, 1949), pp. 16-18. A brief description of social group work as a process of social work was given in Chapter 6.

dances, singing, festivities and other activities for many centuries. But group work, in the new professional term mentioned above, dates its beginning to only about twenty-five years ago. Organizations with a planned purpose of meeting the needs of young persons, especially in big cities, began their work a century ago. The first society of this type was founded, in 1844, in England by a minister, George Williams, who attempted to bring the young drapers of London back to a Christian way of life and with this purpose founded the first Young Men's Christian Association (YMCA).

A retired American sea captain, J. V. Sullivan, who had founded the Marine Mission for seamen, was impressed by the success of the London YMCA, gathered together young men and established in Boston, in 1851, the first American YMCA, which spread in a few years to many other cities of the United States. The purpose of this organization was the improvement of the spiritual and mental conditions of young men, the establishment of living quarters at low price with decent, sanitary facilities, particularly for young men who came to the large cities to find work in business, commerce, and factories, and who could not afford to pay room and board in more expensive homes.

In 1860, the first Boys' Club was founded in Hartford, Connecticut, under the title of "Dashaway Club" by a church women's group, in order to give young boys an opportunity to pursue games and sports, music, dancing, and dramatic activities. Other Boys' Clubs spread quickly over the country, frequently under the auspices of church groups or other civic organizations which desired to attract the children by games, play, and crafts, rather than leaving them to the doubtful influences of city streets. The Jewish Center movement traced its origin to the "literary societies of young people," in the 1840's, who wanted to get together for lectures and discussions.

The first Young Women's Christian Association (YWCA) in the United States was founded in Boston, in 1866, under the leadership of Lucretia Boyd, and another YWCA in New York, in 1867, by Grace Dodge. They provided clean, low-rent housing and a cultural center to girls and young women who came to the cities from other parts of the country in order to work in shops, factories, and commercial enterprises. Girls found it difficult to rent rooms in a decent neighborhood for prices they could afford to pay. Similar reasons led, in New York, to the opening of a boarding home for young women by the Ladies' Christian Union, in 1866. In Boston, in 1885, the first supervised playground was established at the suggestion of Dr. Marie Zakrzewska by the Massachusetts Emergency and Hygiene Association, which wanted to help young children find some possibility of recreation and games without the danger of accidents in the streets or of bullying by older youngsters.

A very important stimulus in the development of social services, including group activities, recreation, and informal education was brought to the United States by the settlement houses.[2] As was discussed above, the first settlement houses were set up in 1886 under the name "Neighborhood Guild" in New York by Stanton Coit, and in 1889 Hull House in Chicago, by Jane Addams, Ellen Starr, Graham Taylor and their friends. The aims of settlement houses were to improve the physical and health conditions and to utilize the religious and educational capacities of the underprivileged, of ignorant exploited people, and of immigrants and unskilled workers who came to industrial centers and large cities. Social settlements did not believe that relief societies could achieve this goal, since they limited their activities to material and medical help. Settlement houses, therefore, attempted to develop among the poor and the low-paid working class a feeling of self respect; their resident staff let the neighborhood share the advantage of higher education, culture, and knowledge by living and working together in the settlement house.

Hospitality, friendliness, education, information, and getting acquainted with one another in the neighborhood was the main pattern of their activities. They pioneered in slums and congested areas in an endeavor to demonstrate by life experience the firm belief of their members in democracy, human equality, and dignity. They fought for equal opportunities for the poor and handicapped and for the abolition of prejudice and discrimination against people because of their skin, religion, race, and foreign birth.[3] Important tools in this fight for human values, education, and cultural development of the underprivileged were various activities of the settlement houses:

[2] For the historical development of settlement houses see Chapter 4 and Lorene M. Pacey, *Readings in the Development of Settlement Work* (New York: Association Press, 1950), pp. 69-73, and 245-260.

[3] L. Pacey, *ibid.*, pp. 2-3; Helen I. Clarke, *Principles and Practice of Social Work* (New York: Appleton-Century-Crofts, Inc., 1947), pp. 90-101; and Arthur E. Fink, *The Field of Social Work* (New York: Holt, 1949), pp. 431-437.

boys' and girls' clubs, playgrounds, kindergartens, adult education classes in languages, economic and legal problems, hygiene, labor relations, handicraft, the study of American history and its institutions, and discussion groups. These activities with children, adolescents, and adults emphasized the need of adjustment of the immigrant groups arriving from many countries. They were organized to acquaint newcomers with their new environment and to help them understand the morals, customs, and laws of the United States. Other informal study groups were devoted to cultural and civic affairs, to economic and health problems, and to the development of creative abilities in art classes and workshops, dramatic and literary groups. New York was the first city to permit the use of school playgrounds and school facilities for recreational activities of young people and adults, thus broadening the possibilities for adult education which had been started before in classes and courses in settlement houses, churches, and private schools.

Following the example of the English foundation of the Boy Scouts through Sir Baden-Powell, the American Boy Scouts were organized in 1910; a few years later a similar movement for girls was created by Juliette Low in 1912 under the title of "Girl Guides." The Campfire Girls were established in 1911 following the planning of a group of educators, under the leadership of Dr. Luther Gulick; their activities were not limited to outings and hiking, but included, as did most of the other youth organizations, games, singing, workshops, and educational and cultural activities in meetings and club discussions. The American Junior Red Cross is composed of nearly twenty million school children, engaged in health, safety, and recreational programs. The 4-H Clubs, sponsored by the U.S. Department of Agriculture, state colleges and counties, develop in rural youth ten to twenty years of age, ideals and high standards for farming, home skills, and cultural life in the rural community.

The motives for the foundation of these organizations were, of course, different. Frequently, there were religious reasons with the idea of strengthening in children and adults in poor neighborhoods the interest and the devotion to a religious life and to counteract the demoralizing influences of slums, filth, and crime. Many organizations started with such motivation, but all agencies in this field had also the sincere desire to advance the moral, intellectual, spiritual, as well as the physical and social, well-being of children, young people, and adults whom they invited to join their activities. In fact, all aimed to develop a sound body and a healthy character in their members, the will of working together with others toward a socially desirable goal through their participation in recreational, cultural, and educational activities. They wanted to help underprivileged children and young people to have social pleasure and recreational advantages which they were lacking in their families in a poor neighborhood, and tried to overcome limitations, prejudice, and injustices based upon low economic status and difference in race, color, and religion.

The settlement houses, in particular, are working toward a rebuilding of understanding and cooperation of neighbors in city quarters, where there is frequently lack of good will, hostility, disunity, and bitter competition, aggravated by low wages, poor working conditions, and neglect of sanitary and housing facilities. Immigrant groups in these neighborhoods arrive with unrealistic, exaggerated ideas about American opportunities and wealth. They have to go through difficult periods of economic deprivation, discrimination because of their language and foreign background, dangers in health, and humiliation until they become settled in the new country. The settlement houses assist the immigrants to go through such trying periods by strengthening their feelings of being welcome and accepted in the new country, by maintaining some of their native skills in arts and crafts, and by encouraging their pride in cultural values which they brought from their homes.

Essential contributions to the work in recreation and leisure time activities were made by the scientific development of psychology, particularly social psychology, sociology, anthropology, and psychiatry. They spread new light on the important elements of group behavior, cultural background, and the significance of group dynamics in their influence on the individual and the group. The philosophy of progressive education showed the importance for human growth by creative free activities in groups.

The development of a scientific technique in individual and group studies as experienced by Mary Follett, Grace Coyle, Gertrude Wilson, Clara Kaiser, Harleigh Trecker, Dorothy Sullivan, Charles Hendry, Gisela Konopka, Susanne Schulze, and others proved the possibilities of new experimental work in group discussions, workshops, and conferences, and the cultural and educational value of planned-for operation in group activities. Recently, the concept of group dynamics, which was inherent in a good deal of the earlier group activities, has been emphasized by Kurt Lewin, Ronald Lippitt, Fritz Redl, Leon Festinger, Norman Polansky, Harold H. Kelley, David Jenkins, Gordon Hearn, Alexander R. Martin, and others, mainly for research in group behavior and development of programs of applied research and cooperation between social scientists and social workers.[4]

Another aspect in the development of group work with sports, recreation, folk arts, folk dancing and craft, as well as informal education, is that this field has been organized in the United States with the same flair for systematic organization and perfection as the industrial machinery of our country.[5] This trend has been strengthened by the fact that during the short period of one or two generations an out-of-door people were herded into metropolitan areas and overgrown cities. It is only natural that they turned to highly organized sports and athletics and to cultural forms of recreation as a substitute for the quiet life and open space on the farm. Baseball and football games have become spectator sports, satisfying millions as a social ritual. They afford a release of tension for many who cannot actively participate in such other sports as hunting, fishing, skiing, boating, and swimming.

II. BASIC CONCEPTS OF SOCIAL GROUP WORK

Social casework is a helping relationship between an individual (the caseworker) with another individual (the client). Social group work, however, is characterized by the fact that it is carried out in a group setting, and the helping process deals with individuals in their relationship as members of a group.

We are aware that human beings do not grow up isolated from others. Children are born into a family; later they join with other children in informal groups. Adolescents and adults usually join a church, lodge, or other social group, following the natural desire for

[4] Ronald Lippitt, "Applying New Knowledge About Group Behavior," *Selected Papers in Group Work and Community Organization* (National Conference of Social Work), 1951, pp. 7-17.

[5] Frederick W. Cozens and Florence S. Stumpf, "Sports and American Culture," *Idea and Experiment*, Vol. 2, No. 2, December, 1952, pp. 12-15. See Helen L. Witmer and Ruth Kotinsky, *Personality in the Making* (New York: Harper, 1952), pp. 273-289.

companionship, belonging, and recognition. In most instances, social casework also is concerned not exclusively with the individual client, but with his family and environment because they play an important role in causing or alleviating personal problems of the individual. The caseworker himself has to function as a member of a group, just as everyone else in our society.

The social group worker, however, is primarily concerned with the relationship among the members of the group and between the members and himself. The group worker functions mainly through his participation in the interacting process between the individuals in the group, but he is not a regular member, identifying himself with the others, absorbed by the activities of the group as such. The worker's functions are guided by his professional understanding of group life and by the individual members' need for his help or for withholding his assistance. This knowledge permits the group worker to give professional service to the group as a whole and to each individual member of the group. In order to be able to assume this responsibility, the group worker needs to be aware of his professional self. He has to control his personal impulses, values, and preferences, and to concentrate upon making it possible for the members of the group to obtain the achievements and personal as well as cultural satisfactions which the group and its activities offer.[6]

Methods of working with groups may be classified into five categories:

1. The *dictatorial or authoritarian method:* The leader orders, the members obey and carry out what they are told.
2. The *personification method:* The members imitate the group worker and attempt to be like him, but they do not explore and find their own abilities.
3. The *preceptive method:* The worker gives instructions, the group members carry them out, learn skills, but they are not detecting their own resources and capacities.
4. The *manipulative method:* The group worker goes with the group through a phase of planning and decision making, but, in fact, the group is only accepting a prearranged program of the leader, but is deceived into believing that they themselves came to the decision.

[6] A. Fink, *op. cit.,* pp. 432-33; G. Wilson and G. Ryland, *op. cit.,* p. 28.

5. The *enabling method:* The group worker helps the members to participate with full responsibility in the life of the group, in its planning and program, in developing their own ideas, skills, and personal attitudes, and to make their own decisions regarding the purposes and actions of the group.[7]

In a democratic society only the last of these methods is the desirable way of achieving the aims of positive, constructive group life. It helps the individual members receive the satisfaction to be accepted as a part of the whole, to express themselves, and to participate in the collective action of the group.[8]

The desire to play and to enjoy the pleasure of games and sports, reading, dramatics, and creative art is fundamental to children and adolescents. First, religious and philanthropic societies made provisions for the recreational interests of their members. Recently, city and county recreation commissions and community centers have taken over a part of the responsibility for providing such opportunities for recreation as playgrounds, tennis and golf courts, tournaments, ball games, and swimming pools. But many private clubs and agencies still are very active in recreation work and carry on for their members a program of informal education for sports, hiking, sailing, fishing, nature study, first aid, and literature; and courses on government, health, economic and labor problems, community planning, and foreign policy.[9]

The settlement houses and international institutes assist immigrants in their adjustment to the new country, but they no longer urge them to abandon their former customs, culture, and language, but rather encourage them to be proud of the customs of their native land which contribute to American culture.

Recreation does not serve primarily the underprivileged, but rather the entire population. The early decades of recreation work were dependent upon the type of programs the agencies were able to offer.

[7] G. Wilson and G. Ryland, *op. cit.,* pp. 60 and 61.

[8] See Chapter 6; Alan F. Klein, *Society—Democracy—and the Group* (New York: The Woman's Press, 1953), and Grace L. Coyle, "Social Group Work," *Social Work Year Book, 1954,* pp. 480-481.

[9] See A. Fink, *op. cit.,* pp. 444-445; G. Wilson and G. Ryland, *op. cit.,* p. 65; Charles K. Brightbill, "Group Work in Public Recreation," in Charles Hendry, *A Decade of Group Work,* pp. 17-25, and "Recreation," *Social Work Year Book, 1954,* pp. 439-448; and Louis H. Blumenthal, "Group Work in Camping, Yesterday, Today, and Tomorrow," *A Decade of Group Work* (New York: Association Press, 1948), pp. 9-16.

The first groups were young people and adolescents, and they still represent the largest group participating in recreational activities. Recently, however, the "senior citizens" and certain handicapped groups, such as blind, deaf, and crippled persons, also take advantage of the possibilities of recreation and group life, its stimulation and its social gratifications; older and handicapped citizens thus obtain satisfaction, pleasure, and knowledge from group activities.

III. PRACTICE OF SOCIAL GROUP WORK

The practice of social group work is determined by the nature and the objectives of the social agency which provides the service, and by the needs which the group and its individual members want to satisfy in their group experience. There are four different levels of group work in which the group worker is active:

1. "Basic" social group work, the practice with "primary groups," such as children, adolescents' and adults' clubs, sport and recreation groups, and study and discussion societies.
2. Supervision of social group workers, professionals and volunteers.
3. Administration of social group work agencies or divisions of other organizations through which group work is offered.
4. Community organization, planning, and coordination for group work activities.[10]

We shall discuss, in this chapter, mainly the first type of group work, the activities of primary social groups which is the common practice of group workers whereas the functions of supervision, administration, and community organization in the realm of group work are assigned to a smaller number of experienced and professionally trained people.[11]

Agencies in the field of recreation may be classified into four categories according to their activities:

1. Agencies with programs providing primarily recreation and informal education, such as public recreation and adult education in schools, extension divisions of colleges and universities, and libraries, YWCA, YMCA, boys' and girls' clubs, and similar private organizations.

---

[10] G. Wilson and G. Ryland, *op. cit.*, pp. 27, 69-78.
[11] *Ibid.*, p. 73; Louis H. Blumenthal, *Administration of Group Work* (New York: Association Press, 1948); Harleigh B. Trecker, "Community Planning for Group Work," in Charles Hendry, *op. cit.*, pp. 124-132.

2. Agencies conducting recreational and educational programs combined with religious, ideological, and social purposes, such as church, young people's and women's groups, clubs interested in civic information, adult and workers' education societies.

3. Agencies primarily concerned with other objectives which conduct recreational and educational programs as a support of their main functions, such as settlement houses and community centers (whose main purpose is the establishment of constructive, cooperative, neighborhood relations, improvement of living and health standards), public housing projects, clubs of labor unions, of factories, and those youth groups like the 4-H Clubs, which fundamentally want to function as "character-building," vocational, or occupational organizations.

4. Agencies which provide therapy to patients in need of physical, mental, and emotional adjustment (hospitals, rehabilitation centers, mental and child guidance clinics)[12]; they use recreation and education as one of the means for achieving their therapeutic objective.

Social group work usually is thought of primarily in connection with leisure time and recreational activities. It is of particular importance, however, in the setting of an institution, such as a children's home, an orphanage, an industrial school, or an old-age home. In institutions the daily life requires a large scale of understanding of human behavior, establishing personal ties with all members of "living groups" as well as of "interest groups" or clubs which may form themselves in the institution.[13] Houseparents, teachers, instructors, and administrators assist children or adults to adjust to the demands of group living, and at the same time to develop or to preserve their own personality and cultural satisfaction. The trained social group worker is able to assist in an institutional setting in developing the constructive aspects of group living, encouraging the individual members to present their ideas, ingenuity, skills, and abilities. He is aware of the dangers of "boss-rule," or dictatorship, and of uncooperative leaders, who subdue other members and make them lose their individuality or exclude those whom they do not like.

[12] See Grace L. Coyle, *Group Work with American Youth* (New York: Harper, 1948), pp. 6-18; Gisela Konopka, "Group Work and Therapy," in Charles Hendry, *op. cit.,* p. 41.

[13] A stimulating discussion of such functions in children's homes is to be found in the chapter "The Group Worker in a Children's Institution" by Netta Berman, in Susanne Schulze's *Creative Group Living in a Children's Institution* (New York: Association Press, 1951), pp. 117-125.

Special problems arise for disturbed and overaggressive members of an institution, frequently found in correctional settings, where there are increased difficulties in planning and carrying out of leisure-time activities, recreational and educational programs, and of bringing to the staff an understanding of group dynamics and group therapy.[14] The group worker should take the initiative in developing staff recreation whenever the institution is not close enough to other resources of leisure time and cultural activities that meet the needs of the staff.

The following examples may illustrate the practice of group work and the responsibilities of the social group worker.

The Dukes[15]

The Acton Community Center is located in one of the overcrowded, blighted areas of the city. The facilities are rather limited for the number of people which it serves, having only a rather small gymnasium, one large hall—used for dances, parties, and occasional banquets—and some smaller meeting rooms. Its executive, Mrs. Lee, has a real feeling and understanding for the needs and desires of the heterogeneous racial groups who live in the area and use the center.

The Dukes are a social club of boys ranging in age from twelve to fifteen years and are representative of the population of the community. The boys live very close to each other and many of them attend the same school. Racial groups represented in the club include: Filipino, Mexican, Negro, and Chinese. The club president, Joe Bass, is a tall, slender Negro youth, fifteen years of age, who is well liked and respected by the other club members. Joe is rather quiet and unassuming in manner and is the indigenous leader. Juan, a handsome Filipino boy, fourteen years old, is the club secretary. The other members include: Chin, a Chinese boy; Morales, a Mexican-American; and Jim, Teddy, Pete, and Chuck, all Negroes.

I began working with them about four months ago and helped them form the club from the neighborhood friendship basis of the group. The activities of the group have been, for the most part, shooting pool in the agency, going on outings to the various local parks, and playing games in the gym. The boys are proud of their group and have purchased jackets alike and had the club name stenciled on them. They have been of great assistance to the agency by helping out at parties and shows for the younger children and acting as waiters and bus boys for the dinners of some of the older groups. There is a tendency for them to feel very

---

14 See S. Schulze, *op. cit.*, pp. 5-10.

15 This case study has been presented by Mrs. Melissa Clark of the Central YWCA in San Francisco and Miss Doreen Moorhead, to whom the author is indebted.

important and to consider themselves deserving of special attention and privileges for this service.

Prior to today's meeting, Mrs. Lee called me into her office to discuss an incident which had occurred with the boys some days previous. It seems that the boys had been playing very noisily in the showers and locker room. Jack, the agency's maintenance and handy man, had gone down to investigate. When he discovered what was going on, he asked the boys to be more orderly and not play tag in the locker room. The boys became offended and exchanged some remarks with him. Jack then called Mrs. Lee and reported the boys to her. She talked to them about their conduct and, when several of the boys seemed to be somewhat impertinent to her, she asked them to leave. All left but Joe Bass, who said that his membership was paid up and he had a right to use the building. After some discussion a settlement was reached. Mrs. Lee felt that the boys would have ill feelings toward her for her part in the incident and wanted worker to find out how they felt. The Dukes had been of great assistance to the agency during the holiday activities and had been highly commended by the staff for this. Mrs. Lee felt that the above incident might start some hostile feelings on the part of the boys toward the agency if it was not straightened out. Worker promised to investigate.

After the usual formalities of the meeting were over, worker opened the subject of the locker room incident by asking just what had occurred. Remarks came thick and fast as to how unjustly they had been treated. It seems that they had been playing a game of tag or hide-and-seek, hiding inside the lockers in the locker room. They thought this was all right as there was nothing down there that they could break, and besides the gym was locked and there was no place else they could play. Joe said, "Jack is just the janitor around here, what right has he to put anybody out?" and Morales said, "That's the way they treat us after all the work we did for 'em around here. We aren't going to do anything else." The other members seemed to share this attitude. Worker listened to similar expressions for some few minutes until each had aired his opinion and all seemed to be waiting for some indication of what worker thought.

Worker reiterated the appreciation of the staff for the splendid work the Dukes had done during the holidays and added his personal commendation to the boys for this evidence of cooperation. Worker then added that he was pleased that the boys could see beyond themselves as a club and lend a helping hand to others. He pointed out that the agency was there for their use and pleasure, and whenever they helped the agency they were indirectly helping themselves. The boys agreed that this was true. Worker then pointed out that playing in the locker room in that manner could result in damage to the equipment which would then have to be used in that state or money spent for its repair that might have been used for something else of a more useful nature. He agreed with them that it was unfortunate that the gym was not available for use as that was really the place for such activity. Worker asked the boys to keep these things in mind in their future behavior around the agency.

Worker then asked the boys how they felt about the work they had done for the agency. They all said it was fun and they didn't mind it at all. They did say they had worked hard however. Worker then asked if they thought they should have been paid for what they had done, and the unanimous reply was, "No!" Worker pointed out that to expect special consideration for any volunteer work done was just like asking for pay, and that rules of conduct made by the agency were not made to restrict any particular group's activity but rather to enable all to gain the maximum benefit from its facilities. Worker called for any further discussion or questions on the matter. There were none and the meeting was turned back into the hands of Joe Bass.

Comments

Worker is aware of the feeling of importance which the Dukes are now experiencing. They are proud of themselves for having their organization and want to make their presence known. They have a desire to set themselves apart from the general body at the agency which worker feels is all right if it can be guided into the proper channels and not developed to too great a degree. Worker feels that the need for recognition, which is permeating the group, was the primary cause for the incident contained in this record. He intends to explore the possibility of some responsibility being delegated to the club by the agency to make use of this feeling.

A Teen Age Council[16]

Representatives of clubs of boys and girls within the age range of 13-18 years form the Teen Age Council of a community center located in Westmoreland, a mobile section of a large city. While many families were moving out of the area, youth from these families returned to the center to participate with their friends in the clubs.

Newspaper accounts about activities of teen agers from this area had given the neighborhood a bad reputation, and the members of the Teen Age Council were concerned about the implications that all youth from this section of town are delinquent. The social group worker encouraged them to discuss their concern in their club meetings, and as a result each representative came to the next council meeting prepared to present the problems as seen by the several clubs represented. In the week preceding the meeting the following two incidents occurred which served to intensify their feelings about the malignment of their neighborhood.

[16] This case illustration has been contributed by Miss Gertrude Wilson, Professor of Social Welfare, University of California, Berkeley.

A popular name band was playing at a public dance, which was held in the public auditorium. A fight occurred, resulting in a general riot. Numerous teenagers were involved from many sections of town, but the newspaper accounts related to Westmoreland only.

An invitational teen age dance was in progress at a community center in the Lorraine Area. The dance was invaded by a gang of boys from Lorraine and Point Star who had not been invited. The disturbance caused by this invasion resulted in eight boys being injured. The police authorities assumed that the youth were from Westmoreland and this was reported in the newspapers.

The representatives came to the council meeting determined that something must be done to let the public know that all teen agers in Westmoreland are not participating in gang activities and, on the contrary, that some young people were concerned about the behavior of their peers. (The social group worker met with the officers of the Council prior to the meeting and helped them to prepare for the discussion which each knew would involve a great deal of feeling). The secretary was at the blackboard, and the president who led the discussion asked each person to suggest what could be done about the situation they were presenting. The secretary wrote the suggestions on the board. After the board had been filled, the social group worker helped the Council to see that all of the discussion of the evening really centered around two questions—(1) Why do youth become delinquent? What causes kids to get "side tracked"? and (2) What can we do to help other young people and ourselves to make this a better community to live in?

The solutions suggested included some improvements in their school, relationships with the police, relationships with parents, quantity and type of opportunities for recreation, and health problems with particular emphasis on need of teen agers for more understanding of sex. Several people suggested that the Council could sponsor a community conference to which they would invite adults in responsible positions not only from Westmoreland but also from the city. The Council voted to undertake such a project. Committees were formed to formulate the questions for such a conference, and each club took a responsibility for some aspect of the conference. After three months the conference was held to which City, School and Social Agency leaders were invited. The response was good and the newspaper publicity favorable.

IV. GROUP WORK IN OTHER SETTINGS

A. COOPERATION BETWEEN CASEWORK AND GROUP WORK AGENCIES

That in the interest of the people whom social work serves a close working together of caseworkers and group workers is most desirable, frequently indispensable, is an accepted idea by now. But it took a long time until this concept took hold among social workers.[17] Caseworkers often turn to group work agencies, such as the "Y's," girls' or boys' clubs, and the 4-H Clubs, for help in behalf of individual children in need of recreation, of companionship, or of developing art and music skills. Group living experience assists the child or youngster who has difficulties in his family or school, who is lonely or frustrated, or suffers from excessive sibling rivalry to find new friends in the group, to feel accepted, to develop his ability to get along with others, and to gain initiative and self-reliance.

The referral of the individual child or adolescent by his caseworker to a group work agency requires careful consideration of his personality, his environment, and his age as to what type of group or camp will be the most helpful experience for him. In an "interest group" the child is attracted by the specific activities carried out in the group, for instance, camping, hiking, sports, radio construction, music, folk dancing. In the "club group" the referred child may find other children of his age who with the help of the worker are willing to accept him into their society. A successful referral requires that the group worker have a keen understanding of the personality and emotional needs of the child, knowledge of symptomatic behavior, the skill to deal with sympathy with the individual child as well as with the group as a whole. Such referrals of individual children are made by children's and family welfare agencies, public welfare departments, hospitals, child guidance clinics, and churches. In making a referral, the group worker finds out which available group in its composition and leadership will best serve the needs of the child, and where he promises to be an asset to the other members. Under such circumstances group experience may function as a succssful adjustment of the referred child.

On the other hand, the group worker becomes aware that one or the other member of the group is in need of a personal, intensified relationship and individual assistance which exceed the possibilities in time and efforts that he may give to him without neglecting his relation to the group as a whole. In such instances the group

[17] Gertrude Wilson, *Group Work and Case Work—Their Relationship and Practice* (New York: Family Welfare Association of America, 1941); Gordon Hamilton, *Theory and Practice of Social Case Work* (New York: Columbia University Press, 1940), pp. 235-236, 242-244; Grace Coyle, *op. cit.*, p. 234; and Harleigh B. Trecker, *Group Work—Principles and Practice* (New York: The Woman's Press, 1948), pp. 101-102.

worker will, with the consent of the child or adolescent, and if need be of the parents, refer him to a casework agency for individual treatment. The child remains in the group as long as he is able to enjoy his participation. A cooperative relationship between the group worker and the caseworker may be of help to the child where he desires help from both workers and proves to be able to use it.

In other cases of referral, it may be indicated that only the social worker of the agency to which the child is referred maintains the immediate relationship with the child, be it a casework or group agency, to permit the child to attach himself fully to the new worker without a rival position of the referring worker. The latter restricts himself in these cases to follow up the development of the child by an occasional conference with the new worker.[18]

It is obvious that neither group work nor casework, nor the coordination of both methods, presents a panacea that will abolish all cases of maladjustment and asocial behavior and cure deeply disturbed and twisted personalities. But it may be hoped that by critical research into methods and approach to young persons, and conscientious professional practice, we shall find more effective ways of satisfying human needs.

B. GROUP WORK WITH ADULTS AND WITH AGED PERSONS

Work in groups with young adults and with middle-aged adult persons has gained importance. It has been practiced in neighborhood groups, meeting at settlement houses and community centers, churches and fraternal lodges; in adult education programs, university extension work; in workers' education, clubs, union committee meetings; and public housing projects. Professionally trained group workers are not often employed in these programs now, but there is increasing recognition that skilled group work process would make these programs more valuable and effective for their members.[19]

---

[18] A. Fink, *op. cit.*, pp. 451-454; H. Trecker, *op. cit.*, pp. 105-107; Rosemary Reynolds, "Services to Individuals Within a Group Work Setting," *Selected Papers in Group Work and Community Organization* (Raleigh, N.C.: Health Publications Institute, 1951), pp. 32-42.

[19] See Leland P. Bradford, "Adult Education as Group Work," L. K. Hall, "Group Work in Religious Education," and Eleanor G. Coit and Orlie Pell, "Group Work in the Workers' Education Setting" in Charles Hendry (editor), *op. cit.*, pp. 52-76.

During recent decades, the proportion of the older generation, over sixty-five years of age, among the total population has steadily increased due to the progress in medical science, geriatrics, and improved living standards. Our country has developed its cultural and recreational institutions with strong emphasis on the needs and habits of children and youth and, until recently, has given little attention to the leisure-time needs of older persons. The growing importance of the older citizen's group requires more consideration, not only in measures of social and economic security,[20] but also in cultural activities and recreation.

With the introduction of old-age insurance and of old-age retirement provisions in industrial health and welfare plans, an increasing number of older persons will be unable to obtain jobs in industry. Their life threatens to become dull and lonely without work so that satisfactory recreational facilities become more and more important for them. The first awareness of this change of emphasis was shown, when William Hudson Center in New York City and settlements in Chicago, primarily Olivet Institute, in 1940, organized the first "Golden Age Clubs" for elderly people. Other cities, Cleveland, Cincinnati, Philadelphia, followed, and at present recreational facilities for older citizens are offered in many cities.[21]

The organization of leisure time for the aged may be planned by a group of oldsters in cooperation with a settlement house, a family welfare agency, a church, or a community center which is ready to provide the meeting place and the facilities for group activities. Lists of the names of older people living in the selected neighborhood will be collected. Personal visits to the aged, a personal letter of invitation, or announcements in the local press may start the work. As in other recreational activities, programs will be arranged according to the interests and preference of the members of the group after it has been organized. They may include games, such as chess, dominos, cards, or checkers; music, movies, or television; a discussion of topics of actual cultural or political importance; or just

[20] These aspects are discussed in Chapters 7, 8, and 9; see also *Man and His Years: An Account of the First National Conference on Aging* (Raleigh, N.C.: Health Publications Institute, 1951); G. Wilson and G. Ryland, *op. cit.*, Chap. 14, and pp. 648-649.

[21] Oskar Schulze, "Live Long and Like It—A Brief Description of Recreational Services for Older People," address given at the National Association of the Associated Lutheran Charities at Minneapolis, Minn., 1947; and Arthur Williams, *Recreation for the Aging* (New York: Association Press, 1953).

an opportunity of getting socially together and talking with people of like situation. Simple refreshments are important because the old folks sometimes rarely have an opportunity of enjoying meals in the company of others. Members of the clubs are sixty years of age or older, many of them widows or widowers, or couples without children or relatives in the community. There should be no discrimination according to sex, faith, or race, nor as to financial status.

Group activities in homes for the aged have also become an important factor in modern institutional care. They are necessary for the well-being of older people who choose an institution as the most satisfactory form of living. Their own active participation is essential in the program, and the total group as well as individual interests shape the activities as in other group settings. But in a home for the aged the question of health sets limitations to recreational activities, discussions, and dramatic performances.[22]

V. GROUP THERAPY

The term "group therapy" is frequently used but not clearly defined. A great variety of activities, including group discussions with psychiatrists or psychiatric social workers, groups meeting in mental hygiene clinics or psychopathic hospitals, or psychodrama, are called group therapy. Careful selection of a suitable group of companions by the group worker is an essential condition for success and consideration of the probable mutual influence of the members of the group upon one another.

The primary objective of such groups is to function as a method of therapy for their members. Such groups have been composed of individuals who were unable to participate in normal group activities with others of the same age, who could not relate to people and were either too shy and withdrawn or so hostile and aggressive that they could not function in a normal group.

Group therapy has its own value in therapy, is not just a simpler, quicker process than individual treatment. It is based upon the curative or socializing effect of a group, upon the development of

[22] Herbert Shore, "Group Work Program Development in Homes for the Aged," *Social Service Review*, Vol. XXVI, No. 2, June, 1952, pp. 181-194; Jerome Kaplan, *A Social Program for Older People* (Minneapolis: University of Minnesota Press, 1953), and James H. Wood, *Helping Older People Enjoy Life* (New York: Harper, 1953).

friendly contacts with the security of help by the group leader in a controlled environment. In this interaction of the patients with each other, everyone feels more secure as he discovers that other members of the group have similar or even worse problems, and that his own difficulties are not caused by a unique failure or inadequacy. This recognition permits the patient to identify himself with other members of the group, lessens his anxiety, and develops his readiness to try to help the others while at the same time adjusting himself to the group. This experience encourages the patient, gives him a feeling of solidarity and of getting along with other people. The entire process is made possible through the relationship between the group therapist and the members of the group.[23] In general, group therapy develops a feeling of unity between the group members. Therapists, as a rule, are careful to avoid patients' expressing their feelings of suppressed hostility, aggression, and related drives too forcefully, because it would distort the climate of the group, and has to be left to individual treatment.

Changes in the environment are disturbing to adults and to children with whom group therapy has been practiced. Samuel R. Slavson, one of the outstanding pioneers in the field of child guidance and group therapy, characterizes his method as "activity group therapy," in which the therapeutic effect is produced by the active participation of disturbed or neurotic children or adults in such a group which permits them to act out or talk about their anxieties, fears, or aggressive feelings. The patient is encouraged to do so because of the uninhibited expression in words or acts of other group members, whereas he repressed his spontaneity before because of fear of being rebuked or losing prestige. In order to achieve such results, the group needs to be composed of a small number of patients of the same sex and of the same age level.[24] The group therapy setting must be informal; it must permit a confidential relation between the therapist and the members of the group.

[23] Robert Plank, "An Analysis of a Group Therapy Experiment," *Human Organization*, Fall and Winter, 1951, Vol. 10, Nos. 3 and 4, pp. 5-21, 26-36; Gisela Konopka, "Group Work and Therapy," Charles Hendry, *op. cit.*, pp. 39-43; and Dorwin Cartwright and Alvin Zander, *Group Dynamics: Research and Theory* (Evanston, Ill.: Row, 1953).

[24] See Chapter 11; also Samuel R. Slavson, *Creative Group Education* (New York: Association Press, 1937), and *An Introduction to Group Therapy* (New York: Commonwealth Fund, 1943), pp. 1-2.

In such therapeutic groups, even children of preschool age play out their anxieties, tensions, and fantasies. They use for their expression various toys and materials, such as animals, dolls, figures of families, wood blocks, plastics, water colors, and finger paints, and the social worker or psychiatrist gives them interpretations of their actions and plays. More intensive psychotherapy is used for disturbed children of elementary school age for whom different materials are offered in order to permit them in their play group to express their feelings.

The success of group therapy with children and adults depends upon a competent group therapist who needs at least the qualifications for individual therapy. Since World War II psychiatric patients have been treated by group therapy in military and veterans hospitals and clinics. In 1943, the American Group Therapy Association was founded, and provides for its members—psychiatrists, psychiatric social workers, group therapists, and clinical psychologists—information on research and new experiences, conferences, and exchange of ideas.

VI. VOLUNTEERS IN SOCIAL GROUP WORK

Because volunteers play a dominant role in the practice of recreation and leisure time activities, we may discuss the function of the volunteer at this point. However, we are aware that volunteers have been the pioneers in all fields of social work, not only in group work, but also in casework, in health services, and in community organization (preceding professional, paid social workers). They began to assist people in financial stress who did not want to ask for poor relief; they founded relief societies, health organizations, schools for the blind and deaf, children's homes, day nurseries, recreation services, settlement houses, family welfare agencies, and the charity organization societies. They laid the foundation on which modern social work is built, and they recognized the need for the professional training of social workers in a complex society.[25]

The first paid employees in social agencies were volunteers who had formerly served without compensation. With the increase in numbers of trained, paid staff, volunteers began to play a less im-

[25] See Chapters 4 and 5 above; Norma Sims, "Volunteers in Social Work," *Social Work Year Book, 1951*, p. 537 ff.; A. Fink, *op. cit.*, pp. 436-437; G. Wilson and G. Ryland, *op. cit.*, pp. 11-13, 600-602.

portant role in social agencies, particularly in casework and health agencies. During a later phase, professional social workers questioned the need and the value of volunteers on their boards and committees and were afraid that they might interfere with their professional operations. More recently, however, this skeptical opinion has changed, and the genuine, intrinsic contribution of volunteers serving on the board of a social agency in interpreting its work to the public and in carrying out its program has been recognized again. An honest partnership between volunteers and professional workers is developing. This partnership proves to be essential in the field of public relations (explaining the agency's work to the people), in the collection of money at fund-raising campaigns, in establishing policies on boards and committees, and in direct services to people with whom the agency deals.[26]

The new relationship between volunteers and professional workers is based upon mutual respect and upon a sharing of responsibility between both. In order to do an efficient job, the volunteer needs to be sincerely interested in the work, must be willing to accept guidance, training, and supervision, and must feel responsible for carrying out the assignment given to him, so that he is no less dependable than a paid worker. On the other hand, the professional staff should express recognition of the value of the volunteer's work—respect for his desire to contribute his time and effort without demanding monetary compensation. The staff should show this appreciation in careful advice, information, and supervision.

In large cities, volunteer bureaus under the auspices of the local community welfare council and special committees in smaller communities examine where volunteers are needed. They encourage the application of volunteers at the bureau and promote their recruitment and training. They recommend the volunteers to those social agencies for which they are best suited.

Both women and men, and an increasing number of young people, individually and in groups, serve as volunteers in private and public social agencies. There are many types of service, such as child care and hospital aids, group leaders, arts and craft instructors, clerical or typist help, automobile drivers, receptionists, entertainers, and

---

[26] Norma Sims, *op. cit.,* pp. 537 and 540; and Violet M. Sieder, "Volunteers in Social Work," *Social Work Year Book, 1954,* pp. 541-542.

librarians.[27] They are especially important in civil defense planning for emergencies because here services cannot be staffed with only trained, professional workers.

Particularly essential is the participation of volunteers in the field of recreation. Recreation agencies have to meet such a broad demand for leadership and guidance that they never are able to engage sufficient paid personnel. The executives in recreation also are willing to use services of volunteers on a broader scale than health and casework agencies do. Finally, recreational activities lend themselves conveniently to the participation of volunteers in games, sports, gymnastics, arts and crafts, camping, and discussion groups. In leisure-time work, the large number of volunteers makes their effective selection, training, and supervision an increasingly important task for the trained professional worker.

VII. TRENDS IN SOCIAL GROUP WORK PRACTICE

Among new elements in the development of social group work, we may emphasize the following trends:

1. The democratic principle of self-determination is recognized as the genuine American method of social group work. The older form of authoritarian leadership is more and more in the process of being discarded. Democracy implies respect for the personal dignity of each group member. It precludes enforcing the leader's own ideas and aims upon the group as long as these ideas are not accepted by the majority of the group.

The professional staff of the group work agency needs to have faith in the idea of democracy and in human dignity, as well as in people's ability to learn and to decide for themselves what they want to do. This democratic idea also requires that the group workers work *with* the group, not *for* the group.

2. Certain group work methods are applied to the expanding program of mass recreation, frequently under the guidance of public recreation departments, schools, and colleges. On the other hand, the need for the setup of smaller groups is recognized in order to

---

[27] The important function of volunteers as board and committee members, sponsors of fund-raising campaigns, and promoters of social service projects is discussed in Chapter 21.

offer individualized services for people who desire personal attention and help.

3. Recreational agencies accept the need for employment of trained, professional social workers who are able to give competent supervision to volunteer leaders and to work with such groups which need skill, understanding, and experience.[28] The development of group work agencies in their administration and their community relations also requires professional skills.

4. Under professional leadership, individual members in groups receive more attention based upon the group worker's understanding of psychiatric concepts of human needs. A new teamwork is developed in which group workers join together with caseworkers, psychiatrists, psychologists, and sociologists in order to help solve personality problems of group members.

5. Professional leadership has already stimulated a broad literature in the field of social group work and the development of scientific research in which social psychology, sociology, and sociometry contribute to a critical evaluation of the validity of group work methods.

6. The specific tasks and objectives of leisure-time and recreational agencies are clarified. An adjustment of the program of recreational agencies is under way according to the actual, essential needs of the community.

7. In many communities, a sincere concern about desirable interracial and intergroup relations is established. It leads to an emphasis on cultural dynamics and mutual respect among different ethnic and religious groups. Organizations are encouraged in which membership is open to everyone regardless of creed, race, color, sex, and economic status.

8. The dynamic forces of interaction find recognition in new, related provinces: in groups of the aged; in churches, factories, labor unions, cooperatives; and in reformatories, prisons, and institutions for mentally defective patients. Group dynamics begins to play an important role in improving relations between management and workers in industry.

9. Social agencies, professional associations, and schools of social work encourage professional education and attempt to develop the most suitable curriculum for training in group work, as well as criteria for the selection of students.

---

[28] See Paul M. Limbert, "Major Trends and Developments in Professional Aspects of Group Work," C. Hendry, *op. cit.*, pp. 141 ff., 148-149.

10. Professional social workers assume the responsibility for improving their own competence and skill, for assisting the schools of social work in their teaching methods, and for raising the quality of work in recreation and group work. They attempt to achieve a commonly accepted classification of jobs and the establishment of salaries commensurate with their responsibilities.[29]

SELECTED BIBLIOGRAPHY

Addams, Jane, *The Second Twenty Years at Hull House.* New York: Macmillan, 1930.
——, *The Spirit of Youth and the City Streets.* New York: Macmillan, 1909.
American Association of Group Workers, *Group Work—Case Work Cooperation, A Symposium.* New York: Association Press, 1946.
Baxter, Bernice, and Rosalind F. Cassidy, *Group Experience: The Democratic Way.* New York: Harper, 1943.
Bernstein, Saul, *Charting Group Progress.* New York: Association Press, 1949.
——, *et al., Group Work, Roots and Branches.* New York: Social Work Today, 1938.
*Blumenthal, Louis H., *Administration of Group Work.* New York: Association Press, 1948.
——, *Group Work in Camping.* New York: Association Press, 1937.
Busch, Henry M., *Leadership in Group Work.* New York: Association Press, 1934.
Clark, Margaret L., and Briseis Teall, *The Executive Director on the Job.* New York: The Woman's Press, 1947.
*Coyle, Grace L., *Group Experience and Democratic Values.* New York: The Woman's Press, 1947.
——, *Group Work with American Youth.* New York: Harper, 1948.
——, "Social Group Work," *Social Work Year Book, 1954,* pp. 480-486.
——, *Social Process in Organized Groups.* New York: R. R. Smith, 1930.
*——, *Studies in Group Behavior.* New York: Harper, 1937.
Dewey, John, *Art as Experience.* New York: Minton, 1934.
Dimmock, Hedley S., *Rediscovering the Adolescent.* New York: Association Press, 1937.
*——, and Harleigh B. Trecker, *The Supervision of Group Work and Recreation.* New York: Association Press, 1949.
Duffus, R. L., *Lillian Wald: Neighbor and Crusader.* New York: Macmillan, 1938.
Du Vall, Everett W., *Personality and Group Work: The Individual Approach.* New York: Association Press, 1943.

[29] G. Wilson and G. Ryland, *op. cit.,* pp. 600-609; and V. Sieder, *op. cit.,* pp. 542-545.

Elliott, Harrison, *The Process of Group Thinking*. New York: Association Press, 1928.

*Follett, Mary Parker, *Creative Experience*. New York: Longmans, 1924.

Gardner, Ella, *Development of a Leisure-Time Program in Small Cities and Towns*. U.S. Children's Bureau, Publication #241, 1937.

Hall, Frances A., *Statistical Measurement in Group Work*. U.S. Children's Bureau, Publication #248, 1939.

Hawkins, Gaynell, *Educational Experiments in Social Settlements*. New York: American Association for Adult Education, 1937.

*Hendry, Charles, *A Decade of Group Work*. New York: Association Press, 1948.

———, *The Role of Groups in World Reconstruction*. New York: The Woman's Press, 1952.

Hiller, Margaret, *Leadership in the Making*. New York: The Woman's Press, 1936.

Hjelte, George, *The Administration of Public Recreation*. New York: Macmillan, 1940.

Jennings, Helen Hall, *Leadership and Isolation (A Study of Personality in Interpersonal Relations)*. New York: Longmans, 1943.

Jones, Anna M., *Leisure Time Education: A Handbook of Creative Activities for Teachers and Group Leaders*. New York: Harper, 1946.

*Kaiser, Clara (editor) *The Objectives of Group Work*. New York: Association Press, 1936.

Kellerman, Henry J., *Personal Standards in Social Group Work and Recreation Agencies*. New York: Welfare Council, 1944.

Kilpatrick, William H., *Group Education for Democracy*. New York: Association Press, 1940.

Klapman, Jacob W., *Group Psychotherapy: Theory and Practice*. New York: Grune, Stratton, 1946.

Klein, Alan F., *Society—Democracy—and the Group*. New York: The Woman's Press, 1953.

*Konopka, Gisela, *Therapeutic Group Work with Children*. Minneapolis: University of Minnesota Press, 1949.

———, *Group Work in the Institution*. New York: Whiteside, 1954.

Kroeber, Alfred L., *The Nature of Culture*. Chicago: University of Chicago Press, 1952.

Kubie, Susan H., and Gertrude Landau, *Group Work with the Aged*. New York: International Universities Press, 1953.

Leigh, Robert D., *Group Leadership: With Modern Rules of Procedure*. New York: Norton, 1936.

Lewin, Kurt, *A Dynamic Theory of Personality*. New York: McGraw, 1935.

———, *Resolving Social Conflicts*. New York: Harper, 1948.

*Lieberman, Joshua (editor), *New Trends in Group Work*. New York: Association Press, 1938.

Lies, Eugene T., *How You Can Make Democracy Work*. New York: Association Press, 1942.

Lindeman, Edward C., *Leisure—A National Issue*. New York: Association Press, 1939.

Lindenberg, Sidney J., *Supervision in Social Group Work*. New York: Association Press, 1939.

Lippitt, Ronald, *An Experimental Study of Authoritarian and Democratic Group Atmospheres*. Iowa City: University of Iowa Press, 1940.

———, *Training in Community Relations*. New York: Harper, 1949.

MacIver, Robert (editor), *Group Relations and Group Antagonisms*. New York: Harper, 1944.

Marden, Charles F., *Minorities in American Society*. New York: American Book, 1952.

Menninger, Karl A., *Love Against Hate*. Boston: Harcourt, 1942.

———, *Man Against Himself*. Boston: Harcourt, 1938.

Meyer, Harold D., and Charles K. Brightbill, *Community Recreation*. Boston: Heath, 1948.

Moreno, Jacob L., *Psychodrama*. 3 vols. Boston: Beacon House, 1947.

Murray, William D., *History of the Boy Scouts of America*. New York: Boy Scouts of America, 1937.

Neumeyer, M. H., and E. S. Neumeyer, *Leisure and Recreation*. New York: A. S. Barnes, 1936.

Newstetter, W. I., Marc J. Feldstein, and Theodore M. Newcomb, *Group Adjustment—A Study in Experimental Sociology*. Cleveland: Western Reserve University, 1938.

*Pacey, Lorene M. (editor), *Readings in the Development of Settlement Work*. New York: Association Press, 1950.

Phillips, Helen U. (editor), *Achievement of Responsible Behavior Through Group Work Process*. Philadelphia: University of Pennsylvania, 1950.

Price, Louise, *Creative Group Work on the Campus*. New York: Columbia University Press, 1941.

Reynold, Rosemary, "Services to Individuals Within a Group Work Setting," *Selected Papers in Group Work and Community Organization*, pp. 32-42, Raleigh, N.C.: Health Publications Institute, 1951.

Robinson, Duane M., *et al.*, *The Chance to Belong: Story of the Los Angeles Youth Project, 1943-1949*. New York: The Woman's Press, 1949.

Romney, G. Ott, *Off the Job Living—A Modern Concept of Recreation*. New York: A. S. Barnes, 1945.

*Schulze, Susanne, *Creative Group Living in a Children's Institution*. New York: Association Press, 1951.

Sieder, Violet M., "Volunteers in Social Work," *Social Work Year Book, 1954*, pp. 538-545.

*Sils, Dorothy H., *Volunteers in Social Service*. New York: National Travelers Aid Association, 1947.

Simkhovitch, Mary K., *Group Life*. New York: Association Press, 1940.

——, *Neighborhood: My Story of Greenwich House*. New York: Norton, 1938.

*Slavson, Samuel R., *An Introduction to Group Therapy*. New York: Commonwealth Fund, 1943.

——, *Character Education in a Democracy*. New York: Association Press, 1939.

——, *Creative Group Education*. New York: Association Press, 1937.

——, *Recreation and the Total Personality*. New York: Association Press, 1946.

Stone, Walter L., *Problems in Social Group Work*. Nashville: Informal Education Service, 1938.

*Sullivan, Dorothea F. (editor), *The Practice of Group Work*. New York: Association Press, 1941.

—— (editor), *Readings in Group Work*. New York: Association Press, 1952.

Taylor, Graham, *Chicago Commons Through Forty Years*. Chicago: Cuneo Press, 1936.

——, *Pioneering on Social Frontiers*. Chicago: University of Chicago Press, 1930.

Tead, Ordway, *Creative Management*. New York: Association Press, 1935.

——, *New Adventures in Democracy*. New York: McGraw, 1939.

——, *The Art of Leadership*. New York: McGraw, 1935.

*Trecker, Audrey, and Harleigh B. Trecker, *How To Work with Groups*. New York: The Woman's Press, 1952.

Trecker, Harleigh B., *Group Process in Administration*, 2nd ed. New York: The Woman's Press, 1950.

*——, *Social Group Work—Principles and Practice*. New York: The Woman's Press, 1948.

Wald, Lillian D., *House on Henry Street*. New York: Holt, 1915.

——, *Windows on Henry Street*. New York: Little, 1934.

Whiteside, William B., *The Boston YMCA and Community Needs: A Century Evaluation, 1851-1951*. New York: Association Press, 1951.

Williamson, Margaret, *Supervision—Principles and Methods*. New York: The Woman's Press, 1950.

*Wilson, Gertrude, *Group Work and Case Work: Their Relationship and Practice*. New York: Family Welfare Association of America, 1941.

——, and Gladys Ryland, *A Bibliography on Group Work*. New York: Association Press, 1945.

*——, *Social Group Work Practice*. Boston: Houghton, 1949.

*Witmer, Helen L., and Ruth Kotinsky, *Personality in the Making*. New York: Harper, 1952.

Wittenberg, Rudolph M., *So You Want To Help People*. New York: Association Press, 1947.

Woods, Eleanor H., *Robert A. Woods: Champion of Democracy*. Boston: Houghton, 1929.

Woods, Robert A., *City Wilderness*. Boston: Houghton, 1898.

——, and Albert J. Kennedy, *Settlement Horizons*. New York: Russell Sage Foundation, 1922.

——, *Neighborhood in Nation-Building*. Boston: Houghton, 1923.

15. Crime, Delinquency, and Corrections

I. CAUSES OF DELINQUENCY AND CRIME

Social services to children, youth, and adults who violate laws are an important part of modern social work. These services developed only after criminal courts punishing the lawbreaker already had a long history. Thus court authorities have been reluctant to recognize the value of the contribution of the services of social workers in probation staffs, family and children's organizations, whose techniques and skills had not yet taken definite form. We shall discuss first the social services rendered to children and young persons who have difficulties in abiding by the legal rules of community life, and then proceed to social services for the adult offender.

Maladjustment and delinquent behavior of children and youth are among the most serious problems of our present society.[1] From the point of view of social work it seems necessary to help children and adolescents to avoid breaking rules, whether or not they are brought before a court or are pronounced delinquent. Social work assists young people in their efforts to abide by the rules of social conduct required by tradition or statute. These efforts include the development of social attitudes and modes of behavior which are not necessarily embodied in legal provisions.[2] Thus juvenile protection in social work is concerned with maladjusted children and youth whose difficulties bring them before the law, but also with those who while

---

[1] For a full discussion of the topic the reader is referred to Negley K. Teeters and John Otto Reinemann, *The Challenge of Delinquency: Causation, Treatment, and Prevention of Juvenile Delinquency* (New York: Prentice-Hall, Inc., 1950), Chap. I; and to John R. Ellingston, *Protecting Our Children from Criminal Careers* (New York: Prentice-Hall, Inc., 1948), Chaps. 1 and 2.

[2] Helen L. Witmer, *Social Work: An Analysis of a Social Institution* (New York: Farrar and Reinhart, 1942), p. 383.

not violating laws prove to be hard to educate in the family or who are disturbing others in school and in the streets.

Such different behavior cannot be treated alike in all children because of the different circumstances under which it occurs. One difficult child may be accepted or even encouraged in his delinquent behavior by his family and neighbors, according to the mores and values in a certain area or community; another child under the same conditions may be brought to a social agency or referred to a child guidance clinic; and still another may be denounced to the police, arrested, and cited before the juvenile court. The economic status of the parents, customs of the local community, and cultural patterns of the social group to which the child belongs are essential factors in determining what happens to a delinquent child. The White House Conference of 1930 defined "delinquency" as juvenile misconduct that might be dealt with under the law. But from the point of view of social work it seems desirable to help the child before he gets in trouble and police authorities and juvenile courts are forced to interfere with his life.

No exact statistical data on the extent of juvenile delinquency in our country are available. But it is estimated that about six in every 1,000 children under eighteen years of age are involved in some type of juvenile delinquency which brings them to the attention of a juvenile court.[3] These figures amount to about 1,000,000 children each year in the United States.

The causes of delinquency are analyzed by different theories. Cesare Lombroso, the noted Italian anthropologist and criminologist, taught that the criminal was born, doomed by certain biological characteristics to lead a life of crime. Today only few scientists adhere to this "constitutional school of criminality." Most students of criminology are convinced that crime and delinquency are not caused through any single source, whether it be heredity, biological structure, or environmental influences, but usually by the working together of several factors. (This school is termed the "Multiple Causation Theory.") Among these various factors may be hereditary

[3] N. Teeters and J. Reinemann, *op. cit.*, p. 18; Fred J. Murphy, Mary M. Shirley, and Helen L. Witmer, "The Incidence of Hidden Delinquency," *American Journal of Orthopsychiatry*, Vol. 16, No. 4, October, 1946, pp. 686–696; and Edward F. Schwartz, "Statistics of Juvenile Delinquency in the United States," *The Annals of the American Academy of Political and Social Science*, Vol. 261, January, 1949, pp. 9–20 (particularly, p. 12).

and biological elements, such as poor health, physical handicaps, abnormalities, glandular disturbances, various degrees of mental deficiency or even psychosis, emotional instability, insecurity, uncontrolled sexual drives, or neurotic behavior. Other factors may be contributed by environment, neglect or rejection by parents, siblings and friends, detrimental influences by a broken home, criminal attitudes of the family, neighbors, or predatory gangs in a slum area. There may also be poverty in the family, gambling, bad companions, irregular or poor education, lack of healthy recreation, excitement through the radio, television, the newspapers, crime stories, comic books, and movies.[4]

Research studies, particularly those of Sheldon and Eleanor Glueck and Clifford Shaw, have shown that certain young persons may become delinquent while others remain law-abiding citizens under the same hereditary conditions and in the same environment.[5]

Since human behavior is determined by the customs and the culture in which we live, a substantial part of delinquency is based upon the conflicting values within and between cultural groups. As an example of such a conflict, the difference between the customs of foreign-born parents and their native-born children is frequently mentioned. Children are ashamed of the "strange" habits and values of their parents while they themselves, as a rule, accept those of their play companions and classmates in school. In fact, our present civilization is not ruled by a single set of cultural and ethical values, but by several conflicting systems. This conflict is more evident in the United States than in other countries due to the wide mobility of its population, its different ethnic background, and the lack of a strict class system.[6]

Cultural anthropology explains the divergence in sexual customs; in approval or disapproval of street fighting, gang rule, stealing of money, food, or automobiles; in fraud, cheating in measures and

---

[4] Henry H. Goddard, *Feeblemindedness: Its Causes and Consequences* (New York: Macmillan, 1919); N. Teeters and J. Reinemann, *op. cit.*, p. 89. See also Herbert Blumer, *Movies, Delinquency, and Crime,* and *Movies and Conduct* (both, New York: Macmillan, 1933).

[5] Sheldon Glueck and Eleanor Glueck, *One Thousand Delinquents* (Cambridge: Harvard University Press, 1934); Clifford Shaw, *Delinquency Areas* (Chicago: University of Chicago Press, 1929); *Brothers in Crime* (Chicago: University of Chicago Press, 1938); and Miriam van Waters, *Youth in Conflict* (New York: Republic Printing Co., 1925).

[6] H. Witmer, *op. cit.*, p. 385; J. Ellingston, *op. cit.*, pp. 13-27.

weights, gambling and betting, riding freight trains, trucks and busses; and in truancy from school, illicit manufacture of liquor, and sex habits among various minority groups and economic classes of our population. Whenever youngsters act in conformity to the customs of their own group, but in violation of the written law or the habit of other groups, the lawbreaker and his family and friends often consider it merely an unfortunate accident to be caught by the police and reprimanded by the court.

More general and not dependent upon the particular customs of minority groups is the conflict existing between the teaching of religious and moral ethics on one hand, and on the other the practical demands of the economic rules of our society. Religious teaching and social philosophy ask the individual to love others, and praise mutual aid and cooperation. In sharp conflict with this humanitarian ideal, the principle of economic competition and individual achievement in terms of success, wealth, property, and high income as measurement of efficiency urge the child to excel others in school and to aim at economic success, even when damaging others. It is obvious that many children and youngsters find it difficult to establish a balance between these conflicting theories.[7]

II. THE JUVENILE COURT

Since the French Penal Code under Napoleon provided for a minimum age at which children could be made responsible for offenses, and for a different treatment of young lawbreakers, the postulate of such differentiation spread in most countries of Western civilization. The English Courts of Chancery already protected the interests of young children under seven years of age who were considered to be incapable of "criminal intent." Children between seven and fourteen years of age could be punished by the courts, provided the prosecutor was able to prove their capacity of entertaining criminal intent. Children over fourteen years of age were punished as adult criminals.

In the United States the press and charity societies complained

[7] Karen Horney, *The Neurotic Personality of Our Time* (New York: Norton, 1937); Franz Alexander and William Healy, *The Roots of Crime* (New York: Knopf, 1935); Bernard Lander, *Toward an Understanding of Juvenile Delinquency* (New York: Columbia University Press, 1953); and Milton L. Barron, *The Juvenile in Delinquent Society* (New York: Knopf, 1954).

that children begging in the streets, or pilfering, needed protection
and reformation, but that the criminal courts punished them for offenses like adult criminals and sent them to jail or prison. It
became evident that harsh punishment, particularly the death sentence, against children was out of proportion to the child's responsibility, and that children placed in jails or prisons with adult criminals were really trained in crime and vice by the older inmates.

In the 1820's New York, Boston, and Philadelphia established
"houses of refuge" for wayward or delinquent children and youngsters in order to separate them from adult criminals. The penal code
of Illinois, in 1831, ruled that for certain crimes penalties for minors
were different than those for adult offenders.[8]

The first juvenile court was created in Chicago on July 1, 1899.
Since 1891 a group of citizens under the leadership of Jane Addams,
Julia C. Lathrop, Lucy L. Flower, Judge Harvey B. Hurd (who
drafted the law), Mary B. Bartelme, Judge Julian W. Mack, Dr. F. H.
Wines (secretary of the Illinois State Board of Charities), and Has-
tings H. Hart (director of the Illinois Children's Home and Aid Society) urged the Chicago Bar Association to encourage the state
legislature to enact legislation for the protection of children and for
their segregation from adult offenders. The law was adopted on
April 14, 1899 with the aim of treatment and control of dependent,
neglected, and delinquent children.[9] The juvenile court judge was
to combine legal skill with the knowledge of human behavior in
order to help the child in his adjustment.

The law established the jurisdiction of circuit and county courts
over children's cases. It based the entire process of investigation,
court hearing, and judicial disposition upon the idea of rehabilitation of the juvenile delinquent. The juvenile court is not a criminal
court; it does not make charges against the child who therefore is
not in need of a defense lawyer. There is no jury to determine the
guilt or innocence of the child. Rather, the court attempts to understand the causes for the behavior of the child or adolescent and orders the measures necessary for his adjustment and rehabilitation.

In the same year in which the Chicago Juvenile Court was established, 1899, Judge Benjamin B. Lindsay organized a special children's court under the Board of Education in Denver, Colorado,

[8] N. Teeters and J. Reinemann, *op. cit.*, pp. 282-283.
[9] Grace Abbott, *The Child and the State, II* (Chicago: University of Chicago
Press, 1938), pp. 303-331.

which developed into a juvenile court in 1903. Other states followed the Illinois example so that by now all states, as well as the federal government, the District of Columbia, Alaska, Hawaii, and Puerto Rico have juvenile courts.[10]

The operation of the juvenile court may be best characterized by its comparison with the adult criminal court. An adult who has committed an offense is, as a rule, arrested and after a hearing before a magistrate either summarily punished by a fine or jail sentence, or held for trial in jail, or released under bail or upon his pledge to appear in court. After a criminal investigation the prosecuting attorney submits the evidence to a jury requesting an indictment of the accused. If the jury finds that the evidence does not justify an indictment, the accused is released. If the indictment is pronounced by the jury, the trial proceeds. The defendant is entitled to have an attorney to represent him. At the arraignment he pleads "guilty" or "not guilty"; in the latter case, a trial jury of twelve members brings in, upon examination of the facts and cross-examination of the witnesses by the prosecuting officer and the defense lawyer, a verdict of "guilty" or "not guilty."

Quite different is the procedure of the juvenile court. Its jurisdiction covers, in the majority of states, youth under eighteen years of age, in some states under seventeen or sixteen years, and in two states minors under twenty-one years. As a rule, neglected and dependent children also are under the jurisdiction of the juvenile court, and in some states placed under adoption, guardianship, or commitment to institutions for handicapped and mentally defective or ill children. The action of the juvenile court usually is initiated by petition; no jury is asked for an indictment.

If a juvenile offender is arrested after violating the law, he is placed in a detention home, not in a jail with adults.[11] In spite of the knowledge that children and youthful offenders are trained in

---

[10] The last state to enact a juvenile court law was Wyoming in 1945. The *Federal Juvenile Delinquency Act* of 1938 provides juvenile court procedure for youths under eighteen charged with violation of federal law, but the transfer of all young offenders under twenty-one years of age to state authorities willing to receive them has been possible since 1932. (See N. Teeters and J. Reinemann, *op cit.*, p. 291.) In 1951, about 500,000 children came to the attention of juvenile courts, 350,000 of them for delinquency cases.

[11] N. Teeters and J. Reinemann, *op. cit.*, pp. 231-237; Florence M. Warner, *Juvenile Detention in the United States* (Chicago: University of Chicago Press, 1933); Austin H. MacCormick and James H. Dooling, "Keeping Children out of Jails: It Can Be Done," *Federal Probation*, September, 1949, pp. 40-45.

crime, distrust society, and become more hostile to good citizenship by being kept in jail, prohibition of jail detention varies widely among the states. Often exceptions are possible for older youth or by order of the juvenile court judge, and whenever no detention is available. Frequently the young offender is heard before a referee or a probation officer at once or the next day, and released upon his promise of good behavior (sometimes termed "adjusting the case") or held for the juvenile court session in the detention home. Many juvenile courts place the child under the supervision of a probation officer when the youngster is released before the final court hearing.

III. THE DETENTION HOME

The detention home, or "juvenile hall," receives children who may be classified into three main categories: (1) children in need of protection, such as dependent and neglected children without proper care, lost children in need of an emergency shelter, mental defectives awaiting commitment, and habitual school truants that are returned to their parents; (2) children in temporary custody, such as children who are runaways from their own or foster families and from children's institutions, and children who serve as witnesses to secure their presence in court; and (3) children awaiting trial before the juvenile court, and delinquent children awaiting transfer to a training school or another institution after court decision.

In some detention homes dependent and neglected children are kept separate from delinquent children. Many children remain only a day or a night in the detention home until they return to their families, but for three types of children frequently a longer placement in the detention home is necessary: (1) children and youngsters beyond the control of their parents, foster parents, and guardians who cannot be prevented from committing new delinquencies, such as serious assault, sexual attacks, burglary, armed robbery; (2) children who are in physical or moral danger in their own families or are without a home; and (3) children whose attendance or uninfluenced testimony at a court hearing or whose placement in an institution can only be assured by detention.[12]

---

[12] See Sherwood Norman and Helen Norman, *Detention for the Juvenile Court: A Discussion of Principles and Practices* (New York: National Probation Association, 1946); Sherwood Norman, "The Detention Home," *The Annals of the American Academy of Political and Social Science*, Vol 261, January, 1949, pp. 158-165; N. Teeters and J. Reinemann, *op. cit.*, pp. 237-246.

The detention home is administered either (1) by the juvenile court (sometimes the chief probation officer is superintendent of the home), (2) by the county authorities (board of supervisors or commissioners), (3) by a local public welfare department, (4) by the state's Department of Social Welfare, or (5) by a private child welfare agency.

Services to the child in the detention home include good physical and custodial care, medical and dental treatment, recreation, instruction according to the age of the child and the length of his stay, and religious services. Although a certain security against escape is necessary, the detention home should avoid an atmosphere of fear and repression. More recently the need of professional casework and clinical services for emotionally disturbed children is acknowledged as well as stimulating, cheerful group activities in workshops, play, and recreation so that the children are occupied and socially interested. However, many detention homes are still far from meeting these standards, which require employment of trained personnel, a superintendent, teachers, caseworkers, group workers, and supervisors. The observation of the child in the detention home regarding his health, mental abilities, and behavior renders valuable information for the court, the probation staff, and social agencies which may later help the child.

The following case study of a boy who remained for a few days in a detention home illustrates some of his reactions toward his being held in the institution. They show the "social climate" and the attitudes of superintendent, caseworker, and group worker when the child's behavior creates difficulties. In this case, however, no special medical, psychiatric, and religious services were made available to the children during a short stay. Recreational activities play an important role during this period. The case describes the achievement of some confidence of the children in the professional staff, a beginning of "treatment," as well as the discipline and limitations of an institution of this type.

The Case of Jack[13]

April 8, 19—: Jack, age 15, was brought in by the court worker of the Juvenile Court at 10 A.M. as an incorrigible. The court worker said that Jack does not want to stay with his parents and is here pending placement.

[13] The case of "Jack," by Ray Studt and Mrs. Elliot Studt, is based upon experiences in the Denver (Colorado) Detention Home.

Interview, 11:30 A.M.: Jack is a tall, dark boy who was very well-dressed when he was first brought in. He is good-looking, though his face is immature and slightly sulky. His thick hair is neatly cut and swept back in a long pompadour. He has a smooth courteous manner, and an air of superiority, which sets up barriers to a genuine relationship.

Jack told me he is here because he can't get along with his parents. When I asked him how he felt about being here, he said, "It looks good enough for me." Since it was getting late I asked him immediately if he would like to come down for lunch. He said, "I am not particular," but decided to come down.

Jack's only request was whether or not he could smoke. He said he is used to a package a day and felt it would be very hard to get along with only one. He agreed to the conditions regarding smoking privileges. When I commented I was sorry that we couldn't arrange for more cigarettes a day he said in a grand manner, "That's all right."

Miss S, the group worker, reported that Jack was contemptuous at lunchtime about the food. Almost immediately he began pestering the worker about when he could have his first cigarette.

April 9, 19—: Jack was caught smoking in the bathroom before breakfast. Eight matches were found in his shoes. He was kept in his room until the caseworker could see him.

Interview, 3:15 P.M.: I could feel that Jack was pretty resentful about this period of isolation. Verbally he was eager to explain away his share in the smoking. He was quick to tell me that another guy brought him the matches. He had only half of a cigarette and was sure that at the time he had accepted the agreement he had only promised not to smuggle matches upstairs. Another guy had brought them. He assured me that he did not know that I had asked him not to pester the boys' worker about cigarettes. I explained the agreement again and said, "You feel we are being pretty mean about this." He said, "No, that seems fair." I said that since he had already had a cigarette today I would not include him again in the smoking group until the following day.

Jack asked if he might write a letter and I explained that he could ask the boys' worker for writing material; also that all letters go over my desk before they are mailed. Then Jack wanted to know if he could go down and play ping pong.

At dinner Jack was show-off and contemptuous. He was the center of much underhanded laughing and whispering. Following dinner he was seen by the superintendent in the office and told that he would have to change his behaviour if he wished to remain in program. Because of the problem he made in the group, the boys' worker had him remain in his room instead of coming to game hour.

April 10, 19—: The boys' worker reported that Jack seemed to be making some attempt to get along during the work period, but by lunch time he was again smarty and openly contemptuous of the food.

At smoking period, Jack asked if he might go to the jail. I asked why he would like to and he answered that he could smoke there all of the time. When I explained that we really had nothing to say about it and since it was Saturday afternoon it would not be possible to reach his court worker to get him moved, he began quickly to cover up his feeling with much talk, saying things like, "I really like it better here," and "You get more privileges here."

Jack began boasting to the boys about his past. He said that he can't get along with his parents and hasn't lived with them for the last twelve years until the last few weeks. He likes West Virginia best. He got a lot of money there, acting as a broker for hill-billy moonshine.

The workers have found Jack "an undisciplined brat." He seems to have no training in work habits and approaches every situation with the attitude of getting the most out of it for himself in an underhanded fashion. The workers have followed the policy of keeping the limits firm.

April 12, 19—: Jack ran away with Lloyd on the way in from the play-yard. The court worker reports that Jack went home, ransacked the place and left a threatening note for his parents, saying that he would never forgive them for filing on him in court.

May 11, 19—: Jack was brought in by the police at 1:45 A.M. for difficulties with his parents. The superintendent reported that Jack was intensely angry. Most of his feeling was focused against his father, who, he says, lies around drunk while his mother works. He said he despised his father, and the superintendent said he had never seen a kid so completely bitter.

Jack had breakfast and lunch on trays.

The boys' worker reports that Jack has been sleeping heavily all day. She found a pack of cigarettes on him, although when the superintendent took him in at night, he found one package and had stripped him and taken away all his clothes.

Interview, 1:45 P.M.: Jack looked bad this time. His hair was tousled and his face white, almost grey. There were shadows under his eyes and his lips were very red and sulky. This was the first time I had seen Jack unkempt, and he made no attempt to appease or fool me. He showed no embarrassment about having run away. He was simply bitter and resigned. (How do you feel about being here?) "I'd still rather be at the jail." (What are you going to do about it?) "Nothing I can do, I guess." I asked what he wanted to do while he was here—stay in his room or go into the group. It was all the same to him. He would just as soon stay in his room. It might be fun to come downstairs once in a while but he would like to stay upstairs most of that time. I asked if he found the program too young for him. He said, "No." (What bothers you most about it?) "Lights off at 8:30 P.M." He likes to sit up and read books. He asked me if he could have a cigarette today. (What do you think about it?) "It is up to you." (You know our rules—referring to the smuggled package). "Then I guess I don't get any." (I told him they don't let them smoke at all at the jail since the new ordinance was passed, and he was surprised at this.)

I said, "You look tired." He answered, "I am tired. I was all over town last night." (Running from the police?) "Yes, some fellow called them up." There was a set resentful look on his face. (You are pretty mad at him.) "Yep." (You are pretty much mad at all the world today.) "No, not quite that bad." I said I was interested to know whether he was so mad at us that he would run away again. He said, "No." He had tried that. "There is no use in running away if you have no place to go."

He has been living with his folks since he ran away from here. It didn't work out well this time either. (Tears welled up in his eyes but he set his teeth and didn't cry.) He had tried working part of the time as a bootblack, part of the time in a Coffee Bar. "I didn't do so bad though," he said. He was waiting for a call to go out on farm work while he was bootblacking. He wanted to know when the trial was likely to be and I told him I didn't think it would be before Friday. I said, "I tell you what Jack. Suppose you stay in your room until tomorrow after breakfast and then I'll see you again about what you want to do. You know our rules and our kind of program. If you would rather stay in your room and have it be like a jail then we can do it that way. If you want to come into the group we will expect you to follow our way of doing things. You can make your choice. We will see how you feel about it tomorrow." He was agreeable about this and even seemed a little relieved.

Jack gives the impression of being completely unhappy. He is full of a feeling of revenge. He seems to have no pattern of identification with other people and he sees everything in terms of his own drives.

Half an hour later the police officer telephoned to say that Jack was wanted with a gang of ex-industrial school boys who had been burglarizing wealthy homes.

A police officer from the Juvenile Police Department came to interview Jack.

May 12, 19—: The boys' worker reported that Jack is more friendly in his manner than ever before. I tried to see him in the morning but he was still sleeping so he had lunch on a tray.

Interview, 2:30 P.M.: Jack seemed to be feeling very much better and his hair was slicked up. He said he would like to go into the group because he is "all slept up now."

Later in the afternoon Jack had a cigarette with Harry. Jack began by saying, "Boy, I'm never going to run away from here again." (Jack, you worry me when you start talking that way. That's what you said last time you were here.) "Did I talk about running away last time?" (You kept saying you never would run away. That's why you worry me.) "I don't blame you any. You don't need to let me go out of doors if you don't think you can trust me." (What do you think? Can I trust you?) "It is up to you whether or not you let me go out." (But what do you think I should do about it?) "I promise you I won't run away."

Then Harry began to talk about how they treat kids in the X-city Detention Home. He said, "They sure treat kids here better than they deserve." Jack talked about how terrible it used to be when Mr. P was here. Then he asked about Lloyd. I told him Lloyd had given himself up at the jail, had been held there a week, had his trial, and was then released to his father to get a job. Jack said, "I sure wish I could have a job, but I bet they won't let me. (What do you think is going to happen?) "If they send me to the Industrial School, it will be my own fault I know that. Last night I realized my mother and father were my best friends in this world. When I was out I didn't know that."

May 13, 19—: Jack is getting into all kinds of trouble today. He fooled with the girls too intimately, teased William until he cried, and used a razor, which he had sneaked from the shop, to enlarge a hole in his door. Both the teacher and the boys' worker reported that Jack was the center of difficulty in the group. After lunch I asked to see him and gave him his cigarette while we talked. (At lunchtime Jack had been overheard saying, "If I could have all the cigarettes I wanted, even half a pack a day, I could stay here for the rest of my life.")

Interview, 2 P.M.: I asked Jack what the trouble this morning was about. He asked if I meant the little boy who cried. (That and other things.) He started to tell me about William. "William tries to make out he is better than other guys. He tries to run the place." Jack thinks he was like that when he came in the first time but now he knows better. "All the guys in here are the same and one isn't better than the other. Jack doesn't mind saying that he doesn't like William but he didn't do nothing to him. When William got hit in the eye, Jack followed him to see what was the matter, and William wouldn't let him in the bathroom. William was crying." About the girls—they were just horsing around, having a good time. Of course, the girls had asked him to tell them some stories about the first World War during the keep-away game. "You wouldn't be getting the wrong ideas, would you?" I said, "I had a good view of what was going on." (I had walked into the mat room during the school program when the boys and girls were playing keep-away at a time when Jack was mauling one of the girls.)

About shaving the door—"I didn't think I was doing anything wrong. I just wanted to talk to the other guys, so I made the hole bigger." (You knew you weren't supposed to have a razor up there.) "No, m'am." (Jack, you and I seem to have different ideas about what is a good way to act. Why do you do all these things? Throw clay, and shave doors? Are they fun? Or do you like to make us mad?) "No, m'am. I just don't think when I am doing it that I am doing anything wrong. It just doesn't come to mind."

About Delbert and Jack getting off in corners by themselves—"We were just talking. We aren't planning no escape." I said, "Jack, I am not asking you to fix up stories for me. I am not saying, 'Jack is a bad boy and has to be locked up,' but I am curious. Twice it has happened that we have had a bunch of guys who were getting along with us pretty well and then when you go into the group, all of a sudden they are all mad at us and don't get along well. What happens?" Jack said, "Do you think I do all of it?" (No, but I do wonder what it is when twice this kind of thing happens when you go into a group.) Well, he didn't know. He thinks, "I and that girl were responsible for William." I interpreted William to him a little. (He is smaller than you and he has had some hard breaks. Maybe you could help him.)

I asked Jack if he felt he could be more careful of property. He would try. I said I thought he should do a repair job to make up for the destruction he had caused. He asked if that meant he couldn't go out of doors today. I said I would check with the superintendent about that but that the work could be done after 3 P.M. Not necessarily during play period.

I told the superintendent that I felt we were getting somewhere with Jack and that we should show him some trust while expecting improvement in behavior. There had been more relationship evidences in this interview than ever before. He had looked me straight in the eye and had talked to me some of the time out of his own feelings. He had evidently lied at some points but had given me his picture of things freely, rather than hunting around for what he thought I wanted him to say. Since the other boys' play period was over, the superintendent took Jack out of doors and pitched horseshoes with him.

The boys' worker discovered Jack turning his light off and on after lights-out by poking a piece of his bed through the hole in his door.

May 14, 19—: Jack and Harry got to talking at smoking period. Jack said, "I am sure sorry I ran away from here. I must have worried you folks a lot." He and Harry in a rush of noble feeling decided they were treated just too good here for boys like them.

Later at the ironing period Jack did an excellent job and the worker commented. He said, "I'm trying to learn to be a good ironer so I can help my grandmother. She is eighty-three years old. When I was with her before I came here, I was sure a mean kid. I've been thinking of the things I could do to help her."

Jack stopped me in the hall and asked if he could call his father. He seemed to want to make up with his father and also to know what was being planned for him. I called the court worker and said I felt it might be helpful for Jack to talk to his father at this time, but the court worker refused permission on the basis of lack of cooperation from the parents.

May 15, 19—: Jack asked at smoking period if I thought he could go to No. 9 Pearl. He would like to go there and work and earn money to go back to his grandmother. He also asked if he might be moved in the dorm with the other big fellows. I explained that that would be up to the boys' worker.

The boys' worker reports that Jack is all of a glow with being cooperative and "good."

May 17, 19—: Jack went out to Juvenile Court hearing at 1:30 P.M. At the time I asked him if he had been involved in the cigarette smoking on the day before. He said, "Yes," that he had gotten it from Thomas, whose father had given him a pack during the visiting period. Jack said, "I like it here now. I wish I could stay."

Because most children are held only a few days or weeks in a detention home, little systematic, academic, or technical education and personality adjustment is possible. The children are of different age groups. Most of them are sent home or are placed in a foster home or another children's institution before they get well acquainted with the detention home staff.

An accepting, friendly attitude of the staff toward the child sometimes is able to break through the fearful, resentful, hostile, emotional defense which most children bring to the detention home when they are arrested. The establishment of a contact between the child and the caseworker, group worker, or counselor may be the beginning of a treatment process. An intensive influence on corrective adjustment of the child can seldom be exercised during such a short period. But the child is protected against destructive influences, is well cared for physically, and the family and society are protected against the child's delinquent actions for the period of detention. Whenever the child feels that the staff takes a sincere interest in his well-being and is willing to help him, a start in his adjustment is made in the detention home.

IV. JUVENILE COURT PROCEDURE

A major characteristic of the juvenile court procedure is the social investigation, conducted by the probation officer attached to the juvenile court. It supplies the data for an understanding of the personality of the young offender, his family, social and economic conditions, the motive of the offense in order to determine the plan for treatment and rehabilitation. The probation officer will clear with the Social Service Exchange (see Chapter 21) whether the family is known to social agencies so that essential facts about the family and the behavior of the child may be incorporated into the investigation.

The probation officer needs knowledge of human behavior and personality for his interview with the child and his family. It is not easy to find contact with delinquent children because they frequently carry over toward the police, the probation officer, and social worker their resentments against their parents or against authority in general, which may have failed to recognize the child's needs. The delinquent child also is often unable to deal directly with his problems and avoids revealing too much to adults. Sometimes he has been hurt by others and has been inconsistently treated by his parents or teachers. Then the child is distrustful and fears being betrayed and punished. To cover this fear, delinquent children cloak themselves with an air of reckless bravery and of callous hardness.[14] In cases of juvenile delinquents, the probation officer, as a rule, will have to make a home call to see the youngster and his family. He will not wait until the youth comes into his office. He studies the nature and circumstances of the offense, former delinquencies of the child, the family background with analysis of personal, educational, and economic conditions, the question of employment, housing and moral conditions, as well as the health status of the child and of the family. In the child's history his relation to parents, siblings, and neighbors; personality traits, conduct, and behavior, the physical and emotional effect of illness, his religious and school experiences; his work records, recreational activities, and his outlook for the future need explanation. The probation officer evaluates these data under consideration of the cultural and social conditions in which the youngster is living and presents his recommendations to the court with the aim in view of finding measures which will be most helpful to the child. Physical as well as mental examinations of the young offender are desirable to interpret his personality. Mental tests by a psychologist or a psychiatric diagnosis are dependent upon local facilities available to the juvenile court. A large number of different psychological tests may be used in order to explain the child's intelligence, the areas of his maladjustment, and the possibilities of rehabilitation and adjustment.[15]

The National Probation and Parole Association recommends the following standards for the juvenile court:

1. Exclusive jurisdiction of the juvenile court over delinquencies of children, and jurisdiction over adults in children's cases.
2. A judge chosen for his sympathetic understanding of children and parents.

---

[14] National Social Welfare Assembly, "Juvenile Delinquency and the Relationship of the Police to Social Agencies" (New York: 1953); and N. Teeters and J. Reinemann, *op. cit.*, pp. 319-328.

[15] See N. Teeters and J. Reinemann, *op. cit.*, pp. 268-273, and pp. 319-336.

3. Private, friendly court hearings and informal, noncriminal procedure.
4. A sufficient number of professionally trained probation officers, both men and women.
5. Facilities for physical examinations and for psychiatric study of problem children.
6. A well-equipped detention home, or selected boarding homes for temporary care of children.
7. An efficient record and statistical system, and adequate clerical help.
8. Cooperation with other agencies and community support through interpretation of the court's function to the public.

Juvenile courts frequently dispose of minor cases of delinquency informally without filing a petition, without preparing a court record, and without a court hearing being held. The arrangement of such an informal adjustment may be assigned to a probation officer, the chief probation officer, or to a referee by the judge, sometimes even to a juvenile bureau or crime prevention division of the local police department.[16] At the court hearing often the child meets the judge of the juvenile court for the first time. The meeting should be dignified, but free from judicial technicalities which frighten the child and his parents. The court hearing is centered around the questions of why the child has become delinquent and what measures may be most effective in preventing further delinquencies and in assisting the child in his readjustment. The establishment of the facts of the specific delinquency is less relevant.

As a rule, the juvenile court hearing is private; the general public and the press are excluded. The presence of spectators is harmful to the youngster because in an open court hearing he either finds himself the center of attraction and is inclined to act as a hero, therefore appearing tough and nonrepentent, or he risks losing the respect of his fellows and neighbors by showing regret of his behavior. The parents of the child, necessary witnesses, and the probation officer are present; representatives of social agencies and of the school authorities may be admitted. The atmosphere of the court hearing should create confidence in the child and his parents that the judge is willing to help them in the solution of the youth's problems.

[16] J. Ellingston, *op. cit.*, pp. 214-215; and Alfred J. Kahn, *A Court for Children* (New York: Columbia University Press, 1953).

The disposition of the juvenile court may be one of the following measures:

1. The child may be placed with a reprimand of the judge under supervision of his parents in his own home.
2. The child may be placed on probation.
3. The child may be taken away from his own home and be placed in a foster family, either through a social agency or under the auspices of the juvenile court.
4. The judge may order the medical or psychiatric examination of the child and place the child for this purpose in a hospital, a children's institution, or a suitable family.
5. The judge may order the commitment of the child to the custody and guardianship of a public or private social agency or children's institution, frequently of a "training school" or "industrial school."
6. The judge may order restitution or reparation of damage caused by the child's delinquency.

The adjudication in juvenile court is not a penal conviction of the child and does not constitute a criminal record. However, many juvenile court laws have not yet statutory provisions to the effect that the disposition of the juvenile court shall not disqualify the young person in any future civil service appointment.

The decision of a criminal court against an adult offender may be changed only by another sentence of an appellate court, but the disposition of the juvenile court may be modified by the judge according to the needs of the child. The right to appeal the decree of the juvenile court to an appellate court is limited in several state laws to questions of law, errors of fact, or certain decisions, such as commitment to a training school or removal from the custody of the parents.

In a few instances adolescent courts or boys' courts have been established in order to separate the trial and treatment of young persons between seventeen and twenty-one years of age from that of adult offenders.[17] The development of adolescent courts has been hampered by a hostile attitude of the public toward a mild or "sentimental" treatment of nearly adult offenders.

[17] N. Teeters and J. Reinemann, *op. cit.*, pp. 328-333, and 344-354; see also Clyde B. Vedder, *The Juvenile Offender* (New York: Doubleday, 1954).

V. PROBATION

"Probation is a process of treatment, prescribed by the court for persons convicted of offenses against the law, during which the individual on probation lives in the community and regulates his own life under conditions imposed by the court (or other constituted authority) and is subject to supervision by a probation officer."[18]

Characteristic of probation, therefore, is the postponement of either the final judgment or the postponement of the execution of the sentence combined with certain conditions imposed by the court, under the guidance and supervision of the probation officer. In practice it is not uncommon that an adult offender is ordered first to serve a certain period in jail or prison and then, under suspension of sentence, to live in the community on condition of good behavior during a period of freedom under supervision. For juvenile delinquents the probation order of the juvenile court allows the youth to live at liberty in his own home or in the custody of a relative, friend, foster parents, or under supervision of the probation officer, instead of a commitment to a correctional institution or training school.[19]

The social elements of probation are threefold: (1) Probation permits the probationer to live a normal life in the community and to readjust to socially acceptable attitudes without being confined, during this period, to a penal or correctional institution; (2) it is granted on the basis of a social investigation by the court on the assumption that the probationer will be able to live a lawful life and may be expected to do so; and (3) it is a process of adjustment through the supervision of a probation officer.

Probation has its legal background in the authority of the court under common law to suspend sentence and to allow the convicted offender to remain at liberty upon condition of good behavior. As a practical method, probation was introduced in the United States as early as 1841 by John Augustus, a Boston shoemaker. He pro-

[18] National Commission on Law Observance and Law Enforcement, *Penal Institutions, Probation and Parole* (Report No. 9, Wickersham Report), 1931, p. 184.

[19] John Otto Reinemann, "Probation and the Juvenile Delinquent," *The Annals of the American Academy of Political and Social Science*, Vol. 261, January, 1949, p. 109; in English common law, probation may be traced to the institution of formal "recognisance," an obligation entered before the court to keep the peace.

vided bail for a poor drunkard who was threatened to be sentenced to the house of correction, and assumed his supervision during a period of "probation." John Augustus, encouraged through the success of his first case, continued to bail, supervise, and assist about 2,000 adults and juveniles until his death in 1859. He also advocated the establishment of an asylum for the treatment of alcoholics.

The first probation law for adult offenders was enacted in 1878, in Massachusetts, and by 1950, forty-two states and the District of Columbia had such probation laws, as well as the federal judiciary system.[20]

The use of probation varies between the states and even among the individual courts. As a treatment, probation is not just leniency, but it is treatment of an offender through supervision in the general community. The cost of probation is only a small fraction of that of institutional commitment. Its advantages are as follows: The probationer remains in his home; his social status is not impaired; he continues to support himself and his family; he is able to pay restitution to the victim of the offense; and he may be rehabilitated with the aid of the probation officer, under use of the resources of the community while his probation status discourages new offenses.

Probation for juvenile delinquents has the same advantages, permits individual casework with the young person, and leaves the child in his normal home. It enables adjustment through preventative and protective services of the local community, avoids the stigma of correctional or training schools, and is much less expensive than institutional commitment.

Condition for an effective probation system is the employment of skilled social workers trained in casework, in the use of community resources, in understanding the behavior of juvenile and adult offenders, and in the necessary cooperation with psychiatrists and psychologists. During recent years standards for probation officers have risen, and in some states civil service requirements and merit systems have been set up. Much still remains to be done.[21]

---

[20] N. Teeters and J. Reinemann, *op. cit.*, pp. 384-386, 391. In 1952, there were 3,716 local probation and parole officers employed for the supervision of juveniles in the United States. Not all of them, however, work full time as probation officers. About one-half of the counties in the United States still have no juvenile probation service.

[21] N. Teeters and J. Reinemann, *op. cit.*, pp. 389-390; Miriam Van Waters, "Adult Offenders," *Social Work Year Book, 1951,* pp. 35-44, particularly pp. 39-40.

Usually the probation service is attached to the court, and the appointment of the probation officers is made by the judge. But there are some recent exceptions when the probation service is established as an independent agency, such as the Los Angeles County Probation Department, or on a state-wide level, such as the California Youth Authority, the Youth Conservation Commission in Minnesota, the Youth Service Commission in Wisconsin, the State Department of Correction in New York, and the State Department of Public Assistance (Division of Child Welfare) in West Virginia.[22]

The probation officer begins with a social investigation in the case of a juvenile court hearing, but for the criminal court the investigation, as a rule, is ordered only after a verdict of guilty is rendered against the adult offender, particularly if the judge is considering not sending the offender to a penal institution. The investigation requires that the probation officer understand the motivations, feelings, and attitudes of the offender, and the influences which the neighborhood, gangs, and other elements may have had on his behavior. The probation officer cannot apply his own standards of life and morals to the offender; his function is to help a person who has got into trouble with the law. He will consider the offender's personality, his physiological equipment, his mental and intellectual capacities, life experiences, cultural background, and setting.

When the probation officer interviews the young person, he gives him a chance to express his difficulties, and discuss his social and personal situation. The probation officer explores with him possibilities of changes in work, environment, or social relations, and the joining of church or group activities which may be helpful in his adjustment. In presenting data on the young delinquent collected in the family, school, and neighborhood, the probation officer has to distinguish between objective facts and his own interpretation of the situation and of the young offender's personality.

For juvenile delinquents, as well as for adult offenders, the probation officer recommends probation to the court only if he is convinced that the offender will be able to use it constructively for his adjustment. If he feels that the offender is not ready to adjust himself in the community, he suggests commitment to an institution.

After the court has placed an adult offender or a juvenile delinquent under probation, the probation officer supervises him as a

---

[22] N. Teeters and J. Reinemann, *op. cit.*, pp. 392-394.

helping service, but under the authority of the court. Whether it is good practice to have the same probation officer carry out the social investigation and the supervision, or whether these two main activities should be separated and assigned to different groups of probation officers, has been the subject of discussion.[23]

In general, girls' supervision and often that of boys under twelve years of age is assigned to women probation officers, and cases of boys over twelve years of age to men. The regional principle that a certain geographical area is assigned to the individual probation officer who supervises the children and young persons in this area is considered economical and practical.

The probation officer recognizes the positive possibilities of authority and its implications for the probationer. He knows that this authoritative element is a necessary function of the judiciary system and of the probation process. On the other hand, he should be free of the traditional feeling of vindictiveness and moral superiority toward the probationer, which would prevent him from objectively interpreting the court decision and the meaning of probation to the probationer in a way which is acceptable to him. He will explain that the court's requirements, such as making regular reports to the probation officer or to the court, planning permanent work, and avoiding drugs and excessive drinking, have to be strictly followed. The probation officer will make it clear that the probationer is free to use his help, but that the responsibility for complying with these court orders is his own, and that it depends upon his attitude and behavior whether the probation process is successfully completed. During this period the probation officer assists the probationer in his personal, emotional difficulties as well as in environmental matters, housing, employment, schooling, and group and cultural relations. Despite the authoritative element in probation, the probation officer should not direct the life of the probationer, depriving him of the responsibility for his decisions.

The probationer has to be educated to make decisions and to assume responsibility without shifting it back to the probation officer, who will not always supervise his life. The relationship between

[23] Walter C. Reckless, "Significant Trends in the Treatment of Crime and Delinquency," *Federal Probation*, March, 1949, pp. 6-11; N. Teeters and J. Reinemann, *op. cit.*, pp. 400-401; and Jay Rumnay and Joseph P. Murphy, *Probation and Social Adjustment* (New Brunswick, N.J.: Rutgers University Press, 1952).

probation officer and probationer must be based upon mutual understanding, respect, sincerity, and confidence, which are possible in
the sphere of authority that is a part of the court's jurisdiction. Rev-
ocation of probation will be recommended by the probation officer if he is convinced that the probationer cannot profit from a
continuation of the probation service, and if he violates the rules of
probation so seriously that institutional treatment seems necessary.
However, the probation officer should be well aware that failure of
probation should not be caused by his own inability to find the
right contact with the probationer or to mobilize other resources
of the community, because such reasons would not justify the rev-
ocation of probation.[24] The support of the community is badly
needed for the probation service.

VI. TRAINING SCHOOLS

Children and adolescents who are not granted probation by a juvenile court because their adjustment cannot be achieved in their own
home or in a foster family are committed to a "training school," frequently also called "industrial school" or "reform school."[25] The
first local school of this type in the United States was the New
York City House of Refuge, founded in 1825 by the Society for
Reformation of Juvenile Delinquents, in order to save neglected,
idle, vagrant, and delinquent children from the vicious influence of
the adult prisons.[26] Other schools in Boston, Philadelphia, and New
Orleans followed, but it was only in 1847 that the first state reform
school was established in Massachusetts. Since this time, the number
of training schools has greatly increased. There were, in 1951, 210
national, state, and local public training schools and 140 private
training schools providing care for dependent, neglected, truant,

---

[24] Arthur Fink, *The Field of Social Work* (New York: Holt, 1949), pp. 389-
400; N. Teeters and J. Reinemann, *op. cit.*, pp. 418-422; and Sara G. Geiger,
"Counseling Techniques in Probation Work," *Federal Probation*, March, 1954,
pp. 26-32.

[25] Though the terminology is not unanimously accepted, we want to speak of
"reformatories" only as penal institutions for young offenders sentenced by
the criminal court, or prisons for adult offenders sentenced for the first time.
Some schools for truant children are called "parental schools."

[26] The inspiration for this concept of child protection had been given by
Professor John Griscom, a Quaker, who had studied the work of Johann Hein-
rich Pestalozzi in Switzerland and Jean Frederic Oberlin (N. Teeters and J.
Reinemann, *op. cit.*, pp. 429-431).

and delinquent children and youths ranging from six to twenty-one years of age.

Some of these institutions have maintained certain practices of the former prisons from which the schools were separated long ago, such as mass treatment, a repressive attitude, and even corporal punishment. Others offer little more than physical and custodial care; they accept the widespread opinion that the school is the place where troublesome and disturbing children may be removed to, primarily for the safety of the population of their home community, and that such children and adolescents should be controlled in the school by the denial of their liberty, enforcement of some general education and vocational training, and strict regulation of their activities. A third type of training school, however, has developed an integrated program of rehabilitation for these children and youths by providing a positive plan for group living under educational guidance. They provide medical and mental health supervision, spiritual, religious, academic and vocational training, recreation, and leisure-time activities, permitting as much of freedom and choice as possible. This type of school still represents a controlled environment in which the children have to accept limitations in their freedom and have to conform to the rules of group living, but they contribute to a constructive development of the children and prepare them for the return to life with their family or in their home community.[27]

Only the last type of training school will achieve a real change of personality and rehabilitation in children and adolescents committed to the school. Many schools suffer from their geographical isolation, which makes it difficult to teach the children how to live in a normal community, how to get along with other groups, how to participate in community activities, and how to use recreational, library, and health services outside the school. The isolation also makes it difficult to use for education other sources of the community, such as workshops, schools, youth centers, and health services, and to find competent personnel interested in professional growth and in the adjustment of young persons. On the other hand, there often is pressure of the population to remove training schools, particularly for older, aggressive boys, from the metropolitan cen-

---

[27] N. Teeters and J. Reinemann, *op. cit.*, pp. 449-408; and J. Ellingston, *op. cit.*, pp. 127-134 and 146-152.

ters in order to protect themselves from new dangers by escapees. In the interest of the readjustment of difficult and disturbed children, the purpose of protection of the community should be considered only of secondary importance, and the construction of new schools in isolated regions should be abandoned.

The diversity of children in their ages, character, physical and mental abilities, and in their various social, psychological, and behavior problems presents a difficult task for institutions of which the majority still are large schools. Most of them are no longer prison-like buildings with huge dormitories, but are organized according to the "cottage system" into small units of about fifteen to twenty-five children in a separate building under the guidance of "cottage parents" or a "cottage mother." But it is still difficult for them to set up and carry on an effective program of individual treatment and adjustment of the children.

One of the main obstacles is the lack of trained and competent personnel. There are yet, in many institutions, employees who have no proper training for their challenging job—former guards in jails or custodians without educational background or skill. Others, however, are well prepared by education, studies, and experience in child development, social work, and psychology to work with children in need of understanding and readjustment. There is in many training schools a trend toward the selection of a superintendent and staff with the point of view of finding really qualified persons who as a team will be able to help the children to overcome the difficulties in personality and behavior which brought them into the training school. There are still other training schools so reluctant as to discourage objective evaluation of their methods, and investigations of deficiences in their operations. Progressive schools are careful in the selection of qualified staff, in the orientation of new workers, and in establishing in-service training programs for the improvement of the services of the school.[28]

After-care (or post-institutional care or parole) is an important factor for securing the effect of the institutional treatment of children and adolescents in training schools because, as a rule, they return to homes and neighborhoods which are far from ideal. There

[28] N. Teeters and J. Reinemann, *op. cit.,* pp. 450-451; see also Albert Deutsch, *Our Rejected Children* (Boston: Little, 1950), which describes conditions in many training schools, good and bad.

is no full agreement as to who should be responsible for after-care, what the content and procedure of after-care should be, and what training is necessary for this service, nor are there, in general, sufficient funds available. After-care might be carried on by a parole officer of the training school, or by a state-wide central after-care agency for released children and adolescents, or by a child or family casework agency in the local community. Of utmost importance is also the employment of well-trained and qualified personnel, which is possible only if adequate salaries, professional in-service training, and possibilities of promotion are secured.[29]

VII. YOUTH CORRECTION AUTHORITIES

After World War I, widespread juvenile delinquency had aroused the interest and concern of many legislators, judges, social workers, and sociologists. In New York, a study by Leonard V. Harrison and Pryor McNeill Grant, *Youth in the Toils*, published in 1938, criticized the destructive effect of committing adolescent youth with hardened adult criminals in reformatories and prisons. In lieu of retributive punishment, which had failed, the American Law Institute, composed of outstanding lawyers, criminologists, and judges, suggested a new approach in educating and treating youthful offenders. It published in 1940 a model *Youth Correction Authority Act*, proposing that the state legislatures establish preventive protection and correctional treatment of young offenders. The American Law Institute suggested that a Youth Correction Authority in the state should coordinate all facilities in educational, medical, and rehabilitation work for juvenile delinquents carried on in social agencies, children's institutions, training schools, clinics, and hospitals. Whenever necessary, the authority itself should establish and operate detention homes, observation clinics, and corrective institutions.

The first state to write the suggestion of the American Law Institute into law was California. In 1941, the legislature enacted the Youth Correction Authority Act, which embodied all essential features of the model act.[30] Professor August Vollmer of the University

[29] Richard Clendenen, "After the Training School—What?" (Washington, D.C.: U.S. Children's Bureau, 1950).

[30] An analysis of the development of the California Youth Authority and its operation is presented in J. Ellingston, *op. cit.*, pp. 55-345; and N. Teeters and J. Reinemann, *op. cit.*, pp. 354-368.

of California, president of the California Prison Association, was mainly responsible for this legislative action. It had been prepared by a citizens' conference, invited by the California Prison Association, in which legislators, educators, police officers, judges, club-women, and social workers took part. In 1943, the name of the organization was changed to "Youth Authority." It was authorized to offer consultation services to local communities, conduct research on the causes of juvenile delinquency, and develop preventive services, diagnostic and treatment facilities.

One of the Youth Authority's major objectives is to protect society more effectively against the danger of crime by substituting for the old unsuccessful methods of retribution and punishment measures of education, correction, and rehabilitation of young offenders. The other major objective is prevention of new delinquency.

The first program of rehabilitation begins with a clinical diagnosis in several reception centers of all young offenders referred to the Youth Authority by the juvenile courts. Studies by a physician, dentist, psychiatrist, psychologist, social worker, and teacher obtain an understanding of the personality and motives of the adolescent, and of the factors which brought the young person to his antisocial action. On the basis of clinical observation, the youngster then is classified according to his age, sex, mental capacities, emotional stability, aptitudes, and personal interests, and the treatment is determined upon these factors. The subsequent therapy and adjustment is carried on under a specialized program of re-education and work assignments which is formulated to meet the individual needs and capacities of the youth. After adjustment of the young person in a selected institution is achieved, parole supervision is provided with careful preparation of the adolescent's return to his family or to the community. Before the release of the young offender, the Youth Authority contacts his family, his employer, and sometimes other people in the community to insure his acceptance when he returns. Parole service offers positive guidance for the young offender in the beginning of his new life in the community.

The second objective, delinquency prevention, is pursued by the systematic development of facilities for sports, recreation, and leisure-time activities for children and young persons on the community level. The program includes the establishment or improvement of probation departments, police juvenile bureaus, and detention homes (in California called "juvenile halls") in order to secure services for children and adolescents who get into trouble. Another aspect of the preventive activities is the creation of community councils and similar civic groups for the coordination of the various social services to youth. Youth groups are invited to take the initiative to participate in recreation work in community and youth centers and other constructive culural group action.

The California Youth Authority is headed by a board of three members appointed by the governor with approval of the Senate for overlapping four year terms.[31] The Board is responsible for the decision on classification and assignment to the desirable school, and on release and parole of young offenders. Under the Board of the Authority a Division of Diagnosis and Classification administers clinics for observation of the young offender, his classification, and commitment to the best-suited institution. The Division of Training and Treatment administers the various training schools and camps to which the youngster is referred for education, vocational training, and adjustment.

The Youth Authority succeeded in decreasing the large numbers of young offenders who formerly overcrowded the various correctional schools of the state and in establishing special smaller schools and forestry camps for the different age groups, with consideration of their character and behavior problems. Classification considers maturity, behavior, and vocational and personal aptitudes of the children. The necessary isolation of children in correctional schools is alleviated by contacts with the surrounding communities so that the children are prepared for their return to the family. Forestry camps for older boys acquaint the youngster with normal work habits in forestry projects, forest fire and blister rust control, road construction, and lumber mill work. Younger boys are placed in several ranch schools whose program is applied to the needs of their age, including instruction in farming and animal husbandry.

The number of girls with delinquency records is, in California as in other states, much smaller. In the schools, the girls are divided according to age groups; special techniques are used for adjusting mentally retarded children. Recreation, art craft, and hobby programs supplement vocational and social adjustment in class work.

---

[31] Two members are appointed from a list proposed by the presidents of the various professional organizations, the third at the discretion of the governor.

Home making, garden work, and housekeeping are used as teaching objects, but gifted girls are encouraged to prepare themselves for higher education. Free medical and dental care are included in the program.

The Division of Field Services is in charge of delinquency prevention and parole. The Delinquency Prevention Section assists the communities in their efforts to prevent and to reduce juvenile delinquency. Preventive work is more effective than punishment, but it has to be done on the local level in the community and neighborhood. The Youth Authority encourages community programs of social agencies, civic groups, youth groups, and individuals for attractive sports and recreation, which divert youth from criminal actions. Consultants are sent to the counties to help in the coordination of recreational facilities with detention homes and juvenile control.

The Youth Authority Board has the final decision for the release of the youngster, but the Parole Section prepares the return to the community by securing in advance a job in business, industry, or agriculture, an apprentice position, or the possibility of entering school. If the family is not able to take the youth back, a foster home might be necessary. After the return of the adolescent, the parole officer of the Division of Field Services is responsible for counsel, advice, and supervision until discharge of the youth from parole. Sometimes a return to one of the institutions of the Youth Authority for further education and training is necessary.

In its activities the California Youth Authority is assisted by an advisory committee of lay citizens apointed by the governor. The Authority has arranged numerous conferences, meetings, and workshops on youth welfare and delinquency prevention throughout the state in cooperation with universities and civic groups. In its legal structure the Youth Authority Board is part of the State Board of Corrections and therefore participates in the program of fighting crime and delinquency.

The integrated program of the California Youth Authority has demonstrated substantial gains. It has resulted in broader public understanding of the modern concept of rehabilitation of maladjusted youth, in a wider unification of correctional facilities in the communities, the counties, and the state, and in a cooperative, working relationship between the Youth Authority, the juvenile courts, detention homes, county probation departments, law enforcement agencies, social agencies, and civic groups.

But California is not the only state which has assumed broad centralized responsibility for prevention and treatment of juvenile delinquency. Similar arrangements have been made in Minnesota by the creation of the Youth Conservation Commission in 1947, and in Wisconsin by the establishment of the Youth Service Commission in the same year under the Department of Public Welfare. In Massachusetts, the Youth Service Board deals with offenders of juvenile court age, and Texas formed in 1949 a State Youth Development Council to conduct research and administer state institutions for delinquent children. It seems that the advantages of a united state authority in the field of juvenile delinquency are becoming recognized. But it might be seriously considered whether such state agencies would not be even more effective if they were coordinated under the Child Welfare Division of the state's Department of Public Welfare. Such an organization could use all the facilities in the field of child welfare and maintain the contact with counties and communities without being limited to the specific field of juvenile delinquency.

VIII. DELINQUENCY PREVENTION
AND CONTROL

During the past decades the knowledge of the variety of delinquency causes has grown and proved the necessity that people in the community must understand that children are not "born to become criminals." We have seen that the causes of delinquency are complex and variable. They may be classified into three groups: individual factors, home factors, and neighborhood factors.[32]

Among the individual factors which lead a child into difficulties are biological conditions, such as glandular disorders, physical handicaps, and biological weakness, conducive to abnormal development or behavior. Mentally retarded children and youth below average intelligence and psychopathic, nervous, unpredictable, and irresponsible adolescents easily fall prey to asocial actions, and the mentally ill may endanger themselves and others. A third set of individual

[32] Charlotte Elmott, *Aspects of a Community Program for Delinquency Control and Youth Protection* (Sacramento: California Youth Authority, 1945); and J. Ellingston, *op. cit.*, pp. 337-342.

factors leading to delinquent behavior are emotional instabilities caused by inferiority complexes, inner conflicts, temperamental disorders, and sex abnormalities. A fourth section is early childhood habits which create anxieties, truancy, run-away tendencies, and the abuse of alcohol or narcotic drugs.

Influences of family and home life are a second group of factors leading to crime. They include the disorganized, divorced, or separated family in which children are mistreated or neglected; illegitimate children growing up without love and proper care are also a part of this group. Families with quarreling, disunited parents who are in disagreement about education and discipline; living in inadequate housing without sufficient privacy for the members of the family; with the lack of leisure time and recreation, and with too heavy work and responsibilities make children tired or rebellious and drive them into the streets. Other causes of conflict in the family are the differences of values and customs between the generations, particularly of parents of foreign descent, and the lack of spiritual and religious attachment to a church or an ethical philosophy.

The third group of neighborhood factors is particularly dangerous in "blighted areas" where the "gang hero" easily becomes the model for young children and where "street corner associations" are the rule. The examples of drunkenness, vice, and adult crime influence the young. In rural regions the lack of healthy recreation and of a community center may induce youths to make the "highway night spot" their gathering place with gamblers, prostitutes, and other dubious acquaintances. In such neighborhoods, schools and churches should open their meeting halls and playgrounds for sports, recreational, and cultural activities; youth organizations and citizens' groups should assume the responsibility for carrying on these programs. Harmful commercial amusements appealing to sexual drives of adolescents, unsupervised dance halls where teen-agers and adults mix and where liquor is sold, and certain obscene movies, magazines, and books will bring youths into troublesome adventures. Other neighborhood factors contributing to juvenile delinquency are neglect of child labor legislation, inducement of truancy, and general lawlessness in the community.

To counteract these dangers which lead youths to crime, a wholehearted teamwork of public and private agencies devoted to the task of crime prevention is necessary. These include schools, churches, parent-teachers associations, youth organizations, group work agencies (such as YMCA, YWCA, YMHA, boy scouts, girl scouts, and boys clubs), probation officers of the juvenile court, social workers, and policewomen and officers of juvenile bureaus of police departments.[33] If all the members of these groups assist parents and guardians in locating difficult children in danger of maladjustment, in recognizing early symptoms of unhappiness, conflict, and insecurity, help can be found.

Careful training of members and staffs of all organizations concerned with delinquency control is essential in order to enable them to recognize the danger and bring parents and youths in contact with the agency which has the facilities to help them. Child guidance clinics and mental hygiene clinics are important,[34] but frequently diagnostic facilities are at present better developed than urgently needed resources for the treatment of seriously disturbed and maladjusted children.

An effective program of delinquency prevention strengthens the family by conscientious casework of public and private social agencies, education for family living and social hygiene, and counseling. It requires the establishment of wholesome recreational facilities (sports, playgrounds, community centers, concerts, drama, puppet shows), and develops social group work and youth groups. Schools, churches, and other character building agencies should be encouraged to serve underprivileged children of poor areas, and to assist law enforcement agencies, including juvenile police bureaus.

An important part in delinquency control may be taken by newspapers, magazines, radio, television, and motion pictures in interpreting juvenile delinquency in terms of honest reports about causes and protection of youths, rather than stressing the sensational aspects, scandals, and a false heroism in delinquent behavior.

IX. ADULT DELINQUENCY AND SOCIAL WORK

The vast majority of adult offenders sentenced for felonies or minor crimes is kept in prisons or penitentiaries, segregated for years

---

[33] N. Teeters and J. Reinemann, *op. cit.,* pp. 577, 580-582, 600-602, 608-609, 612-621; Thomas A. Rowe, "A Youth Council in Action," *Survey Midmonthly,* December, 1948, p. 361; and Herbert G. Blumer and Philip M. Hauser, *Movies, Delinquency and Crime* (New York: Payne Fund Studies, 1933), p. 17.

[34] See Chapter 13; also C. Elmott, *op. cit.,* pp. 7-13; and N. Teeters and J. Reinemann, *op. cit.,* pp. 575-596.

from normal life and left without responsibility for themselves and their families. Only a minority of younger prisoners is assigned to open institutions, such as prison farms and camps where life is less abnormal and the inmates become accustomed to the return to regular community life, which is the final goal of commitment. In fact, just the opposite distribution would be desirable. Only a small percentage of offenders committed to penal institutions are hardened criminals who have to be kept in prison for the protection of society. Long confinement within prison walls brings the prisoner into a state of mind which makes it rather difficult for him to accept a normal human attitude toward life and toward society, although he is expected to react in this way upon his release from prison. In particular, young offenders, maladjusted or misled by gangs and older fellows, are often bedeviled by hard-boiled criminals in prison whenever they are not strictly separated from such elements, as they are in reformatories. Homosexuality is frequent in many penal institutions, a difficult problem for the administration, which is unable to provide outlets for normal drives of young, vigorous men. Much of the nervous tension, unrest, disorder, or violence is caused by sexual frustration and perversion. Many inmates of prisons attempt to escape from the unbearable situation of hopeless times ahead by withdrawal into daydreaming and fantasies.[35]

The honor system, used in some prisons, permits the offender to move up according to his attitude and cooperation, to live in sections which offer better opportunities to learn self-control, and to get acquainted with the outside community. The prisoner usually is assigned to work in a shop or on a farm similar to the type he will experience after his discharge. With privileges accorded to him based upon his adjustment to social demands, he accepts responsibilities for himself and for his neighbors. Open institutions are still rare, but they begin to adjust the prisoner to normal life and do not foster convicts who desire to go back to prison once they have been released.

The oldest, but most neglected, type of our penal system are the county and city jails, of which there are 3,900 in the United States.

[35] For further study of adult crime and its treatment, see Harry E. Barnes and Negley K. Teeters, *New Horizons in Criminology* (New York: Prentice-Hall, Inc., 1949); Max Grunhut, *Penal Reform, A Comparative Study* (New York: Appleton-Century-Crofts, 1948); and Kenyon J. Scudder, *Prisoners Are People* (New York: Doubleday, 1952).

Courtesy California Adult Authority.

CALIFORNIA STATE PRISON AT SAN QUENTIN

The jail serves as a place of detention (1) for adult offenders after arrest, pending trial or release on bail; (2) for witnesses who otherwise may not appear in court or who have asked for protection before the hearing; (3) for convicted offenders before they are brought to a prison or penitentiary; and (4) for offenders sentenced to jail as place of commitment. About three million citizens annually spend some time in jail.

The basic problems of the jail are threefold: (1) its lack of rehabilitation—its failing to understand and influence the convicted offender and, therefore, to prevent recidivism. It is a widespread experience that many offenders are going to jail and back again. The jail confinement does not deter most adult offenders from new violations of the law, nor does it change their attitudes or behavior; (2) its lack of adequate health facilities, medical and dental care, mental hygiene, and treatment of alcoholism, and the high cost of jail confinement measured against its poor results; (3) the loss of society because of the wasteful burden upon public and private social agencies to support the families of persons confined to jail who could maintain their families.[36]

[36] Ralph M. Kramer, "Suggestions for a Rehabilitation Program in City and County Jails," California East Bay Chapter of the American Association of Social Workers, Berkeley, 1946; see also Myrl E. Alexander, "Let's Look at Our Jails," *Federal Probation*, September, 1952, pp. 14-19.

The emotional situation of a convict is well described in the following excerpt from someone who experienced prison life:

From the very day he enters the county jail or the local prison, the prisoner is subjected to a comi-tragic, well-directed, and ruthless campaign to reduce him to the silent and lowest common level of prisondom. Once reduced, unquestioning obedience to orders and absolute subordination of individuality is the prime essential—that is, unless he has powerful friends, which the average prisoner has not. That such orders may be the spawn of archaic rules makes no difference whatsoever.

He is made to feel from the moment he enters the prison gates that he is an outcast, unclean—that he is but one of so many animals to be counted at certain times of the day and herded into place. He would not be human unless every atom of resentment, every antisocial instinct smouldered in sullen hatred.[37]

Under such circumstances, the usual results of a prison or jail experience are not rehabilitation, readjustment, and change of basic attitude toward society, but a retardation in maturity (like a sense of being suspended in time) and frequently actual regression, because the prisoner experiences the confinement as a replica of the state of child dependency.[38] It is a well-known fact that less than 40 per cent of all major crimes in our country lead to prosecution and arrest of the law offenders, and that only 14 per cent finally are convicted for their crime. For this reason, other means than prison and penitentiary confinement have to be sought in order to solve the social problem of crime. A most stimulating account of the Chino Institution for Men, an open institution for adult offenders that prepares them for the return to the community and to decent civilian life, is given in Kenyon J. Scudder's, *Prisoners Are People*, which is recommended to the reader interested in understanding the prison problem.

The most advanced type of penal institutions is the reformatory, primarily for the reception of young adult male offenders and of offenders sentenced for the first time, and frequently limited to persons up to twenty-five or thirty years of age. The Elmira, New York, reformatory served as the first example for this type of institution, and at present there are one or more reformatories in every

[37] "The Prisoner Speaks," *The Annals of the American Academy of Political and Social Science*, Vol. 157, September, 1931, pp. 138-140.

[38] Robert M. Lindner, *Stone Walls and Men* (New York: Odyssey Press, 1946), pp. 418-422; and K. Scudder, *op. cit.*, pp. 5-6, 273-282.

state. Some of these institutions are built on the cottage plan, permitting individual treatment, but this system is not applied in all states. Several reformatories still are using the cell-block system and mass treatment; to help prevent the inmates from escaping some have watch towers that house sharpshooting guards. Progressive reformatories develop a conscientious program of clinical diagnosis, classification, and systematic adjustment similar to the process of treatment of juvenile delinquents which we discussed, using the example of the California Youth Authority.[39]

One of the essential elements in developing the reformatory to an institution of rehabilitation is to supplement the present technical, industrial facilities by programs for personal adjustment. This avoids herding together many offenders and emphasizes therapy rather than punishment.

Penal institutions of all types are classified according to their construction and their equipment into prisons, penitentiaries, and reformatories of maximum, medium, and minimum security. Most city and county jails, prison farms, and forestry camps are of medium or minimum security type.

Religious services by chaplains are offered in most penal institutions. Frequently the chaplains participate in the classification process and assist in educational activities for the prisoners, library, and counseling.

Most penitentiaries, prisons, and reformatories are equipped with prison industries, including several types of workshops with modern machinery, as well as facilities for agricultural work. Usually the agricultural products and goods manufactured in prison industry are exclusively used for public institutions, such as hospitals, schools, and correctional facilities, in order to avoid competition with "free labor" and private industries on the open market ("state use system").

The modern concept of rehabilitation makes it necessary to give up the outdated approach of retaliation and of punishing the offender to take revenge for his attack against society. Rehabilitation is, in fact, neither punishment nor retaliation, but social adjustment, education, and preparation of the offender for living a normal citizen's life. In order to achieve such re-education, social casework in correctional institutions is indispensable. We recognize that this postu-

[39] N. Teeters and J. Reinemann, *op. cit.*, pp. 521-530, 533-535; and J. Ellingston, *op. cit.*, pp. 98-118.

late has not been achieved in many penal institutions, but at least the need for casework with prisoners is theoretically accepted. Offenders in prison or jail have, in general, a deep need for personal attention and help.

The nature of the penal institution certainly makes individual work with prisoners rather difficult, and it sets definite limits to the personal contact, which is the essential tool of social casework. In spite of these limitations, there are possibilities for individual work with the convict, provided that skilled, competent social workers are available. A number of state prisons and reformatories, and most federal penal institutions, have social service departments with trained personnel, which offer the inmates not only medical care, psychological tests, general education and vocational training, but also social services. These facilities are important for achieving the goal of rehabilitation of the prisoner.

Intelligent wardens and superintendents of penal institutions accept the social worker as a vital part in the team of institutional personnel. There is no doubt that walls and bars of the prison are not conducive for letting the inmate cooperate in counseling and casework. But the social worker in the prison still may function successfully in such an authoritative setting if he is skilled enough to overcome the barriers which are erected by the prison environment. This applies for work with inmates who express the desire to consult the social worker, but also with those who are referred to him by the medical officer, the psychologist, or by the classification clinic, when intensive casework seems necessary.

In fact, the best time for the social worker to make contact with a prisoner is the period when he has just entered the prison or jail. The initial shock of the first day or night in the prison and of meeting with the other inmates, when the prisoner is bewildered and scared, often even hateful of everyone, seems the right time for the social worker to get in touch with him. The social worker will give him a chance to discuss the hard realities of prison life, its possibilities for his future, and its educational and vocational opportunities, limited as they might seem to the prisoner. The social worker has to determine how much help the inmate needs, and whether he is able to use social casework assistance at this time. Frequently the prisoner might hide his real feelings, and the social worker has to understand that he needs time before he is able to take advantage of casework service. The social worker should certainly not overwhelm him with suggestions and offers of assistance until the prisoner is really asking for his service. Sometimes he will need advice and help with specific problems, such as contact with his family, arrangements of obligations he left behind, changes in the prison, assignment to a specific training unit, or transfer to other living quarters.

The main task of the social worker in prison is to help the convict in his own attitude towards his crime, sentence, and confinement. He will try to help him clarify his thinking about his own action, change his attitude toward society, and develop new plans for his future life. In this respect, the social worker might well be helpful in advice about the use of the prison library, vocational training and studies, as well as adaptation to the rules of the prison. He will assist him in maintaining contacts with his family and friends when he needs aid for this purpose.

Finally, the social worker will have a substantial role in preparing the convict for his release and his return to the community. He helps him to take an honest attitude toward prison regulations, toward the request for work, and also attempts to explain to him that an important element for permitting his release is a new outlook toward society and its laws. Often it is difficult for the social worker to convince the prisoner that he himself has the responsibility for his change and readjustment. It is easier for the convict to conform on the surface with official rules, but to remain unchanged in his mind. The social worker tries to bring the prisoner to the insight that a release with chance of success requires a definite improvement of his behavior, which alone results in a positive experience of his confinement to prison.

X. PAROLE

Parole may be defined as the release of a prisoner under supervision before the expiration of his sentence, with the provision that he might be returned to the prison if he violates the conditions of his parole. Whereas probation, as we saw, is a judicial decision of the court, parole is an administrative act usually made either by the parole board or the board of directors of the prison.

Parole was first developed in a convict colony in Australia in 1837, and was adapted in England and Ireland in 1840 under Sir Walter Crofton, the director of the Irish Convict Prisons. In the

United States, the first parole system was introduced at Elmira Reformatory (New York) in 1877, and since that time almost all states have developed programs of parole.

Parole requires that the prisoner be returned to the prison to finish his sentence if he commits a new crime or a technical violation of his parole. Examples are failing to report to the parole officer, changing his job or home, leaving the community without permission of the parole authority, or indicating that he might commit another criminal act.

The decision on parole, which is of such vital importance for the prisoner, should be based upon an impartial, careful investigation of his personality and conduct. It should consider reliable information about the prisoner's background, his life experiences, family and neighborhood, his health, and the situation that will confront him after his release. In preparation of the release, the parole officer tries to ascertain whether the family of the prisoner and his neighbors will welcome him back and assist him in adjusting himself to normal life; he will enlist cooperation of social agencies, or other groups which may help the prisoner in this adjustment, especially in obtaining employment, so that he maintains his self-respect and becomes again part of the community.

The supervision of the released prisoner through the parole officer is a responsible job. The case load of the parole officer should not be too large so as to prohibit conscientious supervision. It requires trained and skilled personnel acquainted with human behavior, social casework, and conditions in correctional institutions, plus having the ability to encourage the parolee to assume responsibility for his life in the community. The parole officer also has to interpret the parolee's situation to the community, and he must be familiar with laws and regulations. At present, many parole officers do not meet these requirements, but it may be hoped that courts and parole authorities will increasingly require adequate education and professional training for parole officers who carry such a heavy responsibility.[40] There has been, during recent years, a tendency to centralize the supervision of the parolees under the various state departments of public welfare or state departments of corrections. A combined parole and probation system has been set up in Florida and Virginia.

[40] Russell G. Oswald, "Correctional Treatment," *Social Work Year Book, 1954*, pp. 135-142; and Kenyon J. Scudder, "Prisons Will Not Solve Our Crime Problem," *Federal Probation*, March, 1954, pp. 32-39.

It is essential for a workable parole system to have parole laws which permit an indeterminate sentence so that the parole authority may set the date and the conditions of parole according to the individual development of the prisoner.

The advantages of parole are that the public receives a better protection through the supervision of the parolee, that it gives the prisoner an incentive for good behavior, and that it sends him into the community with the goal of being a law-abiding citizen, rather than with a score of settling with society. Parole permits a choice as to the time for release when favorable conditions are found and acts as a bridge between the abnormal environment of the segregated prison and life under own responsibility in the community. Parole makes our system of treatment of the offender less expensive than does long detainment in penal institutions and offers an opportunity to correct mistakes and injustices which have happened in judgment.[41]

The particular difficulty of parole lies in the fact that the parolee, after serving part of his sentence in a prison or penetentiary, returns to the community with a great handicap. Family, neighbors, employer, and co-workers learn that he has "served time." In addition to this shame, the parolee is pressed by the threat of being returned to the prison for violation of parole conditions. Sometimes parolees are returned to the prison for minor transgressions, such as forgetting to report to the parole officer, changing a job, drinking, or marrying without special permission. There is some question whether minor violations should not be overlooked by a capable parole officer and the return ordered only if a serious offense is commited. Often parolees are very lonely and looking for companionship. The parole officer assists in finding such connections, but in most instances he has to supervise so many people of different needs that it is hard for him to help the individual efficiently.

There are about 40,000 persons released each year on parole from penal institutions in the United States, and the number who have to be returned to the prison varies between 15 to 40 per cent of this group.[42]

[41] Sanford Bates, *Prisons and Beyond* (New York: Macmillan, 1936), pp. 250-251.
[42] Miriam Van Waters, "Adult Offenders," *Social Work Year Book, 1951*, p. 41; and Frank T. Flynn, "Courts and Social Work," *Social Work Year Book, 1954*, pp. 150-154.

Parole boards are in some states politically appointed. In California, Minnesota, and Wisconsin, the Adult Authority serves at the same time as the parole board; in several other states a single commissioner is in charge of prison policies and parole.

Prisoners under parole or after final discharge are assisted in many larger communities by private organizations which provide casework and usually material assistance. The oldest of these organizations is the Pennsylvania Prison Society. The social workers of these voluntary agencies help the released prisoner, particularly women who have been in prison, by giving counsel, clothes, and financial assistance, and securing employment. Their work frequently includes the re-establishment of constructive relations with the family of the former convict. Private organizations have in this respect the advantage of being less distrusted by the offenders and his family, and being more flexible in their policies of assistance and help.

Prison societies, which sometimes assume a neutral name, such as "Service League," assist in gaining the cooperation of the community to give a hand to the returned prisoner and to offer him a chance for normal work and life. They provide information services and conduct research and studies and participate in suggestions for the improvement of legislation and penal institutions. Especially well known in this reform work is the Osborne Association, which for many years has organized important research and surveys of correctional institutions in the United States; it has stimulated penal legislation of the federal government and the states. The American Prison Association, founded in 1870, also improves by forums, conferences, and professional proposals the standards of our penal institutions. In addition to social workers, probation and parole officers, religious groups and civic organizations advocate further reform of the treatment of the adult offenders and the introduction of methods of effective rehabilitation in our correctional system.

SELECTED BIBLIOGRAPHY

*Aichhorn, August, *Wayward Youth*. New York: Viking Press, Inc., 1935.
Alexander, Franz, and William Healy, *Roots of Crime*. New York: Knopf, 1935.
———, and Hugo Staub, *The Criminal, the Judge, and the Public*. New York: Macmillan, 1931.
Banay, Ralph S., *Youth in Despair*. New York: Coward, 1948.

Barnes, Harry Elmer, and Negley K. Teeters, *New Horizons in Criminology,* 2nd ed. New York: Prentice-Hall, Inc., 1953.
*Bates, Sanford, *Prisons and Beyond.* New York: Macmillan, 1936.
Blumer, Herbert, *Movies, Delinquency, and Crime.* New York: Macmillan, 1933.
Cantor, Nathaniel, *Crime and Society.* New York: Holt, 1939.
Carr, Lowell, *Delinquency Control.* New York: Harper, 1941.
Clemmer, Donald, *The Prison Community.* Boston: Christopher, 1940.
*Cohen, Frank J., *Children in Trouble.* New York: Norton, 1952.
*Deutsch, Albert, *Our Rejected Children.* Boston: Little, 1950.
*Ellingston, John R., *Protecting Our Children from Criminal Careers.* New York: Prentice-Hall, Inc., 1948.
Elmott, Charlotte, *Aspects of a Community Program for Delinquency Control and Youth Protection.* Sacramento: California Youth Authority, 1945.
Flynn, Frank T., "Courts and Social Work," *Social Work Year Book, 1954,* pp. 149-154.
Friedlander, Kate, *The Psycho-Analytical Approach to Juvenile Delinquency.* New York: International Universities Press, 1947.
Fromm, Erich, *Escape from Freedom.* New York: Rinehart & Company, Inc., 1941.
Glueck, Sheldon (editor), *Probation and Criminal Justice.* New York: Macmillan, 1933.
———, and Eleanor T. Glueck, *After-Conduct of Discharged Offenders.* New York: Macmillan, 1945.
———, *Criminal Careers in Retrospect.* New York: Commonwealth Fund, 1943.
———, *Delinquents in the Making; Paths to Prevention.* New York: Harper, 1952.
———, *Juvenile Delinquents Grown Up.* New York: Commonwealth Fund, 1940.
———, *Later Criminal Careers.* New York: Commonwealth Fund, 1937.
———, *One Thousand Juvenile Delinquents.* Cambridge: Harvard University Press, 1934.
———, *Preventing Crime.* New York: McGraw, 1936.
———, *Unraveling Juvenile Delinquency.* New York: Commonwealth Fund, 1950.
*Goldberg, Harriet L., *Child Offenders: A Study in Diagnosis and Treatment.* New York: Grune, 1948.
Harrison, Leonard V., and Pryor McNeill Grant, *Youth in the Toils.* New York: Macmillan, 1938.
Healy, Wiliam, *The Individual Deliinquent.* Boston: Little, 1915.
———, and Benedict S. Alper, *Criminal Youth and the Borstal System.* New York: Commonwealth Fund, 1941.
———, and Augusta F. Bronner, *New Light on Delinquency.* New Haven: Yale University Press, 1936.
———, *et al., Reconstructing Behavior in Youth.* New York: Knopf, 1929.

LaRoe, Wilbur, *Parole with Honor*. Princeton: Princeton University Press, 1939.

Lindner, Robert M., *Rebel Without a Cause*. New York: Grune, 1944.

*———, *Stone Walls and Men*. New York: Odyssey Press, 1946.

Merrill, Maud A., *Problems of Child Delinquency*. Boston: Houghton, 1947.

Midcentury White House Conference on Children and Youth (A Digest of the Fact Finding Report), *A Healthy Personality for Every Child*. Washington, D.C.: Health Publications Institute, 1951.

National Probation Association, *Standard Juvenile Court Law*. New York: 1943.

Norman, Sherwood, and Helen Norman, *Detention for the Juvenile Court*. New York: National Probation Association, 1946.

Panken, Jacob, *The Child Speaks: The Prevention of Juvenile Delinquency*. New York: Holt, 1941.

Pigeon, Helen D., *Probation and Parole in Theory and Practice: A Study Manual*. New York: National Probation Association, 1942.

*———, *et al.*, *Principles and Methods in Dealing with Offenders*. New York: National Probation Association, 1949.

Plant, James S., *Personality and the Cultural Pattern*. New York: Commonwealth Fund, 1937.

*Polier, Justine W., *Everyone's Children: Nobody's Child*. New York: Scribner, 1941.

Porterfield, Austin L., *Youth in Trouble*. Fort Worth: L. Potishman Foundations, 1946.

* Reckless, Walter C., and M. Smith, *Juvenile Delinquency*. New York: McGraw, 1932.

*Redl, Fritz, *Understanding Children's Behavior*. New York: Columbia University Press, 1949.

———, and George Sheviakov, *Discipline for Today's Children and Youth*. Washington, D.C.: National Education Association, 1944.

*———, and David Wineman, *Children Who Hate*. Chicago: Free Press, 1951.

*Reinemann, John Otto, "Probation and the Juvenile Delinquent," *The Annals of the American Academy of Political and Social Science*, Vol. 261, January, 1949, pp. 109-119.

*Scudder, Kenyon T., *Prisoners Are People*. New York, Doubleday, 1952.

Shaw, Clifford R., *The Jack Roller: A Delinquent Boy's Own Story*. Chicago: University of Chicago Press, 1930.

———, *The Natural History of a Delinquent Career*. Chicago: University of Chicago Press, 1931.

———, and H. D. McKay, *Juvenile Delinquency and Urban Areas*. Chicago: University of Chicago Press, 1942.

Tannenbaum, Frank, *Crime and the Community*. New York: Ginn, 1938.

Tappan, Paul, *Contemporary Correction*. New York: McGraw, 1951.

———, *Delinquent Girls in Court*. New York: Columbia University Press, 1947.

————, *Juvenile Delinquency*. New York: McGraw, 1949.

*Teeters, Negley K., and John Otto Reinemann, *The Challenge of Delinquency*. New York: Prentice-Hall, Inc., 1950.

Thom, Douglas A., *Normal Youth and Its Everyday Problems:* New York: Appleton-Century-Crofts, Inc., 1932.

Thurston, Henry W., *Concerning Juvenile Delinquency*. New York: Columbia University Press, 1942.

Van Waters, Miriam, *Youth in Conflict*. New York: Republic Printing Co., 1927.

Wessel, Rosa (editor), *A Casework Approach to Sex Delinquents*. Philadelphia: Pennsylvania School of Social Work, 1947.

Williamson, Margaretta, *The Social Worker in the Prevention and Treatment of Delinquency*. New York: Columbia University Press, 1935.

Wood, Arthur, and John B. Waite, *Crime and Its Treatment*. New York: American Book Co., 1941.

*Young, Pauline V., *Social Treatment in Probation and Delinquency*, 2nd ed. New York: McGraw, 1952.

16. Veterans' Services

Legislation for the welfare of veterans was known in Colonial times. Numerous laws, which were changed after each major war, provided land grants, homestead privileges, medical care, and various types of pensions and monetary grants to veterans, their survivors, and dependents.[1] At present veterans' services have two main goals: (1) to compensate the veteran and his family as much as possible for the sacrifice he has made for his country and to prevent his suffering economic loss from his military service; and (2) to demonstrate to the veteran and his family recognizance of gratitude of the nation for risking life or health in the service.[2]

The first group of measures includes compensation to disabled veterans and to survivors, medical care and hospitalization, vocational rehabilitation, educational aid, and job reinstatement. The second category comprises mustering-out pay, preference in civil service positions, bonuses, priorities in housing, and loans for purchasing of homes, farms, and businesses. Recent emphasis in veterans' services is rehabilitation—helping the veteran to regain his position in the community.

The social and economic benefits granted to veterans and their families may be divided into five categories: (1) medical care, hospitalization, and social services; (2) compensation and pensions to disabled veterans and to survivors of deceased veterans, life insurance, and social insurance benefits protection; (3) education, training, and

[1] The history of veterans services in the United States has been discussed in Chapter 5.

[2] See Eveline M. Burns, *The American Social Security System* (Boston: Houghton, 1949), p. 266; Gustavus A. Weber and Lawrence F. Schmeckebier, *The Veterans Administration* (Washington, D.C.: Brookings Institution, 1934), pp. 4, 5, 320; Omar N. Bradley, "The Veterans' Administration," *National Conference of Social Work, Proceedings, 1946*, pp. 353-359.

vocational rehabilitation; (4) job reinstatement, preferences in civil service positions, and employment services; and (5) economic privileges, including mustering-out pay, readjustment allowance, and loan guarantees for the purchase of a house, a farm, or a business.

There are nearly twenty million veterans (including about 350,000 women), and the veterans' families (together with veterans) make up one-third of our nation. The benefits discussed below have been made available by Public Law 550, in 1952, to veterans who have been serving during the conflict in Korea; there are a few minor modifications for unemployment, educational, and training benefits.

The major part of veterans' benefits is provided by the federal government, because veterans, since the independence of our country, have been the principal group of "federal wards." Our main discussion, therefore, will be concerned with the federal program. But most of the states also have established veterans' departments supplementing the federal aid whose activities are briefly indicated below.

I. MEDICAL CARE, HOSPITALIZATION, AND SOCIAL SERVICES FOR VETERANS

In accordance with the present emphasis of veterans' services on rehabilitation, the federal program provides free hospitalization and medical and dental care to veterans in need of treatment for service-connected illnesses and disabilities.[3] The honorably discharged veteran may be admitted to a Veterans Administration hospital or to another authorized hospital. For nonservice connected illnesses, the veteran may be also admitted to a hospital if he is unable to pay the cost of hospitalization and confirms this under oath, when beds are available. In emergencies immediate hospitalization is granted. The treatment comprises prosthetic and other appliances, chaplaincy, library facilities, recreational activities, rehabilitation, and social services. In 1954, the Veterans Administration operated 159 of its own hospitals, twenty of them for tuberculosis, thirty-five for neuropsychiatric, and one hundred and six for general and surgical treatment. Eighteen hospitals, in addition, were under construction.[4] Vo-

[3] See E. Burns, *op. cit.*, pp. 267-268; and Roger Cumming, "Veterans' Benefits and Services," *Social Work Year Book, 1954*, pp. 521-528.

[4] *Annual Report of Administrator of Veterans Affairs, 1952* (Washington, D.C.: Government Printing Office, 1952), pp. 1-2; and R. Cumming, *op. cit.*, p. 526.

cational training and special rehabilitation centers have been set up for blind, deaf, and hard-of-hearing veterans. Blind veterans also are entitled to seeing-eye dogs and electronic and mechanical equipment; legless veterans to payment up to $1,600 for purchase of a special automobile.

The social worker has the function of helping the veteran in his rehabilitation by enabling him to use to his best advantage the various benefits to which he is especially entitled, and other community resources. Casework with the veteran who is ill or disabled deals with personal and family problems, employment, economic questions—particularly, with his attitude and feelings regarding his handicap, his relationship with others, and questions of his adjustment. The caseworker helps the patient to understand the nature of his illness and treatment, and to face obstacles within himself and in his environment which stand in the way of his rehabilitation. The patient is made familiar with the facilities of occupational and physical therapy, vocational guidance and training, and opportunities in general education. The social worker explains to the patient the doctor's advice and prescriptions regarding medication, proper diet, rest, and life habits and helps him to leave the hospital with confidence in his ability to re-establish himself.

In neuropsychiatric hospitals the psychiatric social worker helps the veteran and his family to become familiar with the nature of his nervous disease, the expectation of length of treatment, and time of discharge. Particularly important here is to make patient and family understand how essential the complete treatment is for the cure and the future life of the veteran.

Domiciliary care in special institutions is available for veterans who, because of their disability, are so severely incapacitated that they are unable to earn a living or are unwilling to live in the community.[5] Veterans in need of medical and dental treatment for service-connected ailments which do not require hospitalization are cared for at outpatient clinics. There they receive medical, psychiatric, and dental treatment and medical supplies and appliances.[6] In order to avoid strenuous travel of veterans and to relieve the crowded hospitals and clinics, Hometown Medical Care Plans have been author-

[5] In 1954, there were seventeen institutions for domiciliary care maintained by the Veterans Administration, three of them separate domiciliary centers, which took care of 17,000 veterans.

[6] There were, in 1954, sixty-four mental hygiene clinics operated by the Veterans Administration for psychoneurotic patients.

ized in most states under which veterans may be treated by private physicians and psychiatrists.

Social services are available to veterans in domiciliary institutions and outpatient clinics, as well as in hospitals. Our American system of veterans' aid is characterized by the fact that large expenditures for veterans will be due when they become old and are in financial need, often forty years and longer after a war.[7]

II. ECONOMIC COMPENSATION FOR DISABLED VETERANS AND THEIR FAMILIES

Compensation for service-connected disabilities for veterans who have lost at least 10 per cent of their earning capacity is based upon degree of wartime disability and period of military service. The monthly compensation ranges from $18 to $190, but additional compensations for severe disabilities, such as blindness, loss of a hand, foot, or eye, permit a monthly compensation of $47 up to a maximum of $440. Veterans with disabilities rated as 50 per cent or more receive additional allowances for a wife, children, and dependent parents. When the veteran dies as a result of the service-connected disability, his widow, children, and dependent parents are also entitled to monthly survivors' compensations. In peacetime all compensation rates are 80 per cent of wartime rates.

For nonservice-connected disabilities a veteran with a permanent and total disability may receive a pension of $100 a month, provided that he is in economic need when his annual income does not exceed $1,400 if he has no dependents, or $2,700 if he is married or has minor children. For regular pension and attendance aid $135 is paid per month. Pensions are also paid to the widow and minor children if need is proved. The difference between compensation and pension lies in the fact that the first is paid for all incapacities and is independent of income and financial status of the veteran, whereas pensions are paid only for total nonservice-connected disability and only to veterans or survivors whose income is lower than a statutory limit.

Veterans of World War I were protected through life insurance ranging from $1,000 to $10,000, and veterans of World War II were entitled to purchase the same amounts by National Service Life In-

[7] See Mildred Maroney "Veterans Benefits" in Lewis Meriam and Karl Schlotterbeck, *The Cost and Financing of Social Security* (Washington, D.C.: Brookings Institution, 1950), pp. 96-97.

surance policies. There are more than six million policies in force; both systems are administered by the Veterans Administration.

Survivors of veterans discharged before July 26, 1951, who passed away within three years after their discharge were entitled to their full social insurance benefits under the Old-Age and Survivors Insurance,[8] whereby the veteran is deemed to have had monthly wages of $160 during his military service. Burial expenses for a deceased veteran are reimbursed to relatives or friends up to a maximum of $150.

III. EDUCATION AND VOCATIONAL REHABILITATION

Under the *Servicemen's Readjustment Act* of 1944 (so-called "G.I. Bill of Rights") and its amendments, a program of general *education and training* was made available to honorably discharged World War II veterans with ninety days or more of service. The period of subsidized education varies from one to four years; it is computed one year plus a time equal to active military service; maximum time is four years. For education in approved schools and institutions tuition, supplies, books, and equipment up to $500 a year is paid; subsistence allowances of $75 monthly is given to the veteran without dependents, $105 to the married veteran, and $120 to the veteran with more than one dependent. Training may be performed in industry, business, and workshops providing apprentice or on-the-job training. The allowances for vocational training are $65 for the veteran alone, and $90 for the veteran with dependents, with maximum amounts under consideration of the income earned by the trainee.

Education and training must have an educational or employment objective; no payments are made for purely recreational or avocational courses. As a rule, these benefits expire July 25, 1956.[9]

Vocational rehabilitation is provided under the "Act Providing Vocational Rehabilitation of Disabled Veterans," of 1943 (Public Law 16) in order to restore the employability of disabled war veterans. The training period for vocational rehabilitation is not limited,

[8] See Chapter 9; and James Kutcher, *The Case of the Legless Veteran* (New York: Pioneer Publishers, 1953).

[9] E. Burns, *op. cit.*, pp. 280-285; and Roger Cumming, "Veterans Services," *Social Work Year Book, 1954*, pp. 522-528.

but after four years an approval of the Veterans Administration is required. The vocational training for veterans of World War II terminates July 25, 1956. The training allowance of disabled veterans is paid in addition to disability compensation and retirement pay; compensation and training allowance amount to $105 a month for a veteran without dependents, $115 for a veteran with one dependent (plus $10 for the first and $7 for each additional child), and $15 for dependent parents. The vocational rehabilitation plan is carefully supervised; courses have to be continued so that the benefits will not be wasted and the training will suit the individual needs of the veteran. In hospitals of the Veterans Administration and of the Navy, vocational guidance is provided so that disabled veterans may prepare their rehabilitation training in advance.

IV. JOB REINSTATEMENT AND PREFERENCE IN CIVIL SERVICE

Before the end of World War II, there was uncertainty whether the returning armies would find sufficient jobs available after discharge. For this reason, the *Veterans Readjustment Act* provided the right of the veteran to be re-employed in his former job with special regulations of conflicting interests. Fortunately employment conditions after 1945 were so favorable that little difficulty was faced, in general, by the returning veterans.[10]

In civil service examinations and tests a special priority of 5 per cent for veterans and of 10 per cent for disabled veterans made the eligibility for, and the appointment of, veterans and their widows to civil service positions easier. These priorities were secured for federal civil service, but they were applied in most states also to state and local government civil service jobs.

Special job counseling and placement services are available to veterans and widows of deceased veterans in order to compensate the veteran for the loss of job and to help him to find again his place in the labor market. Policies for effective placement of veterans were

[10] A study of the Research Council for Economic Security, "Employment of Male World War II Veterans," June, 1948 (Publication No. 44, November, 1948, p. 2) found that the chief problem was finding suitable employment for disabled veterans, and that many had a tough time finding jobs. The cost of vocational rehabilitation, in 1948, was only 1.1 per cent of the total expenditures of the veterans' program.

established through the Veterans Placement Service Board, whose chairman is the veterans' administrator. Veterans' employment representatives serve in all state employment organizations and many local employment services. Particular attention is given to counseling and placement services for physically handicapped veterans who had been prepared by vocational rehabilitation.

V. ECONOMIC PRIVILEGES

At the time of honorable discharge, the veteran received a mustering-out pay of $100 when he had had less than sixty days active service, of $200 when he had had at least sixty days but no overseas service, and of $300 when he had had sixty or more days service, including some overseas duty.

In order to assist the serviceman in the transition from military to civilian life, a special type of federally financed unemployment benefit, called "Readjustment Allowance," of $20 a week was paid during World War II and until 1952 to unemployed veterans.[11] Wages or income earned in excess of $3 a week were deducted. The allowance was paid for a period graded upon length of active service, for the first ninety days, eight-weeks' allowance, for each additional month of service, four weeks of allowance, with a maximum of fifty-two weeks of readjustment allowance after discharge.

Since October, 1952, unemployment insurance benefits have been paid to veterans under two different programs: (1) Under the general state unemployment insurance laws, benefits are paid to veterans who have established benefit rights after their return to civilian life or, in twenty states where unemployed veterans receive insurance benefits, on the basis of "frozen wage credits" earned before their military service. (2) Unemployed veterans with active service after June 27, 1950, including veterans of the Korean conflict, receive weekly benefits of $26 for a period of twenty-six weeks, or until they have exhausted a maximum total allowance of $676 under the *Veterans Readjustment Assistance Act* of 1952. A veteran must first claim benefits for which he is eligible under a state unemployment compen-

---

[11] For more details see E. Burns, *op. cit.*, pp. 271-273; for most veterans of World War II readjustment allowances terminated July 25, 1949. More than nine million veterans received these allowances. For the present protection of veterans against unemployment see Ruth Reticker, "Unemployment Compensation for Veterans," *Employment Service Review*, Vol. 21, No. 2, February, 1954, pp. 42-44.

sation law or the Railroad Unemployment Insurance Act. If his benefits under this legislation are less than $26, they are supplemented by federal funds up to $26 a week. The program is administered by the state employment security agencies (Unemployment Compensation Board, Employment Stabilization Commission, Department of Labor, and so on), but the expenditures based upon the Veterans Readjustment Assistance Act of 1952 are reimbursed by the Bureau of Employment Security of the federal Department of Labor.

Self-employed veterans in trade, business, profession, or other vocations are also entitled to readjustment allowance if they had net earnings of less than $100 in the previous month. The allowance equals the difference between actual earnings and $100, the maximum length is 10.4 months.

Veterans and widows of deceased veterans receive help in building a home, establishing a business, or buying a farm by *guaranteeing* up to 60 per cent of the loan from private lending societies or individuals. The maximum guaranty limit is $7,500 for a real estate loan and $2,000 for other loans. When private loans are not available in certain areas, the Veterans Administration is entitled to make direct loans, limited to $10,000, for homes and farms.

When war surpluses and rare housing materials were disposed of after World War II, veterans received priority in purchasing these supplies for business or construction purposes.

Veterans also receive priorities in housing located in public housing projects built with funds of the Lanham Act of 1950, and in securing homesteads on public land.

VI. ORGANIZATION OF VETERANS ADMINISTRATION

Veterans' benefits are administered by the Veterans Administration. The policy-making body is the Central Office in Washington, D.C., which also is responsible for the supervision of the entire program. The various fields of the administration, such as legal problems, claims, appeals, vocational rehabilitation, education, and life insurance, are assigned to staff units. Social services are a subdivision of the Department of Medicine and Surgery in the central, district, and regional offices. Social services are available to veterans under medical treatment and care.

Operating functions are decentralized and delegated to five district offices, to fifty-seven regional offices, and over five hundred field stations. They handle disability and death awards, training and education, and other benefits.[12] Readjustment allowances are paid by the state unemployment compensation agencies, which are also reimbursed for their administrative costs incurred by this cooperation.

A. STATE VETERANS' PROGRAMS

Although the federal government assumes the basic responsibility for veterans' services, nearly all the states provide additional benefits to veterans. These services supplement the federal benefits or continue them after their expiration.[13] The benefits include information and counseling centers, preference in civil service or public employ-

TABLE IV

EXPENDITURES FOR VETERANS' PROGRAMS IN THE U.S.*

Year	Federal Funds	State and Local Funds†	Total
1936-37	$ 485,000,000	. . . . . .	$ 485,000,000
1937-38	494,100,000	. . . . . .	494,100,000
1938-39	513,200,000	. . . . . .	513,200,000
1939-40	535,000,000	. . . . . .	535,000,000
1940-41	534,900,000	. . . . . .	534,900,000
1941-42	537,500,000	. . . . . .	537,500,000
1942-43	555,900,000	. . . . . .	555,900,000
1943-44	622,900,000	. . . . . .	622,900,000
1944-45	914,200,000	. . . . . .	914,200,000
1945-46	2,966,900,000	$ 47,400,000	3,014,300,000
1946-47	6,530,300,000	158,900,000	6,689,200,000
1947-48	6,263,600,000	616,000,000	6,879,600,000
1948-49	6,488,800,000	520,100,000	7,008,900,000
1949-50	6,063,400,000	471,100,000	6,534,500,000
1950-51	5,171,400,000	334,700,000	5,506,100,000
1951-52	5,987,208,319	. . . . . .	. . . . . .
1952-53	5,098,458,094	. . . . . .	. . . . . .

* Derived from Ida C. Merriam, "Social Welfare Programs in the United States," *Social Security Bulletin*, Vol. 16, No. 2, February, 1953, p. 8, Table 1; and Veterans Administration, *Annual Report, 1953* (Washington, D.C.: Government Printing Office, 1954), pp. 1-7.

† Statistics are of preliminary character; no complete data on state and local expenditures for veterans' services before 1945-46 are available. Federal bonus payments, appropriations to government life insurance trust fund, and accounts of several small revolving funds are not included.

The figures indicate the tremendous increase of expenditures at the end of World War II, amounting in 1945-46 to more than 300 per cent, and in 1946-47 to over 200 per cent of the previous annual expenditure.

[12] *Ibid.*, pp. 287-290; U.S. Veterans Administration, *Reorganization of Veterans Administration*, Exhibition IV.

[13] See *Problems of the Veterans*, 1945, University of California, Bureau of Public Administration, Berkeley, Calif., 1944; Franklin Aaronson and Hilda Rosenbloom, "State Aid to Veterans," *Social Security Bulletin*, February, 1945, pp. 12-20.

TABLE V

VETERANS' SERVICES AND THEIR COST, AS OF JUNE 30, 1953*

Veterans' Population		*Services for Veterans*	
		A. Number of Recipients	
World War I	3.311,000	1. Compensations and Pensions	2,504,257
Other wars	152,000		
World War II only	14,712,000	2. Dependents:	
World War II and Korea conflict	1,963,000	(a) Widows	455,328
		(b) Children	310,172
Total veterans in civilian life	20,138,000	(c) Parents	323,818
		Total	1,089,318

B. Expenditures

1. Compensations and Pensions	$1,764,941,718	
2. Dependents' Benefits	608,081,037	
3. Total Expenditures, including medical care and administration	5,098,458,094	
Appropriations	4,354,220,485	
Trust Funds	744,237,609	

* Source: Administrator of Veterans Affairs, *Annual Report, 1953* (Washington, D.C.: Government Printing Office, 1954), pp. 1-4, 7.

ment, tax and license fees exemptions, and additional domiciliary care in state soldiers' homes. Other state benefits are financial aid to needy veterans, bonuses, pensions, and burial expenses to indigent veterans. Several states supply guarantee for loans to veterans for the purchase of homes, farm, or business, sometimes up to a higher maximum than the federal program allows. Educational benefits may permit the veteran to complete studies or training after the federal aid has been exhausted. In other state programs land settlement, homesteads, or institutional care for children are available to veterans and their families.

The state veterans' departments or commissions administer or supervise these services for veterans, but in a few instances, private veterans' organizations or the various state departments of public welfare are charged with providing benefits.

B. COMMUNITY SERVICES FOR VETERANS

Among social agencies some are particularly active in services for veterans. Through its local chapters, the American National Red

Cross assists veterans in the presentation of claims for their legal benefits. Through the home service division of the chapters, it offers casework services, and in special instances, financial aid to veterans and their families. Several veterans' organizations, such as the American Legion and the Veterans of Foreign Wars of the United States also help veterans in their claims and in rehabilitation, in securing housing, loans for purchasing homes, farms and business, in obtaining employment or hospitalization, and in family and child welfare services.[14]

Beyond the federal and state programs, local community services are needed to assist the veteran and his family because the veteran should also receive the consideration and aid given to other citizens. Such services are offered by public and private agencies, such as the local health and welfare departments, the employment service, vocational rehabilitation centers, family and child welfare agencies, and mental hygiene and child guidance clinics.

SELECTED BIBLIOGRAPHY

Aaronson, Franklin and Hilda Rosenbloom, "State Aid to Veterans," *Social Security Bulletin*, Vol. 8, No. 2, February, 1945, pp. 12-20.

Bradley, Omar N., "The Veterans Administration," *National Conference of Social Work, Proceedings 1946*, pp. 353-359.

Burns, Eveline M., *The American Social Security System*, Chap. X, "Income Security Measures for Veterans," pp. 265-292. Boston: Houghton, 1949.

Cohen, Wilbur J., "Federal Government's Program for Servicemen," *Annals of the American Academy of Political and Social Science*, Vol. CCXXXVIII, March, 1945, pp. 63-70.

Cumming, Roger, "Veterans' Benefits and Services," *Social Work Year Book, 1954*, pp. 521-529.

Doherty, William Brown, and Dagobert D. Runes, *Rehabilitation of the War Injured*. New York: Philosophical Library, 1943.

Federal Security Agency, Office of Vocational Rehabilitation, *Restoring the Handicapped to Useful Employment*. Washington, D.C.: Government Printing Office, 1944.

Gray, Carl R. Jr., "The Veterans' Administration," *The American Annual* (1st ed.), 1952.

Hinshaw, David, *Take Up Thy Bed and Walk*. New York: Putnam, 1948.

Krieghbaum, Hillier, "Rehabilitation by Self-Help," *Survey Graphic*, January, 1948.

[14] R. Cumming, *op. cit.*, pp. 527-528.

Magnuson, Paul B., "Medical Care for Veterans," *Annals of the American Academy of Political and Social Science*, Vol. 263, January, 1951.

Mallen, Frank, *You've Got It Coming to You*. New York: McKay, 1952.

Maroney, Mildred, "Veterans' Benefits," in Lewis Meriam and Karl Schlotterbeck, *The Cost and Financing of Social Security*, pp. 96-119. Washington, D.C.: Brookings Institution, 1950.

Mayo, Katherine, *Soldier, What Next?* Boston: Houghton, 1934.

Menninger, Karl, "The Veteran—and Don't Forget," *Survey Graphic*, Vol. 37, No. 7, July, 1948.

Ross, Elizabeth H., "Social Work's Responsibility for Veterans," *National Conference of Social Work, Proceedings, 1946*, pp. 336-341.

Stipe, Jack H., "Social Services in the Veterans Administration," *Journal of Social Casework*, Vol. XXIX, February, 1948, pp. 43-48.

———, "Veterans' Benefits and Services," *Social Work Yearbook, 1949*, pp. 521-528.

United States Veterans Administration, *Reorganization of the Veterans Administration*. Washington, D.C.: Government Printing Office, 1953.

Weber, Gustavus A., and Lawrence F. Schmeckebier, *The Veterans Administration: Its History, Activities, and Organization* (Service Monographs of the U.S. Government, No. 66). Washington, D.C.: Brookings Institution, 1934.

17. *Industry and Social Welfare*

In the field of modern industrial operations four aspects seem of particular importance from the point of social welfare. First, there are the arrangements made (recently described as "industrial health and welfare plans") in plants, mines, and commerce in order to establish or to improve social security, health, and general welfare of the employees and their families. Second, there is the function of public employment services in finding the best-suited worker for employers and the right jobs for workers seeking employment. Third, there is the use of social workers in industrial and commercial companies in order to assist the employees and their families in personal, health, and financial problems and difficulties. Finally, there is the relation of organized labor to social work and its participation in the responsibility for development and maintenance of community welfare services.

I. INDUSTRIAL HEALTH AND WELFARE

The very nature of modern industry with its concentration of large populations in industrial centers around mills and mines has challenged both workers and employers in regard to measures of protecting life, health, and well-being of the workers. A number of older labor unions started as fraternal mutual aid societies; they made provisions to help their members during periods of sickness and unemployment by grants and loans, and to aid the survivors in case of death of the breadwinner. Some employers established medical clinics, pension plans, and life insurance protection for their employees. But only a very small proportion of workers were covered by one or the other type of social protection before World War II. Organized labor had been first opposed to company welfare plans because they endangered the organization of workers in labor unions and curtailed labor's mobility and bargaining strength. When union leaders during the 1930's succeeded in organizing mass-production industries, they were forced to promise their newly recruited members that health, recreational, and retirement benefits which had earlier been introduced by some companies would be maintained.

During World War II rapidly enlarged production created a hunt for manpower while wage increases were restricted by the government's wage stabilization policy. Thus, many companies established pension and health service plans in order to attract workers. This factor seemed even more important because under Old-Age and Survivors Insurance the benefits were rather inadequate having been left at the 1935 level while the cost of living had greatly risen.[1] That was relatively simple because the cost of the plans in the face of excess profit taxes was nominal and could be written off as business expense, whereas the recruitment advantage was an essential one.

The first plans were set up voluntarily by industry. After the federal government completed a bargaining agreement with the United Mine Workers in 1946, which included a pension and welfare plan, such "fringe benefits" became a widespread pattern in collective bargaining because other unions felt they had to prove that they were able to obtain the same concessions from the employers as the mine workers. Before this change, some welfare plans had been financed by the workers themselves. The new pattern which started with a collective agreement of the United Auto Workers at Toledo, Ohio, in 1935, meant that the welfare plans were financed entirely (in some cases, at least in part) by the employers. Finally, in 1948 the National Labor Relations Board ruled that industrial pensions were "conditions of employment" and might be included in all collective bargaining contracts.

Since this development, health and welfare plans play an important role in our industry. As their title indicates they are of three main types: (1) pension or retirement plans providing annuities for workers retired after long service with the company, (2) voluntary health insurance plans, providing prepaid medical care and hospitali-

---

[1] U.S. Department of Labor, *Collective Bargaining Provisions, Health Insurance, and Pensions*, pp. 1-4; and Clark Kerr, *Social and Economic Implications of Private Pension Plans* (Berkeley: University of California, 1949), pp. 2-4. The Amendments of 1950, 1952, and 1954 brought a certain adjustment of old-age and survivors' benefits to actual living costs.

zation for illness not covered by workmen's compensation protection, and (3) a combination of retirement annuities and health services.

There is a great variety in structure, conditions, benefits, methods of administration, and financing among the more than 10,000 existing health and welfare plans. Numerous research studies have analyzed various features of these plans,[2] and labor unions have accepted them as part of a broader concept of social security for their members.

Retirement or pension plans often are combined with a life insurance policy, ranging from $1,750 to $4,000, which is paid by the employer. During and immediately after World War II, 42 per cent of retirement plans were wholly financed by the employer; for the remaining 58 per cent, worker and employer shared the cost. An analysis of 346 retirement annuity plans by the Social Security Administration in October, 1952, revealed that only in 25.4 per cent of the plans the employer alone paid the premiums, whereas in 74.6 per cent both workers and employers shared the expense for the annuity insurance. In nearly all plans, membership was dependent upon a longer period of work in the firm, most commonly five years, less frequently one year. The majority of plans required a minimum age of thirty years and had maximum ages of fifty-five to fifty-nine, sixty, and usually sixty-five years. Frequently, employment may be continued with consent of employer beyond the fixed retirement age; in this case, 18 per cent of the plans provided an increased annuity amount. The annuity is determined in various rates by a percentage of annual earnings and the length of service with the company.

Wages and salaries often are considered up to $3,000 a year. In those plans in which the workers contribute, their payment premiums often amount to 2 to 3 per cent of the first $3,000 annual wages and 2 to 5 per cent of the excess earnings. A large majority of private plans permits the employee who leaves the company before retire-

[2] Some examples are John W. Whittlesey, *Welfare Plans and Collective Bargaining* (Washington, D.C.: Chamber of Commerce of the United States, 1950); Wiltha Van Eenam and Martha E. Penman, *Analysis of 346 Group Annuities Underwritten in 1946-50*, Social Security Administration (Actuarial Study No. 32), 1952; U.S. Department of Labor, *Health, Insurance, Welfare, and Retirement Plans Under Collective Bargaining* (Washington, D.C.: 1950); Research Council for Economic Security, *Employee Benefit Plans Providing Hospital, Surgical, Medical Care* (Chicago: 1951); Social Security Administration, *Independent Plans Providing Medical Care and Hospitalization Insurance in the United States* (Washington, D.C.: 1952).

ment to maintain his annuity rights at this stage (vesting) or to request a cash refund.

Frequently annuity plans provide at the death of the insured worker before his retirement that his own contributions, sometimes with interest, be paid back to his widow and orphans. The most frequent type of annuity plan is the "definite benefit" plan with payments deferred to retirement at a specified age, usually sixty-five years. Many plans allow for an earlier retirement, beginning at fifty-five years of age under a reduced annuity. Frequently permanent disability is a condition of early retirement, and certain plans allow the payment of disability or invalidity benefits without age limit for employees unable to work. The trend in recent agreements has been to postpone annuity payments until actual retirement with an increased pension amount.

The relation of private industrial retirement plans to the benefits of Old-Age and Survivors Insurance is an important question.[3] Some retirement annuity plans provide benefits computed by including old-age insurance benefits received under the federal Old-Age and Survivors Insurance; others pay benefits in addition to whatever old-age insurance is drawn by the retired worker. Both supplement the public social insurance benefits, but the second type grants a larger additional monthly amount to the retired worker. In the financing of plans in which the employees share the expenses, an integration with federal benefits is achieved by classifying a uniform benefit rate on the first $3,000 or $3,600 of annual earnings, with a higher rate on the excess amount. It is widely argued that private annuity plans should include federal social security benefits so that they may be developed into a sound system. They will then secure additional benefits to supplement the rather modest amounts guaranteed under the public old-age insurance system, or may secure benefits at a lower age, or grant benefits to dependents otherwise not protected, such as to a wife or a widow under sixty-five, without young children. Due to the present lack of a federal permanent disability insurance program, private invalidity pension plans are a valuable substitute as long as no general coverage under public legislation can be obtained.

[3] Arthur J. Altmeyer, "Social Security and Welfare Funds," in William Haber and Wilbur J. Cohen (editors), *Readings in Social Security* (New York: Prentice-Hall, Inc., 1948), pp. 132-136.

There are, however, definite limitations in private retirement plans. They cover only a certain percentage of workers, leaving out usually the unorganized—those working in small firms, casual workers, and self-employed persons who may need most a supplementation of federal old-age insurance.[4] They limit the mobility of labor because, particularly under noncontributory plans, workers become eligible for benefits only if they remain for long years in the same industry or serve with the same employer. Thus, workers lose the initiative to change jobs for better conditions, higher pay, and promotions, which are considered vital elements in a well-functioning, fluid labor market. A private plan may bring the older worker into strong pressure to keep his job and stay with his union because of fear of losing his pension.

Another critical point is that private pensions are likely to vary from company to company, and among industries, due to the rhythm of regular employment, wages, age composition of workers, and financial reserves. Equalization of benefits is difficult under these circumstances.[5]

The sound organization of pension plans in collective bargaining is difficult because their technical, financial basis is complicated and requires special statistical experts. It also remains doubtful whether pension plans, especially of smaller firms, are able to guarantee the payment of annuities in case of insolvency, mass dismissal of workers, and other failures. Special provisions are needed to insure that private pension plans do not hinder the older worker in his search for a more satisfying job.

Private pension plans contribute to the social security of those employees who happen to be covered by these plans, but they are not the final solution of general security in old age. Organized labor and students of social security agree that a universal, complex, and adequate public system of old-age insurance is necessary for the protection of the total population. Without such a system the demands of special groups and labor unions for particular benefits under spe-

[4] C. Kerr, *op. cit.*, pp. 4-5; in 1953, of 2,600 collective bargaining agreements only twenty contained the guarantee of an "annual minimum wage," thus providing security for regular employment for some 20,000 workers. The psychological aspects of retirement are well illustrated in a study by Jacob Tuckman and Irving Lorge, *Retirement and the Industrial Worker: Prospect and Reality* (New York: Columbia University, 1953).

[5] Ewan Clague, *The Background of the Pension Problem*, U.S. Department of Labor, Bureau of Labor Statistics, 1949, pp. 5-6.

cific conditions exercise pressure and threaten to result in unbalanced, unfair, overlapping, and competing arrangements which lack equity and are wasteful. The AFL and the CIO consider private pension plans under collective bargaining only as a step to a governmental, comprehensive, and adequate public social security program.[6]

Health benefit plans are the second main type of private security programs developed in industry either by labor unions, collective bargaining, or companies under their own initiative. One of the first medical care plans was founded in New York by the International Ladies' Garment Workers' Union which, as early as 1912, established a union health center with free medical care for its members. Under collective bargaining during and after World War II numerous medical care and hospital plans have been set up. They usually insure all employees of a company in a prepaid medical care and hospital plan, negotiated either with one or several hospitals, physician panels, or with a private insurance company, which assumes the payments for medical care, medicines, and hospitalization in case of illness and accidents not covered by workmen's compensation. Sometimes medical care plans are preceded by exploratory studies such as those of the United Automobile Workers-CIO in Cleveland in a Medical Research Institute in 1940. The benefits of industrial medical care plans are not uniform. In general, medical and surgical care, medicines, appliances, and hospitalization are provided free of charge or for a nominal fee. Less frequently 50 to 60 per cent of the wage is paid during illness up to a maximum period, usually up to one year. Other health agreements limit the services of medical care to preventive measures, medical examination, and diagnosis; encourage the workers to join at their own expense a prepaid medical and surgical care program; or refer them for treatment to their own private physician. A number of prepaid medical care systems with clinic and hospital facilities is sponsored by unions or by cooperative societies. We mentioned already that in four states a temporary disability insurance plan is established under unemployment compensation laws, but these provisions are limited to workers covered by unemployment insurance, and do not include their families.[7]

[6] C. Kerr, *op. cit.*, pp. 9-10; Kermit Eby, "Labor's Drive for Security," *Social Service Review*, Vol. 24, No. 1, March, 1950, pp. 17-18.

[7] See Chapter 9, p. 284; Harold S. Vance, "Industry Looks at the Problem of Financing Health Services," President's Commission on the Health Needs of the Nation, *Building America's Health* (1952), Vol. 4, pp. 121-124.

The cost of health, medical care, and hospital plans usually is shared between employers and workers, but some companies assume the entire payment of contributions, e.g., in chemical and metal industries.[8] As a rule, medical treatment is limited to a maximum amount of expenses for surgery and delivery service, ranging from $25 to $100, and to a maximum hospitalization period ranging from twenty-one to seventy days (sometimes with the assumption of a discount of 50 per cent of the expense up to thirty, ninety, or one-hundred-eighty days of further hospitalization).

The largest voluntary health insurance system in our country is the "Blue Cross Plan." It is fundamentally a hospital insurance, but sometimes it includes services of medical treatment. Commercial insurance companies underwriting sickness insurance are the second group in order of magnitude, but their benefits are frequently limited to cash allowances for a certain number of days of illness or to a contribution to hospital costs. Rarely is comprehensive medical care offered. The third group consists of surgical-medical plans, such as the Blue Shield, sponsored by state medical associations and used under contract by companies, labor unions, and consumer groups for securing medical treatment.

Independent medical care and hospitalization plans are organized either as industrial or nonindustrial plans. The first group comprises prepaid health care arrangements, financed either by the employer, or employer and workers, or employer and union, or by the union, or the workers alone. Nonindustrial health plans are organized by consumers, medical societies, and private medical group clinics or are community-wide institutions, such as the Health Insurance Plan of Greater New York.

Because our country has no compulsory health insurance program, voluntary prepaid medical care plans in industry and under nonindustrial auspices have an important function in meeting the medical needs of the population and in providing health education of the public, research, and experience. They may be pioneers for a general health insurance or public-health service system, which probably will be considered necessary in the future. The voluntary plans also may develop preventive dental care, dental clinics, home-

---

[8] Research Council for Economic Security, *Employee Benefit Plans* (Chicago: 1951); Agnes W. Brewster, *Independent Plans Providing Medical Care and Hospitalization Insurance in 1949 in the U.S., 1950 Survey* (Chicago: 1952), pp. 21-22, 95-99.

nursing services, long-time hospitalization for patients in need of such treatment, and particularly expensive hospital accommodations which may not be included in a general health insurance program.

Retirement annuity, medical care, and hospitalization plans have been combined so that the employees receive substantial protection for their health and old age. An example of such a coordination is the program established for the soft coal industry, administered by a Welfare and Retirement Fund and a Medical and Hospital Fund[9] that have been set up under collective bargaining. In general, about one-half of the unions organized under the American Federation of Labor and under the Congress of Industrial Organization have a health and welfare plan. Their benefits include, as a rule, provisions for life insurance, accidental dismemberment insurance, sick-leave benefits, wage-loss benefits for the period of incapacity due to illness or nonindustrial accident, hospital expense benefits, medical care benefits, maternity benefits, and certain benefits for dependents. But the full program of these benefits serves only 5 per cent of the employees covered under the various health plans.[10]

An analysis of 299 prepayment medical care organizations in 1945 revealed that of 1,512,148 employees protected by these plans for medical and partial dental care 752,786 (50 per cent) paid the full expenses of the plan, 546,772 employees (36 per cent) shared with management in the cost, and for only 212,590 employees (14 per cent) the financial burden of the medical and dental care plan was fully assumed by the employer.[11]

II. PUBLIC EMPLOYMENT SERVICES

One of the social institutions which is of paramount importance for industry and labor is the public employment service. Local, and a few state, employment offices were established as early as the nineteenth century, the first state offices in Ohio (1890), in New

[9] See Margaret C. Klem and Margaret F. McKiever, "Program Developments and Benefit Trends in Voluntary Health Insurance," *Social Security Bulletin*, Vol. 11, November, 1948, pp. 4-5.

[10] Julia Carlson, *Employee Benefit Plans in the Electric and Gas Utility Industries* (Washington, D.C.: Federal Security Agency, 1952), p. 3.

[11] Margaret C. Klem, Margaret F. McKiever, and Walter J. Lear, *Industrial Health and Medical Programs* (Washington, D.C.: Government Printing Office, 1950), p. 295, Table 124.

York (1896) and in Wisconsin (1901).[12] The particular employment problems of new immigrants which were emphasized by the Immigrants Protective Society under Grace Abbott in Chicago led to the setting up of an information service for immigrants in the U.S. Bureau of Immigration in 1907, which was changed into an employment office in 1914. The manpower problems of World War I led, in 1918, to the establishment of the U.S. Employment Service in the federal Department of Labor, with operating offices in each state and 854 local offices. Unfortunately, Congress was not aware of the value of these services for the demobilization of the army; the curtailment of appropriations, in 1919, prevented the activities of the employment offices for veterans and farm workers just when they were badly needed, so that many had to make their living by "apple-selling" and peddling.

It was only in the height of the Depression, after the New Deal government had assumed responsibility, that the public employment services were reactivated. The *Wagner-Peyser Act* of June 6, 1933, developed again a national system of public employment services with financial support of federal funds and with special emphasis on placement of war veterans and agricultural labor. Federal grants permitted the states to organize their employment bureaus and to introduce modern methods of placement with the use of aptitude and vocational tests for occupational classification, by employing qualified personnel. In 1939, the U.S. Employment Service was incorporated as "Bureau of Employment Security" into the Social Security Administration, but after Pearl Harbor, in December, 1941, the state employment offices were merged with the federal service, because of the need of a uniform policy for war needs and, in 1942, were transferred to the War Manpower Commission. After the war, in November 1946, the public employment services were returned to the states, and are operating hence as state agencies, usually under the Department of Employment and in close cooperation with the state unemployment insurance administration. The Bureau of Employment Security, including the U.S. Employment Service,

---

[12] William H. Stead, "Employment Services," *Social Work Year Book, 1941,* pp. 186-195. Local offices were established in New York and in San Francisco in 1860. Private, commercial, fee-charging agencies preceded the public services, but they were usually specialized, and were accused of malpractice, sometimes encouraging employers to fire workers in order to gain new fees, or of sending bad workers.

was attached to the U.S. Department of Labor in 1950. It is not a part of the U.S. Department of Health, Education and Welfare, but cooperates with the Veterans Administration.

The function of the employment services is "to bring workers and employers together." They assist in the effective recruitment and placement of labor, helping workers to find suitable and, if possible, stable employment, and helping employers to find qualified employees. This function is carried out by registration and classification of workers desirous of finding jobs upon consideration of their vocational capacity. Employment services obtain from employers information on job openings and their requirements, and they refer job applicants, if necessary, to other employment offices where workers are needed. The employment service thus is the connecting link between the employer in need of labor and the worker in need of a job. Only seldom do employment services attempt to develop special training or retraining courses or to assume a role in the task of channeling the flow of labor to areas with better placement facilities.[13]

III. SOCIAL WORKERS IN INDUSTRY

During World War I industrial social work in the United States developed under the name "industrial counseling" in a number of plants, particularly in war factories. Between the world wars a few large companies—the Metropolitan Life Insurance Company, the Hawthorne Works of the Western Electric Company in Chicago, and the department store R. H. Macy in New York—employed industrial counselors. Their main function was to help the employees with personal and family problems, in questions of health, care of children, marital problems, and financial difficulties. Other companies followed these examples. Whenever immediate help cannot be given by an interview or advice, the employee is informed about health clinics and hospitals, family service agencies, loan associations, and recreation and adult education facilities and is referred to those community resources which meet his need. Sometimes the industrial

---

[13] Whether a unified, federal employment service with local branches or a state system is preferable is highly controversial. It seems that the quality of service and personnel is more important than the organizational form of the service. See Meredith B. Givens, "Employment Services," *Social Work Year Book, 1949*, pp. 186-187; Helen L. Witmer and Ruth Kotinsky, *Personality in the Making* (New York: Harper, 1952), pp. 290-307; and Arthur W. Motley, "Employment Services," *Social Work Year Book, 1954*, pp. 185-192.

counselor in cooperation with the shop steward will be able to adjust the difficulties the worker may have in relation to his supervisor, his fellow workers, or in regard to the type of his work assignment.[14] Although these activities require professional social work skill and thorough knowledge of social agencies, health facilities, and recreation in the community, only few industrial counselors are trained social workers,[15] the majority being factory operators who get along well with people or come from employment services, vocational guidance, and personnel work.

With the development of defense production and the ensuing spread of war industries in World War II, many plants, yards, and docks engaged industrial counselors, particularly for women. Organized labor became concerned that industrial counselors in the plants might be biased in their approach to personal and work problems in favor of the employer who had hired them, and might lack understanding of, and sympathy for, labor unions. In some instances the counselors or "welfare workers" even were accused of serving as labor spies for management so that the workers had no confidence in them. Therefore, both CIO and AFL developed, with the cooperation of local welfare councils, a new program of "union counselors" under their own sponsorship and control.[16] Social workers of the staff of the Welfare Council, or Council of Social Agencies, or of one of the affiliated organizations were asked to offer training to selected rank-and-file workers, who had the confidence of their fellow workers. The training courses do not attempt to make social workers out of rank-and-file union members in six, or a few more, meetings of two hours each. They aim, however, to give the volunteers an understanding of simple interviewing technique and of classification methods of social problems. The trainees are taught that grievances of a fellow worker about his work and his supervisor belong to the shop steward as representative of the union, and that questions of family disturbances and personal, social, psychological, and health problems should be referred to the proper

[14] Mary Palevsky, *Counseling Services for Industrial Workers* (New York: Family Welfare Association of America, 1945), p. 4; B. A. Kogan, "Some Labor Union Enterprises in Public Health Economics," *American Journal of Public Health*, Vol. 38, July, 1948, pp. 945-946.

[15] There is no specialization in industrial social work here such as has developed in France.

[16] Robert L. Kinney, "Union Counseling Bridges a Gap," *Survey Midmonthly*, April, 1945, pp. 106-108; M. Palevsky, *op. cit.*, pp. 5-8, 35-36.

social and health agencies in the community. The training courses, for this reason, include instruction about the public and private social agencies in the community, their function in the field of family and child welfare, health treatment, and relief, and about their policies and limitations.

The union counselors will be able to answer simple legal and jurisdictional questions themselves. The active participation of union members in the counseling process is of significance. It represents a new, positive approach to their concern in social welfare. Serious social and personal problems, however, should be referred to the social agency best suited to help. The most advisable arrangement is that a union staff member or a social worker who enjoys the full confidence of labor serve on the staff of the Welfare Council or of the Community Chest so that any difficult questions may be referred to him. He contacts then the special social agency which is able to help the person or family in need of service. In some places, a central referral bureau for all inquiries of union counselors and their "clients" has been set up, but in other cities the union counselor (union community service director) refers the inquiring workers directly to the competent social agencies. This integration of social services with labor union counseling has proved of value to union members to overcome family disturbances, to receive neglected medical and dental care, and to replace oppressing debts by reasonable loans. It also has helped to avoid unnecessary duplication of available community services by special institutions of labor unions.[17]

Many problems brought to the attention of industrial counselors are the same as those encountered in family casework, frequently marital difficulties and health and child adjustment questions.[18] The short period of training of union counselors limits their information basically to a survey of community welfare and health organizations and to an understanding of the necessity of referring serious problems to a central, experienced representative, if possible a trained social worker.[19] Only careful in-service training and refresher

[17] R. Kinney, *op. cit.*, p. 108.
[18] M. Palevsky, *op. cit.*, pp. 36-37; Judson T. Landis and Mary G. Landis, *Building a Successful Marriage*, 2nd ed. (New York: Prentice-Hall, Inc., 1953), Chap. 3.
[19] For example, in San Francisco, California, union representatives are on the staff of the Community Chest and of the Industrial Office of the California State Department of Employment.

courses for the union counselors, and a conscientious consultant service by a trained social worker, guarantee reliable operation of this new system of making social agencies available to the bulk of the industrial working population.

The difficulty of preparing rank-and-file workers in plants sufficiently within a short course period for counseling has led to another approach in which professional social workers assume the task of industrial counseling. This has been experienced in the Workers Personal Service Bureau, organized through the Brooklyn Council for Social Planning in cooperation with eighty New York unions. In the factories, individual workers in need of advice, casework, or other services were approached by a group of union members and leaders who had been prepared by the social agency in a training course and in discussion groups.[20] The emphasis in this approach was upon the fact that counseling of the workers and referral to community agencies should be the responsibility of professional social workers who were well familiar with the methods of interviewing, casework, and the resources of the community.

In a number of industries, "in-plant counseling" either by industrial counselors employed by management or by union counselors who advise fellow workers with the consent of management during certain hours on working time, during lunch hours, or after work has been continued. However, industrial counseling does not play such an essential role in the stabilization of the labor force and in the improvement of workers' morale in peacetime as it did during the war.

In some instances, trained professional social workers have volunteered to set up counseling services in union halls in regular evening hours, or at plant premises after agreement with the union and management. Such experiments were carried on in Chicago by the Social Service Employees Union at the stock yards in cooperation with the United Packinghouse Workers, and in similar experiments in Cleveland, New York City, Brooklyn, Columbus, Seattle, Philadelphia, and Detroit, but have not been followed up on a broad basis after World War II.

One labor union has established professional social work under its own auspices. The National Maritime Union (CIO), in cooperation with the United Seamen's Service, has organized a Personal Service

[20] See Alfred H. Katz, "Reaching Out to New Clients," *Survey Midmonthly*, March, 1947, pp. 74-76.

Department as a casework agency in New York. During World War II branch units were operating in New Orleans and San Francisco. Casework is available to members of the American Merchant Marine in regard to family and other personal and health problems, and referrals are made to other social agencies when they may be of help to the seamen.

Trained, experienced social workers are also employed in some of the health and welfare plans administered under union auspices, for example, in the rehabilitation service of the United Mine Workers of America Welfare and Retirement Fund.[21]

IV. ORGANIZED LABOR AND SOCIAL WORK

Labor unions in the United States have historically favored protective legislation with regard to child labor and women's work, workmen's compensation, and old-age insurance. However, prior to the Depression of the 1930's when the pressing need for unemployment insurance as well as for wage and hours legislation was clearly demonstrated, their attitude was one of ambivalence toward this type of social legislation.[22] Since the Depression a positive endorsement of social legislation, including collective bargaining, social security provisions, and extension of social insurance, has become the unanimous attitude of organized labor in our country.[23]

Originally, labor unions manifested substantial suspicion of, and very little sympathy for, public and private social work. Even when industrial workers during World War I substantially contributed to Community Chest drives, they were indifferent about the aims and methods of charitable agencies and the programs that the drives supported. The social worker still was considered as a person doling out largesse and being a representative of a wealthy, superior class,

[21] Constance Kyle, "Case Work in the National Maritime Union," *The Family*, October, 1944, p. 217; Kenneth E. Pohlmann, "Group Techniques in Rehabilitation Counseling," *Journal of Rehabilitation*, July and August, 1951, and "Rehabilitation of Disabled Miners," *American Journal of Public Health*, July, 1952, pp. 791-794.

[22] John A. Fitch, "Samuel Grompers and the Labor Movement," *The Survey*, June, 1950, pp. 291-292; and Albert Deutsch, "Get Together, Labor and Social Work," *Social Work Today*, April, 1942, p. 13.

[23] William H. Davis, "From Strikes to Reasoning," *The Survey*, June, 1950, pp. 285-288; and Wayne McMillen, "Broadening the Base of Social Work," *The Compass*, Vol. 27, No. 3, March, 1946, pp. 11-14.

instead of helping neighbors on a plane of equality. The rank-and-file workers criticized their employers for paying low wages but boasting of the generous contributions they donated to charities. They found that private social agencies sometimes were used to discourage persons in financial need from joining labor unions, and that relief even was abused as a tool in order to break strikes. During World War II a change in this attitude took place. It began with the organization of war relief drives by both the AFL and the CIO in order to help the suffering people of those countries which had been attacked by the Axis powers. When these contributions reached an annual amount of about $50,000,000, in 1942, the National War Fund and the American Red Cross recognized the need of integrating this important source of income into the general welfare campaign. It was evident that several competing drives would result in discontent and conflict among the population, and that only a unified, concerted appeal for war relief as well as domestic health and welfare services would be successful. Organized labor decided to join forces and to cooperate in the National War Fund, through special war relief committees of the AFL and the CIO. Representatives of labor groups were employed in Community Chests, and labor began to play a more significant role in social work.

This role was not limited to aiding the local, state, and national Community Chests and the Red Cross in the united fund raising appeals in factory, plants, docks, and union meetings. In view of the essential efforts of organized labor in raising the high amounts needed for domestic and foreign war relief activities, it was only natural that labor leaders were no longer satisfied with mere "window dressing" representation of labor on boards of social agencies, Community Chests, and welfare councils.[24] Their participation in fund raising campaigns, social welfare planning, and policy development of individual agencies led to understanding and a sincere interest among labor unions and their membership in social work. Labor representatives were able to interpret to union members the need for, and the value of, health and welfare services for their own families

[24] Howard Keeler, "Unions in Social Work," *Social Work Year Book, 1951,* pp. 518-519; Brent Taylor, "Labor Becomes a Big Giver," *Survey Graphic,* February, 1943, pp. 47-48. A significant picture of labor's contribution is presented by Prof. Arthur Hillman, "Labor Joins the Chicago Council: Social Work and Labor Explore Their Common Ground," *Community,* Vol. 22, No. 3, November, 1946, pp. 48 ff.

and for the whole working class, as well as for the sick, old, infirm, and needy children of the community.

In the postwar era, the interest of labor unions in the support of social services through participation in Community Chest campaigns has continued.[25] Closely connected with this active help in raising the necessary funds for voluntary welfare and health agencies is the participation of labor representatives in community welfare councils, which are concerned with the planning of development, concentration, or expansion of social welfare, health and defense facilities. Labor feels that these services should not be handled by a few wealthy people alone, but by representatives of the common man as well. The third result of this sharing in participation of union representatives in policy-making boards and committees of social agencies (though it usually is only a modest participation in view of the economic and social importance of labor) is that union members and their families are better aware of, and more willing to use, the services of health and welfare agencies. Union members are independent people who are little accustomed to turning to public or private social agencies in time of difficulties. Union counselors have recently been able to dissipate the distrust of union members against social agencies and enable them to use services of the community. The experience of union representatives in social agencies has developed mutual respect between labor and social workers. The participation of organized labor in social work is increasingly accepted as a method for more effective interpretation of social work to the public, and as a fair and constructive relationship. Finally, the cooperation of unions in social work planning will bring into focus unmet needs of the community so that Community Chests and Welfare Councils will more easily realize where essential, actual health and welfare needs require new or expanded services.

During the Depression years of the 1930's social workers and clerical and technical employees of social agencies began to join labor unions which were interested in organizing staffs of social agencies into their membership. The aim of the so-called "rank-and-file movement" was to improve working conditions and wages, to gain influence in the professional organizations, and to stimulate

---

[25] In 1950, one to five labor representatives were employed in thirty-five Community Chests in order to maintain the financial support of the workers to social welfare and their responsibility in its activities.

———, *Union Health and Welfare Plans* (Bulletin No. 900). Washington, D.C.: 1947 and 1949.

U. S. Federal Security Agency, *Counseling Services for Workers*. Washington, D.C.: Government Printing Office, 1944.

U. S. Federal Security Agency, Office of Community War Services, *A Guide for Establishment and Operation of In-Plant and Community Information and Counseling Services for Workers*. Washington, D.C.: Government Printing Office, 1944.

Van Eenam, Weltha, and Martha E. Penman, *Analysis of 346 Group Annuities Underwritten in 1946-50*. Washington, D.C.: Social Security Administration, 1952.

Van Kleeck, Mary, "Social Work on the Industrial Frontier," *The Compass*, November, 1944, pp. 3-7.

Weinerman, E. Richard, *Labor Plans for Health: The San Francisco Survey*. San Francisco: Labor Council, 1952.

18. Public Housing and Social Welfare

Social welfare is deeply concerned with adequate housing; next to food and clothing, housing is one of the basic necessities of man, particularly for the maintenance of family life. Housing is a social, an economic, and a civic problem. All three aspects of housing need full consideration. Two movements during the nineteenth century directed public attention to the problems of housing. The first movement was caused by the conditions of the slums and was aimed at housing reform. In New York, the Association for Improving the Condition of the Poor began, in 1842, to describe the dangers of filthy, dark, ill-ventilated slum dwellings. It fought for tenement-house reform and statutory controls of unsafe, unsanitary buildings. In England, Octavia Hill organized rent collection in workers' quarters through volunteer women who were eager to help the residents by advice and practical guidance in home management. In the 1890's the settlement houses in the United States followed this example and tried to improve living and housing conditions, particularly for poor immigrant families in the neighborhood. The social reformers called to the attention of city councils and state legislatures the dangers for health and morale that were created by slums and unsanitary, overcrowded city tenements without sufficient light, heat, air, and plumbing. They asked for regulations which would secure water and sanitary facilities, light, ventilation, and adequate space.

The second movement, "city planning," had as its objective the protection of good residential neighborhoods from the intrusion of factories and substandard construction. It attempted to relate new dwellings to their sites, providing adequate space, privacy, sanitation, water, light, air, gardens, and an attractive exterior in order to de-

516

velop healthy living quarters. It also considered the relation-ship of the neighborhood to the entire community—transporta-tion, communications, hospitals, schools, and recreational facilities.[1] During the last decades both movements have found a joint objective in striving for the construction of healthy, comfortable houses in decent neighborhoods, in urban and rural areas, at a reasonable price, thus providing adequate housing for the entire population.

Housing needs are determined by two main factors. The rapid growth of cities in our industrial age has caused a deficit in the actual dwelling supply in relation to the increasing size of the popu-lation. This shortage was aggravated by the lack of civilian, residen-tial construction during World War II. The other aspect of housing needs is a qualitative one. Millions of urban and rural dwellings are lacking running water, toilet, and private bath. They have become outmoded, overcrowded, unsafe, unsanitary, or are in need of major repairs or replacement. The U.S. Housing Census of 1940 revealed that 6,200,000, or 28.6 per cent, of all urban dwellings, 5,150,000, or 63.9 per cent, of rural residential dwellings, and 6,900,000, or 90 per cent, of rural farm homes were deficient in these facilities or were in need of major repairs.[2]

Increased wages and full employment in World War II brought indirectly some improvement in housing conditions. A sample sur-vey of the U.S. Census Bureau in 1947 showed an increase of dwell-ings to 41,625,000; urban and non-farm dwellings had increased to 34,133,000; family homes decreased to 7,492,000. Sanitary conditions of residential housing had improved. But still 27 per cent of urban and rural non-farm dwellings and 80 per cent of farm homes were classified as below standard. In spite of some progress, there are still many dwellings overcrowded (where more than 1.5 persons live in one room); married couples have to live "doubled-up" with other families, and over 100,000 families are without an apartment or

[1] See Edith Elmer Wood, *Housing of the Unskilled Wage Earner* (New York: Macmillan, 1919); Hugh R. Pomeroy, "Housing and City Planning," *Social Work Year Book, 1949*, pp. 233-244; Wilson S. Borland, "Housing and City Planning," *Social Work Year Book, 1951*, pp. 229-238; Arthur Hillman, *Community Organization and Planning* (New York: Macmillan, 1950), pp. 111-129; and Bryn F. Hovde, "Housing and City Planning," *Social Work Year Book, 1954*, pp. 257-266.

[2] National Housing Agency, *Reference and Source Material on Housing and Housing Needs* (1947), pp. 4-5.

house.[3] In cities environmental deficiencies are found due to the lack of organized, planned development: overuse of land, outmoded street patterns, "shack towns" in suburban areas, poor traffic conditions, and lack of adequate transportation, parks, playgrounds, and other recreational facilities.

Thomas photo. Courtesy National Child Labor Committee

HOT SHACKS—LITTLE VENTILATION

Legislation in the field of housing began on the local level in New York City and a few metropolitan cities[4] in the 1860's, with regulations that required building practices for fire protection, and correction of the worst slum conditions. Land and building speculators, however, continued in big cities and industrial regions the business practice of constructing substandard tenements and of purchasing exemption from regulations by political corruption.[5] Practical experience proved that private enterprise on a competitive market

[3] W. Borland, *op. cit.*, p. 230.

[4] State legislation in the realm of public housing with subsidies for low-rent construction was first passed in New York. In England, the *Housing of the Working Classes Act* as early as 1890 enabled cities and towns to construct sanitary dwellings and to eliminate slums.

[5] Langdon W. Post, *The Challenge of Housing* (New York: Rinehart, 1938), pp. 81, 119-123.

could not produce decent, sanitary, and sufficiently spacious housing for low-income families without tax exemptions and substantial government subsidies for low-rent dwellings. Housing legislation, therefore, approached the social need of adequate housing for families of low income through (a) restrictive regulations, building codes, condemnation procedures for unsafe, unsanitary buildings, and zoning; (b) tax exemptions for adequate housing at low rents; (c) subsidies to private builders, corporations, and housing societies for the construction of good, low-rent dwellings in replacement of slums; (d) government intervention through financing of private construction by loans or guarantees; and (e) governmental housing construction of low-cost housing units.

In the Depression of the 1930's federal housing legislation started with the *Home Loan Act* of 1932. It established the Federal Home Loan Bank Board (renamed in 1947 the "Home Loan Bank Board") as a credit institution to savings banks and loan societies in order to rescue desperate farm and home owners. In 1933, the Home Owners' Loan Corporation was founded in order to aid individual home owners through refinancing of mortgage debts on long-term, low interest amortization. In 1934, the *National Housing Act* established a system of mortgage insurance, administered by the Federal Housing Administration, as an important stimulus to private home construction. From 1934 to 1949 it insured, at modest interest, twelve million mortgages, amounting to $18 billion and encouraged high standard construction. But this program scarcely secured housing improvement for the low income group.[6]

Direct action in order to build decent housing for low-income groups started under the Public Works Administration (PWA) in 1933, primarily set up in order to povide jobs for the unemployed. In 1937, the *United States Housing Act* created a permanent program for planning, construction, and management of public housing projects under local housing authorities, approved by state laws. It was administered by the U.S. Housing Authority, now renamed "Public Housing Administration," and provided long-range loans and annual contributions to approved projects. During World War II additional war housing projects were financed under the Lanham Act, which created residential facilities for eight million persons. After the war, in 1947, the Housing and Home Finance Agency replaced the Na-

[6] W. Borland, *op. cit.,* pp. 230-232.

tional Housing Agency. It consists of four divisions: (1) the Federal Housing Administration, (2) the Public Housing Administration, (3) the Home Loan Bank Board, and (4) the National Housing Council as coordinating body for all activities in this field with representatives of other federal agencies, and it is now the federal organization in the field of public housing. Its policies comprise research, financial assistance to private enterprise, and modest public housing programs. In Congress the *Wagner-Ellender-Taft Bill* of 1945 and the *Taft-Ellender-Wagner Bill* of 1947 were not passed due to the influence of opponents of public housing. However, a number of states and over two hundred cities appropriated funds to construct public housing or assist private building, usually with preference for war veterans.

In 1949, the federal *Housing Act* announced, as a "Declaration of National Housing Policy," that the general welfare and security of the nation and the health and living standards of its people require housing production and related community developments sufficient to remedy the serious housing shortage. It also demanded the elimination of substandard and other inadequate housing through the clearance of slums and blighted areas, and the realization as soon as feasible of the goal of a decent home and a suitable living environment for every American family. In order to achieve this goal in the future, previous public activities should be continued: slum clearance and urban redevelopment with federal assistance to local communities, subsidies for low-cost housing, special aid to large families, stimulation of private investment in public housing developments, research in housing costs, methods, and standards, and aid to farm construction. Development of public housing projects for middle-income families with annual earnings from $2,800 to $4,400 have been facilitated by the *Housing Act of 1950*.

City planning—the thoughtful, scientific development of cities along rational lines devised to contribute to the health, amenity, convenience, and security of the citizens and to further commerce and employment[7]—is carried on by local and a few regional planning commissions in more than 2,000 cities and four hundred counties. These agencies are in charge of zoning, street and highway construction, and urban redevelopment, but they often are hampered by inadequate budgets and stubborn resistance of special interest groups.

[7] *Ibid.*, p. 236; and Catherine Bauer, "Housing in the United States," *International Labor Review*, July, 1945, pp. 18-21.

	United States	Urban and Rural Non-Farm			Rural Farm
		Total	Urban	Rural Non-Farm	
Total dwelling units	45,983,398	39,625,455	29,569,073	10,056,382	6,357,943
Number reporting	44,502,192	38,367,616	28,762,804	9,604,812	6,134,576
Not dilapidated:	40,162,719	35,222,966	26,909,029	8,313,937	4,939,753
Private toilet and bath, hot running water	28,102,478	26,671,966	22,371,438	4,300,528	1,430,512
Private toilet and bath, only cold water	1,435,345	1,307,310	934,740	372,570	128,035
Running water, no toilet or bath	5,491,491	4,570,600	3,033,928	1,536,672	920,801
No running water	5,133,405	2,673,090	568,923	2,104,167	2,460,315
Dilapidated:	4,339,473	3,144,650	1,853,775	1,290,875	1,194,883
Private toilet and bath, hot running water	626,997	596,555	510,102	86,453	30,442
Lacking hot water, private toilet, bath	3,712,476	2,548,095	1,343,673	1,204,422	1,164,381
Condition or presuming facilities not reported	1,481,206	1,257,839	866,269	451,570	223,367

Percentages

	United States	Total	Urban	Rural Non-Farm	Rural Farm
Total dwelling units	....	....	....	....	....
Number reporting	100.0	100.0	100.0	100.0	100.0
Not dilapidated:	90.1	91.3	93.5	86.6	80.5
Private toilet and bath, hot running water	63.1	69.5	77.8	44.8	23.3
Private toilet and bath, only cold water	3.2	3.4	3.2	3.9	2.1
Running water, no toilet or bath	12.3	11.4	10.5	16.0	15.0
No running water	11.5	7.0	2.0	21.9	40.1
Dilapidated:	9.7	8.2	6.5	13.4	19.5
Private toilet and bath, hot running water	1.4	1.6	1.8	0.9	0.5
Lacking hot water, private toilet, bath	8.3	6.6	4.7	12.5	19.0
Condition or presuming facilities not reported	....	....	....	....	....

It should be noted that the term "dilapidated" does not mean the same as "major repairs," which was used in the 1940 census. These figures were taken from the 1950 census; the definitions for the terms used are considerably different, and a comparison cannot be made with the 1940 census because of this.

The recognition that a foresighted and constructive housing policy is one of the essential requirements in the cultural program of the nation is slowly making progress in the population. Housing reform was first the concern of a small group of social reformers and social workers, but at present legislative bodies, business, industry, labor, and veterans take part in the shaping of housing policy. From the beginning of housing reform, such social workers as Jane Addams and her friends at Hull House and in other settlement houses[8] have been among the pioneers of slum clearance, tenement house legislation, and better housing. They were especially aware of the dangers of unsanitary, unsafe housing for all aspects of family life and were among the most active fighters for the development of sound housing concepts and policies, for the building of decent homes for low-income families, and for sound city planning.

Family and children's agencies and leisure-time and recreation organizations cooperate with housing authorities and offer their services to families residing in housing projects. They are helpful in developing new constructive forms of neighborhood life—recreation centers for children and young people, adult discussion groups, and art and drama clubs. In a setting very different from the old slums surrounding the settlement houses, they apply some of their creative social ingenuity.

Special housing needs exist for the older generation.[9] Old-age and survivors' insurance benefits, private annuities, public service retirement allowances, and industrial pensions establish a certain economic security for many of our senior citizens so that they do not have to look forward to a sad end in the poorhouse. However, the amount of monthly income derived from these programs is, in general, so modest that their free choice as to where they live still is rather restricted whenever their health conditions make it difficult to climb narrow stairs, or to use old-fashioned heating, kitchen, and bathroom equipment. Their failing strength will prevent many old couples or single widows and widowers from maintaining a clean household and getting adequate food, so that they will be endangered by malnutrition and illness. For the older generation housing costs have been disproportionally high as was shown by research studies of

[8] Jane Addams, *Twenty Years at Hull House* (New York: Macmillan, 1910), pp. 98-100, 289, 294-296.

[9] See Hertha Kraus, "Housing Our Older Citizens," *The Annals of the American Academy of Political and Social Science*, January, 1952, pp. 126-130.

the Social Security Administration in 1946-1948. This research in eight large cities found that older people spent from 37 to 51 per cent of their total budget on rent, heating, and light.[10] This high expense limits their purchase abilities for nutritious food, adequate clothing, medical care, medicines, and cultural and recreational needs. It also makes it more difficult for the aged to invite and to visit with relatives and friends, although often they have a deep yearning to maintain personal friendships and social contacts to relieve their loneliness.

As we discussed above, present community services are not sufficient. One essential improvement would be created if the present supply of low- and medium-cost housing facilities would be enlarged and improved in order to meet the particular needs of older persons. New housing projects should include single story units without stairways, and well-lighted, airy apartments with modern home-management facilities. Homemaker and nursing services should be kept ready in cooperation with community welfare agencies to make it simple for old people in such housing units to secure proper care, food, and medical attention in order to preserve their health and limited strength. The experiments of cottage colonies or special apartment houses for the aged in New York, New Jersey, California, Florida, Colorado, and Connecticut deserve careful attention and research followup. Most older people prefer to live in their own homes, in familiar surroundings with their furniture and personal belongings. But many are in need of long-time domestic help, nursing care, and medical supervision which may be provided by social agencies if the homes of the aged are not too widely scattered in the community, are readily accessible, and if housing arrangements permit the old people to care for themselves as much as possible and to assist other companions in such an environment.

Senior citizens should not be forced to live in any specific type of residence. It may be expected, however, that many older people prefer quiet housing facilities of low-rent type to a mixed surrounding with noisy children and teen-agers whose habits are not conducive to the rhythm of life of the old. Such facilities also need good transportation so that relatives and friends may visit them easily. The planning of good housing facilities for older couples or

[10] *Ibid.*, p. 127; "A Budget for an Elderly Couple," *Social Security Bulletin*, Vol. 11, No. 2, February, 1948, pp. 4-12; New York State Joint Legislative Committee on Problems of the Aging, *Age Is No Barrier*, (1952), pp. 10-17, 117-119.

single persons could be included in public housing projects or in units financially supported by government. Senior housing group apartments or cottages and companion apartments have been suggested as possible types which would be economical, would accommodate substantial numbers of older persons, and may be easily coordinated for housekeeping, cleaning, and laundry services provided by the management of such units.[11]

Similar special public housing needs exist for handicapped, blind, and crippled persons, who cannot obtain normal housing at prices they are able to pay. In some public housing projects the rights of racial and religious minority groups have been protected by "no discrimination" clauses and a policy of management that gives particular consideration to their needs so that they are accepted as well as other families.

The setting up of a social service department in larger housing units under the public housing authorities has been made in some instances with success. Social workers serve as counselor, as family caseworker, and as group worker in this setting if they are professionally trained to perform such a variety of functions. In England and France social workers are employed more frequently by housing authorities in large projects than here. It may be possible, however, to assume some of the preventive action in preserving good family relations and developing sound recreational and cultural life in housing projects by an intensive use of available social agencies in the community which may give special attention to the social needs of senior residents in new housing units.

Social workers know that decent housing is a fundamental requirement for wholesome family living. Suitable housing opportunities need to be provided throughout the country for the entire population under conditions that are within the financial capacity of all citizens. For the lowest income groups, the government will have to assume the responsibility for an adequate supply of public housing facilities, because private construction cannot build with profit for their needs. In order to secure good housing, a comprehensive program of loans and grants-in-aid for public low-rent housing projects is necessary. Slums, shack towns, and similar substandard areas show a much higher incidence of disease, infant mortality, crime, juvenile

11 H. Kraus, *op. cit.*, pp. 132-137; and Wilbur C. Hallenbeck, *American Urban Communities* (New York: Harper, 1951).

delinquency, and fire as compared with normal residential neighborhoods and are a danger for the entire community.

The development of adequate housing for low- and medium-income groups of citizens requires construction by private builders and under public auspices. Human needs for health, comfort, privacy, and safety must be satisfied; rents or purchase prices should be based upon the ability of the families to pay. Cooperation of surrounding communities is needed to afford education, worship, employment, safety from traffic and other hazards, health protection, recreation, welfare services, and shopping facilities. No discrimination as to creed, race, color, national origin, or class status should be permitted. Families with several children, persons with special health problems, and migratory workers need special consideration and protection.[12] Rural housing reform is a particular problem because of the reluctance of farmers to make changes, and because of the high cost of rural construction. Under the *Housing Act of 1949*, the Department of Agriculture is entitled to give loans to farmers for housing improvement for which they are unable to obtain loans from banks or loan cooperatives (credit unions). The distribution is made through the Farmers Home Administration, and the loans may be used for adequate housing of the farmers and of their farm workers.

SELECTED BIBLIOGRAPHY

Abbott, Edith, *The Tenements of Chicago: 1908-1935*. Chicago: University of Chicago Press, 1936.

Abrams, Charles, *The Future of Housing*. New York: Harper, 1946.

American Housing: Problems and Prospects. New York: Twentieth Century Fund, 1944.

Aronovici, Carol, *Housing and the Housing Problem*. Chicago: McClurg, 1920.

———, and Elizabeth McCalmont, *Catching Up with Housing*. New Jersey: Beneficial Management Association, 1936.

Bauer, Catherine, *A Citizen's Guide to Public Housing*. Poughkeepsie, N.Y.: Vassar College, 1940.

———, "Housing in the United States, Problems and Policy," *International Labour Review*, Vol. LII, No. 1, July, 1945.

[12] American Association of Social Workers, *Statement on a National Housing Program*, May, 1946, pp. 1-2; Catherine Bauer, *op. cit.*, p. 5; Clayton C. Jones, "Group Work in the Low-Rent Housing Setting," in Charles Hendry, *A Decade of Group Work*, (New York: Association Press, 1948), pp. 77-85, and Morton Deutsch and Mary Evans Collins, *Interracial Housing* (Minneapolis: University of Minnesota Press, 1951).

*————, *Modern Housing.* New York: Houghton, 1934.

Blandford, John B., *Our Postwar Housing Problem.* Chicago: National Association of Assessing Offices, 1944.

*Borland, Wilson S., "Housing and City Planning," *Social Work Year Book, 1951*, pp. 229-238.

Breese, Gerald, and Dorothy E. Whiteman, *An Approach to Urban Planning.* Princeton: Princeton University Press, 1953.

Churchill, Henry S., *The City Is the People.* New York: Reynal, 1945.

Dahir, James, *Communities for Better Living; Citizen Achievement in Organization, Design and Develoment.* New York: Harper, 1950.

————, *The Neighborhood Unit Plan, Its Spread and Acceptance.* New York: Russell Sage Foundation, 1947.

Ebenstein, William, *The Law of Public Housing.* Madison: University of Wisconsin Press, 1940.

*Fitch, James Marston, *American Building: The Forces That Shape It.* Boston: Houghton, 1948.

Foley, Donald L., *Neighbors or Urbanites?* Rochester, N.Y.: University of Rochester, 1952.

Ford, James, *Slums and Housing.* Cambridge: Harvard University Press, 1936.

Gold, Henry R., *Sociology of Public Housing.* Dallas: Housing Authority, 1940.

Goodman, Percival, and Paul Goodman, *Communitas: Means of Livelihood and Ways of Life.* Chicago: University of Chicago Press, 1947.

Gray, George H., *Housing and Citizenship; A Study of Low-Cost Housing.* New York: Reinhold, 1946.

Gutheim, Frederick A., *Houses for Family Living.* New York: The Women's Foundation, 1948.

Hill, John G., "Fifty Years of Social Action on the Housing Front," *Social Service Review*, Vol. XXII, No. 2, June, 1948.

Hovde, Bryn J., "Housing and City Planning," *Social Work Year Book, 1954*, pp. 257-266.

Klutznick, Philip M., "Public Housing Charts Its Course," *Survey Grahic*, Vol. XXXIV, No. 1, January, 1945, pp. 15-18.

Kraus, Hertha, "Housing Our Older Citizens," *Annals of the American Academy of Political and Social Science*, Vol. 279, January, 1952, pp. 126-138.

————, "Older Persons Have Special Housing Needs," *Journal of Housing*, January, 1950.

Mumford, Lewis, *City Development; Studies in Disintegration and Renewal.* New York: Harcourt, 1945.

————, *The Culture of Cities.* New York: Harcourt, 1938.

National Associations of Housing Officials, *Community Services and Public Housing.* Chicago: 1947.

Perry, Clarence A., *Housing for the Machine Age.* New York: Russell Sage Foundation, 1939.

*Pomeroy, Hugh R., "Housing and City Planning," *Social Work Year Book, 1949*, pp. 233-244.

Post, Langdon W., *The Challenge of Housing*. New York: Rinehart, 1938.

Reed, William V., and Elizabeth Ogg, *New Homes for Old*. New York: Foreign Policy Association, 1940.

Reiss, Richard L., *British and American Housing*. New York: National Public Housing Conference, 1937.

Robbins, Ira S., "Housing Our Aging," New York State Legislative Committee on Problems of the Aging, *Age Is No Barrier* (1952), pp. 117-119.

Sanders, S. E., and A. J. Rabuck, *New City Patterns; the Analysis of a Technique of Urban Reintegration*. New York: Reinhold, 1946.

Schnapper, M. B., *Public Housing in America*. New York: Wilson, 1939.

Sharp, Thomas, *The Anatomy of the Village*. Baltimore: Allen Lane, Penguin Books, 1946.

Straus, Nathan, *The Seven Myths of Housing*. New York: Knopf, 1945.

——, *Two-Thirds of a Nation: A Housing Program*. New York: Knopf, 1952.

United States Housing Authority, Federal Works Agency, *Housing and Welfare*. Washington, D.C.: Government Printing Office, 1940.

Watson, Frank, *Housing Problems and Possibilities in the United States*. New York: Harper, 1935.

Wood, Edith Elmer, *Introduction to Housing: Facts and Principles*. Washington, D.C.: U.S. Housing Authority, 1940.

*——, *Recent Trends in American Housing*. New York: Macmillan, 1940.

19. International Social Welfare

International social work is the youngest branch of social welfare activities. It is based upon the recognition that international cooperation in social welfare is needed in order to assure the well-being, social and economic security, and good health for human beings everywhere which are indispensable for securing world peace and stability.

Intergovernmental action to develop a peaceful world comprises the activities of the United Nations in regard to world trade, international courts, communication, and education. Social work contributes to these efforts its awareness of human needs and suffering, its respect for human dignity, and its skill in helping human beings, particularly in relief of hunger and disease, in fighting catastrophes, and in rehabilitation services.

International social welfare organizations may be classified into four groups:

1. Government agencies of international character (for example, the United Nations, World Health Organization, UNESCO, International Labor Organization).

2. Private international organizations (for example, the International Conference of Social Work, International Red Cross, International Child Welfare Union, World YWCA, World Federation of Mental Health, World Assembly of Youth).

3. National government agencies extending their work to other countries (for example, the U.S. Children's Bureau, U.S. Public Health Service).

4. National private agencies extending their social service to other countries (for example, the Danish or Swedish Red Cross, Swiss Aid to Europe, the Dutch Interchurch Aid, American Friends Service Committee, American Joint Jewish Distribution Com-

mittee, Church World Service, Catholic Community Service Council, Unitarian Service Committee).[1]

I. HISTORY OF INTERNATIONAL SOCIAL WELFARE

The first international activities in social welfare developed about the mid-nineteenth century when representatives of private and public charities began to organize international conferences in order to share their experiences and thereby to learn of effective new methods in the field of social services. These conventions met at various cities of Europe, frequently in Paris, Brussels, London, Frankfurt-am-Main, Milan, Stockholm, later in the United States in Chicago, and in Washington, D.C. The content of the conventions was related to special problems which were reflected in their titles: International Congress of Charities, Corrections and Philanthropy; Penitentiary Congress; International Penal and Prison Congress; Universal Congress for the Improvement of the Fate of the Blind; International Congress of Public and Private Relief; and International Congress for the Protection of Discharged Prisoners.

After World War I, the International Conference of Social Work met for the first time in Paris, in 1928, and became the international forum of comprehensive character for the exchange of experiences and ideas in social welfare. The purposes of the International Conference are to bring social workers of all countries of the world together with the aim to improve, by mutual exchange of knowledge, social welfare systems and methods of social work. Conferences were held after the founding conference in Paris at Frankfurt-am-Main, in 1932, and in London, in 1936. After interruption by World War II, the fourth conference met in Atlantic City and New York in 1948, the fifth in Paris, in 1950, the sixth in Madras, India, in 1952 and the seventh in Toronto, in 1954. The first proposal of an International Conference was made by Dr. Clotilde Mulon of Paris, but the real organizer and founder of the International Conference was Professor René Sand of the University of Brussels (Belgium).

The first large-scale organization of many nations which is re-

[1] A similar classification is suggested by George L. Warren, "International Social Work," *Social Work Year Book, 1943,* pp. 232-249; and Savilla Millis Simons, "International Social Work," *Social Work Year Book, 1951,* pp. 245-247.

lated to social welfare was the International Red Cross.[2] Its foundation was inspired by the vision of Henri Dunant, a young banker of Geneva. By accident, he came to the battlefield of Solferino in 1859 and was so shocked by the suffering of the wounded and dying soldiers on both sides that he wrote a book describing these horrors entitled "Un Souvenir de Solferino." He asked for humane treatment of the wounded. This book stirred public opinion in many countries and led to the Geneva Convention of 1864, at which the International Red Cross was founded. Its articles provide that under the guidance of an International Committee, composed of Swiss citizens, principles of humane treatment and medical care of wounded soldiers were to be established, and that hospitals, ambulances, doctors, and nurses caring for these patients should be respected as neutral institutions. The International Committee recognizes new national societies of the Red Cross, encourages all civilized nations to join the Geneva Convention, and attempts to secure the observance of this international law. The International Committee also organizes, if necessary, special agencies in periods of war for the relief of civilian populations, the communication with prisoners of war, including the sending of letters and parcels to these prisoners from their families. It arranges for visits and inspection of prisoner of war camps, and conducts special relief actions in case of major natural catastrophes.

After World War I, in 1919, the League of Red Cross Societies was formed as a federation of the national organizations, aside from the International Committee. The League consists of sixty-eight national Red Cross societies, promotes voluntary national Red Cross work, and encourages collaboration for the improvement of health, prevention of disease, and relief in case of epidemics, earthquakes, floods, and fires.

During World War I, Red Cross societies began to conduct large-scale relief actions. The American and British Red Cross organized hospitals, convalescent homes, dispensaries, and infirmaries in France, Belgium, Italy, and Greece. After the war, international relief actions were continued under the auspices of the International Red Cross, as well as by various national Red Cross societies and other relief organizations. A children's fund for the feeding of under-

2 Martin Gumpert, *Dunant, The Story of the Red Cross* (New York: Oxford University Press, 1938); and Ernest P. Bicknell, *With the Red Cross in Europe* (Washington, D.C.: American National Red Cross, 1938).

nourished children and for the establishment of child welfare centers, summer camps, kindergartens, and various schools in many European countries characterizes a development of international welfare service.[3]

Red Cross societies were joined in this effort during and after both world wars by other relief organizations, such as the American Friends Service Committee, the British Service Committee (Quakers), the American Jewish Joint Distribution Committee (A.D.C.), the International Save-the-Children Fund (now called the "International Child Welfare Union"), the American Relief Administration, the Near East Foundation, the European Children's Fund, and other philanthropic and humanitarian organizations.

During the period between the two wars, the International Save-the-Children Fund was particularly active in developing child health and welfare services in Ethiopia, Central Africa, and the Balkan countries. The Near East Foundation assisted in the rehabilitation of Greece by setting up hospitals, orphanages, and schools. The Joint Distribution Committee continued its work for children, orphans, and medical care in eastern Europe. It was assisted by another international organization, "O.S.E.," an international federation for the provision of medical care, hospitals, and dispensaries and for the training of Jewish doctors, nurses, and health personnel. Another international organization which developed at the end of the first World War was "O.R.T.," which is devoted to the vocational training of young Jewish persons to prepare them for immigration and resettlement.

During World War I, recreational services were developed by the American Young Women's Christian Associations in various European countries. The international organization of the YWCA, called "World's YWCA," had already been founded earlier in England, in 1894, and helped after and during World War I in refugee and immigration aid. In 1921, it organized a nondenominational International Migration Service (now called "International Social Service") as an independent agency with headquarters in Geneva. The national YMCA's founded an International Committee in 1879 and carried on an extensive program of international service, mutual visits, and conferences; a YMCA committee for war prisoners' aid was active in both world wars.

[3] John Maloney, *Let There Be Mercy* (New York: Doubleday, 1944).

A new stimulus to international cooperation was given by the foundation of the League of Nations.[4] The League had a standing committee on social welfare, and its secretariat established a section on "Social Questions and Opium Traffic." The Committee on Social Questions was particularly concerned with protection of women and children against prostitution ("Traffic in Women and Children"). This committee dealt also with methods of protection of children in the field of child labor, with measures for young people in periods of unemployment, and with the suppression of obscene publications. The committee published reports on child marriage, the status of illegitimate children, the setup of child welfare councils, guardianship for illegitimate children, and work in institutions and foster families for children. In the field of health protection the Health Organization of the League published information on epidemics in cooperation with the International Office of Public Health in Paris and set up special bureaus in Singapore and Rio de Janeiro for protective measures against communicable diseases and epidemics. With a permanent world-wide service for the dissemination of epidemiological information, the Health Organization assisted governments in the development of public health systems by interchange of experts and technical personnel and the assignment of specialists to other countries.

II. THE UNITED NATIONS RELIEF AND REHABILITATION ADMINISTRATION (UNRRA)

The United Nations Relief and Rehabilitation Administration (UNRRA) became the most dynamic force in the development of international social welfare. Founded on November 9, 1943, in Washington, D.C., by forty-four nations, it was an international organization, preceding the United Nations, that was called upon to solve relief problems of tremendous magnitude. The aggression of

[4] See Harriet E. Davis (editor), *Pioneers in World Order* (New York: Columbia University Press, 1944); Martin Hill, *The Economic and Financial Organization of the League of Nations* (Washington, D.C.: Carnegie Endowment, 1946); Arthur Sweetzer, "The Non-Political Achievements of the League," *Foreign Affairs*, October, 1940; League of Nations, Economic Department, *Europe's Overseas Needs, 1919-1920, and How They Were Met* (Geneva: 1924); and Carlile A. Macartney, *Refugees, the Work of the League* (London: League of Nations Union, 1936).

the Axis powers had in three years overrun thirty-five countries in Europe and Asia, destroying their economic and political system. It left them in semistarvation, ravaged by hunger, diseases, epidemics and despair, without sufficient food, clothes, and shelter, and lacking care for the sick and homeless. To assist the victims of the war and to restore, after their liberation, normal living conditions, morale, health, and hope was a task which could be undertaken only through the cooperation of all countries of the free world.

As early as in August, 1940, Winston Churchill had announced that after the defeat of the Nazis, supplies of food, medicine, raw materials, and the means for reconstruction would be provided to the liberated countries by interallied collaboration. The Leith-Ross Committee (Allied Committee on Post-War Requirements) in London started work for relief and rehabilitation in Europe. The Middle-East Relief and Refugee Administration (MERRA) in Cairo, Egypt, established camps for refugees from the countries attacked by the Axis powers (Poland, Greece, Yugoslavia, Czechoslovakia). In the United States, President Franklin D. Roosevelt, in 1948, established the Office of Foreign Relief and Rehabilitation Operations under the able leadership of former Governor Herbert Lehman, of New York, which began relief work for civilians in North Africa in cooperation with the Allied armies.

The creation of UNRRA became a promise to the people in the invaded countries and to their underground fighters, giving them assurance that the nations of the free world would share their resources in food, clothing, medicine, and emergency supplies as soon as help possibly could be brought. The basic idea was that victory was not enough, that peace also had to be won.

When UNRRA was able to go into action, it curbed widespread starvation, prevented epidemics, and averted moral and economic collapse in all seventeen war-warped countries where its assistance was requested.[5] It took over the refugee camps in the Middle East and began to bring food, clothing, medicine, and shelter for the hungry, sick, and homeless populations. This relief spelled the difference between life and death for millions of men, women, and

[5] United Nations Relief and Rehabilitation Administration, *The Story of UNRRA* (Washington, D.C.: 1948), p. 3 ff; National Planning Association, *UNRRA: Gateway to Recovery* (Washington, D.C.: 1944), pp. 12-17; Harold H. Hutcheson, "International Agencies for European Reconstruction," *Foreign Policy Reports*, Vol. XXIII, No. 9, July 15, 1947, pp. 110-120.

children. It was the more urgent as the war was a global one spreading to Europe, Asia, the South Pacific, the Near East, and Africa. The entire population of the war-devastated countries was affected. Strategic bombing destroyed vast areas; the "scorched earth" policy of the Nazis increased the suffering of the civilian population terrorized by concentration camps, and their inhuman, criminal "biological extermination" murdered millions of innocent human beings.

UNRRA's resources, though they amounted in total to more than three billion dollars, never were large enough to restore fully the shattered economy of the occupied countries. They could not rebuild the destroyed cities, public utilities, factories, mines, ports, railroads, and fishing fleets. But UNRRA put back into operation the segments of the national economy that were indispensable for the survival of the people, for the carrying out of the relief program, and for the start of rehabilitation. In order to prevent starvation, UNRRA furnished food and medicine, doctors, nurses, and hospitals. In order to repair roads, bridges, and communications, it provided trucks, bulldozers, freight cars and repair supplies. Millions of refugees and slave laborers captured by the Axis powers were cared for in camps, children's homes, and reception centers.

The main principle of UNRRA was not only to provide relief but also to lay the groundwork for the economic and social recovery of the occupied countries, in order *to help people to help themselves.*[6] UNRRA's tasks were gigantic. It was the greatest of all relief and rehabilitation undertakings ever attempted in human history. It worked at a time when the world was in chaos and the supplies and materials that UNRRA urgently wanted for its work were almost nonobtainable because the fighting armies needed them also: food, clothing, medicine, ships, trucks, railroads, other supplies. UNRRA also had to struggle against the shortage of manpower because in all Allied countries men were needed for the armed forces. It often faced jealousy and mistrust on behalf of the military authorities who thought that they could administer relief themselves. In order to carry on this difficult task more effectively, UNRRA created an international administration, which formed a

[6] Herbert H. Lehman, "UNRRA on the March," *Survey Graphic*, Vol. 33, No. 11, November, 1944, pp. 436-440, 470-471; *UNRRA: Gateway to Recovery*, p. 15; Martha Brandscombe, "The Children of the United Nations—UNRRA's Responsibility for Social Welfare," *Social Service Review*, Vol. XIX, No. 3, September, 1945, pp. 310-323.

loyal staff deeply devoted to the challenging cause of international aid.

At the end of the war, most nations were desperately in need of the means for survival and rehabilitation. UNRRA accepted the challenge to see to it that nations without foreign exchange would not be left without an adequate share in these rare supplies so that they could avoid starvation and economic collapse.

At first, aid was limited to the invaded Allied countries without foreign exchange—Albania, Byelorussia, China, Czechosolvakia, Greece, Poland, the Ukraine, and Yugoslavia—then it was extended to Austria and Italy. Limited help also was given to Ethiopia, Finland, Hungary, Korea, and the Philippines. The occupied western European countries, France, the Netherlands, Belgium, Luxembourg, Denmark, and Norway, owned foreign exchange and did not ask UNRRA aid so that UNRRA could not arrange a relief action for them.

The administration of UNRRA was directed by a Council composed of one representative of each of the forty-eight nations which subscribed to the organization; the Council decided the policy of the agency. A Central Committee composed of representatives of nine governments acted as executive board and made emergency decisions between Council sessions. The executive responsibility and the appointment of the staff was vested in the Director-General—first, Herbert H. Lehman (now United States Senator), then, Fiorello H. LaGuardia (former Mayor of New York), and Major General Lowell W. Rooks. The staff included members of forty nations and totaled, at its peak, over 12,000 persons scattered around the globe. There were experts in administration, food and agriculture, transportation, construction, social welfare, public health, medicine, nursing, communications, finance, and accounting.

In contrast to other international agencies before UNRRA, such as the League of Nations or the International Labor Organization, which had only recommended measures and legislation to their member governments, UNRRA was operating as an "action organization." It also became the testing ground for the collaboration of the Allies. The vast dispersion of its activities throughout the world made their administration and coordination difficult.

Starving, sick, and desperate people wanted quick action where UNRRA could not draw upon tradition and former experience.

UNRRA's international staff was willing to work under trying conditions and sacrifices. There was a wide delegation of authority from the executive branch to the missions and welfare teams.

UNRRA was financed by its member nations which had not been occupied by the enemy. They were asked to contribute 2 per cent of their national income for relief and rehabilitation, while all members agreed to share in the cost of administration. Other nations, private agencies, and individuals made voluntary contributions. The largest contributors were the United States with $2,700,000,000 (about 70 per cent), United Kingdom with $624,650,000, and Canada with $138,738,739.[7] Most contributions were made in the form of commodity credits and supplies.

In order to carry on its program, UNRRA bought three billion dollars worth of food and supplies in many parts of the world, packed and shipped them in more than 6,000 cargo ships over every ocean. It moved into country after country when the Axis forces retreated. It seldom had enough of the many commodities the liberated countries were pleading for, and prompt delivery frequently was delayed by military obstacles, procurement decisions by national agencies, legislative actions in many countries, strikes, changing international policies, changes in government authority, and civil war.

The Council had established the principle that UNRRA supplies should be distributed without regard to politics, race, or religion. It was ordered that food and other supplies should be given without charge to anyone in distress who could not pay for them. But governments were permitted to sell goods to those who were able to pay for them in local currency so that the countries could rebuild their health, welfare, and community services. About one-half of UNRRA's total activities was spent for distribution of food. There was severe hunger in Europe and Asia, widespread malnutrition and hunger diseases. But actual starvation and threatening famines and epidemics were averted through UNRRA food (mostly bread grain, rice, fat, oils, dairy products, canned or powdered milk, sugar, meat, and vegetables). UNRRA furnished agricultural tools, seeds, farm animals, and fertilizer to restore production.

[7] United Nations Relief and Rehabilitation Administration, *op. cit.*, p. 10; and George Woodbridge, *The History of UNRRA* (New York: Columbia University Press, 1950).

UNRRA organized the largest international health program, so far known, which curbed epidemics across Europe and, with the exception of one cholera epidemic, in Asia. The medical staff counseled and assisted the governments of the liberated countries in the rehabilitation of their public health services, with the use of modern medical and sanitary methods, and installed UNRRA's own medical care only in the displaced persons' (DP) camps. UNRRA's health services averted typhus, and other widespread contagious diseases, reduced malaria in Greece and Italy, and stopped cholera epidemics in China and Egypt in 1946 and 1947. Hospitals, nursing schools, and sanitary systems were established with modern medical supplies, and UNRRA taught doctors, nurses, and technicians how to use them.

The care of the refugees and displaced persons became a major task of UNRRA.[8] By May, 1944, UNRRA had taken care of 40,000 Yugoslav, Greek, and Polish refugees, partisans and their families, in tent camps in the Middle East and Northern Africa. In Germany, Austria, and Italy, UNRRA assisted the Allied military forces in the reception of about eight million refugees and slave laborers in assembly centers, and in their repatriation to their home countries. UNRRA also coordinated the work of voluntary social agencies of many countries, which provided refugee aid and immigration services. It set up a Central Tracing Bureau in order to find lost relatives, husbands, wives, children, and parents, and organized the repatriation of displaced persons and slave laborers who wanted to return to their native countries. Many needed hospitalization, medical and psychiatric treatment, and rehabilitation. Special children's centers were established for children who had lost their families. Many of them had seen their parents killed before their eyes. There were over 10,000 children in these centers in Germany (Aglasterhausen, Munich, Feldafing, and so on), and other thousands were brought back from German families where the Nazis had placed them.

There were among the refugees and displaced persons more than

[8] Fred K. Hochler, *Europe's Homeless Millions* (New York: Foreign Policy Association, 1945), and "Displaced Persons," in George B. de Huszar, *Persistent International Issues* (New York: Harper, 1947), pp. 41-68; National Planning Association, *Europe's Uprooted People* (Washington, D.C.: 1944); and Jane Perry Clark Carey, *The Role of Uprooted People in European Recovery* (Washington, D.C.: National Planning Association, 1948).

500,000, however, who for political or religious reasons could not or did not want to return to their homeland. UNRRA did not force them to go back against their desire and, in June, 1947, turned them over to the International Refugee Organization which had been set up for this purpose by the United Nations. In the DP camps over forty private agencies worked with UNRRA in refugee aid. UNRRA was not responsible for the repatriation of prisoners of war or displaced persons who refused to be brought back to their native land. The International Red Cross Committee in Geneva and the Intergovernmental Committee on Refugees, created at the Evian Conference in 1938 in cooperation with the League of Nations High Commission for Refugees, had been organized before for these tasks.

In August, 1946, the United States and the United Kingdom requested that UNRRA's activities should be brought to a close; they did not want to continue relief and rehabilitation on an international basis. Thus UNRRA's work was terminated at the end of 1947.[9]

When UNRRA had to cease its work, other international agencies took over important phases of it with the assistance of substantial residual funds and some of UNRRA's trained personnel. These were the International Children's Emergency Fund (created upon the urgent request of the UNRRA Council by the United Nations), the International Refugee Organization, the World Health Organization, and the United Nations Food and Agricultural Organization.[10]

III. SOCIAL WELFARE UNDER THE UNITED NATIONS AND INTER-GOVERNMENTAL AGENCIES

Under the provisions of the United Nations Charter, approved in 1945, the Economic and Social Council (ECOSOC) was authorized to develop a comprehensive system of international social welfare, dealing with humanitarian and social problems. It was to become "the international machinery for the promotion of the economic and social advancement of all peoples." This goal was to be accomplished by the promotion of higher standards of living, by attempting to

[9] Roy F. Henderson, "Relief and Rehabilitation," in G. de Huszar, *op. cit.,* pp. 15-40.
[10] W. Hardy Wickwar, "UNRRA in Retrospect," *The Social Service Review,* Vol. XXI, No. 3, September, 1947, pp. 363-374; Donald S. Howard, "After UNRRA—What?" *Survey Graphic,* Vol. 36, April, 1947, pp. 236-239, 264-269.

secure full employment, by the development of conditions of economic and social progress, and by international cooperation among nations in solving problems of economic, social, health, and related character.

The Council promotes international cultural and educational cooperation, and it encourages universal respect for, and observance of, human rights and fundamental freedoms for all human beings without distinction as to race, sex, religion, or language. Within the framework of the Council, health and welfare questions are primarily the concern of the Social Commission. The Commissions on Human Rights, Economics and Employment, Status of Women, and Narcotic Drugs assume responsibility in related fields of importance for the health and welfare of people through community services.[11] The Council prepares draft conventions for international cooperation and makes recommendations to the General Assembly of the United Nations as well as to member governments with reference to social legislation, education, and health and cultural progress. The Council has the responsibility for coordinating the activities of the specialized agencies in the field of welfare, cultural relations, and health.[12]

In the United Nations Secretariat, the Division of Social Welfare in the Department of Social Affairs is the staff unit which administers social service projects under the direction of ECOSOC and with the advice of its Social Commission. The work of the Division of Social Welfare and of the Technical Assistance Administration are the most important practical activities of the United Nations in international social welfare operations. They include research studies and reports on social problems, assistance in social welfare programs and social administration, consultant service to governments, information on social welfare practice, collection and provision of literature and films, scholarships for studies in foreign countries and fellowships for observation of social services in other countries, help in social welfare training, and increasing knowledge and skill in services for families, children, handicapped persons, correctional serv-

---

[11] The organizational structure of ECOSOC is shown in Chart 6, p. 540; see Donald S. Howard, "International Govermental Social Work," *Social Work Year Book, 1949*, pp. 244-252.

[12] See pp. 541-542, and Savilla M. Simons, "International Social Work," *Social Work Year Book, 1951*, pp. 245-259; Frances K. Kernohan, *et al.*, "International Social Work," *Social Work Year Book, 1954*, pp. 266-285.

CHART 6: STRUCTURE OF THE ECONOMIC AND SOCIAL COUNCIL

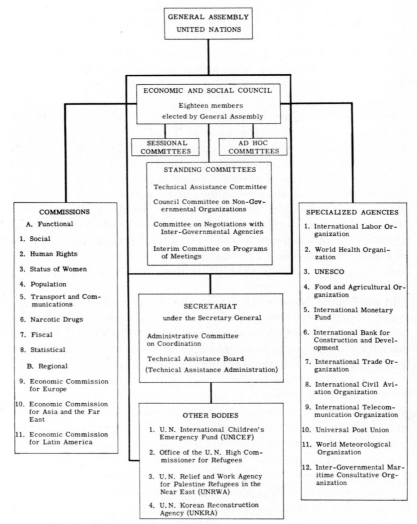

GENERAL ASSEMBLY
UNITED NATIONS

ECONOMIC AND SOCIAL COUNCIL

Eighteen members
elected by General Assembly

SESSIONAL
COMMITTEES

AD HOC
COMMITTEES

STANDING COMMITTEES

Technical Assistance Committee

Council Committee on Non-Governmental Organizations

Committee on Negotiations with
Inter-Governmental Agencies

Interim Committee on Programs
of Meetings

COMMISSIONS

A. Functional

1. Social

2. Human Rights

3. Status of Women

4. Population

5. Transport and Com-
   munications

6. Narcotic Drugs

7. Fiscal

8. Statistical

   B. Regional

9. Economic Commission
   for Europe

10. Economic Commission
    for Asia and the Far
    East

11. Economic Commission
    for Latin America

SPECIALIZED AGENCIES

1. International Labor Organization

2. World Health Organi-
   zation

3. UNESCO

4. Food and Agricultural Organization

5. International Monetary
   Fund

6. International Bank for
   Construction and Development

7. International Trade Organization

8. International Civil Aviation Organization

9. International Telecom-
   munication Organization

10. Universal Post Union

11. World Meteorological
    Organization

12. Inter-Governmental Mar-
    itime Consultative Org-
    anization

SECRETARIAT

under the Secretary General

Administrative Committee
on Coordination

Technical Assistance Board
(Technical Assistance Administration)

OTHER BODIES

1. U. N. International Children's
   Emergency Fund (UNICEF)

2. Office of the U. N. High Commissioner for Refugees

3. U. N. Relief and Work Agency
   for Palestine Refugees in the
   Near East (UNRWA)

4. U. N. Korean Reconstruction
   Agency (UNKRA)

Source: Yearbook of the United Nations, 1953, "Functions and Organization of the United Nations," p. 24.

ices, and housing. International seminars on social security, rural welfare, child welfare services, and teaching of social casework have been arranged under the auspices of the United Nations with the aid of the participating countries on various continents. At the request of governments, experts are sent to those countries which desire advice on such matters as child welfare, rehabilitation of handicapped persons, public assistance, casework or group work techniques, social insurance legislation and administration, prevention and treatment of delinquency, and community organization for health and social welfare.[13]

Courtesy United Nations and World Health Organization

PROTECTION AGAINST TUBERCULOSIS IN INDIA THROUGH WORLD HEALTH ORGANIZATION

Among the specialized international agencies, the following operate programs which are related to social welfare and health:

1. The *International Refugee Organization* (IRO), which was discontinued in 1952.
2. The *United Nations Children's Fund* (UNICEF), which was originally called United Nations International Children's Emergency Fund," and which is now working within the framework of the United Nations.
3. The *International Labor Organization* (ILO).

[13] The activities of the High Commissioner for Refugees and of the United Nations Relief and Works Agency for Palestine Refugees in the Near East are discussed on pp. 542 and 543-544.

4. The *World Health Organization* (WHO).
5. The *Food and Agricultural Organization* (FAO).
6. The *United Nations Educational, Scientific, and Cultural Organization* (UNESCO).

The last four organizations are independent in their administration and operation, and are directed by their own boards and councils. Their governing bodies, however, work in close cooperation with the United Nations.

1. *The International Refugee Organization.* In 1947 it took over from UNRRA the care of about 700,000 displaced persons and refugees, mainly placed in assembly centers and camps in Central Europe in order to repatriate or resettle them. Both activities met serious difficulties. The composition of the families of refugees with small children or older dependents and the age of others prevented many from emigrating to countries which were willing to receive only single, young, healthy men or women suited for rural or industrial labor. Others were excluded from emigration by health conditions, particularly by tuberculosis, crippling and contagious diseases, or vocational limitations. There were not sufficient funds to pay transportation even for those refugees who wanted to emigrate and had found a country willing to receive them. IRO adhered to the principle that no refugee should be compulsorily repatriated. The so-called "hard core" refugees, particularly old, handicapped, and sick persons, who with few exceptions were nowhere admitted and could not migrate to other countries, finally had to be left where they were—mainly in Germany, Austria, and Italy.[14]

When IRO terminated its operations in 1952, the United Nations assumed the responsibility for the remaining 400,000 refugees and displaced persons who had neither been repatriated nor resettled, as well as for new religious and political refugees. In order to provide aid and international protection for these refugees, the Office of the United Nations High Commissioner for Refugees (UNHCR) was created in 1951. The High Commissioner has headquarters in Geneva and attempts to reach the conclusion of agreements between various nations to secure the rights and the legal status of refugees and emi-

---

[14] See Edward B. Marks, Jr., "The Hard Core DP's," *The Survey*, Vol. 85, No. 9, September, 1949, pp. 481-486; Marie Dresden Lane, "Who Share Our Concern for These People: The Resettlement of Unwanted Refugees by the International Refugee Organization," *Social Service Review*, Vol. XXVI, No. 3, September, 1952, pp. 270-283.

grants. The Office attempts to facilitate the settlement of refugees in the country where they have sought asylum, to integrate them into this country's economy, and to make them self-supporting. When it proves impossible for the country of residence to absorb the refugees, migration is considered. The High Commissioner is not engaged in direct migration and settlement services, but he negotiates with governments and voluntary agencies to enable the refugees to migrate to countries where they may find a new home.

Because the budget of the High Commissioner is not sufficient to supply financial aid even to the most needy groups of refugees, the United Nations General Assembly authorized the High Commissioner to issue a special appeal for a Refugee Emergency Fund. Refugees in need of help, in 1954, were still living in camps in Shanghai, Hong Kong, Palestine, Turkey, Greece, Italy, Trieste, Austria, and Germany. Their total number was estimated at three million; not included in this number were seven million refugees in India who fled from Pakistan after the partition of the country. A difficult problem are the new refugees in Western Germany who escaped from the territory behind the Iron Curtain and for whom international help seems urgently required.[15]

The High Commissioner has set up branch offices in Washington, D.C., London, Paris, Brussels, Rome, Bad Godesberg (Germany), Vienna, Athens, Bogota (Columbia), and Hong Kong to work for the legal, economic, and social protection of refugees, provision of certificates, and for their admission to countries which are willing to receive them and their resettlement there.

Another serious problem of an international nature developed in 1948 when nearly 800,000 Arab refugees who had fled from Israel were in gravest need in the surrounding Arab countries and in Arab-controlled areas of Palestine. IRO was not able to assume responsibility for their care. The International Red Cross and the American Friends Service Committee organized emergency aid for food, clothes, houses, health services, and some vocational training. The United Nations finally were forced to set up a *Relief and Work Agency for Palestine Refugees in the Near East* (UNRWA), whose

[15] Some of these refugees will come as immigrants to the United States, under the provisions of the Refugee Immigration Act of 1953 (see p. 124). See also, Walter A. Friedlander, "The New Refugees in Germany: A Challenge to Social Work," *Social Work Journal*, Vol. XXXIV, No. 4, October, 1953, pp. 157-160, 178.

director is appointed by the Director-General of the United Nations, in consultation with the government members of an Advisory Commission composed of the representatives of France, Turkey, the United Kingdom, and the United States as permanent members, and of Jordan and Syria. In 1954, there were still over 700,000 refugees, one-third of them living in camps and tents, near Gaza in southern Palestine and in Jordan, Lebanon, and Syria.[16]

2. *United Nations Children's Fund.* Under its original title "United Nations International Children's Emergency Fund" this agency was established in 1946 at the urgent request of the UNRRA Council in order to carry on child feeding and child welfare services that could not be discontinued without grave damage to millions of children, pregnant women, and nursing mothers. The United Nations Assembly adopted provisions stipulating that UNICEF was to operate for the benefit and rehabilitation of children and adolescents in war-devastated countries, in those countries which received UNRRA assistance, and finally for child-health purposes where they were needed in general. The distribution of aid was to be on the basis of need, without discrimination because of race, creed, nationality status, or political belief.

UNICEF received first over $32 million from UNRRA, and it is now financed by voluntary contributions of governments and private resources. The Fund is administered by an Executive Board composed of representatives of twenty-six nations and by an Executive Director who is appointed by the Secretary-General of the United Nations. After the war the Fund first was concerned with emergency measures through mass feeding of children and expecting mothers. In 1950, the program was changed to children's aid of long-term nature, child health projects, particularly antituberculosis and antisyphilis vaccination, and training programs for child welfare personnel.[17] UNICEF applies the "matching principle": It requires

[16] *United Nations Bulletin*, Vol. 14, No. 5, March 1, 1953, p. 185; and Vol. 16, No. 9, May 14, 1954, pp. 354-357. An analysis of this difficult problem is presented in Sibylla G. Thicknesse, *Arab Refugees: A Survey of Resettlement Possibilities* (London: Royal Institute of International Affairs, 1949), and Joseph B. Schechtman, *The Arab Refugee Problem* (New York: Philosophical Library, 1952).

[17] See United Nations International Children's Emergency Fund, *UNICEF— A Compendium*, Vol. III, New York, 1952; Samuel K. Jacobs, "The United Nations International Children's Emergency Fund: An Instrument of International Social Policy," *Social Service Review*, Vol. XXIV, Nos. 2 and 3, June, 1950, pp. 143-172; September, 1950, pp. 347-373.

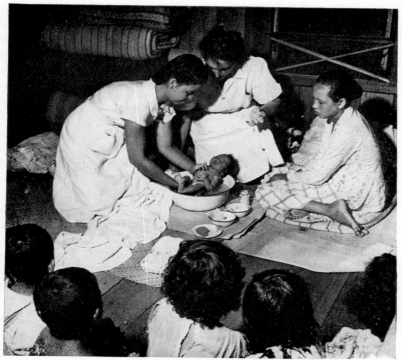

Courtesy United Nations and World Health Organization

MOTHER AND CHILD HEALTH IN SARAWAK, BORNEO

that the government or voluntary agencies in the country where aid is given provide indigenous supplies, such as flour, potatoes, vegetables, fruits, sugar or fats, transportation, as well as the staff for distribution of UNICEF supplies and medical or child welfare services. The Fund thus operates on a cooperative basis with the country receiving aid and encourages initiative for the development of effective child protection, child welfare services, and the training of competent personnel, doctors, nurses, social workers, midwives, and health visitors who can improve conditions immediately.

The Fund assisted in the establishment of the International Children's Center, in Paris, which provides training, research, and demonstration projects in maternal and child services for doctors, nurses, social workers, and other professional personnel. UNICEF also supports the setup of a postgraduate training center for nurses and physicians at the All India Institute for Health and Public Hygiene in

Calcutta. Its most spectacular actions after the end of World War II were mass feeding programs and the testing and antituberculosis vaccination of nearly forty million children in Europe, Asia, the Near East, Africa, Latin America and the Philippines which still are going on. UNICEF provides food, clothing, and drugs for children in natural catastrophes, such as famines, droughts, floods, earthquakes, and volcanic eruptions.[18]

The following experience of a health worker on the island of Borneo in 1952 illustrates international welfare services under the auspices of UNICEF. In the tropical region near Simanggang, he discovered a seventeen-year-old boy, in a wooden cage suspended under the longhouse where the villagers live. The child was totally crippled with yaws, his body raw all over with sores. For seven hopeless years he had been caged in this way in order to protect the parents and other members of the family and the inhabitants of the village from contagion and from the intolerable smell of his rotting flesh. No medical treatment for this cruel disease was known in the isolated village. The cage was just big enough for the boy to sit in, but he could not get up or walk a bit. Food was passed through a small opening of the cage.[19]

The fate of this child is a brutal, cogent example of what a case of untreated yaws can do to an unhappy human being suffering from this disease. The young Dayak was moved with the help of a jeep to the Kuching Hospital. There, elaborate plastic surgery has cured his continuous pain and helped him regain some use of his limbs. Today one single shot of UNICEF penicillin, at a price of only fifteen cents, is needed in order to cure a case of yaws provided the disease is caught in time. In June 1953, vaccination campaigns under the auspices of UNICEF in Asia passed the one million mark of immunization against this contagious illness.

On October 6, 1953, the United Nations decided that UNICEF should continue on a permanent basis as an international child welfare organization.

---

[18] *UNICEF, Addenda to Compendium,* November, 1952, p. 2; see also, Katherine F. Lenroot, "International Children's Emergency Fund," *Social Security Bulletin,* Vol. 10, No. 4, April, 1947, pp. 7-10; and Maurice Pate, "UNICEF, A Year of Achievement in 80 Countries," *United Nations Review,* Vol. 1, No. 2, August, 1954, pp. 11-15.

[19] *United Nations Bulletin,* "News of the World's Children," Vol. XIV, No. 12, June 15, 1953, p. 439.

3. *The International Labor Organization.* This agency was organized in 1919, after World War I, and has assisted in the improvement of labor-management relations and social legislation and in the development of social security systems in many countries. The ILO recommended social insurance laws, the replacement of outdated poor relief by modern social assistance statutes, maternity and infant protection, child labor laws, and the protection of unmarried women and illegitimate children. When ILO began its work, only a few countries in western and central Europe had social insurance laws on their statute books; in 1953, thirty-eight member nations of ILO had workmen's compensation laws; thirty, health insurance; fourteen, unemployment compensation; thirty-six, general old-age insurance programs; and seventeen, family allowance schemes.[20]

The basic aims of the ILO are to improve labor conditions and living standards through international understanding and cooperation, to promote economic and social stability, and to contribute to international peace by promoting social justice.

The administration of the ILO is vested in a body of delegates of sixty-six nations, representing not just governments, but also labor and management. The International Labor Conference is its parliament to which annually each member country sends four delegates: one employer, one worker, and two government representatives. The "governing body" is the executive council of ILO; the International Labor Office, its secretariat, has its headquarters in Geneva. The ILO is financed by its government members and has been accepted as a "specialized agency" by the Economic and Social Council of the United Nations. Both the ILO and the United Nations share the interest in the strengthening of social security and the improvement of living standards and health conditions. ILO works in closest cooperation with ECOSOC for the protection of child and woman labor, and the development of social insurance, public assistance legislation, and family allowances.

4. *World Health Organization.* During the Conference in San Francisco in 1945, which created the Charter and founded the organization of the United Nations, Brazil proposed to include the protection of health into the goals of the United Nations. After prep-

[20] Daniel S. Gerig, "The International Labor Organization and Social Welfare," *National Conference of Social Work, 1948*, pp. 50, 52, and 57; and Carl H. Farman and Veronica Marren Hale, *Social Security Legislation Throughout the World* (Washington, D.C.: Social Security Administration, 1949).

aration in Paris, an International Health Conference convened in New York in June, 1946, invited by the United Nations, and approved the Constitution of the World Health Organization. It is the first world-wide health agency, comprising seventy-five nations as members, a specialized agency of the United Nations.[21] Its principal organs are the World Health Assembly, composed of representatives of all member countries and meeting each year, the Executive Board with eighteen members elected by the Assembly, and the Secretariat under the Director-General.

The WHO carries on the work of international health activities formerly organized by the International Office for Public Hygiene in Paris, the League of Nations, and UNRRA. Its objective is the attainment of the highest possible level of health for all the people on earth. The preamble of the WHO constitution defines health as "the state of complete physical, mental, and social well-being and not merely the absence of disease or infirmity." Six major programs of action include the promotion of maternal and infant hygiene, of nutritional diets, and of environmental hygiene, as well as campaigns against malaria, tuberculosis, yaws, typhus, trachoma, and venereal diseases. Many of these health programs are operated jointly with UNICEF when they are aimed at the protection of children, mothers, and youth, and with other organizations.

WHO also takes an active part in the technical assistance program of the United Nations.[22] Its main emphasis is directed towards the development of efficient public health services (including demonstration projects), toward control of endemic diseases, fight against communicable disease, improvement of sanitation, and training of health personnel. An interesting type of work was done in India. The government constructed a penicillin factory. UNICEF imported the equipment and machinery, and WHO provided the technical advisors and the facilities for training of Indian personnel.

In 1948, a private international organization in the field of mental hygiene, the World Federation for Mental Health, was founded in London at the World Congress for Mental Health. The Federation supports the work of the United Nations, of the World Health Or-

---

[21] C. E. A. Winslow, "International Cooperation in the Service of Health," *Annals of the American Academy of Social and Political Science*, Vol. 273, January, 1951.

[22] See Walter R. Sharp, *International Technical Assistance* (Chicago: Public Administration Service, 1952), pp. 73-77; and H. L. Keenleyside, "Education or Catastrophe," *Adult Leadership*, Vol. 2, No. 7, December, 1953, pp. 4-7.

ganization, and of the UNESCO, in cooperation with governments, professional associations, and private mental hygiene societies. Its goal is the promotion of mental health, in fostering the ability to live harmoniously in a world of tensions, and in providing information, popular education, and the training of professional personnel in the field of mental hygiene.

5. *Food and Agricultural Organization.* The United Nations Food and Agricultural Organization (FAO), with headquarters in Rome, was established in 1945 with the purpose of abolishing famines and malnutrition by promoting health and welfare through increased food production and a better distribution of agricultural products. As progress in sanitary facilities and medical care reduces mortality rates and therefore increases the population, it becomes necessary to augment the agricultural production by the use of scientific methods. In 1953, sixty-three nations were members of the organization. FAO furnishes technical information and instruction and conducts research and demonstration projects in crop and animal improvement and forest and fishery development. FAO assists countries on their request by improving methods of conservation, processing, and marketing of food.[23]

The aim of the United Nations and its specialized agencies to secure to all mankind basic human rights, a decent standard of living, and health, social and economic security, can be achieved only if above all every man has sufficient food. For this reason the work of FAO is of such vital importance to human welfare.

6. *United Nations Educational, Scientific, and Cultural Organization.* As a specialized agency of the United Nations, UNESCO was established in 1945 in order to contribute to peace and security by international cooperation in the fields of education, science, and culture. Its organization is composed of a General Conference with representatives of all member nations (fifty-nine in 1953), an Executive Board of eighteen members, and the secretariat under a Director-General with headquarters in Paris. UNESCO strives to promote mutual understanding among peoples by the distribution of cultural, scientific, and educational information—through libraries, radio, movies, periodicals, and newspapers.[24] It encourages exchange

[23] United Nations Food and Agricultural Organization, *Essentials of Rural Welfare* (Washington, D.C.: 1949); W. Sharp, *op. cit.*, pp. 71-73.

[24] U.S. National Commission for UNESCO, *United States—United Nations Information* (Washington, D.C.: U.S. Department of State, 1946), Series 14.

of students, artists, scientists, international children and youth conferences, seminars, and research studies in philosophy, humanities, history, art, social, and natural sciences.

UNESCO is mainly concerned with the development of education, human values, and social behavior.[25] UNESCO attempts to realize the idea of a world community by promoting special projects, such as international youth conferences, camps, schools, and children's villages. In a program of promotion of welfare in a rapidly changing world its task is the emphasis on constructive, peaceful use of technical improvements. UNESCO's function is to apply the teachings of cultural anthropology, psychology, and sociology to the improvement of education, the abolition of illiteracy, the development of adult education and the encouragement of creative art and scientific research with full respect for indigenous cultural and religious values.[26]

IV. THE TECHNICAL ASSISTANCE PROGRAM

Assistance in periods of mass distress—famine, flood, earthquakes, fire, and volcanic eruptions—has been the object of international relief for a long time. The rapid development of technology and natural science, however, has focused our attention upon the fact that more than half of the people of our world are living under conditions of hunger, poor health, and economic deprivation. For many decades, therefore, religious missionary groups, private philanthropy, and more recently, national and international public agencies have brought education, technical training and skills, and child and health services to countries in need of help.[27] During World War II,

---

[25] Charles S. Ascher, *Program-Making in UNESCO, 1946-1951* (Chicago: Public Administration Service, 1951); W. Sharp, *op. cit.*, pp. 77-80; and Harold E. Snyder, *When People Speak to People* (Washington, D.C.: American Council on Education, 1953).

[26] Other specialized agencies which are less oriented toward health and welfare policies are the World Bank for International Reconstruction, the International Monetary Fund, the Universal Postal Union, the International Trade Organization, the International Telecommunications Union, the International Civil Aviation Organization, and the Inter-Governmental Maritime Consultative Organization. (See Chart 6, p. 540.)

[27] W. Sharp, *op. cit.*, pp. 1-23; F. Kernohan, S. Simons, and C. Owen, *op. cit.*, pp. 274-278, and 282-283; William A. Brown, Jr., and Redoers Opie, *American Foreign Assistance* (Washington, D.C.: Brookings Institution, 1953), and Robert T. Mack, Jr., *Raising the World's Standard of Living* (New York: Citadel, 1953).

UNRRA brought organized methods of technical assistance to countries willing to accept such aid in order to help themselves. As we discussed above, some of the main activities of the United Nations Secretariat in the field of social welfare and those of the specialized agencies in connection with the United Nations are devoted to the objective of assisting the peoples of the so-called "underdeveloped areas of the world" (which we might rather design as "developing areas") to defeat the threat of hunger, disease, and want by production of more food, more clothing, better housing, and sanitation.

In his inaugural address, January 20, 1949, President Truman emphasized the need for raising living standards in underdeveloped countries by helping them to increase their production by technical improvement of their material resources, agriculture and industries, and of the productive capacity of their people. This *Point Four Program* suggested the investment of capital for the economic development of these countries through private, governmental, and international resources (for example, the International Monetary Fund) and the establishment or expansion of technical assistance so that the exchange and the application of scientific and professional knowledge, techniques, and skills would help the people to raise their living standards. The program was conceived as a cooperative enterprise of all countries through the United Nations and its specialized agencies.

President Truman's initiative was highly praised, but the realization of his idea was delayed by Congress. In 1950 the *Foreign Economic Assistance Act* approved the basic objective "to aid the efforts of the peoples of the underdeveloped areas to develop their resources and improve their working and living conditions by encouraging the exchange of technical knowledge and skills and the flow of investment capital."[28] Business pressure urged special treaties with foreign countries in order to secure capital protection for private investors. The *Act for International Development* (1950) attempted to achieve a compromise between aid to underdeveloped areas for the development of their resources, by exchange of technical knowledge and skills, and by the investment of capital in these areas. The government was authorized to participate in international projects

[28] S. Simons, *op. cit.*, p. 256; and Frances K. Kernohan, "Organization for Foreign Social Policy," *Social Work Journal*, Vol. 34, No. 4, October, 1953, pp. 147-150, 173-176.

of technical assistance under the auspices of the United Nations and
its specialized agencies or to conclude bilateral agreements with individual countries. The administration of the Point Four Program
was vested in the Technical Cooperation Administration (TCA) in
the Department of State, and, in 1953, was transferred to the Foreign
Operations Administration, in the Office of the Director of Mutual
Security. Requests for technical assistance were made from countries
in Europe, Asia, the Near East, Latin America, and Africa. After the
approval of a project to which the foreign countries always contribute their own share in materials, supplies, personnel, and maintenance, other federal agencies, such as the Department of Health,
Education and Welfare or the Department of Agriculture, assume
the execution of the project, usually in cooperation with a field mission of the Foreign Operations Administration. Projects are divided
into the categories of (1) agriculture and natural resources development, (2) health, education, and welfare, and (3) industry and government services. [29]

Characteristic of many of the projects, especially from the point
of view of social work, has been the cooperation among members
of different nations and various professions in these "field teams."
They are frequently composed of an agriculturist, an engineer, a
doctor, a nurse, a plant pathologist, and a social worker, as well as
indigenous experts in some of these professions. The particular contribution of the social worker in the team is his professional experience and ability to recognize the most urgent needs of the population and to assist people to find for themselves the best-suited solution
for their problems. The social worker's qualification for this function is based upon his knowledge of human behavior and his understanding of the specific mentality of the people with whom he works.
This concept makes him accept the religious and cultural customs of
people, which may be very different from his own. It enables him
to help a foreign community to determine the extent and urgency
of its problems and to activate all possible resources for their solution.

The development of such a program of technical assistance services, therefore, needs to be done in cooperation with the people of

---

[29] A penetrating analysis of the structure, organization, and administration of
the projects is to be found in W. Sharp, *op. cit.*, pp. 25-58; and United Nations,
Technical Assistance Board, *The Expanded Programme of Technical Assistance
for Economic Development of Under-Developed Countries* (New York: 1953).

the community and in consideration of the importance of their religious and cultural values and their human dignity. The specific assignment of a social worker in the team is the awakening of a sincere interest in the population for the betterment of their living conditions, to make them desirous for the changes which may be brought about in the program.[30] In cooperation with the other members of the team, the social worker has to use all his skill to explore and enlist the resources in the community which may help to solve urgent health and welfare needs. He has to evaluate their emotional, as well as their health and economic, implications so that the team may establish a working program for economic development, child health and welfare, delinquency prevention, rehabilitation of the handicapped, or whatever is an urgent need of the community. Some technical assistance projects of this type already have demonstrated remarkable progress in control of malaria, tuberculosis, yaws and other diseases, in food production as to quality and quantity of nutrition, and improvements in educational methods, housing conditions, sanitation, water supply, and industrial development.

The same type of technical assistance projects has been carried on under the auspices of the United Nations and its specialized agencies with financial and technical aid of the United States. In 1949, ECOSOC submitted a program for international technical assistance to the General Assembly of the United Nations, which approved the proposal. Projects are carried on through the Food and Agricultural Organization, the World Health Organization, the United Nations Children's Fund, the International Labor Office, and UNESCO. Most of them are oriented toward the promotion of rural welfare; the organization of "social centers" or "community centers"; the improvement of production methods, and village and water development; the founding of cottage handicrafts and small-scale industries; and progress in education, vocational training, rehabilitation, public hygiene, and communications. In rural settings of developing nations, such as India, the Arab countries, and Egypt, the success of

[30] Melvin A. Glasser, *The Role of Social Service in Raising the Standard of Living* (New York: American Association of Social Workers, 1953), pp. 28-34; Charles I. Schottland, "Social Work Issues in the Political Arena," *Social Welfare Forum, 1953*, pp. 18-33; and Hertha Kraus, "Identifying Professional Requirements for Social Service Abroad," *Social Casework*, Vol. 35, No. 4, April, 1954, pp. 147-152.

technical assistance depends essentially upon whether the people in the village can be encouraged to assume the responsibility for social change as their own project.[31] In 1954, almost 2,000 experts were sent to 70 countries by the United Nations and the specialized agencies in technical assistance.

Neither foreign aid nor measures arranged by the national central government will be of lasting value, unless there is in the village itself the enthusiasm and the spirit of self-help and of cooperation necessary to rebuild the economy, and to improve social and health conditions. To achieve this is the task of the social worker in a technical assistance team. In most countries of the Far and Near East and Africa the education of social workers for work in rural villages has just begun. They are prepared for various skills—to aid in public assistance, child welfare, elementary and health education, home economics, sanitation, midwifery, and nursing service. They need personal qualities, such as resourcefulness, maturity, ingenuity, dedication to their people, and a deep sense of devotion to their work. In India, for example, in several demonstration projects, women workers live in villages in teams of three. One worker gives nursing and midwife service; the second teaches craft, assists in general school education, and organizes adult classes; and the third works with children, especially with those of "toddler" age.[32] Efficient supervision of such women workers requires trained, professional social workers to inspire and guide women and men workers in village improvement activities.

At its meeting in May, 1953, the Social Commission of the Economic and Social Council of the United Nations characterized the following as essential elements in social welfare functions in the technical assistance programs: the training of professional, technical, and auxiliary personnel for social service; community organization; the encouragement of self-help activities for the improvement of living standards; and the strengthening of public social welfare programs and statistical and research services. It called for demonstra-

[31] See Karl de Schweinitz, *Social Security for Egypt* (Washington, D.C.: Social Security Administration, 1952), pp. 61-64; Dorothy Moses, "Welfare in India—Village Life and Social Work," *The Survey*, Vol. 88, No. 5, May, 1952, pp. 210-213; and United Nations, *Program of Concerted Practical Action in the Social Field of the United Nations and Specialized Agencies* (New York: 1953).

[32] D. Moses, *op. cit.*, p. 213; see also Dewey Anderson and Stephen Raushenbush, *A Policy and Program for Success* (Washington, D.C.: Public Affairs Institute, 1950), pp. 17-22.

tion projects for proving the value of a simultaneous approach to social, economic, educational, and health problems.[33] Experience in international social service confirms this emphasis on interprofessional teamwork as an important condition for successful work.

V. INTERNATIONAL EXCHANGE OF
SOCIAL WORKERS

The exchange of experts in various disciplines is an important part of the technical assistance program under the auspices of the United Nations and under those of the United States, but has been also supported by other international and national private organizations. In this connection, we merely want to mention the important contributions which physicians, public health officers, sanitary engineers, agricultural, transportation, industrial, and food experts, specialists in the treatment and prevention of diseases and epidemics, and laboratory technicians and nurses made toward the improvement of economic, social, and health conditions in developing areas. In the field of social welfare, the United Nations are primarily interested in the development of adequate services for family, youth, and child welfare, rehabilitation of handicapped persons, and housing and community planning. The specialized agencies of the United Nations have devoted their primary action to the improvement of physical and mental health, maternal and child care, education, rural welfare, employment security, and social insurance. In order to achieve progress in social welfare programs, many countries request that expert advisers be sent to assist them in the establishment and improvement of social services, assist them in organization and administration, and assume teaching and demonstrations. These activities are designed as International Advisory Social Welfare Services. They play an important role for the planning and development of welfare and health services, programs of public assistance and social insurance, rehabilitation and village centers, and social legislation. Consultants are selected on the basis of a request of the government, which wants to use their services and has the right of approval.[34] Experts are pro-

[33] See "The Social Commission Report," *United Nations Bulletin,* June 1, 1953, p. 396; and Margaret Mead, *Cultural Patterns and Technical Change* (New York: UNESCO, 1953).

[34] See United Nations, Department of Social Affairs, *International Advisory Social Welfare Services* (Lake Success, N.Y.: 1949).

vided by the United Nations, the specialized agencies, governments, and voluntary social welfare organizations.

Another aspect of this exchange are Fellowship Programs under the auspices of the United Nations, national governments, and private agencies which enable social workers and students to observe or to study methods, organization, and operation of social welfare in another country. This International Exchange of Social Welfare Personnel provides opportunities for experienced, as well as young, social workers and students to broaden their understanding, knowledge, and skills.[35] Three methods of exchange are used: (1) fellowships for travel and observations of social agencies and institutions varying between three and nine months, (2) scholarships for formal academic education in schools of social work, as a rule for one or two years, and (3) a direct exchange of teachers, administrators, research or other specialists; experts in correctional work, directing settlement houses, training schools, children's institutions, and in training youth leaders.

For American social workers and students of social work some opportunities for teaching, study, and research are provided by the Fulbright Educational Exchange Program. Such experiences strengthen mutual understanding between nations, professional knowledge, and cooperation in social welfare from which all countries benefit, the visitor as well as the host country. Careful preparation and professional and cultural orientation for international exchange deeply enhances its value.

An important role in the interpretation of our concepts and programs of social welfare on the international level is assigned to the social welfare attachés, who have been appointed by the Department of State since May, 1948. Their function is to inform government and private agencies regarding important development in legislation and experiences in social welfare and in international welfare organizations. They also assist public and private social agencies in their overseas relief and welfare programs and serve as consultants of the Embassy to foreign social welfare organizations.[36] Social welfare

[35] See United Nations, Department of Social Affairs, *International Exchange of Social Welfare Personnel* (Lake Success, N.Y.: 1949), pp. 1-7; and Marguerite V. Pohek, "What Can Casework Contribute to European Social Services?" *Social Work Journal*, Vol. 35, No. 1, January, 1954, pp. 15-18.

[36] See Frances K. Kernohan, "Social Welfare Attaché Program," *Survey Midmonthly*, Vol. 84, December, 1948, pp. 355-356, and "Organization for Foreign Social Policy," *op. cit.*, pp. 149-150, 173.

attachés have been appointed on the staff of the Embassies in Paris, New Delhi, and Cairo, but are not maintained at present. It may be hoped that this constructive, valuable service be continued and extended to other embassies and legations.

VI. VOLUNTARY AGENCIES IN INTERNATIONAL SOCIAL WELFARE

Our discussion has already shown that the work of private social agencies of either international or national character engaged in overseas work is an important part of the present international social welfare activities. During the war and the period of emergency relief abroad, they were coordinated in the United States under the President's War Relief Control Board and its successor, the Advisory Committee on Voluntary Foreign Aid. Most of these agencies are also members of the American Council of Voluntary Agencies for Foreign Service, which includes religious and non-sectarian organizations and the relief services of AFL and CIO. The relief work in Germany after the end of the war was carried on by the Army, the High Commissioner, and voluntary agencies that were admitted under a "Council of Relief Agencies Licensed for Operations in Germany" (CRALOG). Of particular importance proved to be the "Neighborhood Centers" supported by the American Friends Service Committee, Church World Service, and the Unitarian Service Committee. The latter organization also conducts training institutes for social workers and teachers with the aid of the High Commissioner and of German social agencies. Similar relief activities in Japan, Korea, and Okinawa are performed by organizations combined in LARA, "Licensed Agencies for Relief in Asia." These activities include the feeding of children and nursing mothers, clothing aid, and assistance in the reconstruction of welfare services, hospitals, orphanages, and schools. Very essential is the rehabilitation work in Korea, where the "United Nations Korean Reconstruction Agency" (UNKRA), financed from voluntary government contributions, is working together with various private organizations, including the American Korean Foundation, American Friends Service Committee, the Unitarian Service Committee, World Church Service, American Relief for Korea, "Houses for Korea," and the American Education Mission. In the United States, the National Social Welfare Assembly serves as coordinating body between public and private agencies devoted to international social services and develops cooperative programs in this area.

The International Conference of Social Work whose seventh conference was held in Toronto in 1954, is an international forum for the discussion of welfare, health, and education issues. The members of the International Conference are organized under thirty national committees which plan the international meetings and assist in recruiting membership and in the exchange of information. Headquarters of the Conference are in Columbus (Ohio) and in Paris (France).[37]

In 1929 an International Committee of Schools of Social Work, which arranges for international and regional meetings in order to promote the standards of social work education throughout the world, was established. Finally, an International Federation of Social Workers, which enlists as members national professional associations of social workers, was formed in connection with the International Conference of Social Work in Paris, in 1950. This international federation aims at the promotion of high standards of service and professional cooperation between social workers in all countries of the world.

VII. INTERNATIONAL ASPECTS IN SOCIAL WORK EDUCATION

Throughout the world social work is performed within the framework of cultural, religious, economic, and social conditions which determine the different values and customs of the people who use social services. Most countries are convinced that the performance of social welfare functions requires special preparation and training.[38] But the basic responsibility for the care of people in need is not everywhere placed upon the community, or a government au-

[37] See Charlotte E. Owen, "International Voluntary Social Work," *Social Work Year Book, 1949,* pp. 252-260; Lyman C. White, *International Non-governmental Organizations* (1951); and Joe R. Hoffer, "Conferences of Social Work," *Social Work Year Book, 1954,* pp. 132-133.

[38] Sir Raphael Cilento, "The World Moves Toward Professional Standards in Social Work," *Social Work Journal,* Vol. 29, No. 3, July, 1948, pp. 99-107; Walter A. Friedlander, "Some International Aspects of Social Work Education," *Social Service Review,* Vol. 23, No. 2, June, 1949, pp. 204-210; Katherine Kendall, "International Developments in Social Work Education," *Social Work Journal,* Vol. 32, No. 2, April, 1951, pp. 70-77.

thority; in some countries it still rests with the family, the wider circle of relatives, with the church, or other religious or charitable agencies. Under these circumstances, it is difficult to establish a uniform definition of "Social Work" or "Social Worker" which would be recognized everywhere. But certain characteristics of social work are world-wide: (1) as a "helping process" for individuals, families, and groups, helping them to solve their economic, health, or personal problems; (2) as a "social function" for the benefit of the individual and the community, not the agency; (3) as an "enabling process," encouraging the use of community facilities and the development of sources for the betterment of the community.[39]

Social service being so closely interrelated with the economy and culture of the nation, the principles, methods, and concepts of social work in the United States discussed in this book cannot be applied rigidly in countries whose customs, values, and resources are different from our own. Social work has to be adapted to the cultural, economic, and climatic setting. Dean Donald S. Howard, speaking at the National Conference of Social Work, in 1952, explained these differences but emphasized that everywhere social work is the discipline, based upon a combination of a philosophy, knowledge, attitudes, and skills, that helps individuals, groups, communities, and societies attain the highest possible level of well-being, primarily by "helping them to help themselves." Social welfare, of course, also assists people who cannot help themselves—children, the aged, the crippled, the blind, and the sick.[40]

As we have seen, international social work agencies are aware of the necessity of training social workers, and they assist countries that have no or too few facilities for the training of social workers and auxiliary personnel. The social workers' and students' exchange program and the delegation of teachers and instructors to foreign countries are part of the process of education for social welfare. The United Nations has considered founding a research center or an international school of social work, but this project has not been car-

[39] K. Kendall, *op. cit.*, pp. 73-74; and Edward H. Spicer (editor), *Human Problems in Technological Change: A Casebook* (New York: Russell Sage Foundation, 1952).

[40] Donald S. Howard, "The Common Core of Social Work," *The Social Welfare Forum, 1951*, pp. 14-36; Lester B. Granger, "Basic Human Needs," *Social Work Journal*, Vol. 34, No. 2, April, 1953, pp. 65-70, 87-88.

ried out.[41] Such a school would provide the opportunity to compare the philosophy and methods of social welfare of various nations.

The experiences of persons engaged in various aspects of foreign relief, rehabilitation, and international social welfare cooperation, as discussed in this chapter, have created a new spirit of mutual understanding, respect, and good will. The finding of a "common core of social work" has strengthened the conviction that all peoples of the world, whether rich or poor, have their right to self-respect, human dignity, self-determination, and freedom from want and fear. Social workers are conscious that in helping peoples abroad to overcome hunger, disease, and suffering, the well-being of all peoples is directed toward the development and maintenance of world stability and peace. Social welfare has become an integral part of the worldwide efforts for the advancement of human progress.[42]

SELECTED BIBLIOGRAPHY

Abbott, Edith, "International Social Welfare," *The Compass,* Vol. 28, No. 4, May, 1947, pp. 3-36.

Anderson, Dewey, and Stephen Raushenbush, *A Policy and Program for Success.* Washington, D.C.: Public Affairs Institute, 1950.

Barr, Stringfellow, *Let's Join the Human Race.* Chicago: University of Chicago Press, 1950.

Baster, James, and Willard Thorp, "Point Four: Development of Backward Areas," *American Economic Review,* Vol. 41, May, 1951, pp. 399-417.

Bicknell, Ernest P., *With the Red Cross in Europe.* Washington, D.C.: American National Red Cross, 1938.

Blelloch, David, "Technical Assistance: Programmes and Policies," *International Affairs,* Vol. 28, January, 1952, pp. 49-58.

Brooks, Howard L., *Prisoners of Hope.* New York: L. B. Fischer, 1942.

Brugger, Florence, "What Are Profitable Imports for the United States," *National Conference of Social Work, Selected Papers in Group Work and Community Organization, 1952,* pp. 80-90.

Carey, Jane P. Clark, *The Role of Uprooted People in European Recovery.* Washington, D.C.: National Planning Association, 1948.

*Cilento, Sir Raphael, "The World Moves Toward Professional Standards in Social Work," *Social Work Journal,* July, 1948, Vol. 29, No. 3, pp. 99-107.

Condliffe, J. B., and A. Stevenson, *The Common Interest in International*

---

[41] W. Friedlander, *op. cit.,* p. 206; some international schools of limited character or special goals function in France and India.

[42] American Association of Social Workers, "Platform Statement on International Cooperation for Social Welfare," 1953.

Organization. Montreal: International Labor Office, 1944 (Ser. B., No. 39).

Crowne, S. A., "Technical Assistance and Economic Aid," *Journal of International Affairs*, Vol. 6, Winter, 1952, pp. 58-64.

*Daniels, Walter M. (editor), *Point Four Program.* New York: Wilson, 1951.

Davis, Harriet E. (editor), *Pioneers in World Order.* New York: Columbia University Press, 1944.

de Jongh, Jan F., "A European Experiment in Casework Teaching," *Social Casework*, January, 1953, Vol. 34, No. 1, pp. 9-17.

*de Schweinitz, Karl, *Social Security for Egypt.* Washington, D. C.: Social Security Administration, 1952.

Eliot, Martha M., "Child Feeding in Europe Under the ICEF," *American Journal of Public Health*, Vol. 28, January, 1948, pp. 8-18.

———, "Need of the Children," *Survey Graphic*, Vol. 37, March, 1949, pp. 140-142.

Ellis, Howard S., *The Economics of Freedom.* New York: Harper, 1950.

Farman, Carl H., "World Developments in Social Security," *Social Security Bulletin*, Vol. 13, No. 3, March, 1950, pp. 3-12.

———, and Veronica Marren Hale, *Social Security Legislation Throughout the World.* Washington, D.C.: Social Security Administration, 1949.

Finer, Herman, *The United Nations Economic and Social Council.* New York: World Peace Foundation, 1946.

*Friedlander, Walter A., "International Aspects of Social Work Education," *Social Service Review*, Vol. XXXII, No. 2, June, 1949, pp. 204-210.

Fry, Varian, *Surrender on Demand.* New York: Random House, 1945.

Gerschenkron, Alexander, and Berthold F. Hoselitz, *The Progress of Underdeveloped Areas.* Chicago: University of Chicago Press, 1952.

*Glasser, Melvin A., "Social Service in Underdeveloped Areas: A Report on the International Conference," *Social Work Journal*, Vol. 34, No. 2, April, 1953, pp. 59-64.

Granger, Lester B., "Basic Human Needs," *Social Work Journal*, Vol. 34, No. 2, April, 1953, pp. 65-70, 87-88.

Gumpert, Martin, *Dunant: The Story of the Red Cross.* New York: Oxford, 1938.

Harris, Seymour E., *The European Recovery Program.* Cambridge: Harvard University Press, 1948.

Hill, Martin, *The Economic and Financial Organization of the League of Nations.* Washington, D.C.: Carnegie Endowment, 1946.

Hoffman, Paul G., *Peace Can Be Won.* New York: Doubleday, 1951.

Howard, Donald S., "Foreign Relief and Rehabilitation," *Social Work Year Book, 1947*, pp. 190-203.

*———, "International Governmental Social Work," *Social Work Year Book, 1949*, pp. 244-252.

*———, "The Common Core of Social Work," *Social Welfare Forum, 1951*, pp. 19-36.

Huxley, Julian S., *UNESCO, Its Purpose and Its Philosophy.* Washington, D.C.: Public Affairs Press, 1947.

Hyman, Joseph P., *Twenty-Five Years of American Aid to Jews Overseas.* New York: American Jewish Joint Distribution Committee, 1939.

Jones, Rufus M., *A Service of Love in Wartime.* New York: Macmillan, 1920.

*Kasius, Cora, "Casework Developments in Europe," *Social Casework*, Vol. 32, No. 7, July, 1951, pp. 281-288.

*———, "Are Social Work Principles Emerging Internationally?" *Social Casework*, Vol. 34, No. 1, January, 1953, pp. 23-29.

Kendall, Katherine A., "International Developments in Social Work Education," *Social Work Journal*, Vol. 32, No. 2, April, 1951, pp. 70-77.

*———, "Social Work Education: A Responsibility of the Total Profession," *Social Casework*, Vol. 34, No. 1, January, 1953, pp. 17-23.

*Kernohan, Frances K., Savilla M. Simons, and Charlotte E. Owen, "International Social Work," *Social Work Year Book, 1954*, pp. 266-285.

Kraus, Hartha, *International Relief in Action: 1914-1943.* Scottdale, Pa.: Herald Press, 1944.

Lally, Dorothy, "Comments on the International Fellowship Program," *Social Welfare Forum, 1952*, pp. 104-117.

*———, "Gains in International Social Welfare," *Social Casework*, Vol. 33, No. 6, June, 1952, pp. 227-233.

Lane, Marie Dresden, "Public Assistance Concepts in an International Agency," *Social Security Bulletin*, Vol. 14, No. 5, May, 1951, pp. 3-9, 30.

*Learned, Ruth, "International Social Work," *Social Work Year Book, 1947*, pp. 233-240.

Lenroot, Katherine F., "Development of a Long Range International Program for Children," *U.S. Department of State Bulletin*, Vol. 26, June 16, 1952, pp. 962-965.

Lie, Trygve, *Peace on Earth.* New York: Hermitage House, 1949.

Lubin, Isadore, "The Revolution in Human Affairs," *Social Welfare Forum, 1952*, pp. 75-83.

Maloney, John, *Let There Be Mercy.* New York: Doubleday, 1941.

Marks, Edward B., Jr., "The Hard Core DP's," *The Survey*, Vol. 85, September, 1949, pp. 481-486.

Nicholson, James T., "Effective Development in International Social Welfare Programs," *National Conference of Social Work, Selected Papers in Group Work and Community Organization*, 1952, pp. 73-79.

Owen, Charlotte E., "International Voluntary Social Work," *Social Work Year Book, 1949*, pp. 252-260.

Potter, Pitman B., *The Social Services of the League of Nations.* Geneva, Switzerland: Geneva Research Center, Special Studies, Vol. 6, No. 9, 1935.

*Rees, Eltan, "The Refugees and the United Nations," *International Conciliation*, June, 1953, No. 492, New York.

Rockefeller, Nelson A., "Building the Economic Basis for Better Living Throughout the World," *Social Welfare Forum, 1952*, pp. 84-94.

Roosevelt, Eleanor, and Helen Ferris, *Partners—The United Nations and Youth.* New York: Doubleday, 1950.

Sayre, Wallace S., and Clarence E. Thurber, *Training for Specialized Mission Personnel.* Chicago: Public Administration Service, 1952.

*Sharp, Walter R., *International Technical Assistance.* Chicago: Public Administration Service, 1952.

Simons, Savilla M., "Current Developments in International Social Welfare," *The Compass*, Vol. 28, No. 2, January, 1947, pp. 13-17.

*———, "International Social Work," *Social Work Year Book, 1951*, pp. 245-259.

Staley, Eugene, *World Economic Development.* Montreal: International Labor Office, 1944.

United Nations, Department of Social Affairs, *International Advisory Social Services.* Lake Success, N.Y.: 1949

———, *International Exchange of Social Welfare Personnel.* Lake Success, N.Y.: 1949.

———, *Preliminary Report on the World Social Situation.* New York: 1952.

*Warren, George L., "International Social Work," *Social Work Year Book, 1947*, pp. 232-249.

White, Lyman C., *International Non-governmental Organizations.* New Brunswick, N.J.: Rutgers University Press, 1951.

Wickwar, W. Hardy, "Relief Supplies and Welfare Distribution: UNRRA in Retrospect," *Social Service Review*, Vol. XXI, No. 3, September, 1947, pp. 363-374.

Wilson, Francesca M., *In the Margins of Chaos.* New York: Macmillan, 1945.

*Woodbridge, George, *The History of UNRRA.* 3 vols. New York: Columbia University Press, 1950.

PART III. *Social Welfare Administration*

20. *Principles of Social Welfare Administration*

The administration of public and private social agencies is designed and organized to achieve the full effect of the services for which they have been established. The principles that rule the administration of social welfare organizations will be discussed in this chapter. We shall emphasize the administration of public welfare agencies, but keep in mind that similar principles and methods are applied in the management of private social agencies as well. Administration of social agencies translates the provisions of social legislation and the aims of private philanthropy and religious charities into the dynamics of services and benefits for humanity. Management of social agencies is oriented to aid people in the most efficient way possible; it has been briefly described as the art of human relations.[1]

The skills of administration have not been limited to social welfare settings. They are derived from public administration in general and from the techniques of business management. But the special objective of social services—to help human beings—is an element which distinguishes the management of social agencies from that of commercial and industrial enterprises and, to a lesser degree, from other public services that do not directly deal with human beings.

Administration of public social agencies in our country is complicated by the specific roles legally assigned to the three levels of government: federal, state, and local. It is similar to the management

---

[1] Karl de Schweinitz, *People and Process in Social Security* (Washington, D.C.: American Council on Education, 1948), p. 20. Other definitions are "facilitating activities necessary and incidental to the giving of direct service by a social agency" (Arthur Dunham) or "the process of transforming social policy into social service" (John C. Kidneigh); Harold Silver, "Administration of Social Agencies," *Social Work Year Book, 1954,* p. 19.

of other branches of government, such as that of public works, schools, or highways. The administration is determined by laws and statutes, its budget by decisions of the legislative body that allocates the annual appropriations and indirectly influences the appointment of personnel. Our constitutional principle of the separation of powers has not always been observed in the administration of public welfare, because courts frequently have assumed administrative functions, such as the disbursement of mothers' pensions, orphans' allowances, and workmen's compensation. The trend, however, is toward an assignment of such executive functions to administrative bodies, no longer to the courts.

Policies in public welfare administration are primarily established at the state level by state departments of public welfare, either by the board of the agency or by the executive director or commissioner. The policies and regulations for those public welfare programs that are carried on by federal agencies (such as veterans' services, old-age and survivors' insurance) or for which the federal government shares the expenses are determined either fully or in part by federal agencies. Public welfare administration, like other government operations, requires clear objectives, functions, policies, an efficient organizational structure, coordination of services, precise staff organization, sound methods of selection, recruitment and promotion of personnel, decent working conditions, and fiscal accounting and control as guarantees of efficient management.

There are, nevertheless, very important differences from other types of government functions. The objective of social service requires efficient management, thorough experience, and familiarity with the philosophy, the structure, and methods of social welfare, including knowledge of social legislation and sound welfare practice. Above all, public welfare administration requires a sincere appreciation of and devotion to the specific objectives of public welfare and its inherent social philosophy. This identification with the aims and function of social welfare is required not only of the executive of a social agency and his assistants, but of the entire staff.

I. FUNCTIONS OF WELFARE ADMINISTRATION

It is possible to group the main administrative activities of social agencies into the following seven functions. Luther Gulick invented a kind of "magic formula," "*POSDCORB*," for this classification, which we follow here because of its simplicity. *P* means planning, *O* organizing, *S* staffing, *D* directing, *CO* co-ordinating, *R* reporting, and *B* budgeting.[2] But many other authorities prefer a somewhat different classification.

1. *Planning* is the process of envisioning the future structure and operation of the social agency. It includes the determination and clarification of the objectives, functions, and policies to be pursued. The objectives of the agency are its immediate tasks and its long-range goals; operative functions are the way the agency intends to pursue its objectives; policies are the general rules that determine the work of the agency. The various services of the agency form its program. The planning function makes it necessary to observe the operation of these services, which should be flexible and dynamic so as to meet the changing needs of the population, and to improve standards and techniques by applying professional experience.

2. *Organizing* provides the administrative structure of the agency. It determines the functions of the "group of ultimate control," such as the entire population of a county for the public welfare department or the members of a private family welfare society, of the "governing board" (for example, a board of county commissioners or a lay board of directors in a child protective agency), of the executive, and of the staff.

3. *Staffing* refers to personnel administration. It is an important function because the composition, the size, and the competence of the staff determines the quality of the agency's services and their value. Personnel administration includes the realization of the agency's personnel policies on recruitment and employment, tenure, salaries, vacations, and working conditions. Standards of personnel are based upon criteria for performance, promotion, and compensation. Part of the personnel administration is the evaluation of the performance of the members of the staff to ensure efficient service and fair treatment. Personnel practices include in-service-training, grievance

---

[2] Luther Gulick and L. Urwick, *Papers on the Science of Administration* (New York: Columbia University Press, 1937), p. 13; Arthur Miles, *Introduction to Public Welfare*, pp. 329-338; Arthur Dunham, "Administration of Social Agencies," *Social Work Year Book, 1949*, pp. 15-16; H. Silver, *op. cit.*, pp. 20-21; Lewis Meriam, *Public Service and Special Training* (Chicago: University of Chicago Press, 1936), pp. 2-3.

procedure, rules of retirement, dismissal of personnel, and supervision. Frequently, unions of social workers participate in establishing regulations for personnel administration and personnel practice.

4. *Directing* is the function of the executive, involving the responsibility for final decisions and for the supervision of the administrative process of the agency. Direction requires creative leadership able to enlist the willing and enthusiastic cooperation of the staff. It includes the ability to share professional thinking with the staff, to improve methods and operations, and to give confidence through fair evaluation and treatment. Under the direction of the executive or his assistants the regular activities of the social agency are carried out. In a public welfare department they would include the reception of applicants, aid in filling out applications, home calls and social investigations, determination of eligibility, forwarding of an assistance check, and other services. For routine procedure of this type, the term "processing" frequently is used.

5. *Coordination* requires a distinct determination of each staff member's assignment and the establishment of lines of responsibility and authority. Within this setup the executive should give each staff member the opportunity to exercise his initiative, and the feeling that he performs a job which is important to the total program of the agency. Because the executive is best informed about the social policy developed by the board, he is responsible for sharing with the staff his insight into the essential elements and possibilities of effective service and into community relations.

6. *Reporting* is the administrative function of rendering to the governing board, to the membership or legislative body, and to the public an account of the agency's work. It requires a system of recording and accounting, statistics, and research upon which the reports are based. Reports are not limited to the statistical and formal accounts that frequently are ordered by legal provisions. They include statements to the public through newspapers, radio, television, and addresses to citizens' groups. Reports are an effective way of interpreting the agency's work to the public so that it is able to recognize the value of the agency's services. These effects of well-formulated, readable reports are part of the maintenance of good public relations. Friendly, cooperative ties with other social agencies and community facilities result in mutual assistance and supplementation of social services rather than in rivalry and mistrust and are valuable to the clients of the agency.

7. *Budgeting* is the function of mobilization, disbursement, and control of the financial resources of the agency. In public agencies, the administration of the budget requires negotiations for the allocation of funds by the federal, state, or local government; in private welfare organizations, the raising of money by special campaigns or the participation in the distribution by the community chest (see Chapter 21). It also involves the setting up of proper accounts, fiscal records, and controls to guarantee that the received money is spent wisely and in accordance with the policies and rules of the agency. Budgeting also means the allocation of the funds available to the branches and divisions of the agency in such a way that each of them can operate most effectively.

II. ORGANIZATIONAL STRUCTURE

The structure of public social agencies is part of the federal, state, or local government setup. The organization, as a rule, is determined by law or statute and by the functions based upon legal provisions as well as upon the size of population and the territory served by the social agency. The legislative body influences the organization, personnel, and content of services by appropriating or witholding funds for their operation. In private social agencies, either the members or a board of directors exercises the power of ultimate control.

Usually the governing board is a commission, such as the board of a state public welfare department, a county welfare commission, or the board of directors of a voluntary family welfare agency. Sometimes a single administrator replaces the governing board (for example, the Commissioner for Social Security as head of the Social Security Administration in the U.S. Department of Health, Education and Welfare). He may be supported by an advisory board. In private agencies, the board of directors usually is composed of lay persons. The board and its committees decide upon policies, support the mobilization of the necessary resources, and assist in public relations.

The *executive* is the chief administrative officer of the agency. Usually he is appointed by the board or by another authority, such as the governor of the state, the county board of supervisors, or the city council. He is responsible for the management of the agency and for carrying into effect the program and the policies of the agency that are adopted by the board or by statute. The executive represents the authority of the governing board, but, as the chief of the staff, he also maintains the interrelation between the board and the personnel of the agency. The executive is responsible for presenting to the board all essential information so that it can decide upon realistic policies.

The *staff* varies according to nature and size of the agency. In larger agencies, the staff consists of one or more assistant directors, supervisors, social workers, clerical and maintenance workers, and sometimes other professional personnel, such as physicians, nurses, accountants, lawyers, teachers, psychologists, and home economists. In many social agencies volunteers are engaged in various activities.

The executive is responsible for the establishment of subdivisions of the social agency, such as departments and district or branch offices, and for coordination and cooperation among divisions. It is also his duty to distribute the agency's functions into line, staff, and auxiliary services.

Another element of the agency's organization is the management of offices, buildings, or institutions, of equipment, procurement, storage, and issuance of supplies. This element is particularly important when residential facilities, such as a children's home, a settlement house, a senior citizens' residence, or a correctional institution, have to be maintained, but the proper management of recreational buildings and community centers is also essential. Location and equipment of the agency should meet the needs of the people who use its services. An example of the organizational structure of a state public welfare department is given in Chart 7.

III. PERSONNEL ADMINISTRATION

Competent, reliable, conscientious personnel is the most important factor in social agency administration[3] as it is in other professional services, medicine, nursing, law, and teaching. Only a well-trained staff of adequate size can perform social services as they are required for the welfare of the people. In this sense "adequate staff" means "economy," because too few or untrained workers cannot perform qualified casework or group work. Personnel policy of the social agency requires three basic elements: (1) clearly formulated, writ-

[3] R. Clyde White, *Administration of Public Welfare* (New York: American Book, 1950), p. 327; A. Miles, *op. cit.*, pp. 340-362; Elwood Street, *A Handbook for Social Agency Administration*, (New York: Harper, 1947), pp. 210-212.

ten standards of employment for specific positions, based upon competence; (2) provisions for fair dealing on grievances; and (3) delegation of final authority to the executive in dealing with matters of competence and discipline.[4]

A. METHODS OF APPOINTMENT OF PERSONNEL

For a long time in public and private social agencies personnel was employed without legal requirements and without specific qualifi-

CHART 7: ORGANIZATION OF THE WISCONSIN STATE DEPARTMENT OF PUBLIC WELFARE

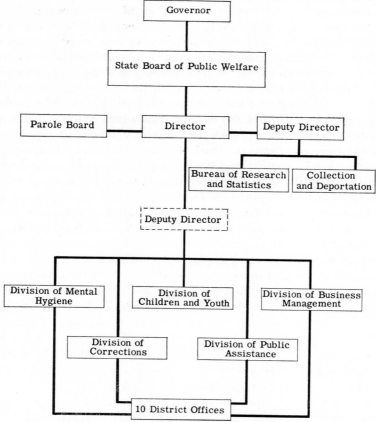

Source: Wisconsin State Department of Public Welfare, Division of Children and Youth, Biennial Report, 1950-1952, Chart II, p. 4.

[4] H. Silver, *op. cit.,* p. 23-24.

cations. Frequently appointments were based upon personal acquaintance with influential people, family relations, favoritism, or upon political affiliations. In 1829, President Jackson established political patronage, the so-called "spoils system" under the title of "administrative reform" as a system of rotation-in-office. This type of unregulated appointment remained in practice in federal, state, and local government for over fifty years.[5] It was only after the assassination of President Garfield by a frustrated applicant for public office, in 1881, that the *Pendleton Act of 1883* changed the spoils system. It created the United States Civil Service Commission composed of three members appointed by the President. Not more than two members of the Commission may belong to the same party. The selection of federal employees was to be made upon the basis of open competitive examinations. Vacancies also were to be apportioned among the states according to the size of population. The Pendleton Act established the fundament of *civil service* for the federal government. In 1883, New York passed the first state civil service law. Many other states and municipalities also enacted civil service systems, but some of them neglected to provide the necessary funds for proper administration, or frequently tried to abuse the system. Despite certain faults and inconsistencies, the principle of civil service has found acceptance in the federal service, in most states and in many cities, but only in a limited number of counties.

The main responsibilities of civil service administration are: classification of positions, establishment of qualifications and of rates of compensation, recruitment of applicants, and preparation and evaluation of examinations. Job classification includes an analysis of the functions performed in the position. The duties of each position are grouped according to their similarities and dissimilarities. Positions that have a sufficient number of similar elements are combined into a class of occupations that warrants common treatment and compensation. The job classification determines the requirements (age, education, experience, and so on) that must be fulfilled to take the examination. Qualifications are higher for jobs requiring independent work and supervisory responsibility. In social welfare it is important that supervisors and persons in responsible positions complete two years of graduate studies at a recognized school of social work.[6]

[5] A. Miles, *op. cit.*, pp. 340-343; R. C. White, *op. cit.*, pp. 332-338.
[6] See Chapter 22, and Karl de Schweinitz, *op. cit.*, pp. 129-140.

B. MERIT SYSTEMS

A variation of the civil service principle is the special merit system for the selection and appointment of personnel in public welfare services. Whereas civil service methods are used for the appointment of personnel in various branches of public government, the merit system is particularly related to the needs of public welfare administration.[7] A few state merit systems were set up after the enactment of the Social Security Act of 1935. When the Amendment to the Act of 1939 required that the states introduce an approved merit system of personnel as a condition for receiving federal grants-in-aid, all states established such merit systems. The standards announced by the federal government followed those used in federal and state civil service procedures. They require that the states adopt open competitive examinations as a basis for employment in order to give all qualified persons a fair and equal opportunity for an appointment and to administer a job classification and equitable pay plan. Under the Hatch Act and many state laws public employees are barred from participating in political activities. Discrimination because of religious, racial, and political affiliations is prohibited. Promotions are based upon length of service and capacity. Where no civil service commissions operate, state merit councils are organized to administer the system.

Under many state merit systems, the state department of public welfare is authorized to determine the qualifications of candidates to be appointed not only in its own administration but also in county and city welfare agencies. Frequently a *joint state merit system* is organized, which selects employees for public assistance, child welfare services, public health services, and unemployment insurance administration.

The provision of the Social Security Act Amendment of 1939, which is the foundation of state merit systems, has greatly contributed to the employment of competent personnel and has reduced political interference and personal favoritism in social welfare appointments. Merit systems have the potentiality of reducing the

---

[7] R. C. White, *op. cit.*, pp. 338-340; A. Miles, *op. cit.*, pp. 343-345; Marietta Stevenson, *Public Welfare Administration*, (New York: Macmillan, 1938), pp. 326-332; National Resources Planning Board, *Security, Work, and Relief Policies* (Washington, D.C.: Government Printing Office, 1942), p. 539.

high turnover of staffs, inadequate standards of personnel, substandard compensation, and unfair treatment of personnel. They encourage adequate education and training of applicants and enable public welfare agencies to adopt reasonable standards of work, salary, and promotions and to transfer personnel from one welfare program to another. Above all, merit systems develop a professional attitude and a spirit of service in public welfare administration which is of decisive importance for the public.

The U.S. Civil Service Commission, state and local civil service agencies, and public employment services cooperate in recruiting personnel. In order to make recruitment effective, for example, the California State Personnel Board has established procedures which include (1) timely notices of examinations, (2) wide publicity, (3) prompt notification of qualified candidates, (4) enumeration of all pertinent data on notices, and (5) flexibility for new classifications. Many states, counties, and cities use radio programs for announcements of civil service examinations and of job opportunities. Recruiting problems sometimes arise because of competition between the public agencies of the three levels of government, private industry and social agencies. Local coordinating committees have assisted in solving conflicts.[8]

Specified examinations are given only for certain civil service positions and promotions. In theory, these examinations should secure the recruitment of the best qualified candidates. Many state and local positions, however, limit the candidates to those who have lived a certain period (usually one year) in the state or county, and some even limit positions to persons born in the county or city. It is obvious that such residence requirements are inconsistent with the goal of civil service selection. Other limitations are caused by minimum and maximum age and certain educational conditions.

Civil service examinations are designed to eliminate unfit candidates and to determine the best qualified persons. They take into consideration statements of education and occupational experience, and consist of written and oral tests, which are graded and scored. For positions that require professional skills professional education should be a minimum qualification. In practice there has been a tendency to consider occupational experience as a substitute for graduate education in social work; however, this is incompatible with the developing concepts of the professional character of social work.

The written tests in civil service examinations are the so-called "short answer type." They include true-false questions, multiple-choice questions, and completion tests where the candidate has to supply significant words which were omitted to test the candidate's familiarity with the subject. Sometimes the examinations also present a few questions of the short-essay type, which permit the candidate to express his knowledge and opinions. The grading of the written examination is performed with the help of a "key," which contains the correct answers or which weighs the items that must be included in essay questions.

The following is an example of an announcement of a civil service examination:

United States Civil Service Commission
January 14, 1953

Examination for "Social Worker" in hospitals and regional offices of the Veterans Administration.

Requirements:

Education: Applicants must be U.S. citizens and must have successfully completed graduate study equivalent to all the requirements for the master's degree or diploma of graduation from the second-year curriculum of an accredited school of social work. This study must have included courses in case work, and in psychiatric and medical information. The applicant must have completed all the supervised field work required for the second-year curriculum by the school of social work which he attended. The accredited schools of social work are those accredited by the National Council on Social Work Education.

Experience: For Social Workers (Grade GS-7). No experience is required of applicants whose training in an accredited school of social work included three quarters or two semesters of supervised field work in case work. However, applicants whose training did not include this amount of case work must have had 1 year of case work experience.

Salary: $4,205 per year, periodic increase $125, maximum basic salary $4,955.

Probationary appointments become permanent upon satisfactory completion of a probationary period of 1 year.

Oral examinations are given to candidates who have completed all other requirements. They are usually given by an examining committee of three persons; the members of the committee are in most instances volunteers, well experienced in social welfare. The oral interview is primarily designed to evaluate the candidate's personality and his qualifications for the position. The validity of the oral test is disputed because of its subjective nature, but it is an important means of appraising the personality of the candidate, his bearing, dress, speech, reactions, alertness, response, tact, and flexibility. The weight of the oral interview in the total examination should be small.[9]

For leading positions, "unassembled examinations," which include high entrance requirements as to experience in responsible assignments and permit the civil service commission an individual treatment of the candidates, are often preferred. In such examination references of past performance, recommendations, personal qualities, and oral interview play a decisive role. Professional candidates like this type of examination because of its personal atmosphere and formal dignity, but it might easily be abused.

In addition to the written examination, the civil service commission evaluates the background, education, and practical experience of the candidate. In order to evaluate objectively, the background, education and occupational experience are scored on the basis of a predetermined table of values. General and specialized education are weighed according to the character of the schools and institutions. Occupational experience is classified according to its value in the position for which the candidate is examined.

After civil service examinations are completed, all candidates who passed are "certified" for a given position and arranged in the *Eligible List* in order of their grades. For each position a special eligible list is set up which according to law may expire within a certain period, usually two years. Veterans and incumbents may have preferential rights, and disabled veterans in some instances are placed on the top of the eligible lists if they pass with the assistance of their priority treatment. The appointing officer sometimes has to select the person at the top of the list. However, more frequently he may select one of the first three on the list. Usually appointments are made for a probationary period, during which the candidate may be dismissed.

[9] John M. Pfiffner, *Public Administration* (New York: Ronald Press, 1935), p. 188; R. C. White, *op. cit.*, p. 353-358.

In the case of dismissal the candidate may ask the civil service commission to restore him to the eligible list, but he may not be re-certified to the same agency from which he was discharged.

If a new civil service system is introduced, usually temporary employees are appointed and examinations are given after a certain period. Sometimes incumbents are "blanketed in," they are not required to take the regular examination; this method, as well as preference for incumbents, is dangerous because it defeats the principle of appointment according to ability.

C. SALARIES

Under civil service and merit systems, compensations are set up in proportion to the requirements for the positions. The positions are classified, as a rule, as clerical, professional, and administrative. In each class the compensation scale aims to attract competent personnel. In many agencies the clerical salaries of certain employees are higher than those of some professional workers, but some professional salaries may exceed those of certain administrative positions.

The federal government and certain states, such as California and New York, divide positions into only two categories: (1) the clerical-administrative-fiscal, and (2) the professional—with promotional possibilities in each of these classes.

Examples of salaries under the California Merit System in 1953 are the following: "Social Worker I," beginning salary from $210 to $258 per month. Required 3 years college or 3 years full-time paid employment in social welfare or related fields, such as teaching, nursing, employment service with contact to the public; "Social Worker II," beginning salary from $230 to $288 per month, requiring one year graduate school of social work and 6 months probationary employment.[10]

One of the characteristics of the spoils system was the uncertainty about length of service. Under the merit system, however, an employee may be dismissed only "for cause." He is entitled to defend himself against charges and to be heard before an impartial referee, a commission, or a board. As an example of the establishment of tenure, we may refer to the *California State Civil Service Act of 1936*. It permits the removal of a civil service employee for incompe-

[10] California Merit System Examining Agency, March, 1953; see also U.S. Bureau of Labor Statistics, *National Survey of Salaries and Working Conditions in Social Work* (Washington, D.C.: 1951).

tency, inefficiency, insubordination, dishonesty, intemperance, immorality, profanity, discourteous treatment of the public or other employees, improper political activity, willful disobedience, violation of the Civil Service Act, or of the rules and regulations of the State Personnel Board, for any other failure of good behavior or other acts which are incompatible with, or inimical to, the public service.[11]

Tenure requires that an employee be entitled to appeal to an impartial body when he is dismissed, regardless of the cause. The hearing must permit presentation of evidence and careful consideration and decision by the appeal body with some formal procedure, although no court routine is necessary.

On the other hand, tenure should not result in the retention of uninterested, mediocre, inefficient employees. This practice has caused severe criticism of bureaucracy. When reductions in staff because of budget cuts or of legislative changes make separations necessary, seniority alone should not be the decisive factor, but the agency should rather retain the employees who are most efficient and best qualified for the job.

D. PROMOTION

Promotion is the assignment of an employee to a position of higher rank, more responsibility, or greater compensation. To encourage young people to go into public welfare service there must be opportunity for advancement. Promotions should not be based exclusively upon seniority, but also on the service record. This record should evaluate the specific qualities in an accurate analysis of the employee's performance. Promotions may also require special examinations. Such examinations should be open to agency personnel as well as to outsiders, because incumbents already have the advantage of experience in service. The agency should have an opportunity to hire exceptionally good persons from outside. If there is no competition from outsiders, a close bureaucracy is in danger of becoming self-sufficient, uncritical, indifferent to public opinion, and apathetic in its service to clients. Public welfare personnel should not be recruited solely for the lowest positions and should not be promoted exclusively through the ranks.[12]

[11] *The Law Governing Civil Service in California* (Sacramento: 1936), p. 19; R. C. White, *op. cit.*, pp. 340-342; and A. Miles, *op. cit.*, pp. 357-358.

[12] R. C. White, *op. cit.*, pp. 358-360; and A. Miles, *op. cit.*, pp. 357-358.

E. IN-SERVICE-TRAINING AND STAFF DEVELOPMENT

In-service-training serves as an orientation of a new employee to the organization, the technical set-up, the routine work, and rules and procedures of the agency. It aims at refreshing the skill and knowledge of the staff with regard to methods of work, new developments, changes in legislation and policy, and new professional points of view.[13] However, it is no substitute for education for social welfare.

In-service-training is carried on by regular staff meetings, either for the entire staff or certain groups of workers (such as caseworkers, group workers, supervisors, field staff), or by special courses or institutes. Institutes should require serious study and permit staff preparation and follow-up conferences. Study courses usually continue over a longer period and should encourage active and critical participation of the staff members.

Staff development intends to improve the capacity and effective work of public welfare personnel. It uses in-service-training and primarily conscientious *supervision* as its principal means. It seeks to secure continued professional growth of all staff members and to strengthen their skill and interest in performing the best possible service for the public. Staff development leads to an improvement of the quality of work performed in the social agency.

Private social agencies do not have to use civil service or merit systems. They establish their own employment practices, which are approved by their governing boards. In most private agencies personnel standards are equal or even higher than in public services. Frequently standards of recruitment and personnel practice are developed under the auspices of national organizations in which the individual agencies hold membership, such as the Family Service Association of America, and the Child Welfare League of America.

IV. BUDGET AND FINANCE

The financial resources of public welfare agencies are mainly derived from taxes, those of private social agencies from allocations of the local Community Chest, from membership contributions, and from individual donations and bequests.

---

[13] A. Miles, *op. cit.,* pp. 358-360; E. Street, *op cit.,* pp. 271-275; and R. C. White, *op. cit.,* pp. 370-371.

In order to determine the necessary resources of a social agency, a budget is prepared. This is an estimate of the expenditure required for the year to carry on the services of the agency. The budget contains a detailed analysis of the services of the agency, of expenditures for aid to clients, for personnel to render services, and expenditures for office management, buildings, repair, replacement, or expansion when the services of the agency make such expenses necessary.

In general, the budget is prepared for one fiscal year. But its preparation is a function of long-time planning under the agency board, in public as well as in private agencies.

In a public welfare agency, the budget serves three functions: (1) It is a financial plan of operations for the next fiscal year (sometimes for two years); (2) it serves as a means of obtaining the necessary funds from the legislature (state assembly, county board of supervisors, and so on); and (3) it renders the basis for control of financial transactions.[14]

In preparing the budget, the agency presents the data for the expenditures of the current year and frequently of several preceding years, organized according to the major items of the budget to show the statistical trends. Conditions of change in population, in rates of assistance, in number of persons served, in staff, and in salaries and other factors are analyzed. Classification of expenditure is not uniform in the states or in the counties of the same state. In some instances a so-called "line-item-budget" is required, which does not permit use of remaining balances for any other item in the budget. This type of budget is economical, but its lack of flexibility easily interferes with efficient welfare administration.[15] The purpose of the budget is to present an accurate and intelligible survey of the expected income and of the proposed expenses of the agency.

In public welfare agencies, central budget control has produced sound business management and increased efficiency, and central-purchasing may lead to savings. Budget control should not interfere with the responsible management of the social welfare program in which the agency is engaged, and line-item-budgets should be avoided.

Public welfare is mainly paid for by three classes of taxes: (1) property taxes; (2) excise taxes; and (3) income taxes.

1. *Property taxes* have been for a long period the main financial

---

[14] R. C. White, *op. cit.*, pp. 415-417; and E. Street, *op. cit.*, pp. 345-354.
[15] A. Miles, *op. cit.*, pp. 405-406; and R. C. White, *op. cit.*, pp. 423-428.

resource of local government, towns, cities, and counties. Property taxes are primarily taxes on real estate, buildings, and land, and on personal property, such as jewelry, stocks, bonds, mortgages (liens), and automobiles. Regular household goods and clothes usually are exempt, since a reasonable amount of personal property is not assessable. Property taxes are classified according to levels of assessed value in many states. Real property of small value is left tax free; other property classes are taxed with increasing rates in order that real property which cannot be concealed is not too heavily burdened, and to assure that "intangible property," such as bonds and stocks, is properly assessed. The goal of such legislation is to levy property taxes on those people who are most able to pay. For local welfare expenditures property taxes are the primary financial resources, especially where the full burden of general assistance is carried by counties or cities.

2. *Excise taxes* are domestic taxes on consumption, mainly sales taxes, which are paid directly by the consumer. They include taxes on liquor, tobacco, cigarettes, cosmetics, theatre and sport tickets, and special sale taxes. In many states there is a general state tax which provides part of the revenue for the welfare expenditures of the state.

3. *Income taxes* are those levied primarily on net income of individuals, self-employed persons and wage earners, and of corporations. They are graduated so that individuals and corporations in higher income brackets pay a higher tax. Because of certain deductions and exemptions for dependent children the lowest income group frequently is not taxed. Income taxes provide resources for the federal and many state governments and serve as revenue for federal and state welfare expenditures.

In addition to these three main classes of taxes there are other taxes and fees for deeds and mortgages that do not play a major role as resource for the welfare budgets of federal, state, and local governments, but sometimes are used to raise revenue for public welfare expenses.[16]

In a number of states, specific taxes such as liquor, gasoline, poll, motor or store license, sales, luxury, inheritance, beer and wine, fuel, dividends and property taxes, are assigned to cover fully or in part the expense of public assistance. Special taxes raised for the social insurance programs have been discussed in Chapter 9. The "assigned

---

16 For a more detailed analysis of taxation and public welfare revenues see R. C. White, *op. cit.*, pp. 393-414; A. Miles, *op. cit.*, pp. 407-411; and Alfred G. Buehler, *Public Finance* (New York: McGraw, 1936), pp. 219-225.

tax" may easily result in insufficient revenues in a depression period, and appropriations from general taxation are preferable to secure the means for public welfare programs.

Every social worker in a public welfare agency should be well acquainted with the tax structure and the means of raising the resources for the administration of the welfare services in his community and state. The social worker must have an understanding of the tax structure and of the reactions of the population toward the taxes involved to be able to discuss intelligently the social and economic factors involved and to interpret the social effects of the agency's services.

The financing of private social agencies is part of the community organization process which we shall discuss in the subsequent chapter.

V. TRENDS IN SOCIAL WELFARE
ADMINISTRATION

1. Social workers have shown an increasing interest in welfare administration during the past decade. This interest is based partly upon the recognition that social welfare administration is a vital element in the quality of services rendered by social agencies and that effective leadership in social agencies under public and private auspices requires full understanding of, and experience in, social work. No longer is the belief valid that a successful businessman or a railroad executive is well equipped to direct a social agency. Since social agency administration begins to be identified with social work, students and professional social workers demonstrate sincere interest in this area of social welfare.

2. Schools of Social Work are assuming an increasing responsibility in teaching social welfare administration and in integrating the knowledge of this topic with skills in community organization, casework, and group work. Knowledge of social welfare administration embodies the understanding of (a) relationship principles applying to individuals and groups, (b) the totality of the process of social agency administration, and (c) the various kinds of program characteristics of social agencies.[17]

[17] John C. Kidneigh, "Social Work Administration; An Area of Social Work Practice?" *Social Work Journal*, Vol. 31, No. 2, April, 1950, pp. 57-61, 79; H. Silver, *op. cit.*, pp. 24-25; and Eveline M. Burns, "The Role of Government in Social Welfare," *Social Work Journal*, Vol. 35, No. 3, July, 1954, pp. 95-102, 124-125.

3. There is an increasing realization that theoretical formulations and practical principles of social welfare administration need further clarification and scientific analysis. The interest of social workers seems to go beyond the questions of external organization and structure of agencies to an exploration of the dynamics of effective social welfare administration.

4. There is a growing belief that the responsibility for the administration of public welfare functions in our country rests primarily with the states, counties, and cities. The federal government, however, is obliged to aid state and local governments in providing the funds for adequate welfare services, in equalizing the financial base for public welfare so that the poorer states may carry on satisfactory programs, and in developing national standards and goals.[18] Administration of social welfare should be community centered.

5. Personnel in social welfare is being selected, promoted, and retained increasingly on a basis of merit. Workers in social welfare administration are qualified by professional education and social work skills, by their human convictions, and by a sense of responsibility toward the clients and toward those who finance welfare services.

6. In personnel administration, progress is evident in greater job security, sometimes in collective bargaining agreements with unions in social work or as part of civil service and merit rating systems. The increasing number of retirement annuity provisions in public welfare agencies and the partial inclusion of social workers on a voluntary basis in federal old-age and survivors' insurance are signs of this trend. The National Health and Welfare Retirement Association also has developed private retirement plans for the security of social workers.

7. With regard to the responsibility for public funds, the conviction is wide-spread and growing that public monies should be administered only by a public agency. Public welfare departments are entitled to use private social agencies in behalf of individuals and groups and to compensate them for such services. In such instances agreements should secure full protection of the clients and guarantee the proper use of public funds.

[18] There is a difference of opinion among students of public welfare about the desirable participation of the federal government in welfare services. See Robert T. Lansdale, "A Major Problem of Public Welfare: The Growing Complexity of Administering Public Assistance," *Public Welfare*, Vol. II, No. 1, January, 1953, pp. 7-12.

8. There is an increasing recognition that public welfare owes to the people and to its representatives a full accounting regarding the purposes, policies, methods of operation, and a breakdown of the expenditures. However, such information should protect the privacy of individuals who receive public welfare services.

9. The development of higher standards of social agency administration is furthered by national, state, and local agencies of both public and private character.

10. There is a growing recognition that Public Welfare has a responsibility for promoting scientific research. Such social research is designed to improve the quality and the effect of social welfare administration, and to help to alleviate or prevent conditions which result in the need for social services.[19]

SELECTED BIBLIOGRAPHY

Abbott, Edith, *Public Assistance, Select Documents,* Vol. I. Chicago: University of Chicago Press, 1940.

American Public Welfare Association, *Adequate Staff Brings Economy.* Chicago, 1939.

*Atwater, Pierce, *Problems of Administration in Social Work.* Minneapolis: University of Minnesota Press, 1940.

Baker, Helen, and Mary S. Routzahn, *How to Interpret Social Welfare.* New York: Russell Sage Foundation, 1946.

Barnard, Chester I., *The Function of the Executive.* Cambridge: Harvard University Press, 1938.

———, "The Nature of Leadership," *Human Factors in Management.* Parkville, Mo.: Park College Press, 1946.

Blumenthal, Louis H., *Administration of Group Work.* New York: Association Press, 1948.

Breckinridge, Sophonisba P., *Public Welfare Administration in the United States, Select Documents,* 2nd ed. Chicago: University of Chicago Press, 1938.

Buehler, Alfred G., *Public Finance.* New York: McGraw, 1936.

Chase, Stuart, and M. T. Chase, *Men at Work; some democratic methods for the power age.* New York: Harcourt, 1945.

*Cohn, Martin, and Elizabeth Wallace, *Some Problems of Administration in Social Work.* Toronto: University of Toronto Press, 1944.

*de Schweinitz, Karl, *People and Process in Social Security.* Washington, D.C.: American Council on Education, 1948.

Dimock, Marshall E., *The Executive in Action.* New York: Harper, 1945.

[19] "Essentials of Public Welfare," A Statement of Principles Prepared by the Welfare Policy Committee of the American Public Welfare Association, *Public Welfare,* Vol. II, No. 1, January, 1953, pp. 5-6.

Dunham, Arthur, "Administration of Social Agencies," *Social Work Year Book, 1949,* pp. 15-22.

Follett, Mary P., *Creative Experience.* New York: Longmans, 1924.

———, *The New State.* New York: Longmans, 1918.

*Gulick, Luther, and L. Urwick (editors), *Papers on the Science of Administration.* New York: Institute of Public Administration, Columbia University, 1937.

*Hanchette, Helen W., *et al., Some Dynamics of Social Agency Administration.* New York: Family Service Association of America, 1946.

Harlow, Rex F., and Marvin M. Black, *Practical Public Relations.* New York: Harper, 1947.

Hosch, Florence I., "Personnel Standards in Social Work," *Social Work Year Book, 1949,* pp. 346-354.

*Johnson, Arlien, "The Administrative Process in Social Work," *National Conference of Social Work, Proceedings 1946,* pp. 249-258.

*Kidneigh, John C., "Social Work Administration; An Area of Social Work Practice," *Social Work Journal,* Vol. 31, No. 2, April, 1950, pp. 57-61, 79.

Klein, Alice Campbell, *Civil Service in Public Welfare.* New York: Russell Sage Foundation, 1940.

Landis, J. D., *The Administrative Process.* New Haven: Yale University Press, 1938.

Lee, Porter R., *Social Work as Cause and Function and Other Papers.* New York: Columbia University Press, 1937.

Leirfallom, Jarl, and Russell P. Drake, *Organization and Administration of Local Public Welfare Services.* Chicago: American Public Welfare Association, 1943.

Macdonald, J. H., *Practical Budget Procedure.* New York: Prentice-Hall, Inc., 1939.

McLean, F. H., and Ralph Ormsby, *Organizing a Family Agency.* New York: Family Welfare Association of America (now Family Service Association of America), 1944.

Marcus, Grace F., *The Nature of Service in Public Assistance Administration.* Washington, D.C.: Social Security Administration, Public Assistance Report No. 10, 1946.

Martz, Helen E., *Citizen Participation in Government; A Study of County Welfare Boards.* Washington, D.C.: Public Affairs Press, 1948.

Meriam, Lewis, *Public Personnel Problems from the Standpoint of the Operating Officer.* Washington, D.C.: Brookings Institution, 1938.

Metcalf, Henry C., and Mary P. Follett, *Business Management as a Profession.* New York: McGraw, 1927.

———, and L. Urwick (editors), *Dynamic Administration: The Collected Papers of Mary Parker Follett.* New York: Harper, 1942.

*Miles, Arthur P., *An Introduction to Public Welfare.* Boston: Heath, 1949.

Mosher, W. E., and J. D. Kingsley, *Public Personnel Administration,* 2nd rev. ed. New York: Harper, 1941.

*National Resources Planning Board, *Security, Work, and Relief Policies.* Washington, D.C.: Government Printing Office, 1942.

Pfiffner, J. M., *Public Administration.* New York: Ronald Press, 1935.

Routzahn, Evart G., and Mary S. Routzahn, *A Study in Public Relations.* New York: Russell Sage Foundation, 1943.

*Silver, Harold, "Administration of Social Agencies," *Social Work Year Book, 1954,* pp. 19-26.

Simon, H. A., et al., *Determining Work Loads for Professional Staff in a Public Welfare Agency.* Berkeley: University of California, 1941.

*Stevenson, Marietta, et al., *Public Welfare Administration.* New York: Macmillan, 1938.

Stillman, C. C., *Social Work Publicity.* New York: Century Company, 1927.

*Street, Elwood, *A Handbook for Social Agency Administration.* New York: Harper, 1947.

————, *The Public Welfare Administrator.* New York: McGraw, 1940.

Swift, Arthur L., *Make Your Agency More Effective: A Manual for Institutional Self-Study.* New York: Association Press, 1941.

Tead, Ordway, *Democratic Administration.* New York: Association Press, 1945.

*Trecker, Harleigh B., *Group Process in Administration.* New York: Woman's Press, 1946.

Urwick, L., *The Elements of Administration.* New York: Harper, 1944.

Vasquez, Charles B., *Courses in Administration in Schools of Social Work.* Denver: University of Denver, 1947.

Weigel, John C., and Fletcher C. Kettle, *The Illinois Plan of Fiscal Control.* Springfield: Illinois State Department of Public Welfare, 1940.

White, Leonard D., *Introduction to the Study of Public Administration,* 3rd ed. New York: Macmillan, 1948.

*White, R. Clyde, *Administration of Public Welfare,* 2nd ed. New York: American Book, 1950.

Withers, William, *Financing Economic Security in the United States.* New York: Columbia University Press, 1939.

21. Community Organization

I. PRINCIPLES

We defined "Community Organization" as "the social work process of establishing a progressively more effective adjustment between the social welfare needs and the community resources within a geographic area."[1] In our discussion here we consider those phases of community life that are devoted to social welfare. We are aware, however, that the life of the local community includes the planning and coordination of education, housing, transportation, water and sewage supply, and other necessities of human living as well as social and health services, and that an integration of these essential elements in community planning is indispensable. Instead of the term "Community Organization" some social workers prefer "Social Welfare Planning," "Social Inter-Group Work Process," "Social Welfare Organization," or "Social Engineering." The three main objectives of community welfare organization are (1) to determine the social needs, (2) to arrange for careful and conscientious planning to meet the needs of the population, and (3) to mobilize the forces of the community in the best way to achieve this goal.

Clarence King[2] has emphasized that all social work programs in our country can accomplish their purpose only if they are accepted by the majority of the people. This is one of the tasks of community organization; citizen participation in welfare organization is the essential factor in this process of social work. We already discussed in

[1] See page 187. Various definitions are discussed in Wayne McMillen, *Community Organization for Social Welfare* (Chicago: University of Chicago Press, 1949), pp. 20-22. See also Herbert H. Stroup, *Community Welfare Organization* (New York: Harper, 1952), pp. 138-148; and Arthur P. Miles, *American Social Work Theory* (New York: Harper, 1954), pp. 181-187.

[2] *Organizing for Community Action* (New York: Harper, 1948), p. 22; see also Arthur Hillman, *Community Organization and Planning* (New York: Macmillan, 1950), pp. 13-14.

Chapter 17 how important the active cooperation of organized labor is in community organization. Democracy, indeed, requires the working together of all groups of the population in the development, maintenance, and the reorganization of institutions for health, welfare, and recreation. This principle applies to all types of social work, but particularly to community welfare organization. Because citizens have broad insight into the social needs of their communities and are able to oversee the various problems, and because their permanent support of a new or an expanded program of services is indispensable, their genuine, responsible initiative in the planning and in the setting up of welfare and health services is necessary.

To mobilize the citizens for social welfare programs requires the knowledge and skills of the "community organizer," the professional workers, and the volunteers engaged not only in the community organization process but also in other phases of social work which are related to activities in community organization. The social and psychological elements that influence citizens in their decisions about participation in community projects are of vital importance in a democracy.[3] The increased interest in volunteer services which we discussed above[4] is an indication of the growing concern of citizens about the welfare needs of the entire population and of their willingness to offer their time and energy in order to assist in meeting social needs. Such interest must be recognized and encouraged.

It is necessary to distinguish the underlying social philosophy, which is the same in community organization as in casework or group work, from the special skills or techniques applied to achieve an efficient coordination and integration of community resources for health and welfare. Community organization is an inter-group process. When it is concerned with specific objectives, such as the enactment of social legislation, the establishment of new welfare policies, or the creation of a necessary social agency, we call these activities "social action." We shall discuss this kind of activity later.

The objectives of community organization are (1) to help citizens in finding the ways best suited for the provision of health and

[3] Among many studies which investigate these elements, the reader is referred to Helen E. Martz, *Citizens Participation in Government* (Washington, D.C.: Public Affairs Press, 1948); A. Hillman, *op. cit.,* pp. 135-137; Ordway Tead, *The Art of Leadership* (New York: McGraw, 1935).

[4] See Chapter 14.

welfare services, for the improvement of the social environment, and for prevention and aid of suffering; (2) to encourage cooperative efforts of the population for the purpose of common human welfare; (3) to construct for individuals and groups the channels of mutual understanding on problems of health and welfare and the means of communication essential to common action.

Community organization does not relieve citizens as individuals or as civic groups from their social responsibilities. It rather attempts by exchange of ideas and experiences to clarify the social responsibility of the community, citizens, and government authorities regarding the necessary measures to be taken to meet social and health needs.

Within the framework of community organization the social worker has the task of contributing his professional knowledge, skill, and experience.

(a) From his awareness of social conditions, the social worker is able to share with other citizens the recognition of health and welfare needs.

(b) He is qualified to stimulate in the community the necessary surveys and research in order to establish facts and prepare a plan for improving conditions.

(c) The social worker is able to assist in the interpretation of social needs to his clients, to the neighborhood, and to social groups in the community.

II. HISTORY OF COMMUNITY ORGANIZATION

Community organization has its main roots in the English Charity Organization Societies and the subsequent charity organization movement in the United States.[5] The need for coordination of the work of charities and philanthropic societies had been recognized earlier, but its realization became first one of the objectives of the Association for Improvement of Conditions of the Poor which was founded in New York City in 1843. The Association divided the city into districts and assigned visitors to investigate family needs and to determine where improvements in housing, health, and living conditions were needed. Charity Organization Societies whose development in

[5] See Chapters 2, 4, and 6; certain earlier attempts of coordination of charitable work were made by Juan Vives, the Hamburg-Elberfeld system in Germany, and Count Rumford in Munich.

this country began in Buffalo, in 1877, recognized that their principal goal was to coordinate the existing charities and relief societies, to avoid overlapping and duplication of services, and to encourage co-operation between social agencies instead of rivalry and competition for donors and for the care of clients. To find solutions for these problems, special councils or boards were established in Charity Organization Societies of Rochester, N.Y., Elmira, N.Y., and in New York City as early as 1882. These councils were composed of representatives of the major charities in the city. Francis H. McLean favored the idea that a separate body assume the responsibility for coordination of welfare agencies and planning of programs, and his idea was carried out when in 1908 the Associated Charities of Pittsburgh, Pa., organized a community welfare council.[6] Similar councils, usually called "council of social agencies," were set up in Milwaukee in 1909, in St. Louis in 1911, in Cincinnati and Cleveland in 1913, in Minneapolis in 1916, and in Chicago in 1917. In 1954, 450 community welfare councils were members of the national federation, "Community Chests and Councils." Their objectives are coordination of social welfare activities and inter-agency cooperation between public and private social agencies, the raising and maintaining of standards of service, development of community leadership in the promotion of health and welfare, and social planning. Because the quality of service often varies among agencies, community welfare councils are able to raise these standards by requiring a certain level of performance as a condition of council membership. Since individual social agencies and institutions developed according to the initiative of individual philanthropists or of independent religious and humanitarian groups, social welfare councils now provide the means of investigating social needs of the community and of coordinating agency efforts, with agreement on division of work and on basic policies.

The financing of charities was from the very beginning a major interest of the Charity Organization Societies. The vast and increasing number of relief societies, charitable institutions, and other social agencies in large cities led to continuous solicitation of donations and contributions from well-to-do citizens. Almost every day bank-

[6] Frank Bruno, *Trends in Social Work* (New York: Columbia University Press, 1948), p. 194; W. McMillen, *op. cit.*, pp. 416-417, considers the Milwaukee council the first independent council because the Pittsburgh organization remained part of the Associated Charities for a year.

ers, businessmen, lawyers, and physicians were approached by one or another group of citizens, hospitals, dispensaries, or orphanages, which competed for the favor of the donors. They could not understand why such a vast array of agencies was necessary since many of them seemed to do the same work. Some donors became hostile and refused contributions, others asked for a change in agency collection policies. This demand of the public was made for still another reason. A number of fraudulent, unscrupulous "entrepreneurs" asked for donations for charities with impressive titles and betrayed the trust of the benevolent people they approached. Some social agencies that hired skillful fund raisers were able to collect substantial contributions, often much more than their services warranted, whereas others of vital importance to the community had to operate on a starvation level because they lacked efficient fund-raising facilities.[7]

Some early attempts at combined fund-raising for charities had been made in Liverpool by Reverend A. Hume in 1873, by the Associated Charities of Denver, Colorado in 1887, by federations of Jewish Charities beginning in Boston in 1895, and by the Charity Organization Society of Elmira, N.Y. in 1910. Still earlier the YMCA's had introduced a community-wide campaign for raising money for their activities. Another element in the development of joint financing of social agencies was the "charity work endorsement committees," which at the turn of the century were sponsored by chambers of commerce and commercial associations. But in Cleveland, in 1913, the first "Community Chest," as a special organization for the financing of social work, was founded under the title "Federation for Charity and Philanthropy" on the initiative of Major N. D. Baker. It substituted one organization and one campaign for fifty-three drives and collections, and succeeded in tripling the number of donors to charity. In a few years fifteen metropolitan cities introduced similar community chests, and during both world wars many war chests followed the same pattern. In 1954, 1250 community chests carried membership in "Community Chests and Councils."[8] The main objective of the community chest is to procure the necessary funds for the operations of its member agencies. But it also aims at a fair and constructive distribution of the collected

[7] W. McMillan, op. cit., pp. 414-417.

[8] Lyman S. Ford, "Community Chests," Social Work Year Book, 1951, p. 117; and Allen T. Burns, Community Mobilization for Human Needs (New York: Community Chests and Councils, 1938).

funds so that the participating agencies may best serve the interests of the population and improve and expand their services as needed. In order to carry on its campaign successfully and to obtain the necessary contributions for private agencies, the chest has to interpret for the public the programs and policies of social agencies.

The development of the Social Service Exchange is closely related to that of community welfare councils and community chests; it will be discussed briefly below.

III. STRUCTURE OF COMMUNITY ORGANIZATION

The agencies that carry on the process of community organization may be divided into two groups: those operating on the local level, and those active on a state, national, or even international level. For the purpose of our discussion only the first group needs a full analysis.

In a city or large county of metropolitan character, community organization, as a rule, is performed by the following organizations: (1) community welfare council, (2) community chest, (3) coordinating council, (4) neighborhood council, (5) the social service exchange, and (6) individual social agencies.[9]

1. *A Community Welfare Council* or *Council of Social Agencies* exists in almost every city with a population of 100,000 or more for the purpose of community-wide planning and coordination of the local health, welfare, and recreational services. The organization of the councils is not uniform, but the following features are characteristic of most of them. They are composed of representatives of all social agencies in the area of welfare, health, and recreation which maintain standards acceptable to the council, and often of some individual members, such as the mayor of the city and outstanding persons in the field of philanthropy, health, welfare, and culture. The social agencies represented usually include public agencies, such as the department of public welfare, the public health department, the recreation and park commission, the board of education, and the juvenile court. Because public agencies are maintained by taxes, they participate in the work of the community welfare council without

[9] W. McMillen, *op. cit.*, pp. 317-328, 417-428; and A. Hillman, *op. cit.*, pp. 135-137.

an interest in receiving financial support from money-raising campaigns. However, some private agencies also may be members of the council without sharing in general collections for health and welfare purposes. Each social agency participating in the council is usually represented by two members, one the president or another member of the board of directors, the other a professional social worker, in most instances the executive of the agency. In large cities or counties the council establishes a number of divisions, such as family welfare, child care and adoption, recreation, health and medical care services, and care for the aged, with committees to direct each division. Sometimes the council conducts a separate "Social Planning Bureau," a statistical and research bureau, and a public information division. An example of the organization of a council is presented in Chart 8. The functions of a community welfare council are frequently classified into the following six activities:[10]

(a) *Coordination.* The meetings of the council with its lay board and staff members and of its committees present to the public and private social agencies and to the citizens a full picture of the health and welfare work performed in the community. Usually the council distributes a bulletin and other pertinent information among its members. In these ways, members have an opportunity to share experiences, to develop mutual understanding, and to work together. Meetings and conferences permit them to identify common problems, to explore unmet needs of the population, and to eliminate duplication of effort. Thus the council operates as a clearing house, permitting better service for the community.

(b) *Fact-Finding.* Often social and health conditions in the community must be investigated to determine the causes and the size of problems, the available resources for health and welfare services, and the cost and distribution of such services. Therefore social research and surveys are necessary to acquire reliable knowledge of conditions that need social change. Sometimes it is advisable to request "outside" experts or consultants to conduct such a survey because they are not biased in regard to the conservation of the existing social services and are able to compare conditions with those in other cities or regions. Committees in charge of evaluation of social

[10] Merrill F. Krughoff, "Councils in Social Work," *Social Work Year Book, 1947,* pp. 132-133; and Rudolph T. Danstedt, "Councils in Social Work," *Social Work Year Book, 1954,* pp. 142-145.

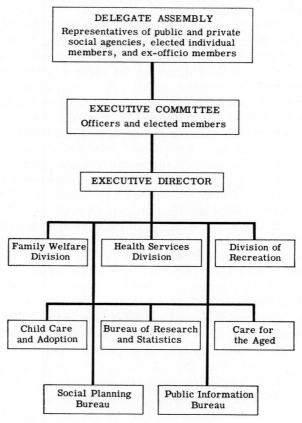

surveys should be composed of laymen and of professional workers. They should convey the findings and recommendations of the survey not only to the members of the council but also to the general public.

(c) *Joint Action.* The advantage of a community welfare council is that it combines a large number of organizations and mobilizes through its board and lay members important forces in the community. As a result, it is able to conduct careful planning on the basis of research and examination of the prevailing conditions, and to enlist the support of many groups in carrying out the measures recommended by its fact-finding committee. For example, the committee may recommend the consolidation of two children's homes or the conversion of one into a nursing home for chronically ill patients, or the closing of an agency that is no longer needed, or the establishment of a new service, such as a mental hygiene clinic.

(d) *Improving the Quality of Service.* The observation and evaluation of the quality of services rendered by the social agencies of the community is an important function of the council. The council attempts to improve inadequate services by consultation with board members and by providing intensive staff training courses.

(e) *Common Services.* There are certain welfare activities that are of value to the entire community, not limited to just one or the other social agency. Such activities are the proper function of a community welfare council, as in case of a central index, usually called "social service exchange," or a central volunteer bureau, which encourages volunteers to apply for participation, advises them about opportunities, selects and prepares them for their work, and refers them to agencies where they are needed. Other common services are a central information bureau which contacts the press, radio and television companies, and movie theatres to enlist broad public interest in health and welfare facilities and to advise individuals about recreation, health, and welfare agencies; or a research and statistical bureau or institute, which carries out some of the social surveys and studies mentioned above or which often with the aid of citizens' groups and foundations, encourages such studies by other organizations.[11] Further possibilities are a joint intake bureau for casework, child care, or guidance services.

(f) *Developing Public Understanding.* One of the essential objectives of the community welfare council is to bring the value of the work of social agencies to the attention of the people and to enlist their understanding, concern, and active participation in these services.[12] We mentioned already certain activities of the council,

[11] The reader is referred to Professor Ernest Greenwood's "Echo Park Study" as an illustration of such a community research and fact-finding project (see Appendix); see also Lucy P. Carner, "The Youth and Government Project," *National Conference of Social Work, Selected Papers in Group Work and Community Organization,* 1952, pp. 12-16.

[12] A. Hillman, *op. cit.,* pp. 166-177; Davis McEntire, *Leisure Activities of Youth in Berkeley, California* (Berkeley Council of Social Agencies, 1952); examples of research studies conducted under the auspices of community welfare councils are cited in Chapter 6, pages 195-197.

the information bureau, and the central volunteer bureau, which serve this purpose. But the council's responsibility goes beyond these special methods of reaching the people of the community. Social surveys have shown that a large percentage of the citizens have a very vague notion of what social agencies do and why they are necessary. To bring the facts to the people and to impart to them clear, objective, basic information about health and social conditions and the role of social and health agencies is a real challenge for the community welfare council. Such councils may be very effective in developing community leaders—lay persons who have a clear understanding of the need for health and welfare services and who are able to convey their knowledge to civic organizations, church and service clubs, women's associations, and youth groups.

2. *The Community Chest* was formed because private social agencies depend to a large extent upon voluntary contributions for the financing of their services and their personnel. A cooperative method of raising the necessary funds for these activities is required to avoid dissatisfaction and hostility among the people who are called upon for contributions to private social agencies and to secure a fair support to all essential welfare organizations.[13] As a rule the community chest is governed by a board of directors which represents not only all social agencies that are members of the chest but also citizens constituting a broad cross-section of the population of the area. Boards of directors usually are made up of the presidents and the executives of the social agencies, representives of the chamber of commerce, of large industries, merchants associations, service clubs, church groups, professional associations, and organized labor. In large cities these representatives form a delegate association of the community chest and elect a board of directors, which supervises the operations of the chest and sets up its policies. The management of the chest is directed through an executive committee and its officers (president, secretary, and treasurer) as well as through the executive director who usually is appointed by the board of directors. There are laymen and representatives of other social agencies on both the board of directors and on the executive committee of the chest. Frequently they represent the public welfare department, the board of education, the health department, and the recreation commission, advise about the population's need for voluntary health, recreation,

[13] See pages 109 and 188.

and welfare services, and support the endeavor to raise funds for private agencies. The most important work of the chest is entrusted to the budget committee and to the campaign committee. The budget committee is composed of some members of the executive committee, other lay persons and representatives of the community welfare council. Prior to the annual campaign, usually in September, all participating social agencies submit a detailed budget for the subsequent year and request a certain share in the funds to be raised by the chest drive. The budget committee carefully studies the requests, compares them with former budgets, and discusses each agency's request with its representatives. The budget committee then estimates the total amount of money that may be raised by the campaign and revises, in view of this estimate, the plan for the allocation of funds to the individual agencies. The adjusted budget is submitted to the executive committee or to the board of directors for approval.

The campaign committee is in charge of the preparation of the annual drive. It invites church, civic, and youth organizations to enlist volunteers for a house-to-house canvass. It appoints special subcommittees and captains for individual contributions and special drives among industries, department houses, service clubs, banks, professional associations, and organized labor groups. The committee supervises the campaign which usually lasts no longer than one month or six weeks. An illustration of the pattern of chest organization is shown in Chart 9.

In order to carry on a successful campaign, the community chest has to interpret to the population the year around the necessity as well as the extent and quality of recreational, health, and welfare services offered in the community. That a close working relationship with the community welfare council is necessary in this respect is obvious from the same objectives of both agencies. The chest's interpretation is a cooperative effort with the public information task of the council and is usually carried on with joint planning and in mutual agreement. From the financial point of view, the community chest promotes health and welfare of the citizens by requiring the most efficient, coordinated, and well-integrated services. The chest works with this goal by avoiding duplications of work, conducting or stimulating research regarding the social and health needs, and encouraging careful planning and evaluation of projects and welfare operations.

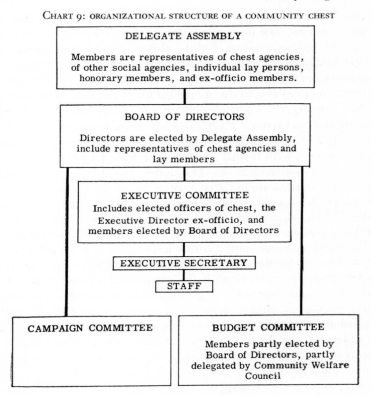

CHART 9: ORGANIZATIONAL STRUCTURE OF A COMMUNITY CHEST

DELEGATE ASSEMBLY

Members are representatives of chest agencies, of other social agencies, individual lay persons, honorary members, and ex-officio members.

BOARD OF DIRECTORS

Directors are elected by Delegate Assembly, include representatives of chest agencies and lay members

EXECUTIVE COMMITTEE
Includes elected officers of chest, the Executive Director ex-officio, and members elected by Board of Directors

EXECUTIVE SECRETARY

STAFF

CAMPAIGN COMMITTEE

BUDGET COMMITTEE

Members partly elected by Board of Directors, partly delegated by Community Welfare Council

When the community chest assumes the responsibility for the financial support of private social agencies, for the fund-raising campaign, and for a fair distribution of the collected contributions, the community welfare council is free to concentrate its attention upon social surveys and research, coordination of health, welfare, and recreation services, and program planning.

The principle of joint fund-raising for welfare purposes as represented by the community chest has proved to be successful. This fund-raising has resulted in the collection of larger amounts of money than were contributed to all local social agencies prior to a federated campaign. After World War II, in most cities the total result of the annual campaigns could be maintained and even a slight increase in contributions reached, but not always as much as extension of social services and increasing cost required.

There are, however, serious problems which face the community chests. A number of important health and welfare agencies, especially the American Red Cross, the National Tuberculosis Association, the National Foundation for Infantile Paralysis, the American Heart Association, the National Society for Crippled Children and Adults, and the American Cancer Society, have not joined in the local drive of the community chests and have insisted in carrying on their own campaigns. Citizens have been dissatisfied by near-monthly independent appeals of major health or welfare organizations made in addition to the annual campaign of the community chest. This situation requires a change in policy. In a number of cities, beginning in Detroit and Flint, Michigan, a so-called "United Health and Welfare Fund" has been set up which combines the local community chest and the agencies which managed their own drives into only one yearly campaign. The success of such a new type of federation depends mainly upon the energy with which industry, commerce, and labor unions insist upon unity of fund-raising. Other chests attempt to reduce the number of independent campaigns by an "open door policy," inviting local, state, or national agencies to participate in the local campaign. Unfortunately the good will of the local chests has so far not changed the fund-raising policies of the large national organizations mentioned above.[14] In the California East Bay a Federation of community chests has been set up in order to integrate the work of several chests, to avoid duplication of solicitations, and to achieve an over-all, united campaign.

In general, community chests welcome special donations and bequests which are made independent of the regular, annual campaign. In some metropolitan cities a separate Community Fund has been organized in order to receive and administer such donations and bequests for charitable purposes and health and welfare services. The Fund has its own by-laws, a board of directors which determines the policy of the agency, and an executive who is responsible for the administration and the allocations of the money, stocks, bonds, and other properties. Usually there is planned cooperation between the Fund and the local chest.

In some cities the community welfare council and the community chest are combined in a single organization. An example of the struc-

[14] L. Ford, *op. cit.*, pp. 119-122; see also W. McMillen, *op. cit.*, pp. 448-457, 461-462.

ture of such a joint agency is given in Chart 10. In other instances where a separate Council and Chest operate, the necessary teamwork is secured by the employment of one executive and staff for both the Council and the Community Chest. Both organizations share office and other facilities and have common research and public relations committees. The Community Welfare Council usually participates in the selection of the members of the budget committee of the community chest.

3. *The Coordinating Council* is a citizens' group created for co-ordinating the social forces of a municipal district in order to deal with specific social problems (primarily juvenile delinquency). The first coordinating council was founded in 1919, in Berkeley, California, by Professor August Vollmer, then Chief of Police, in co-operation with Dr. Tau Don Ball, psychiatrist of the police department, and Dr. Virgil Dickson, member of the Board of Education. A preceding social survey at an elementary school had revealed that 90 per cent of these children were in families under economic stress, and that a coordination of the sources of the community was needed in order to prevent juvenile delinquency by proper care, treatment, and guidance. The head of the public welfare department and of the city health department and executives of social agencies joined the group on invitation for regular weekly meetings. In 1924, the Berkeley Coordinating Council for Child Welfare was officially estabished for the following reasons:

1. To improve the physical, moral and mental welfare of the children in the community.
2. To co-ordinate the activities of existing agencies, preventing duplication.
3. To promote personal acquaintance and esprit de corps among the executives of various agencies.[15]

The coordinating council achieved successful cooperation of public authorities and private social agencies in the area and developed a child guidance clinic and vocational counseling, a social service exchange, and broad educational programs. Following this example, similar coordinating councils were established in San Francisco, Los

[15] Unpublished material of the Berkeley Coordinating Council, in the possession of Professor August Vollmer; see also Katherine F. Lenroot, "Delinquency Prevention Through School and Social Agency Coordination," *Educational Forum*, November, 1943, pp. 11-15; and Kenneth S. Beam, *Coordinating Councils in California* (Sacramento: Department of Education, 1938).

CHART 10: JOINT COMMUNITY CHEST AND WELFARE COUNCIL

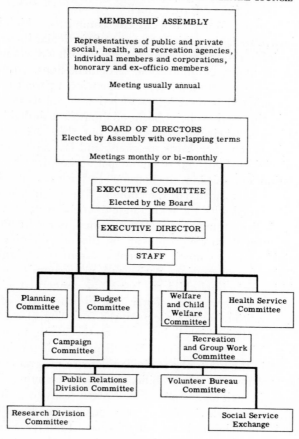

Angeles, and other cities in California. Later, coordinating councils were organized in New York, Illinois, and St. Paul, Minnesota, but no national federation has been set up. Coordinating councils maintain a cooperative relationship with the local community welfare council, and are represented at its delegate body or board of directors. Their main objective is the prevention of juvenile delinquency, but some coordinating councils have given attention to other social problems. They differ in their functions from community welfare councils by emphasis on specific social questions, and by enlisting the participation of local civic groups and individuals who are not members of the community welfare council.[16]

4. *Neighborhood Council* is a citizens' committee which is organized to improve social conditions that are of particular importance to a certain neighborhood. Some of the neighborhood councils have grown from planning committees in settlement houses; others have been encouraged by a council of social agencies, a parent-teacher association, or other civic or religious societies. Social workers usually participate in the work of neighborhood councils as individuals or as representatives of their social agencies, but they are a minority; usually businessmen, merchants, teachers, and lay representatives of service and civic groups and of municipal authorities, such as park and recreation commission or housing authority, and of various churches form the majority of the council. The neighborhood council is not concerned with the wide range of social welfare and health questions as is the community welfare council, nor with just one or a few very urgent special problems as the coordinating council.

The neighborhood council frequently attempts to improve the local facilities for recreation, parks and playgrounds, or summer camp facilities for school children. It may be concerned with the establishment of a community center, the improvement of sanitary or housing conditions within the area, the founding of a consumers' cooperative to restrict high living costs, or the setting up of garbage collection policies. During World War II many neighborhood councils took part in the work of the civilian defense program and shared with other groups the responsibility for social planning. The local character of the neighborhood council often leads to a sincere and intensified interest of its members.[17] In some cities, such as Pittsburgh, Pennsylvania, all neighborhood councils have founded a federation, and use the professional staff of the federation for their programs and activities.

[16] W. McMillen, *op. cit.*, p. 324; H. Clarke, *op. cit.*, pp. 138-139; A. Hillman, *op. cit.*, pp. 218-227; August Vollmer, "Crime Can Be Checked," *Community Organization*, Vol. VII, March-April, 1939, pp. 3-4; Sybil A. Stone, Elsa Castendyck, and Harold B. Hanson, *Children in the Community* (Washington, D.C.: U.S. Children's Bureau, Publication No. 317, 1946); and Elise H. Martens and Helen Russ, *Adjustment of Behavior Problems of School Children* (Washington, D.C.: U.S. Office of Education, 1932).

[17] W. McMillen, *op. cit.*, pp. 325-326; and Helen Clarke, *Principles and Practice of Social Work* (New York: Appleton, Century-Crofts, Inc., 1947), pp. 138-139.

A few neighborhood councils have developed a highly critical attitude toward social agencies and have accused them of being undemocratic, condescending, and of having neglected the real needs and wishes of the people.[18] It is doubtful, however, whether these criticisms are not exaggerated, and whether the suggested social action is not rather a real concern to all elements in a conscientious community organization.

5. *The Social Service Exchange* is a centralized registration, a cooperative clearing service which lists all persons known to health and welfare agencies. Sometimes the title "social service index" or "confidential exchange" is used. The concept of the exchange was brought to our country with that of the Charity Organization Society from England, where a confidential index had been established as an important element in coordination of services. It seems that the first social service exchange in the United States was the Registration Bureau in Boston, established in 1876.[19] The purpose of the social service exchange is to provide clearance so that each social agency knows whether or not persons applying for aid or service receive similar or other care by another organization, thus avoiding fraud, duplication of efforts, and waste. The social service exchange has three functions: (1) to register social agency records as referred to the exchange; (2) to supply, on request of a member agency, information about previous registrations of the person or family in the index; and (3) to notify the member agencies, previously aiding the person, of the new inquiry. Thus the social service exchange promotes cooperation and exchange of information among social agencies serving the same person or family. Criticism of the exchange has recently advocated that it might be abolished, but rather a revision of its functions may be needed.

The social service exchange is organized either by the community welfare council, the community chest, or an individual public or private agency (for instance, the public welfare department or a

---

[18] Saul Alinsky, *Reveille for Radicals* (Chicago: University of Chicago Press, 1946), describes the "back-of-the-yards" organization near the stockyards of Chicago.

[19] Margaret F. Byington, *The Confidential Exchange: A Form of Social Cooperation.* (New York: Russell Sage Foundation, 1912); Morton I. Feicher, "Let's Abolish the Social Service Exchange," *Social Work Journal,* Vol. 33, No. 1, January, 1952, pp. 28-31; and Daniel R. Elliott, "Social Service Exchanges," *Social Work Year Book, 1954,* pp. 496-500.

private family service agency), or it is established as an independent organization. In 1951, the organizational structure of the 291 social service exchanges was as follows:

(a) 131 under auspices of a community welfare council,
(b) 54 under auspices of a community chest,
(c) 8 under joint auspices of community chest and council,
(d) 57 under auspices of a public welfare agency,
(e) 16 under auspices of private social agencies,
(f) 30 exchanges operating as an independent agency.[20]

The financing of the social service exchange is either assumed by the sponsoring agency, such as the community chest, the community welfare council, a public welfare department or a private agency, or by member agency fees. The latter may be arranged according to size of work load of agencies so that the budget of the exchange is assessed in advance or according to the prorate use of the exchange by each agency.

The technical process of the exchange is simple. Its equipment consists of a card index to the case records of the member agencies. A separate card for each family contains surname, first names, woman's maiden name, birth dates of parents and children, the address, and a note on cross references. There also is usually a street and house card for all registered persons. Inquiries and information are exchanged on simple, printed forms.

The material of the exchange is confidential, and its value depends upon the cooperation of all member agencies in keeping the register up to date and conforming with the policies of the exchange. The structure of a typical exchange is illustrated by Chart 11.

Most social service exchanges serve a city or a county, but a few systems have been developed for a larger area, several counties, a state, or more than one state.

6. *Community Organization by Individual Social Agencies* is executed by many high-standard agencies, such as family welfare agencies, child protective or child care agencies, adoption societies, and health services. This is, of course, only a secondary function of these agencies. Community organization may concern the development of recreational facilities in cooperation with lay groups and public authorities, establishment of a mental hygiene clinic or other

---

[20] Gertrude N. Horney, "Social Service Exchanges," *Social Work Year Book, 1951*, pp. 483-486.

joint treatment facilities, or the raising of funds for such special goals as the construction of a clinic or hospital. Individual agencies are particularly active in community organization where no community welfare council has been established or where it does not function properly.

We have discussed so far the structure of local community organization. On the state level only a few state councils of social work coordinate the forces of public and private welfare and health agencies. But there are a variety of advisory committees and commissions (such as a recreation commission) and state conferences of social work in which representatives of public and private social agencies work together with lay persons for the purpose of coordination and better use of resources. Certain organizations have been set up on a regional basis, comprising several states, such as the

CHART 11: ORGANIZATIONAL STRUCTURE OF A SOCIAL SERVICE EXCHANGE

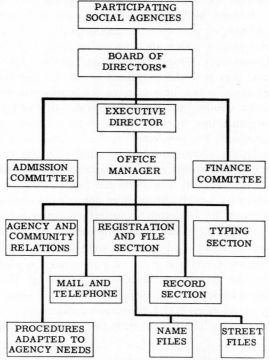

Source: Adapted from Edith King, *The Social Service Exchange* (Washington, D.C.: Social Security Board, Bureau of Public Assistance, Bureau Circular 16, 1943).
* Determines policies and standards.

Regional Conferences of the Child Welfare League of America and the Southern Regional Council, which attempts to improve civic, economic, and racial conditions of the Negro population in the southern states.

A new type of community organization under public auspices has recently been developed in North Carolina. The State Board of Public Welfare appointed a consultant on community services, in the fall of 1951, with the assignment of helping counties and communities in organizing social and health services in relation to the needs of the population. The first area of work undertaken by the consultant was the development of a widespread plan for welfare services in civil defense in cooperation with representatives of county superintendents of public welfare and the State Council for Civil Defense. A manual on welfare services in civil defense was prepared to supplement the general program. The consultant works with the staffs of public and private welfare agencies regarding the establishment of services for children, such as day-care centers and recreation facilities, and in enlisting private clubs and organizations to help those social welfare agencies which are directly working for civil defense, the United Community Defense Service and the associated agencies. The consultant also provides a trained social worker for a survey in the Indian reservations of the state for improvement of living standards, health conditions, and the economy of the Indian tribes.

National organizations in the field of social welfare under public and private auspices are interested in the process of coordinating services, developing adequate standards, and enlisting broad public support. Their large number makes integration and coordination on the national level difficult. The National Social Welfare Assembly represents voluntary health and welfare agencies as their central national organization. Its functions include facilitating cooperation of public and private social welfare programs, and developing cooperative planning and coordination of field services with states and local communities. Certain aspects of community organization are carried on by the American Association of Social Workers and other professional social work organizations,[21] by various national organizations of religious and humanitarian character, and by such special organizations as the American Public Welfare Association, the

[21] See Chapter 22, and Ray Johns, *The Co-operative Process Among National Social Agencies* (New York: Association Press, 1946), pp. 112, 253-254.

Child Welfare League of America, the Family Service Association of America, and the Community Chests and Councils. The U.S. Department of Health, Education and Welfare attempts to assist in a process of coordination and improvement of standards of service by studies, research, publications, and conferences.

On the *international level* the functions of most organizations of an international character are concerned with welfare and health services in foreign countries and devoted to achieving international cooperation and integration of methods, skills, and resources.[22] The activities of UNRRA during and after World War II, the United Nations, Department of Social Affairs, the Economic and Social Council (ECOSOC), the World Health Organization, and UNESCO are examples of agencies, active in international community organization.

IV. PRINCIPAL AREAS OF COMMUNITY ORGANIZATION

Community welfare organization has the task of promoting and developing social and health services designed to protect the people against four major human problems: (1) dependency, (2) ill health, (3) unmet recreational and cultural needs, and (4) maladjustment that comprises emotional and mental disturbances, child neglect and misbehavior, juvenile delinquency, and adult crime. These four problems frequently are closely interrelated so that in one family several, or all of them, are prevailing—a fact that leads to increased suffering of the family members.

1. The main protection against dependency is provided by public assistance and social insurance programs analyzed in Chapters 8 and 9. Community organization[23] wants to improve, simplify, and consolidate the services for the prevention of destitution, and for aid in case of economic insufficiency. It hopes to avoid duplication of effort, red tape, and delays, and to determine where and which private social services are needed to supplement the public assistance and social insurance program.[24]

In urban communities, private social agencies spend an average

[22] These organizations and activities have been analyzed in Chapter 19.
[23] This comprehensive classification has been suggested by Bradley Buell, *Community Planning for Human Services* (New York: Columbia University Press, 1952), pp. 11-12.
[24] *Ibid.*, pp. 61-62, 64-67.

of from 5 to 10 per cent of the funds spent by public welfare agencies on assistance payments. It is essential that relief rendered by private organizations supplement, but not duplicate, public assistance. One of the largest groups in need of economic assistance is the chronically ill for whom private institutions, which formerly served as children's homes or old-folks' homes, might well be converted into chronic-nursing homes. Another group that depends upon private social agencies when in economic distress is the one not eligible for public assistance for reason of residence, nationality, or danger of deportation (particularly migrants and new immigrants). As we discussed in Chapter 6, family and children's casework agencies use money grants partly as tools of treatment in order to achieve personal adjustment and rehabilitation.

2. The protection of people against ill health is the second major objective of community organization. This protection is carried on through three systems: (a) public health programs under local, state, and federal government; (b) communal services for medical care, clinics, and hospitals under both private and public auspices; and (c) private medical and dental care. Community organization is concerned with the first two programs only; although private practice of medical and dental treatment greatly influence the two other programs, the community requires merely that doctors and dentists be duly licensed.[25] Public health services include health protection programs which were developed by private health agencies. The community program of health services is composed of hospitals, clinics, dispensaries, and visiting nurses services, which are partly provided by private social agencies, partly by government, and partly (especially hospitals) as a private, commercial enterprise. Originally these services were organized to secure medical and hospital care for indigent people who could not afford to pay for physician's treatment or hospital care; at present, they serve the entire population. The emphasis on reduction of mortality has shifted from communicable, infectious diseases to maternity and infant mortality, chronic diseases, heart ailments, and cancer. Health education, disease control, and preventive service are important aspects of community health planning; another is the expansion of the control and treatment of chronic disabilities.[26]

[25] *Ibid.*, pp. 125-135; see also Chapter 12.
[26] *Ibid.*, pp. 232-234.

3. The industrial, urban development of the twentieth century has changed the typical recreation of the idyllic countryside, in woods and hills, to the need for playgrounds and parks, sport facilities, swimming pools, tennis and golf courses, summer camps, gymnasiums, and community centers. Even in rural communities these recreation services have become an accepted part of public and private agencies' activities. A great variety of commercial leisure-time opportunities are offered at consumer expense: movies, theater, athletic contests, races, amusement parks, bowling alleys, billiard games, and certain tennis courts and golf courses. Restaurants, commercial dance halls, some bathing beaches, riding academies, swimming pools, and vacation camps also are commercial enterprises. For those recreational facilities which are open without charge to the general public, municipal and county recreation and park commissions assume an increasing responsibility. These public recreation programs are an essential element in community organization, as well as the leisure-time activities of many voluntary recreation agencies, such as the YWCA, YMCA, and Girls' and Boys' Scouts.[27] The funds for the support of recreational and "character building" activities are largely derived through the Community Chest.

The goal of community organization in recreation programs is less clearly defined than that of economic assistance or health services. Three types of services seem necessary: (a) provision of large-scale facilities for general public use, such as playgrounds, parks, and auditoriums; (b) the organization of activity interests, such as sports, arts, cultural and social facilities, and informal education; and (c) the organization of youth groups, such as Boy Scouts, Girl Scouts, Camp Fire Girls, 4-H Clubs, and clubs in community centers and neighborhood houses.[28]

These recreational services, in large urban communities, may be organized under district patterns which consider the particular needs of the specific areas. Research and careful planning have to establish the criteria for the decision where various types of recreation are most needed.

4. Social services which protect and aid people who have difficulties in adjusting to the demands of social living or who suffer from mental deficiencies or disorders are an important section of

[27] The reader finds a discussion of their activities in Chapters 7 and 14.

[28] B. Buell, *op. cit.*, p. 378; and Charles K. Brightwell, "Recreation," *Social Work Year Book, 1954*, pp. 446-448.

community activities. They comprise (a) protective and correctional services, (b) mental and child guidance clinics and institutions, and (c) social casework services. Community organization aims to obtain adequate facilities for the prevention and treatment of maladjustment in the form of delinquency and crime, mental disturbance, or personality disorders. These facilities include probation, correctional and parole services, diagnostic and treatment clinics, institutions for mentally disturbed patients, and casework services for families, children, and adults. The integration and effective cooperation of these services for all types of maladjustment is a challenge for community planning.[29]

The findings of the St. Paul study confirmed that in a small group of families (exactly 6,466 representing only 6 per cent of the total population) several major social problems converged. Over 5,000 of these families were in financial need, over 5,000 showed evidence of serious personal maladjustment, and nearly 5,000 had one or more members in a grave state of ill health. Chronically ill persons were found in more than one-third of these families, persons handicapped by chronic diseases in more than one-quarter. Almost one-third of the family group had at least one member with official records of criminal or antisocial behavior. About 20 per cent of the same families had one or more members in treatment or in institutions for mental deficiency. Among these families 40 per cent were suffering from lack of economic support by the father or breadwinner or his failure to meet major social responsibilities.

Of the mentally defective patients found in these families over one-third were family heads who should have been responsible for the maintenance of the family. Of the people with serious crime or antisocial behavior records, nearly half were fathers or at least the "titular heads" of the family; their destructive influence upon children and adolescents in these families seems obvious.

The cumulation of social maladjustment was characterized by the finding that of the 6,466 families there were in 1,940 families people with both serious physical illness and crime or behavior disorders. In one-half of all these families the person so afflicted was the head of the family. On the other hand, only less than one-tenth of all these families participated in any of the sound recreation programs organized by the community.

[29] B. Buell, *op. cit.*, pp. 334-341, 412-413.

V. SOCIAL ACTION

Within the framework of community organization, social action means the activities which are designed to bring about constructive social legislation, social reform, and administrative measures for the improvement of social conditions. Kenneth Pray defined social action as "the systematic, conscientious effort directly to influence the basic social conditions and policies out of which arise the problems of social adjustment and maladjustment to which our services as social workers are addressed."[30]

Social action wants to achieve the changes in statutes and programs, which are required, in order to help people to lead healthy, decent, and satisfactory lives. Social workers are well acquainted with social conditions, which need a change, and with their effect upon human beings. For this reason social workers have the competence, but also the moral obligation, to assist in spreading public understanding and awareness of the need for social reform and social legislation. In settlement houses and neighborhood councils the discussion of social legislation and measures of improving health, housing, and living standards plays an essential role. When legislative changes are needed and the call for measures is raised either in church or citizens' groups, in a neighborhood center, or in a family welfare agency, a community welfare council may be the organization best equipped for coordinating the forces in the city to submit the request for legislative measures.

Social action is directed toward promotion of social legislation, but not exclusively limited to this aspect. It may involve the formation of a pressure group that discusses the necessary changes with legislators, government officials, and other citizens. Frequently, social action requires a patient campaign of public information and education on specific social, health, or legal conditions. A typical form of social action is the "legislative council," an organization formed by representatives of various civic and church groups, labor unions, and social workers.[31] These councils perform two functions: They

[30] Kenneth Pray, "Social Work and Social Action," *National Conference of Social Work, Proceedings 1945*, p. 346; see also, Grace Coyle, "The President's Report," *The Compass*, June, 1944, pp. 3-8; and Eveline M. Burns, "Social Action and the Professional Social Worker," *The Compass*, May, 1947, pp. 37-40.

[31] James Sidel, "The State Legislative Council—A Median for Social Action," *The Compass*, March, 1945, pp. 8-11.

serve as a clearing house for all groups concerned with social legislation, and they organize citizens and organizations for the support of
essential measures of social legislation.

Professional organizations of social workers and unions of social
workers employed in public and private agencies have taken an
active part in encouraging or fighting proposed legislation on the
local, state, and federal level.[32]

SELECTED BIBLIOGRAPHY

Andrews, F. Emerson, *Philanthropic Giving*. New York: Russell Sage
Foundation, 1950.
———, *Corporation Giving*. New York: Russell Sage Foundation, 1952.
*Baker, Helen Cody, and Mary Swain Routzahn, *How To Interpret So-
cial Welfare*. New York: Russell Sage Foundation, 1947.
Beam, Kenneth S., *Coordinating Councils in California*. Sacramento:
California Department of Education, Bulletin No. 11, 1938.
———, *Coordinating Councils: How Shall They Be Organized?* New
York: National Probation Association, 1937.
Benjamin, Paul L., "Techniques of Social Action: Securing Social Legis-
lation," *National Conference of Social Work, Proceedings 1945*, pp.
326-366.
Bond, Elsie M., *Methods of Securing Social Welfare Legislation*. New
York: State Charities Aid Association, 1941.
Brander, J. P., *Community Chest*. London: G. Allen, 1941.
Browning, Grace, "Social Work and the Public," *Social Service Re-
view*, Vol. XXIII, No. 2, June, 1949, pp. 211-217.
*Buell, Bradley, and Associates, *Community Planning for Human Serv-
ices*. New York: Columbia University Press, 1952.
Carner, Lucy P., "The Youth and Government Project," *National Con-
ference of Social Work, Selected Papers in Group Work and Com-
munity Organization*, 1952, pp. 12-16.
Colcord, Joanna C., *Your Community; Its Provision for Health, Education, Safety, and Welfare*. New York: Russell Sage Foundation, revised by Donald S. Howard, 1947.
Community Chests and Councils, *Community Organization for Health
and Welfare on a State-Wide Basis*. New York: 1946.
———, *Health and Welfare Planning in the Smaller Community*. New
York: 1945.

[32] Dorothy Kahn, "Social Action from the Viewpoint of a Professional Organization," *National Conference of Social Work, Proceedings 1940*, pp. 498-
507; Harry L. Lurie, "Social Action: A Motive Force in Democracy," *Proceedings, 1941*, pp. 631-641; Benjamin Youngdahl, "Social Workers: Stand Up
and Be Counted," *The Compass*, March, 1947, pp. 21-24; and "The Role of Social
Agencies in Social Action," *Social Work Journal*, Vol. 33, No. 3, July, 1952,
pp. 146-148.

——, *Labor Participation in Organized Health and Welfare Activities Other Than Fund Raising.* New York: 1943.

——, *Teamwork in Our Town: Through a Community Welfare Council.* New York: 1950.

——, *The Neighborhood Approach to Community Planning,* Bulletin No. 94. New York, 1937.

——, *What Councils of Social Agencies Do,* Bulletin No. 100. New York, 1939.

Coyle, Grace L., "Group Work and Social Change," *National Conference of Social Work, Proceedings 1935,* pp. 353-405.

Dahir, James, *Communities for Better Living: Citizen Achievement in Organization, Design and Development.* New York: Harper, 1950.

Danstedt, Rudolph T., "Councils in Social Work," *Social Work Year Book, 1954,* pp. 142-148.

——, "Current Conflicts in the Approach to Community Organization," *Social Service Review,* Vol. XXIV, No. 1, March, 1950, pp. 67-73.

Davison, Owen R., "Community Chests," *Social Work Year Book, 1954,* pp. 115-121.

Dewey, John, *Liberalism and Social Action.* New York: Putnam, 1935.

Dimock, Marshall, *The Executive in Action.* New York: Harper, 1945.

*Eldridge, Seba, *The Dynamics of Social Action.* Washington, D.C.: Public Affairs Press, 1952.

Embree, Edwin R., and Julia Waxman, *Investment in People; The Story of the Julius Rosenwald Fund.* New York: Harper, 1949.

Fenton, Norman, "Educational Possibilities of the Coordinating Council," *Community Coordination,* Vol. VII, March-April, 1939, pp. 7-8.

Fisher, Jacob, *The Rank and File Movement in Social Work, 1931-36.* New York: New York School of Social Work, 1936.

Fitch, John A., "The Nature of Social Action," *National Conference of Social Work, Proceedings 1940,* pp. 485-497.

Glenn, John M., Lilian Brandt, and F. Emerson Andrews, *Russell Sage Foundation, 1907-1946.* New York: Russell Sage Foundation, 1947.

Guild, J. P., and A. A. Guild, *Social Work Engineering: An Outline of Topics for Survey, Planning, and Appraisal.* New York: Harper, 1940.

Gunn, Selskar M., and Philip S. Platt, *Voluntary Health Agencies: An Interpretive Study.* New York: Ronald Press, 1945.

Harrison, Shelby M., and F. Emerson Andrews, *American Foundations for Social Welfare.* New York: Russell Sage Foundation, 1946.

Hawkins, Gaynell, *Education for Social Understanding.* New York: American Association for Adult Education, 1940.

Hayes, Wayland J., *The Small Community Looks Ahead.* New York: Harcourt, 1947.

Hiller, Robert I., *The Education and Work Experience of Community Organization Practitioners.* New York: Community Chests and Councils of America, 1949.

*Hillman, Arthur, *Community Organization and Planning*. New York: Macmillan, 1950.

Hopely, Russell J., *Civil Defense for National Security*. Washington, D.C.: U.S. Civil Defense Planning Office, 1948.

*Howard, Donald S., *Community Organization: Its Nature and Setting*. New York: American Association of Social Workers, 1947.

Jenkins, Edward C., *Philanthropy in America*. New York: Association Press, 1950.

Johns, Ray E., *The Cooperative Process Among National Social Agencies*. New York: Association Press, 1946.

*King, Clarence, *Organizing for Community Action*. New York: Harper, 1948.

————, *Social Agency Boards and How to Make Them Effective*. New York: Harper, 1938.

King, Edith Shatto, *The Social Service Exchange; A Device for Facilitating the Exchange of Confidential Information Among Welfare and Health Agencies*. Washington, D.C.: Social Security Board, Bureau of Public Assistance, 1943.

Kinneman, John A., *The Community in American Society*. New York: Appleton-Century-Crofts, Inc., 1947.

Klein, Philip, et al., *A Social Study of Pittsburgh*. New York: Columbia University Press, 1938.

Kraus, Hertha, "Community Organization in Social Work: A Note on Choices and Steps," *Social Forces*, October, 1948.

Krughoff, Merrill F., "Councils in Social Work," *Social Work Year Book, 1947*, pp. 130-138.

Landis, Benson Y., *Rural Welfare Services*. New York: Columbia University Press, 1949.

Lee, Porter, *Social Work as Cause and Function*. New York: Columbia University Press, 1937.

Lindeman, Eduard C., *Wealth and Culture*. New York: Harcourt, 1936.

Lyon, Yolande, *Stepping Stones to a Health Council*. New York: National Health Council, 1947.

MacIver, R. M. (editor), *Group Relations and Group Antagonisms*. New York: Harper, 1944.

*McMillen, Wayne, *Community Organization for Social Welfare*. Chicago: University of Chicago Press, 1945, 5th impression, 1949.

McNeil, C. F., "Community Organization for Social Welfare," *Social Work Year Book, 1954*, pp. 121-128.

Martz, Helen E., *Citizen Participation in Government*. Washington, D.C.: Public Affairs Press, 1948.

Matthews, William H., *Adventures in Giving*. New York: Dodd, 1939.

Morgan, Arthur E., *The Small Community: Foundation for Democratic Life*. New York: Harper, 1942.

National Social Work Council, *Health and Welfare Services in the National Defense*. New York: 1940.

Neumeyer, Martin H., "The Los Angeles County Plan of Coordinating

Councils," *Sociology and Social Research*, Vol. 29, May-June, 1935, pp. 460-471.

Nisbeth, Robert A., *The Quest for Community*. New York: Oxford University Press, 1953.

North, Cecil C., *The Community and Social Welfare: A Study in Community Organization*. New York: McGraw, 1931.

Norton, William J., *The Cooperative Movement in Social Work*. New York: Macmillan, 1927.

Ogden, Jean C., and Jess Ogden, *Small Communities in Action*. New York: Harper, 1946.

Olds, Edward B., *Use of Research Methods in Studying St. Louis Day Nurseries*. St. Louis: Research Bureau, Social Planning Council, 1951.

Paradise, Viola, *Toward Public Understanding of Casework*. New York: Russell Sage Foundation, 1948.

Parsons, Talcott, *The Structure of Social Action*. Glencoe, Ill.: Free Press, 1952.

Pettit, Walter W., *Case Studies in Community Organization*. New York: Appleton-Century-Crofts, Inc., 1928.

Philips, Wilbur C., *Adventuring for Democracy*. New York: Social Unit Press, 1944.

Reid, J. T., *It Happened in Taos*. Albuquerque: University of New Mexico Press, 1946.

Rich, Wilmer Shields, "Foundations and Community Trusts," *Social Work Year Book, 1954*, pp. 233-241.

Routzahn, Mary B., and Evart G. Routzahn, *Publicity for Social Work*. New York: Russell Sage Foundation, 1928.

Ruml, Beardsley, and Theodore Geiger, *The Manual of Corporate Giving*. Washington, D.C.: National Planning Association, 1952.

Sanderson, Dwight, and Robert A. Polson, *Rural Community Organization*. New York: Wiley, 1939.

Seymour, Harold J., *Design for Giving; The Story of the National War Fund, Inc., 1943-47*. New York: Harper, 1947.

Sieder, Violet, and John McDowell, *Evaluation of Neighborhood Center and Neighborhood Council*. Montclair, N.J.: Council of Social Agencies, 1948.

*Sills, Dorothy H., *Volunteers in Social Service*. New York: National Travelers Aid Association, 1947.

*Sorensen, Roy, *The Art of Board Membership*. New York: Association Press, 1950.

Steiner, Jesse F., *Community Organization*. New York: Appleton-Century-Crofts, Inc., 1930.

*Stroup, Herbert Hewitt, *Community Welfare Organization*. New York: Harper, 1952.

Taylor, Eleanor K., *Public Accountability of Foundations and Charitable Trusts*. New York: Russell Sage Foundation, 1953.

Tolleris, Beatrice K., *Radio; How, When and Why to Use It*. New

York: National Publicity Council for Health and Welfare Services, 1946.

Vollmer, August, "Crime Can Be Checked," *Community Coordination,* Vol. VII, March-April, 1939, pp. 3-4.

Young, Erle Fiske, "The Coordinating Council Plan in Los Angeles County," *Journal of Criminal Law and Criminology,* Vol. 26, May, 1935, pp. 34-40.

Youngdahl, Benjamin, "Social Workers: Stand Up and Be Counted!" *The Compass,* March, 1947, pp. 21-24.

YWCA, National Board, *The Role of the Board in Community Y.W.C.A.'s; Responsibilities, Characteristics, and Functions.* New York: 1948.

22. *Professional Aspects of Social Work*

I. DEVELOPMENT OF THE PROFESSION

The forerunners of social work, individual citizens giving alms to people in need, and charities under auspices of the churches, were known in ancient times. But social work as a profession is young. It grew mainly from the Humanitarian Movement of the nineteenth century which attempted to improve the desperate conditions of the poor, to achieve social reform by legislation, and to awaken the social conscience of the public. For the first time the need for professional education in social work was emphasized in 1893, by Anna L. Dawes at the International Congress of Charities, Correction, and Philanthropy, held in Chicago.[1] In the Charity Organization Societies the necessity of preparation for charitable work was recognized, but it was not before 1898 that the first six-weeks' training course was set up by the New York Charity Organization Society. It later was extended to six months and developed into the New York School of Social Work.

In Chicago, the Institute of Social Science opened in 1901 under the leadership of Graham Taylor, Sophonisba P. Breckinridge, and Edith Abbott, then became the School of Civics and Philanthropy, and later the School of Social Service Administration of the University of Chicago. Boston, Philadelphia, and St. Louis established similar schools of social work in 1904 and 1908. Since that time the recog-

---

[1] Esther Lucile Brown, *Social Work As a Profession,* 4th ed. (New York: Russell Sage Foundation, 1942), pp. 25-30; a full analysis of the history of social work education is presented by Edith Abbott, *Social Welfare and Professional Education,* Rev. ed. (Chicago: University of Chicago Press, 1942), and by Ernest V. Hollis and Alice L. Taylor, *Social Work Education in the United States* (New York: Columbia University Press, 1951), pp. 3-52.

nition of social work as a profession has made remarkable progress. Until the beginning of academic education, social workers were trained under an apprenticeship system without systematic, scientific knowledge. Their technical skill depended upon the executives of the charity agencies where they served as volunteers. During the first decade of this century the necessity of social reform as well as of competent individual service became evident in connection with social problems caused by mass emigration from European countries. The rapidly developing industrialization and urbanization of our country created social problems and human suffering that called for skillful personnel to administer social services. The great Depression of the 1930's finally brought unexpected economic distress to large masses of the population and showed that trained social workers were indispensable. There were in most professions, for example, in law, ministry, medicine, three stages in the development of professional education: (1) an apprenticeship under an experienced practitioner, (2) the establishment of private schools, and (3) the recognition of universities that a professional school should be part of their academic program. At the fiftieth anniversary of the New York School of Social Work, in 1948, Sir Raphael Cilento, then Australian Director of Social Activities of the United Nations, could pronounce that there is not the slightest doubt in the United States that social work is a profession.[2]

The criteria for any profession have been stated as the following:

1. Special competence, acquired through intellectual training, which develops skills and requires the use of independent, responsible judgment, not merely mechanical skills.

2. Distinct techniques capable of communication through an orderly and specialized educational discipline, with application of knowledge and skills based upon academic learning.

3. Practitioners who become conscious of common bonds and organize as a professional association for the promotion of high standards and of common interests.

4. The professional association has concern for the development of standards of service for the profession as a whole as expressed by a code of ethics, provision for specialized education, and the use

---

[2] "The World Moves Toward Professional Standards in Social Work," *Social Work Journal*, Vol. 29, July, 1948, p. 102; see also Clyde E. Murray, "Social Work as a Profession," *Social Work Year Book, 1954*, pp. 505-508, 513-516.

of specialized knowledge and skill in order to apply them in the public interest.

5. A professional person has a sense of personal responsibility and accountability to others in the same field for the kinds of standards he sets for himself.[3]

It was not until the end of World War I that social work began to be recognized as a profession. There is a marked difference in this respect from other professions, such as law, medicine, teaching, and the ministry. The changes in the attitude of the people toward public relief and charities, which we discussed earlier, led to new positive concepts with regard to the persons who performed new types of services. This historical fact explains the delay of the acceptance of social work as a profession in our country.

There is no more doubt today that social work satisfies the criteria for a profession. The social worker has to study the scientific principles of human behavior and the structure and organization of social institutions. With these principles before him, he has to develop under his own responsibility knowledge and skill in working with people under specific social, economic, and emotional conditions. Social work has organized professional associations which maintain standards of performance and behavior. Social work recognizes its responsibility for competent service and for the welfare of human beings whom it serves.

The number of graduate schools of social work in the United States and Canada has increased, by 1954, to fifty-nine (seven of them in Canada) which now are accredited by the Council on Social Work Education (formerly by the American Association of Schools of Social Work). About 7,000 graduate students were, in 1953, enrolled in schools of social work in the United States and Canada.

The youth of the social work profession explains the fact that at present more than half the persons employed in social work positions have not received professional education in social work. The study, *Social Work Education in the United States*, by Ernest V. Hollis and Alice L. Taylor, raises the question whether it might be necessary to classify the functions in social agencies into activities

[3] Arlien Johnson, "Certification as an Aim of a Professional Association," *Compass*, Vol. 26, September, 1945, p. 8; R. Clyde White, *Social Work* (Boston: Bellman, 1941), p. 6; Benjamin E. Youngdahl, "Social Work as a Profession," *Social Work Year Book, 1949*, pp. 497-498; and "Social Work at the Crossroads," *Social Work Journal*, Vol. XXXIV, No. 3, July, 1953, pp. 111-113.

which require graduate, professional training, and such activities which may be performed by persons who do not have graduate education, but are prepared for simpler, technical work.

In fact, the proportion of trained social workers is steadily increasing, and there is a growing awareness by social agency boards and public welfare commissions, as well as by the public, that professionally trained social workers are needed for the responsible, competent performance of social services.[4] Thus social work gradually is being accepted alongside the older professions—the ministry, law, teaching, and medicine.

II. SOCIAL WORK EDUCATION

A. UNDERGRADUATE EDUCATION

Preparation for social work requires high school study with the qualifications to enter college. In the college, undergraduate study includes a broad course in liberal arts with emphasis on social sciences, sociology, social welfare, history, philosophy, economics, psychology, political science, cultural anthropology, and physical and biological science.

Because the number of social welfare positions exceeds by far the present total amount of professionally trained people in social work, a substantial group of social agencies employs students already upon graduation from college. These positions are mainly junior positions in public welfare departments, in recreation and leisure-time organizations, in probation services of juvenile courts, in institutions for children and adults, in personnel work in commerce and industry, in social security administration, unemployment compensation, workmen's compensation, and in public employment services. The completion of four years in college in a social welfare major or in a related program, including courses in the field of social welfare, public assistance, child welfare, criminology, community life, history of

---

[4] E. Hollis and A. Taylor, *op. cit.*, pp. 88-96, 141-152; Ernest F. Witte, "The Role of a Professional Social Work Association," *Social Work Journal*, Vol. XXXI, No. 1, January, 1950; Benjamin Youngdahl, "Social Work as a Profession," *Social Work Year Book, 1951*, p. 491; John Kidneigh, "Education for Social Work," *ibid.*, pp. 163-165; Katherine A. Kendall, "Education for Social Work," *Social Work Year Book, 1954*, pp. 170-185; and Melvin A. Glasser, "Social Work in 1954: Potentialities and Pitfalls," *Social Work Journal*, Vol. 35, No. 3, July, 1954, pp. 103-106, 126-127.

philanthropy, and social statistics, gives the student an orientation to the social services and a cultural and educational background that is needed for successful work in the positions mentioned above.

The undergraduate program acquaints the student with the basic concepts and major findings of the social sciences, psychology, sociology, and economics. It also gives him an understanding of the importance of biology, genetics, history and principles of government, social philosophy, public health, and family problems. The undergraduate student gains a broad background of present society and of man as an individual and as a member of various groups. He then learns to arrive at some integrated perspective of the relations between human behavior and the demands of our society. He studies to be able to state his opinion clearly and interpret the facts and his ideas to other people so that they comprehend what he wants to communicate to them. Finally, the undergraduate student masters the process of learning with the significance of spiritual growth.[4a] On the basis of these studies, the student has the choice (1) to apply for advanced, graduate, professional training in social work; (2) to use his preparation for accepting employment in a position which does not require graduate training; or (3) to consider this undergraduate program as preparation for informed, intelligent citizenship which brings him an understanding of social welfare concepts, the wide range of social problems, and the motivation to help solve them. The last group may be businessmen, housewives, local officials, state legislators, teachers, labor leaders, and citizens in many other occupations.

A typical, undergraduate social welfare major program includes the following courses:

(1) In lower division (two first years of college)—general psychology, general economics, elementary statistics and research, introduction to sociology, history, biology, and anthropology.

(2) In upper division (junior and senior year)—concepts, history and system of social welfare, methods of social work, public as-

[4a] Karl de Schweinitz, *People and Process in Social Security* (Washington, D.C.: American Council on Education, 1948), pp. 111-123; E. Hollis and A. Taylor, *op. cit.*, pp. 173-186; J. Kidneigh, *op. cit.*, p. 165; Arlien Johnson, "Social Work Education in the United States," *Social Work Journal*, Vol. 33, No. 3, July, 1952, pp. 132-137; and Harold E. Wetzel, "Educational Priorities As Seen by the Undergraduate Department," Council on Social Work Education, *Education for Social Work, Proceedings, 1953*, pp. 58-61.

sistance, child welfare, social security, social problems and social institutions, social legislation and reform, social philosophy, child and adolescent psychology, mental deficiency, abnormal psychology, social psychology. It also may comprise introduction to clinical psychology, municipal and state government, public administration, problems of poverty, labor economics, public finance and taxation, and crime prevention and correction.

Other courses may deal with problems of juvenile delinquency, race relations and culture, migration, study of group behavior, community recreation, dynamics of culture, medical sociology, child hygiene, and housing and planning.

Some colleges offer in their programs facilities for making observations in social agencies in order to acquaint the student with the methods and the practice of social welfare under the name of "field work." The value of these courses is disputed. The graduate schools of social work find that field work as clinical practice of social work processes is a vital part of graduate education but is successful only through integration with academic courses in casework, group work, and community organization and by very responsible supervision. The attempt to provide practical experience of sufficient breadth and intensity in the undergraduate program poses the problem of securing conscientious and reliable field supervision, and of curtailing unduly the time required for a broad liberal education and a background in the social sciences and the humanities. Social agencies, on the other side, use in-service training, as well as seminars, institutes, and extension courses of universities, in order to supplement knowledge and skills of staff members who have no professional training. Numerous workers in social agencies recognize in their practical experience that they need professional education and apply to a graduate school of social work for professional study.

An example of positions not requiring graduate training is the following, listed as a typical job in Joseph P. Anderson, *Opportunities in Social Work* (New York: Vocational Guidance Manuals, 1952), p. 71.

Visitor.   Salary: $2,328-$2,700 per annum.

Duties: Under supervision, in accordance with well-defined policies and procedures, to determine the eligibility and extent of need of applicants for and recipients of public assistance, and to perform related duties as required. To be responsible for a case load of assistance recipients; to determine financial and other needs of recipients and applicants; to determine eligibility of recipients and applicants for assistance, through planned home and office interviews; to evaluate the resources of applicants and recipients, determine the extent of their need, prepare family budgets and authorize assistance grants, subsequent changes, and discontinuances of grants; to cooperate with and refer clients to appropriate community service organizations; to interpret the public assistance program to individuals and organizations in the community; to prepare correspondence and reports, as required; to maintain accurate and current case and other records; and to perform related duties as required.

Requirements: Five years of full-time paid employment, within the last 15 years, including three years of special experience as defined below: Special experience is employment, related to the duties and responsibilities of this position, in one or more of the following fields: public or private welfare work, teaching in an accredited school, registered or public health nursing, vocational counseling, credit investigation, personnel placement, or rehabilitation; or any equivalent combination of experience and education derived by substituting one year of high school education for one-half year of employment and one year of college education for one year of employment, with the restriction that only appropriate college education may be substituted for special experience.

Private agencies usually grant a two-week vacation period after the completion of one year of work and arrange for sick leave. State, county, and city regulations usually permit twelve days' vacation and fifteen days' sick leave each year, whereas under federal civil service twenty-six days' vacation after the first year and fifteen days' sick leave are the rule.

B. PROFESSIONAL EDUCATION FOR SOCIAL WORK

Graduate training for social work requires, as a rule, the successful completion of two academic years of study in an accredited school of social work leading to the granting of the master's degree.[5] Prerequisite for the entering of the graduate school is the bachelor's degree, preferably in social welfare or in the social sciences, and personal quality for the profession of social work. Most schools accept students older than thirty-five years only if they have demon-

[5] A number of social work positions are available to students who have completed one year of studies in an accredited school of social work. Certain schools grant a "certificate" after the successful completion of one year's study, and five of the fifty-nine accredited schools, in 1953, offered only one year of professional education.

strated good capacity for social work. Graduate social work education is characterized by its close integration of academic courses in the school with practical field work in a selected social agency under careful supervision.

In the development of social work education, the schools considered eight areas of particular importance which are often called "The Basic Eight":

1. Social casework (generic and specialized).
2. Social group work.
3. Community organization.
4. Social research and statistics.
5. Social welfare administration.
6. Public welfare and child welfare.
7. Medical information.
8. Psychiatric information.

The aims of professional education in social work are to develop competence in three major areas: (1) conceptual and perceptual understanding; (2) skills in methods, procedures, and processes; and (3) personal professional qualities.[6]

1. The first category includes understanding of individual and group behavior, of the significance of human behavior in relation to social environment, and of the historical perspective of social welfare development and of religious, economic, political, and social movements. It requires a grounding in the social sciences, covering such matters as structure and philosophy of government, nature of social change, causes and effect of cultural factors, and principles of social security. It also demands the knowledge of the principles, objectives, and processes in social casework, group work, community organization, supervision, intergroup relations, public administration, social planning, and social research. The education includes the study of public relations, standards of social legislation; the administration of social welfare, community structure, dynamics, and resources; the study of human growth; and the development of physical, social, and emotional deviations from normal features and behavior.

[6] E. Hollis and A. Taylor, *op. cit.*, pp. 220-225; Charlotte Towle, "The Distinctive Attributes of Education for Social Work," *Social Work Journal*, Vol. 33, No. 2, April, 1952, pp. 63-72, 94; and Council on Social Work Education, *Education for Social Work* (Proceedings), 1953.

2. The skills of professional social work are the ability to establish and maintain purposeful and constructive relationships with individuals, groups, and communities. The main skill in the helping process is that of enabling an individual, a group, or a community to identify and clarify problems and needs, and to solve them by their own initiative in a socially desirable way. The social worker learns to use his own resources in professional relationships based upon self-understanding, control of personal needs and feelings, and warmth of response. Other skills are those of social administration, planning, social action; use of scientific methods in research and practice; skill in teamwork with other professions; ability in communication, staff development, supervision, and volunteer and student training; and preparation for social work teaching, and social statesmanship.

3. The personal, professional qualities that graduate training aims to develop include genuine warmth, sensitivity to, and liking for people, and the capacity to identify with a variety of persons. A professional philosophy comprises a high degree of social conscience and conscientiousness, emotional, mental, and physical stability, maturity, self-security, imagination, resourcefulness, flexibility, as well as personal integrity, courage, and a sincere conviction about the values of social work. Professional concepts make the student capable of standing up for the rights of people even against hostile attitudes of the public. These qualities, furthermore, encompass conceptual thinking, open-mindedness, clarity of purpose, accuracy, ability to share, courtesy in professional relationships, and a belief in the value of citizen participation and in the right of the individual, the group, and the community to make their own decisions within the framework of a democratic society.

It is easy to understand that these three areas of professional competence can be fully developed only by an integration of academic classwork and clinical supervised field instruction. Field work requires, as a rule, two full days weekly for the first graduate year and three days weekly for the second year. Supervisors are either members of the university faculty or are staff members of the social agency where the student receives his field work training. In both instances an intensive cooperation between the teaching faculty and the field supervisor in observing the student's professional development and learning is maintained. Field work is designed to integrate the academic knowledge, practical understanding, and professional skill of the student by personal contact and direct work with clients.

Beyond the level of the master's degree, a number of schools of social work have set up an advanced program. This has been classified either as "the third year" with the aim of strengthening the professional skills of the student or as "the doctoral program," leading to a Doctor of Social Work or a Doctor of Philosophy degree.[7] The latter program, as a rule, requires two more years of postgraduate studies, which offer a deepening and refinement of knowledge and skill, new knowledge directed toward definition and solution of professional problems (with the evaluation and testing of social work methods and hypothesis), and the broadening of professional perspective. The doctoral program integrates social work knowledge and methodology with other scientific disciplines; develops independent critical professional thought, and interprofessional relationships; and prepares primarily for teaching of social work, for the administration of education programs, and for social work research.[8]

For many years the graduate schools of social work were organized as the American Association of Schools of Social Work (AASSW), while other colleges which offered undergraduate programs had formed the National Association of Schools of Social Administration (NASSA). Since 1952, the Council on Social Work Education coordinates the activities of both associations. It now represents also social work executives, social workers, social work educators, and citizens interested in social work. The functions of the Council on Social Work Education are to establish standards and to accredit schools of social work, to aid in better selection and education of students and social workers, to improve social work education, to interpret social work to the public, and to help in continuing professional growth of employed social workers. The organizational structure is a Council consisting of seventy-eight delegates, a Board of Directors, and four standing committees on (1) accreditation; (2) program, services, and publications; (3) schools and departments of social work; and (4) research.[9]

<hr />

[7] In 1954, eleven schools had doctoral programs in the United States. K. Kendall, *op. cit.*, pp. 175-176.

[8] Charlotte Towle, Eveline Burns, and Eleanor Cockerill, *Social Work Education in the Post Master's Program* (Guiding Principles) (New York: Council on Social Work Education, 1953), pp. 9-11, 23-29.

[9] The Council's address is 345 East 46 Street, New York 17, New York; its present Executive Director is Dr. Ernest F. Witte; see also Swithum Bowers, "Evaluating the Structure and Content of Social Work Education" (Council on Social Work Education: *Education for Social Work, Proceedings, 1953*), pp. 22-28.

III. REGISTRATION OF SOCIAL WORKERS

Other professions, such as medicine, teaching, law, and nursing, are recognized by an official license, certificate, or registration, which is required for performing professional service. In several European countries (France, Switzerland, Germany, Austria, and Sweden), social workers need a license in order to practice their profession. In the United States, however, no license has yet been introduced, but suggestions have been made that licensing should be required or that the practice of social work should be restricted.

In 1933, the California Conference of Social Welfare organized registration on a voluntary basis, requiring the passing of a carefully prepared examination. The registration aimed to confirm the status of a competent professional person, the identification with other members of the profession working for high standards and the best service to the public, the affiliation with others seeking to improve the status of social workers, and the assurance of belonging to a professional group that inspires public confidence.

In 1945, a statutory system of official registration and certification for social workers replaced the voluntary program in California. The State Board of Social Work Examiners, consisting of seven members who are appointed by the governor, administers the registration system. Applicants who have completed successfully one year at an accredited graduate school of social work and who pass a written examination receive a certificate authorizing them to the title "Registered Social Worker" (R.S.W.). The members of the Board of Social Work Examiners include at least two lay persons; the professional members must be registered social workers. The Board maintains a register of social workers, conducts research, prescribes qualifications, gives examinations, and issues certificates. A certificate is suspended or revoked if a registered social worker is convicted of an offense involving moral turpitude, is a habitual drug addict who would endanger the public, is declared insane or incompetent, advocates the overthrow of government by force, violence or other unlawful means, or has committed a dishonest or fraudulent act as a social worker resulting in substantial injury to others.[10]

[10] Runo E. Arne, "California Registers Its Social Workers," *Compass*, Vol. 28, July, 1947, pp. 11-14, and "Protection of the Public Through Licensing of Social Workers," *Social Work Journal*, Vol. 33, No. 4, October, 1952, pp. 184-190; and Donald V. Wilson, "Status by Statute," *Compass*, Vol. 26, September, 1945, pp. 11-15.

The value of the registration for the protection of the public and for the self-respect of professional workers depends partly upon the personnel practices of social agencies. In Los Angeles and in San Diego, the County Civil Service Commission uses registration as a basis for position classification, and the County Bureau of Public Assistance of Los Angeles, the largest single social work employer in California, requires registration for initial employment. Another decisive factor for the value of registration is the continuing and increasing interest in the measure on the part of the public, the employing social agencies, and social workers themselves.

Puerto Rico enacted registration and certification of social workers in 1934 and strengthened the law in 1940. Missouri experimented with voluntary registration in 1934 but found no response among the employing agencies. Indiana introduced voluntary registration in 1949.[11]

Registration of social workers achieves the purpose of improving standards of social work and of assuring the public that social work practitioners are qualified to give professional service. It achieves the first step of legal recognition of the profession of social work. It does not restrict practice to those registered and holding the title, "Registered Social Worker." First, it is necessary that sufficient qualified registered social workers will be available to administer social service functions requiring professional knowledge and skill.

There is no doubt that the present social services must be maintained and extended according to the changing needs of the people. The number of adequately trained social workers must be increased. The public will gradually recognize their own stake in competent social work practice.[12] After these requirements have been met, it seems desirable to introduce a licensing system, as in medicine, and to restrict social work practice to trained, competent, licensed practitioners.

11 Eleanor M. Hack and Fred M. Steinberger, "Registration of Social Workers in Indiana," *Public Welfare in Indiana*, Vol. 59, July, 1949, pp. 8-9; Celia N. Bunker, "Licensing Law for Social Workers in Puerto Rico," *Compass*, Vol. 23, January, 1942, pp. 8-9; and Susan Pettes, *Licensing and Registration of Social Workers* (New York: American Association of Social Workers, 1953).

12 John McDowell, "Methods of Regulation of Professional Practice," unpublished paper, American Association of Social Workers, New York, 1946.

IV. PROFESSIONAL ORGANIZATIONS IN SOCIAL WORK

The largest and general professional organization in social work is the American Association of Social Workers (AASW). It comprises men and women who are professionally concerned with problems of social organization and adjustment. The Association serves as a clearing house for professional social work activities and promotes social legislation, social research, and interpretation of social work. Originally organized in 1916 as the National Social Workers Exchange, the Association was set up in 1921. In 1954, it had 131 chapters with 13,605 members.[13]

Membership is open to persons who have completed at least two years of college, three years of additional preparation, and two years of accredited experience, which must include the equivalence of a college major in social and biological science and credits for one year's work in a school of social work. Instead of this seven-year requirement, candidates are entitled to membership after receiving a bachelor degree of an approved university and completing a two-year graduate course in an approved school of social work.

A junior membership is open to persons with one-year graduate training in social work, and a student membership to all students in an accredited school of social work. The Association has given excellent leadership in the development of professional standards, in social work education, and in the attempt to combine the various professional organizations in social work. It publishes a quarterly, the *Social Work Journal* (formerly called the *Compass*), and the *Social Work Year Book*, since 1951.[14]

There are several other specialized professional organizations of social work. The oldest is the American Association of Medical Social Workers (AAMSW), which was founded in 1918 under the title of "American Association of Hospital Social Workers." It com-

---

[13] Its present Executive Secretary is Joseph P. Anderson, its headquarters 1 Park Ave., New York 16, New York, where more detailed professional information may be obtained.

[14] Clyde E. Murray, "Social Work as a Profession," *Social Work Year Book*, *1954*, pp. 505-516; and President's Commission on the Health Needs of the Nation, Vol. 3, *America's Health Status, Needs and Resources* (Washington, D.C.: Government Printing Office, 1952), pp. 221-222.

prised, in 1954, 2,291 individual and corporate members and had sixteen districts and five regional organizations.

The National Association of School Social Workers (NASSW) was organized, in 1919, as the American Association of Visiting Teachers. It had, in 1954, about six hundred members, most of them practicing school social workers.

A third specialized organization is the American Association of Psychiatric Social Workers (AAPSW). It was founded in 1926 and had, in 1954, 1,889 active and associate individual members.

The American Association of Group Workers (AAGW) was founded, in 1936, under the name of "American Association for the Study of Group Work." It has thirty-three chapters throughout the country and in 1954, 2,150 individual members.

In addition to these four specialized professional associations, there are two other study groups, the first of which is not of purely professional character. The Association for the Study of Community Organization was founded, in 1946, as a professional interest group. It was composed, in 1954, of 555 members, and conducts a number of discussion groups. The Social Work Research Group was organized, in 1949, in order to stimulate the development of research in social work. It had in 1954, 261 members who teach, practice, or administer social work research. Finally, there is an International Federation of Social Workers composed of national organizations of professional social workers in many countries.

The six national professional social work membership organizations (with the exception of the Association for the Study of Community Organization) have set up a Temporary Inter-Association Council (TIAC) which submitted, in December, 1952, a plan for a single organization of social workers which would mean an integration and strengthening of all professional associations in social work. It is expected that an agreement between the membership organizations will lead, in 1955, to a unified association entitled to speak for the entire profession of social work.

V. STANDARDS OF PROFESSIONAL PRACTICE

The principles of American social work arise from the beliefs in a democratic society. Foremost among them are the following:

1. Firm faith in the dignity, worth and creative power of the individual;
2. Complete belief in his right to hold and express his own opinions and to act upon them, so long as by so doing he does not infringe upon the rights of others;
3. Unswerving conviction of the inherent, inalienable right of each human being to choose and achieve his own destiny in the framework of a progressive, yet stable, society.[15]

Professional social work is built on an integrated body of knowledge distilled from physical, medical, psychological, and social science, and on technical methods derived from both this scientific knowledge and the tested experience of skilled practitioners.

Principles of ethical conduct of the social worker direct his relationship to the clients, to the social agency, to his colleagues, to the community, and to the profession of social work. These principles are embodied in a Code of Ethics, which together with standards for professional practice was adopted by the Delegate Assembly of the American Association of Social Workers in 1951.

Since social work is founded on belief in the value of the individual, it has a special responsibility to protect civil rights based upon democratic principles. Only in doing so, social work is able to discharge its professional obligations with intellectual integrity. The professional social worker has the moral responsibility to work toward the abridgement of discrimination because of race, color, religion, sex, marital status, national origin, residence, citizenship, political beliefs, union affiliation, or involvement in labor disputes. Civil rights of the clients served by social workers and those of social workers themselves have to be protected in order to preserve their human dignity and self-respect.[16]

VI. SOCIAL WORK LITERATURE

The growth of the young social work profession is reflected in the substantial number of books and periodicals to which we have referred in the selected bibliographies. The current developments of

[15] American Association of Social Workers, *Standards for the Professional Practice of Social Work* (New York: 1952), p. 3. (Supplement to *Social Work Journal*, Part II, of July, 1952).

[16] *Ibid.*, pp. 14-15; Louis H. Towley, "Professional Responsibility in a Democracy," Council on Social Work Education, *Education for Social Work*, *Proceedings 1953*, pp. 10-21.

social welfare are analyzed in the *Social Work Year Books*, the proceedings of the National Conference of Social Work, published recently under the title *The Social Welfare Forum* and *Selected Papers* in casework, in group work, and community organization. Other annual proceedings and year books are published by the Church Conference of Social Work, the National Conference of Catholic Charities, the National Conference of Jewish Communal Service, the National Probation and Parole Association, the U.S. Department of Health, Education and Welfare, and many other federal, state, and local organizations and private health and welfare associations.

The following alphabetical list of periodicals in the United States contains current information on social welfare:[17]

American Child, National Child Labor Committee.
American Journal of Economics and Sociology.
American Journal of Mental Deficiency.
American Journal of Orthopsychiatry, American Orthopsychiatric Association.
American Journal of Psychiatry.
American Journal of Sociology.
American Sociological Review.
*Annals (of the American Academy of Political and Social Science).
**Bulletin of the American Association of Medical Social Workers.*
**Bulletin of the National Association of School Social Workers.*
Catholic Action, National Catholic Welfare Conference.
Catholic Charities Review, National Conference of Catholic Charities.
Channels, National Publicity Council for Health and Welfare Services.
Child Development Abstracts and Bibliography.
Child Study: Journal of Parents' Education.
*Child Welfare, Child Welfare League of America.
*Children, U.S. Children's Bureau, Department of Health, Education and Welfare.
*Community, Community Chests and Councils of America, Inc.
Employment Service Review, U.S. Employment Service, Department of Labor.
Federal Probation, U.S. Bureau of Prisons.
*Focus, National Probation and Parole Association.
**Group: In Education, Recreation, and Social Work, The*, American Association of Group Workers.
Highlights, Family Service Association of America.
Impact, United Nations Educational, Scientific and Cultural Organization (UNESCO).

[17] Periodicals of oustanding importance for students and practitioners are marked (*).

Jewish Center, National Jewish Welfare Board.

Jewish Community, Councils of Jewish Federations and Welfare Funds.

Jewish Social Service Quarterly, National Conference of Jewish Communal Service.

Journal of Abnormal and Social Psychology, American Psychological Association.

Journal of Criminal Law and Criminology.

Journal of Educational Sociology.

Journal of Exceptional Children.

Journal of Gerontology.

*Journal of Psychiatric Social Work, American Association of Psychiatric Social Workers.

Journal of Rehabilitation, National Rehabilitation Association.

Journal of Social Hygiene, American Social Hygiene Association.

Journal of Social Issues, Social Science Research Council.

Law and Contemporary Problems, Duke University.

Marriage and Family Living, National Conference on Family Relations.

*Mental Hygiene, National Association for Mental Health.

Monthly Labor Review, U.S. Bureau of Labor Statistics.

Nervous Child.

Occupational Therapy and Rehabilitation.

Personnel Administration.

Prison Journal, Pennsylvania Prison Society.

Prison World, American Prison Association.

Probation, National Probation and Parole Association.

Psychiatry: Journal of the Biology and the Pathology of Interpersonal Relations.

Psychoanalytic Quarterly.

Psychoanalytic Review: An Educational American Journal of Psychoanalysis Devoted to an Understanding of Human Conduct.

Psychological Abstracts, American Psychological Association.

Psychosomatic Medicine: Experimental and Clinical Studies, National Research Council.

Public Administration Review, American Society for Public Administration.

*Public Welfare, American Public Welfare Association.

*Recreation, National Recreation Association.

Rural Sociology: Devoted to Scientific Study of Rural Life, Rural Sociological Society.

Smith College Studies in Social Work.

Social Forces, University of North Carolina Press.

Social Research, New School of Social Research

*Social Security Bulletin, U.S. Department of Health, Education and Welfare.

*Social Service Review: A Quarterly Devoted to the Scientific and Professional Interests of Social Work, University of Chicago Press.

*Social Work Journal, Official Publication of the American Association of Social Workers.

Sociology and Social Research, University of Southern California.

Sociometry: A Journal of Interpersonal Interpretation.

VII. OUTLOOK

Social work as a dynamic profession is subject to changes that are influenced by the development of our society, our religious, cultural and sociological values, and by scientific progress. Certain trends which we illustrated in this book indicate important phases of the present situation, which may be here briefly summarized.

1. Social work is in need of a clarification of its purpose and philosophy.[18] It tries to gain a full agreement among social workers in this respect and develops a program of interpretation of its aims so that the public might become aware of what social services mean for our society. The development of codes of ethics, personnel practice, and civil rights is a significant proof of the strength of professional ideas in social work.

2. With the increasing recognition of social work and its contribution in solving social problems of our society, not only public and private social agencies but also industry, labor unions, commercial firms, hospitals, health agencies, churches, and the courts employ social workers and take advantage of their skill. In some instances individual social workers operate in private practice as family or marriage counselors or in cooperation with psychiatrists or psychologists.

3. Characteristic of present-day social work is its commitment to teamwork with other professions. Because social workers derive their knowledge from the sociologist's concept of the social process, the political scientist's knowledge of government and administration, the psychologist's comprehension of human behavior and mental functions, the anthropologist's understanding of cultural factors and personality differences, the geneticist's knowledge of hereditary influences, the economist's insight into the process of our economy, the psychiatrist's cognition of emotional illness and health, and the physiologist's observation of physical and nervous functions they

[18] B. Youngdahl, op. cit., pp. 497-500; and Herbert Bisno, The Philosophy of Social Work (Washington, D.C.: Public Affairs Press, 1952), pp. 111-123.

integrate their work with that of other professions. The interdisciplinary approach, the cooperation of several professions, in the prevention of pathological conditions in individuals and groups and in the treatment process promises further progress in the results of diagnosis and cure.

4. Social workers also are on the way to coordinating their own professional activities. They attempt to clarify the common generic basis of the various types of social work, to unify their professional organizations, and to establish a comprehensive system of social work education and accreditation of its institutions.

5. Social work gives increasing attention to social work research. It no longer relies solely on research done by the social sciences, medicine, psychology, and anthropology but proceeds to assume responsibility in developing its own critical research, testing its methods and the results of its operations. The multi-discipline idea accepted in social work requires social workers to draw from the social and biological sciences basic data on human beings (their nature and behavior), on our society, and economic structure. However, social workers are contributing to this research their own concepts, observations, and experiences. This contribution includes an examination of the potentials and dynamic forces in the social group and in the community, the willingness to measure social needs and trends, and the effect of social work practice with an application of methods and knowledge of related scientific fields.

6. Also, the international scene has been opened to social work. It is developing world-wide concepts, has begun to recognize the impact of social problems in faraway countries, and is assuming responsibility for contributing its professional ideas, knowledge, and skills to the well-being of people everywhere. Social work is aware that in such an international climate, and under cultural, social, economic, and health conditions often very different from our own, new concepts and new approaches are necessary.[19] From the observation of foreign nations and from visitors to our country, social workers are learning other ways of meeting human problems and are re-evaluating our own methods and philosophy of social work. So-

---

[19] Edward H. Spicer, *Human Problems in Technological Change* (New York: Russell Sage Foundation, 1952), pp. 16-18, 277-280; and Florence Brugger, "What Are Profitable Imports for the United States?" *National Conference of Social Work, Selected Papers in Group Work and Community Organization, 1952,* pp. 80-90.

cial work has, through its international experiences, strengthened its conviction that the most effective and satisfactory way of helping people is to assist them to help themselves.

SELECTED BIBLIOGRAPHY

*Abbott, Edith, *Social Welfare and Professional Education*, Rev. ed. Chicago: University of Chicago Press, 1942.

American Association of Social Workers, *Social Work as a Profession*, Rev. ed. New York: 1947.

*Anderson, Joseph P., *Opportunities in Social Work*. New York: Vocational Guidance Manuals, 1952.

*Bisno, Herbert, *The Philosophy of Social Work*. Washington, D.C.: Public Affairs Press, 1952.

Bower, Chester L., "Social Workers and the Community: A Challenge to Education," *Social Work Journal*, April, 1953, pp. 71-73.

*Brown, Esther Lucile, *Social Work as A Profession*, 4th ed. New York: Russell Sage Foundation, 1942.

Bruno, Frank J., *Trends in Social Work as Reflected in Proceedings of the National Conference of Social Work, 1874-1946*. New York: Columbia University Press, 1948.

Carr-Saunders, A. M., and P. A. Wilson, *The Professions*. Oxford: Clarendon Press, 1933.

Clarke, Helen I., *Principles and Practice of Social Work*. New York: Appleton-Century-Crofts, Inc., 1947.

*de Schweinitz, Karl, *People and Process in Social Security*. Washington, D.C.: American Council on Education, 1948.

Devine, Edward T., *When Social Work Was Young*. New York: Macmillan, 1939.

Fink, Arthur E., *The Field of Social Work*, Rev. ed. New York: Holt, 1949.

*Goodall, Frances, "Personnel Standards in Social Welfare," *Social Work Year Book, 1951*, pp. 342-350.

*Hamilton, Gordon, "Helping People—the Growth of a Profession," *Social Work as Human Relations*, pp. 3-18. New York: Columbia University Press, 1949.

———, *et al.*, *Social Work as Human Relations*. New York: Columbia University Press, 1949.

Hathway, Marion, "Twenty-five Years of Professional Education for Social Work," *Compass*, Vol. 27, June, 1946, pp. 13-18.

*Hollis, Ernest V., and Alice L. Taylor, *Social Work Education in the United States*. New York: Columbia University Press, 1951.

Howard, Donald S., "New Horizons for Social Work," *Compass*, Vol. 28, No. 6, November, 1947, pp. 9-13, 28.

*Kidneigh, John C., "Education for Social Work," *Social Work Year Book, 1951*, pp. 158-170.

Klein, Philip, "Social Work: General Discussion," *Encyclopaedia of the Social Sciences*, Vol. 14, pp. 165-173. New York: Macmillan, 1930-35.

Lee, Porter R., *Social Work as Cause and Function*. New York: Columbia University Press, 1937.

Miles, Arthur P., *An Introduction to Public Welfare*. Boston: Heath, 1949.

———, *American Social Work Theory*. New York: Harper, 1954.

Murray, Clyde E., "Social Work as a Profession," *Social Work Year Book, 1954*, pp. 505-517.

Pray, Kenneth L. M., *Social Work in a Revolutionary Age and Other Papers* (edited by Jessie Taft). Philadelphia: University of Pennsylvania, 1949.

*Reynolds, Bertha C., *Learning and Teaching the Practice of Social Work*. New York: Farrar & Rinehart, 1942.

Steele, Evelyn, and H. K. Blatt, *Careers in Social Service*. New York: Dutton, 1946.

Steiner, Lee R., *Where Do People Take Their Troubles?* Boston: Houghton, 1945.

Stroup, Herbert Hewitt, *Social Work: An Introduction to the Field*. New York: American Book, 1948, 1953.

Towle, Charlotte, *The Learner in Education for the Professions*. Chicago: University of Chicago Press, 1954.

Tufts, James H., *Education and Training for Social Work*. New York: Russell Sage Foundation, 1923.

Wessel, Rosa, and Goldie Basch Faith, *Professional Education Based on Practice: Two Studies in Education for Social Work*. Philadelphia: University of Pennsylvania, 1953.

*Witmer, Helen Leland, *Social Work: An Analysis of a Social Institution*. New York: Farrar & Rinehart, 1942.

Youngdahl, Benjamin E., "Shall We Face It?" *Social Work Journal*, Vol. 29, No. 2, April, 1948, pp. 63-69.

*———, "Social Work as a Profession," *Social Work Year Book, 1949*, pp. 497-506; and *1951*, pp. 491-500.

Appendix

AN EXAMPLE OF SOCIAL WELFARE
RESEARCH

Social welfare research has several goals which were analyzed in Chapter 6. The following example describes a social survey in a specific location for exploring the needs of the population in order to avoid incidences of the social problem of juvenile delinquency prevalent in that area. The research investigates the adequacy of the social services available which might counteract the spread of juvenile delinquency by exploration of the causes of this incident. The study analyzes recreation and leisure-time activities by a careful, objective inquiry, which is described in detail. It evaluates the present results of social agencies and recreational activities in the area with regard to the need of the population for protection against disturbances, riots, and destruction of property.

The excerpt of this research does not attempt to assess the specific professional skills in social work methods which have been mentioned in Chapter 6, but it describes the research methods applied, in order to obtain an objective picture of the existing conditions, and submits recommendations for necessary social change.

THE ECHO PARK STUDY[1]

Background of the Study

The Echo Park Murder. Early one morning in March of 1948 a forty-nine year old man was stabbed and killed in a vacant lot at Alvarado and

[1] The author is indebted to the writer of this research study, Dr. Ernest Greenwood, Associate Professor, School of Social Welfare, University of California, Berkeley, and to Mr. Ralph W. Fisher, Executive Secretary, County of Los Angeles Youth Commission, for their permission to describe, in its main parts, this research project.

Temple Streets in Los Angeles. The dead man's empty wallet was found beside him. A few hours later the police arrested four youths and charged them with the murder. Of the four, two youths were of Mexican, one was of Syrian, and one was of Yugoslavian descent. All four lived in the general area where the body had been found. In ages they were seventeen, eighteen, nineteen and twenty. The youths admitted having beaten the victim and having taken from the latter a bottle of whisky. At the time of their arrest, however, they denied having stabbed or robbed the dead man.

In May of 1948 the Los Angeles County Grand Jury submitted an indictment for murder in the case and handed the youths over to the District Attorney for prosecution. The boys pleaded guilty to a manslaughter charge and in July of 1948 were committed to the California Youth Authority which, after individual study of each, placed them in appropriate retraining schools where they are at present.

Request for Study. Upon handing down its indictment of the four youths, the Grand Jury addressed to the County Board of Supervisors a request for a study of "the social factors which . . . contributed to the moral breakdown and entrance upon crime" of the four indicted youths.

The County Youth Committee, in its 1948-49 budget, had provided funds for "research by contract." In September of 1948 it therefore contracted with the Research Department of the Welfare Council of Metropolitan Los Angeles to conduct a sociological study of the Echo Park area. The Research Department gathers facts about the socio-economic conditions and needs of the Los Angeles community which are used by the functional divisions of the Welfare Council in their program planning.

Method of the Study

In the autumn of 1948 the Research Department submitted to the County Youth Committee an outline of study which the latter approved. The outline consisted of a three-pronged approach.

Quantitative Area Analysis. Part I of the proposed study was to consist of an area analysis drawing primarily from quantitative data. It called for the presentation of such facts about the study area as its history, physical description, population composition, occupational groupings, educational level, housing, ecological factors, and social services. The aim of this section was to present the environmental picture which usually forms the backdrop against which the more dynamic factors play to produce anti-social phenomena. Chapter II of this report contains the quantitative area analysis.

Very valuable information was derived from *The Social Areas of Los Angeles,* a recent publication of the Haynes Foundation by Eshref Shevky and Marilyn Williams, which describes the census tracts of the county in terms of their social position in our urban scheme. By means of it the study area could be tested for internal homogeneity. Physical description of the study area was secured through field visits by Research Department staff members. Again, much descriptive, as well as historical, information was derived from reports of other investigators who have in the past studied the area; particularly helpful were the reports of Marion Flad "The Echo Park Community" and Ruth Morgan "Alvarado-Temple-Echo Park Area Process Record."

Cultural Neighborhood Analysis. Part II of the proposed study called for an examination of those cultural factors operating in the study area which might have generated the outbreaks of juvenile violence. It was to deal with those aspects of the area's culture which might be related to juvenile delinquency in general and to the crime of the indicted four youths in particular. Such facts as inter-group tensions, social structure of the community, social values of the area's youth, community patterns of aggressive behavior, gang phenomena, were to be included in this section.

Technical Advisory Committee. Some of the more important aspects of the method employed in the collection of the cultural data bear brief mention. The data constituting the cultural analysis of the study area were secured through interviews with persons working and living there. To assist the Research Department in matters relating to the number and types of interviewees and the content and conduct of the interviews, a Technical Advisory Committee was set up whose personnel contained social scientists from local universities. The Committee considered the employment of group interview method for securing cultural data about the study area and decided against it. The group interview method would have involved convening those individuals working or residing in the study area, who were to have been interviewed individually; a group interview would then have been conducted by a competent discussion leader. The intent was to reduce the costs usually incurred by lengthy individual interviews. The Advisory Committee decided that, for the type of information sought by the study, the group interview was inferior to the individual interview and that there was no adequate substitute for the searching one-to-one relationship of the individual interview.

Conducting Interviews. The interviewing process began with a series of ten interviews with professionals working in the study area. The latter included school principals, recreation workers, a probation officer and a librarian. While professionals are not the most dependable source of information about the culture of a community, they are easily identifiable and readily accessible to other professionals. Hence they constitute a convenient entree into an area. The aim of the interviews with professionals was two-fold: (1) to acquire a picture of the social situation in the study area as seen by them, and (2) to secure the names of non-professional persons who might subsequently be more intensively interviewed. Every professional interviewed was asked to suggest the names of lay residents who were informed on social conditions in the study area and who would agree to being interviewed. In this manner an initial panel of nineteen names of non-professional persons was secured. When interviewees from among the latter were visited, they, in turn, were asked to suggest the names of other prospective interviewees on the non-professional level. This procedure permitted a fanning out and digging deeper into the study area netting a final panel of thirty-seven non-professional persons.

Since budgetary limitations imposed upon the study rendered it difficult for the Research Department staff to conduct the interviews with non-professionals, advanced social science students from two local colleges were enlisted for the purpose. Before students began interviewing, every prospective interviewee was first visited briefly by a Research Department staff member, the purpose of these preliminary visits being twofold: (1) to secure the interviewee's consent for the interview, and (2) to appraise him as a likely source of information. This screening process resulted in a fifty per cent shrinkage in the interviewee panel.

In order to standardize the interviews and render the interview records relatively comparable, the student interviewers were supplied with a set of categories around which to build their interviews. These were subjects intended to serve as pegs around which to focus the conversation so that the interview would not wander into irrelevant tangents. The categories included such items as: identifying information about the interviewee; social-psychological factors operating within his family; economic status of the family; relation of the family to the community and society. Interviewers were instructed to memorize the list of categories, to conduct their interviews in a free, informal manner and not to resort to note-taking during their visits. Each interviewer was assigned one interviewee who was revisited several times until the desired information was secured.

Interview Data. Of the total number of interviews conducted by the students only eleven were usable. The composition of the eleven persons represented by these interviews is as follows: six males, five females, two Negro, three Mexican-American, six Anglo-American; eight married, three single; four youths under twenty-five, seven adults over twenty-five; five active in community organizations, six inactive. The ratio of effective and fruitful interviews out of the total proved to be no poorer than usually encountered in community cultural studies. Past experience in community studies have amply demonstrated that it takes literally dozens upon dozens upon dozens of lengthy individual interviews to yield even a small but relatively dependable residue of cultural data. A community survey of such proportions could not be contemplated on the very limited budget at the disposal of this investigation.

Community Resources

Educational and Religious. There are ten schools in the Echo Park Area, of which six are public elementary schools. The remaining four schools are: Lady of Loretto Catholic grade and high school, the Belmont

Senior High School and two special schools, the Mary E. Bennet and
Custer Avenue schools. Virgil Junior High School, located on Vermont
Avenue and outside the study area, draws the students of junior high
ages residing in the Echo Park Area. The Echo Park Branch Library,
one of the older and smaller branches in the city system, is located on
the corner of Glendale and Temple at the foot of Echo Park.

There are thirteen churches in the study area, three of which are
Negro churches. Of the thirteen churches, three are Catholic and ten are
Protestant, and of the latter one is Episcopalian.

Recreation Facilities. The schools located in the study area have each
some play space. These are limited both in size and equipment and, except for Belmont High School, are primarily intended to accommodate
the elementary age groups. The chief recreational resource is Echo Park,
operated by the municipal Recreation Department. This playground,
established in 1906, is the oldest one in the municipal system and is the
center of community activity in the study area. The recreation center
has two full-time recreation directors and a number of part-time workers. Its program is year round and embraces all age groups. Average
daily attendance at the playground is about 500, of whom half are adults,
and the other half are children and youth. Teen age clubs of both sexes,
athletic teams, hobby classes, and special interest groups for adults comprise the range of activities. Construction of the new Hollywood
Freeway has cut through the Echo Park recreation area separating the recreation building from the recreation grounds. This renders supervision
somewhat difficult inasmuch as the supervisory offices are located in the
recreation building.

Los Angeles Youth Project. In the fall of 1947 the Youth Project Area
Coordinator working in the Echo Park Area received reports of tension
and unrest evident among the youth of the study area. Gang fights and
minor infractions of the law were increasing.

A number of Echo Park Area residents, who felt more than ordinary
concern over these events, met several times together with the Youth
Project Area Coordinator and representatives of schools and youth serving agencies operating in the study area. The group eventually constituted itself into a continuing committee known as the Youth Project Advisory Committee for the Rosemont Area with the stated purpose of
obtaining better youth services for the community.

As a direct result of the efforts of this Committee, several youth serving agencies increased their services in the study area. However, agencies which are dependent on volunteer leadership could do little, because
they encountered minor success in recruiting volunteers. The Committee's investigation uncovered the need for leadership for youth groups
as well as for additional facilities, specifically for meeting places, club
rooms, a gymnasium and swimming pool and space and equipment for
large muscle outdoor games. The endeavors of the Youth Project Advisory Committee with the cooperation of the Board of Education made

available the facilities of Rosemont Elementary School for evening activities for teen-agers. The Board of Education also supplied supervision through its Youth Services Division. During the early part of 1949 several co-ed clubs for teen-agers were formed, one under the leadership of a Church Welfare Bureau group worker and the others under the volunteer leadership of local residents. The Youth Project Advisory Committee is presently engaged in stimulating the organization of scout troops for the younger age groups and in recruiting additional volunteer leaders.

Some Aspects of the Culture of the Echo Park Area

Examination of the interview records revealed that only seven principal topics were mentioned with sufficient frequency to warrant their treatment. Thus, where only one or two interviews alluded to a category, that category was omitted.

Intercultural Relations

The interview data reveal some discrepancy of opinion regarding the relationship to one another of the various cultural groups in the Echo Park Area. Some of the interviewees indicated that these groups exhibit considerable harmony and cooperation, while others felt that the situation in the area is characterized by disharmony and subtle conflict. Occasionally the same respondent gave contradictory testimony in the same or in successive interviews.

Intergroup Harmony. Those who assert the existence of intergroup harmony do so on the basis of the following types of evidence. Many cultural groups live side by side without apparent strife. They are represented on the membership of various community organizations, such as the local P.T.A.'s and the like. Whenever community social affairs are planned by the adult societies which meet at the Echo Park Recreation Center, the numerous population groups usually respond cooperatively. The young children using the playgrounds in the area mix well, playing together in small groups or forming teams, without regard to race and religion. If a Negro youngster performs well on the athletic field or in the recreation hall, the Anglo youngsters applaud him and vice versa. There are also numbers of amorous friendships between Anglo- and Mexican-American youths.

One educated Negro informant remarked that Negroes are well accepted by the Anglo community, and a Mexican-American youth stated that, in contrast to some other areas where he has resided, he has noticed remarkably little tension among the minorities in Echo Park. The respondents also allude to the mixed racial composition of some of the youth gangs in the area which operate without internal friction.

Intergroup Tensions. On the other side is the contention that although the many cultural groups live side by side in Echo Park, there is no real amity and social intermingling among them. The members of the groups keep to themselves and that is the reason for the absence of open conflict. Some tension between the Anglo-American and Mexican-American children has manifested itself on the school playgrounds in the form of sporadic arguments and fights. It is the writer's interpretation that the interview data tend to bear out the existence of a cleavage between Anglo-Americans on the one hand and Mexican-Americans and Negroes on the other hand, as well as the existence of a lesser cleavage between Negroes and Mexican-Americans, the former regarding themselves as of higher status than the latter and the latter tending to resent it.

The interviews pointed to occasional adolescent associations between Anglo-American girls and Mexican-American boys which are frowned upon by the Anglo group of all ages and even by some of the Mexican-Americans themselves. One professional worker who was interviewed contended that these "affairs" do not have a healthy basis in that they are not the effect of the mutual acceptance of each other of the two cultural groups. Rather they are defense reactions on the part of those engaging in them. Thus, the Anglo girl who engages in a flirtation with a Mexican-American boy is usually one who is not well adjusted to her own cultural group.

Some interviews underlined the point that the parents are responsible for the underlying tensions among the population groups. The very young children of all backgrounds play together freely on the school yard and playground. When the Anglo parents hear about it, they forbid their children to associate with youngsters from other groups. These children cease their attendance at the interracial activities of the Recreation Department giving spurious reasons for their inactivity.

The Negroes of Echo Park

Socio-Economic Status. Economically it is one of the better Negro residential sections. A number of the Negro families own their own homes wholly or partially. In many families both parents are working with the aim of raising their economic standards. They work at such jobs as chauffeurs and maids in the better residential areas of West Los Angeles and as maintenance workers in public buildings. School authorities stressed the physical cleanliness of the Negro children.

The Negroes of Echo Park exhibit a marked urge to rise socio-economically. Their homes are immaculate and often tastefully furnished; they have aspirations for their children and exhibit the values of middle class Anglo-American culture. It is the writer's interpretation drawn from the interview data that there is a tendency on the part of the Negroes of Echo Park in certain situations to identify with the Anglo-Americans as against the Mexican-American group and, further, that this has aroused the resentments of some of the latter.

Community Relations. The interview data are contradictory regarding inter-group relations involving the Echo Park Negroes. Some interviewees stressed the existence of an alliance between Negro and Mexican-American versus the Anglo population, while others pointed to an antagonism between Negro and Mexican-American schoolmates. Some interviews underlined a relative absence of antagonism between Anglos and Negroes as particularly exemplified by the fact that there has not been any great exodus of Anglos resulting from a recent increase in Negro population. The Negroes were described by one professional as quiet, well-behaved, keeping to themselves, and "watching" what goes on.

The school principals claim to have made attempts with varying degrees of success to activate the Negroes in community affairs. Negro mothers, unlike the Mexican women, are eager to participate in these activities and regard the endeavor as a mark of status. The same informants add, however, that there is at the same time a diffidence to take on real responsibilities and a tendency to assume minor roles. Thus Negro women will readily assist at social functions by baking, cooking, cleaning and the like, but will shy off occupying offices. In this respect the younger Negroes have shown considerable progress over their parents.

The Mexican-American Home

The Mexican-American home, as the term is here employed, is one where one or both parents have been born in Mexico while the children are native-born. The family is a patriarchal one with the father exercising the authority and the mother occupying a secondary but respected position. Spanish is spoken in the home; the parents speak poor English while the children are bilingual.

The Conflict of Cultures. Because depreciation of old-world values, except perhaps the Anglo-Saxon and Scandinavian, is characteristic of our American culture, the children of Mexican-born parents reject the values of the homes in which they were born and reared. This point was repeatedly emphasized by the professionals interviewed. The interview data do not distinguish between the normal conflict which customarily characterizes the relationship of successive generations and that which is the peculiar result of a clash of cultures. This distinction aside, the result of this conflict, as summarized by the writer from the interview data, is a break between the generations evidenced by such things as: a rebellion and disregard of parental authority (which probably carries over in their attitude toward all authority); difficulty on the part of parents in controlling their children; a lack of mutual understanding between parents and children; independent rather than cooperative and mutual participation by both children and parents in leisure-time activities; an occasional feeling of confusion and defeat by parents, expressed in the form of complete indifference with a resultant laxity of behavior on the part of the children. This conflict of cultures is regarded by several professionals interviewed as a chief source of youth problems in the area.

Community Participation. The interview data point to the fact that Mexican-born parents, unlike the Anglo-Americans, are not "joiners." They participate less in community activities and show less interest in local organizations. The school principals claim to have made repeated attempts to draw those parents into the P.T.A. but little headway has been achieved. The Mexican-born are somewhat baffled by the intricacies of the American culture and their attention is apt to be focussed upon their own cultural group rather than upon the larger community. It is our interpretation that this fact has deprived the Mexican-American youth of the socially beneficial example of community participation and community loyalty on the part of their elders.

Economic Conditions. The economic conditions of the Mexican-American families are poor, although not so bad as those of some Mexican-Americans who live in the East side of the city. Homes are overcrowded; there is considerable doubling up in sleeping quarters; an appreciable number of homes are without private baths and inside toilets, and have inferior plumbing; apartment houses are often rundown, dirty and neglected. The small frame homes are of better appearance. The flowered wallpaper, old and worn furniture, the clashing colors and the dime-store statuary on the tables, all display low economic status. But there is all the evidence of an attempt at cleanliness and some comfort. In the area there are to be seen considerable numbers of cheap second-hand automobiles which are kept running as a result of the mechanical ingenuity of their owners. When there are jobs available, both parents work in order to enable families to get along.

Mental Outlook of Mexican-American Youth

The interviews contain important bits of scattered information which enable us to piece together a picture of the outlook of the youth of the study area. The details below apply primarily to the Mexican-American youth although to a lesser degree to the Negro and other minority groups.

Insecurity. The youth are characterized by self-consciousness, lack of self-assurance, diffidence, insecurity, frustration and unrest. Interviewers were received with reserve, distrust and a reluctance to give information. Individual youths interviewed questioned whether the interviewer represented the law enforcement authorities. One youth responded during the first interview, but during the second interview resisted and spoke little. It later came out that he had related his interview experience to his companions who had cautioned him not to talk any more.

The professionals interviewed complained that the youth of the area lack initiative and that they do not wish to shoulder responsibility in their clubs which therefore languish. They are described as loud, ostentatious in dress and easily victimized by passing fads. The professionals claim that the Mexican-American youth, having rejected the culture of their foreign-born parents, are attracted to the more blatent and raucous elements of the American scene which promise thrills and excitement. The result, as interpreted by the writer, is mental confusion and emotional disturbance. The gap between the generations is also evidenced by the fact that parents and children do not spend time together engaging in activities, as, for example, recreation, which have a cohesive influence. It is the writer's interpretation drawn from the interview data that, cut off from their own families and not completely accepted by the Anglo-American group, the Mexican-American youth are isolated and lonely.

Anti-Education Bias. Many of the young people drop out of school early as a result of a number of factors. There are heavy economic pressures operating in their homes, and the prospect of an additional breadwinner is welcomed by their parents. The prospect of having to face discrimination in the sphere of economic competition operates to dissuade them from acquiring a maximum of education. Some complain of hostile attitudes on the part of school teachers which also tend to discourage them from remaining at school. As a defense, the youth often express an anti-education bias, they refer derisively to those of comparable age who want to stay at home and read books, and they look forward to leaving school as early as possible.

Aggressiveness. The school and recreation workers who were interviewed repeatedly referred to the fact that many of the Mexican-American youth exhibit an aggressive hostility which might well be a consequence of their basic insecurity. According to these professionals, they relish conflicts of any sort whether they be physical or psychological. They vie among themselves and match wits and strength with teachers and people in authority. They are apt to destroy property and break up orderly groups at play. They often irritate the local merchants by their hooliganism in front of their stores, and they have indulged in rowdyism inside the local theatre. They are constantly seeking to test "how much they can get away with," how much tougher they can be than the other fellow or the other group, and they are constantly sensitive to situations and opportunities which would permit such tests.

General Outlook. The economic outlook for the area's Mexican-American youth is not bright and they express concern about their own future. They come out of school untrained in any occupations, and they have not received the vocational guidance enabling them to make maximum use of their limited education. They are unable to find jobs, and the idle hang around pool halls and saloons, congregate on street corners and crowd the limited recreation facilities. They complain of having nothing to do but apparently lack the inner resources to devise the creative recreation which will absorb their energies. They spend much of their time roaming about in the streets and occasionally getting into scrapes. There is substantial evidence to the effect that some of the teenagers among the Mexican-Americans smoke marijuana when they can get it.

Attitude Toward Authority

The interviews unfold a difference in the attitudes toward the law enforcement authorities on the part of the respondents. School authorities and Anglo-American residents are favorably disposed and express some sympathy for the difficulties encountered by law enforcement officers in an area of conflict such as Echo Park. Mexican-Americans, however, are very critical of the authorities accusing them of unfairness, discrimination, lack of sympathy and occasional brutality.

Pro Attitudes. Those who are favorably disposed toward the law enforcement officers point out the difficulties surrounding their work. The Echo Park youth have a record of violence and the police assume great risks in patrolling the area. In self-protection they must make a show of force and occasionally resort to it. However, the use of force is usually a last resort and persuasion and reason are invariably initially employed. Police officers have, on the whole, established a sound and friendly relationship with the youth of the area. Individual officers have befriended youths who are known to be gang leaders, calling them by their first names and have spent long hours conversing with the latter with a view of favorably influencing them. It is claimed that this individualized attention has reaped beneficial results.

From the professional workers particular praise was forthcoming for the work of the juvenile detail of the police force. They are credited with breaking up or minimizing the detrimental activities of the youth gangs. The Group Guidance Unit of the County Probation Department is also mentioned favorably in connection with their effective supervision of social functions at the Echo Park Recreation Center which has resulted in a decrease of rowdyism and violence. Some of those who speak well of the law enforcement authorities deny the charge that the latter are brutal and say that, in reality, they are apt to be too generous and lenient with youths who, perhaps, should be treated with greater severity.

Contra Attitudes. On the other side is expressed fear, resentment and disrespect for the law enforcement authorities, directed not against the County Probation Officers or the Police Juvenile Detail, but against the regular uniformed police. In instances where the latter are not resented outright, they are regarded as a nuisance, because they are constantly engaged in stopping youths, particularly the Mexican-Americans, warning and searching them and in other forms of harassment. Youths claim that they cannot converse innocently on the streets, because their groups are always questioned and broken up by the police without cause or provocation. It has often happened that a police car will circle about for hours keeping watch on a group of youths, following them around wherever they might wander with the obvious intent of driving them off the streets.

Some of the youths interviewed indicated that very often police behavior becomes violent. Youths have received mild beating, rough handling, coarse treatment accompanied by uncouth language. It is claimed that the police are often inconsiderate in that they will book youths on minor infractions whereas these might be just as easily dispensed with paternal warnings. However, once an official charge is filed against the youth, he has a record. One professional admitted that the police are not always tactful in their treatment of the youths, which has earned them an unfavorable reputation in the area. The result is that the youth fear them and view them as symbols of autocratic authority. Another professional pointed out that there is an avid consumption by the area's youth of newspaper stories of police corruption and implication in vice rackets. It is our interpretation that such news has the effect of reenforcing an already prevalent disrespect for the law enforcement authorities.

The Phenomenon of Gangs

The Setting. The Echo Park Area has a history of juvenile gang conflict and violence. However, the event which precipitated the present study was an isolated incident unrelated to the gang violence that from time to time has flared up in the area. There is nothing to indicate that the four indicted youths constituted a gang or had carried out the crime as part of gang activity. They were friends who probably happened to have been together at the time of the crime which was apparently spontaneous on their part. On the other hand, it should be pointed out that the setting in which the event occurred was one which has a history of violence and that the four youths had been reared in an environment in which extreme manifestations of aggressive behavior are not unusual.

Existence of Gangs. The informants who were interviewed for this study offered contradictory opinions regarding the existence of gangs. Professional workers and housewives claim that they have heard that gangs exist, but they have never had any contact with the phenomenon and are apt to doubt its existence. It is the writer's view that unscientific news reporting of sporadic fights between Anglo-American and Mexican-American youths has the effect of inflating the incidents into gang proportions and the public acquires the impression of the existence of roving gangs. At the same time, however, the evidence drawn from the interview data is that gangs do exist in the Echo Park Area. Thus, a number of our youth informants had actually been members of gangs and been involved in gang fights. One youth who was interviewed stated that he still cannot wander into the eastern portion of the study area, because he might be spotted as a member of a rival gang and beaten up.

History of Gangs. The interviewees who were visited were in general agreement that violent gang activity has recently subsided. But the last ten years had seen violence between rival gangs marked by shootings and stabbings as a consequence of which a number of youths were seriously injured. The war years, with their zoot suit riots in the East side of the city, were likewise violent in the study area. The informant mentioned the last flare-up as having occurred in the fall of 1947 when two gangs fought a series of battles for the possession of the Echo Park playground in which skulls were fractured and lungs punctured. The altercation resulted in court action, with a number of youths being sent to state schools and forestry camps.

The study area has therefore been generally known as a violence area. The professionals stated that for a time parents would accompany their children to and from school as a protection against possible violence, and those residents who live in the western portion of the study area are still somewhat apprehensive about allowing their children to frequent the Echo Park playground which has in the past been the scene of violence. The locale of gang fights which occurred in the past has been the southeast portion of the study area.

Cross-Cultural Composition of Gangs. While there are no distinctly Negro gangs, there are some smaller gangs consisting of entirely Mexican-American youths or entirely Anglo-American youths. However, these internally homogeneous groups are very few and most gangs are of heterogeneous cultural composition. Thus the West-Temple gang is made up of Mexican-Americans, Anglo-Americans and Negroes. The East-Temple gang consists predominantly of Mexican-Americans with a small number of youths of Filipino extraction. Most of the lesser gangs are likewise of mixed cultural composition. Usually a Mexican-American youth assumes leadership, although occasionally the leader might be a Negro as was the case recently in the West-Temple gang. While some gangs do cut across geographic lines, drawing their members from scattered portions of the study area, most gangs, and certainly the two principle ones, are geographically defined. Therefore, the gang battles in the study area have been primarily between gangs living to the east of Echo Park versus those living to the west of it. They have also involved gangs living outside the study area.

Causes for Gang Warfare. It is the writer's interpretation drawn from the interview data that the real underlying causes of the gang fights in the study area are to be found in the aggressive behavior patterns of the area's youth flowing from the basic insecurities that characterize their lives. Although there is no actual hunger and gross physical want among the minority groups living in Echo Park, there is considerable frustration and deprivation. The milieu nurtures harshness and aggressiveness as defenses against the frustration and insecurity.

At this juncture we can only enumerate the spark-setting incidents which, according to our informants, usually generate these outbursts. In view of all the facts that have been thus far detailed about the study area's culture, it seems to the writer that the opportunities for gang conflict in the area are legion and any relatively inconsequential incident is sufficient to set fire to a fight. The following are some actual incidents which, according to our interviews, have resulted in gang fights.

For example, during a basketball game at the Echo Park playground one of the players was accused by his opponents of playing contrary to rules. The former resisted the accusation and he was beaten up. Next day the victim of the violence returned to the playground with his gang, who came to avenge the beating, and a free-for-all ensued. Teams are organized or spontaneously formed along gang lines. This injects an element of seriousness into an otherwise innocent pastime and makes every bit of friction during the game a cause for trouble. Another incident laden with conflict is where one gang will come upon the playground, see another gang using a court or a diamond or a set of athletic equipment, and will proceed to take it away from the latter. Gangs have been known deliberately to go forth with the intent of breaking up an orderly game in process and one gang battle was generated by just such an incident.

One very vital social area around which conflict often occurs is the heterosexual one. As one young informant put it, when, at a dance, a fellow makes a pass at another's girl, the former is not going to let him get away with it. A heated argument between two youths as to who should dance with a girl can end violently if they are members of different gangs. Such an incident actually caused one outburst. Several flare-ups occurred at the Friday night dances which were once held regularly at the Echo Park Recreation Center. When one culminated in a stabbing, they were discontinued.

Echo Park, Focus of Conflict. Echo Park proper, since it is a meeting place of the many conflicting groups residing in the study area, has been the scene of much of the violence described above. But Echo Park has been more than just the scene; it has also been the immediate cause of these outbursts. The gangs have used the playground as a hangout. The members of the West-Temple gang live in closer proximity to Echo Park itself than do the East-Temple gang, and so the former consider the Park and its playground as their quasi-private property. Invasion of Echo Park by members of the East-Temple gang has in the past been a cause for violent retaliation by the West-Temple gang. One particularly violent fight took place when the Temple-Beaudry gang invaded Echo Park en masse and were repulsed by their antagonist only to return reenforced and be repulsed again.

The Echo Park recreation ground is probably the most attractive one for miles around, and it has drawn youths from sections beyond its immediately surrounding area. The informants state that a number of fights have resulted from "invasions" by gangs from outside the study area. Several adult informants insisted that the entire series of gang fights was caused by outsiders who came from the Civic Center district, the East side and from sections north of Sunset Boulevard.

Decline of Gang Violence. The consensus among the respondents is that the last year or more have witnessed a decline in gang activity in that there have been no violent incidents during that time. A number of reasons is given by them for this decline. It is claimed by some that the commitment to state schools and forestry camps of a number of youths who participated in the last gang fight has removed the ringleaders who spark plugged the fights. Some refer to the excellent work done by the Police Juvenile Detail whose salutary influence upon some gang leaders, to which we have referred before, has tended to calm things down. The recreation workers refer to the efforts of the Group Guidance Unit of the County Probation Department. Probation Officers have organized athletic teams and have managed to draw in gang members, singly or in groups, into their organized programs. These same probation officers appear in a supervisory capacity at social functions held on the Echo Park Recreation Center and their presence has a favorable effect. How long the present quiet will last, none was willing to say.

The Role of Recreation

The fact that the Echo Park playground has been both the scene and the occasion for much of the gang fights that have earned a stigma for the Echo Park Area compels that brief attention be given to the problem of recreation in the study area. That the subject of recreation is an integral part of a cultural analysis will be presently apparent.

Need for Recreation Facilities. The respondents who were interviewed were almost unanimous in their agreement that the Echo Park Area is in great need of additional recreation facilities. This sentiment was universally expressed by all respondents, professionals and lay people, young as well as old. First priority was placed upon recreation space and adequate equipment, including a swimming pool; next was the emphasis on proper professional supervision. There was no implication in any of the interviews that such improvements would affect basically the socio-economic factors generating the aggressive behavior patterns found among the study area's youth. It was, however, claimed that additional recreation facilities would alleviate conditions by removing one of the "incidents" which in the past has set off conflict. It is significant that the most violent gang fights had occurred at the Echo Park playground.

The Role of Recreation. It is the writer's interpretation drawn from the interview data that recreation facilities assume a role in the Echo Park Area which is different from that in more privileged districts. Recreation facilities are much more intensely used in an area such as Echo Park than in, let us say, Beverly Hills. Homes in the study area are more apt to be overcrowded and their smaller yards do not provide for adequate play space. Mothers work and are not at home to supervise children during their after school hours. The only places they can spend their spare time are the street, the public recreation ground or the commercial facilities such as pool halls and movies. However, lower economic standards and unemployment among the youth mean less money available for commercial amusements and hence a greater reliance upon public recreation. In an area of social deterioration it is important to draw the youth off the streets. Ruth Morgan reports Echo Park Residents as stating that this section along Temple Street beween Douglas and Alvarado is becoming a skid row with winos and derelicts in evidence. This renders the streets a morally hazardous environment for the youth of the study area. It seems to the writer that attempts to draw the youth off the streets will result in even more intensive use of existing recreation facilities.

Echo Park Overtaxed. The Echo Park playground is the only properly equipped recreation center serving an extensive area. There are playgrounds at both the eastern and western periphery of the study area, but these are attached to elementary schools, are small, overcrowded, and poorly equipped. They are fit for use by very young children, but the recreation workers assert they are not inviting to the older youth of gang age. The result is that the area's youth all converge upon the Echo Park Playground.

Augmenting the difficulty is the influx of youth from adjacent areas with recreation shortages. Recreation workers claim that even if no youth from other neighborhoods frequented it, the Echo Park playground would still encompass a sufficiently large service area. They also point to the fact that the new freeway bisects the playground, involving some loss of play area and rendering more difficult the task of proper supervision. Hence they suggest large, well-supervised playgrounds at both the eastern and western ends of the study area. They claim that freeway construction has resulted in displacement of much needed play space, a fact which is bound to add to already existing sources of difficulty.

In view of the findings of this study and in the light of the basic principles of human behavior which they illustrate, the following practical steps are suggested.

1. For service in schools, playgrounds and social agencies located in areas predominantly populated by economically underprivileged, minority groups, the attention that has to date been given toward selecting professionals who are sympathetic to these groups and appreciate their personal and social problems should be continued and intensified. Endorsement and active encouragement should be given to educational, recreational, and law enforcement agencies to augment their in-service training programs by means of intercultural institutes so that persons working in areas populated by minorities can become periodically reacquainted with the problems of the latter.

2. There is a need for more and better equipped recreational facilities in the Echo Park Area to provide for the displacement of play space resulting from freeway construction. However, even more important than facilities or equipment is well-trained, sympathetic personnel to work understandingly with the Area's youth.

3. Most of us already recognize that, while recreation programs are valuable and should be promoted, they do not constitute the cure for juvenile delinquency. Recreation is not an antidote for the defensive attitudes bred by the frustrations of belonging to a minority group. Efforts on the part of agencies conducting intercultural education and organization should be continued and intensified toward bringing about a more successful integration of minority youths in general and Mexican-American youths in particular into, and their greater acceptance by, the dominant culture. The work of the Los Angeles Youth Project in this area is worthy of note. Because of the importance of this intercultural emphasis, if recreation is to be promoted, work with small groups, utilizing

the social group work approach, should be favored over mass recreation. Although more expensive, social group work is more individual-centered and hence more desirable in the case of youth who are victims of rejection and deprivations.

4. Attention should be focussed upon the employment problems and economic opportunities of minority youth in general and Mexican-American youth in particular. An agency with an intercultural orientation should undertake studies in this area. A vocational training and guidance center for minority youth should be set up in the Echo Park Area, perhaps privately financed, to assist them in meeting realistically their vocational problems. It is strongly urged that the County Youth Committee appoint a small committee to implement this recommendation at the earliest moment.

5. To counteract the disintegrating influences of the urban environment as these impinge upon the Echo Park Area, community sentiment and cohesiveness should be generated by fostering local community groups in the study area. People can acquire community roots and a sense of belonging only if they undergo common experiences. In this manner the residents of Echo Park can be activated into assuming greater concern for the problems of their community and greater initiative in their solution. The task of community organization should not be left to "the other fellow" to undertake, but should be lodged in some experienced agency which would bring to bear upon the problem the type of skills characterized by the Los Angeles Youth Project. In this context the churches and schools are in a position to achieve much. In leisure time and in adult education programs the adults of a community can meet in small interest groups and lay the basis for further cooperative endeavors.

6. Although the Echo Park Area has attracted attention because of past events, there are other similar districts in the Los Angeles metropolitan area which, though dormant, are potential tension spots. We have sufficient techniques at our disposal to identify such spots. These areas should be studied before rather than after the tensions have exploded and assumed violent forms. All too often our studies are inspired by individual crises and tied to sporadic eruptions. Long-time studies are needed for anticipating these crises and forestalling the eruptions. In the Los Angeles community there is no agency engaging in systematic and long-time studies of juvenile delinquency in all of its aspects. Such studies should comprise not only investigations into the causes of delinquency, but also analyses into the effectiveness of current treatment methods and available community services for handling delinquents. The present study might be considered as only a first step on the part of the County Youth Committee toward such a comprehensive research program. It is recommended that the County Youth Committee, as the agency authorized to deal with the county wide problems of youth, should undertake the sponsorship of such long-time, well-planned studies.

Name Index

Subject Index